T0330978

Edited by Alec Schmidt, this book is a comprehensive compilation featuring insights from leading academic and practitioner authorities in the field of sustainable finance. This book explores a wide range of topics, from ESG ratings to impact investing, from regulation to practical implementation, from sustainable mutual funds to climate indexes, and from ESG preferences to ESG performance and reporting. In particular, it addresses current and complex hot topics such as net-zero investing, Scope 3 emissions, 3D investing, and the application of AI and machine learning to sustainable finance. Covering listed equities, fixed-income instruments, and real assets, this book is a must-have for anyone looking to deepen their understanding of ESG and climate investing.

— Thierry Roncalli, *Head of Quantitative Research, Amundi,* and *Professor of Finance, University of Paris-Saclay*

This book provides a very nice and thorough overview of sustainability investing by combining research with practice. It covers a wide range of topics from net-zero investing to analyzing ESG data, which gives readers a broad understanding of sustainable investment strategies. Its excellent contributors also offer balanced and insightful views on the different facades of the subject. This book is an excellent guide for students and practitioners interested in incorporating sustainability into financial decisions.

— Aaron Yoon, *Assistant Professor, Kellogg School of Management, Northwestern University*

Sustainable Investing: Problems and Solutions offers an innovative exploration of ESG investing, blending cutting-edge research with practical insights. This book covers a range of topics, from ESG data analysis to the impacts of sustainable investment strategies. The contributors, with their diverse backgrounds, offer a well-rounded perspective on the field, addressing challenges and suggesting solutions for sustainable finance practitioners. This book is a valuable resource for anyone looking to understand and integrate sustainability into financial decision-making.

— David Carlin, *CEO of Cambium Global Solutions, Senior Advisor to UNEP Finance Initiative,* and *Visiting Fellow at King's College London*

SUSTAINABLE INVESTING
Problems and Solutions

SUSTAINABLE INVESTING
Problems and Solutions

Editor

Anatoly B Schmidt
New York University, USA

World Scientific

V JERSEY · LONDON · SINGAPORE · BEIJING · SHANGHAI · HONG KONG · TAIPEI · CHENNAI · TOKYO

Published by

World Scientific Publishing Co. Pte. Ltd.

5 Toh Tuck Link, Singapore 596224

USA office: 27 Warren Street, Suite 401-402, Hackensack, NJ 07601

UK office: 57 Shelton Street, Covent Garden, London WC2H 9HE

Library of Congress Control Number: 2024031469

British Library Cataloguing-in-Publication Data
A catalogue record for this book is available from the British Library.

SUSTAINABLE INVESTING
Problems and Solutions

ISBN 978-981-12-9777-9 (hardcover)
ISBN 978-981-12-9778-6 (ebook for institutions)
ISBN 978-981-12-9779-3 (ebook for individuals)

For any available supplementary material, please visit
https://www.worldscientific.com/worldscibooks/10.1142/13972#t=suppl

Desk Editors: Nandha Kumar/Sandhya Venkatesh

Typeset by Stallion Press
Email: enquiries@stallionpress.com

Printed in Singapore

About the Contributors

Alexander V. Chernokulsky is a Senior Researcher at the A. M. Obukhov Institute of Atmospheric Physics of the Russian Academy of Science and Associate Professor at the Higher School of Economics (Moscow). He is also Director for Analysis and Management of Climate Risks at CarbonLab LLC and serves as Scientific Secretary of the Scientific Council of the Russian Academy of Sciences on Earth's Climate Problems. Alexander is the Principal Investigator of eight projects and (co-)author of over 30 articles in peer-reviewed climatic journals and six book chapters.

Anatoly (Alec) B. Schmidt is an Adjunct Professor at the Finance and Risk Engineering Department of the NYU Tandon School. He also taught for many years at Stevens Institute of Technology and was a visiting professor at Nanyang Technological University and Moscow Financial Academy. Alec holds a Ph.D. in Physics and has worked in the financial industry for more than 20 years, most recently as Lead Research Scientist at Kensho (a market data analytics company, currently part of S&P Global). Alec has published three books, *Quantitative Finance for Physicists* (Elsevier 2004), *Financial Markets and Trading: Introduction to Market Microstructure and Trading Strategies* (Wiley 2011), and *Modern Equity Investing Strategies* (World Scientific 2021), as well as multiple papers on agent-based modeling, portfolio management, asset pricing, ESG investing, and trading strategies.

Antoine Bonelli is a Consultant at AI Builders, a consulting firm specializing in the definition and deployment of data and AI strategic plans for large corporations. He graduated from EMLYON Business School in France with a specialization in data science, focusing mainly on ESG data as well as corporate strategy.

Aston S. K. Chan is the Head of Investment Solutions at Impact Cubed, a London-based sustainability investment advisor and data provider that specializes in sustainability and ESG integration using advanced portfolio engineering frameworks. Aston has led an industry-first effort to research and operationalize 3-dimensional portfolio construction, a framework to target outcomes in terms of risk, return, and sustainability simultaneously. Aston has over 20 years of experience in investment management and quantitative research. He started his career at the Quantitative Strategies Group at Deutsche Bank in 2002. Aston later joined Auriel Capital Management LLP, a global macro and long/short equity hedge fund, followed by co-founding GLC Global Macro as a portfolio manager. Prior to joining Impact Cubed, Aston founded AMAC Research, a portfolio management and quantitative research consultancy advising hedge funds and family offices. Aston has a master's degree in finance from the London Business School.

Bruno G. Kamdem is a Co-Founder of a minority-owned consulting start-up Lepton Actuarial where he serves as the Principal and Sustainable Finance Practice Leader. Bruno is also an adjunct faculty member at the Department of Finance and Risk Engineering at the NYU Tandon School of Engineering where he teaches Sustainable Investments. Concomitantly, Bruno is a part-time lecturer of Mathematical Finance at the Johns Hopkins University, department of Applied Mathematics and Statistics, where he teaches Commodity Markets and Green Energy Finance. Bruno has published articles in the *Journal of Fixed Income, Energy Policy*, and *Renewable and Sustainable Energy Reviews*. He has presented at various conferences and seminars such as the International Federation of Operational Research Societies, the Peter Carr Brooklyn Quant Experience (BQE) Seminar Series, the Bloomberg BBQ Seminar, the John Hopkins University Financial Mathematics Seminar, and the University of Toronto Fields Institute Seminar. Bruno obtained his Ph.D. in Operations Research from the School of Engineering and Applied Science at George Washington University, an M.S. in Applied Mathematics, and a B.S. in Mathematics and Economics, both from the University of Maryland, Baltimore County.

Budha Bhattacharya is the Head of Systematic Research at Lombard Odier Asset Management where he leads quantitative research on the sustainability side, maintaining, improving, and scaling existing systematic models and launching new ones, as well as leading data- and technology-related innovations within sustainability. Budha has 20 years of experience in capital markets with Goldman Sachs and UBS. He previously founded and served as CTPO of ESG IQ, a big data analytics platform at KPMG UK. Alongside his corporate career, Budha is an Industrial Professor of Finance at UCL's Institute of Finance and Technology. He pursued his doctoral studies in quant finance at UCL, and holds an Executive MBA from INSEAD and an M.Sc. in Financial Economics from the University of Exeter.

Costanza Consolandi, Ph.D., is an Associate Professor of Corporate Finance at the University of Siena and Adjunct Professor at LUISS University. Her research activities focus primarily on finance and sustainability.

Cynthia Hanawalt is the Director of Climate Finance and Regulation at Columbia University's Sabin Center for Climate Change Law. Prior to joining the Sabin Center, Ms. Hanawalt served as Chief of the Investor Protection Bureau for the New York State Office of the Attorney General. Previously, she was a litigation partner at the firm Bleichmar Fonti & Auld LLP.

Dimitar Trajanov, Ph.D., is a Visiting Research Professor at Boston University and Head of the Department of Information Systems and Network Technologies at the Faculty of Computer Science and Engineering at Ss. Cyril and Methodius University in Skopje, North Macedonia. From March 2011 until September 2015, he was the founding Dean of the Faculty of Computer Science and Engineering. During his tenure, the faculty became the largest technical college in N. Macedonia. Dimitar is the leader of the Regional Social Innovation Hub, established in 2013 jointly by the UNDP and the Faculty of Computer Science and Engineering. His professional experience includes working as a senior data science consultant for one of the largest pharmaceutical companies, a data science consultant for UNDP in North Macedonia, and a software architect in a couple of start-ups. Dimitar is the author of more than 170 journal and conference papers and seven books. He has been involved in more than 70 research and industry projects, being project leader on more than 40 projects.

Egor M. Muravev is a master's program student in low-carbon development at the Higher School of Economics in Moscow. He holds a bachelor's degree in international economic relations from the Financial University under the Government of the Russian Federation.

Emma Elizabeth (Bessie) Antin Daschbach is a Partner at Hinshaw & Culbertson LLP. Bessie spearheads ESG at Hinshaw & Culbertson. She holds a certificate in Sustainable Capitalism and ESG from Berkeley Law School, an LLM in International and Comparative Law from Columbia Law School, and a JD from Tulane Law School, where she is also a longstanding adjunct professor of environmental law and policy. Bessie accumulated more than twenty years of experience in high-risk litigation before turning to ESG and she applies that experience to orient clients toward proactive ESG solutions.

Fei Liu is a Professor at IPAG Business School, Paris, with a background in econometrics and the application of artificial intelligence techniques to financial time series.

Gorgi Lazarev is a fourth-year student at the Faculty of Computer Science and Engineering at the Ss. Cyril and Methodius University, Skopje, majoring in Software Engineering and Information Systems. During his studies, he expressed interest and gained knowledge in various fields, including web development and web services, backend development, data science, and DevOps, and has put the knowledge into practice by developing diverse projects and applications, utilizing numerous programming languages and technologies. On the academic side, he has also worked on research projects in the fields of artificial intelligence and data science, focusing on climate change and the ESG (Environmental, Social, and Governance) framework, and has co-authored three research papers in these focus areas.

Guillaume Coqueret is an Associate Professor of finance and data science at EMLYON Business School. He holds a master's degree in finance from the University of Paris I, a master of science degree in management from ESSEC Business School, and a master's degree in probability and finance from Sorbonne University. He completed his education with a

Ph.D. from ESSEC Business School in Finance and Applied Mathematics. His research has been published in journals such as *Journal of Banking and Finance, Annals of Operations Research, Journal of Portfolio Management, Quantitative Finance, Journal of Mathematical Economics, and European Journal of Operational Research.* In 2020, he co-wrote *Machine Learning for Factor Investing* (CRC/Chapman Hall), and in 2022 his book *Perspectives in Sustainable Equity Investing* was released by the same publisher.

Hans-Jörg von Mettenheim is a Professor and Director of the Finance and Economics Department at IPAG Business School, Paris. He is Co-Founder of Keynum Investments and AiData, and is passionate about implementing machine learning applications in big data contexts.

Heiko Bailer, a seasoned investment professional, brings over 20 years of expertise to the field, with an investment style that integrates sustainability, regulatory considerations, and diversified alpha. His career spans well-known companies, family offices, and fintechs across Europe, Asia, and the United States, with significant contributions to institutions such as Deutsche Bank, ABN AMRO, and Credit Suisse. Engaging actively in academic research, Dr. Bailer holds a Ph.D. in Statistics and a degree in Computational Finance from the University of Washington.

Irena Vodenska, Ph.D., is a Professor of Finance, Director of Finance Programs, and Chair of the Administrative Sciences Department at Metropolitan College, Boston University. Her research focuses on sustainability in finance and macroeconomics, using Large Language Models (LLMs) and Artificial Intelligence (AI) to leverage big data analytics. She conducts theoretical and applied interdisciplinary research using quantitative approaches for modeling interdependencies of financial networks, systemic risk, and global economic crises. She studies the effects of media on financial markets, corporations, financial institutions, and related global economic systems. She uses Natural Language Processing (NLP) to text-mine important factors affecting corporate performance, Environmental, Social, and Governance (ESG) corporate reporting, and global economic trends, primarily related to climate change and social responsibility. She teaches Derivatives Securities and Markets, Financial Regulation and Ethics, and ESG Investing at Boston University. She is also a Chartered Financial Analyst (CFA) charter holder. As a Principal Investigator (PI) for Boston University, she has won interdisciplinary research grants from the European Commission (EU), the US Army Research Office, and the National Science Foundation (US).

Jim Hawley, Ph.D., is Professor Emeritus at the School of Economics and Business, Saint Mary College of California. He is the author/co-author of four books, most recently *Moving Beyond Modern Portfolio Theory: Investing that Matters* (with Jon Lukomnik), and editor/co-editor of three handbooks on corporate governance and responsible investment, in addition to numerous scholarly articles and papers on topics including corporate governance, responsible and sustainable investment, the international monetary and financial system, and environmental issues. Jim has been a guest professor at the University of Cambridge, Université de Paris, Université de Montpellier, Maastricht University, St. Gallen University, and the Kennedy School, Harvard University. He has spoken at numerous professional investor conferences and is frequently quoted in the media. He has previously worked at Wells Fargo Bank, TruValue Labs, and Factset.

Lindsey Stewart is the Director of Investment Stewardship Research at Morningstar Europe. Lindsey analyzes asset managers' sustainable investing policies and practices with a focus on their engagement, proxy voting, and public policy outreach activities. Lindsey joined Morningstar in April 2022 from the Financial Reporting Council — the UK regulator responsible for audit, accounting, corporate governance, and investment stewardship — where he was head of stakeholder engagement. He has over 20 years of experience in investor relations consulting, equity research, and financial reporting and regulation at KPMG and Makinson Cowell. Lindsey is a Chartered Global Management Accountant and also holds the CFA Institute's Chartered Financial Analyst® designation.

Lou Chitkushev, Ph.D., is an Associate Professor of Computer Science at Boston University. He is the Founding Director of Boston University's Health Informatics Program and serves as a Senior Associate Dean for Academic Affairs at BU's Metropolitan College. Professor Chitkushev is best known for his computational and AI-based models for analyzing health and economic data and systems, focusing on privacy, ethics, and sustainability. He has also contributed to the areas of new Internet architectures, cybersecurity, and digital forensics investigation. Professor Chitkushev is a Co-Founder of Boston University's Center for Reliable

Information Systems and Cyber Security (RISCS) and the RINA Lab, where Recursive Inter-Network Architecture (RINA) has been introduced as an efficient, scalable, and secure approach to Internet architecture. His research has been supported by grants from the European Commission (EU), the National Security Agency (US), and the US Department of Justice. He has served as a reviewer at the US National Science Foundation. He holds a B.S. in Electrical Engineering, an M.S. in Biomedical Engineering, and earned his Ph.D. in Biomedical Engineering from Boston University.

Marcin Kacperczyk is a Professor of Finance at Imperial College London with research interests in the areas of investments, information economics, financial intermediation, and artificial intelligence. His research has been published in leading academic and practitioner journals, including *Econometrica, Quarterly Journal of Economics, Journal of Finance, Journal of Financial Economics, Journal of Monetary Economics*, and *Review of Financial Studies*. Marcin has completed his Ph.D. in finance at the University of Michigan. He has previously worked at the NYU Stern School of Business and the UBC Sauder School of Business. He is a Research Associate at the Center for Economic Policy Research and a former Faculty Research Fellow at the National Bureau of Economic Research. He is the Editor of the *Review of Finance* and Associate Editor for *Financial Management*, the *Journal of Financial and Quantitative Analysis*, and *Management Science*. Marcin's work has been widely covered by the media, such as *CNN, CNBC, Bloomberg, WSJ, FT, NYT, Business Week, U.S. News*, and *Washington Post*. Two of his papers have been nominated for the Smith Breeden Prize and one received the Spaengler IQAM Award for the best paper published in the *Review of Finance*. He is a current holder of the European Research Council research grant and former President of the European Finance Association. He is also a research advisor at the European Central Bank.

Mathieu Joubrel is a graduate of École Polytechnique and HEC Paris, with a master's degree specializing in data science and artificial intelligence. Mathieu is an entrepreneur who worked as a firefighter, data scientist, and GHG emissions modeler. These experiences taught him that the environmental and social challenges in modern economy cannot be dealt with separately. He thus co-founded ValueCo to develop tools to accelerate the sustainable transition through responsible investment.

Maxime Kirgo is a Quantitative Analyst in the Lombard Odier Systematic research team, where he contributes to maintaining and developing new ITR metrics. Before joining Lombard Odier in 2023, he completed his doctoral studies at Ecole Polytechnique (France) and EDF R&D (French electricity provider). His research focused on geometry processing and geometric deep learning. Maxime also holds a Master of Science degree from the Technical University of Munich (Germany) and an engineering degree from CentraleSupélec (France) with a background in computer science and machine learning.

Risto Trajanov is a Data Science graduate student at Rice University in Houston, sponsored by the Fulbright Program. Risto graduated from the Faculty of Computer Science and Engineering, Ss. Cyril and Methodius University, Skopje, with a "High Achievement" award for completing with a GPA higher than 9.5 (out of 10). Since 2021, he has been a data scientist, developing a product that would help investors detect greenwashing by providing a platform for monitoring a company's ESG behavior. His professional career started as a teaching mentor for high schoolers learning the programming language Java, followed by a machine learning internship at the Macedonian Academy of Sciences and Arts. He conducted two machine learning internships at Loca Inc., a Silicon Valley start-up, and Netcetera, a tech company. He was also active in the non-governmental sector, having volunteered as a computer science assistant at Smart-Up Innovation Lab, an NGO in Skopje. Risto has co-authored several research papers about optimization, machine learning, and explainable AI published in prestigious conferences including IEEE SSCI, EVO Apps, and PPSN.

Ron Große is the Head of Private Banking at the Brunswick Savings Bank (Braunschweigische Landessparkasse). He manages portfolios according to quantitative and sustainable principles.

Shaheen Contractor, CFA, is a Senior ESG Research Analyst for Bloomberg Intelligence. Her research efforts include analyzing ESG performance and its impact on risk, return, and valuations across industries; drivers and challenges for ESG funds; and the impacts of a low-carbon transition. Mrs. Contractor has a Master of Science degree in Sustainability Management from Columbia University.

Tensie Whelan is a Clinical Professor at the NYU Stern School. Tensie is also the Founding Director of the NYU Stern Center for Sustainable Business.

Her previous experience includes serving as President of the Rainforest Alliance, Executive Director of the New York League of Conservation Voters, Vice President of the National Audubon Society, and Managing Editor of Ambio, a journal of the Swedish Academy of Sciences. She has also been a journalist in Latin America. She has sat on numerous boards, including the Nespresso and Unilever advisory boards. Tensie holds a B.A. from New York University, an M.A. from American University, and is a graduate of the Harvard Business School Owner President Management (OPM) Program. She was awarded the Stern Faculty Excellence Award in 2020.

Thomas Kuh joined Morningstar Indexes as Head of ESG Strategy in January 2022. He was the first Global Head of ESG Indexes at MSCI from 2010–2017, where he led the launch of the first low-carbon indexes and initiated the strategic partnership with Bloomberg Barclays on the first suite of ESG fixed-income indexes. More recently, Thomas was Head of Index at Truvalue Labs (now part of FactSet), integrating real-time ESG signals from unstructured data into index design. Earlier in his career, he was Managing Director of Indexes at KLD Research & Analytics and creator of the first ESG index, where he collaborated with Barclays Global Investors on the launch of the first ESG ETFs. He was also Head of Indexes at RiskMetrics Group prior to its acquisition by MSCI and is the Founder and President of Benchmark ESG Consulting LLC. Thomas earned his M.A. and Ph.D. from the University of Massachusetts at Amherst and has a B.A. from Hampshire College. He is on the Advisory Board of the Journal of Impact and ESG Investing.

Ulf Erlandsson is CEO and Founder of the Anthropocene Fixed Income Institute, a research organization empowering companies to utilize fixed-income investment to drive the climate transition. Ulf previously focused on global credit; sovereign, supranational, and agency debt; and total return alpha strategy at the Swedish state pension fund, AP4. Prior to that, he was a quantitative strategist at Barclays Capital. Ulf has published a number of books and articles on the topics of credit and sustainable fixed income. Ulf was named Environmental Finance's Bond Personality of the Year in 2022 and awarded CFA Sweden's ESG Prize in 2021. He earned his Ph.D. in Economics from Lund University.

Umachander Balakumar is the Net Zero Data Lead at U.S. Bank. He was a subject-matter expert on ESG and Climate Risk at KPMG, and a former Research Scholar at the NYU Stern Center for Sustainable Business.

Chander's works include a chapter within the *Global Handbook of Impact Investing* on the topic of constructing multi-asset class emission reduction portfolios and the development of portfolio/risk analytics at Dynamo Software, a cloud platform for alternative investments. He also consulted on ESG and impact 401K portfolio strategies, and has developed various tools for helping financial firms collect, manage and report on their Scopes 1, 2, and 3 emissions data. Chander can be reached at ubalakum@gmail.com.

Viet Hoang Le is a Ph.D. student at Paris-Saclay University and has a strong interest in machine learning technology. He is a quantitative researcher at Keynum Investments.

Contents

Introduction

Anatoly B. Schmidt

Finance and Risk Engineering, NYU Tandon School,
New York, USA

Classical finance treats investors as rational agents "who always prefer more wealth to less" (Miller & Modigliani, 1961). This statement not only represents academic interest but also directly relates to Friedman's famous claim (1962) that has become the motto of many corporate CEOs: "There is one and only one social responsibility of business — to use its resources and engage in activities designed to increase its profits so long as it stays within the rules of the game, which is to say, engages in open and free competition without deception or fraud."

Yet, according to the extensive research in behavioral finance, investors are generally not completely rational in the way that classical finance expects them to be. This happens because humans are often driven by their cognitive errors and emotions (see, e.g. Statman, 2019). Also, numerous investors have been demonstrating their social responsibility. Indeed, a total of 4,375 investors managing $121 trillion had signed the Principles for Responsible Investment (PRI, 2023) by the end of 2021, which is a dramatic increase since 2006 when the 63 investors overseeing $6.5 trillion started this initiative (Edmans, 2023). Socially responsible investing may include various activities:

- Thematic investing — investing in products and practices that reflect social values, e.g. solar energy, clean air, and water technology.

- Screening out the products and practices that are inconsistent with the investor's values, e.g. so-called "sin" (tobacco, weaponry) and "brown" (energy, utility) industries. There are some indications, however, that the optimal divestment strategy from "brown" industries is to hold the best-in-class "brown" companies rather than their blanket exclusion (Edmans *et al.*, 2022).
- Sustainable investing — incorporating environmental, social, and governance (ESG) factors in the investment selection process.

The ESG factors can be treated as the business non-pecuniary risks. There has been intense debate on whether the ESG framework implies only a "single materiality" that addresses the shareholder interests, i.e. focuses only on the ESG impact on corporate performance and outlook (see, e.g. Eccles, 2023; Edmans, 2023). An alternative, so-called "double materiality" includes corporate impact on the world (climate, environment, and society), which is a matter of concern for the stakeholders (i.e. all of us, including the shareholders). I think this debate is somewhat misguided since the harmful corporate impact, whether it is water and air pollution, child labor, neglecting employee well-being, etc., can result in expensive lawsuits, consumer boycotts, and employee strikes, which may significantly hurt the corporate bottom line.

Several examples of the ESG taxonomy are present in the literature. A popular single materiality classification is reflected in the Sustainability Accounting Standards Board categories (SASB, 2023). Double materiality is embodied in the United Nations Sustainable Development Goals (SDGs) (see United Nations, 2023). While there are differences in objectives and effects of ESG integration and SDG investing, it was found that about 98 percent of the industry-specific topics included in the SASB standards are related to one or more SDG (Guillot, 2020). Still, in terms of average ratings, the ESG-sorted and SDG-sorted portfolios may not overlap significantly (De Franco *et al.*, 2021).

This book covers multifaceted problems and their possible solutions in sustainable investing. It includes 18 chapters written by 30 experts in the field from academia and industry. The collection includes three main topics. The general problems of sustainable investing are addressed in Part 1. It starts with an overview of the current state in this field by Consolandi and Hawley in Chapter 1 ("From ESG to Sustainable Impact Finance: Moving Past the Current Confusion"). Dashbach and Hanavalt discuss the existing ESG legal framework in Chapter 2 ("ESG Legislation,

Regulation, and Legal Implications"). Whelan and Balakumar focus on the ESG specifics for private equities in Chapter 3 ("Framework and Tools for Responsible Private Equity That Drives Societal and Financial Value"). Kuh and Stewart offer reviews of the sustainable investment indexes and funds in Chapter 4 ("The Indispensable Role of Indexes in the Evolution of Sustainable Investing") and Chapter 5 ("Sustainable Funds: Drivers of Progress or Expressions of Preference?"), respectively. Vodenska, Chitkushev, R. Trajanov, and D. Trajanov describe the AI methods for capturing information relevant to ESG reporting and sustainable investing in Chapter 6 ("Navigating Global ESG Investment Regulations Using AI"). The machine learning techniques for deriving and analyzing the ESG data are discussed by Bhattacharya and Kirgo in Chapter 7 ("A Sneak Peek into Machine Learning Methods for ESG Factor Score Computation") and by Contractor in Chapter 8 ("Challenges Discovered Analyzing ESG Data and Their Potential Solutions").

Part 2 (Chapters 9–12) addresses the global problem of climate change. It starts with an overview of net-zero portfolios being the means of reducing the investment carbon footprint by Kacperczyk ("Net-Zero Investing") in Chapter 9. A challenging problem of estimating Scope 3 greenhouse gas emissions is discussed by Bonelli and Coqueret in Chapter 10 ("The Determinants of Scope 3 Disclosure among Large Corporations"). Muravev and Chernokulsky address the current status of venture investments in carbon dioxide removal technologies in Chapter 11 ("Venture Investment in Carbon Dioxide Removal Technologies: Current State and Outlook"). Kamdem formulates the optimization problem of fuel production in carbon trading in Chapter 12 ("Optimizing Fuel Production in Carbon Trading: A Karush–Kuhn–Tucker Framework for Sustainable Balance").

Part 3 (Chapters 13–18) is devoted to sustainable investing strategies. In particular, Große, Le, Liu, and von Mettenheim describe a strategy based on the proprietary sustainability sentiment in Chapter 13 ("Portfolio Management with News-Based Sustainability Scores"). Bailer examines the profitability of portfolios derived using traditional asset-pricing factors and sustainability factors in Chapter 14 ("Optimizing Sustainable Performance: A Strategic Approach to Value Creation and Impactful Investing"). Chan explores the impact of sustainability measures on portfolio risk and return in Chapter 15 ("Portfolio Costs of Sustainability and Three-Dimensional Trade-offs"). Jubriel describes the practices that investors can use to improve the impact of their investments in Chapter 16

("Post-investment Strategies for Impact Investing"). Erlandsson discusses the perspectives of applying sustainable investment preferences in fixed-income portfolios in Chapter 17 ("Fixed-Income ESG Strategies"). Finally, Schmidt introduces new portfolio performance measures that are relevant for sustainable investing in Chapter 18 ("Portfolio Performance Measures for Sustainable Investing").

The book is aimed at academics and practitioners working in sustainable finance. It will also be useful for college students majoring in this field.

References

De Franco C., Nicolle, J., & Tran, L.-A. (2021). Sustainable investing: ESG versus SDG. *The Journal of Impact and ESG Investing*, 1(4), 45–62.

Eccles, R. (2023). Seeking common ground in the politicized debate about ESG. Retrieved from https://corpgov.law.harvard.edu/2023/08/10/seeking-common-ground-in-the-politicized-debate-about-esg/ (Accessed on November 30, 2023).

Edmans, A. (2023). The end of ESG. *Financial Management*, 52, 3–17.

Edmans, A., Levit, D., & Schneemeier, J. (2022). Socially responsible divestment. ECGI Working Paper Series in Finance, Working Paper 823/2022. European Corporate Governance Institute, Brussels.

Friedman, M. (1962). *Capitalism and Freedom*. University of Chicago Press. Chicago.

Guillot, J. (2020). What is the connection between SASB and the SDGs? SASB. Retrieved from https://www.sasb.org/blog/what-is-the-connection-between-sasb-and-the-sdgs/ (Accessed on November 30, 2023).

Miller, M. & Modigliani, F. (1961). Dividend policy, growth, and the valuation of shares. *Journal of Business*, 34, 411–433.

PRI. (2023). About the PRI. Retrieved from https://www.unpri.org/about-us/about-the-pri (Accessed on November 30, 2023).

SASB. (2023). SASB conceptual framework. Retrieved from https://www.sasb.org/wp-content/uploads/2019/05/SASB-Conceptual-Framework.pdf?source=post_page (Accessed on November 30, 2023).

Statman, M. (2019). *Behavioral Finance. The Second Generation*. CFA Institute Research Foundation. New York.

United Nations. (2023). Sustainable development. Retrieved from https://sdgs.un.org/goals (Accessed on November 30, 2023).

Part 1

General Problems in Sustainable Investing

Chapter 1

From ESG to Sustainable Impact Finance: Moving Past the Current Confusion

Costanza Consolandi* and Jim Hawley†

*Associate Professor of Corporate Finance,
Department of Business and Law,
School of Economics and Management,
University of Siena, Italy*

†*Professor Emeritus, School of Business and Economics,
Saint Mary's College of California, USA*

Abstract

In this chapter, we argue that environmental, social, and governance (ESG)/sustainability is moving from being based primarily on ESG ratings and rankings, which has caused significant confusion, to being based on mandated disclosure and analysis of externalities. We briefly examine the basis of ESG ranking and rating confusion, concluding that the current methodologies of major providers result in neither significant change nor accurate disclosures by firms. Alternatively, we suggest that an integration of externality data will significantly modify Modern Portfolio Theory as it does not account for externality effects on "systems" (think market beta) or the interactive effects of firms' actions on other firms in various types of portfolios, both directly and indirectly. These dynamics are qualitatively important given the growth and dominance of universal owner-type portfolios. Not accounting for externalities leads to sub-optimal economic system performance, reducing the financial return both absolutely and sometimes relatively. In turn, these dynamics redefine what financial "materiality" means. Finally, we place these concepts and developments into the context of global emerging regulatory standards and debates about them.

1. Introduction

Environmental, social, and governance (ESG) factors in investing have become increasingly significant globally, although, in recent years, they have received considerable political blowback in the U.S. from the Republican right (Berg *et al.*, 2023b, p. 1). Yet, as ESG becomes ever more influential, for investment decision-making, even in the U.S., as Edmans (2022) argues, it is "not ESG investing; it's investing" using ESG factors and analysis. This is an important distinction which goes to the heart of the globally widespread ESG confusion.

The first element of this confusion is that there is no consensus about defining, measuring, weighting, and thus analyzing these three sets of factors (each one, especially the E and S factors, having multiple components) as they are sourced using numerous rating agencies and datasets competing across a large variety of paradigms. The result is as follows: increasing "ESG confusion" among practitioners, academics, and other analysts caused by both friends and foes of "ESG investing" or investing considering ESG factors.

The second element of the confusion concerns the definition of materiality and what metrics capture various definitions. We look at the rating and ranking confusion first. Below are a few recent examples (as of this writing, late 2023) give a flavor of the analysis of "ESG confusion" and some attempts to bring some standards and order as well as move past what we see as the inherent ESG ratings muddle.

2. Confusion 1: Ratings and Rankings — Clarification and Limitation

In an attempt to make sense of the ESG ratings muddle, the "Aggregate Confusion Project" at Massachusetts Institute of Technology (MIT) pulled together research that critiqued the ESG "confusion." The project is one of many research undertakings that focused on ESG ratings and rankings (e.g. MSCI, Sustainalyics, and Refinitiv), the lack of correlation among raters and rankers, how they are used (or misused), and the implications for equity or bond prices and portfolio construction. All analysts agree that there is little correlation among ratings, especially on S issues, but on the E and G ones as well. For example, LaBella *et al.* (2019) found low correlations among major raters and rankers both in the U.S. and the world, with a low correlation of 0.16 (U.S. and global) for governance a correlation of 0.19 (U.S.) and 0.23 (global for social, and 0.29 (U.S.) and only a correlation of 0.31 (global).[1]

The MIT project provides one perspective on possible solutions to analyze six major ESG ratings providers, attempting to remove the noise inherent in these ratings while drawing on each raters' useful information (Berg *et al.*, 2023a). The project concludes that ESG firm ratings can be made useful by adjusting for geographical locations and the nature of specific portfolios.

The approach of Berg *et al.* (2023a) develops an earlier approach from a highly influential paper (Berg *et al.*, 2022) focused on the problem of inherent noise in ESG ratings, summarizing the problems of major ESG raters, individually as well as when compared with each other, in addition to proposing a methodological way of dealing with the divergence and noisy data problems.

One example of how such a diffusion of ratings might be used to find alpha or what Cremers *et al.* (2023) call "materiality" (meaning narrowly defined financial materiality) is by creating a metric called "Active ESG Shares," which measures the relative importance of ESG information in portfolio construction and goes beyond the traditional approach — labeled by Cremers *et al.* (2023) as "Directional ESG" — which assesses the impact on fund performance based on investing in stocks with high vs. low ESG ratings. Active ESG Shares are calculated using a variety of ESG ratings (given low correlations) by comparing the total fund's portfolio weights of ratings against the fund's ESG benchmark. Cremers *et al.* show that ESG funds that deviate from simply following ESG ratings perform better, with the strongest results for funds that hold stocks with a high level of ESG ratings disagreement. The hypothesis is that active funds with specialized and knowledgeable ESG managers will be able to

---

[1] LaBella *et al.* (2019, 4) suggest that the dispersion among ESG raters and rankers should be viewed as more akin to sell-side stock analysts' buy/sell recommendations rather than credit ratings.

use their expertise to sort through the diffusion of ratings to outperform others. Active ESG considers the entire distribution in a portfolio, while directional ESG considers the average ESG rating and is the more useful metric for ESG outperformance. The underlying focus on ESG ratings is the idea that they in themselves have little "material" information but that active ESG shares can produce significant alpha when one invests in stock with significant ratings disagreement. The point of this quick summary by Cremers *et al.* (2023), and there are others as well attempting to find alpha from the ESG confusion, is that ratings and rankings not only present complexity but are also at best indirect indicators of underlying ESG information. This underlying information, we argue, is overwhelming based on economic externalities although mostly absent in the ESG confusion literature. This is a striking omission.

Against this increasingly well-trod line of research on ESG ratings and rankings, our purpose in this chapter is to suggest that while the discussion has been useful, albeit at times "confusing" and complex, the focus on ESG ratings of individual firms needs to move on in two key ways. The first returns to the classic economic concern about externalities rather than ratings and rankings per se. The second, building on the first, focuses especially on large, highly diversified investors' portfolios, rather than a firm-by-firm focus on nearly all ESG analyses to date. The latter looks for alpha opportunities, which we consider useful at the margins for some investors and useful for price discovery under some conditions, but irrelevant for most large and indexed investors.

In short, we foresee that ESG will move beyond a firm-by-firm idiosyncratic risk approach to a focus on a whole portfolio, universal owner system risk approach. We think this is already underway among many large institutional investors, and to a degree practice is leading both theory and fully developed empirical analysis.

The historical background to this ESG muddle is analyzed succulently by the High Meadows Institute. It divides sustainable finance (ESG) into three historical phases, socially responsible investment, ESG, and systemic investment and impact management, all of which are parts of sustainable finance (respectively labeled stages 1.0, 2.0, and 3.0 of sustainable finance) (High Meadows Institute, 2021, p. 3). Implicitly, it argues that continuing to focus on ESG from a purely individual firm view based on equity (and/or bond) ESG performance (stages 1.0 and 2.0) misses critical systems interactions and effects (stage 3.0). This is what we call Sustainable Impact Finance (SIF), a systems approach to sustainability. Several other terms capture this as well, such as systems investing (The Investment Integration Project

(TIIP), 2021) and holistic portfolio analysis/universal owner perspectives (Hawley & Williams, 2001).

Thus, the MIT Aggregate Confusion Project and other analyses of ESG ratings and rankings, while useful in looking at stages 1.0 and 2.0, are far less helpful when thinking about sustainable finance 3.0: how firms interact with systems and how systems affect firms. A system is used to mean both beta (the market as a whole) and the underlying economic (or more broadly socio-economic) system upon which all financial markets are both dependent and with which they interact (Lukomnik & Hawley, 2021, pp. 88–94).

In other words, the MIT approach and similar approaches, focusing on market equity/bond movements, ignore whether ESG (however measured) makes a difference in what firms over time do in terms of E, S, and G outcomes or impacts. They are restricted to how individual firms perform in a narrow financial sense, that is, how individual equity and bonds are valued even if with a focus on relevant "material" ESG metrics (High Meadows Institute, 2021, p. 9).[2] A similar approach in a more comprehensive study focused on E and S ratings finds that financial performance is not harmed and may be helped (Henisz *et al.*, 2019). Yet, this study like many others is not rigorously focused on outcomes and changes over time, that is, on impact especially financial impacts on portfolios.

Financial performance in relation to the impact problem is well summarized by a University of Zurich study. The authors write the following:

> For ESG metrics to reflect company impact, the focus should be on impact materiality. Historically, most ESG ratings have emphasized financial materiality, which is legitimate when the purpose is to identify companies that will do well in a changing environment. However, when the purpose is to drive change (rather than benefit from change), ESG ratings should focus on impact materiality. An easy way to think about it: If the company's ESG score improves, does the world become a better place? If the answer is yes, the score may serve as a reasonable proxy for company impact. (Heeb *et al.*, 2022)

---

[2] It should be noted that the High Meadows' approach is at its root a stakeholder one: Its Sustainable Finance 3.0 relies on stakeholder views to make the case, but we believe it misses the following: (1) feedback loops regarding dynamic materiality; (2) holistic portfolio effects; and (3) lumping all stakeholders/society into one category. In terms of the last point, it might be more realistic to look at 'material' stakeholders by firm, industry, etc. These issues are discussed in the chapter.

The following is their conclusion as to whether ESG integration (one ESG method) affects the real economy: "maybe a little bit." Yet, even with the emergence of "impact materiality" (as discussed in the following) as a focus of "change," this approach appears to implicitly assume that portfolio long-term risk-adjusted values are separate from "change." An SIF or systems perspective argues that both are intimately connected. It is critical to connect "finance" to impact.

We think this is because these are still early days of focusing on impact materiality, by both analysts and more importantly by market actors who are otherwise focusing on ESG and financial materiality. From our perspective, the limitation of the sustainable finance 2.0 approach is that it remains focused on how firms individually perform solely in terms of stock returns or bond ratings. As we discuss in the following, this approach assumes a modern portfolio theory and a Fama–French factor approach to idiosyncratic risk mitigation along with an efficient frontier, even when it becomes an ESG-efficient frontier. While useful, we argue that this approach is too restricted: It is unable to confront the challenges of sustainability as it does not consider economic externalities, especially in the context of highly diversified portfolios. Additionally, it ignores the real-world connection between the financial system (e.g. ESG performance measured solely by equity values and based primarily on ratings and rankings by leading providers such as MSCI and Sustainalytics) and the larger socio-economic system.

This systemic approach has been rapidly developed since about 2015. The relation between impact, finance, and the larger socio-economic system is captured by the Impact Management Platform (2023, p. v) statement: "The economy's reliance on the viability and stability of environmental and social systems is demonstrated by … climate change [and by other factors that are the foundation] of social systems … upon which business and finance depend." The statement argues that a narrow financial approach focused on single entities is insufficient because "… it does not take into account the *contributions* that enterprises make to the accumulation of system-wide risk …."

Hart and Zingales (2017, pp. 3–5) consider an element of the relation between what they call "shareholder welfare" and market value. Their focus is primarily on firm-specific market value, although they do mention the problem of universal owners (without using that term). They also note that there is some, perhaps significant, overlap between stakeholders and shareholders. Stakeholder in this formulation as consumers, for example, or stakeholders impacted by various externalities. Their paper is important for its focus on externalities in relation to the social responsibility of firms, specifically as a critique of Friedman (1970) for ignoring externality effects.

3. Confusion #2: Materiality and Impacts on Emerging Standards

Emerging standards are moving from relying (solely or primarily) on ratings and rankings to a more empirically based focus on "impacts," although that term, too, is used in many different and often contradictory ways.

The CFA Institute, the Principles for Responsible Investment (PRI), and the Institute for Global Sustainable Investment Alliance (CFA Institute, 2023) (hereafter, CFA) issued a white paper focusing on five areas of responsible (for our purposes, ESG) investment: screening, ESG integration, thematic investing, stewardship, and impact investing. We briefly focus only on a few points central to this chapter: risk-adjusted returns; impact investing; and stewardship.

A core point the white paper makes is that most ESG analyses focuses on risk-adjusted returns, which is quite different from a single focus, for example, on equity prices or bond prices and ratings, on which to judge a firm's ESG performance. This, too, is significantly different from discounted cash flow (DCF), advocated, for example, by Edmans (2022 and 2023). The distinction is that different investors often have very different definitions of risk, ways of measuring it, and investment time horizons. Aside from time horizons, risk metrics are not explicitly considered in DCF analysis.[3] Moreover, even when DCF analysis incorporates ESG performance by adjusting the discount rate, it could lead to double counting if a company's higher (lower) risk attributable to a low (high) ESG performance is widely known in the market and already incorporated in the discount rate through a higher (lower) company beta (Bos, 2014).

The CFA paper discusses impact investing which we deal with in the following section. Most important in our view is the CFA's discussion of

---

[3]The factors in DCF are (estimated) cash flow over *x* periods of time and the discount rate, which is often a company's weighted cost of capital.

stewardship, which is also the most detailed of the five elements of ESG that the paper discusses.

Our purpose in this chapter is not to survey or analyze these ESG conceptual frames, methodologies, or data inputs as this ground has been well covered by others. Rather, we suggest that an entirely different approach is needed, elements of which are, in fact, emerging among investors, regulators, lawmakers, and analysts. These concerns are often embedded in the stewardship concept.

What we suggest is twofold: First, without explicitly incorporating the impacts of externalities, any ESG analysis falls short both economically and financially. Second, even when externalities are taken into account and valued (a difficult and inexact task by its nature), the financial models that most of these data are "plugged into" fall short. Thus, there is a data and model problem.

We think the reason is straightforward: the models are based on modern portfolio theory (MPT) which, in a partial equilibrium framework, excludes the often-complex feedback loops between individual firm (and/or industry and/or sector) behavior and systemic risk. MPT assumes that non-diversifiable risk (e.g. global warming or some market macro crises) is unaffected by investments in the firms which create externalities. This is despite the findings that 75–90% of variations on return are explained by the market as a whole by beta (Ibbotson, 2010, pp. 18–20).

In turn, as all large and most small and medium-sized investors hold diversified portfolios (à la MPT), they are inherently exposed to and unwittingly to contribute to systemic effects of their investments. Specifically, externalities affect various E and S factors, in addition to financial risk factors (too often excluded in most ESG analyses). Furthermore, as portfolio companies contribute to (negatively or positively) systemic (and sub-system) risk/opportunity, such risk feeds back into portfolios, creating systematic (portfolio-wide) risks/opportunities (TIIP, 2023, pp. 15–21).

Indeed, the impact of the partial equilibrium framework becomes increasingly significant when externalities are taken into account. As highlighted by Edmans (2023), a company has the ability to improve its ES metrics at the expense of other firms, resulting in a net effect on aggregate externalities that is either neutral or negative. This observation also applies to investors, as many asset managers express their commitment to decarbonize their portfolios or align them with net-zero objectives. However, it is important to recognize that decarbonizing one's portfolio does not automatically lead to the broader decarbonization of society or indeed of other investors' portfolios. For example, the sale of shares in an energy company depends on another investor acquiring those shares, highlighting the complex dynamics and limitations involved in the pursuit of sustainable financial practices. It should be evident that in these circumstances there is an overlap of (self) interests between holders of large portfolios (and some smaller ones as well) and "society," or significant specific stakeholders.

We thus suggest that to move beyond the current muddled state of ESG, it is imperative to develop what we call a SIF perspective.[4] This begins with a focus on externalities in the context of highly diversified, universal owner-type portfolios.[5] It involves quantifying and assessing how externalities impact financial return, which is linked to the "real" non-financial economy.

The focus on the impact of externalities on the portfolio of universal owners has at least two levels. Taking a cue from climate change analysis, Scope 1 is the direct and financial impact of externalities. Scope 2 is the indirect but in many cases no less important impact on (longer-term) financial performance, e.g. on supply chains and social, natural, and human capital formation (and maintenance). Taken together, these constitute a socio-economic and financial focus on capital formation in the context of externalities over the long term.

4. SIF, "System Investing," and Stakeholders/ Stockowners

The concept of sustainability that we adopt in this chapter posits sustainability as the pathway to sustainable development, defined by the 1987

---

[4]Similar approaches use a variety of terms, e.g. system-level investing (TIIP); impact stewardship (UK); and Active ownership 2.0 (Principles for Responsible Investment). We think SIF focuses meaning and attention on finance in relation to impact by naming them specifically.

[5]A universal owner has broadly diversified holdings (e.g. equities, debt instruments, and private equity) such that to a large degree they represent a cross section of these asset markets. Universal owners have come to dominate almost all developed market economies and many middle- and low-income markets as well. Estimates of market dominance vary among analysts, but all agree that they own in a range of 70–80% of assets. See Amel-Zadeh *et al.* (2022) for a low estimate based on their analysis of blockholders (vs. universal and common owners).

U.N. Bruntland Report as follows: "Meeting the needs of the present without compromising the ability of future generations to meet their own needs" (U.N.). Although this is the explicit and sometimes implicit goal of ESG investors, the implications of sustainability are far too often overlooked, as most ESG investing focuses on a firm-by-firm evaluation of E, S, and G factors. Sustainability inherently demands both a firm (or industry or sector) evaluation and a systems approach looking at how individual firms, industries, and sectors contribute to systems effects, and in turn how the system affects feedback. One must trace and calculate externality impacts as well as model how these are valued (including on a net present value basis) in financial terms. That is the "S" and "I" in *SIF*. While the term "systems investing" (and sometimes stewardship) is increasingly used to capture these issues, our approach to systems emphasizes the role of finance, albeit necessitating a broader view of what finance (and accounting) must become (See TIFF on system investing).

The SIF perspective focuses on the financial implications of externalities. Indeed, there are a multitude of studies focused on externality effects, both in the S and E of ESG. There are some studies that attempt to value (in financial and economic terms) externality impacts (see, for example, Impact Weighted Accounts; Serafeim and Trinh (2020)). But, to our knowledge, there are only selected case studies that look at these externality effects from the angle of whole portfolio impacts, which has been called "systems materiality" by one observer.[6] This means that from a portfolio-wide perspective, the whole is greater than the sum of its (ESG externalities) parts.[7]

4.1. *Impact Investing is not SIF*

In the context of ESG investing focused on financial materiality (Sustainable Finance 2.0 in the High Meadows Institute's framework), and in the body of literature on the relationship between ESG and

---

[6]Private communication.

[7]It could be argued that this would result in "soft" data for financial accounting, but we suggest that it has always been an illusion that "hard" financial accounting does not include large elements of "soft" data, e.g. intangibles such as goodwill and valuation of human capital. It has been long noted that the growth of service and human capital-intensive economies makes financial valuation more difficult as intangibles are more difficult to value than tangible assets.

financial performance. In this regard ESG often *adopts* a Fama-French model (see, for example, Bennani *et al.* (2018), Khan *et al.* 2016). In sum, ESG investing has uses a mean-variance perspective (a la Fama-French) based on outside-in effects of ESG factors as they affect financial performance. The inclusion of ESG factors in investment decisions has transformed the sustainability component from a distinct variable to an integral part, resulting in an "ESG-adjusted mean–variance" framework.

Indeed, Rober Eccles and Daniel Crowley wrote the following: "Modern portfolio theory allows investors to maximize expected return for a given level of risk. Of course, portfolio theory continues to evolve. Forty years ago, most business schools taught that the best way to manage portfolio risk is through diversification among equities with different return profiles (i.e. their covariance). Before long, it was observed that by adding other asset classes, the risk associated with a particular level of return could be reduced. Asset allocation models are growing ever more sophisticated, and many now include an ESG overlay. As the world becomes increasingly complicated, fiduciaries are compelled to adopt new analytic techniques. These developments have nothing to do with public policy debates. Instead, they pertain to investor need for material information about their investments" (Eccles & Crowley, 2022).

The term "Impact" is often associated with "impact investing," that is, whether at market or below market rates of return (however calculated), an investment intended to have a very specific "impact" that is explicitly focused on a defined purpose and outcome. We, however, use the term "impact" quite differently: *impact investing is not impact finance.*

Indeed, it should be obvious that *all* finance has impact, for good or ill depending on one's viewpoint and standards. In adding sustainability to impact finance (SIF), there are at least two elements. The first important but limited step is to develop (based on MPT) an impact/externality-adjusted mean–variance perspective (EAMVP) to the financial performance of a portfolio, which considers the financial impact of externalities. By adjusted, we mean consideration of relevant E, S, or G factors, which are not just financially "material" but are also material because of their impact (see below).

In this regard, Farzamfar *et al.* (2022) show that firms, under pressure to enhance environmental performance, concurrently experience a decline in social status, evidenced by an elevated frequency of compliance violations in areas such as employment, healthcare, workplace safety, and consumer protection. The study reveals a consistent trend where companies, on average, offset a complete elimination of environmental penalties with a 23% increase in social violations. Moreover, the propensity to reduce social responsibility is larger when firms operate in high-emission industries (for which emission reduction is therefore financially material).

But, it should not stop there as EAMVP, like its underlying MPT frame, accounts for neither a portfolio's own systemic effects nor feedback loops (Lukomnik & Hawley, 2021). Indeed, within the confines of most MPT models, while systemic risk can affect portfolios, portfolios or their component parts do not affect systemic and other risk (in MPT terms, the focus is on idiosyncratic risk leading to an efficient frontier). Alternatively, SIF analysis goes beyond EAMVP by also accounting for the financial impact of externalities created by a specific firm (sector/industry), an inside-out approach, complementing an outside-in analysis.

While an outside-in MPT approach leads to a firm-by-firm portfolio analysis, which does not consider externalities created by the firm (sector or industry), an inside-out approach recognizes the elementary yet critical and well-established economic analysis of externality effects, that is, impacts, both pecuniary and non-pecuniary. Traditional finance models entirely ignore this long-established economic insight, especially from a portfolio-wide, holistic perspective, that is, a universal owner viewpoint. From this angle, a proportion of externality impacts (direct and secondary) is internalized within the portfolio itself, meaning sub-optimal economic performance by the internalizing firm if the externality is negative. Sub-optimality of a firm, or more realistically of many firms and sectors, logically suggests that the market as a whole (beta) operates in economic terms sub-optimally. As a universal owner portfolio is a representation of the market, of beta, the portfolio performs sub-optimally. This has a host of important implications as discussed at the end of this chapter (Lukomnik & Hawley, 2021, pp. 28–45).

In a systemic approach, the logic is elementary yet surprisingly far too often ignored. If one considers only an outside-in approach (that is, the impact), the "outside" comes primarily from other firms' externalities. Hypothetically and simplistically, if one owns a portfolio of only two firms, if firm A internalizes some proportion of a negative externality produced by firm B (outside in), it is operating sub-optimally. If the market or significant subset of it (a "reasonable investor") recognizes this impact, it is material. But, what should the owner of the two firm portfolios do if it cannot either hedge or sell?[8] At minimum, one should pressure firm B to document its externality so that firm A can know the extent of its internalization and attempt to value its damage. Additionally, the two firm portfolio owners can take other actions to attempt to get firm B to mitigate its negative externality through, for example, regulatory advocacy, public pressure campaigns, governance engagement, or a push, in this case for a Coaseian negotiation based on tort liability law, if other conditions are satisfied (i.e. no or very low transaction costs) (Coase, 1960).

Thus, both outside-in and inside out analyses are essential for one to understand how a portfolio in the long run (but also in the medium and in some cases the short run) will behave financially. This is what we mean by "impact finance." It is two-sided: dynamic and systemic, both contributing to systems effects (risks or de-risking) and absorbing externalities. It is dynamic because it changes over time.

There is thus a need for inside-out and outside-in accounting (e.g. Serafeim and Trinh (2020). This still-developing approach is the logical outgrowth of both cost and financial accounting. It focuses on the direct impact (think of it as the pecuniary impact) of externalities created by portfolio companies. Yet, there are also indirect and secondary impacts (non-pecuniary externalities). Externalities, of course, affect more than portfolio companies; that is, they impact non-companies, e.g. communities, the environment, and employees. In turn, these have both direct and often complex indirect effects as economic inputs on human, social, and natural capital. From a socio-economic point of view these factors are essential to current and especially future economic activities, and of course, all human activities. The European Union's formulation of double or dual materiality attempted to capture some elements of these points, as we discuss in the following. From our point of view, however, while dual materiality captures important elements of the relation between the financial and what is characterized as "stakeholders" (basically all of society), it is both incomplete and too general, hence somewhat misleading. For example, the World Benchmarking Alliance (2023, p. 16) list fully seventeen different stakeholders. The general use of the term "stakeholder" is too general making it difficult to understand outside of a specific context.

---

[8]This is typically the case for large, long-term diversified, often indexed or shadow-indexed investors who dominate the market.

5.　Materiality(ies)

Materiality is an established financial, accounting, and legal term, about which is there much debate, important jurisdictional differences, and, indeed like ESG, also much confusion in the use of the term. The OECD defines materiality from a very high and general level as follows:

> Material information can be defined as information whose omission or misstatement can reasonably be expected to influence an investor's assessment of a company's value. This would typically include the value, timing and certainty of a company's future cash flows. Material information can also be defined as information that a reasonable investor would consider important in making an investment or voting decision. (OECD, 2023, p. 27)

Note the implicit assumption: This is an outside-in perspective. The term "reasonable investor" originates from a U.S. Supreme Court decision in 1976, reaffirmed in 1999, that is based on the long-standing U.S. "reasonable person" standard dating back to the 1933 Securities Act. (The "reasonable investor" standard for defining and judging "materiality" is widely used in other jurisdictions (e.g. EU, U.K., and Canada) and among various standard setters (e.g. ISSB and GRI)[9] (Katz & McIntosh, 2021). While in the U.S. the "reasonable investor" is black-letter law, as with all black-letter laws, specific meanings and contexts are contested and change over time. From our perspective, there are two key elements. The first is that markets have always had and must have different views on what is "reasonable" or else buy-and-sell functions would decline and, *reductio absurdum,* cease entirely. Thus, what may be material for one investor's need (e.g. long-term E factors) would for another be less important or not important (e.g. short-term traders or hedge funds). The second element is more important. The growth in almost all markets of large, diversified, universal owner-type investors has come to dominate markets. These highly diversified investors are changing the basis for what is "reasonable" by taking into account the impact of externalities on their

---

[9]Despite widespread use, there is some criticism of the legal standard of "reasonable investor(s)" in its relation to materiality in U.S. legal commentary. See, for example, Oesterle (2011) and Lin (2015).

portfolio. In doing so they have also expanded the definition of what is material to their portfolios.

Thus, structural changes in markets due to large, diversified investors have created a demand for additional disclosure beyond what was previously seen as "financial." Indeed, what from a regulatory point of view is "financial" has itself been ever-changing. What has been labeled "non-financial" has often become "not yet financial or pre-financial" and then "financial" (that is, material even in a narrow sense) (See World Economic Forum (WEF), 2020, p. 14). For example, prior to the turn of the last century, corporate governance was not seen as "material," and was neither (accurately) reported on nor reported on at all. Regulatory action (e.g. Sarbanes-Oxley in the U.S.) was a response to governance demands by (many) investors and others. Thus, neither governance nor more recently carbon disclosure is an "extra" or "non-" financial factor, but both have become necessary inputs into the financial analysis of a firm and a portfolio (International Auditing and Assurance Standards Board (IAASB), 2011). A parallel response in the U.S. (and prior to that in the EU and other jurisdictions) to governance regulation is the S.E.C.'s proposed enhancement to and standardization of carbon disclosure as material (United States Security and Exchange Commission (USSEC), 2022).

In the sustainability reporting space, the concept of materiality is far more complex given the multiple stakeholders — sometimes with conflicting interests — who can be interested in the information of a company's sustainability report, as we discuss in the following. Current approaches to ESG materiality within various frameworks and guidance fit into the following two perspectives. The simple business case perspective (outside-in) posits that an ESG issue is considered material when it exerts a substantial (either positive or negative) influence on the financial performance of the company. Conversely, the societal impact perspective (inside-out) contends that a subject is deemed material when it holds significance for both society and the company, with the latter significantly affecting this subject.

The two perspectives are reflected in the differences between two major non-governmental standard-setting organizations: the Global Reporting Initiative (GRI) and the International Sustainability Standard Board (ISSB) and its parent organization, the International Financial Reporting Standards (IFRS). In general, the GRI gravitates to an inside-out materiality view and defines as "material" "those topics that have a direct or indirect impact on an organization's ability to create, preserve or erode economic, environmental and social value for itself, its stakeholders and society at large" (GRI, 2011, p. 3). This definition has been recently revised to the following: "the organization prioritizes reporting on those topics that reflect its most significant impacts on the economy, environment, and people, including impacts on human rights" (GRI, 2020, p. 8). To date, the GRI has not developed a viewpoint on the relationship between the financial aspect and its impact on various stakeholders nor has it focused on the implications of structural changes in markets dominated by large, diversified, universal owner-type investors.

The ISSB has its origins in the U.S.-based Sustainability Accounting Standards Board (SASB) and has focused on an outside-in single financial materiality from the point of view of the individual firm. This is formulated by the ISSB in its S1 standard: "This Standard requires an entity to disclose information about all sustainability-related risks and opportunities that could reasonably be expected to affect the entity's cash flows, its access to finance or cost of capital over the short, medium or long term …. Sustainability-related risks and opportunities that could not reasonably be expected to affect an entity's prospects are outside the scope of this Standard." Its climate standard, S2, has similar language — as it is capital market focused (ISSB, 2023) (See ISSB, 2018 for a background to this language) — but it calls for disclosure on Scope 2 and 3 emissions, which are clearly impact focused. It is not clear how ISSB reconciles this implicit difficulty with its generic definitions and its focus in its S2 standard.

Until recently, with the introduction of the concept of "double materiality" by the EU Corporate Sustainability Reporting Directive (CSRD), the two approaches to materiality were considered to be competing. Double materiality recognizes the outside-in and inside-out natures of externalities, and in this regard moves beyond the generally accepted interpretation of U.S. (single) materiality. However, as noted, some interpretations of "single" materiality recognize the inside-out/outside-in importance of data disclosure even if this is implicit as in the 2023 S.E.C. carbon proposal.

The EU view is summed up nicely in the CSRD, which requires companies to disclose information "to the extent necessary for an understanding of the development, performance, position and impact of (the company's) activities." This means companies should disclose not only how sustainability issues may affect the company but also how the company affects society and the environment (European Commission, 2020, p. 3). In particular, the European Sustainability Reporting Standards (ESRS)[10] include a definition of these two materiality dimensions:

(1) "an impact perspective when it pertains to the undertaking's material actual or potential, positive or negative impacts on people or the environment over the short-, medium- and long-term. Impacts include those connected with the undertaking's own operations and upstream and downstream value chain, including through its products and services, as well as through its business relationships" (ESRS 1, paragraph 43).
(2) "a financial perspective if it triggers or could reasonably be expected to trigger material financial effects on the undertaking. This is the case when a sustainability matter generates or may generate risks or opportunities that have a material influence, or could reasonably be expected to have a material influence, on the undertaking's development, financial position, financial performance, cash flows, access to finance or cost of capital over the short-, medium- or long-term" (ESRS 1, paragraph 49). In this document, the terms "risks and opportunities" are used to identify the financial risks and opportunities that are in the scope of financial materiality.

The often-complex processes by which financial material changes are beyond the scope of this chapter. But, it is nevertheless important to note that one element of change comes from the development of social norms, which is considered right and wrong, acceptable or not acceptable. Such norm advocacy (the form it usually takes) also has an impact on regulatory and legislative rules and laws. From our perspective, while all norm changes may not be financially material at any given point (indeed the majority may never be), some will affect what is financially material. There is no clear demarcation between what is often called Values (norms) and value (financial) (Lukomnik & Hawley, 2021, pp. 62–62).

Stark (2023) took a different approach in her important presidential address to the American Finance Association, focusing on the confusion between what she called value and values, the former focusing on the pecuniary and the latter on the non-pecuniary. As discussed in the following, both approaches have not looked at, or looked at in any analytical

---

[10]Brief note on EFRAG and ESRS.

depth, the relation between values (social norms) and value: what in a different context Milton Friedman called the "rules of the game" (Friedman, 1970). The point (which Friedman, too, did not consider) is that rules (both legal and norm-based) change over time and place and these changes can and do lead to the dynamic nature of financial materiality (Stark, 2023, p. 1845).

This nature of useful and necessary investor information is ever-changing. This is nothing new. There is debate about whether the term "dynamic" or "emerging" materiality is necessary under the U.S. reasonable investor standard as reasonableness itself is considered dynamic by some, and therefore materiality is as well (Katz & McIntosh, 2021). These legal and definitional debates aside, the important aspects are the content changes themselves. What is apparent is that ESG is moving from overwhelmingly using rating and ranking data to a focus on externalities and their impacts based on mandated, self-disclosed firm data along with reliable third-party data. Obviously, this can only occur with mandated standardization. Along with mandated disclosure will come mandated assurance functions.

Additionally, reflecting a view that materiality is dynamic, there is a limited if yet a highly abstract and ill-defined feedback mechanism between "society" (i.e. stakeholders) and financial materiality. This attempts to capture the "net yet financial" process as it may become directly financial (Lukomnik & Hawley, 2021, p. 70).[11]

For example, if a norm shifts about animal rights due to stakeholder activities and general societal belief changes, as in the U.K., these belief changes can provide feedback for risks and opportunities for various firms, a classic outside-in effect. This has also been called a Value-to-value shift, or a norms (Values) transmutation into financial functions (value) (Lukomnik & Hawley, 2021, pp. 62–63; Starks, 2023, 1840 et seq). These shifts typically occur along with regulatory and legislative actions, changing what Milton Friedman called "rules of the game" (Friedman, 1970). Stark does not address the question of whether in her view and analysis Values can morph into value. For her, there is a clear

---

[11] In the EU context, the dynamic characteristic of materiality is well incorporated in ESRS1: "(...) In general, the starting point is assumed to be the assessment of impact materiality, as a sustainability impact may become financially material when it translates or is likely to translate into financial effects in the short-, medium-, or long-term. (...)" ([Draft] ESRS2, 2.2 par. 47).

(and apparently not changing) divide between stakeholders (affected by externalities) and firms themselves, and by extension investors who hold assets in these firms. In this sense, the important question of the relation between some stakeholders and value creation or destruction is avoided.

What is missing in the EU and some other dual-materiality formulations is the impact that universal owners have on the financial system itself, as they typically incorporate some stakeholders (and sometimes stakeholders' Values) as investors. That is, these large, diversified investors represent citizens who invest for retirement, as savings for children's education, or to buy a house. These goals are clearly financial but organically tied to citizens' status as both "stakeholders" and investors (including beneficiaries of defined benefit pensions). We might call them "financial stakeholders" as they wear (at least) two hats. In short, what is too often presented as a demarcation line between financial and societal is in fact a porous membrane: It leaks both ways and there are numerous feedback loops. These feedback loops are often the core of the "becoming material" process. Ignore them at one's peril.

How both the GRI and ISSB do and do not conform to existing EU (and some other regions') disclosure regulations, as well as ongoing and emerging standards (e.g. in the U.S. regarding climate change disclosure at the S.E.C.), is beyond the scope of this chapter. However, what is clear is that mandated disclosure standards, as well as some substantive mandates, focus on inside-out and outside-in types of materiality, often using the term impact materiality. The discussions between GRI and ISSB (and others, especially regulators) about this are ongoing, adding to confusion about the definition and uses (and use cases) of "materiality."[12]

Despite their differences, what is striking about both the ISSB and GRI approaches is that both accept a divide between the financial and the larger, in the GRI's words, "… economy, environment and people for the

---

[12]On September 4, 2023, EFRAG and GRI published a joint statement on the high level of interoperability achieved between the ESRS and the GRI Standards. "(…) In keeping with the requirement formulated in the CSRD to adopt a double materiality approach and to take account of existing standards, the ESRS have adopted the same definition for impact materiality as GRI and have leveraged GRI's expertise. ESRS and GRI definitions, concepts and disclosures regarding impacts are therefore fully or, when full alignment was not possible due to the content of the CSRD mandate, closely aligned" (EFRAG-GRI Joint statement of interoperability, https://efrag.org/news/public-444/EFRAG-GRI-Joint-statement-of-interoperability-?AspxAutoDetectCookieSupport=1).

benefit of multiple stakeholders" (GRI, 2022, p. 2). An SIF approach closes this gap as it emphasizes a direct financial focus (in this regard, similar to ISSB/IFRS), but with an inside-out/outside-in analysis, which especially recognizes the importance of universal owner-type investors. An SIF focus thus also intersects with a GRI approach but is focused on externalities as financial factors, again going beyond idiosyncratic risk single-firm focus to a holistic portfolio approach as well. In effect, an SIF approach broadens the ISSB/IFRS view while focusing more narrowly than on a GRI perspective. In doing so, it transforms both. To put it slightly differently, SIF connects the dots missing in both approaches by expanding the financial (to better reflect what we see as real-world finance and where trends in finance and accounting are going). Driving this is a paradigm shift with the rise of highly diversified universal owners and with this shift comes the recognition that stakeholders may also have an influence on what becomes financial and material.

While a comprehensive survey of what different types of corporates and investors focus on regarding materialities is beyond the scope of this chapter, two surveys of large investors and corporates provide some indications that a stakeholder "dual materiality" (EU definition) orientation is emerging among practitioners. An S&P study of firms found that 54% were interested in material issues for "external shareholders," 52% had metrics for that purpose, and 71% were reporting on any form of materiality (S&P Global, 2023, pp. 19–20. See p. 4 for methodology). Of those corporates tracking external impacts, 43% were reporting publicly. As would be expected, there is significant variation by sector and by "material" issue.

A survey by Institutional Shareholder Services (ISS) of large investors (asset managers, asset owners, and others, in order of numbers surveyed) and corporates fills in the picture of emerging materialities' scopes. About 75% of investors responded that materiality assessments should include a company's "… expected impact on the environment and society … [and] the largest part of that group (44%) said that these impacts can be expected to impact the company's financial performance in the medium- to long-term …." Although there was a significant regional difference, about 90% of non-U.S. firms responded that E and S impacts should be reported, and 58% of U.S. firms stated that impacts should be reported as well (ISS, 2023, p. 7).

Both the S&P and ISS surveys did not ask or discuss attempts to value either the external impacts or the value these impacts have on the firms themselves. This could be done, for example by using methods such as

Monte Carlo similations or scenario analysis. Valuing externalities remains a significant, relatively unexplored yet critical dimension of the next phase of ESG/sustainability. For example, Schoenmaker and Schramade (2023, pp. 408–424) provide both discussion and initial quantitative models of impact integrated into risk and the cost of capital analysis and models. Such models and analysis are a move away from ESG rating and ranking in order to confront the challenges of impact and externality integration into financial theories and models.

Additionally, Harris (2023: pp. 2–3, 5, 47) developed a model (with some empirical evidence) which attempts to provide "…a foundation for quantitative models that address topics like universal ownership and impact investing including defining the concepts of contribution multipliers, prices of impact, impact returns, and impact frontiers." (1) While Harris focuses on what he calls "non-pecuniary preferences," suggesting that dominant existing asset pricing models need to evolve, his treatment of externalities (and to a degree their internalization) is an important contribution to pricing externalities, even if his primary focus is on what he sees as non-pecuniary aspects of "impacts."

However, Stark (2023, pp. 1854–1855) appears to assume that it is values investors alone (e.g. non-pecuniary focused) who are most (or entirely) concerned about E and S externalities as they affect "communities and society," despite, for example, the survey data just discussed. Her discussion moves from a brief mention of externalities into whether firms individually have significant tail risk if they create negative externalities, concluding that some research suggests that they do, whether or not the market at a particular moment price these in (e.g. in bond ratings and prices). This approach while useful is nevertheless static, missing the multiple effects that Values may have on value; although Stark recognized reputational and other forms of risk, this is not integrated into nor developed in her conceptual framework.

6. Conclusion

As a SIF approach begins to replace older schools of ESG thought (based on ratings and rankings), logically, this will lead to a holistic portfolio framework contrasted against a firm/sector/industry approach, as in an MPT idiosyncratic risk framework. A SIF perspective accounts for (and must develop calculation methods for) two-sided externality effects, the "impact" of finance: inside-out and outside-in. This quantification of these externality impacts remains an important challenge going forward. From this perspective, we suggest that "impact finance" brings us back to the original and core meaning of sustainability yet viewed from a financial return perspective that we have called SIF.[13]

In this regard, both inside-out and outside-in externality effects imply that some proportion of externalities impact a single portfolio while these effects also (by definition) affect other portfolios. That is, externalities have firm- as well as portfolio-specific effects in addition to beta (whole-market) effects. As highly diversified portfolios tend to be representative of the market, they are beta portfolios, subject more to the performance of the whole market rather than to the sum of its components as analyzed by MPT or by EAMVP.

The Principles for Responsible Investment formulation captures these ideas well in "Active Ownership 2.0" defined as follows:

> Systemic issues require a deliberate focus on and prioritization of out-comes at the economy or society-wide scale. This means stewardship that is less focused on the risks and returns of individual holdings, and more on addressing systemic or "beta" issues such as climate change and corruption. It means prioritizing the long-term, absolute returns for universal owners, including real-term financial and welfare outcomes for beneficiaries more broadly. (PRI, n.d., 11)

References

Amel-Zaheh, A., Kasperk, F., & Schmalz, M. (2022, September). Marvricks, Universal and Common owners — The largest shareholders of U.S. public firms. CESIFO working papers. Retrieved from https://papers.ssrn.com/sol3/papers.cfm?abstract_id=4059513.

Bennani, L., Le Guenedal, T., Lepetit, F., Ly, L., Mortier, V., Roncalli, T., & Sekine, T. (2018). How ESG investing has impacted the asset pricing in the equity market. Retrieved from https://ssrn.com/abstract=3316862 or http://dx.doi.org/10.2139/ssrn.3316862.

---

[13] This formulation is different from the term "investing for sustainability impact" as used in Freshfields Bruckhaus Deringer (2021, 11), which suggests intentionally attempting investments yielding sustainability results.

Florian Berg, Julian F. Koelbel, Anna Pavlova & Roberto Rigobon. https://www.nber.org/people/anna_pavlova

Berg, F., Heeb, F., & Koelbel, J. F. (2023b, March 31). The economic impact of ESG ratings. Retrieved from https://papers.ssrn.com/sol3/papers.cfm? abstract_id=4088545 (Accessed December 14, 2023).

Berg, F., Koelbel, J. F., Pavola, A., & Rigobon, R. (2022). ESG confusion and stock returns: Tackling the problem of noise. Retrieved from https://www.nber.org/papers/w30562.

Berg, F., Lo, Andrew, W., Rigobon, R., Singh, M., & Zhang, R. (2023a). Quantifying the returns of ESG investing: An empirical analysis with six ESG metrics. Retrieved from https://papers.ssrn.com/sol3/papers.cfm? abstract_id=4367367.

Bos, J. (2014). Using ESG factors for equity valuation. *CFA Institute Magazine*, November/December. Retrieved from https://www.cfainstitute.org/-/media/ documents/article/cfa-magazine/2014/cfm-v25-n6-5.ashx (Accessed January 1, 2024).

CFA Institute. (2023, November). *Global Sustainable Investment Alliance, and Principles for Responsible Investment, Definitions for Responsible Investment Approaches.* Retrieved from https://www.gsi-alliance.org/wp-content/uploads/ 2023/10/ESG-Terminology-Report_Online.pdf (Accessed December 15, 2023).

Coase, R. (1960). The problem of social costs. *Journal of Law and Economics*, 3(1), 1–44.

Cremers, K. J., Martjin, R., Timothy, B., & Zambrana, R. (2023 July). The complex materiality of ESG ratings: Evidence from actively managed ESG funds. Retrieved from https://papers.ssrn.com/sol3/papers.cfm? abstract_id=4335688.

Eccles, R. &, Crowley, D. F. C. (2022, September 1). Turning down the heat on the ESG debate: Separating material risk disclosures from salient political issues. Harvard Law School Forum on Corporate Governance. Retrieved from https://corpgov.law.harvard.edu/2022/09/01/turning-down-the-heat-on-the-esg-debate-separating-material-risk-disclosures-from-salient-political-issues/ (Accessed December 30, 2023).

Edmans, A. (2022). The end of ESG. *Financial Management.* Retrieved from https://onlinelibrary.wiley.com/doi/full/10.1111/fima.12413 (Accessed November 22, 2023).

Edmans, A. (2023). Applying economics — Not gut feel — To ESG. *Financial Analyst Journal*, 79, 4.

European Commission. (2020, June 8). Consultation document, review of the non-financial reporting directive. Retrieved from https://ec.europa.eu/info/law/ better-regulation/have-your-say/initiatives/12129-Revision-of-Non-Financial-Reporting-Directive/public-consultation_en (Accessed December 21, 2023).

Farzamfar, A., Foroughi, P., & Ng, L. (2022). The hidden cost of going green: Evidence from firm-level violations. Retrieved from https://ssrn.com/ abstract=4081186.

Freshfields Bruckhaus Deringer. (2021). *A Legal Framework for Impact: Sustainability Impact in Investor Decision Making.* Retrieved from https://www.unepfi.org/industries/investment/a-legal-framework-for-impact-sustainability-impact-in-investor-decision-making/ (Accessed December 15, 2023).

Friedman, M. (1970). The social responsibility of business is to increase profits. Retrieved from https://www.nytimes.com/1970/09/13/archives/a-friedman-doctrine-the-social-responsibility-of-business-is-to.html (Accessed December 12, 2023).

GRI. (2011). *Technical Protocol: Applying the Report Content Principles.* Amsterdam: GRI. Retrieved from https://www.plateformeco2.ch/portal/documents/10279/17373/GRI_Technical+Protocol.pdf/0e1294be-ce1b-4c31-9943-4904c06240fd (Accessed January 1, 2024).

GRI. (2020, June). GRI universal standards: GRI 101, GRI 102, and GRI 103 — Exposure draft. Retrieved from https://www.globalreporting.org/standards/media/2605/universal-exposure-draft.pdf (Accessed January 1, 2024).

GRI. (2022, February 22). The materiality madness: Why definitions matter. *The GRI Perspective.* Retrieved from https://www.globalreporting.org/media/r2oojx53/gri-perspective-the-materiality-madness.pdf (Accessed December 15, 2023).

Harris, J. (2023, November 9). Pricing investor impact. Retrieved from https://papers.ssrn.com/sol3/papers.cfm?abstract_id=4263206 (Accessed December 15, 2023).

Hart, O. & Zingales, L. (2017). Companies should maximize shareholder welfare not market value. *Journal of Law, Finance, and Accounting*, 2, 247–274.

Hawley, J. P. & Williams, A. T. (2001). *The Rise of Fiduciary Capitalism.* University of Pennsylvania Press, Philadelphia, PA.

Heeb, F., Kellers, A., & Kolbel, J. (2022). *Does ESG Integration Impact the Real Economy?* University of Zurich, Center for Sustainable Finance and Private Wealth. Retrieved from https://www.csp.uzh.ch/dam/jcr:ac4406e3-ae17-43c0-8fa1-f967cd5abacb/BAFU%20Report_DIGITAL_pages.pdf.

Henisz, W., Koller, T., & Nuttall, R. (2019). Five ways ESG creates value. *McKinsey Quarterly.* Retrieved from https://www.mckinsey.com/~/media/McKinsey/Business%20Functions/Strategy%20and%20Corporate%20Finance/Our%20Insights/Five%20ways%20that%20ESG%20creates%20value/Five-ways-that-ESG-creates-value.ashx (Accessed December 29, 2023).

High Meadows Institute. (2021). Sustainability in capital markets: ESG integration and impacts. Retrieved from https://www.highmeadowsinstitute.org/projects/future-of-capital-markets/.

Ibbotson, R. C. (2010). The importance of asset allocation. *The Financial Analysts Journal*, 66(2), 18–20.

Impact Management Platform. (2023, June). *The Imperative for Impact Management: Clarifying the Relationship between Impacts, System-wide Risk and Materiality.* (Accessed January 3, 2024).

Impact Weighted Accounts. Retrieved from https://www.hbs.edu/impact-weighted-accounts/Pages/research.aspx. (Accessed December 13, 2023).

Institutional Shareholder Services (ISS). (2023, October 31). *2023 ISS Global Benchmark Policy Survey.* Retrieved from https://www.issgovernance.com/file/policy/2023/2023-ISS-Benchmark-Survey-Summary.pdf (Accessed December 5, 2023).

International Auditing and Assurance Standards Board (IAASB). (2011). *The Evolving Nature of Financial Reporting: Disclosure and Its Audit Implications.* Retrieved from https://www.iaasb.org/publications/evolving-nature-financial-reporting-disclosure-and-its-audit-implications (Accessed December 13, 2023).

International Sustainability Standards Board (ISSB). (2023, March 22). ISSB delivers proposals that create comprehensive global baseline of sustainability disclosures. Retrieved from https://www.ifrs.org/news-and-events/news/2022/03/issb-delivers-proposals-that-create-comprehensive-global-baseline-of-sustainability-disclosures/.

International Sustainability Standards Board (ISSB). (2018, October). Definition of materiality: Amendments to IAS 1 and 8. Retrieved from https://www.ifrs.org/content/dam/ifrs/project/definition-of-materiality/definition-of-material-feedback-statement.pdf.

Johnston, I. (2023). Oil and gas firms face virtually no extra borrowing costs, S&P finds. *Financial Times*, November 6. Retrieved from https://www.ft.com/content/830e3ae6-0c3c-4da9-87e7-4ff72aa3e249 (Accessed December 2, 2023).

Katz, D. A. & McIntosh, L. (2021, May 1). *Corporate Governance Update: "Materiality" in America and Aboard.* Harvard Law School Forum on Corporate Governance. Retrieved from https://corpgov.law.harvard.edu/2021/05/01/corporate-governance-update-materiality-in-america-and-abroad/ (Accessed December 5, 2023).

LaBella, M. J., Sullivan, L., Russel, J., & Novikov, D. (2019, September). *The Devil is in the Details: The Divergence in ESG Data and Implication for Responsible Investing.*

Lin, T. C. W. (2015). Reasonable investor(s). *Boston University Law Review*, 95, 460–518.

Lukomnik, J. & Hawley, J. P. (2021). *Moving Beyond Modern Portfolio Theory.* Routledge, London and New York.

Oesterle, D. A. (2011). The overused and underdefined notion of 'materiality' in securities law. *University of Pennsylvania Journal of Business Law*, 14(1), 167–207.

Organization for Economic Cooperation and Development (OECD). (2023). *G20/OECD Principles of Corporate Governance*. Retrieved from https://www.oecd.org/publications/g20-oecd-principles-of-corporate-governance-2023-ed750b30-en.htm (Accessed December 24, 2023).

Principles for Responsible Investment (PRI). (n.d.). Active ownership 2.0: The evolution stewardship urgently needs. Retrieved from https://www.unpri.org/download?ac=9721.

S&P Global. (2023). *Annual Scoring & Methodology Review*. Retrieved from https://www.google.com/url?sa=t&rct=j&q=&esrc=s&source=web&cd=&ved=2ahUKEwjbxbL8mOiEAxUIGtAFHcMpB0QQFnoECBAQAQ&url=https%3A%2F%2Fportal.s1.spglobal.com%2Fsurvey%2Fdocuments%2FAnnual_Scoring_Methodology_2023.pdf&usg=AOvVaw2ZIfKlTQ4foIb3NdTzrFn0&opi=89978449 (Accessed December 17, 2023).

Schoenmaker, D. & Schramade, W. (2023). *Corporate Finance for Long-Term Value*. Springer. open access book, Retrieved from https://link.springer.com/book/10.1007/978-3-031-35009-2 (Accessed July 7, 2023).

Serafeim, G. & Trinh, K. (2020). A framework for product weighted accounts. Retrieved from https://www.hbs.edu/impact-weighted-accounts/Documents/Preliminary-Framework-for-Product-Impact-Weighted-Accounts.pdf.

Starks, L. T. (2023 August). Presidential address: Sustainable finance and ESG issues-value versus values. *The Journal of Finance*, LXXVIII (4), 1937–1872.

The Investment Integration Project (TIIP). (2021). In W. Burkhart & S. Lydenberg (eds.), *21th Century Investing: Redirecting Financial Straggles to Drive System Change*. Berrett-Koehler, Oakland CA.

The Investment Integration Project (TIIP). (2023). *(Re)Calibrating Feedback Loops*. Retrieved from https://tiiproject.com/wp-content/uploads/2023/12/12-6-23-ReCalibrating-Feedback-Loops-FINAL.pdf (Accessed November 29, 2023).

United Nations Sustainability. Retrieved from httpsi://www.un.org/en/academic-impact/sustainability#:~:text=In%201987%2C%20the%20United%20Nations,to%20meet%20their%20own%20needs (Accessed December 2, 2023).

United States Security and Exchange Commission (USSEC). (2022, March 21). *SEC Proposes Rule to Enhance and Standardize Climate-Related Disclosures for Investors*, Press Release. Retrieved from https://www.sec.gov/news/press-release/2022-46 (Accessed November 19, 2023).

World Benchmarking Alliance. (2023, September). *Corporate Accountability: Closing the Gap in Pursuit of Sustainable Development*. Retrieved from https://www.worldbenchmarkingalliance.org/research/white-paper-corporate-accountability/ (Accessed December 9, 2023).

World Economic Forum (WEF). (2020). *Measuring Stakeholder Capitalism: Toward Common Metrics and Consistent Reporting of Suitability Value Creation*. Retrieved from https://www.weforum.org/stakeholdercapitalism/ (Accessed November 26, 2023).

https://doi.org/10.1142/9789811297786_0002

Chapter 2

ESG Legislation, Regulation, and Legal Implications

Emma Elizabeth Antin Daschbach*
and Cynthia Hanawalt†

*Hinshaw & Culbertson LLP, New Orleans, USA

*†Sabin Center for Climate Change Law,
Columbia Law School, New York, USA*

Abstract

There are reams of legislative and regulatory frameworks in the United States (U.S.), Europe, and elsewhere addressing matters of environmental and social concern. But, in referring to Environmental, Social, and Governance (ESG) legal frameworks, the narrower sets require (or at least encourage) in-scope companies to either (i) make some disclosure about how those companies are addressing environmental or social issues or (ii) address how in-scope companies do that, including, for example, what terminology they use to signal where those companies stand on environmental or social issues. This chapter covers some of the most prominent examples of both sets of legal frameworks with discrete attention to those relevant to the financial sector. This chapter also covers some of the key tests on those frameworks and ESG more generally, including legislation aimed at prohibiting the use of ESG factors in the U.S.

29

There are reams of legislative and regulatory frameworks in the United States (U.S.), Europe, and elsewhere addressing matters of environmental and social concern. In fact, the challenge might be in identifying a legal regime that does not address one or both in some measure. But, in referring to Environmental, Social, and Governance (ESG) legal frameworks, the narrower sets do one of two things: The first set requires (or at least encourages) in-scope companies to make some disclosure about how those companies are addressing environmental or social issues. The second set addresses how in-scope companies do that, including, for example, what terminology they use to signal where those companies stand on environmental or social issues.

This section covers some of the most prominent examples of both sets of frameworks with discrete attention to those relevant to the financial sector. This includes frameworks already in place and others still pending as of the publication of this section. It bears emphasizing that there are a multitude of ESG frameworks beyond those noted here — frameworks in place, pending in other jurisdictions, and extending beyond those having singular relevance to the financial sector.

Overall, the body of ESG frameworks is evolving so quickly that any research should assume the information provided here is but a starting point for understanding those in place and what they require of companies generally or the financial sector especially. Note further that in an increasingly global market, frameworks can have extra-jurisdictional impact. In some instances, frameworks may require (either expressly or as a practical matter) that companies reach into their value and supply chains for disclosure data. They may also establish (again, either expressly or as a practical matter) an effective bar to market access in any given jurisdiction for any company that does not comply. Given that, it is advisable to consider frameworks beyond the bounds of a company's home jurisdiction.

1. United States

1.1. *Biden Administration's "Whole-of-Government" Approach*

Discussion of U.S. ESG legal frameworks relevant to the financial sector starts at the top — with the advent of the Biden Administration in 2021. At that juncture, ESG considerations (especially climate-related considerations) became a central component of federal policy in the U.S. On

May 20, 2021, President Biden issued his *Executive Order on Climate-Related Financial Risk*. The Executive Order acknowledged both the physical risks presented by the "intensifying impacts of climate change" and the transition risks presented by the "global shift away from carbon-intensive energy sources and industrial process." It warned that "[t]he failure of financial institutions to appropriately and adequately account for and measure these physical and transition risks threatens the competitiveness of U.S. companies and markets, the life savings and pensions of U.S. workers and families, and the ability of U.S. financial institutions to serve communities."

Against that backdrop, the Executive Order directed arms of the federal government to take enumerated steps toward mitigating climate-related financial risk. As summarized by the Fact Sheet distributed at the White House Briefing on the Executive Order, the aim was to accomplish five overarching objectives, with concrete action items for each:

Develop a Whole-of-Government Approach to Mitigating Climate-Related Financial Risk: The Executive Order requires the National Climate Advisor and the Director of the National Economic Council to develop a comprehensive government-wide climate risk strategy to identify and disclose climate-related financial risk to government programs, assets, and liabilities.

Encourage Financial Regulators to Assess Climate-Related Financial Risk: The Executive Order encourages the Treasury Secretary to work with Council members to assess climate-related financial risk to the stability of the federal government and the stability of the U.S. financial system. Additionally, the Treasury Secretary should work with member agencies to consider issuing a report on recommended actions to reduce risks to financial stability.

Bolster the Resilience of Life Savings and Pensions: The Executive Order directs the Labor Secretary to consider suspending, revising, or rescinding any rules from the prior administration that would have barred investment firms from considering ESG factors, including climate-related risks, in their investment decisions related to workers' pensions.

Modernize Federal Lending, Underwriting, and Procurement: The Executive Order directs the development of recommendations for improving how federal financial management and reporting can incorporate climate-related financial risk, especially as that risk relates to federal lending programs and major federal suppliers.

Reduce the Risk of Climate Change to the Federal Budget: The Executive Order directs that the federal government develop and publish annually an assessment of its climate-related fiscal risk exposure. It also directs the Office of Management and Budget to reduce the federal government's exposure through the formulation of the President's Budget and oversight of budget execution.

Following President Biden's Executive Order, federal regulators followed suit, resulting in guidelines and rules addressing climate-related financial risk and other ESG considerations.

1.2. *OCC, FDIC, and Federal Reserve Guidelines for Climate-Related Financial Risk*

Federal banking regulators led the U.S. federal government's approach to ESG considerations (and, again, climate risk in particular) over the course of 2021 and 2022 with the release of principles addressing climate-related financial risk management for large financial institutions. Those regulators include the Office of the Comptroller of the Currency (OCC) (*Principles for Climate-Related Financial Risk Management for Large Banks*, October 24, 2023), the Federal Deposit Insurance Corporation (FDIC) (*Statement of Principles for Climate-Related Financial Risk Management for Large Financial Institutions*, October 24, 2023), and the Federal Reserve (*Principles for Climate-Related Financial Risk Management for Large Financial Institutions*, October 24, 2023).

The OCC described the intent behind the set of principles as follows:

The Office of the Comptroller of the Currency…today announced draft principles designed to support the identification and management of climate-related financial risks by banks with more than $100 billion in total consolidated assets.

All banks, regardless of size, may have material exposures to climate-related financial risks. These principles are targeted, however, at the largest banks, those with over $100 billion in total consolidated assets.

The principles are intended to support banks' efforts to focus on key aspects of climate-related financial risk management ... [and] provide a high-level framework for climate-related financial risk management consistent with existing OCC rules and guidance.

The OCC went on to outline and explain the kinds of risks it sought to address:

Weaknesses in how banks identify, measure, monitor, and control the potential physical and transition risks associated with a changing climate could adversely affect banks' safety and soundness. Banks are likely to be affected by both the physical risks and transition risks associated with climate change (referred to in the principles as climate-related financial risks). Physical risks refer to the harm to people and property arising from acute, climate-related events, such as hurricanes, wildfires, floods, and heatwaves, and chronic shifts in climate, including higher average temperatures, changes in precipitation patterns, sea level rise, and ocean acidification. Transition risks refer to stresses to certain banks or sectors arising from the shifts in policy, consumer and business sentiment, or technologies associated with the changes necessary to limit climate change. While many banks already consider these risks, the principles support banks' efforts to focus on key aspects of climate-related financial risk management, allowing bank boards of directors and management to identify risks and develop and implement appropriate strategies to mitigate those risks.

The FDIC's stated basis for, and description of, its set of proposed principles echoed that of the OCC. And, the Federal Reserve's set of principles, in turn, were self-described as "substantially similar" to those of the OCC and FDIC.

Overall, these principles align with the Task Force on Climate-Related Financial Disclosures (TCFD) and call for enhanced governance, strategic planning, risk management, and oversight, as well as data collection, measurement, and reporting with regard to climate-related financial risk. (For context, note that the TCFD was created by the Financial Stability Board in 2015 in an effort to improve and increase climate-related financial reporting, and it has since become a foundational framework referenced by many global regulators in their efforts to address climate risk.) The collected proposed principles were finalized in late 2023, and the finalized guidance was similar to the proposed versions. The Federal Reserve went a step further, launching a Pilot Climate Scenario Analysis Exercise and beginning work with six large U.S. banks to measure climate-related financial risks. Taken together, the collected principles may signal a direction for future financial regulator inquiry, supervision, and enforcement with regard to climate-related risk and are, thus, a responsible starting point for beginning compliance efforts.

1.3. *The Securities and Exchange Commission on ESG-Related Topics*

The U.S. Securities and Exchange Commission (SEC) has taken the most significant steps of any federal agency toward addressing ESG and implementing related legal frameworks. Some of those steps predate the Biden Administration's sweeping Executive Order and the directives therein.

Human Capital Disclosures: In August 2020, the SEC introduced amendments to its disclosure rules requiring registered companies to disclose "a description of the registrant's human capital resources to the extent such disclosures would be material to an understanding of the registrant's business." As per the SEC's summary of the amendments, the aim was to "modernize the description of business, legal proceedings, and risk factor disclosures that registrants are required to make pursuant to Regulation S-K … to account for developments since [the underlying rules'] adoption or last revision, to improve disclosure for investors, and to simplify compliance for registrants." Subject to a noted materiality test, the amendments require registered companies to disclose "the number of persons employed by the registrant," "a description of the registrant's capital resources," as well as "a description of any human capital measures or objectives that the registrant focuses on in managing the business," including, for example, "measures or objectives that address the attraction, development, and retention of personnel."

Approval of Nasdaq Board Diversity Rule: In August 2021, the SEC approved a board diversity rule proposed by the Nasdaq Stock Market. As per that rule, any Nasdaq-listed company is required to either have or explain why it does not have at least two members of its board of directors who are diverse, including at least one director who self-identifies as female and at least one director who self-identifies as an underrepresented minority or LGBTQ+. In support of the rule, the SEC indicated the rule would make "consistent and comparable statistics" regarding board diversity widely available to investors and that the rule would provide increased transparency on the topic — regardless of any given investor's ultimate view on the topic as those views may vary. In considering the reach of this rule, note that as of the publication of this section at least 5,000 companies were listed and traded on the Nasdaq on a daily basis. And, in terms of market capitalization shares traded, the Nasdaq ranked second only to the New York Stock Exchange.

GHG Emissions and Climate-Related Disclosures: As of the publication of this section, the most notable development from the SEC on ESG was its proposed rules regarding greenhouse gas (GHG) emissions and climate-related risk disclosures and the finalization of the rules in March 2024. Released in 2022, the SEC's proposal would have required publicly traded companies and other companies with at least $700 million worth of shares in the hands of public investors to make certain specified emissions and climate-related disclosures. Specifically, the proposed rules would have required these companies to disclose their direct GHG gas emissions ("Scope 1"), their GHG emissions related to the energy and electricity they purchase ("Scope 2"), and GHG emissions across their upstream and downstream value chain ("Scope 3"). Scope 3 upstream activities included purchased goods and services, capital goods, waste generated from operations, and employee business travel and commuting. Scope 3 downstream activities in turn, included the transportation and distribution of products, a third party's use of those products, and its investments. As such, the reach of Scope 3 would have been extensive. In addition to emissions disclosures, the proposed rules would have required companies to describe board oversight of climate-related risks, including the names of board members and committees responsible for climate oversight, the process by which the board is informed about climate risks, and the frequency of discussion about such matters. Additionally, boards would have to identify members with expertise in climate-related risks and describe the nature of their expertise.

The SEC's proposal provoked intense reactions upon release, including both significant support and fierce criticism. From the outset, legal challenges were anticipated, including legal challenges as to whether the proposed rules go beyond the SEC's rulemaking authority and/or whether they might infringe on free speech protections to the extent that their disclosure requirements could amount to "compelled speech" — a recurring contention made by ESG opponents as discussed in more detail later in this section. Much of the most intense criticism focused on the Scope 3 requirement. As intimated, Scope 3 reaches a wide range of indirect emissions sources, and some contended that any mandate requiring capture of those data — much less accurate capture of those data — would be unworkable and unduly burdensome. Opposition to the Scope 3 provisions of the SEC's proposed rules originated even from some of those advocating for the rules overall.

As noted, in March 2024, nearly two years since its initial proposal, the SEC finalized its rules. The final rules include significant revisions from the 2022 proposal. Most notably, Scope 3 emissions disclosure requirements were removed from the rules; Scope 1 and 2 emissions disclosures are required only if material; and smaller reporting companies, emerging growth companies, and non-accelerated filers are exempt entirely. The final rules also eliminated the requirement to describe board members' climate expertise. As of the publication of this chapter, the SEC's final rules are the subject of litigation consolidated in the United States Court of Appeals for the Eighth Circuit.

Names Rule: In September 2023, the SEC finalized amendments to "enhance and modernize" the Investment Company Act "Names Rule." The SEC's Press Release announcing the amendments summarized them as follows:

> The Names Rule currently requires registered investment companies whose names suggest a focus in a particular type of investment (among other areas) to adopt a policy to invest at least 80 percent of the value of their assets in those investments (an "80 percent investment policy"). The proposed amendments would enhance the rule's protections by requiring more funds to adopt an 80 percent investment policy. Specifically, the proposed amendments would extend the requirement to any fund name with terms suggesting that the fund focuses in investments that have (or whose issuers have) particular characteristics. This would include fund names with terms such as "growth" or "value" or terms indicating that the fund's investment decisions

incorporate one or more environmental, social, or governance factors. The amendments also would limit temporary departures from the 80 percent investment requirement and clarify the rule's treatment of derivative investments.

While somewhat limited in their scope, the amendments are noteworthy even beyond their immediate application as they may signal regulator attention to financial products other than investment funds, including other sustainability-linked products emerging in financial markets.

Climate and ESG Task Force: Finally, note the SEC's institution of its Climate and ESG Task Force in the Division of Enforcement in 2021. As described by the SEC, "Consistent with increasing investor focus and reliance on climate and ESG-related disclosure and investment, the Climate and ESG Task Force will develop initiatives to proactively identify ESG-related misconduct." This section does not address activity by the Task Force but does counsel attention to its enforcement actions for insight into SEC's scrutiny of ESG-related representations.

1.4. *A Note on Carbon Offsets*

The U.S. Commodity Futures Trading Commission has also tuned into ESG representations, establishing its Environmental Fraud Task Force aimed at deceptive practices in voluntary carbon markets. As with the SEC's Climate and ESG Task Force, this section will not address activity by the Environmental Fraud Task Force but recommends attention to its activity for insights into how it might address claims based on carbon emissions offsets.

Relatedly, note the update by the Federal Trade Commission (FTC) to its guidelines for Use of Environmental Marketing Claims. Often referred to as the "Green Guides," these strive to prevent unfair or deceptive marketing, applying to "claims about the environmental attributes of a product, package, or service" (16 C.F.R. §260.1(c)). They have been the subject of attention since December 2022, when the FTC announced that it was seeking public comment on updates. The guides might well extend to representations regarding "carbon-neutral" or "net-zero" characteristics, including those based on carbon emissions offsets and, as such, also warrant attention.

1.5. *Emerging Frameworks at the State Level*

The U.S. federal government has not been alone in its attention to ESG and the implementation of ESG frameworks. There have also been significant developments at the state level. This section addresses the frontrunners as of writing this section: California and New York.

1.5.1. *California's recent laws on GHG emissions and climate-related disclosures*

In the midst of the wait and debate around the SEC proposal, California forged ahead with its own emissions and climate-related disclosure rules in 2023. Most notably, California did so with a Scope 3 requirement included in its emissions rule and without a materiality threshold. As of the publication of this section, two rules have now been approved in California — California's Senate Bill 253 (SB 253) and Senate Bill 261 (SB 261) — both signed by California Governor Gavin Newsom in the fall of 2023, and known together as the California Climate Accountability Package.

SB 253 addresses emissions. Upon signing the bill into law, Governor Newsom expressed concerns about the implementation deadlines for the law. But, as passed, the law directed the California Air Resources Board to issue regulations mandating GHG disclosures by the end of 2024, with reporting requirements to kick in later in 2026. Those disclosure requirements extend to anyone meeting the definition of a "reporting entity" under the law, which means the following: (1) a partnership, corporation, limited liability company, or other business entity formed under the laws of California, the laws of any other state of the U.S. or the District of Columbia, or under an act of the Congress of the U.S.; (2) with total annual revenues over $1 billion; and (3) that does business in California.

The law largely mirrors the proposed SEC rules. Scope 1 emissions are defined as "all direct GHG emissions that stem from sources that a reporting entity owns or directly controls, regardless of location, including, but not limited to, fuel combustion activities." Scope 2 emissions are defined as "indirect GHG emissions from consumed electricity, steam, heating, or cooling purchased or acquired by a reporting entity, regardless of location." And, Scope 3 emissions include "indirect upstream and downstream GHG emissions, other than scope two emissions, from sources that the reporting entity does not own or directly control," which may include "purchased goods and services, business travel, employee commutes, and process and use of sold products." Thus, as with the SEC's proposal, California's rule covers an extensive breadth of emissions sources. Also of note are the additional directives that SB253 outlines for the form and content of disclosures requiring that disclosures conform with the GHG Protocol developed by the World Resources Institute and the World Business Council for Sustainable Development, and requiring independent third-party assurances as to disclosures. Finally, failure to comply with SB 253's reporting requirements and timely filing of the required annual report could result in administrative penalties of up to $500,000 per reporting year. While it remains to be seen how SB 253 is applied, including how the threshold element of "does business in California" is interpreted, it is expected that SB 253 will cover a vast number of companies. Given the anticipated reach of California's emissions disclosure requirements, the implications of the rules are significant. California is an enormous market where most major companies operate and, thus, will qualify as reporting entities under the law. And, importantly, there is no distinction in SB 253 between private and publicly held businesses as is inherent in the SEC rules. Even with its $1 billion threshold requirement, at signing, SB 253 was expected to apply to approximately 5,000 companies.

SB 261 has a lower revenue threshold of $500,000. With that, at signing, it was expected to apply more broadly than SB 253 — to as many as 10,000 companies. And, again, Governor Newsom expressed concerns upon signing SB 261 regarding its implementation deadlines because, as passed, the law requires all 10,000 in-scope companies to deliver biennial climate risk reports to the California Air Resources Board starting January 1, 2026. The law defines "climate-related financial risk" as "material risk of harm to immediate and long-term financial outcomes due to physical and transition risks, including, but not limited to, risks to corporate operations, provision of goods and services, supply chains, employee health and safety, capital and financial investments, institutional investments, financial standing of loan recipients and borrowers, shareholder value, consumer demand, and financial markets and economic health." And, reports addressing these risks must be prepared in keeping with the TCFD, with administrative penalties for failure to comply of up to $50,000 per year.

As with the SEC's rules, implementation of California's new rules could be slowed by legal challenges. Opponents contend that the rules are preempted by federal law and that the rules violate the dormant commerce clause and the protections that doctrine affords against undue burdens on interstate commerce through extraterritorial regulation. However, California's ability to regulate out-of-state businesses was significantly strengthened when the U.S. Supreme Court found in 2023 in *National Pork Producers Council vs. Ross* that there was no commerce clause violation with regard to California's Proposition 12 addressing treatment of pigs for livestock so long as the law did not discriminate between in-state and out-of-state entities.

1.5.2. *California's recent law on carbon emissions offsets and climate-related claims*

In October 2023, Governor Newsom also signed into law Assembly Bill 1305 (AB 1305), known as the Voluntary Carbon Market Disclosures Act. The law imposes detailed annual disclosure requirements on companies participating in carbon emissions offset markets as well as companies making climate-related claims more generally. And, like SB 253 and SB 261, AB 1305 applies to both public and private companies. Section 44475 of AB 1305 outlines the disclosure requirements for any "entity that is marketing or selling voluntary carbon offsets within the state." Section 44475.1 outlines additional disclosures required if any "entity purchases or uses voluntary carbon offsets that makes claims regarding the achievement of net zero emissions, claims that the entity, related entity, or a product is "carbon neutral," or makes other claims implying the entity, related entity, or a product does not add net carbon dioxide or greenhouse gases to the climate or has made significant reductions to its carbon dioxide or GHG emissions." And, section 44475.2 outlines disclosures for any "entity that makes claims regarding the achievement of net zero emissions, claims that the entity, a related or affiliated entity, or a product is 'carbon neutral,' or makes other claims implying the entity, related or affiliated entity, or a product does not add net carbon dioxide or greenhouse gases … to the climate or has made significant reductions to its carbon dioxide or GHG emissions."

1.5.3. *New York's guidelines for climate-related financial risk and disclosure*

The New York Department of Financial Services issued guidance on managing climate crises specific to banks and insurance companies that aims to align with the principles issued by federal regulators as discussed previously. And, in addition to those guidelines, New York also proposed its own climate corporate accountability act requiring certain companies within the state to annually disclose Scope 1, 2, and 3 emissions, though as of yet no such law has been passed (Senate Bill S897A).

2. Key International Frameworks

2.1. *ESG Reporting Requirements in the European Union*

The Corporate Sustainability Reporting Directive (CSRD) is a relatively new reporting regime governing the European Union (EU), though many non-EU companies are required to comply as well, making the disclosure requirements relevant for major U.S. businesses with multinational operations. The European Parliament adopted the CSRD in November 2022, replacing the previous regulatory framework for ESG reporting in Europe, the Non-Financial Reporting Directive (NFRD), and in so doing, significantly expanded the scope of covered companies subject to reporting requirements in the EU, from 11,700 to an anticipated 49,000. The CSRD will apply to all large companies incorporated in an EU member state that meet certain financial and/or employee thresholds. They will meet these if they cross at least two of three size thresholds on a solitary or consolidated basis. The thresholds are (i) 250 employees, (ii) €20 million in assets, and/or (iii) €40 million in annual revenues. These values will be adjusted to reflect inflation. Non-EU parent companies of EU corporations that meet these thresholds, and controllers of EU branches with over €40 million in annual revenues, when the group collectively generates at least €150 million in annual revenues within the EU, must also comply with the CSRD. Further, issuers of EU-listed securities will be subject to CSRD regime requirements no matter where they are incorporated, including small and medium-sized companies. Current estimates suggest that over 3,000 U.S. businesses will have to comply with the CSRD. Compared to the California laws with respect to climate disclosure, as well as the U.S. SEC rules, the CSRD sets remarkably low size thresholds overall. Furthermore, these thresholds apply on a consolidated basis, meaning that turnover, asset, and employee figures must be added across the entity group (or EU sub-group, in the case of groups that are headquartered abroad) when determining the company's size for CSRD reporting purposes.

The CSRD will be phased in over five years and will require detailed information across a broad range of sustainability topics, including climate, nature, governance, working conditions, and diversity. Companies will have to report on their business strategy, targets and metrics, products and services, and business relationships up and down the value chain. In total, over 1,000 discrete data points are covered. The first phase of European Sustainability Reporting Standards (ESRS), which applies to companies subject to the CSRD, was issued in the summer of 2023. The ESRS provide a common reporting standard for sustainability metrics. There are twelve points in the ESRS, which cover the gamut of sustainability issues organized under four pillars: cross-cutting, environment, social, and governance. The ESRS will begin to come into force for select entities on January 1, 2024, with initial reports due in 2025 for the 2024 fiscal year. Sector-specific reporting standards will be released by mid-2024.

Under the Environmental Pillar with respect to climate, the disclosure requirements are generally focused on a company's policies related to climate change mitigation and adaptation, the company's energy consumption, disclosures of Scope 1, 2, and 3 emissions, GHG removal and mitigation projects, and internal carbon pricing. Companies will also have to disclose how climate-related risks and opportunities may have materially affected their financial performance, financial position, cash flows, as well as risks and opportunities, including those instances in which there is a significant risk of material adjustment to the carrying amounts of assets and liabilities within the next reporting period. Companies will need to reconcile their disclosures to financial statement line items if significant amounts of their assets, net revenues, and liabilities are impacted by climate risks. That said, the CSRD climate-related disclosures are subject to a materiality determination. Importantly, this means that Scope 1, 2, and 3 emissions data are only due if they are deemed material. However, the EU rules incorporate a "double materiality" principle (which looks at both ESG risks to the firm and the broader negative societal impacts). This stands in contrast to the U.S. approach, which is focused purely on "financial materiality" (that is, the ability of ESG risks to ultimately impact the issuers' financials). If a company concludes that climate change is not a material topic for its business (from either a financial or an impact perspective, in accordance with the EU's "double materiality" framework), and therefore does not report in accordance with that standard, it must instead provide a detailed explanation of the conclusions of its materiality assessment with regard to climate change. With respect to any auditing requirement, only limited assurance is required on all reported data initially. This will potentially scale up to reasonable assurance in the future, with the EU Commission set to evaluate this need by 2028.

The Sustainability Pillar focuses on the people associated with the enterprise, be they workers, consumers, or other stakeholders. For the "workers in the value chain" ESRS, the disclosure focuses on how to understand the enterprise's material impact on the value chain workers. This requires looking at working conditions, how employees are treated equally or unequally, and other worker-related rights such as child labor or adequate housing. In keeping with the double materiality standard, the disclosure focuses not only on the impact of the value chain workers on enterprise value but also the enterprise's impact on the value chain work force.

The Governance Pillar has only one ESRS: business conduct. The goal is to encourage transparent and sustainable business practices. Business conduct includes a variety of aspects of a company's behavior such as corporate culture, management of relationships with third parties, methods for avoiding corruption and bribery, the company's political engagement, and payment practices, including those payment practices to other, smaller enterprises covered by the CSRD.

The ESRS will begin to apply in 2024 when the CSRD comes into force. Large companies will have to comply with the CSRD in their annual reports for 2024, with smaller businesses reporting two years later. This means that the first reports will be available in 2025 for large EU-listed issuers, financial sector firms, and other "public interest entities" already in scope of the NFRD. The year 2026 will bring about the first reports for large (non-listed) EU companies and parents of large EU groups, and 2027 for EU-listed small and midsize enterprises (SMEs). Finally, non-EU parent companies with significant activity in the EU will be required to report for financial years on or after January 1, 2028, meaning that the final initial round of reports for covered entities will be due in 2029. For the first three years, the application of the requirements will be on the same rationale disclosure basis, meaning that corporations must comply or explain why they cannot comply with the requirements. This is meant to provide flexibility as companies may limit disclosures on their value chain where information is insufficient.

Importantly, the CSRD will have an equivalency mechanism that could exempt an entity from reporting requirements under the "substantial compliance" doctrine. It has not yet been established whether disclosures under other pending frameworks, like the state of California's new emissions disclosure laws or the SEC's proposed climate disclosure rules, would be deemed equivalent. But, several key differences between the EU and U.S. approach are worthy of mention. With respect to sustainability coverage, while the CSRD addresses all aspects of E-S-G, the U.S. disclosure rules are exclusively focused on the "E," specifically climate (though, as noted earlier, there are separate SEC rules and proposals relating to other ESG matters, including human capital management and board diversity, that call for other means of compliance by companies).

2.2. *The ISSB: A Voluntary Standard Poised for Widespread Adoption*

The International Sustainability Standards Board (ISSB), launched in 2021 at COP26 in Glasgow, published its first two finalized standards in 2023: S1, General Requirements for Disclosure of Sustainability-related Financial Information and S2, Climate-related Disclosures. These standards are only the first two of a comprehensive set of standards that ISSB is planning to issue with respect to ESG disclosures. The ISSB is part of the International Financial Reporting Standards (IFRS), which were developed by the International Accounting Standards Board (IASB). While these parent organizations are not critical to understanding how the ISSB works, what is important to note is that the ISSB is part of a larger network of reporting standards designed to facilitate global comparability of financial information. Companies and countries may adopt these standards voluntarily or through regulatory action.

The ISSB standards build on the TCFD framework, which many multinational companies already comply with to varying degrees. The sustainability-related financial information disclosure standard requires companies to share both the risks and the opportunities they foresee over the short, medium, and long term with an eye to providing investors with information relevant to decision-making. For matters other than climate, which is covered by S2, it refers to sources to assist companies in identifying sustainability-related risks, opportunities, and information. It is also designed to be used in conjunction with any system of accounting requirements, for example, Generally Accepted Accounting Principles (GAAPs), which are used in the U.S. Like the ESRS, the standards are interconnected, meaning that in identifying sustainability-related risks and opportunities that could impact company prospects, they must refer to any other ISSB standard (currently just climate-related, but with more standards to come). They also must consider any industry-specific standards and may consider extrinsic guidance from other standard-setting bodies whose aims align with generating information for financial report users. The report should take the company's entire value chain into consideration when viewing the risk and opportunity set. The climate disclosure standard also requires information about governance, transition and adaptation strategies, risk management, and specific metrics and targets, which are the pillars of the TCFD architecture. Scope 1, 2, & 3 emissions are required in various forms. The climate-related disclosure requirements include the physical and transition risks a company faces, as well as the climate-related opportunity set, if any. The ISSB borrows its definition of materiality from the IFRS Accounting Standards. Entities must disclose information that is material, which means information that could reasonably be expected to influence decisions that the primary users of general-purpose financial reports make based on those reports.

The ISSB standards were designed to achieve baseline global comparability for financial markets. They fulfill the same role as the ESRS under the CSRD. Aware of this overlap, the EFRAG has issued comparative guidance explaining the interoperability of standards of the ISSB and ESRS for companies that need to navigate between the two and understand the incremental differences. One of the underlying goals of the ISSB drafters was removing duplicative reporting requirements for multinational companies that are subject to oversight in a variety of jurisdictions. The cooperation between the IFRS, EFRAG, and the European Commission supports this goal.

Note that the ISSB S2 standard requires an entity to use scenario analysis to assess its climate resilience. It also requires disclosure of Scope 3 emissions, including details about the calculation methodology, inputs, and assumptions. The ISSB does not require disclosure within audited financial statements; rather, it requires that a covered entity draw connections between disclosures and the financial statements within the general-purpose financial reports. Assurance is not required by the ISSB; it is up to adopting jurisdictions to choose what level of assurance, if any, is required. The ISSB materiality standard also differs from the EU standard: the ISSB standard focuses on what is material to primary users of the financial information and does not consider affected stakeholders like employees or the community.

Note again that the ISSB standards are voluntary, and do not take the force of regulation unless they are adopted by specific jurisdictions. Brazil was the first country in the world to adopt these standards, when it announced in October 2023 that it had adopted the ISSB's inaugural sustainability standards (IFRS S1 and IFRS S2) for voluntary reporting from the start of 2024. The standards will be incorporated into the country's mandatory regulations two years later, when ISSB-aligned disclosures become mandatory for all listed companies starting January 1, 2026. Once the standards become mandatory in 2026, reasonable assurance will be required on ISSB-aligned sustainability reports. Commonwealth nations such as Canada and the United Kingdom have indicated an interest in adopting the ISSB standards as well.

3. Anti-ESG in the U.S.

Dubbed "woke" capitalism by its fiercest opponents, ESG has come under fire in the U.S. Critics argue ESG advances environmental and social agendas but not necessarily financial aims and, as such, is out of bounds for businesses. This section will address some of the tactics employed by the opposition as of publication, including state anti-ESG legislation and antitrust arguments. This section will also address litigation responses to ESG and anti-ESG legislation. Note again the rapidly evolving landscape; developments will continue to emerge and demand attention.

3.1. *State Anti-ESG Legislation*

State legislatures became a key forum for the debate over ESG in the U.S. in 2023. While the 2022 state legislative season saw only a few dozen proposed bills across the U.S. aimed at restricting ESG, that number was up to approximately 100 by 2023 — an increase highlighting the roiling political division around ESG in the U.S. Most of the bills proposed were modeled on resolutions advanced by either the American Legislative Exchange Council or the Heartland Institute (both conservative interest groups) and can be subdivided into a few categories. The first category has been referred to as "divestment bills," calling for state divestment from financial institutions and other companies that use ESG factors or that "discriminate" against certain sectors. A second category has been referred to as "ESG ban bills" with the aim of eliminating use of ESG factors outright. In addition to these general categories, other approaches have emerged. This section will address key examples across the two noted categories as well as others. Regardless of the approach, the balance of state anti-ESG legislation through 2023 was trained on financial institutions and those institutions' use of ESG factors.

Overall, state anti-ESG legislation has drawn pointed censure from legal and economic analysts alike. From the legal perspective, concerns have been raised as to whether legislation affords sufficient clarity as to whom it applies to and how it applies. For example, some legislation relies on terms such as "pecuniary" or "non-pecuniary," the boundaries of which critics argue are not entirely clear. And, from the economic perspective, concerns have been raised as to whether legislation and its impact on financial institutions could result in depressed returns on investments managed by those institutions, increased climate-related risk exposure for those investments, and even a winnowing of markets for financial products, giving way to increased costs to consumers and taxpayers. In particular, analysts have cautioned that taxpayers could be saddled with millions, if not billions, in increased interest rates as the range of financial institutions servicing municipal bonds narrows and costs correspondingly increase.

Texas: Addressing "Boycott": In 2021, Texas passed a pair of laws that prohibit government entities, including public retirement funds, from doing business with financial institutions that do not support the oil, gas, and gun industries. Senate Bill 13 (SB 13) requires the Texas Comptroller to issue a "blacklist" of financial institutions that boycott oil and gas companies. Comptroller Glen Hager released such a list in 2022. Senate Bill 19 (SB 19) requires any company with 10 or more employees and that enters into a contract of $100,000 or more with a government entity to attest that the company does not boycott the oil, gas, and gun industries and will not do so for the duration of the contract.

Kentucky: Prohibiting Government Use of ESG Factors Outright: Kentucky aimed to restrict the use of ESG considerations by government entities directly. In March 2023, Governor Andy Beshear signed into law House Bill 236 (HB 236). The law addresses state-administered retirement funds, prohibiting fund managers' use of ESG considerations in investment decisions and requiring that they consider only "pecuniary" factors. Such factors are defined as those having a "direct and material connection to the financial risk or financial return of an investment."

Florida: A Combined Approach: Florida's House Bill 3 (HB 3) was signed into law by Governor Ron DeSantis in the spring of 2023 and was set to go into effect on July 1, 2023. Entitled *An Act Relating to Government and Corporate Activism*, the law prohibits government entities from doing business with companies that use ESG factors and addresses company activities directly. Enrolled at 51 pages long, HB 3 was also the most far-reaching of state anti-ESG legislation. The checklist of entities and activities falling within HB 3 extends to financial institutions generally and more specifically to the following: banks; savings banks and savings associations; money services businesses; licensees; issuers of bonds; plan administrators, fiduciaries, and boards of trustees of retirement systems or plans, including municipal and firefighters plans; deposits and investments of state money, including trust investments and securities; investment managers contracting with governmental entities as well as government investors themselves; and citizen support and direct support organizations. In addition to those financial entities and activities, the law extends to state contracts and local government contracts, as well as Florida College System institutions and state universities.

The practical effect of HB 3's application varies to some degree among the various types of entities covered. But, at a high level, the law advances a few tenets. Foremost, it requires reliance only on "pecuniary factors," which it defines as factors that are "expected to have a material effect on the risk or returns of an investment based on appropriate investment horizons consistent with applicable investment objectives and funding policy." It prohibits the use of "non-pecuniary factors" as well as "the consideration of … any social, political or ideological interests." The law also prohibits "unsafe and unsound practices," which it defines as including the denial or cancellation of services to a person on the basis of a long list of considerations not qualifying as "quantitative, impartial, and risk-based." Among the list of considerations the use of which would be considered unsafe and unsound practice are the following: political opinions, speech, or affiliations; religion; manufacture, distribution, sale, purchase, or ownership of firearms or ammunition; exploration, production, utilization, transportation, sale, or manufacture of fossil fuel-based energy, timber, mining, or agriculture; and support of the state or federal government in combating illegal immigration, drug trafficking, or human trafficking.

Also included in the list of considerations the use of which would be considered unsafe and unsound practice is the failure to meet, commit to meet, or expected failure to meet the following: environmental standards, including emissions standards, benchmarks, requirements, or disclosures; social governance standards, benchmarks, or requirements, including, but not limited to, environmental or social justice; corporate board or company employment compensation standards, benchmarks, requirements, or disclosures based on characteristics protected under the Florida Civil Rights Act of 1992; and policies or procedures requiring or encouraging employment participation in social justice programming, including, but not limited to, diversity, equity, or inclusion training. In several instances, HB 3 also requires some form of attestation or assurance as to compliance with its terms and even provides for sanctions, penalties, and recovery of attorney fees and costs in the event of violation and enforcement. At least one provision in the law regarding licensees equates a violation of this law with a violation of the Florida Deceptive Trade Practices Act.

Missouri: Requiring Attestation: The concept of an attestation was also implemented by Missouri, but notably at the impetus of its Secretary of State Jay Ashcroft. There were 13 anti-ESG bills introduced in the Missouri legislature in 2023, all of which were bundled into one piece of legislation, House Bill 863 (HB 863), which ultimately failed in the senate. Following that failure, however, Secretary Ashcroft relied on his own authority to implement a rule on the topic. The rule went into effect in July 2023 and requires financial advisors and institutions to disclose to clients the incorporation of any environmental or social consideration used in investment advice (15 CSR 30-51.170). Clients must in turn sign an acknowledgment and consent to incorporation of any such environmental or social consideration as to their investments. As discussed in the following, Missouri's rule is the subject of litigation pending as of the publication of this section.

A Note on Insurance: Texas Governor Greg Abbott signed Senate Bill 833 (SB 833) into law in the summer of 2023, aimed exclusively at insurers. The law prohibits insurers from using any "environmental, social, or governance model, score, factor or standard" to charge different insurance rates unless those differing rates are relevant and related to the risk being insured; based on an ordinary insurance business purpose, including the use of sound actuarial principles, or financial solvency considerations reasonably related to loss experience for the different types of risks and coverages made available by a particular insurer; or if application of the law would require "a material change in insurer's business plans." Similarly, North Dakota enacted House Bill 1429 in April 2023, prohibiting insurers operating in the state from refusing coverage or changing rates based on ESG considerations.

3.2. *Antitrust Challenges to ESG Initiatives*

Within ESG initiatives, climate collaborations in particular have drawn antitrust scrutiny. As the private sector has become increasingly engaged in the effort to combat climate change, debates have emerged about the impact and legality of collaboration among firms — particularly those in the same industry. Hundreds of business climate collaborations have begun in recent years, with goals ranging from the establishment of shared net-zero targets to the development of frameworks for carbon accounting. As these groups have proliferated, antitrust questions have arisen regarding joint standard setting and information sharing in industry-wide collaborations, as well as coordinated engagement by investors and financial institutions. Increasingly, antitrust challenges are said to be chilling necessary engagement and the mobilization of private actors to fight the accelerating harms of climate change.

3.2.1. *Antitrust threats*

For decades, antitrust has actually been underenforced in the U.S., under both Republican and Democratic administrations. During that time, the nation has seen the rise of monopolies and oligopolies across the economy, in industries as diverse as technology, healthcare, airlines, retail, and defense contractors. Many analysts point to this consolidation as a significant driver of inequality, and those concerns have led to a surge of enforcement activity from the FTC and Department of Justice (DOJ) under the Biden Administration. But, while prosecutors aim to reinvigorate the anti-monopoly origins of antitrust, some politicians pursuing an "anti-ESG" agenda have attempted to use antitrust theories as a tool against ESG initiatives.

The effort began in earnest in the fall of 2022, when 19 Republican state Attorneys General (AGs) announced an investigation into six large

U.S. banks involved with the Net-Zero Banking Alliance, a group of global banks with a shared goal of financing the transition to net zero. In April 2023, 21 Republican state AGs published an open letter to more than 50 large asset managers, claiming potential violations of fiduciary duty obligations and state consumer protection laws due to the managers' ESG investment activities. That summer, Congress expanded its own anti-ESG agenda, and the House Judiciary Committee issued a subpoena to Ceres, a nonprofit that works with capital market leaders to focus on sustainability, claiming that the shareholder group "appears to facilitate collusion" through its involvement with Climate Action 100+. Later, the House Judiciary Committee sent investigative letters reciting similar climate and antitrust concerns to two top proxy advisory firms, Glass Lewis and Institutional Shareholder Services, as well as the activist investor Trillium Asset Management and the hedge fund Engine No. 1. By fall 2023, the House Judiciary Committee had expanded its effort when it issued subpoenas to an umbrella of industry-specific climate alliances known as Glasgow Financial Alliance for Net Zero (GFANZ) and a leading shareholder advocacy group, As You Sow, accusing them of antitrust violations. The subpoenas marked an escalation of the past year's efforts by Congressional Republicans and Republican AGs to use antitrust laws to stymie financial institutions' ESG practices. Although climate alliances with net-zero goals were the initial target, those theories of antitrust violations largely failed to gain traction, and an expanded set of firms that engage in shareholder advocacy and proxy advice on any ESG-related matters were targeted.

3.2.2. *Antitrust principles*

Three primary U.S. federal antitrust statutes govern agreements among competitors. First, the Sherman Act of 1890, in Section 1, establishes the foundational prohibition of monopolization and unlawful trade restraints. Second, the Clayton Act of 1914 identifies additional prohibited conduct, including with respect to mergers and acquisitions and interlocking directorates (when the same director — or even limited partner firm — sits on the boards of two or more competing firms). And third, the FTC Act, in Section 5, bars unfair methods of competition. States can enforce the federal laws and in many cases have their own antitrust laws. These statutes proscribe unlawful conduct in general terms, establishing broad principles as to how markets should operate fairly and competitively, leaving courts and regulatory authorities to inquire into the specific details of any challenged business practice. Under these antitrust laws, certain types of agreements among firms — such as price fixing and market share allocation — are deemed so likely to harm competition that they are considered *per se* unlawful, and antitrust violations will be assumed without the consideration of any potential benefits from the agreements. By contrast, other agreements — such as mergers or vertical arrangements — may have both anti-competitive effects and pro-social benefits and thus are analyzed under a "rule-of-reason" framework to assess the overall effect of the behavior, including "pro-competitive" effects that may be beneficial to consumers. In practice, most antitrust cases are resolved in courts under "rule of reason," which means assessing the facts of each case and weighing the harms against the benefits.

3.2.3. *An example: Antitrust allegations against GFANZ and as you sow*

Industry associations have always faced scrutiny under federal and state antitrust laws: These groups are designed to facilitate communication among competitors and thus naturally invoke the specter of potential antitrust violations. Competitor coordination runs contrary to the broad consumer protection goals of antitrust law to deliver competitive prices while ensuring businesses operate at high levels of quality and efficiency. Agency guidelines, as well as robust case law, have been developed to direct the behavior of trade associations and standard-setting organizations. GFANZ, Climate Action 100+, and other climate alliances fall within this tradition of industry trade groups. GFANZ is a global coalition of leading financial institutions committed to accelerating decarbonization in line with the goals of the Paris Agreement. GFANZ alliances are built around information sharing and voluntary standard setting, among other collaborative activities between members. These attributes of independence and voluntariness are important to establish that, under traditional antitrust principles, the coalitions are not vulnerable to group boycott claims. Moreover, their behavior is not unusual: Voluntary industry standard-setting organizations and trade associations — like the American Petroleum Institute (API) — have long been permissible under U.S. antitrust laws. Indeed, the FTC and DOJ offer guidelines to support the practices of trade associations and standard-setting organizations, clearly distinguishing between collaborative, often pro-competitive, practices and behavior that violates antitrust law. It is important to remember that a corporate boycott under antitrust law is not the same as a consumer "boycott" or protest movement to stop purchasing from a specific entity. Rather, a corporate boycott is a specific type of horizontal agreement among competitors, where firms agree to take joint action against another competitor. The intent of a collective boycott must be anti-competitive — like excluding a rival from the market — to raise antitrust concerns. Industry coalitions with shared commitments, such as targeting net-zero goals, do not fit this legal definition. Indeed, in the GFANZ alliances, the member financial institutions do not compete with the companies they finance.

There is no case law suggesting that climate alliances are vulnerable under any of these theories, and, to date, no cases have yet been filed. This may be because, given the legal risks, trade associations typically take precautions to ensure that prohibited topics — like sharing information on pricing or other competitively sensitive information — are kept out of bounds. The fossil fuel industry itself is attuned to these risks. The API, for example, publishes extensive antitrust guidance for its members and emphasizes in its literature that lobbying is the API's main function. Joint lobbying efforts are among the main functions of many trade associations, as these efforts to influence legislative or executive action enjoy First Amendment protection.

When professional associations have been found to violate antitrust laws, it is often because the conduct in question veers too close to cartel behavior. The phrase "ESG cartel" does appear in the allegations recited in the subpoenas' cover letters. However, the term "cartel" invokes specific meaning under antitrust law. In short, it refers to a group of producers who coordinate (illegally) to fix prices, divide markets or customers, limit production, or otherwise restrain trade. Further, the use of the term "ESG" is problematic. It has become casual shorthand for a range of divergent ideas, including not only rigorous portfolio risk analysis but also aspirational strategies for investors to "do well and do good." It is also often used simply as a marketing tool. This unfortunately means the term easily lends itself to misrepresentation. In any event, it is unclear here what specific market "ESG" is referring to in the subpoenas — an antitrust violation would depend on a precise definition of the market: for a type of fossil fuels, perhaps, a renewable energy source, or an investment product. Further, there is no group of "ESG" producers that appear to be conspiring here, nor is there an indication of which prices have allegedly been inflated.

Similarly, there does not appear to be merit to the other allegations against As You Sow, a nonprofit organization that engages with companies on behalf of shareholders to reduce GHG emissions. One implicit theory in the subpoena is that As You Sow may function in a "hub-and-spoke" model, where the group engages on topics around climate action with multiple firms in the same industry. But, there is nothing illegal about that model. Such behavior is only prohibited by antitrust laws if it facilitates another type of anti-competitive practice like facilitating market collusion by sharing data among competitors or encouraging monopolization. That does not seem to be the claim here. Furthermore, As You Sow does not compete with the companies it engages with, making the legal arguments for anti-competitive behavior difficult to craft.

3.2.4. *Another example: Antitrust challenges to DEI initiatives*

Corporate practices aimed at increasing diversity in workspaces and institutions have also come under antitrust fire for being discriminatory and a restraint on trade, echoing the language of antitrust. In 2023, a pair of cases — *Students for Fair Admissions, Inc., (SFFA) vs. President & Fellows of Harvard College* and *SFFA vs. University of North Carolina* — made affirmative action illegal in school admissions, finding that it discriminates on the basis of race, which the U.S. Supreme Court held violates the Fourteenth Amendment. In the wake of these decisions, anti-DEI actors have been emboldened.

The antitrust argument against DEI initiatives is that diversity-based employment or contracting decisions are an unlawful restraint on trade because they allegedly discriminate unfairly against qualified individuals or firms based on immutable characteristics and are ultimately harmful to consumers. For example, a stated preference for partnerships with minority-owned corporations has been portrayed as an unreasonable restraint on trade. Proponents of these and other related diversity-based practices argue that they are not discriminating against a group but rather trying to expand their reach to traditionally underrepresented groups and that these efforts ultimately benefit consumers. As antitrust is focused on consumer impact, any challenge brought under antitrust theory will likely fail unless opponents can show a demonstrable harm.

3.3. *Litigation Responses to Anti-ESG Efforts*

As a focus on ESG has gained traction among corporations and other entities interested in bolstering their social credentials, and in "doing good" while turning a profit, anti-ESG sentiment has also strengthened among opponents, resulting in a proliferation of anti-ESG legislation and regulation, including the brand of state-level anti-ESG legislation discussed previously. This dynamic has resulted in a volatile space with a variety of ongoing litigation. Opponents of *ESG* practices — particularly with respect to climate and DEI policies — have focused attention on what practices are required or prohibited by fiduciary duty, fighting against deference to agency decision-makers, and seeking expansive First Amendment protections for companies. Many of these challenges are brought in the U.S. Court of Appeals for the Fifth Circuit, where the judges are typically more receptive to a deregulatory agenda. Proponents of ESG have also sought relief in the courts from anti-ESG legislation, especially disclosure requirements. Given all the legislative activity and heated public debate, litigation is a logical outgrowth.

3.3.1. *Fiduciary duty*

Fiduciary obligations have been under heightened scrutiny due to increased ESG activity. Fiduciary duties are legally owed by fiduciaries to shareholders, and possibly to other stakeholders, depending on the jurisdiction. Under U.S. state laws, and particularly Delaware where a majority of corporations are registered, fiduciary duties are owed by trustees to beneficiaries of pension plans, and by directors and officers to their corporations. There is debate about these duties as they relate to ESG — are they exclusively a duty to maximize profit for shareholders or can they be something more, such as a duty to preserve the future interests of beneficiaries? The terminology "pecuniary" has become important, as investors seek to take a holistic view about the way the companies they invest in are managed. As intimated earlier, opponents argue that ESG considerations are inherently not pecuniary, asserting that they are divorced from the economic well-being of a company. Proponents disagree, pointing to statistics about the financial benefits that are concomitant with a company being sound from an ESG perspective.

Recent litigation has addressed the types of considerations that may be included in fiduciaries' investment analysis. One case in New York pending as of publication of this section, *Wong et al. vs. New York City Employees Retirement System et al.* (NYCERS), is testing the waters. Brought on behalf of several NYCERS beneficiaries by a conservative law firm, the case focuses on a decision by several pension funds to divest from fossil fuels. NYCERS trustees assert that their decision to divest from the fossil fuel industry, which was only 3% of the total portfolio, was predicated on analysis that showed that the headwinds facing the industry due to the clean energy transition made it an unattractive investment moving forward. The trustees assert that their decision was driven by pecuniary considerations and not an overarching social agenda. Plaintiffs and their attorneys counter, pointing to statements made by politicians and several fiduciaries that proclaim their goal to put New York at the forefront of the clean energy movement and pursue net-zero policies; plaintiffs allege that this shows the trustees are putting broad social goals above the interest of the plans' beneficiaries. Notably, divestment from fossil fuels has increased momentum in recent years, with over 1,500 institutions committed to divesting their assets, representing over $40.5 trillion dollars. Fossil fuel companies recognize this as a threat to their continued profitability in their own financial disclosures. And, indeed, the industry was in financial decline until Russia invaded Ukraine in February 2022, driving fossil fuel prices back up after nearly a decade in decline. The NYCERS case is not yet resolved, and the judge's assessment of the trustees' decision to divest may set an important precedent for the interpretation of fiduciary duties.

Another case that focuses on fiduciary duties owed to pensioners involves the Department of Labor's (DOL) 2022 Investment Duties Rule. That rule clarified the duties of fiduciaries of Employee Retirement Income Security Act (ERISA) employee benefit plans concerning investment selection and actions. In *Utah vs. Walsh*, 26 states and other parties sued the DOL and Secretary of Labor over the rule. Plaintiffs alleged that the rule was arbitrary and capricious, and also that it violated ERISA's statutory language. Until 2020, under ERISA, fiduciaries were permitted to consider collateral or non-financial benefits of competing investments that had equal economic merit (e.g. expected returns) and strategic merit (e.g. portfolio diversification goals). In 2020, the Trump Administration updated the rule to state that this tiebreaker was only available when fiduciaries were unable to distinguish investments on the basis of pecuniary factors alone. According to the Biden Administration's DOL, this created confusion as to whether ESG factors were pecuniary and had a chilling effect on integrating any ESG factors into the investment selection process. The Biden Administration rolled back the Trump rule by allowing explicit consideration of ESG factors, changed the rule's text to say that decisions must be based on "factors that a fiduciary determines are relevant to a reasonable risk and return analysis," and officially allowed the tiebreaker test. There were also reductions in documentation requirements from 2020 in the 2022 rule. Plaintiffs in the ensuing challenge to the Biden Administration's update alleged that they would have to expend more time and resources monitoring investment advisors and pointed to likely harm to oil and gas companies from restricted capital access, resulting in diminished tax revenues for their states.

The Texas court in *Utah vs. Walsh* applied a *Chevron* analysis to find that ERISA does not foreclose consideration of non-pecuniary factors such as ESG factors because ERISA is silent in the case of a "tie" between investment options. As Congress did not directly speak on the issue, the court deferred to the agency's reasonable interpretation — a fact that was also supported by repeated prior rulemakings. In *dicta*, the court noted that it "is not unsympathetic to Plaintiffs' concerns over ESG investing trends, it need not condone ESG investing generally or ultimately agree with the Rule to reach this conclusion." "All that is necessary is a minimal level of analysis from which the agency's reasoning may be discerned." The case has been appealed, and the type of deference promised by the U.S. Supreme Court's 1984 *Chevron* decision, which has long protected agency decision-making from extreme judicial interference, may soon no longer be applicable, given a pair of cases that will be heard by the Court in 2024. Those cases, *Loper Bright vs. Raimondo* and *Relentless vs. Department of Commerce*, question whether *Chevron* is good law and may make it significantly harder for ESG regulations to survive judicial review if agency deference is stripped at the federal level. The question of whether ESG considerations are officially within the space of "pecuniary" remains open, as does the future of judicial deference to agencies.

3.3.2. *DEI policies*

The U.S. Supreme Court's recent repudiation of affirmative action admissions practices has emboldened anti-DEI activists. But, even before those decisions, a handful of cases had arisen in the space — although so far courts have been resistant to those anti-DEI efforts. These challenges have taken a variety of forms, including a shareholder books-and-records request, a challenge to a stock exchange's disclosure policy, and constitutional and state law challenges in a shareholder derivative lawsuit.

In 2022, a shareholder sued the Walt Disney Company over the corporation's response to Florida House Bill 1557 (HB 1557), commonly known as the "Don't Say Gay" rule. Disney spoke out against HB 1557, drawing criticism from Governor DeSantis and resulting in the revocation of Disney's special tax district, which encompassed the Florida theme parks. The shareholder served a books-and-records demand, asserting that Disney directors and officers may have breached their fiduciary duties to the company and shareholders through their DEI advocacy efforts. However, the legal challenge in *Simeone vs. The Walt Disney Co.* was short-lived, as the court determined that the shareholder's purpose was improper. The court issued a strongly worded rebuke of the shareholder's lawyers, who it said were "entitled to pursue litigation in support of [their] beliefs. But … [this type of suit] is not a vehicle to advance them." The court continued, finding that corporate strategy, including whether to comment on external matters, is vested in the hands of directors and subject to their discretion. The court noted that these types of DEI matters are controversial, and the board's conduct indicated that it took appropriate steps to adopt a stance for the company on "matters of social significance" that might be disagreeable to some shareholders. The shareholder "has every right to [disagree]" with Disney's policy, but Disney's opposition to HB 1557 is protected "business judgment."

Anti-DEI proponents moved into the administrative arena when they sued Nasdaq over the board diversity rule discussed earlier. Again, the court was not receptive to anti-DEI arguments. In a resounding loss for the Alliance for Fair Board Recruitment, the court found that Nasdaq is not subject to any constitutional constraints as a non-state actor (therefore dismissing plaintiffs' First and Fourth Amendment claims) and that the board diversity rule does not violate the Exchange Act by exceeding statutory authority, or the Administrative Procedure Act by being arbitrary and capricious. In a nod of approval for DEI considerations, the court noted that the disclosure rule would likely contribute to investors' investment and voting decisions, given statements made by a variety of stakeholders about their interest in access to corporate DEI information.

3.3.3. *Disclosures*

Just as disclosure requirements form the heart of our securities regulations, they are central to debates within the ESG movement. For investors and other interested parties to know about a company's policies and be able to make informed decisions, they must be able to find out about them. However, not all disclosure requirements are pro-ESG. The noted Missouri rule requires investment advisers who incorporate ESG factors, or any "social objective or non-financial objective," into their analysis to make their clients sign state-mandated forms that indicate their investment process is "not solely focused on maximizing a financial return." In response, the Securities Industry and Financial Markets Association (SIFMA), an industry group representing the securities industry, sued to challenge the rule. Plaintiffs argued that the rule compels politically charged non-neutral speech and forces individuals to adopt the government's position on a controversial topic, and therefore should receive a higher level of scrutiny and be barred by the First Amendment.

Anti-ESG groups frequently leverage the First Amendment to argue against ESG-related disclosures. The National Association of Manufacturers (NAM) intervened in a case against the SEC, *NCPPR vs. SEC*, to argue that corporations should not be forced to include activist shareholder statements in their proxy statements on First Amendment grounds. NAM alleges that those proposals, which often include ESG language, are divorced from shareholder value creation and are too controversial to justify forcing corporations to adopt them as their own speech. The outcome of that challenge is undecided.

However, in another case, *Chamber of Commerce vs. SEC*, the U.S. Court of Appeals for the Fifth Circuit reviewed First Amendment logic to find that these types of rationale disclosures required by state actors (in that case, the SEC) are not in violation of the First Amendment, relying on Fifth Circuit precedent from *NetChoice, LLC vs. Paxton,* a case that addressed state efforts to regulate the online speech of social media platforms. The SEC's rule was struck down on arbitrary and capricious grounds for other reasons, but the rationale disclosure requirement withstood First Amendment scrutiny. The U.S. Supreme Court recently granted *certiorari* in *NetChoice*, but as it stands, pure ESG rationale disclosure does not violate the First Amendment, even in the conservative Fifth Circuit. From both sides of the debate, the mandatory disclosure space has been ripe for legal challenges over ESG policies under the First Amendment.

As should be apparent from the range of frameworks and legal developments covered in this chapter, the approach to ESG varies significantly by jurisdiction, with profound divergences among countries and within U.S. states. A harmonized approach to climate-related risk, DEI initiatives, or other ESG priorities remains as elusive, with corporations and citizens bearing the brunt of that uncertainty.

https://doi.org/10.1142/9789811297786_0003

Chapter 3

Stakeholders at the Gate: Driving Financial Value Through Sustainability in Private Equity

Tensie Whelan and Umachander Balakumar

NYU Stern Center for Sustainable Business,
New York, USA

Abstract

Private equity (PE) funds have become majority owners of hospitals, newspapers, schools, real estate, industrial manufacturers, extractive industries, consumer brands, and retail. Worldwide, approximately 10,000 PE firms enjoy ownership rights in 40,000 portfolio companies, which in turn manage 20 million employees. On that scale, PE has a significant influence on corporate behavior, especially when it has majority or controlling interests.

PE firm policies and approaches can create value for all stakeholders, including the environment, or extract value to the detriment of other stakeholders (and potentially reduce their own returns). Our research aims to identify how PE can avoid doing harm, as well as provide positive impact. We have undertaken a robust academic review of the state of PE in terms of its contribution to creating or extracting value and developed an accountability framework that provides insights into the various categories of PE impact, both positive and negative. The framework lays out the criteria that investors, civil society, regulators, and others can explore to assess the PE firm's performance and includes human capital management, financial engineering, strategy and innovation, and societal impact, among other categories. This chapter will provide examples of positive and negative behavior through the lens of the accountability framework, as well as present insights into how sustainability can drive financial value in PE at the firm level.

1. Introduction

Business leaders and investors are moving to embed sustainability in business and embrace stakeholder capitalism, a system in which corporations aim to serve the interest of all stakeholders (customers, supplies, employees, communities, and shareholders). Increasingly, this approach is seen to be more profitable as well as more resilient in the long term.

These shifts come at a time when private equity (PE), whose goals are generally focused exclusively on shareholder return, has grown its presence globally. PE funds are majority owners of hospitals, newspapers, schools, real estate, industrial manufacturers, consumer brands, and retail, among other sectors. Worldwide, approximately 10,000 PE firms enjoy ownership rights in 40,000 portfolio companies, which in turn manage 20 million employees (Eccles *et al.*, 2022).

On that scale, PE has a significant influence on corporate behavior, especially when it has majority or controlling interests. Therefore, PE firm policies and approaches have the potential to create value for all stakeholders, including the environment, or be extractive and detrimental to other stakeholders. For example, as we will cite later in the chapter, in the hospital sector, PE ownership has been correlated with higher prices, longer hospital stays, and higher death rates. In the newspaper sector, PE firms fire reporters and drop local reporting, leading to lower engagement in the community and lower voting in local elections. In the education sector, PE ownership has been associated with higher costs and higher student loans coupled with poorer outcomes for students (who are often from disadvantaged communities).

On the positive side of the ledger, there are an increasing number of PE firms focused on environmental, social, and corporate governance (ESG) and long-term value creation, as we will see in this chapter. For example, PE is a big investor in renewables and the associated infrastructure, investing $52 billion in 2021, according to Bloomberg (Robertson & Karsh, 2021). To develop this framework, we undertook an academic literature review of more than 70 papers on PE and desk research and interviews with select PE firms that focus on impact and ESG integration, including Carlyle, Kohlberg Kravis Roberts (KKR), and Blackstone, and impact players, such as Developing World Markets (DWM), Summa Equity, and Closed Loop. We also engaged with PE-focused groups, such as UN Principles for Responsible Investment (PRI), Predistribution Initiative, PE Stakeholder Project, CERES, ESG Convergence Initiative, Institutional Limited Partners Association (ILPA), and American Investment Council (AIC), and issued a white paper that covers the findings in extensive detail (Balakumar & Whelan, 2023). We hope the framework will provide needed insights for limited partners (LPs), general partners (GPs), corporates, civil society, and regulators concerning signals of value creation or value extraction strategies.

2. The Responsible Investing Framework Overview

In this section, we present our Accountability Framework, in which we differentiate between management decisions at the **PE firm** level and **portfolio company** level. Though the categorizations are distinct, they are not separate, and practices at the firm level do influence the practices of the portfolio companies as shown in the following:

- At the PE firm level, the framework focuses on PE firm governance, policies, and decision-making and its impact on portfolio companies as well as its own footprint.
- At the portfolio company level, the framework identifies impact categories where PE firm policies and subsequent portfolio firm management can drive negative and positive ESG and financial performance.

While we present the full framework for only GPs in this overview section, readers can find the framework and full report, including the portfolio company framework, on the NYU Stern Center for Sustainable Business (CSB) website.

2.1. *Accountability Framework: Private Equity Firm*

The following impact categorizations were derived through a rigorous academic literature review and expert interviews with PE firms and civil society groups:

(1) Sustainable and Responsible Investment Policies
(2) Management & Human Capital
(3) Fund Management
(4) Strategy and Innovation
(5) Societal Impact.

Specific impact sub-areas are then defined with sample data points to illustrate how users of the framework can measure accountability. The sample data points are to be used as a guide and are by no means an exhaustive list of metrics available. **The data points can be negative or positive.**

3. Diving Into the Accountability Framework for General Partners

3.1. *CATEGORY 1: Sustainable and Responsible Investment Policies*

Crafting a responsible investment policy helps guide operations and management with the goal of ensuring profitable returns based on stakeholder value creation, strategic management of material ESG issues, and positive societal impact. Firms must develop the policy's purpose, scope, governance (how it will be overseen), implementation, reporting, and revision. Poor definition and/or execution of a policy may lead to allegations of greenwashing and reduced investor trust. Carefully defining each component while securing leadership buy-in is an important step to facilitate the long-term implementation and viability of the policy (see Figure 1).

3.2. *Components of a Responsible Investment Policy*

A firm-wide responsible investment policy includes purpose, scope, governance, implementation, reporting, and revision, and should inform and

	Impacts		Sample Data Points	
Sustainable and Responsible Investment Policies *A sustainable and responsible investment policy defined by firm priorities and monitored implementation*	I.	*A robust and credible sustainable investment policy*	i. ii.	A defined purpose, scope with mechanisms for measurement and revision within the policy Ownership and accountability of policies taken by leadership, board and/or investment committees
	II.	*Monitored implementation of the sustainable investment policy*	i. ii.	Key person or persons defined within the policy of educating and promoting the policy across the firm Active ESG due diligence completed on deals (e.g. number of deals rejected due to ESG reasons)

	Impacts		Sample Data Points	
Management & Human Capital *Management approach is guided by a robust responsible investment strategy and diverse and ESG credentialed senior leaders*	I.	*Board, CEO & employee credentials*	i. ii. iii. iv.	Diverse board and deal teams with ESG credentials Regular ESG/RI performance tracking at leadership and board levels Dedicated ESG/RI committees Employee sustainability and stakeholder engagement credentials
	II.	*Firm diversity, culture, and incentives*	i. ii. iii. iv.	DEI of firm employees DEI talent pipeline including recruiting, retention and promotion Pay equity ESG aligned incentives and/or upward earnings incentives

	Impacts		Sample Data Points	
Strategy & Innovation *Describes the firm's capabilities in meeting its sustainable investment policy throughout its pre- and post-investment processes*	I.	*Long-term horizon and investment sourcing alignment with ESG and/or UN SDGs*	i. ii. iii. iv. v.	Sourcing of investments in line with firm's sustainable investment policy with respect to region, timeframe, UN SDG progress, sector/industry focus. Holding periods consistent with driving innovation and returns, e.g. perpetual funds vs shrinking of investment cycles Implementing and adhering to sector-specific sustainability guidelines Duty of care toward public goods (even when privately owned) such as water and forests Responsible exits

Figure 1. PE Firm Responsible Investment Framework

	Impacts	Sample Data Points
Fund Management *Fund management practices with respect to handling dry powder, subscription credit lines, additional fundraises, and reporting.*	I. Reporting and transparency of financial performance	i. Use of PME with consideration of market cap, industry/sector and leverage size ii. Use of Subscription Credit Lines
	II. Fund additions and dilution	i. Number of top-up, annex funds and multiple fund investments
	III. Subscription credit line use	i. Reporting and transparency of subscription credit line use
	IV. Prudent handling of dry powder	i. Dry powder management practices with respect to time horizons (investments in liquid cash & cash equivalents vs. less liquid holdings)
	V. Fees	i. Amount and types of fees charged by the PE firm to the portfolio company
	VI. Tax structuring	i. Domicile of master fund ii. Fee waivers

	Impacts	Sample Data Points
Societal Impact *How well the PE firm and its portfolio companies are contributing to positive impacts and reducing negative societal impacts*	I. Transparent ESG and impact reporting for PE firm and portfolio companies	i. Adoption of credible ESG standards and frameworks (e.g. SASB, IRIS+) ii. Annual reporting of firm and portfolio company impact in line with sustainable investment policy iii. Independent third party audit of ESG iv. Compliance with EU SFDR, SEC and other regulatory ESG labeling requirements v. Financed emissions (Scope 3)
	I. Formal or informal commitments to decarbonization, DEI, living wage, and other impacts	i. Net Zero Asset Managers, SBTI ii. Living wage assessments iii. DEI goals iv. B Corp
	I. Embedded sustainability	i. ESG is embedded in the organization's business strategy along with performance–based KPIs supported by an appropriate level of investment

Figure 1. (*Continued*)

guide a culture of stakeholder value creation and transparency in activities, extending beyond traditional investment mandates to include non-financial key performance indicators (KPIs). The responsible investment policy should clarify if the company is pursuing an impact approach, e.g. investing in firms that have a positive societal impact such as inclusive finance or renewable energy, or a responsible investing approach, which includes integration of ESG principles and practices into a standard portfolio of companies (Nelson, 2021).

A responsible investment policy can be used to validate the deal sourcing, management, and exit of deals beyond simple checkbox criteria. From strategies that focus on creating employee-owned stock ownership plans for portfolio companies to addressing thematic issues (recycling, clean energy, etc.) to prioritizing specific ESG metrics (CO_2 emissions, diversity, etc.), there is a wide range of what can fall under such a policy. While motivation for developing a responsible investment policy can come from investor and regulatory pressure, it can also be a means of differentiation for the firm.

3.3. *Purpose*

The PE firm should define the purpose of its responsible investment policy. Potential elements, derived from the AIC and PRI, could include the following goals (American Investment Council, 2023):

(a) Progress toward an environmental or social goal (which presents a business opportunity) through targeted sectors and deals.
(b) Reducing risk associated with certain environmental or social factors by avoiding certain deals.
(c) Addressing potential or current stakeholder issues through the selection of deals.
(d) Alignment with current or expected regulations.
(e) Risk/return profile: Most PE firms investing in impact, for example, are looking for market rate returns, but some are willing to take concessionary rates.

The purpose of the policy should be clearly identifiable to internal and external stakeholders as well as to investors to avoid charges of greenwashing or reputational damage. A report by Bain & Company and ILPA found that "ESG-related risks and a lack of ESG performance improvement are the most dominant reasons LPs walk away from {PE} investments" with 67% of LPs saying they would walk away from an investment due to the potential risk of negative ESG headlines (Lino *et al.*, 2022). Consider an example from KKR's responsible investment policy, shown in Figure 2, which clearly states its purpose (KKR, 2023).

Responsible Investment Policy

Effective June 2023

1. Purpose

KKR[1] maintains that the thoughtful management of environmental, social, and governance ("ESG"), regulatory, and geopolitical issues is an essential part of long-term business success in a rapidly changing world, and incorporating such business-relevant issues as part of our investment process helps us both create and protect value. We believe it is crucial to our ability to deliver results on behalf of clients and shareholders, and consistent with our fiduciary duties and efforts to maximize returns, for us to understand and take into account the ways in which these issues may impact commercial outcomes for our investments.

We believe geopolitics, supply chain concerns, scarce resources, changing consumer and customer demands, evolving norms, competition for workers and customers, increased regulation, and other similar issues are expected to pose greater challenges and opportunities for companies around the world. KKR seeks to reduce risk and enhance value by building a proactive focus on these issues across the investment life cycle, wherever possible.

Responsible investment reflects our commitment to integrating and managing material[2] ESG considerations in our investment processes globally across asset classes. The purpose of this policy[3] is to articulate KKR's broad framework and approach to that commitment.

For the purposes of this policy, "material" ESG issues are defined as those issues that KKR, in its sole discretion, determines have – or have the potential to have – a substantial impact on an organization's ability to create or preserve economic value. As one input to assessing what is a material ESG issue for each investment, KKR utilizes the industry-specific issue topics identified by the SASB Standards.[4]

Figure 2.   KKR responsible investment policy June 2023

3.4. *Scope*

The responsible investment policy should define scope, e.g. the type of investments (primary, secondary, and co-investments), and timing (current or future funds). GPs should also specify the extent to which their policy applies in minority and/or non-control investments and global/regional business units with respect to their level of investment and influence (Hampole & Komgold, 2021). This may be a key point for GPs with diversified interests in different types of holdings. Not stating the scope related to minority-held investments may cause reputational damage if firms are not clear about their level of influence.

3.5. *Measurement and Revision*

The policy should include a governance structure that ensures accountability, effective implementation, and transparent reporting, with provisions for revisions of the policy. Detailed within the scope should be how the policy is being applied and measured. This includes the description of non-financial KPIs to be utilized before and after investment, along with the specifics of how they will be implemented, reported, and revised. The specific KPIs may vary depending on the portfolio company and the sustainability strategy to be deployed.

This can fall under the purview of the Chief Compliance Officer or another senior role. Taking the size of the firm into consideration, the responsibilities may fall to cross-functional teams rather than a single individual. Additionally, the policy must be accompanied by top-down organizational buy-in for effective implementation or risk being a simple checkbox item with no real firm value.

4. Category 2: Management and Human Capital

A purposeful approach to human capital management and a comprehensive responsible investment policy create the foundation for the successful application of different responsible investment practices. Beginning with human capital management, firms need to prioritize the recruitment and matching of relevant GP skills to deal types. Firms also need to invest in junior-level talent pipelines or risk a talent vacuum in the future, especially for talented women and people from Black, Indigenous, and people of color (BIPOC) backgrounds who have been traditionally underrepresented in the industry. Firms should strive to codify these aspects within their firm purpose and culture. In this section, we will outline practices pertaining to ESG credentials, diversity, equity, inclusion, pay equity, and company culture, and their impact on firm performance.

4.1. *Human Capital*

A purposeful approach to human capital management and a comprehensive sustainable investment policy creates the foundation for the successful application of different responsible investment practices. Beginning with human capital management, firms need to prioritize the recruitment and matching of relevant GP skills to deal types. Firms need to invest in junior-level talent pipelines or risk a talent vacuum in the future. Excellence in human capital management for a PE firm includes hiring and maintaining a diverse employee base with appropriate operational expertise and ESG credentials and supporting them through a positive, inclusive, and equitable organizational culture. As LPs add sustainability measures to their due diligence, data points including relevant backgrounds, skill sets, and diversity are being examined to ensure competency and assess risk.

4.2. *Industry & ESG Credentials*

Some PE firms focus on hiring employees with financial engineering expertise whom they employ to cut costs at portfolio firms, sell real assets, and take on debt. This is a limited set of skills in today's complex world, where LPs and portfolio companies are looking for PE firms with expertise that can help with improving operations and taking on a transformational pivot. In fact, one study found that the careful matching of GP skill sets with deal strategies (organic vs. inorganic) can lead to better performance capture relative to peers, after removing the effects of leverage and observing increases in sales growth; earnings before interest, taxes, depreciation, and amortization (EBITDA); margins (EBITDA/sales); and multiples (enterprise value/EBITDA). High-level, organic deals focus on operational improvements while inorganic deals prioritize merger and acquisition (M&A) strategies. In brief, GPs with operationally honed skill sets through industry experience or management consulting outperformed their peers with financial backgrounds in organic deals while those with non-operational backgrounds were better able to capture value in M&A deals (Acharaya *et al.*, 2010).

Matching skills with needs is essential to capture value across various types of deals, but the practice is not being followed consistently across the industry. To address the issue, firms are targeting individuals with expertise in talent acquisition, capability assessments, and leadership. Coined as "leadership capital partners (LCP)," their responsibilities include the sourcing and support of appropriate partner skill sets to tackle deals (Ulrich & Allen, 2017). Though the title varies, firms are allocating resources to leadership to ensure they are staffing and incentivizing appropriately.

Sustainability credentials, like the Fundamentals of Sustainability Accounting (FSA) of the IFRS, are growing in importance due to the need to assess the materiality of ESG variables on portfolio company performance with respect to revenue, expenses, assets, liabilities, and costs of capital. Consider a firm evaluating the acquisition of a hotel chain with coastline properties. Without proper industry experience or sustainability credentials, those evaluating the deal may overlook concerns such as the hotel chain being in a high water-stressed region with poor energy infrastructure and its exposure to extreme weather events.

Firms like KKR have recognized the importance of dedicated ESG teams and in 2021 tripled their personnel focusing on ESG compliance, integration, data science, and impact measurement (KKR Announces Formation of Sustainability Expert Advisory Council, 2021). Warburg Pincus (2021) similarly created a dedicated ESG committee within its Investment Support Group; its members meet on a quarterly basis to discuss ESG activities and attend conferences for continued learning.

4.3. *Diversity, Equity, and Inclusion (DEI)*

Attention to diversity in the workplace has increased significantly over the past few years and public markets have adapted by increasing the representation of marginalized groups across junior and senior levels. Evidence shows that PE firms are catching up when it comes to diversity at junior levels but are lagging in senior leadership representation. Gender diversity at higher-level positions is lacking at firms, especially for C-suite executives, where women only account for 15% of positions compared with nearly 25% in public corporations. A 2021 McKinsey study also found people of color are also disproportionately underrepresented at senior levels, and more so in PE than corporate America (Nee & Quigley, 2022).

The lack of diversity can affect deal performance. Consider the 2020 study examining the effects of socio-demographic factors, including gender, race, and nationality, and occupational backgrounds of lead partners on deal performance. Firms with higher diversity in lead partners had higher growth rates (EV CAGR) and multiples (EV/EBITDA and EV/Sales), and performed better with complex deals and with deals that occurred in uncertain conditions. In this study, complex deals represented deals following inorganic growth strategies, cross-border transactions, and company size, while uncertain conditions represented the volatility/ risk based on the four drivers of the presence of a crisis period, economic policy uncertainty, industry volatility, and company age/maturity. A 2017 BCG Diversity and Innovation Survey also shows data on diverse leadership correlating with higher innovation revenue (Lorenzo *et al.*, 2018).

Compared to occupation diversity, socio-demographic diversity was more significant in predicting outperformance and adds further evidence that it should be prioritized by firms (Hammer *et al.*, 2021). Unfortunately, socio-demographic diversity within deal teams is lacking, with only 1–2% of members identifying as Black or Latinx, compared to publicly traded companies where the breakdown is closer to 13% (Nee & Yee, 2021).

Figure 3 illustrates the independent analysis of data compiled through Pitchbook, firm websites, and impact reports of the top ten US PE firms by assets under management (AUM), showing female representation in leadership positions ranging from 7% at Apollo to 40% at HarbourVest Partners (Basak & Karsh, 2020).

Firms are strengthening DEI through partnerships and dedicated internal working groups. Palladium Equity Partners prides itself on having a "majority of minority employees." 72% of its workforce identifies as minority and 64% identifies as female. Palladium accomplished its high levels of diversity by developing a pipeline with partners such as the Association of Asian American Investment Managers, Sponsors for Educational Opportunity, and the "I Have a Dream" Foundation, among others. In addition, Palladium is working to increase diversity in its portfolio firms. As a member of the 30% Coalition, Palladium Equity Partners set a goal for every portfolio board to be gender and ethnically diverse by 2021. In achieving its B Corp certification in March 2022, Palladium announced that it had also made progress toward its 30% Coalition goal: "out of 139 total members of its boards of directors, 28% are female, 29% identify as a member of an ethnic minority and 47% identify as a member of an ethnic minority or female" (Palladium Equity Partners, 2022).

The ILPA Diversity in Action brings together GPs and LPs with a common purpose of advancing DEI within the PE industry. To date, the initiative has produced a set of diversity metrics for fund managers, their staff, and portfolio companies and has supplemented its standard ILPA DDQ with the same metrics (ILPA, 2021).

Firms like Summa Equity Partners are tackling the underrepresentation of women in finance by becoming signatories to the Women in Finance Charter to increase the overall proportion of women in leading positions at financial institutions. The charter promotes the recruitment, retention, and promotion of women, as well as an inclusive culture and behavior through meaningful KPI goals. For example, the charter recommends that firms interview 50% women for roles at all levels and create processes for pay transparency and parity (Bain & Company & Aviva, 2022).

Figure 3. Top ten largest US private equity firms and leadership gender diversity

4.4. *Company Culture*

Company culture is defined by the values and purpose of the firm and expressed in the actions and practices of the firm. A positive culture and a sense of purpose are becoming important to key stakeholders, from LPs to employees. When surveyed by EY in 2021, 60% of PE firms reported having some difficulty in recruiting millennial and Gen Z workers while 82% reported difficulty in retaining them (Saenz *et al.*, 2021). Based on what was previously discussed, firms can build a strong firm-wide culture beginning with the following:

(1) Developing and implementing a clear statement of purpose and associated values.
(2) Implementing the purpose and values through the firm's responsible investment policy, ESG initiatives, and aligned pay incentives.
(3) Attracting and retaining a diverse workforce through targeted initiatives, commitments, and partnerships with outside groups like LGBT Great.
   (a) Hire a leadership capital partner whose role will be to help recruit diverse employees with critical operational and sustainability skill sets.
   (b) Ensure a diverse workforce pipeline for senior-level positions.
   (c) Promote internally and provide career progression opportunities for junior-level employees.
(4) Working toward internal pay transparency while correcting any pay inequality.

The very same metrics and policies focused firm-wide, where applicable, ideally would also be applied to portfolio companies, like how Towerbrook (2021) seeks to have its portfolio companies attain B Corp status. This flow-through effect from firms to portfolio companies allows PE firms to act as agents of change in reshaping corporate cultures across industries on a large scale.

5. Category 3: Strategy

After laying the foundation for responsible human capital management practices and a responsible investment policy, firms should develop a strategy to implement these principles through the investment cycle.

To ensure a responsible investing approach that creates value for all stakeholders, PE firms should take a long-term perspective (with associated capital investments), incorporate ESG considerations into deal sourcing, and consider the impact of the exit on the portfolio company's stakeholders and performance.

Beginning with deal sourcing, the process usually starts with due diligence, deal execution, and implementation/value creation and ends at exit. From aligning and tracking ESG metrics, including UN Sustainable Development Goal (SDG) metrics, pre- and post-investment through industry framework, like the Operating Principles of Impact Management (OPIM), there are a myriad of ways to begin marrying a firm's responsible investment policy to its investment decision-making process and strategy. A focus on creating long-term stakeholder value, e.g. worker well-being, customer satisfaction, and environmental protection, should be inherent in the strategy.

The typical PE investment process can be seen in the OPIM guidance in Figure 4. PE firms can be guided by the OPIM, which require firms to define their own strategic impact objectives and monitor impact before, during, and after investment. Some 160 firms have signed on to the

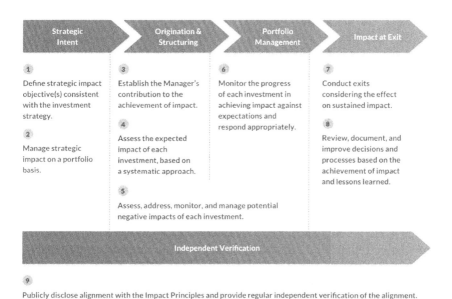

Figure 4. The nine operating principles for impact management

Principles, including companies such as the International Finance Corporation (IFC), Flatworld Partners, and Credit Suisse AG.

Managing impact and ESG is no longer solely the purview of impact-focused firms. Not having a framework or process in place not only exposes the firm to headline risk from its investments but also deters LPs, who have begun adopting more ESG-focused mandates within their investments.

Summa Equity, a Nordic PE firm, has managed to capitalize on its ESG approach to identify unique investment opportunities that other firms may overlook. With an investment approach geared toward addressing natural resource efficiency, changing demographics, and technology-enabled transformations, Summa Equity is investing in companies that solve global issues while generating competitive returns for its investors (We invest to make a change, 2023).

Summa accomplishes this by identifying investment opportunities based on the potential impact as measured by the UN SDGs. For example, Summa invested in Sortera, a Swedish recycling company, and identified SDGs #11 (sustainable cities and communities), #12 (responsible consumption and production), and #13 (climate action) as performance markers. Sortera improved the recycling process and opened an electric recycling facility, which enabled it to reduce its net emissions by 226,000 tons in one year. Furthermore, other initiatives like establishing speed caps on fleet trucks further reduced fuel consumption and costs by 10%. These types of investments led Sortera to quadruple its revenue in the 36 months following its acquisition (Indahl & Jacobsen, 2019). Summa's strategy paid off: Its third fund closed in record time and was oversubscribed with commitments of €2.3 billion in four months (Summa Equity Raises the Largest European Impact Fund to Date — Announcing Final Close of C. €2.3 billion for Third Fund, 2022).

5.1. *Long Termism*

Responsible investing requires a long-term vision even if holding periods are relatively short (Lykken, 2020). In other words, embedding sustainability in a portfolio company to position it for a successful exit (and a good valuation) means looking beyond the typical holding period of between 2 and 10 years. A long-term approach is critical to tackling the important challenges facing businesses and society today, but investors will also need to consider what might eventually become a challenge in the future. For example, PE can be an effective leader in driving the carbon transition across multiple sectors. However, a short-term horizon will reduce the investment needed to transition fossil fuel-reliant industries to meet emission reduction mandates as it is unlikely to pay off in a 3–5-year context, like how development banks are now forced to consider project investments beyond the short term (GermanWatch & NewClimate Institute, 2018).

Furthermore, Partners Group, an evergreen investor, showcases how over 10 years, a typical $1 billion closed-end fund with the same return (IRR) as an evergreen strategy will lag that same evergreen strategy by $2 billion in value creation (Howarth & Ivanac, 2021).

Likewise, JAB Holdings has been managing its portfolio companies through an evergreen strategy geared toward long-term investments in consumer goods and services. JAB Holdings manages more than $50 billion in capital and has had a 20% compound annual growth rate (CAGR) since its inception in 2012, beating the PE average return of 14.2% (Celarier, 2021). JAB Holding Company (2021) has recently begun incorporating ESG considerations into its investment decision-making process as highlighted in its investing approach, making the case that value could be driven higher with attention paid to sustainability factors. Some of its holdings such as Green Mountain Coffee, Panera Bread, and Krispy Kreme are reporting on their sustainability initiatives (Ennis, 2023).

5.2. *Deal Sourcing*

Deal sourcing is the pipeline of potential investments based on the firm's strategy, risk–return expectations, impact objective, and other criteria. Firms with an impact lens would look for companies that contribute (or could contribute) to solving societal challenges, perhaps using the UN SDGs as a framework for identifying opportunities. Bamboo Capital's investment strategy states its strategic intent to target companies that improve the lives of underserved populations in developing countries. Bamboo tracks the performance of its portfolio companies through a UN SDG lens, including outcomes such as jobs supported, strengthened value chains, positive effects on customers, and reduced negative effects on the climate. For example, Bamboo's investments drive SDG impact as follows:

(1) **UN SDG #1 No Poverty:** Bamboo finances 33 microfinance institutions and seven fintech companies, providing 88 million people with access to financial services.

(2) **UN SDG #2 Zero Hunger:** Bamboo's portfolio supports 62,000 smallholder farms through its agribusiness support and financing of three farmer organizations and three agribusinesses.
(3) **UN SDG #3 Good Health and Well-Being:** Bamboo provides services to 3.6 million patients through the financing of four healthcare access investee companies.

Bamboo's theory of change can be found in its annual impact report (Bamboo Capital Partners, 2020, pp. 8–9).

5.3. *Responsible Exits*

When the PE firm sells a portfolio at "exit," it captures the final return on invested capital (ROIC) and demonstrates its ability to generate positive returns for investors. However, its exit strategy should include ensuring that the buyer will set up the acquired company for success, a step that is sometimes deprioritized to maximize returns.

Exits can occur through different mechanisms: initial public offerings (IPOs), secondary buyouts, trade sales (strategic acquisition by a company seeking a complementary business line), management buybacks (Investees buy back shares and control from GPs), and liquidations. Of these, liquidations (bankruptcies) are viewed the least favorably due to their value destruction. Between 2007 and 2018, secondary buyouts and trade sales (selling to a strategic buyer with an aligned business) were the predominant options employed by firms, a consequence of lengthened holding periods (Cazalaa *et al.*, 2019). With lengthened holding periods, GPs must negotiate extensions or find additional liquidity for their investments due to increased fundraising amounts and LP demand for new opportunities. Secondary buyouts and trade deals provide this liquidity for GPs to exit and find opportunities during periods of increased competition, shrinking fundraising cycles and increasing dry powder (capital in search of a target). As firms feel these pressures, those without any defined procedures to assess business resilience and sustainability after an exit may see poorly executed exits that negatively affect the portfolio company.

Table 1 describes the characteristics of different exit strategies. When considering buyers, especially in trade deals and secondary buyouts, firms will need to assess the buying firm or company's motivations for acquisition as well as its ESG history. An inadequate assessment of the goals of

Table 1. Characteristics of Different Exit Strategies

Exit type	Buyer	Timing	Value Narrative	Business Resilience	ESG Considerations
IPO	Public market listing.	Preparation begins 18–36 months before sale; pricing dependent on market sentiment and volatility (Deloitte, 2016).	Brand; value proposition; competitive differentiators.	Increased regulatory reporting including ESG; GPs hold on to a portion of control to show continued confidence in the company.	Compare to industry peers and evaluate potential and current ESG risks and opportunities; current level of disclosure.
Trade deals	Strategic buyer usually with a complementary business line.	Handover period of 12–24 months; dependent on sector/industry landscape and individual company factors.	Business IP; existing relationships and client base; product consolidation.	Dependent on buyer history, market behavior, and value narrative.	Same as IPO; evaluate fit of acquiring company culture and ESG policies.
Secondary buyouts	Another PE firm.	Deals can be completed within weeks; dependent on selling firm's liquidity needs.	Additional untapped value creation opportunities; discounted purchase price.	Potential improvement to operational efficiency (Achleitner *et al.*, 2012); multiple buyouts lead to erosion of value generation; dependent on buyer history, market behavior, and value narrative.	Same as IPO; evaluate previous owner's impact on culture and ESG policy.
Management buyouts	Investee management team or promoters.	Deals can be completed within weeks; dependent on individual company factors.	Limit upside distribution of future earnings to investors.	Dependent on management's long-term vision.	Same as IPO.

the buyer puts acquired companies at risk for mismanagement and eventual failure (Kitzmann & Schiereck, 2009).

The pandemic shed light on the adverse effects of poorly executed buyouts in PE; as of April 2020, 27 of 38 consumer retailers owned by PE firms were revealed to have the weakest credit profiles compared to industry (Louch & Cooper, 2020). Thousands of employees went on unemployment while PE firms filed for bankruptcy and continued to collect dividends.

Research indicates that PE firms, particularly those specializing in leveraged buyouts, can increase the likelihood of bankruptcy in their portfolio companies. A study that tracked 484 public-to-private leveraged buyouts (LBOs) over 10 years found a bankruptcy rate of approximately 20% vs. the control group's rate of 2% (Ayash & Rastad, 2019). This suggests that highly leveraged transactions in PE are not prioritizing the long-term health of their portfolio companies but rather their exit values.

The Global Impact Investing Network (GIIN) provides guidance on how responsible exits should be considered throughout the deal's life cycle, as shown in Figure 5 (Schiff & Dithrich, 2018).

1. PRE-INVESTMENT

- Invest in organizations for which impact is inherent to their business models.
- Understand the investee's plans for growth and likely exit scenarios.
- Invest in mission-driven founders.

2. AT THE TIME OF INVESTMENT

- Co-invest with aligned investors.
- Hardwire impact through shareholder agreements or legal certifications.
- Structure investments to plan for responsible exits.

3. DURING THE INVESTMENT

- Embed impactful practices into company processes that will outlast changes in ownership.

4. AT THE TIME OF EXIT

- Exit at the right time to ensure the company has access to the resources it needs to scale.
- Maintain management in place.
- Select aligned buyers according to various criteria, such as their vision for scaling the company, track record, and experience in the sector.

Figure 5.   GIIN summary of achieving responsible exits

In addition to ensuring a responsible exit with the buyer, PE firms can work with the portfolio companies to share the exit's financial returns more equitably. For example, HCAP Partners incorporates "carrot agreements" into its engagement with its portfolio companies upon acquisition, with the aim of incentivizing and rewarding companies that have made tangible improvements in job quality (a strategic priority for HCAP). The carrot agreement begins with HCAP setting aside a pool of capital upon exit if two conditions are met:

(1) HCAP meets a certain return threshold.
(2) The portfolio company has made meaningful improvements on job quality standards during the tenure of HCAP's investment.

If both conditions are met, the capital is disbursed to employees with a focus on those considered to be low- to medium-income (LMI) workers. HCAP Partners (2020) successfully implemented two carrot agreements in 2020 with its investments in Mission Healthcare and Confirm Biosciences.

6. Category 4: Fund Management

Responsible investing includes transparent financial reporting. PE has experienced less regulatory scrutiny and regulation than public markets, sometimes resulting in lax or opaque fund management and financial reporting. The use of PME and subscription lines of credits (SLCs) may inflate performance and lead to excessive fees which has led to increased scrutiny of GP management activities. In 2022, the SEC proposed new amendments under the 1940 Investment Act, seeking to increase "transparency, competition, and efficiency in the $18-trillion marketplace" from reporting to fees (SEC, 2022).

Our review of fund management practices by PE firms explores the transparency of financial reporting, with a focus on three areas that are most subject to abuse: the use of public market equivalence (PME) valuations, subscription credit lines, and fund fees.

6.1. *Public Market Equivalence (PME)*

PE funds typically provide quarterly, unaudited reports and an audited annual report to investors. The quarterly reports provide snapshots of the firm's operations, cash flows, and investment performance, which LPs use to adjust their tactical asset allocation (TAA) and exposure to sector/ industries and regions. This section will examine the discrepancies that can arise from non-contextual reporting in public market equivalence (PME) values and the remedies that GPs can adopt to fill the contextual gap. PME is considered a better measure than internal rate of return (IRR) and invested capital multiples (TVPI, RVPI, DPI, etc.) because it directly compares how capital might have performed if invested in the public markets using a public benchmark. This provides investors with insight into how much value their private market investments generated relative to comparable public market investments. The use of PME can address the shortcomings of IRR by considering the length of the holding period, the timing of cash flows, and potential reinvestments, giving a more accurate measure of performance.

Unfortunately, a PME fails to account for many financially material factors such as market cap, leverage, sector/industry focus, foreign exchange effects, and other characteristics of the fund. In fact, several studies have shown that the incorrect use of public benchmarks inflates returns, especially for buyout funds that invest in small-cap value companies (Franzoni *et al.*, 2011; Driessen *et al.*, 2012, pp. 511–535). Adjusting for the size premium, the average buyout fund return was found to be similar to small-cap indices including the oldest small-cap passive mutual fund ("DFA micro-cap"). When the benchmark is levered up and changed to small and value indices, returns are lowered by −3.1% per annum (Driessen *et al.*, 2012, pp. 27–230). Overall, when considering market cap, leverage, and sector/industry, the current performance of PE funds has been shown to be near the level of public markets when compared to PE performance two decades ago, as seen in Figure 6 (Ilmanen *et al.*, 2020).

6.2. *Subscription Credit Facilities*

The aggregate volume of SLCs has increased exponentially since 2014, as seen in Figure 7 (Albertus & Denes, 2019, p. 33). A limited partnership agreement (LPA) sets the total value an LP has pledged to invest in the GP's fund or investment vehicle. This committed capital is then called in at periodic intervals or when needed by GPs to make investments. SLCs allow GPs to borrow money like a loan with the LPs' uncommitted capital as collateral instead of calling capital directly from LPs. GPs use SLCs to

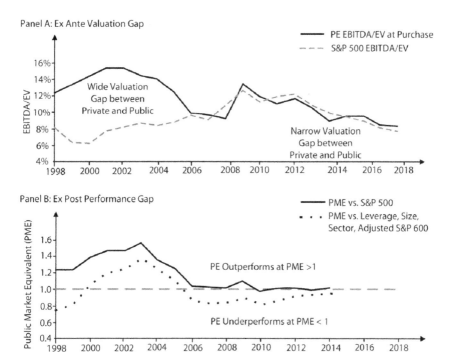

Figure 6. Valuation gap and performance gap between PE and public equities (1 January 1998–30 September 2018)

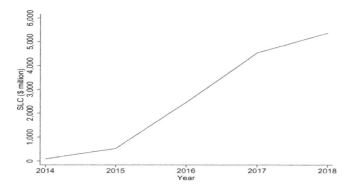

Figure 7. Aggregate use of subscription lines of credit from 2014 to 2018

deploy capital quickly, especially in rapid-paced buyouts. This allows GPs to call capital less frequently, lowering the administrative costs associated with processing capital calls and allowing LPs to maximize the time value of money (TVM) of their investments by placing them in more liquid investments prior to the call (Kazemi, 2020).

Unfortunately, GPs sometimes use SLCs to inflate performance, specifically the IRR of investment vehicles. Consider the example in Table 2 which compares a traditional capital call schedule with the use of a subscription credit line.

Research suggests that use of subscription lines of credit allows funds to delay capital calls from the beginning of the holding period to the middle of the holding period (Albertus & Denes, 2019, pp. 12–15). This allows the fund to push negative cash flows further into the future, increasing overall IRR as distributions are paid out soon after. A recent study using Burgiss data of buyouts found that the annualized IRR for funds using subscription credit lines was increased by 2.6% and that low-performing funds used SLCs to increase the likelihood of meeting their set hurdle rate (Albertus & Denes, 2019, pp. 25–27). Low-performing funds were also able to jump closer to their next performance quartile by using SLCs, thereby skewing the overall asset classes' performance. If this approach continues, defaults could occur during periods of high market stress with limited liquidity.

The ILPA, an industry group dedicated to furthering LP interests, released a series of recommendations to increase the transparency of SLC

Table 2.   Subscription Credit Line Call Schedule Examples

Scenario 1: With no SLC							
Cash Flow Type	**2017**	**2018**	**2019**	**2020**	**2021**	**2022**	**IRR**
GP cash flows	−$60 m	0	0	$15 m	0	$100 m	—
LP cash flows	−$60 m	0	0	$15 m	0	$100 m	14.83%

Scenario 2: With SLC							
Cash Flow Type	**2017**	**2018**	**2019**	**2020**	**2021**	**2022**	**IRR**
SLC	$60 m	0	0	−$75 m	0	0	—
GP cash flows	−$60 m	0	0	$15 m	0	$100 m	—
LP cash flows	0	0	0	−$60 m	0	$100 m	29.10%

Note: m — million.

use with GPs. Broken down by quarterly and annual reporting, GPs should begin reporting information as detailed in ILPA's recommended disclosures on SLC use, including providing Net IRR w/o use of the facility, calculation methodology, and size of the facility (ILPA, 2020).

6.3. *Fund Fees*

The primary fee structure in PE is straightforward; it includes management fees and carried interest traditionally represented by the 2 and 20 rule. The carried interest is 20% of the excess return earned by GPs after meeting a hurdle rate or preferred rate of return agreed upon by LPs. Carried interest is taxed as a capital gain to the GP of the fund. The investment manager of the fund receives management fees in exchange for investment advice typically amounting to 2% of the LP's invested AUM. Investment managers use management fees to cover the cost of a fund's annual operations (Steinman, 2014). A visual breakdown of the typical organizational structure of PE and associated fees can be seen in Figure 8.

The fees are usually listed in a "Management Service Agreement" (MSA) for investors. However, PE firms have found ingenious ways to increase their revenue by charging excessive fees to portfolio companies.

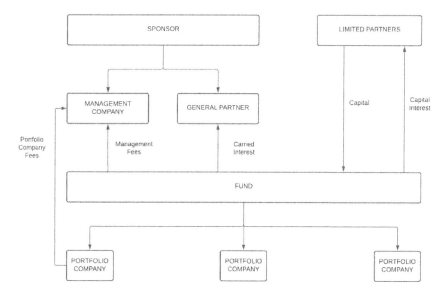

Figure 8.   Typical organization structure of private equity

One paper compiled by the Center for Economic and Policy Research discusses abusive fee allocation and expense practices including double-dipping (charging LPs for back-office expenses that should have been covered by the 2% management fee), failure to share monitoring fee income (the consulting and advisory fees paid to GPs by portfolio companies), and using consultants to avoid sharing fees (hiring outside of the PE firm and billing the services to the portfolio companies) (Appelbaum & Batt, 2016).

Table 3 describes some of the fees charged to LPs and portfolio companies. The offsets column describes fees charged to portfolio companies that are offset by the management fee charged to LPs (Stepstone, 2016). This prevents GPs from generating revenue from simply performing expected fund management services, but these offsets must be clarified in MSAs with respect to the percentage offset and types of fees that can be offset. For example, if a GP manages to collect $1 million in fees from one of its funds with 60% offset, then only $600,000 would be deducted from the management fee paid to the GP.

In addition to the fees listed above, GPs charge additional fees to portfolio companies including monitoring fees to provide oversight after acquisitions and transaction fees upon the completion of a deal. Both fees are dependent on the market cap and earnings before interest, taxes, depreciation, and amortization (EBITDA) of portfolio companies; GPs do offer potential tax incentives for portfolio companies, but excess fees can tilt a company into bankruptcy. The increased bankruptcy risk comes because of the value of fees which restrict a company's ability to use the

Table 3.   Private Equity Fee Types

Fee Types	Limited Partners	Offsets	Portfolio Companies
One Time	• Organizational expenses • Broken deal expenses	• Transaction expenses • Exit fees • Breakup fees	• Legal fees • Due diligence fees • Consulting fees • Financing fees
Annual Fixed	• Audit tax expenses • Fund administration expenses	• Monitoring fees; Accelerated monitoring fees • Director fees	NA
Asset-Based	• Management fees	NA	NA
Performance	NA	• Carried interest	NA

assets for other purposes. Over a 20-year period from 1994 to 2014, 600 portfolio companies in a sample study were charged close to $10 billion in monitoring fees alone, plus another $10 billion in other fees (Phalippou *et al.*, 2016). These fees are traditionally considered offsets, but without being defined as such in MSAs, GPs do not have to report or include these expenses as part of their management fee.

GPs can use fee waivers to lower their taxable income rate by claiming their deferred share of future returns under the lens of long-term capital gains and not ordinary income. The reasoning is that if GPs are forgoing their management fee in the present for a share of future earnings, and since future earnings are subject to market conditions, GPs should be taxed at the long-term capital gains rate to account for market volatility of returns (Ashraf & Pirio, 2013). Issues arise surrounding fee waivers in the recognition of what should be considered ordinary taxable income vs. long-term gains. Current regulatory guidance in the U.S. allows for firms to recognize the waiver of management fees bearing any significant entrepreneurial risk. However, deliberate miscategorization of fee waivers allows GPs to circumvent the underlying risk they are subject to with respect to their fund contributions and allows them to realize greater profit when their returns are considered long-term gains (*Proposed Regulations Issued on Management Fee Waivers — Insights — Prosker Rose LLP*, 2015).

LPs have begun asking GPs to include any additional fees under the umbrella of management fees. Meanwhile, the SEC has also begun to act in 2023, requiring firms to provide investors with quarterly statements on performance, expenses, and fees; prohibiting GPs from collecting certain fees and expenses related to unperformed services, paid back carry, and portfolio company fees; and suggesting limits on GP extensions of credit from LPs (Drew, 2022; SEC, 2023).

7. Category 5: Societal Impact

Responsible investing frameworks should ensure that PE creates value for key stakeholders (including the portfolio firm, employees, communities, and investors). Research supports this outlook. For example, one study evaluated the performance of 16,802 companies that received PE financing and found that there was a positive and significant correlation between receiving PE financing and annual employment and sales growth in the corresponding year (Paglia & Harjoto, 2014). Another study examining whether 772 PE firms contributed to the financial fragility of companies during the 2008 financial crisis showed that PE-owned companies issued less debt and increased capital spending compared to their non-PE-owned peers. PE firms, as a result, increased the value of their investments by 6% relative to other companies in the post-crisis periods (Bernstein *et al.*, 2017).

However, some firms may go further and focus on making profits explicitly through creating positive societal impact, which is the subject of this category. PE is in a unique position, with its deep cross-sector engagement, to embed sustainability as core to investment strategy and report on robust social and environmental KPIs.

Leading the transformation may allow first-movers to capture high-value opportunities and attract more capital, with, for example, early adopters of EU Sustainable Finance Disclosure Regulation (SFDR) expecting better fundraising periods. This will require firms to address material ESG issues and impacts through their investment strategy, design and implement robust ESG/impact implementation with their portfolio companies, make formal or informal commitments to address issues such as DEI or climate change, track ESG-related KPIs, and report their progress in ESG/impact reports.

It is important to note that ESG and impact are two different strategic approaches. ESG aims to manage material ESG risk as well as explore ESG business opportunities. For example, a PE firm that aims to bring Employee Stock Ownership Plans to the employees of its portfolio companies is aiming to improve stakeholder benefits and performance through that strategy, but the companies that it works with may not have an impact focus. PE firms with an impact focus aim to solve societal problems through the purpose of those companies, investing in themes such as renewable energy or inclusive finance. In both cases, KPIs can be assessed and tracked qualitatively and quantitatively using ESG- or UN SDG-based metrics (UNDP, n.d.). All of these become more important as major global regulatory bodies like CSRD require companies to consider double materiality assessments (EFRAG, 2023).

7.1. *Embedding Sustainability*

Sustainability is embedded when the proactive management of material ESG issues and a balanced approach to the needs of stakeholders (including shareholders) are completely and effectively integrated into the company's business strategy with the goal of creating positive societal value which unlocks financial value for the company.

In the past, investors and corporate leaders would often dismiss the negative societal impacts of their businesses as externalities for which they were not responsible. Unfortunately, PE ownership in industries such as healthcare, education, and even newspapers can drive negative societal outcomes for which the PE firm is directly accountable. Academic research into PE ownership of colleges, for example, found lower graduation and loan repayment rates, as well as lower earnings by graduates. The authors found evidence that these detrimental outcomes reflect lower educational inputs and increases in marketing due to firms prioritizing profitability through increased leverage. Students were burdened with rising tuition costs and more debt. In addition to the financial impacts felt by students, the quality and scope of degree programs decreased, leading to a decline in graduation rates by 13% (Eaton *et al.*, 2019).

With the consolidation of local newspapers and reporting outlets by PE (representing 13% of the market in 2019), another study found the focus on the bottom line led to reporters being laid off and local news coverage declining. The study also found that this led to local citizens being less likely to vote in local elections (Ewens *et al.*, 2021).

On the upside, a meta-analysis by NYU Stern CSB of over 1200 academic studies showcased a strong correlation between the performance of ESG factors and positive corporate (58%) and investor (33%) financial returns as seen in Figure 9 (Whelan *et al.*, 2021).

Similarly, after reviewing PE deals in the Asia-Pacific region with social or environmental considerations or in sectors related closely to ESG

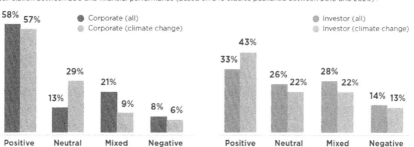

Figure 1. Positive and/or neutral results for investing in sustainability dominate. Very few studies found a negative correlation between ESG and financial performance (based on 245 studies published between 2016 and 2020) .

Figure 9.　NYU Stern CSB ESG meta-analysis

issues such as water, waste, and education, a study found these deals to have higher return multiples than their non-ESG counterparts (Yang *et al.*, 2019).

For the PE firm and its portfolio companies, ESG/sustainability must be a part of corporate strategy, not a stand-alone strategy. That means approaching the sustainability landscape in the same way one tackles corporate planning — start with understanding the relevant ESG trends and associated risks and opportunities. Use the ESG lens to explore — what are the material ESG issues for the PE firm and its investment thesis? The investment strategy will dictate the material ESG factors — for example, manufacturing will have different material ESG risks compared to technology. Other ESG materiality questions will include the following: How do we recruit and retain high-performing employees? Where is the regulation going? What type of technologies might help? What is the competition doing? With whom might we collaborate to meet our goals? The Sustainability Accounting Standards Board (now part of the ISSB — the International Sustainable Standards Board) provides a good guide on material ESG issues for both PE firms and their portfolio companies.

After identifying the firm's material ESG issues, the firm should consult with stakeholders such as employees, regulators, NGOs, and their own portfolio companies to determine what they consider to be the most material ESG issues for the firm. That mapping then can be used to develop a materiality matrix, which provides insight into the importance of various topics for the firm and the stakeholders and becomes a core building block for the firm's embedded sustainability strategy. This learning process will be helpful when working with portfolio companies to require them to develop their own ESG and stakeholder mapping and materiality matrices. A sample firm-wide materiality matrix by Neuberger Berman PE Partners (NBPE) can be seen on page seven of their 2022 Private Markets ESG report, depicting key ESG factors across several industries (Neuberger Cerman, 2022). The proprietary framework helps guide NBPE's due diligence and ESG integration across their direct investments. Though categorized differently, the same level of information is captured compared to traditionally formatted matrices, an example of which can be seen through Bank of America's approach on their website (see Bank of America, n.d.).

The embedded sustainability strategy will inform all aspects of the PE firm's approach, from its own human capital to its investment policy, dealmaking, portfolio company engagement, fund management, and exit strategy. For example, consider EQT, a Swedish firm that in 2019 became the first PE firm to include a statement of purpose, signed by the entire board, showcasing its commitment to the long-term viability or "futureproofing" of its portfolio companies (EQT, n.d.). Its efforts fall in line with its active ownership and include commitments to support multiple stakeholders, diversity, and renewable energy within the scope of the UN SDGs. This has been good business for EQT; in a five-year post-exit study, 70% of its exited portfolio companies were shown to be still growing with an annual average sales and employment growth of 9% and 8%, respectively (Eccles *et al.*, 2020, p. 5). In aligning itself with its statement of purpose, EQT follows an embedded sustainability strategy beginning with a societal impact framework. The framework is similar in design to a materiality matrix focused more on the solutions and practices of a potential investment with respect to sustainability and the UN SDGs. Company operations, both direct and indirect, are analyzed through the environmental and social problems they solve (solutions) with respect to the efficacy and scope of the company's impact (practices) as shown in Figure 10. This two-dimensional framework allows EQT a better in-depth review of its portfolio companies' contributions to UN SDG progress and a better understanding of the risks arising from sustainability factors (Eccles *et al.*, 2020, p. 8).

As discussed in the strategy and innovation section, regular updating of responsible or sustainable investment policies will be necessary, due to the dynamic nature of materiality. Firms that are sector focused are especially vulnerable to disruptive technologies and social trends and need to be able to quickly change course and develop new metrics. Dynamic materiality can be addressed if firms include a scenario-based approach that considers potential sector-wide outcomes (Bancilhon & Park, 2021).

Identifying which products, technologies, or sector-specific practices are reducing ESG risk and driving ESG value can be evaluated by creating

WSAudiology

Global pure play producer of hearing aids and accessories with more than 100 years of experience and a proven track record as an industry innovator

Solutions: Improving lives and reducing inequalities for people with hearing disabilities globally through continuous innovation in hearing aids and educational efforts

Practices: Pushing renewable energy and energy efficiency across operations for reduced negative climate and environmental impact – *Improved bottom line through increased operational efficiency – 32% reduction in electricity consumption between 2017-2018*

Figure 10. Application of EQT societal impact framework to WSAudiology

and tracking performance-based KPIs through proprietary or industry frameworks such as the Sustainability Accounting Standards Board, the ESG Data Convergence Initiative, or the OPIM which was covered in previous sections.

Furthermore, PE firms are increasingly making formal and informal public commitments on material ESG issues such as climate and DEI, supported by industry-wide initiatives.

7.2. *Environmental Commitments*

Formal commitments to groups such as the Net Zero Asset Managers Initiative (NZAM) enable firms to hold themselves accountable as agents of change. Net Zero Asset Managers encourages firms to report emissions, strategies, and progress in reaching net-zero emissions by 2050 or sooner (NZMA, n.d.). Investindustrial, a European and B Corp PE firm, is a member of the Net Zero Asset Managers Initiative and pledged in late 2021 to achieve net zero across all its funds by setting science-based targets for its portfolio company emissions. Additionally, Investindustrial requires portfolio companies to publish their carbon emissions as well as their exposure to climate risks, and results have shown them mostly outperforming their public peers with respect to the MSCI Europe ESG Index. To continue their progress in keeping temperatures below or at 1.5°C by 2030, Investindustrial (2021) provided the following targets based on the Science Based Targets (SBT) initiative in its press release:

- "Investindustrial's direct and indirect emissions to be reduced by 68.5% on a headcount intensity basis and 46.2% in absolute, in accordance with 1.5° mitigation pathways;
- Investindustrial to achieve and maintain 100% renewable energy by 2030 and beyond;
- 100% of the Investindustrial portfolio companies in legacy and future funds will have their own SBTs validated by 2030 onwards;
- Residual emissions by Investindustrial and the portfolio companies to be neutralized by verified emissions removals from nature-based solutions."

The Initiative Climat International (iCI) also aims to help PE firms accelerate the transition to net zero (PRI, 2021). As of May 2022, 160 PE firms representing more than $3 trillion AUM were signed up to ICI, which recently released a report on greenhouse gas (GHG) accounting and reporting for PE firms (PRI, 2022). The report provides guidance and methodologies for firms to calculate portfolio company emissions based on the PE firm's degree of operational and financial control over the portfolio company. Other aspects covered in the report include the calculation of direct and indirect emissions, financed and non-financed emissions, and reporting methodologies (Bone *et al.*, 2022).

PE firms are also making individual climate commitments. Blackstone aims to reduce carbon emissions by 15% in aggregate over three years in new portfolio company investments where it controls the company's energy usage. To support its efforts, Blackstone is developing a carbon accounting system that will allow it to measure, track, and report on Scope 1 and 2 emissions of its investments (the lack of Scope 3 tracking is an important omission, as most corporate emissions are Scope 3).

7.3. *DEI Commitments*

Commitments to DEI, as discussed in the human capital section, should also be part of the firm's focus on positive societal impact — not only for its own employees and portfolio company employees but also in terms of vendors, customers, and communities. Groups and initiatives like LGBT Great, which promotes LGBT + equity and inclusion, and the Women in Finance Charter, which seeks to increase the representation of women in the field, are examples of organizations firms can partner with to address DEI within their firm. Other groups like the Management Leadership for Tomorrow (MLT) have created specific certifications like the MLT Black Equity at Work Certification to encourage firms to "pursue Black equity with the same effort as their pursuit of earnings and other key priorities." Firms that have committed to earning the designation include Ares, Bain, BlackRock, and Wellington Management. The process of earning the certification requires firms to show observable progress toward the following five key areas (more information can be found on mlt.org):

(1) Increasing Black employee representation at every level of the organization, from the Board of Directors and senior leaders to middle management and professionals to the organization as a whole.

(2) Ensuring pay equity between Black and White employees in similar roles and providing just compensation and equitable benefits for positions in which Black employees tend to be overrepresented.

(3) Creating an anti-racist workplace where Black employees feel they belong, are valued, and can advance.

(4) Progressing toward proportionate vendor and supplier spending with Black-owned businesses and proactively utilizing organizational capabilities in support of Black equity.

(5) Providing annual contributions and/or in-kind services to non-profit organizations that increase Black equity and investing in Black equity-focused financial institutions and/or investment products.

7.4. *Reporting*

Top-to-bottom ESG reporting for both the PE firm and its portfolio companies is becoming increasingly important to ensure good management and to attract capital. The lack of a standardized definition of ESG coupled with a lack of audited ESG reporting has increased investor concerns about greenwashing. Public market funds have experienced challenges to their ESG labeling as seen in the 2022 raid of Deutsche Bank and SEC investigation of Goldman Sachs (*Reuters*, 2022; Natarajan & Beyoud, 2022). While the crackdown has begun in public markets, PE firms have also begun increasing the transparency of their own ESG reporting. In fact, some PE firms have demonstrated that transparent reporting of ESG leads to building investor confidence and reducing concerns of greenwashing by LPs (Hamlin, 2022).

ESG reporting standards such as GRI and SASB have already gained a foothold in public markets and are increasingly being adopted in private markets. As occurred with accounting standards, many of the frameworks and standards for ESG are undergoing consolidation. The International Sustainability Standards Board (ISSB), which oversees the International Financial Reporting Standards (IFRS), has further consolidated SASB, and as of 2023, has taken over climate-related disclosures from TCFD. Similarly with 81% of Asia-Pacific companies being GRI aligned, ISSB has been working closely with GRI to identify commonalities in reporting (IFRS, 2023).

The ESG Data Convergence Project, a consortium of LPs and GPs representing over $4 trillion of assets, is seeking to standardize ESG reporting for PE (Buck *et al.*, 2021). Membership is open to any interested LPs and GPs. A summary of the first set of draft ESG metrics released in 2021 can be seen in Figure 11, with the understanding that additional metrics will follow. The latest update in 2023 saw the addition of net-zero metrics measuring portfolio company decarbonization ambitions, strategies, and targets.

Whether or not firms decide to join the ESG Data Convergence Project or other initiatives, best practice requires third-party audited reporting and is increasingly demanded by LPs. According to a McKinsey's Sustainability Reporting Survey, of the 57 investors who responded, 67% said they would like sustainability reports to undergo the same level of scrutiny as financial reports (Bernow *et al.*, 2019). As calls for audits of non-financial information increase, firms need to verify not only their performance against different ESG KPIs but also their processes. Firms such as Bluemark, a Tideline company, provide audit services to verify the progress of non-financial KPIs and the processes which firms use to collect the data in accordance with the frameworks they have adopted.

This differentiation between process and performance-based auditing is a double layer of assurance for investors in confirming the data quality of reported metrics. These non-financial audits help avoid potential headline and regulatory risks related to misleading investors and are essential to a firm's review of its sustainable investment policy and KPIs.

Key Metric	Individual Data Points
Greenhouse gas emissions	• Scope 1 • Scope 2 • Scope 3 (optional)
Renewable energy %	• Total energy consumption • Total renewable energy consumption
Board diversity	• Percentage of women on board of directors • Percentage of under-represented groups on board of directors (optional for non-US companies)
Work-related injuries	• Total number of work-related injuries • Total number of work-related fatalities • Days lost due to injury
Net new hires	• Organic net new hires • Total net new hires • Annual percent attrition
Employee engagement	• Do you conduct an annual employee feedback survey? (Y/N) • Percentage of employees responding to annual survey (optional)

Source: ESG Data Convergence Project.

Figure 11. ESG data convergence draft metrics

7.5. *EU Sustainable Financial Disclosure Regulation*

Recognizing, building, and monitoring a sustainability metric inventory is a prelude to meeting jurisdictional reporting requirements focused on material ESG and climate risk factors. In Europe, the Sustainable Financial Disclosure Regulation (SFDR) acts as a regulatory body to improve transparency in sustainable investment products especially in its claims to combat greenwashing. To accomplish this, SFDR published guidance under numerous articles dealing with different forms of disclosure as they relate to sustainable investment products (The European Parliament, 2019; Maples Group, n.d.).

For PE and other firms, Articles 4, 6, 8, and 9 are important in reporting disclosures related to funds with sustainability characteristics and their accompanying risks. To aid in the classification of funds, the European Supervisory Authority (ESA) published a set of metrics and technical guidance on identifying principal adverse impacts (PAIs) which influence different sustainability characteristics. Of the metrics proposed, 14 were deemed mandatory with the additional being considered opt-in, as shown in Figure 12 (Vanhomwegen, 2021).

The PAIs act as indicators for fund managers to provide contextual environmental and social information on the adverse effects inherent in their fund and holdings. This information will be provided in a PAI Statement disclosed separately per Article 4 requirements. Additional guidance is forthcoming from ESA and European Securities and Markets

MANDATORY ADVERSE SUSTAINABILITY INDICATORS

Climate and other environment indicators	Social and governance indicators
• GHG Emissions (Scope 1,2,3 & Total) • Carbon Footprint • GHG Intensity • Fossil fuel sector • Non-renewable energy consumption and production • Energy consumption intensity per high impact climate sector • Biodiversity sensitive areas • Emissions to water • Hazardous waste ratio	• Violations of UN Global Compact principles and OECD Guidelines • Lack of processes and compliance mechanisms to monitor compliance with UN Global Compact principles and OECD Guidelines • Gender pay gap • Board gender diversity • Exposure to controversial weapons

Figure 12.   ESA metrics

Authority (ESMA) on the technical applications of breadth of coverage for the PAIs, especially focused on emissions (ESMA, 2023).

7.6. *Financed Emissions Reporting*

With climate change driving increased extreme weather events, droughts, coastal erosion, and higher temperatures, market actors have begun to focus on their emissions. The Partnership for Carbon Accounting Financials (PCAF) helps financial services firms calculate, monitor, and report their financed emissions from their investments. Financed emissions dealing with investments pertain to the GHG Protocol's Scope 3 Category 15 (investments) designation and deal with a financial firm's attributable emissions from its underlying investments including corporate loans. Though not directly responsible for these emissions, firms indirectly bear the burden of a portion of the emissions based on the size of their invested capital relative to the value of the asset or loan. PCAF's methodology applies across 7 asset classes, including listed equities and corporate bonds, business loans and unlisted equities, project finance, commercial real estate, mortgages, motor vehicle loans, and sovereign debt.

Current guidance does not include PE, but firms can begin to take steps to prepare for data sourcing and collection. Data sourcing is the most cumbersome step and requires firms to adhere to PCAF's data quality guidance in selecting sources as shown in Figure 13.

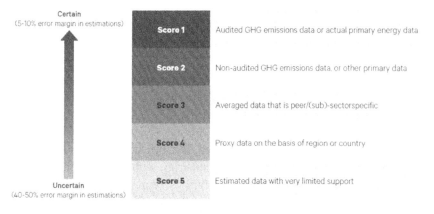

Figure 13. PCAF data quality guidance (2019)

Firms should strive for data sources with a score of 2 or 1, but market limitations in emissions data quality may make it difficult to achieve that goal. To collect audited or unaudited emissions or other primary data, portfolio company investments need systems in place capable of doing so. Technology providers like Novata, Persefoni, and Green Project Technologies exist to facilitate and aggregate the carbon accounting process portfolio-wide, but it will be PE firms who ultimately push the adoption of such processes within their portfolio companies.

7.7. *Benefit Corporation (B Corp) Certification*

Some PE firms have pursued B Corp certification for themselves and their portfolio companies to demonstrate their commitment to positive societal impact. For PE firms, the B Corp standard requires firms to provide transparency on their firm's governance structure, worker impacts, community engagement, environmental impacts, and stakeholder impacts. These are measured through a set of required disclosures which are publicly available on B Lab's website. The requirements are as follows and can be seen on B Corp's website (B Corp, 2023):

(1) "Demonstrate high social and environmental performance by achieving a B Impact Assessment score of 80 or above and passing our risk review. Multinational corporations must also meet baseline requirement standards.
(2) Make a legal commitment by changing their corporate governance structure to be accountable to all stakeholders, not just shareholders, and achieve Benefit Corporation status if available in their jurisdiction.
(3) Exhibit transparency by allowing information about their performance measured against B Lab's standards to be publicly available on their B Corp profile on B Lab's website."

Dozens of PE firms have achieved B Corp certification including Bridge Fund Management and InvestIndustrial, with ratings from B Corp of 145 and 116, respectively. These ratings represent a firm's overall impact and allow it to be benchmarked with peer firms in the industry.

8. Conclusion

The framework provides an assessment tool for LPs, GPs, and stakeholders to review policies, practices, and impacts and advocate for course corrections, if necessary. Forward-thinking and early-moving GPs will be interested in using this framework to guide decision-making, as will LPs who wish to translate the framework findings into tools to drive change and accountability through their due diligence and review.

We hope we have demonstrated that PE has a clear pathway to creating value for stakeholders and the planet while generating superior returns. These goals are not mutually exclusive and, in fact, showcase the sometimes-deleterious consequences of short-term, value-extractive behaviors. It is in everyone's interest — investors, corporations, communities, employees, and GPs — to put in place policies, governance, strategies, and KPIs that drive responsible and sustainable investing in portfolio companies.

Acknowledgments

We would like to thank the funders of this project, an anonymous donor and the US Endowment for Forestry and Communities, as well as Delilah Rothenberg at the Pre-Distribution Initiative, Peter Dunbar at the UN PRI, Jennifer Flood and Serge Younes at InvestIndustrial, as well as the PE firms and myriad other organizations who helped. We would also like to thank NYU Stern interns Lauren Marx and Lia Feng for their research assistance.

References

Acharya, V. V., Gottschalg, O., Hahn, M., & Kehoe, C. (2010). Corporate governance and value creation: Evidence from private equity. *Social Science Research Network*, 24. Retrieved from https://doi.org/10.2139/ssrn.1324016.

Achleitner, A., Figge, C., & Lutz, E. (2012). Drivers of value creation in a secondary buyout: The acquisition of Brenntag by BC partners. *Social Science Research Network*. Retrieved from https://doi.org/10.2139/ssrn.2071247.

Albertus, J. F. & Denes, M. (2019). Distorting private equity performance: the rise of fund debt. *Social Science Research Network*. Retrieved from https://doi.org/10.2139/ssrn.3410076.

American Investment Council. (2022, May 10). Guidelines for responsible Investing — American Investment Council. Retrieved from https://www. investmentcouncil.org/guidelines-for-responsible-investing/. (Accessed December 10, 2023).

An introduction to responsible investment I PRI. (n.d.). PRI. Retrieved from https://www.unpri.org/investment-tools/introductory-guides-to-responsible-investment. (Accessed December 10, 2023).

Appelbaum, E. & Batt, R. (2016). Fees, fees and more fees: How private equity abuses its limited partners and U.S. taxpayers. Retrieved from https://cepr.net/images/stories/reports/private-equity-fees-2016-05.pdf. (Accessed December 10, 2023).

Ashraf, S. & K. Pirio, A. (2013). Management fee waivers: The current state of play. *Journal of Taxation and Regulation of Financial Institutions*, 27(2). Retrieved from https://www.ballardspahr.com/-/media/files/articles/2013-11-management-fee-waivers-current-state-of-play.pdf?la=en&hash=BF0665 08467EB801FF6F456FE9DD83FE.

Ayash, B. & Rastad, M. (2019). Leveraged buyouts and financial distress. *Social Science Research Network*. Retrieved from https://doi.org/10.2139/ssrn. 3423290.

B Corp. (2023, October 6). B Corp Certification demonstrates a company's entire social and environmental impact. Retrieved from https://www.bcorporation. net/en-us/certification/. (Accessed December 11, 2023).

Baboolall, D., Nee, A., & Yee, L. (2021, March 1). How private equity can catalyze diversity, equity, and inclusion in the workplace. McKinsey & Company. Retrieved from https://www.mckinsey.com/industries/private-equity-and-principal-investors/our-insights/how-private-equity-can-catalyze-diversity-equity-and-inclusion-in-the-workplace. (Accessed December 10, 2023).

Bain & Company & Aviva. (2022). Women in finance charter blueprint. Retrieved from https://www.bain.com/contentassets/5a93335e26af4f47a1744a2a823 6de35/women-in-finance-charter-blueprint.pdf. (Accessed December 10, 2023).

Balakumar, U. & Whelan, T. (2023, February). The road to responsible private equity: A responsible investing framework, insights and cases toward a positive pathway. NYU Stern CSB. Retrieved from https://drive.google.com/file/d/1IEY--rCv_OxK83r-5Wg6OrsvYuuGk_3B/view.

Bamboo Capital Partners. (2020). Weathering the crisis, building resilience: Impact report 2020. Retrieved from https://bamboocp.com/wp-content/uploads/Bamboo-Impact-Report-2020-1.pdf. (Accessed December 10, 2023).

Bancilhon, C. & Park, J. (2021, July 22). Dynamic materiality: How companies can future-proof materiality assessments | Blog | Sustainable Business Network and Consultancy | *BSR*. Retrieved from https://www.bsr.org/en/blog/dynamic-materiality-how-companies-can-future-proof-materiality-assessments. (Accessed December 10, 2023).

Bank of America. (n.d.). ESG materiality assessment — Bank of America. Retrieved from https://about.bankofamerica.com/en/making-an-impact/materiality. (Accessed December 10, 2023).

Basak, S. & Karsh, M. (2020, December 9). Apollo finds fewer than 100 Black executives in private equity. *Bloomberg.com*. Retrieved from https://www.bloomberg.com/news/articles/2020-12-09/apollo-finds-fewer-than-100-black-executives-in-private-equity?leadSource=uverify%20wall. (Accessed December 10, 2023).

Bernow, S., Godsall, J., Klempner, B., & Merten, C. (2019, August 7). More than values: The value-based sustainability reporting that investors want. McKinsey & Company. Retrieved from https://www.mckinsey.com/capabilities/sustainability/our-insights/more-than-values-the-value-based-sustainability-reporting-that-investors-want. (Accessed December 11, 2023).

Bernstein, S., Lerner, J., & Mezzanotti, F. (2017). Private equity and financial fragility during the crisis. Working Paper 23626, National Bureau of Economic Research, Cambridge. Retrieved from https://doi.org/10.3386/w23626.

Bone, J., Eddie, M., Hudson, V., Ayles, E., Gregory, D., & Plummer, Z. (2022). Greenhouse gas accounting and reporting: For the private equity sector. Retrieved from https://www.unpri.org/download?ac=16265. (Accessed December 11, 2023).

Buck, L., Brennan, J., Shandal, V., Brigl, M., Fischer, G., Stoffers, M., & Remillard, M. (2021, October 21). How private equity can converge on ESG data. BCG Global. Retrieved from https://www.bcg.com/publications/2021/private-equity-convergence-on-esg-data. (Accessed December 11, 2023).

Cazalaa, G., Hayes, W., & Morgan, P. (2019, August 1). Private equity exit excellence: Getting the story right. McKinsey & Company. Retrieved from https://www.mckinsey.com/industries/private-equity-and-principal-investors/our-insights/private-equity-exit-excellence-getting-the-story-right. (Accessed December 10, 2023).

Celarier, M. (2021, December 4). Is private equity overrated? *nytimes.com*. Retrieved from https://www.nytimes.com/2021/12/04/business/is-private-equity-overrated.html#:~:text=As%20of%20September%202020%2C%20private,industry%2C%20using%20the%20latest%20numbers. (Accessed December 10, 2023).

Commitment — The net zero asset managers initiative. (n.d.). Retrieved from https://www.netzeroassetmanagers.org/commitment/. (Accessed December 10, 2023).

Deloitte. (2016). Private company IPOs: Is timing everything? Retrieved from https://www2.deloitte.com/content/dam/Deloitte/us/Documents/audit/us-audit-private-company-ipos-is-timing-everything.pdf. (Accessed December 10, 2023).

Drew, B. J. (2022, February 9). SEC proposes new rules for private equity. *Journal of Accountancy*. Retrieved from https://www.journalofaccountancy. com/news/2022/feb/sec-proposes-new-rules-private-equity.html. (Accessed December 10, 2023).

Driessen, J., Lin, T., & Phalippou, L. (2012). A new method to estimate risk and return of non-traded assets from cash flows: The case of private equity funds. *Social Science Research Network*. Retrieved from https://doi. org/10.2139/ssrn.2065940.

Eaton, C., Howell, S. T., & Yannelis, C. (2019). When investor incentives and consumer interests diverge: Private equity in higher education. *Social Science Research Network*. https://doi.org/10.2139/ssrn.3371413.

Eccles, R. G., Lennehag, T., & Nornholm, N. (2020, August 17). EQT: Private equity with a purpose. Retrieved from https://ssrn.com/abstract=3652586. (Accessed December 10, 2023).

Eccles, R. G., Shandal, V., Young, D., & Montgomery, B. (2022). 21 Private equity should take the lead in sustainability. In *De Gruyter eBooks: Vol. July-August 2022* (pp. 203–212). *Harvard Business Review*. https://doi.org/ 10.1515/9783111295268-022.

EFRAG. (2023). Implementation guidance for the materiality assessment. Retrieved from https://www.efrag.org/Assets/Download?assetUrl=%2Fsites% 2Fwebpublishing%2FMeeting%20Documents%2F2307280747599961% 2F06-02%20Materiality%20Assessment%20SRB%20230823.pdf&AspxAu toDetectCookieSupport=1. (Accessed December 10, 2023).

Ennis, M. (2023, April 20). How green mountain coffee roasters ensures every cup is packed with goodness. Retrieved from https://www.keurig.com/hub/ lifestyle/gmcr-packed-with-goodness. (Accessed December 10, 2023).

EQT. (n.d.). Statement of purpose. Retrieved from https://eqtgroup.com/about/ statement-of-purpose/. (Accessed December 10, 2023).

ESMA. (2023, August 3). Sustainable finance: Implementation timeline for SFDR | TR | CSRD | MiFID | IDD | UCITS | AIFMD. Retrieved from https:// www.esma.europa.eu/sites/default/files/library/sustainable_finance_-_ implementation_timeline.pdf.

Ewens, M., Gupta, A., & Howell, S. T. (2021). Local journalism under private equity ownership. *Social Science Research Network*. Retrieved from https:// doi.org/10.2139/ssrn.3939405.

Franzoni, F., Nowak, É., & Phalippou, L. (2011). Private equity performance and liquidity risk. *Social Science Research Network*. Retrieved from https://doi. org/10.2139/ssrn.1517044.

Germanwatch & NewClimate Institute. (2018). Aligning investments with the Paris agreement temperature goal. Retrieved from https://newclimate.org/ sites/default/files/2018/09/MDB_WorkingPaper_2018-09.pdf. (Accessed December 10, 2023).

Hamlin, J. (2022, February 17). What one private equity investor calls 'Greenwashing,' another calls ESG. Institutional Investor. Retrieved from https://www.institutionalinvestor.com/article/2bstn31sw3niuqsm641s0/portfolio/what-one-private-equity-investor-calls-greenwashing-another-calls-esg. (Accessed December 11, 2023).

Hammer, B., Pettkus, S., Schweizer, D., & Wünsche, N. (2021). The more the merrier? Diversity and private equity performance. *British Journal of Management*, 33(1), 231–265. https://doi.org/10.1111/1467-8551.12456.

Hampole, N. & Korngold, D. (2021, March 4). ESG in private equity: How to write a responsible investment policy | Reports | sustainable business network and consultancy | BSR. Retrieved from https://www.bsr.org/en/reports/esg-in-private-equity-how-to-write-a-responsible-investment-policy. (Accessed December 10, 2023).

HCAP Partners. (2020). 2020 annual impact report. Retrieved from https://static1.squarespace.com/static/6334ad5adde1f249453ad01a/t/638557cca89b9902cf408f2d/1669683151931/HCAP+2020+Annual+Impact+Report+Rev+05-21-B.pdf. (Accessed December 10, 2023).

Howarth, A. & Ivanac, J. (2021). Evergreen funds: The next frontier for private markets investors? Retrieved from https://www.partnersgroup.com/fileadmin/user_upload/Files/Research_PDF/20220210_Partners_Group_Research_Evergreen_Funds.pdf. (Accessed December 10, 2023).

IFRS. (2023, November 9). IFRS — GRI establishes sustainability innovation lab in coordination with the IFRS foundation. Retrieved from https://www.ifrs.org/news-and-events/news/2023/11/gri-establishes-sustainability-innovation-lab-in-coordination-with-the-ifrs-foundation/. (Accessed December 11, 2023).

IFRS. (n.d.). SASB Standards and other ESG frameworks. SASB. Retrieved from https://sasb.org/about/sasb-and-other-esg-frameworks/#:~:text=Frameworks%20provide%20principles%2Dbased%20guidance,for%20each%20topic%2C%20including%20metrics. (Accessed December 11, 2023).

Ilmanen, A., Chandra, S., & McQuinn, N. (2020). Demystifying illiquid assets: Expected returns for private equity. *The Journal of Alternative Investments*, 22(3), 8–22. Retrieved from https://doi.org/10.3905/jai.2019.1.086.

ILPA. (2020). Enhancing transparency around subscription lines of credit: Recommended disclosures regarding exposure, capital calls and performance impacts. Retrieved from https://ilpa.org/wp-content/uploads/2020/06/ILPA-Guidance-on-Disclosures-Related-to-Subscription-Lines-of-Credit_2020_FINAL.pdf. (Accessed December 10, 2023).

ILPA. (2021). Due diligence questionnaire and diversity metrics template — ILPA. Retrieved from https://ilpa.org/due-diligence-questionnaire/. (Accessed December 10, 2023).

Indahl, R. & Jacobsen, H. G. (2019). Private equity 4.0: Using ESG to create more value with less risk. *Journal of Applied Corporate Finance*, 31(2), 34–41. Retrieved from https://doi.org/10.1111/jacf.12344.

Investindustrial. (2021). Investindustrial announces science based targets and net zero emissions deadline for all funds. Retrieved from https://www.invest industrial.com/dam/Investindustrial/news/Investindustrial-announces-science-based-targets-and-net-zero-emissions-deadline-for-all-funds/Investindustrial%20announces%20science%20based%20targets%20and%20net%20zero%20emissions%20deadline%20for%20all%20funds.pdf.

JAB Holding Company. (2021). JAB — September 2021. Retrieved from https://www.jabholco.com/img/pages/home/JAB-September_2021.pdf. (Accessed December 10, 2023).

Kazemi, H. (2020, September 29). Subscription line of credit: Benefits, risks, and distortions. Retrieved from https://caia.org/blog/2020/09/29/subscription-line-of-credit-benefits-risks-and-distortions. (Accessed December 10, 2023).

Kitzmann, J. & Schiereck, D. (2009). A note on secondary buyouts-creating value or recycling capital. *iBusiness*, 1(2), 113–123. Retrieved from https://doi.org/10.4236/ib.2009.12015.

KKR Announces Formation of Sustainability Expert Advisory Council. (2021, December 1). *Businesswire.com*. Retrieved from https://www.businesswire.com/news/home/20211201005266/en/KKR-Announces-Formation-of-Sustainability-Expert-Advisory-Council. (Accessed December 10, 2023).

KKR. (2023, June). Responsible investment policy. Retrieved from https://www.kkr.com; https://www.kkr.com/content/dam/kkr/sustainability/pdf/responsible-investment-policy.pdf. (Accessed December 10, 2023).

Lino, M., Connolly, L., Overman, D., McCoy, D., Schey, M., & Anders, S. (2022, February 17). Limited partners and private equity firms embrace ESG. Bain. Retrieved from https://www.bain.com/insights/limited-partners-and-private-equity-firms-embrace-esg/. (Accessed December 10, 2023).

Lorenzo, R., Voigt, N., Tsusaka, M., Krentz, M., & Abouzahr, K. (2018, January 23). How diverse leadership teams boost Innovation. BCG Global. Retrieved from https://www.bcg.com/publications/2018/how-diverse-leadership-teams-boost-innovation. (Accessed December 10, 2023).

Louch, W. & Cooper, L. (2020, May 10). Coronavirus unravels private-equity playbook for some retailers. *WSJ*. Retrieved from https://www.wsj.com/articles/coronavirus-unravels-private-equity-playbook-for-some-retailers-11589115600?mod=pls_whats_news_us_business_f. (Accessed December 10, 2023).

Lykken, A. (2020, January 24). PE firms aren't keeping portfolio companies as long as they used to. *Pitchbook.com*. Retrieved from https://pitchbook.com/news/articles/pe-firms-arent-keeping-portfolio-companies-as-long-as-they-used-to. (Accessed December 10, 2023).

Maples Group. (n.d.). EU sustainable finance disclosure regulation: What, when & how for March 2021. Slideshow available here https://maples.com/en/knowledge-centre/2020/11/guide-to-the-eu-sustainable-disclosure-regulation.

Natarajan, S. & Beyoud, L. (2022, June 10). Goldman Sachs facing SEC probe of ESG funds in asset management. *Bloomberg.com*. Retrieved from https://www.bloomberg.com/news/articles/2022-06-10/goldman-sachs-facing-sec-probe-of-esg-funds-in-asset-management. (Accessed December 11, 2023).

Nee, A. & Quigley, D. (2022, March 30). The state of diversity in US private equity. McKinsey & Company. Retrieved from https://www.mckinsey.com/industries/private-equity-and-principal-investors/our-insights/the-state-of-diversity-in-us-private-equity. (Accessed December 10, 2023).

Nelson, R. (2021, September 21). A guide to responsible investment policies for private equity. Conservice ESG. Retrieved from https://esg.conservice.com/responsible-investment-policies-private-equity/. (Accessed December 10, 2023).

Neuberger Berman. (2022). Private markets ESG report 2022. Report hyperlink automatically downloads. Retrieved from https://www.nb.com/en/global/esg/reporting-policies-and-disclosures.

Operating Principles for Impact Management. (n.d.). The 9 principles. Retrieved from https://www.impactprinciples.org/9-principles. (Accessed December 10, 2023).

Paglia, J. K. & Harjoto, M. A. (2014). The effects of private equity and venture capital on sales and employment growth in small and medium-sized businesses. *Journal of Banking and Finance*, 47, 177–197. Retrieved from https://doi.org/10.1016/j.jbankfin.2014.06.023.

Palladium Equity Partners. (2022, March 29). Palladium equity partners announces B corporation certification [Press release]. Retrieved from https://www.palladiumequity.com/media/palladium-equity-partners-announces-b-corporation-certification.

PCAF. (2019). PCAF North America Methodology Launch. In *PCAF*. Retrieved from https://carbonaccountingfinancials.com/files/downloads/1910-PCAF-NA-Methodology-Launch.pdf. (Accessed December 11, 2023).

Phalippou, L., Rauch, C., & Umber, M. P. (2016). Private equity portfolio company fees. *Social Science Research Network*. Retrieved from https://doi.org/10.2139/ssrn.2703354.

PRI. (2021, March 19). Nearly 90 private equity firms representing $700 billion AUM have signed up to a global climate initiative ahead of COP26. Retrieved from https://www.unpri.org/news-and-press/nearly-90-private-equity-firms-representing-700-billion-aum-have-signed-up-to-a-global-climate-initiative-ahead-of-cop26/7383.article. (Accessed December 11, 2023).

PRI. (2022, May). Initiative Climat International publishes new standard for GHG accounting and reporting in private equity. Retrieved from https://www. unpri.org/news-and-press/initiative-climat-international-publishes-new-standard-for-ghg-accounting-and-reporting-in-private-equity/9982.article. (Accessed December 11, 2023).

Proposed regulations issued on management fee Waivers — Insights — Proskauer Rose LLP. (2015, July 24). Proskauer. Retrieved from https://www.proskauer. com/alert/proposed-regulations-issued-on-management-fee-waivers. (Accessed December 10, 2023).

Reuters. (2022, May 31). German officials raid Deutsche Bank's DWS over "greenwashing" claims. *Reuters*. Retrieved from https://www.reuters.com/ business/german-police-raid-deutsche-banks-dws-unit-2022-05-31/. (Accessed December 11, 2023).

Robertson, B. & Karsh, M. (2021, July 7). Private equity is ditching fossil fuels over climate change concerns. *Bloomberg.com*. Retrieved from https://www. bloomberg.com/news/articles/2021-07-06/private-equity-is-ditching-fossil-fuels-over-climate-change-concerns?leadSource=uverify%20wall. (Accessed December 10, 2023).

Saenz, A., Lo Parrino, M., Burrell, K., Foss, J., & Belaief, J. (2021, February 1). 2021 global private equity survey. EY — Global. Retrieved from https:// www.ey.com/en_gl/private-equity/are-you-exploring-the-future-or-just-visiting. (Accessed December 10, 2023).

Schiff, H. & Dithrich, H. (2018). Lasting impact: The need for responsible exits. Retrieved from https://thegiin.org/assets/GIIN_Responsible%20Exits_2018. pdf. (Accessed December 10, 2023).

SDG Impact | United Nations Development Programme (UNDP). (n.d.). Retrieved from https://sdgimpact.undp.org/private-equity.html. (Accessed December 11, 2023).

SEC. (2022, February 9). SEC proposes to enhance private fund investor protection. SEC.gov. Retrieved from https://www.sec.gov/news/press-release/ 2022-19. (Accessed December 10, 2023).

SEC. (2023, August 23). Private fund advisers; Documentation of registered investment adviser compliance reviews. SEC.gov. Retrieved from https:// www.sec.gov/rules/2022/05/private-fund-advisers-documentation-registered-investment-adviser-compliance-reviews. (Accessed December 10, 2023).

Steinman, B. (2014, August). Private equity fund fees. *duanemorris.com*. Retrieved from https://www.duanemorris.com/site/static/private_equity_ fund_fees.pdf. (Accessed December 11, 2023).

Stepstone. (2016). Uncovering the costs and benefits of private equity. Retrieved from https://www.stepstonegroup.com/wp-content/uploads/2021/07/ StepStone_Uncovering_the_Costs_and_Benefits_of_PE.pdf.

Summa Equity raises the largest European impact fund to date — Announcing final close of c. EUR 2.3 billion for third fund. (2022, January 20). Summa equity. Retrieved from https://summaequity.com/readings/summa-equity-raises-the-largest-european-impact-fund-to-date-announcing-final-close-of-c-eur-2-3-billion-for-third-fund. (Accessed December 10, 2023).

The European Parliament. (2019, December 9). Regulation (EU) 2019/2088 on sustainability-related disclosures in the financial services sector. *Official Journal of the European Union.* Retrieved from https://eur-lex.europa.eu/legal-content/EN/TXT/PDF/?uri=CELEX:32019R2088&rid=1. (Accessed December 11, 2023).

TowerBrook. (2021). TowerBrook responsible ownership report 2021. Retrieved from https://www.towerbrook.com/TowerBrook_Responsible_Ownership-2021.pdf. (Accessed December 10, 2023).

Ulrich, D. & Allen, J. (2017, August 11). PE firms are creating a new role: Leadership capital partner. *Harvard Business Review.* Retrieved from https://hbr.org/2017/08/pe-firms-are-creating-a-new-role-leadership-capital-partner. (Accessed December 10, 2023).

Vanhomwegen, H. (2021, December 2). SFDR mandatory indicators & principal adverse impact (PAIS). *greenomy.io.* Retrieved from https://greenomy.io/blog/sfdr-principal-adverse-impact#:~:text=Principle%20Adverse%20Impact%20indicators%20are,certain%20investments%20pose%20sustainability%20risks. (Accessed December 11, 2023).

Warburg Pincus. (2021). Environmental, social & governance report 2021. *warburgpincus.com.* Retrieved from https://warburgpincus.com/wp-content/uploads/2021/08/Warburg-Pincus_2021-ESG-Report.pdf. (Accessed December 10, 2023).

We invest to make a change. (2023, January 27). Summa equity. Retrieved from https://summaequity.com/strategy. (Accessed December 10, 2023).

Whelan, T., Atz, U., V Holt, T., & Clark, C. (2021). ESG and financial performance: Uncovering the relationship by aggregating evidence from 1,000 Plus Studies Published between 2015–2020. *stern.nyu.edu.* Retrieved from https://www.stern.nyu.edu/sites/default/files/assets/documents/NYU-RAM_ESG-Paper_2021%20Rev_0.pdf. (Accessed December 10, 2023).

Yang, K., Akbar, U., Dessard, J., & Seemann, A. (2019, April 17). Private equity investors embrace impact investing. Bain. Retrieved from https://www.bain.com/insights/private-equity-investors-embrace-impact-investing/. (Accessed December 10, 2023).

Chapter 4

The Indispensable Role of Indexes in the Evolution of Sustainable Investing

Thomas Kuh

Morningstar Indexes, Chicago, Illinois, USA

Abstract

New investment strategies call for new benchmarks. The evolution of sustainable investing over the past three decades has demonstrated the validity of this statement. To facilitate investment, indexes are used as the basis of investment vehicles by passive managers and as investment universes by active managers. As benchmarks, they provide an ongoing time series of return, risk, and financial fundamental data. For environmental, social, and governance (ESG), climate, and impact strategies, indexes also play an important role by defining and measuring sustainability standards and characteristics. As sustainable investing has grown in popularity and sustainable investing strategies have expanded beyond ESG analysis to encompass climate and impact, indexes serve a crucial function, establishing sustainability standards and measuring sustainability characteristics. This chapter shows how classical finance theory broadened the use cases of indexes; provides a brief history of sustainability indexes; and explains how sustainability indexes contributed to improvement of ESG research and advancement of sustainability strategies by answering critical questions about ESG risk and opportunity, carbon intensity, and net-zero pathways, in addition to measuring financial performance and risk. Situated at the intersection of the passive and sustainable investing trends, indexes are cornerstones of this maturing and increasingly influential set of investment practices.

1. Introduction

New investment strategies elicit new benchmarks. This axiom applies to sustainable investing, as it does to other strategies like factor investing. This chapter examines the indispensable role of indexes in the growth and legitimacy of sustainable investing. Indexes codify strategies, define standards, facilitate investment, measure financial and sustainability performance, generate new sustainability metrics, and support research. Yet, the nature and scope of these contributions are not widely appreciated in the context of sustainable investing.

During the past several decades, the financial system has experienced the rise of passive investing and sustainable investing. Sustainability indexes sit at the intersection of these two seemingly unrelated trends. These benchmarks have been instrumental in the success of sustainable investment, serving the needs of asset managers as well as institutional, wealth, and retail investors. They systematize sustainable investing strategies, contribute to improvements in data, and help to address critical questions about performance and impacts.

Indexes have become an integral part of the investment value chain since the Dow Jones Transportation Average was launched in 1884. The roots of responsible investing go back to the 17th century, according to Domini & Kinder (1986), though the modern incarnation of sustainable investing began in the late 20th century. Indexes have been instrumental in the ascendancy of sustainable investing practices, and will continue to play a crucial role in its evolution.

This chapter documents how finance theory's definition of the *market portfolio* contributed to the development of indexes and passive investing, and how the intersection of passive and sustainable investing created the opportunity for sustainability indexes. It then reviews the evolution of sustainability indexes — what they are, how they differ from the *market portfolio*, and their evolution during the past three decades. Finally, we examine ways in which sustainability indexes have been indispensable to the advancement of best practices in sustainable investing.

A few caveats. Some people find sustainable investing terminology confusing. In what follows, sustainable investing is treated as a category encompassing multiple strategies, namely, socially responsible investing (SRI); environmental, social, and governance (ESG); climate; and impact investing. Reflecting the historical trajectory of sustainable investing, most of the commentary is about equity indexes, although benchmarks for other asset classes — notably fixed income — have become more common in recent years. Many of the observations made about equity indexes apply to fixed-income indexes. Also, it is worth noting that this analysis focuses on the pivotal role of indexes in shaping the contours of sustainable investment practices, not analyzing investment performance. That is a topic for another day.

2. Why Indexes Matter

Indexes are a through line in classical financial theory and capital markets. They inform the key actors in the investment value chain, fulfilling a range of use cases for market participants. For asset owners, they act as benchmarks for asset allocation and performance measurement. For investment consultants, they inform performance assessments in manager evaluations and reporting to asset owner clients. For asset managers, they are used to measure returns, risk, and performance attribution, and for client and regulatory reporting. Passive managers use indexes to build index-based investment products, while active managers use indexes as benchmarks and investment universes.

An index is a hypothetical portfolio of securities, designed to provide transparent, rules-based exposure to a particular market, strategy, or theme. Indexes provide access to different asset classes, size segments, geographies, themes, and increasingly investment strategies. They exist for a broad range of asset classes, including equity, fixed income, commodity, real estate, hedge fund, and cryptocurrency markets. Within equities, there are indexes for size segments, geographies, industries, and sectors. There are also single and multi-factor indexes as well as benchmarks for thematic exposure. In recent years, SRI, ESG, and climate indexes have emerged as benchmarks and the basis of investable products that are driving the growth of sustainable investing.

Every index methodology articulates a purpose, describing its objective, investment thesis, and utility for investors. The purpose of broad-market capitalization-weighted benchmarks is to deliver diversified exposure to equity markets. The objectives of sustainable investing indexes are variously expressed in terms of exposure to ESG risk and opportunity, climate risk or transition, social or environmental impact, and themes like biodiversity, gender and racial diversity, or renewable energy. The methodology describes an index's intended exposure to sustainability and financial factors, and defines the rules for integrating sustainability data into index construction to achieve this objective.

A good benchmark is representative, reliable, transparent, and subject to clear governance procedures. In this context, representative means a benchmark should accurately portray the economic characteristics of the market or strategy it is intended to describe. Reliable means the index is constructed with quality data and investors can depend on it to achieve its intended purpose. Transparent means the methodology clearly describes the purpose, construction rules, data, and calculation procedures, and that the methodology is publicly available. Effective governance procedures are necessary to ensure the integrity and accountability of the index and avoid conflicts. Adherence to these standards give indexes the imprimatur of objectivity and credibility.

Throughout most of the 20th century, the primary function of an index was to benchmark the performance, risk, and financial fundamentals of a portfolio in relation to those characteristics of the underlying market. Equity indexes almost exclusively reflected a national, regional, or global market, sector, or industry — in other words, various slices of the global economy. Similarly, broad-market fixed-income indexes provided exposure to corporate, sovereign, treasury, government-related, and securitized bonds from developed and emerging market issuers.

The growth of passive investing in recent decades has complemented the benchmarking use case with the function of supporting index-based investment vehicles. This development has made indexes even more important to the investment process and the functioning of financial markets.

2.1. *Finance Theory, the Market Portfolio, and Indexes*

Finance theory in the 20th century advanced our understanding of risk by differentiating market risk from the risk of individual securities and showing that diversification can mitigate stock-specific risk. The theory was founded on a set of simplifying assumptions about the motivations, behavior, and time horizon of investors, the availability and cost of borrowing and lending, and the efficiency of security markets. In addition to offering a framework for managing risk through portfolio construction, the elegant theoretical framework enshrined broad-market capitalization-weighted indexes as a proxy for the *market portfolio*, providing the rationale for index-based investing.

This elevated indexes from their limited role as performance gauges to being fundamental links in the investment value chain and fueling the rise of passive investing. Indexes are valuable because of the transparency, efficiency, and cost-effectiveness they convey to investors. The scope of their influence has grown, driven by advances in technology, data, and fund structures that have deepened demand for portfolio benchmarking and broadened interest in passive investing.

The pillars of finance theory are modern portfolio theory (MPT), the capital asset pricing model (CAPM), and the efficient market hypothesis (EMH). MPT, based on the work of Harry Markowitz (1952), furnished the first rigorous theoretical justification for portfolio diversification. Developed independently by William Sharpe (1964) and others, CAPM builds on Markowitz's MPT framework to explain how to construct portfolios within the constraints of the model's assumptions. Their contributions to finance theory earned Markowitz and Sharpe the 1990 Nobel Memorial Prize in economics.

The framework distinguished two types of risk: systematic risk (market risk or beta) and specific risk (risk associated with an individual stock). Systematic risk cannot be eliminated through diversification. However, CAPM asserts that investors can reduce specific risk through diversification with a portfolio on the efficient frontier. Using mean-variance optimization, investors can determine the highest returns for a given level of risk. The EMH, attributed in its modern form to Eugene Fama, is a theory asserting that security prices reflect all relevant information. Among other things, it implies that active investors cannot systematically outperform passive investors.

A direct link between finance theory, portfolio construction, and investment products fueled the rise of passive investing. CAPM and the EMH defined the concept of the *market portfolio*, a hypothetical diversified basket of all assets weighted in proportion to their size. It is the model for broad-market capitalization-weighted indexes, designed as proxies for equity markets and therefore representing market beta. In turn, these benchmarks are the basis of portfolios used in passive investable products seeking equity market exposure.

In his seminal article "What is an Index?" Andrew Lo (2015) integrates the EMH with his adaptive market hypothesis (AMH), which is grounded in behavioral finance. He observes that index-based investing "democratized personal investing by taking the reins of portfolio management from the active stock-picking gunslingers of the day and handing them over to a broadly diversified index fund, which served as a proxy for the market portfolio." In light of this progress, Lo argues for reconceiving the definition and role of indexes in a contemporary context. From his perspective, the essential qualities of an index are that it is transparent, investable, and systematic. But, they should not be constrained to function simply as representations of the market portfolio.

Lo seeks to reconcile the historical period from which capitalization-weighted indexes emerged with the realities of contemporary portfolio management. "New trading technology has now given us the ability to create indexes that are not necessarily market-cap-weighted, that are not necessarily even 'passive' in the traditional sense." In his view, indexes can be systematic and dynamic rather than passive, for example, representing target risk or target date strategies. He asserts that "one of the most important implications of this new definition ... is that investing and risk management can be decoupled: passive investing need not, and should not imply, passive risk-taking, as it currently does."

These theoretical developments have had profound implications for investment practices. They advanced our understanding of risk and return in the context of portfolio construction. The premise that investors can manage portfolio risk through diversification shifted the framework for risk and return from the level of individual securities to portfolio diversification. They also provided a theoretical justification for index-based investments as an alternative to active management strategies, helping pave the way for passive investing and fueling the growth of exchange-traded funds. Finally, armed with a powerful theoretical justification, they enhanced the influence of index providers, whose benchmarks are now essential tools for capital allocation, in the asset management industry.

2.2. *The Confluence of Passive Investing, ETFs, and ESG Investing*

Passive investing has experienced secular growth in recent decades. A Thinking Ahead Institute (2023) study of the 500 largest global asset owners shows that "Investment in passive strategies [in 2022] accounts for 34.7% of the total, marking a 4% increase in its share of investments ... compared to the previous year." This is up from 8% of global Assets under management (AUM) in passive funds in 2007, according to a BIS study (Sushko & Turner, 2018).

In 1993, the first exchange-traded fund (ETF) was launched in the U.S. to track the S&P 500. As of 2022, there were 8,754 ETFs worldwide, up from 276 in 2003, according to Statista (2023). A vast majority of ETF assets are in the U.S. and Europe. ETFGI (2023) reported that AUM in global ETFs hit a record $10.5 trillion at the end of Q2 2023. The share of assets in passive funds is largest in the U.S., which accounts for more than 60% of the global equity market today. Bloomberg (2021) reported that "It's only a matter of time before passive assets overtake active in U.S.-based mutual funds and ETFs. The 42.9% of assets … managed passively are up from 31.6% … at the end of 2015."

The exchange-traded fund structure is uniquely well suited for passive investors and consequently for index providers. The emergence of ETFs as an alternative to mutual funds stems from advantages related to the vehicle structure, notably real-time trading, transparency, low fees, and tax treatment (which may vary depending on local regulation). Most ETFs, as measured by number of funds and assets, are purely passive although active ETFs have experienced growth in recent years.

Lo observed that "in recent years, indexes have become the preferred structure for investors seeking passive exposure to various investment themes — such as renewable energy — and strategies — serving as blue-prints for approaches such as ESG." Global assets under management in sustainable investment strategies totaled more than $30 trillion in 2022, according to the Global Sustainable Investment Alliance (2022). This represents about 27.5% of the $109 trillion in total global assets under management in 2022 as reported in a McKinsey study (Banani, Kwek, Lai & Torbey, 2023).

Morningstar (2023) calculates that AUM in global sustainable funds totaled $2.7 trillion, as of Q3 2023. Together, Europe (84%) and the U.S. (11%) account for 95% of global sustainable fund assets (see Figures 1–3). Of these, about $643 billion (29%) in Europe and $114 billion (38%) in the U.S. are in passive funds.

Not surprisingly, developments in sustainability indexes mirror the growth in passive sustainable fund assets. The Index Industry Association (IIA), a trade organization for global index providers, tracks the number of indexes in the market. IIA (2022) reports that the total number of ESG

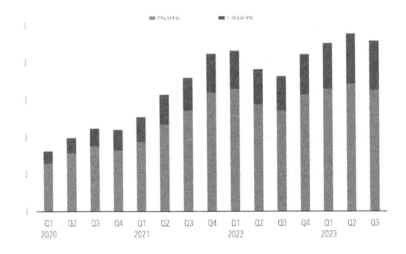

Figure 1.   European sustainable fund assets

Source: Morningstar Direct, Manager Research, Data as of September 2023.

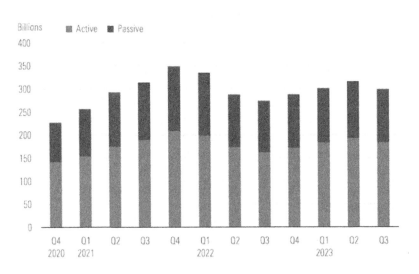

Figure 2.   U.S. sustainable fund assets

Source: Morningstar Direct, Manager Research, Data as of September 2023.

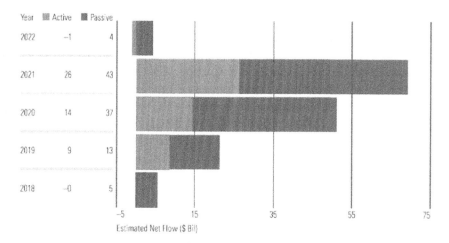

Figure 3. U.S. sustainable fund flows: The shift to passive funds

Source: Morningstar Direct, Data as of December 31, 2022. Includes funds that have liquidated; excludes funds of funds.

indexes exceeds 50,000 and identifies them as the fastest-growing segment in the market at 55%. This figure is up from 43% growth in the prior year and compares with an overall industry growth rate of 4.4%. Fixed-income ESG indexes grew almost 96% and outnumbered equity indexes, which rose by more than 24%, for the first time. These figures tell the story of a robust, rapidly evolving sustainability index ecosystem.

2.3. *Sustainability Indexes*

A sustainability index provides systematic, transparent, rules-based exposure to ESG, climate, or impact factors. These indexes are distinguished from traditional indexes by the information used in sustainable investing strategies and how the data are integrated into the selection and weighting of constituents. It is worth observing that not all sustainability indexes are "pure" versions of what is described here. Many commingle elements of the different approaches, such as combining attributes of an SRI index (exclusion), an ESG index (positive selection), and a climate index (emissions constraints).

Sustainable indexes function as an alternative to traditional market benchmarks, designed to represent sustainable investing strategies, provide systematic exposure to sustainable investing factors, and measure their performance, risk, and financial characteristics. They share the attributes of standard financial benchmarks, distinguished by the integration of sustainable investing criteria into index construction. They use either capitalization or alternative weighting methodologies. However, they do not fit the traditional model of an index as the proxy for the *market portfolio* based solely on the efficient frontier and being weighted based on company size.

Figure 4 illustrates a simplified version of the process for creating and maintaining a sustainable investing index. The starting universe of companies is usually defined by a capitalization-weighted broad-market benchmark. The parent benchmark may be global or represent a specific country, region, size segment, industry, sector, and so on. The salient point is that, since most sustainable indexes are derived from a version of the *market portfolio*, they will almost inevitably be compared when it comes to analyzing performance, risk, and financial fundamentals.

The first step excludes companies that are ineligible for the index, if applicable. This could be because a company provides prohibited products or services, for example, tobacco, firearms, or thermal coal. A second type of exclusion is associated with company actions and behavior, for example, violations of global norms for human rights, labor rights, or environmental stewardship.

The eligible universe for the index is the set of remaining parent index constituents. The next stages in the process integrate sustainability data

Figure 4.   Construction of a sustainable investment index

Source: Morningstar Indexes. Illustrates a simplified version of the process for creating and maintaining a sustainable investing index.

into the index and determine the extent of sustainability exposure based on which companies are selected and the weights assigned to each security. Selection is the outcome of applying index rules to the eligible universe. Some indexes use a threshold criterion, including all companies that meet or exceed a particular standard. Others use a best-in-class approach, which targets companies with the highest ESG ratings in each sector representing a proportion, e.g. 50%, of the market capitalization of that sector. In other cases, the entire eligible universe is included and exposure is achieved through rules that determine constituent weighting.

Following selection, the exposure of an index to a particular sustainability factor is determined by the weights assigned to constituents. Reflecting the influence of the *market portfolio*, most indexes are market capitalization weighted, meaning the weight of each security is based on its market capitalization as a proportion of the total market capitalization of the index. Other approaches include *equal weighting*, *tilt*, and *optimization*.

When constituents of a best-in-class index are capitalization weighted, the index will be sector neutral in relation to the parent. By design, this removes a potential source of systematic risk from the ESG index while increasing stock-specific risk by a factor determined by the targeted percentage of the capitalization of the parent. For example, if a best-in-class index aims for 50% sector representation, it doubles constituent weights relative to the parent index and thereby increases idiosyncratic risk. This is an effective way to provide investors with exposure to high ESG scores. By combining this selection process with capitalization weighting, a best-in-class index can provide exposure to companies with relatively high ESG ratings with fewer unintended biases.

Equal weighting applies a *pro rata* weight based on the number of constituents. This approach places small companies on the same footing as large ones, so it has the effect of giving more sway to small companies than a cap-weighted index. *Tilt* approaches use an algorithm to over- and under-weight constituents, usually in relation to their capitalization weights. In this case, it acts as a form of modified capitalization weighting. Tilt indexes often retain most of the constituents in the parent, rather than reducing the index universe through selection. Companies are reweighted based on key exposure criteria, such as ESG rating, carbon emissions intensity, impact score, or a combination of factors.

Optimization is a quantitative technique used to manage risk and return trade-offs in a portfolio, first applied in a financial context by Markowitz in his work on CAPM. Today, optimization tools enable the construction of portfolios with specific *ex ante* characteristics. Typically used to maximize returns for a given level of predicted risk, sustainable indexes use an objective function that aims to maximize exposure to high ESG ratings or minimize exposure to carbon-intensive companies, subject to a specific *ex ante* tracking error target. Optimization is a powerful portfolio construction tool, though it is sometimes criticized for being a "black box." When applied to index construction, it is not easy to discern the factors that determine the selection and weighting of specific assets. Some investors find that the lack of transparency is problematic.

Once an index is created through the application of its rules for selection and weighting, it is maintained with periodic rebalances and reconstitutions. These can be as frequent as monthly or as infrequent as annually, with most broad-market capitalization-weighted indexes rebalanced quarterly. The trade-off is that more frequent rebalances maintain the purity of the intended exposure but result in a higher turnover, which increases transaction and other costs for investors. Rebalances and reconstitutions are an opportunity to account for changes in float factors, shares outstanding, and other corporate actions, and to make constituent changes based on size, liquidity, or other eligibility criteria. Most constituent changes are made at rebalances or reconstitutions, though rules allow for interim changes due to mergers, acquisitions, bankruptcy, or delisting.

Following the rebalance of a parent index, refreshed sustainability data are employed to screen, rank, and select companies to determine which companies are added or removed. This ensures that the most current sustainability data are integrated into the index. Since ESG, climate, and impact data add a layer of complexity to index construction, sustainability indexes typically have higher turnover than a typical cap-weighted benchmark and thus exhibit tracking errors in relation to the parent. For example, Morningstar Global Markets Sustainability Index, which aims for 50% market cap representation relative to the Morningstar Global Large-Mid Cap Index, had an annualized turnover of 11.5% vs. 4.2% for the parent index in 2023. To limit changes at the margin that would result in higher turnover, index providers apply buffer rules that favor incumbent constituents over companies with similar sustainability characteristics that are not in the index.

3. The Evolution of Sustainability Indexes

This section provides perspective on the historical progression of the different sustainable investing practices as a basis for understanding the evolution and role of sustainability indexes. Sustainable investing is pre-mised on the view that every investment has real-world effects, whether positive or negative. Consequently, investors should be intentional about anticipated effects on society and the environment of their decisions. These diverse approaches share the objective of leveraging capital mar-kets to generate more sustainable outcomes, acknowledging the impact of companies on the world at the same time as the world has an impact on companies.

What distinguishes sustainable investors from investors focused exclusively on financial considerations is their intention to integrate analysis of ESG and climate risks and opportunities, address negative externalities of market activities, and achieve positive impacts. In short, they seek to change the framework and time horizon for investment decision-making, though achieving such ambitious aspirations remains a work in progress. The field of sustainable investing began as an exercise in values alignment and then transitioned to a focus on ESG materiality and impact. In recent years, its attention has been directed to facilitating the transition to a low-carbon economy as a response to the potentially existential threat of climate change, as the objectives of the 2015 Paris Agreement were taken up by investors across the globe and regulators in Europe (see Table 1).

3.1. *Socially Responsible Investing (SRI)*

SRI was shaped by the civil rights movement and the Vietnam war in the 1960s, the anti-apartheid campaign in South Africa in the 1970s, and the Exxon Valdez oil spill in 1989. Kinder *et al.* (1993) state the following:

> For a few investors, the motivation is pure avoidance. Most, however... want their money to move society towards positive objectives: a cleaner environment or a fair employment system...[They] view their invest-ment policies as another means to work toward a just society. Thus, SRI is part of a strategy for achieving change, rather than an end in itself.

This articulation of means and ends laid the foundation for what we now call sustainable investing. Despite the popular perception today that SRI is simply about excluding companies based on personal values, the authors describe it as "a process both of elimination and seeking out." Pax World Balanced Fund (now Impax Sustainable Allocation Fund), the first SRI mutual fund, was launched in 1971.

Table 1.   Evolution of sustainability indexes

Category	Type	Purpose	Selection	Weighting	Example	Date
SRI	Negative screens	Values alignment	Exclude companies with business in South Africa	Market cap	Boston SAFE (South Africa Free Equity) (ceased in 1992)	1986
	Positive selection	Track companies that pass screens & stand out relative to sector peers	Early best-in-class process & exclusion	Market cap	Domini 400 Social	1990
	Corporate Social Responsibility	Track universe of companies that meet CSR standards	Meet minimum inclusion criteria	Market cap	FTSE4Good	2001
ESG	Best-in-Class	Track performance of companies w/ high ESG score relative to sector peers	Best-in-class by count within sector	Market cap	Dow Jones Sustainability	1999
			Best-in-class by market cap within sector	Market cap	KLD Broad Market Social	2001
	Optimized	Maximize exposure to ESG factors while managing risk	Optimization	Optimization	KLD Select Social	2004
	Tilt	Provide ESG exposure through weighting rather than selection	Parent universe with limited exclusions	Tilt	MSCI ESG Universal	2017
Climate	Climate Solutions, Clean Energy & Clean Tech	Exposure to themes like renewable energy & clean technology	Thematic	Modified equal	WilderHill Clean Energy	2004

	Low Carbon	Portfolio decarbonization by reducing exposure to CO_2 emissions & stranded asset risk	Optimization	Optimization	MSCI Low Carbon Target	2014
	Climate Transition	Track trajectory toward net-zero carbon emissions in 2050	Optimization or iterative algorithm	Optimization or iterative algorithm	EU Paris-Aligned & EU Climate Transition Benchmarks	2019
Impact	Green Bonds	Track global green bond market	Green bonds eligible for parent index	Market value	S&P Green Bond	2014
	Social Impact Fund of Funds	Track market-rate private equity & venture capital impact funds	Private closed-end funds w/social impact & market-rate goals	Fund size	GIIN Impact Investing Benchmark	2015
	Impact Revenue	Exposure to companies who address SDGs	>50% of revenues related to SDGs	Impact revenue factor	MSCI Sustainable Impact	2016

Source: Morningstar Indexes.

The early years of SRI were characterized by a rudimentary, academically informed model, scarce data, and limited interest from the financial markets. SRI practices evolved in the pre-digital world. Evaluations of companies were based on an analytical framework that looked at environmental considerations and key stakeholder relationships. Data on issues like the environment, community relations, employee relations, and product quality and safety were hard to come by. There was little information on company policies and behavior since they did not routinely report on these issues. So, the research depended on information gleaned from questionnaires, phone calls, and stories published in print and broadcast media. Additional information was gathered from NGOs, governments, and other specialized data sources.

The research aimed at insights into management, strategy, and culture at companies. Analysts sought to identify company cultures that valued human, social, and natural capital and that exhibited innovative management practices. The research consisted of data collected across a range of stakeholder relations, but there were no overall company-level scores, ratings, or assessments. There was typically little information available except for the largest and most controversial companies. The main types of information used for index construction were product-based exclusions (e.g. tobacco), controversies, and information about positive and negative activities and the impact (categorized as "Strengths" and "Concerns") of companies.

SRI indexes are defined in part by values-based exclusions. The first SRI index excluded companies involved in alcohol, gambling, tobacco, nuclear power, and military weapons as an initial step. Some indexes are defined by a single exclusion like tobacco or fossil fuels. Others use exclusion to align with religious beliefs, such as Islamic indexes which exclude alcohol, pork, and entertainment to be Shariah compliant, and Catholic indexes that mandate exclusion of companies that violate Church doctrine related to pornography and abortion.

The oldest continuously maintained and published sustainable investing index is the Domini 400 Social Index launched in 1990 by KLD Research & Analytics. KLD modeled the Domini 400 on the S&P 500, which was launched in 1957, and delegated index management to a committee. The committee model reflected the state of data and technology in the late twentieth century and was considered the best available index maintenance process at the time. The Domini 400 committee's decisions were based on written guidelines taking account of rules and precedents. In 2010, the index (then named the MSCI KLD 400 Social Index) switched to a rules-based process recognized as best practice today.

The purpose of the index is derived from religious and secular traditions stressing an ethic of responsibility to society and the environment. Following the exclusion of companies with revenues from alcohol, tobacco, gambling, military weapons, and nuclear power, the committee explicitly sought to select a set of companies diversified across industries, sectors, and size segments. This was an early, less systematic prototype of the best-in-class methodology that characterized most ESG indexes.

Another important SRI index is FTSE4Good. Launched in 2001, this index set inclusion standards based on corporate social responsibility (CSR) criteria, aimed at encouraging companies to meet and exceed minimum standards, with the objective of raising these standards over time. At launch, FTSE earmarked some licensing revenues for contribution to UNICEF, hence the name. Though it has evolved into a more traditional ESG index over the years, FTSE4Good was influential because it was one of the first sustainable investing indexes developed by a major index provider.

3.2. *Environmental, Social, and Governance (ESG) Investing*

The term "ESG" was introduced in *Who Cares Wins: Connecting Financial Markets to a Changing World*, published by the United Nations Global Compact (2004). Endorsed by the World Bank and International Finance Corporation along with twenty major financial institutions, the report articulated "guidelines and recommendations on how to better integrate ESG issues in asset management, securities brokerage services and associated research functions." It initiated the development of a framework reflecting institutional investors' beliefs about the risks and opportunities associated with these issues and a rationale for integrating them into their investment process.

Framed in the vocabulary of mainstream finance, ESG catalyzed a transition from the values orientation of SRI to a focus on investment risk and opportunity. It analyzed the materiality of ESG factors and their implications for the fiduciary duties of institutional investors. This framework gave investors and other stakeholders agency to raise specific ESG issues to the level of materiality. According to Kuh *et al.* (2020),

ESG issues become material because they represent negative externalities that businesses may eventually internalize, which has the potential to create additional costs. Alternatively, they may reflect positive externalities that result in the creation of intangible value that later boosts revenue, market share, or profitability.

Climate change, human rights, supply chain management, diversity, and executive compensation are examples of the dynamic materiality of ESG topics.

The Principles for Responsible Investment (PRI) initiative has been both a catalyst for and expression of the rationale for integrating ESG considerations into investment decisions. Founded in 2006, the PRI had 5,381 asset owner, asset manager, and service provider signatories, representing $121 trillion AUM (as of 31 March 2023). The success of the PRI is emblematic of the global uptake of sustainable investing by institutional investors that began in the early years of this century and has driven its integration into mainstream finance.

ESG is a framework for analyzing material sustainability-related risks and opportunities. ESG ratings synthesize data on a broad range of topics and aggregate them into a single metric. Ratings have the virtue of simplifying a complex set of issues into a score or letter grade, offering investors a means to compare a large universe of companies and integrate these data into their investment decisions. In the absence of established regulatory or voluntary standards, research firms developed proprietary ESG ratings frameworks. Critics of ESG ratings, e.g. Brackley *et al.* (2022), have raised questions about the low correlation of ratings among leading rating agencies, data quality, predictive value, and cost.

ESG ratings emerged from the confluence of a new analytical framework, more and better data, and demand for a synthetic analysis of an expanding body of knowledge. The development of ESG indexes coincided with the advent of the Information Age and the transition from data scarcity to abundance. The internet fundamentally changed the economics of data availability and distribution by increasing supply, lowering cost, and making it easier to access. Under pressure from investors, companies began issuing sustainability reports. Clients of SRI research firms were no longer content to simply receive a growing volume of information on sustainability issues. They wanted to know how to interpret it and what it all added up to.

As the primary building blocks of ESG indexes, ratings considerably streamlined index creation at scale when compared with SRI indexes. Controversy scores, which analyze the severity of impactful ESG events at companies, complement the ratings by providing information about events that increase ESG risk at companies. Since ESG ratings are typically assigned annually, controversies provide a mechanism to incorporate relevant information occurring in the interim period between ratings. Many ESG indexes also incorporate product screens that reflect the perspective that some goods and services generate external costs that undermine sustainable development.

Best-in-class analysis is the predominant methodology for ESG indexes. ESG ratings enable comparative ranking of companies on material ESG risks and opportunities. Best-in-class selection typically targets a specific percentage of the market capitalization of a parent index and enables the creation of benchmarks that represent a consistent subset of a national, regional, or global market. This approach enables the creation of highly diversified benchmarks. The degree of exposure to high ESG ratings depends on the target market capitalization representation of the index. Target exposure of the top 20% of companies will provide higher ESG quality, as measured by a weighted average of ESG ratings, than the top 50%. The trade-off is that the index will have fewer constituents, be more concentrated, exhibit higher idiosyncratic risk, and funds based on it will have lower investment capacity than a broader benchmark. In short, it will be riskier and less investable.

The first best-in-class ESG index was the Dow Jones Sustainability World Index (DJSI), launched in 1999 as a collaboration between Dow Jones and Sustainable Asset Management. The DJSI was designed to measure corporate sustainability performance and identify companies whose managements were best prepared for addressing those risks and opportunities. The index methodology targeted the top 10% of companies by count (not market capitalization), based on voluntary responses to questionnaires. Naqvi and Jus (2019) observed that "At first, it was a small, self-selecting group of sustainability pioneers. Transparency was poor [but improved over time]." The index provider encouraged companies to cite their membership as evidence of being sustainability leaders, a model also followed by FTSE4Good.

In 2001, KLD and Russell Indexes collaborated to launch the first broad-market best-in-class index, the KLD Broad Market Social Index.

This index refined best-in-class selection methodologies by targeting proportionate sector representation based on market capitalization rather than number of companies, reducing potential risk from sector bias relative to the parent index. By using the Russell 3000 — a widely used institutional benchmark — as its parent index, the KLD Broad Market Social Index was the first ESG index designed to meet the needs of institutional investors for a broad diversified investment universe. Its original sector representation target of 66% was revised to 50% in 2010. The scale of this index prompted KLD to create systematic scores — precursors of ratings — to aid the index committee in managing index selection.

In 2004, KLD launched the first optimized sustainability benchmark, the KLD Select Social Index. The index methodology was designed to provide diversified exposure to companies with high ESG scores after excluding tobacco companies. Since most sustainable investors are not agnostic about tracking errors, optimization offers the opportunity to trade risk exposure to gain ESG exposure. This index is noteworthy because optimization results in a non-capitalization-weighted portfolio, indicating a willingness to move away from the *market portfolio* model. The objective function of the optimization targeted a 2% *ex ante* tracking error, representing the expected risk budget for gaining exposure to high ESG scores. It is higher than many passive investors expect, though considerably lower than the tracking error of active portfolios. This index was licensed in 2005 for the first sustainable investing ETF, an important milestone in making sustainable investments more accessible to investors.

Tilt methodologies are a way to get sustainability exposure by over- and under-weighting companies based on ESG, climate, or impact metrics. Unless the tilts are dramatic, they result in indexes that track closely to their parent. For example, the MSCI World ESG Universal Index tilts in favor of companies with high ESG ratings and those with improving ESG ratings and has a tracking error under 1%. Broad-market tilt indexes are intended for institutional investors who favor being widely invested in but want some ESG exposure. Large global asset owners, cited as "universal owners," e.g. by Hawley and Williams (2000) and Quigley (2020), may seek this type of exposure.

3.3. *Climate Investing*

The Paris COP21 meetings in 2015 marked a turning point in global ambitions to tackle climate change and for sustainable investing. The Paris

Agreement, an international treaty signed by 196 countries, is a commitment to limit the increase in the global average temperature to well below 2°C above pre-industrial (1850–1900) levels and pursue efforts to limit the temperature increase to 1.5°C above pre-industrial levels. To limit global warming to 1.5°C, greenhouse gas emissions must peak before 2025 at the latest and decline 43% by 2030.

With increasing attention being paid to the effects of climate change, such as extreme weather events and physical climate risk, climate-related investing is emerging as the most compelling strategy for many sustainable investors. In a recent Morningstar Indexes (2023) report, 52% of 500 global asset owners surveyed said that environmental factors have become "More" or "Much More" material in the past year with "net zero" as the most material environmental issue. The report notes that with "the urgency of tackling climate change, it is not surprising that asset owners view the transition to net zero emissions as the environmental factor most material to their decision-making."

Kumra and Woetzel (2023) estimate that the transition to a low-carbon economy will require $275 trillion by 2050, or an annual average of $9.2 trillion spending on physical assets. The urgency to act in the face of climate change has motivated investors to mobilize this massive scale of capital though current levels fall short. Their objective is to allocate capital to reduce greenhouse gas emissions (GHG) emissions from fossil fuels, increase non-GHG-emitting energy sources like renewable and nuclear energy, develop technologies across a range of industries to enable the transition, and get companies to make capital investments to reduce their GHG emissions.

Climate has been on the agenda of sustainable investors and has been addressed in the environmental pillar of ESG research since the 1990s. The publication of "Unburnable Carbon" by Carbon Tracker Initiative (2011) gave analysts, portfolio managers, and asset owners a taxonomy and framework for a science-based understanding of climate-related financial risks and opportunities. As climate change has advanced, physical and transition risks have come into focus as investment considerations. Consequently, investors are developing the tools to address climate risk in their portfolios and engaging with companies and policymakers to hasten the transition to a low-carbon economy.

Climate-related indexes encompass a range of strategies including thematic benchmarks aimed at climate solutions like renewable energy and clean technology. For example, the WilderHill Clean Energy Index was launched in 2004. Among the first broad-market climate-related

Figure 5.   Climate strategies and their roles in portfolios

Source: Morningstar Manager Research.

benchmarks were ex-fossil fuel indexes such as the S&P 500 Fossil Fuel Free Index, launched in 2015. The MSCI Low Carbon Target Indexes, the first indexes designed to significantly reduce carbon exposure in the portfolio, were launched in 2014 using optimization to reduce exposure to carbon-intensive assets and fossil fuel reserves.

These benchmarks set the stage for a new class of climate indexes. In 2020, the European Commission set minimum standards for Climate Transition Benchmarks (CTBs) and Paris-aligned Benchmarks (PABs). Building on the model of reducing carbon exposure pioneered in low-carbon benchmarks, it catalyzed progress on climate-related investment strategies and ushered in the phase of climate transition benchmarks (see Figure 5). Among the perceived shortcomings of PABs is their focus on reducing carbon emissions exposure in portfolios as a risk management strategy. Asset owner groups Net-Zero Asset Owner Alliance (NZAOA) (2022) and the Institutional Investors Group on Climate Change (IIGCC) (2023) have expressed the desire for benchmarks that track the net-zero pathways at companies to support engagement to reduce emissions in the real economy. Climate-related investing will continue to drive interest and innovation, given the risks and opportunities associated with climate change. Net-zero indexes are expected to spearhead the next phase of climate investing.

3.4. *Impact Investing*

While there are direct linkages in the progression from SRI to ESG to climate investing, impact investing can be understood as an offshoot of this lineage. With roots extending back to the 18th century Methodists and Quakers, modern impact investing has roots in a combination of SRI and philanthropy. According to Trelstad (2016),

> It is out of the intersection of [philanthropic] program-related investing and sustainable investing that the concept of 'impact investing' emerged in the 2000s. Impact investors believe that by investing in business models that address social and environmental challenges … they can generate market-rate financial returns while also delivering measurable impact on the targeted problem.

Impact investments are intended to have quantifiable social and environmental benefits, along with financial returns. According to the Global Impact Investing Network (GIIN), among the core principles of impact investing are intentionality (the explicit objective of achieving a particular impact), expectations of financial returns (or at least return of capital), and impact measurement. Organizations like GIIN have developed a taxonomy and measurement standards to support these practices. Broader frameworks for defining impact include the UN Sustainable Development Goals (SDGs) and the EU Taxonomy for Sustainable Activities, but measuring impact at scale has proven to be challenging.

The association with philanthropy contributes to the perception that impact investments generate below-market returns. While some impact investments have concessionary terms, most target risk-adjusted market-rate returns. Many impact investments are associated with small-scale private market projects, which facilitate the measurement of benefits. Although there is debate about whether and how the principles of impact investing apply to public markets, green bonds are considered by many to be an example of how impact investing can achieve its objectives at scale. The Climate Bonds Initiative (2023) estimates the size of the green bond market at $2.33 trillion as of December 2023.

In recent years, the concept behind green bonds has been extended to other sustainability objectives such as social bonds, sustainability bonds (supporting environmental and social targets of governments and corporations, though not earmarked for particular projects), and blue bonds (supporting marine and coastal conservation). The ability to track the use of proceeds and measure the outcomes is critical to impact instruments. There are also a growing number of thematic funds with impact objectives.

S&P launched the first green bond index in 2014. Holdings consist of bonds in the parent index that are qualified as "green" by the Climate Bonds Initiative and meet various financial eligibility criteria. This and similar benchmarks measure the performance of a universe of securities intended to finance environmental impact and are a means to create green bond investment products. However, they do not measure the actual impact of the investments.

The GIIN Impact Investing Benchmark was created in 2015 to provide data on the performance of social impact funds. Unlike any of the other benchmarks discussed here, it is a fund-of-funds index, designed to track the performance of market-rate private equity and venture capital impact funds. In the absence of the transparency that public markets provide, this benchmark is important for helping investors understand the performance of private market impact investments.

Launched in 2016, the MSCI Sustainable Impact Index was the first impact benchmark for public equity markets. It is designed to include companies that generate at least 50% of their sales from products and services that address key social and environmental challenges as defined by the SDGs. It provides exposure by weighting constituents using an impact revenue factor. This thematic index is concentrated, holding 5% of the constituents in the parent global index. Like green bond indexes, it does not attempt to quantify impact, relying instead on revenue metrics as a proxy for impact.

4. The Indispensable Role of Sustainability Indexes

Indexes act as scorekeepers (of performance), validators (of data), and facilitators (of investment). They are indispensable for progress in sustainable investing because they communicate in the lexicon of finance, and their objectivity conveys credibility to analysis based on their data. As they have evolved to represent thematic and strategy investments, indexes act as test cases for validating new data and analytics. Indexes codify investment strategies and provide structured representations of sustainability strategies and practices. The breadth and complexity of this heterogeneous set of investment objectives are embodied in the index ecosystem.

Index providers require a high level of data quality and consistency to ensure the integrity of sustainability benchmarks. Portfolio managers need benchmarks that appropriately reflect their mandates. Asset owners need the tools to develop an asset allocation plan and evaluate performance in the context of their investment policy as it relates to sustainable investment. Sustainability indexes perform these functions by systematically integrating ESG and climate metrics into benchmark construction and objectively tracking financial *and* sustainability outcomes, supporting investable products, and producing information for analysis and reporting on ESG, climate, and impact investing.

4.1. *Benchmarking Sustainable Investing*

As scorekeepers, indexes traditionally track financial metrics: performance, risk, and fundamentals. In addition to traditional financial performance, sustainable investors need to know the impacts of portfolio companies as part of an overall performance assessment. Sustainable indexes spawned a new category of metrics that measure ESG quality, carbon emissions, impact, and product involvement exposure at a portfolio level.

Based on a request from an ETF sponsor in 2005, KLD began calculating portfolio-level sustainability quality scores for the KLD Select Social Index using a weighted-average scoring model. Today, ESG, carbon, impact, and other measures are standard gauges for investors seeking to understand how their investments compare to the market on sustainability criteria in addition to how they perform financially. These data are widely used for reporting and research.

Indexes played a crucial role in legitimizing sustainable investing as it was being adopted by institutional investors, first in Europe and then globally. ESG investing marked an intentional transition away from the values orientation of SRI to align with fiduciary duty by focusing on material ESG issues. If risk-adjusted returns on ESG and climate strategies consistently underperformed the broad market over a long time of period, it would call into question their underlying premise or implementation. This would make the case for sustainable investing more difficult to rationalize from a fiduciary viewpoint. From this perspective, benchmarking sustainable investing performance has profound — potentially existential — implications for sustainable investors. Consequently, developing benchmarks with sound methodologies and appropriate data is not merely an academic exercise.

The performance implications of sustainable investment strategies have been an ongoing subject of debate. Consistent with MPT, the prevailing argument against it is that reducing the investment universe will harm returns. This view has persisted despite evidence to the contrary. A systematic performance comparison across the range of strategies would be challenging without the universe of sustainable investing indexes.

KLD created the Domini 400 Social Index to address questions about the risk and return characteristics of SRI strategies, provide investors with a universe of companies that meet specific criteria, and license the index for passive investable products. At the 30th anniversary of its launch, MSCI (2020) documented that it outperformed its benchmark 10.43% vs. 10.07% over that period. The index's long-term track record has contributed to rethinking the assumption that SRI and ESG strategies will necessarily hurt performance and cost investors.

Over the years, sustainability index data have been used in a growing body of academic and practitioner research. Whelan *et al.* (2021) conducted a meta-analysis of more than 1,000 papers published in 2015–2020. They concluded that "[f]or investment studies typically focused on risk-adjusted attributes such as alpha or the Sharpe ratio on a portfolio of stocks, 59% showed similar or better performance relative to conventional investment approaches while only 14% found negative results." Many of these studies cite sustainable investing indexes for comparison with conventional market benchmarks.

4.2. *Validating Data and Analytics*

Index providers have also been instrumental in validating and improving ESG, climate, and impact data. The stringent data requirements of index providers contributed to the greater precision, discipline, and quality of ESG ratings and data providers. This alignment of interests was most evident in cases where index providers also own the research and data firms.

The quality of sustainability indexes is primarily determined by methodologies and data inputs. Good quality data are complete (with respect to universe coverage), current, and comparable. The integrity of the resulting index may be compromised in the absence of these attributes. So, sustainable investing indexes usually have rules that govern the treatment of parent index constituents that do not have the necessary data. If the information for a particular data point is from different years for different companies, it undermines the quality of the selection process.

When data for different companies are measured inconsistently, the resulting metrics and comparisons are less reliable.

Data quality has been an ongoing priority in sustainable investing. In the 1990s, the absence of reported information on sustainability issues led investors to engage with companies seeking disclosure of ESG policies, practices, and outcomes. If they balked, companies risked facing shareholder resolutions seeking the disclosure of information on ESG issues. Companies began voluntarily publishing ESG reports as that became the norm. The Governance & Accountability Institute (2022) reported that 96% of S&P 500 companies and 81% of Russell 1000 companies published a sustainability report, including 68% of companies in the bottom half of the Russell 1000 in 2021.

From the standpoint of data quality, voluntary disclosure is better than no disclosure, but it leads to very uneven data. As sustainable investing has taken root in mainstream finance, global reporting standards like ISSB and TCFD along with reporting regulations have improved, and will continue to improve, the overall quality of company-reported data.

Index providers have similar data quality standards as analysts and portfolio managers since indexing is a form of systematic portfolio construction, so sustainable investing data must meet these rigorous standards. The data must be accurate and of high quality, meaning that they are relevant to the purpose of the index, current, complete, and comparable to enable accurate implementation of selection and weighting rules.

A period of consolidation among sustainability research and data providers took place starting around 2010. Index providers, including FTSE, S&P, and MSCI, acquired or developed ESG research businesses, building vertically integrated business models. This development enabled them to conform the sustainability data to the needs of their index businesses. The result was universal coverage that matched global benchmarks, along with a greater emphasis on currency, comparability, and relevance.

Conforming ESG research to the discipline and precision of index management contributed to making the data more "fit for purpose" in the hands of analysts and portfolio managers. ESG ratings are a case study of this phenomenon. They entered the lexicon in the late 1990s as tools designed to enable relative comparisons of the sustainability performance of companies. Their principal role is to inform security selection, portfolio construction, and index management. Ratings were originally based primarily on company-reported information, but data sources have broadened considerably in recent years. In the past decade, ratings and data have become more sophisticated as more and better data along with more powerful technology came into play.

Thirty years ago, the Domini 400 Social Index committee developed a disciplined but qualitative process for comparing companies to maintain sector balance in the first SRI index. Over time, the needs of KLD's index business led the research team to create a scoring model to improve the objectivity and scalability of company comparisons. So, while ratings and other ESG data facilitate index development, indexes stress test data inputs, contributing to improvements that benefit all investment practitioners using the data.

Throughout this development, indexes were a proving ground for ratings and other ESG data. Indexes test the efficacy of ESG ratings, providing systematic real-time observations of their financial implications. As the scale of the benchmark universes increased and index methodologies became more rules based, ESG scores or ratings became essential tools for index construction. Industry and sector analysis is used in index management for best-in-class selection methodologies, which require the ability to rank companies against their peers.

CO_2 emissions are another example of how indexes help generate better data. When investors started to take account of carbon emissions as a contributor to climate changes and as a risk consideration from an investment perspective, very little information was available. Few companies reported on Scope 1 and 2 emissions a decade ago. Some reported data were available through the Carbon Disclosure Project, but they were highly variable and most companies did not disclose any data.

Indexes function as laboratories for testing the efficacy and enhancing the data quality, though of course they are not solely responsible for these refinements. Using estimations to fill critical data gaps is standard practice in the index business. When low-carbon indexes were launched, they required values for every company in the benchmark universe, prompting ESG data firms to develop better estimation models to compensate for the low reporting rate. Emissions information has improved dramatically in recent years as regulators promulgated reporting standards, measurement techniques advanced, and more companies opted to disclose.

4.3. *Facilitating Sustainable Investment*

Sustainable indexes facilitate investment by enabling passive investable products and developing benchmarks for new themes and strategies. Passive sustainable fund and asset growth is discussed in Section 2.2.

Sustainable investors seek to change investment practices — analysis, asset selection, and portfolio construction — to generate more socially and environmentally sustainable real-world outcomes. The resulting investment benchmarks vary from the underlying market rather than simply reflecting it. Investors seek alternatives to the *market portfolio* when it does not appropriately represent their investment objectives.

The history of sustainable investing indexes is one of progress from the simple exclusion of alcohol or tobacco companies to complex, highly engineered solutions like PABs designed to decarbonize annually at a rate intended to converge on net-zero emissions in 2050. Net-zero investing strategies exemplify the kind of innovation that characterizes sustainable investing. Though the data and the benchmarks are at an early stage, investors are committed to supporting the process on the premise that it is essential to start to work with what we have today and improve over time as data and metrics allow.

The future of sustainable indexes will be shaped by specialized data enabled by new technology that complements the information disclosed by companies. Artificial intelligence will be increasingly applied to the collection and analysis of information to improve the currency and accuracy of the data used in benchmark construction. External data sources will enable investors to triangulate on risks that companies may not report. For example, geospatial data captured by satellites are now being used to identify potential physical risks from climate change by mapping physical assets to areas vulnerable to severe weather events, flooding, wildfires, and other developments associated with climate change. These developments will animate a new generation of broad-market and thematic indexes focused on climate and intersectional issues like biodiversity, land use, and a just transition.

5. Conclusion

It is not coincidental that sustainable investing took root in mainstream finance during the Information Age. Digital technologies, the internet, and big data led to a transformation that conveys agency to corporate stakeholders, creating opportunities to raise sustainability issues to the level of materiality. Sustainable indexes have been indispensable to this process, providing credible information that helped institutional investors establish the case that ESG and climate considerations are consistent with fiduciary duty.

In this context, indexes function as building blocks for the investment process and catalysts for innovation. For emerging investment practices like sustainable investing, they define the investment thesis, measure performance, support investable products, and assess whether outcomes align with investor objectives. Indexes also enable investors to articulate narratives framed around data that explain how and why investments behave the way they do and the real-world impacts they have. And, they generate an ongoing data series that shapes the story as it unfolds into the future.

This chapter documents how classical finance theory validated passive, index-based investing, transcending the boundary between performance benchmarking and portfolio construction. The history of sustainability indexes started with SRI, transitioned to ESG, and progressed to climate and impact. It reflects advances in data, technology, and fund structures that enable the implementation of investment strategies that deviate from the *market portfolio* into indexes, blurring the line between pure passive and active investing. This environment enabled sustainable investing to flourish, introducing new data, analysis, and investment practices into capital markets. Indexes are — and will continue to be — essential instruments in this ongoing transformation of investment.

Acknowledgments

Some material in Section 2.1 appeared in an article written by the author entitled "Are We in a New Investment Paradigm?" in the Q4 2022 edition of *Morningstar Magazine*. This material is used with written permission from Morningstar Inc.

References

Banani, F., Kwek, J.-H., Lai, J., & Torbey, H. (2023). *Everything Everywhere All at Once: North American Asset Management 2023*. McKinsey & Company. https://www.mckinsey.com/industries/financial-services/our-insights/everything-everywhere-all-at-once-north-american-asset-management-2023.

Bioy, H., Wang, B., Stankiewicz, A., & Biddappa, A.R. (2023). *Investing in Times of Climate Change 2023*. Chicago, IL: Morningstar.

Brackley, A., Brock, E., & Nelson, J. (2022). *Rating the Raters Yet Again: Six Challenges for ESG Ratings*. ERM Sustainability Institute. https://www.sustainability.com/thinking/rating-the-raters-yet-again-six-challenges-for-esg-ratings/.

Carbon Tracker Initiative. (2011). *Unburnable Carbon: Are the World's Financial Markets Carrying a Carbon Bubble?* Retrieved from https://carbontracker.org/reports/carbon-bubble/.

Climate Bonds Initiative. (2023). Retrieved from https://www.climatebonds.net/ (Accessed August 12, 2023).

Domini, A. & Kinder, P. (1986). *Ethical Investing*. Boston, MA: Addison Wesley.

ETFGI. (2023). ETFGI Reports Assets Invested in the Global ETFs Industry Reached a Record US$10.51 Trillion at the End of June. Retrieved from https://etfgi.com/news/press-releases/2023/07/etfgi-reports-assets-invested-global-etfs-industry-reached-record. (Accessed August 12, 2023).

Global Sustainable Investment Alliance. Global Sustainable Investment Review 2022. The report is not attributed to a particular author(s). Retrieved from https://www.gsi-alliance.org/wp-content/uploads/2023/12/GSIA-Report-2022.pdf.

Governance & Accountability Institute, Inc. New York, NY. Report is not attributed to a particular author(s). Retrieved from https://www.ga-institute.com/fileadmin/ga_institute/images/FlashReports/2022/G_A-2022-Sustainability_Trends_Report.pdf?vgo_ee=IirpQr%2FOJGKu5758FjtTyzVOLCk3RmpszkV33qCt%2FtlKa%2F29n%2FmQfhvY%3AXhcooLzBR87zeMsupoebYKsAgbU6DV7A.

Hawley, J. & Williams, A. (2000). *The Rise of Fiduciary Capitalism: How Institutional Investors Can Make Corporate America More Democratic.* Philadelphia, PA: University of Pennsylvania Press.

Index Industry Association. (2022). Sixth Annual Index Industry Association Benchmark Survey Reveals Continuing Record Breaking ESG Growth, Multi-Asset Expansion by Index Providers. Press release dated 11-1-2023. Retrieved from https://www.indexindustry.org/sixth-annual-index-industry-association-benchmark-survey-reveals-continuing-record-breaking-esg-growth-multi-asset-expansion-by-index-providers-globally%ef%bf%bc/.

Institutional Investors Network on Climate Change. The report is not attributed to a particular author(s). Published on 23-5-2023. Retrieved from https://www.iigcc.org/resources/enhancing-the-quality-of-net-zero-benchmarks.

Kinder, P., Lydenberg, S., & Domini, A. (1993). *Investing for Good: Making Money While Being Socially Responsible*. New York, NY: HarperCollins.

Kuh, T. (2022). Are we in a new investment paradigm? *Morningstar Magazine*, Q4, 37–40.

Kuh, T. & Gast, A (2023). Voice of the Asset Owner Survey 2023 — Quantitative Analysis. Chicago, IL: Morningstar. Retrieved from https://assets.contentstack.io/v3/assets/bltabf2a7413d5a8f05/blt933cb07c08fa9f1d/6553b26c0e64b99bd46ecbaf/Voice-of-the-Asset-Owner-Survey-2023-Quant-Analysis.pdf.

Kuh, T., Shepley, A., Bala, G., & Flowers, M. (2020). Dynamic Materiality: Measuring What Matters *AI, Unstructured Data and the Future of ESG Investing*. FactSet White Paper. Published January 17, 2020. Quote from p. 7. Retrieved from https://go.factset.com/hubfs/Website/Resources%20Section/White%20Papers/dynamic_materiality_white_paper.pdf.

Kumra, G. & Woetzel, J. (2022). *What it Will Cost to Get to Net-zero*. New York, NY: McKinsey Global Institute.

Lo, A. (2015). *What is an Index?* Cambridge, MA: Massachusetts Institute of Technology — Laboratory for Financial Engineering. October 12, 2015.

Markowitz, H. (1952). Portfolio selection. *The Journal of Finance*, 7(1), 77–91.

Morningstar Manager Research (2023). Global Sustainable Fund Flows: Q3 2023 in Review. Chicago, IL: Morningstar.

MSCI. (2020). Retrieved from https://www.msci.com/esg/30-years-of-esg (Accessed August 12, 2023).

Naqvi, M. & Jus, M. (2019). *The Benchmark that Changed the World: Celebrating 20 Years of the Dow Jones Sustainability Indexes*. New York, NY: S&P Dow Jones Indices.

Net-Zero Asset Owner Alliance. (2022). Development and Uptake of Net-Zero-Aligned Benchmarks: A Call to Action for Asset Owners and Index Providers. Retrieved from https://www.unepfi.org/industries/development-and-uptake-of-net-zero-aligned-benchmarks-a-call-to-action-for-asset-owners-and-index-providers/.

Quigley, E. (2020). Universal Ownership in Practice: A Practical Investment Framework for Asset Owners. Cambridge, UK: University of Cambridge.

Sharpe, W. (1964). Capital asset prices: A theory of market equilibrium under conditions of risk. *The Journal of Finance*, 19, 425–442.

Stankiewicz, A. (2023). *Sustainable Funds U.S. Landscape Report*. Chicago, IL: Morningstar.

Statista. (2023). Number of Exchange Traded Funds (ETFs) Worldwide from 2003 to 2022. Retrieved from https://www.statista.com/statistics/278249/global-number-of-etfs/ (Accessed August 12, 2023).

Sushko, V. & Turner, G. (2018). The implications of passive investing for securities markets. *BIS Quarterly Review*, 113–131.

The Global Compact. (2004). *Who Cares Wins — Connecting Financial Markets to a Changing World*. UN Environmental Programme Finance Initiative. Geneva, Switzerland. Retrieved at https://www.unepfi.org/fileadmin/events/2004/stocks/who_cares_wins_global_compact_2004.pdf.

Thinking Ahead Institute. The World's Largest 500 Asset Managers. *A Thinking Ahead Institute and Pensions & Investments Joint Study.* October 2023. p. 6. Retrieved at https://www.thinkingaheadinstitute.org/research-papers/the-worlds-largest-asset-managers-2023/.

Trelstad, B. (2016). Impact Investing — A Brief History. SSRN 2886088.

Whelan, T., Atz, U., Van Holt, T., & Clark, C. (2021). *ESG and Financial Performance: Uncovering the Relationship by Aggregating Evidence from 1,000 Plus Studies Published between 2015–2020*. New York, NY: NYU Stern Center for Sustainable Business.

https://doi.org/10.1142/9789811297786_0005

Chapter 5

Sustainable Funds: Drivers of Progress or Expressions of Preference?

Lindsey Stewart

CFA — Investment Stewardship Research, Morningstar, London, United Kingdom

Abstract

Funds with "sustainable" labeling have taken an outsized share of global fund inflows in the 2020s to date. However, there is a lack of clarity on what they actually do, what role they play in investors' portfolios, and whether it is a case of "sacrificing returns for the greater good." Regulators globally are trying to fill the gaps by proposing prescriptive labeling and disclosure frameworks to ensure the investors know what they are buying. But, are the regulations built on the right premise? Are "sustainable" funds designed to drive global progress on issues like climate change and human rights or do they merely cater to investors' ethical preferences on environmental and social topics? This chapter examines the status quo, the existing and proposed regulations aimed at addressing how asset managers treat sustainability themes, and how these regulations fit with the ongoing debate over the role of sustainable funds.

1. Introduction

The rise of investment products labeled as "sustainable funds" has been one of the asset management industry's key developments of the 2020s so far.[1] Capital flows into these products have skyrocketed since the start of the decade, as investors increasingly accepted the significant effect that the environmental, social, and governance (ESG) issues could have on long-term investment performance. This has prompted increased scrutiny over the impact of ESG integration on the wider market, both from proponents and detractors.

Skeptics of the latest wave of "sustainable funds," that focus on ESG risks and opportunities alongside financial returns, believe that the trend inappropriately prioritizes outcomes other than maximizing financial returns and can divert needed capital away from necessary but at times controversial areas of the global economy. But, the proponents highlight their own areas of complaint, often believing that sustainable funds differ too little from their conventional counterparts (either from an allocation perspective or from an investment stewardship perspective) to make the kind of difference to investee companies' sustainability practices that they claim to make.

The debate has focused the attention of regulators and investors on exactly what the purpose of sustainable funds should be.

Are they primarily a means of directing capital toward economic activities that reduce harm to the planet and society? If so, there is evidence that they have a long way to go in achieving that aim.

Are they instead primarily a means of allowing investors to express their ethical preferences and invest in line with their own priorities? If so, then it would appear that the future of sustainable funds looks a lot like their origin over a century ago.

This chapter examines the history underpinning today's sustainable funds and explores the arguments behind the two alternative views of their purpose.

2. Origins of Sustainable Funds

The investment products available today that are labeled as "sustainable funds" have their roots in religious and ethical schools of thought dating back over a century (Martini, 2021).

---

[1] While acknowledging that there is a valid debate to be had over how sustainable funds with a sustainability label actually are, this chapter uses the name "sustainable fund" as is consistent with common parlance.

The late 19th century saw religious groups, such as the Methodists and Quakers, express concerns over social and moral issues in business (*Financial Times*, 2006). This culminated in the Methodist Church's decision to begin investing in the stock market but to avoid taking stakes in businesses that raised ethical objections for them. The exclusion of "sin" sectors, such as alcohol or gambling, plays a prominent role in the thinking behind many sustainable fund methodologies today.

The 1970s saw the dawn of "socially responsible investing" (SRI), building on the thinking behind the religion-led investing principles of the prior decades. Divisive social issues, such as the Vietnam War and apartheid in South Africa, prompted fund providers to create products that avoided exposure to businesses participating in violent conflicts or social injustices.

Through the 1980s to the early 2000s, funds with "ethical" or "socially responsible" labels increasingly moved beyond "negative screening" — excluding perceived wrongdoers — and prioritized "positive" inclusion of businesses seen to drive beneficial changes in the world, such as renewable energy and the circular economy. Committees (either at the fund or at the provider of the SRI index that many such funds used as a benchmark) would decide what the ethical and social priorities of a fund strategy would be.

Much of the thinking behind ethical and SRI funds over the years was incorporated in the UN Millennium Development Goals, launched in 2000 (which in turn, became the foundation for the Sustainable Development Goals set in 2015), as well as the UN-supported Principles for Responsible Investment (PRI) in 2006. These frameworks now form the foundation of many of today's sustainable fund offerings.

The key point here is that for most of the 100-odd-year history of what we would now call ESG-focused funds, such products were primarily intended to cater to the specific ethical and societal priorities of the investors.

3. The 2020s — An Inflection Point

That long-maintained focus appears to have changed recently, with 2020 being a pivotal year. Around the turn of the current decade, the emerging crop of sustainable funds placed less emphasis on the ethical and societal preferences of investors. Instead, more emphasis was placed on ESG factors — particularly climate change — as being central to a fund's investment proposition, *irrespective* of the investor's personal stance on such issues.

Interest among investment managers in sustainability-focused reporting frameworks, like the Taskforce on Climate-related Financial Disclosures (TCFD) and the Sustainability Accounting Standards Board (SASB) standards, moved from the fringe to the mainstream throughout 2019 and 2020. Investment managers were specifically interested in climate change and other ESG themes from the perspective of assessing through a broader lens the material risks and opportunities their investments were exposed to.

This switch to a more universal view of integrating sustainability issues into investing had its defining moment in March 2020, when Larry Fink, CEO of BlackRock, the world's largest investment manager, declared the following in his annual letter to CEOs (Larry Fink, 2020):

> Climate change has become a defining factor in companies' long-term prospects. ... Investors are increasingly reckoning with these questions and recognizing that climate risk is investment risk. Indeed, climate change is almost invariably the top issue that clients around the world raise with BlackRock. From Europe to Australia, South America to China, Florida to Oregon, investors are asking how they should modify their portfolios. These questions are driving a profound reassessment of risk and asset values. And because capital markets pull future risk forward, we will see changes in capital allocation more quickly than we see changes to the climate itself. In the near future — and sooner than most anticipate — there will be a significant reallocation of capital.

In anticipation of this significant reallocation of capital, two key effects are observable among the world's asset managers.

Firstly, the integration of ESG factors into investment portfolios became a firmwide issue, rather than a matter for individual strategies, for most of the capital managed by asset managers. Asset managers sought to reflect this firmwide view by affiliating themselves with organizations seeking to advance sustainable investing and a green economy. For example, in the four years from March 2019 to March 2023, the number of PRI members (PRI, 2024) more than doubled to over 5,000 (see Figure 1).

Secondly, asset managers created a rapidly growing volume of products claiming to prioritize sustainable investing. Inflows into these products grew rapidly in 2020 (see Figure 2). The Global Sustainable Investment Alliance estimates that global sustainable investing assets grew by 55% in the four years to December 2020 (Global Sustainable Investment Review, 2022).

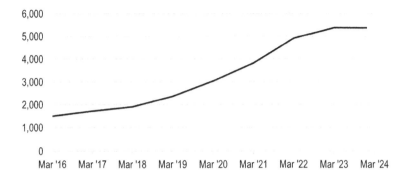

Figure 1. Number of PRI signatories

Source: unrpri.org. Data as of January 15, 2024.

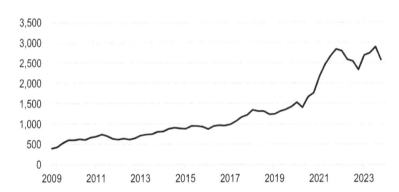

Figure 2. Global sustainable fund assets (USD billions)

Note: Chart shows data for sustainable funds by prospectus for worldwide open-end and exchange-traded funds (excluding money market funds, feeder funds, and funds of funds).

Source: Morningstar Direct. Data as of December 13, 2023.

Data for global exchange-traded and open-ended funds show an even steeper growth rate for products made available to the general investing public. Data from Morningstar show that assets in global open-ended and exchange-traded sustainable funds more than doubled over the same period, hitting USD 1.7 trillion by the end of 2020 (*Reuters*, 2021) and accelerating further in 2021.

As shown in Figure 3, the growth in sustainable fund assets over this period greatly outstripped that of the fund market overall, which grew by around 60% over the four years to the end of 2020.

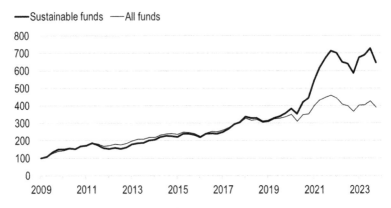

Figure 3.   Global fund assets (indexed)

Note: Chart shows data in USD for sustainable funds by prospectus for worldwide open-end and exchange-traded funds (excluding money market funds, feeder funds, and funds of funds) indexed to 100 as of January 2009.

Source: Morningstar Direct. Data as of December 13, 2023.

However, the sustainable fund market peaked in late 2021. That year was a high-water mark for finance sector participation in sustainability initiatives. The UN COP26 Climate Change Conference held in the UK was a particular focal point, with the International Sustainability Standards Board — keenly anticipated by global investors (Stewart, 2021) as a means of harmonizing a fragmented patchwork of sustainability standards — launched at the event.

However, by the first half of 2022, the Russia–Ukraine conflict and the ensuing energy supply disruption that followed prompted a market rotation toward securities with more defensive characteristics — the energy and aerospace and defense sectors particularly benefited. Asset outflows hit both sustainable and conventional funds as the growth-oriented investments that had underpinned their performance fell out of favour. (This trend reversed in 2023, but not without further volatility, as Figure 3 shows.)

Also starting in 2022, a wave of anti-ESG sentiment took hold primarily in conservative-leaning U.S. states that, it is fair to say, prompted some of the largest investment managers based there to modify their previously more enthusiastic backing for the firmwide sustainability approaches mentioned earlier.

A key indicator of this change in sentiment is observable in proxy-voting data for U.S. investment managers. Morningstar's research on key

ESG resolutions (Stewart, 2024) analyzes manager support over time for environmental or social shareholder resolutions backed by at least 40% of a company's independent shareholders. (Using the 40% support threshold helps ensure comparison of proposals of similar quality, as perceived by the market, from year to year.) The proposals cover a variety of topics, including climate and the environment, but also social issues like labor rights, workplace fairness and safety, human rights, and ethical use of technology.

As shown in Figure 4, large European asset managers have shown consistently high support for key ESG resolutions over the 2021–2023 proxy years — averaging 98% in each year. However, at large U.S. managers, average support for these resolutions has declined from 67% in the 2021 proxy year to 50% in the 2023 proxy year.

Furthermore, support for key resolutions by sustainable funds run by the same U.S. managers has also declined, although their average support sits at a slightly higher level compared with the managers' entire fund range. The average support for key resolutions by the U.S. managers' sustainable funds has fallen from a high of 74% in the 2021 proxy year to 58% in 2023.

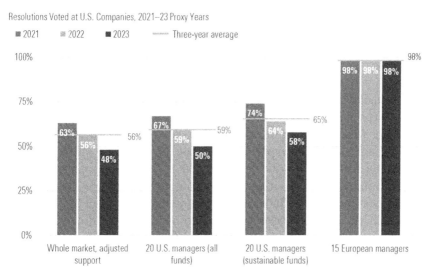

Figure 4. Average support for key ESG resolutions: U.S. and European managers

Note: Chart shows data for proxy years ended June 30.
Source: Morningstar Manager Research. Morningstar Sustainalytics ESG Voting Policy Overlay service. Data as of January 2, 2024.

It is also notable that only some of the firms' sustainable funds make different decisions on ESG proxy voting compared with their conventional funds (Stewart, 2023). Several firms (including the "Big Three" index firms, BlackRock, Vanguard, and State Street) tend to apply the same voting decision across practically all their advised portfolios.

Amid this considerable volatility — in the size of the sustainable fund market, the sustainable fund product offering, and the investment stewardship decisions applied by sustainable funds — it is reasonable to ask what the true role of sustainable funds is in the market and what it should be. Do they do a better job of driving the global economy toward a more sustainable footing or are they better suited toward reflecting the preferences of fund investors?

4. Drivers of a Sustainable Economy?

There is considerable evidence that the success of sustainable funds in delivering impact — driving change in the real economy — is detectable but is often limited.

A recent study (Heath *et al.*, 2023) found that "SRI funds select firms with lower pollution, more board diversity, higher employee satisfaction, and better workplace safety. Yet, both in the cross-section and using an exogenous shock to SRI capital, we find that SRI funds do not significantly change firm behavior. Moreover, we find little evidence that they try to impact firm behavior using shareholder proposals."

Sustainable funds try to achieve their goals either through stewardship activity (primarily engagement and proxy voting) or through investment allocation (often focusing on exclusions and divestment, although recently greater emphasis has been placed on gaining exposure to positive themes).

On the stewardship side, the paper cites evidence that such funds may lack the incentives and stewardship resources to engage with portfolio companies (Bebchuk & Tallarita, 2020), and that the impact of SRI funds on a firm's cost of capital is too small to meaningfully affect corporate investment decisions (Berk & van Binsbergen, 2021). A recent study by S&P Global Ratings (*Financial Times*, 2023) provided an example of this.

Meanwhile, regarding divestment, the paper cites Edmans *et al.* (2022) who argue that outright exclusion of companies causing negative externalities may be less optimal than "tilting" — holding those companies' stocks if they have taken corrective action.

However, Kahn *et al.* (2023) found that "companies reduced their greenhouse gas emissions when stock ownership by green funds increased and did not alter their emissions when ownership by non-green funds changed."

This collective effect may hold signs that the power to deliver impact lies more in collaborative engagement by investors, rather than solely the presence of sustainable funds, as alluded to in Miazad (2023). However, as that paper also notes, "current corporate law and governance framework was not designed for investor collaboration" and attempts to further this aspect of sustainability stewardship have met a degree of resistance, particularly in the United States.

Increasingly, it is becoming clearer to many investors that driving sustainable impact lies more within the power of lawmakers and regulators who can create the conditions for financial sector actors to invest in transforming economies. In light of this, it is possible that the high expectations of 2021 that sustainable finance would lead the transition have receded permanently.

5. Reflections of Investor Preference?

The concept of sustainable funds being primarily a reflection of their investors' own preferences is taking hold again more strongly. This has been reinforced by new regulations in several of the world's major capital markets, aimed at implementing labels for sustainable funds. The proposed labels and disclosures are intended to better inform investors about how sustainable funds' allocation and stewardship strategies help deliver on their ESG objectives.

The U.S. Securities and Exchange Commission's proposed ESG disclosures rule (U.S. Securities and Exchange Commission, 2022) aims to ensure that disclosures in fund prospectuses clearly outline how the stated goals of a fund are matched by the fund's sustainability characteristics:

> Funds focused on the consideration of environmental factors generally would be required to disclose the greenhouse gas emissions associated with their portfolio investments. Funds claiming to achieve a specific ESG impact would be required to describe the specific impact(s) they seek to achieve and summarize their progress on achieving those impacts. Funds that use proxy voting or other engagement with issuers

as a significant means of implementing their ESG strategy would be required to disclose information regarding their voting of proxies on particular ESG-related voting matters and information concerning their ESG engagement meetings.[2]

The goal is to allow investors "to allocate their capital efficiently and meet their needs," which can be understood to mean the investors' own sustainability priorities. The SEC states the following in its proposal:

> Requiring comparable, consistent, and reliable information from all funds and advisers that use an ESG label would reduce the risk of exaggerated claims of the role of ESG factors in investing, thereby increasing the efficiency and reliability with which investors seeking an ESG strategy can find a fund or adviser that meets their investing preferences.

New fund labeling regulation in the UK appears to have similar aims. The Financial Conduct Authority's Sustainability Disclosure Requirements (SDR) (Policy Statement PS23/16, 2023) regulation also intends to implement a labeling scheme for sustainable funds. Outlining its rationale as follows, the FCA states the importance it places on alignment with investors priorities:

> Financial products that are marketed as sustainable should do as they claim and have the evidence to back it up. The regime will support consumers in navigating their investments with trust that the products they are buying do as they say they will.

Both the SEC and the FCA are proposing labels that clearly differentiate between funds that focus on sustainability themes and those that promise to deliver real-world impact, acknowledging the evidence mentioned earlier that impact can often be difficult to demonstrate.

The European Securities and Markets Authority (ESMA) has also bought into this thinking. In its November 2022 Consultation Paper on Guidelines on Funds' Names (European Securities and Markets Authority, 2022), ESMA states the following:

---

[2]https://www.sec.gov/news/press-release/2022-92.

The use of ESG- and sustainability-related terminology in fund names should be used only when supported in a material way by evidence of sustainability characteristics, or objectives that are reflected fairly and consistently in the fund's investment objectives and policy and its strategy.

Alignment has become the key word in sustainable investing circles, which means that sustainable funds are increasingly being measured on how closely their allocation and stewardship decisions match the intentions and preferences of their investors. That focus on the investor's core values would bring today's sustainable funds much closer to their century-old origins.

References

Bebchuk, L. A. & Tallarita, R. (2020). The illusory promise of stakeholder governance. *Cornell Law Review*, 106, 91.

Berk, J. & van Binsbergen, J. H. (2021). The Impact of Impact Investing. *Stanford University Graduate School of Business Research Paper, Law & Economics Center at George Mason University Scalia Law School Research Paper Series No. 22-008.* Retrieved from SSRN: https://ssrn.com/abstract=3909166.

Ethical Funds. *Financial Times*, July 14, 2006. Retrieved January 15, 2024, from https://www.ft.com/content/d603b526-131e-11db-9d6e-0000779e2340.

European Securities and Markets Authority. (2022, November). Consultation paper on Guidelines on funds' names. European Securities and Markets Authority. Retrieved from https://www.esma.europa.eu/press-news/esma-news/esma-launches-consultation-guidelines-use-esg-or-sustainability-related-terms.

Global Sustainable Investment Review. (2022). Global Sustainable Investing Alliance Website. Retrieved from https://www.gsi-alliance.org/wp-content/uploads/2023/12/GSIA-Report-2022.pdf. (Accessed January 15, 2024).

Heath, D., Macciocchi, D., Michaely, R., & Ringgenberg, M. C. (2023, November). Does socially responsible investing change firm behavior? *Review of Finance*, 27(6), 2057–2083. Retrieved from https://doi.org/10.1093/rof/rfad002.

Larry Fink's 2020 Letter to CEOs. (2020). A Fundamental Reshaping of Finance. BlackRock Corporate Website. Retrieved from https://www.blackrock.com/corporate/investor-relations/2020-larry-fink-ceo-letter. (Accessed January 15, 2024).

Martini, A. (2021). Socially responsible investing: From the ethical origins to the sustainable development framework of the European Union. *Environment, Development and Sustainability*, 23, 16874–16890. Retrieved from https://doi.org/10.1007/s10668-021-01375-3.

Morningstar. (2023). Morningstar Asset Flows Quarterly Data: Sustainable Fund by Prospectus. Retrieved from Morningstar Direct. (Accessed December 13, 2023).

Oil and Gas Firms Face Virtually No Extra Borrowing Costs, S&P Finds. *Financial Times*, November 17, 2023, Retrieved from https://www.ft.com/content/830e3ae6-0c3c-4da9-87e7-4ff72aa3e249. (Accessed January 15, 2024).

PRI. (2024). Annual Reports and Signatory Reporting. Principles for Responsible Investment website. Retrieved from https://www.unpri.org/. (Accessed January 15, 2024).

Stewart, L. (2021, March). Global Institutional Investors on the IFRS Foundation's Sustainability Standards. KPMG UK. Retrieved from the Harvard Law School Forum on Corporate Governance. https://corpgov.law.harvard.edu/2021/03/27/global-institutional-investors-on-the-ifrs-foundations-sustainability-standards/. (Accessed January 15, 2024).

U.S. Securities and Exchange Commission. (2022, May). Proposed Rule: Enhanced Disclosures by Certain Investment Advisers and Investment Companies about Environmental, Social, and Governance Investment Practices. U.S. Securities And Exchange Commission. Retrieved from https://www.sec.gov/files/rules/proposed/2022/ia-6034.pdf.

https://doi.org/10.1142/9789811297786_0006

Chapter 6

Navigating Global ESG Investment Regulations Using AI

Irena Vodenska[*,‡]**, Risto Trajanov**[†]**, Gorgi Lazarev**[‡]**,**
Lou Chitkushev[§]**, and Dimitar Trajanov**[§,‡]

[*]*Administrative Sciences Department, Metropolitan College,*
Boston University, Boston, Massachusetts, USA

[†]*College of Data Science, Rice University, Houston, Texas, USA*

[‡]*Faculty of Computer Science,*
Ss. Cyril and Methodius University, Skopje, North Macedonia

[§]*Computer Science Department, Metropolitan College,*
Boston University, Boston, Massachusetts, USA

Abstract

Global initiatives such as the Principles for Responsible Investment (PRI) or the UN Sustainable Development Goals (SDGs) are well poised to catalyze the transition toward climate justice, food security, and agricultural resilience. These initiatives motivate countries to develop frameworks for sustainability reporting to facilitate the transition economy. Globally, policymakers and regulators have proposed regulations to increase the transparency and uniformity of reporting surrounding climate change and corporate social responsibility. We investigate over 100 global documents related to regulatory developments in sustainable taxonomies, climate disclosures, and Environmental, Social, and Governance (ESG) fund requirements reported in the 2023 Sustainable Fitch Tracker of ESG Regulations and Reporting Standards. We propose a model utilizing the power of Artificial Intelligence and Large Language Models to analyze global regulatory documents to capture sustainability-related risks and opportunities defined by the Sustainable Accounting Standard Board (SASB). We compare the performance of keyword-based and ChatGPT-based models and find that the ChatGPT model successfully detects a greater number of global regulatory documents containing the SASB topics. Our results show that the European Union is the leader in having the largest amount of effective and mandatory regulatory coverage of SASB categories, followed by Nigeria and Saudi Arabia. The United States is the leader in effective and non-mandatory regulatory coverage, followed by Malaysia and Mexico.

1. Introduction

In the era of the climate crisis and increased awareness of social responsibility, corporations are at a crossroads in deciding their best transition pathways to the new economy. There is a growing recognition of the urgent need for climate action and preserving natural resources, including agricultural land and water. Social and economic infrastructure and delivery of essential services such as education and healthcare are at the forefront of the transition pathways. Today's corporate world is at an inflection point as countries grapple with the urgency for transitioning away from fossil fuels, which was discussed at numerous previous UN Conferences of the Parties (COPs), and agreed on for the first time at the COP28 held in 2023 in the United Arab Emirates. Besides this seminal agreement, and if every government in the world makes commitments toward sustainability and phasing out of fossil fuels, the world will still fall short on delivering such promises without the commitments of the private sector.

Corporations are essential partners on the journey to greater sustainability. The world needs the public and private sectors to act synchronously through open dialogue to achieve meaningful a triple bottom line (profit, people, and planet). Finance is essential for achieving the Paris Agreement goal of not exceeding the 1.5°C increase in temperature by the end of the century. The investment industry can help by facilitating the issuance of green or blue bonds, obtaining resources to protect the environment, preserving biodiversity, keeping the coral reef alive, and improving air quality. Investment managers can direct significant investments toward innovative green technologies to help them grow and become competitive with their carbon-based counterparts. Investing in long-term profitable and socially responsible sustainability is crucial for the transitioning economy.

1.1. *Socially Responsible Investing*

Socially responsible investing is not a new concept. It dates back to the 1960s when investors started evaluating investments based on companies' impact on social and environmental areas. One of the earlier providers of socially responsible data was Kinder, Lydenberg, and Domini & Co. (KLD), which was established in 1988. KLD offered insights into corporate practices and their impact on the environment and society. The organization developed a framework to assist investors in conducting analytical assessments, aiding in selecting companies for inclusion in socially responsible portfolios. The research was primarily qualitative, as the quantitative data were difficult to obtain or nonexistent (Bender *et al.*, 2023). Responsibility investment is an approach of incorporating investments with specific characteristics in portfolios based on investors' beliefs. For example, investors may be interested in green investments, social impact, and ethical or faith-based investments. Socially Responsible Investing (SRI) evolved into Environmental, Social, and Governance (ESG) to closely describe ESG considerations.

Environmental factors are widely considered in the context of climate and economic risks. The climate is becoming the top global risk, closely followed by geopolitical and societal factors. Companies today face water depletion, lack of natural resources, extreme weather, and rising temperatures. Climate change is becoming an issue of financial stability. The future of the economy and our planet depends on the relationship between business activities and the environment. Climate change is defined as a change in the climate, directly or indirectly, attributed to human activity that alters the composition of the global atmosphere in addition to natural climate variability (Karl & Trenberth, 2003). The main driver of the warming of the planet is rising emissions of greenhouse gases, carbon dioxide being the most significant contributor to the warming effect because of its higher concentration in the atmosphere, currently at levels not seen since before Homo sapiens first appeared (Chartered Financial Analyst (CFA)

Institute ESG, 2022). Climate change mitigation is a human intervention that involves reducing the sources of greenhouse gas emissions to slow down the process of climate change. The goal is to stabilize greenhouse gas levels in a time frame sufficient to allow ecosystems to adapt naturally to climate change. Examples of mitigation strategies include deploying renewable energy sources, retrofitting buildings to become more energy efficient, adopting more sustainable transportation and infrastructure, and improving forest management and reducing deforestation. Mitigation strategies include implementing carbon reduction policies by penalizing heavy emitters and promoting greenhouse gas emissions reduction through either a carbon tax or a cap-and-trade mechanism (CFA ESG, 2022).

When considering the social aspect of ESG investing, we need to be aware of social megatrends and their effects on societies and economies. These megatrends include globalization, increased international trade, growth in global interactions, and the exchange of ideas and cultures. Other important megatrends are automation and artificial intelligence (AI), which are associated with faster production and lower labor costs, affecting many industries, including automotives, healthcare, and financial services. Social factors can be categorized as those impacting external stakeholders, such as customers, local communities, and governments, or they can affect internal stakeholders, like company employees and management.

In the ESG arena, the E is getting most of the attention, closely followed by S, while the G is almost an afterthought. The firm's performance and risk are closely related to corporate governance factors that can either enhance or destroy a firm's value. Factors such as board diversity, inclusion of experts as board members, or independent audit committees are essential considerations. Good corporate governance contributes to better corporate outcomes, socially and financially. At its foundation, governance is about people and procedures. Corporate culture that encourages exceptional business performance without taking undue risks is an example of good governance from which strong performance and long-term prosperity for shareholders and other stakeholders should follow.

Within the ESG investment framework, important elements of portfolio management are stewardship and engagement, describing the responsibility to act in the best interests of the asset owner. Engagement is a component of good stewardship and refers to actions aimed to preserve and enhance long-term value. Stewardship and engagement are beneficial because they boost shareholder value and can be described as an execution of fiduciary duty, a core aspect of responsible investing or acting in the best interests of the investment beneficiaries. According to the Freshfield report, integrating ESG considerations in the investment analysis can more reliably predict financial performance and consider ESG risks (Freshfield, 2005).

Stewardship and engagement encourage enhanced communication and information flow between investors and investees. The principles of responsible investments recognize the importance of (1) communicative dynamics, or the exchange of information; (2) learning dynamics, or enhancing knowledge; and (3) political dynamics, or building relationships. Moreover, the Principles for Responsible Investment (PRI) initiative states that modern fiduciary duties require investment advisors to incorporate **financially material** ESG factors into investment decision-making (PRI, 2023).

What is "material," or how do we define "materiality?" When securities markets lack information, liquidity dries out, trading becomes expensive, markets whither, and investors stay away. When securities markets require too much information, disclosure becomes costly and cumbersome. Companies find alternatives to market financing and markets become less relevant. The concept of materiality comes to the rescue in finding just the right amount of helpful information for investors. The definition of materiality can be summarized as follows: "A fact is material If there is a substantial likelihood a reasonable investor would consider it important in making securities-related decisions." Materiality is typically measured both in terms of likelihood and magnitude of impact. The information is material when a "… substantial likelihood exists that the omitted fact would have been viewed by the reasonable investor as having significantly altered the 'total mix' of information made available" (SEC s.b. 99, TSC v Northway (1976). Basic v Levinson (1988)). The reporting duty of ESG impact relates to the financial materiality of expected and adjusted corporate risk and performance. Disclosing material information ensures that the statements are not misleading and that investors and asset owners have all relevant and vital information to support their investment decisions.

While the history of considering social responsibility in investment decisions is relatively long, only after the 2010s, with the rapid development of technology for data scraping, storage, and processing, was the opportunity presented for taking the social responsibility assessment of corporate behavior to the next level. Several major sustainability data providers merged providing improved availability of sustainability data. KLD was acquired by RiskMetrics, which was acquired by Morgan Stanley Capital International (MSCI) in 2009. MSCI also acquired GMI ratings in 2014, becoming one of the leading providers of ESG ratings. Another ESG ratings provider to join the race was Sustainalytics, which was eventually acquired by MorningStar in 2020. The list of ESG providers was expanded by S&P acquiring the ESG division of RobecoSAM in 2019 and the London Stock Exchange consolidating FTSE, Refintiv, and Beyond Ratings. Moody's, FactSet, ISS, RepRisk, and Vigeo Eiris followed, joining the list of leading ESG data providers (Bender *et al.*, 2023). With the rapid technological developments, eScience was well poised to extract information from qualitative and quantitative sustainability data.

1.2. *History of Science and Artificial Intelligence*

The concept of eScience (Hey, 2009) represents a transformative shift in scientific inquiry, heralded as the fourth paradigm of science (Figure 1). This paradigm follows the historical phases of empirical observation, theoretical formulation, and computational simulation. eScience encompasses the digital collaboration among researchers and the employment of advanced computing capabilities to manage and process large datasets to create data-intensive science. It enables scientists to explore complex phenomena that were previously unattainable due to computational constraints, thus unlocking new frontiers of knowledge and understanding. This approach leverages the vast amounts of data generated by modern experiments and observations, applying sophisticated algorithms and analytics to extract insights, often using resources distributed across high-performance computing networks. eScience augments traditional scientific methodologies and promotes more collaborative interdisciplinary approaches to research, accommodating the increasing need for sharing and analyzing large-scale data across various scientific domains.

Artificial Intelligence is not a new concept but dates back to the 1950s (Buchanan, 2005). In 1956, the Dartmouth Conference gave rise to AI, defined as the "discipline of building machines as intelligent as humans." Herbert A. Simon, a Nobel Laureate in Economics (1978) and an AI pioneer, created the Logic Theory Machine with Allen Newell in 1956 and

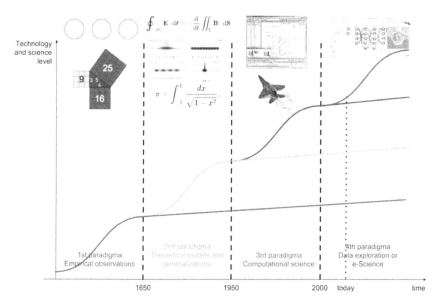

Figure 1. Visual representation of the historical evolution of the four paradigms in science, highlighting the transition from empirical observation to theoretical formulation, followed by computational simulation, and culminating in eScience. Adapted from (Hey, 2009)

the General Problem Solver (GPS) program in 1957. In 1965, he stated, "Machines will be capable, within twenty years, of doing any work a man can do." Since then, AI has continued to go through its busts and booms, and in the 21st century, we already have experiences with pioneering autonomous vehicles and automated personal assistants with remarkable accuracy in understanding, interpreting, and generating human language exemplified by advanced models like OpenAI's ChatGPT.

As data became increasingly available, the providers of ESG ratings tirelessly worked to offer investors metrics to aid in sustainable investment decision-making. However, the correlation among different providers of ESG ratings has been relatively low, and it has become hard to understand whom to trust. Financial institutions turned to in-house research, established ESG analyst positions, and started doing ESG due diligence internally. The problem was no longer a lack of data or metrics; the problem was of too many data-diverse methodologies for assessing the environmental, social, and governance aspects of corporate behavior, a lack of standards, a lack of transparency, and an absence of reporting regulations.

1.3. *Why Regulate Sustainability-related Reporting?*

The backbone of securities regulation in the United States comprises several vital acts. Among them is the Securities Act of 1933 — truth in securities law (Securities Act, 1933) — governing primary offerings of securities by issuers to the public in exchange for capital. There is a requirement for investors to receive significant disclosures about securities offered to the public, with deceit, misrepresentation, and fraud in selling securities being prohibited. The 1933 Securities Act requires securities registration, offering potential investors all the **material** information about the issuer's business.

The Securities Exchange Act of 1934 (Exchange Act, 1934) regulates the secondary trading of securities and market participants. The Securities and Exchange Commission (SEC) was created by the Exchange Act of 1934. The SEC is empowered to register and oversee securities and self-regulatory organizations (SROs), such as the New York Stock Exchange (NYSE), the National Association of Securities Dealers Automated Quotation (NASDAQ), and the Financial Industry Regulatory Authority (FINRA). The SEC requires periodic reporting by publicly traded companies. The company reports contain standardized financial disclosures prepared according to the Generally Accepted Accounting Principles (GAPP).

Investment advisers are regulated by the Investment Advisers Act (IAA) of 1940 (IAA, 1940), which requires advisors to register with the SEC and conform to regulations designed to protect investors in securities. Advisers, unlike broker-dealers, are fiduciaries, defined as providing investment advice considering the **investor's best interests**. Broker-dealers use the suitability of the investment principle when providing investment advice and are not fiduciaries. Fiduciary Duty is a cornerstone of offering investment advice, and it is prudent for investment advisers to consider and disclose all potential risks, including ESG-related risks, when offering investment advice. Companies need to adopt standardized disclosure rules to successfully consider and measure the impact of ESG-related risks and opportunities. The Investment Company Act (ICA) of 1940 regulates the organization of companies, including mutual funds, that invest primarily in securities and whose own securities are offered to the investing public (ICA, 1940).

Investment advisers offering securities to the general public need to consider sustainability directly related to the investment's ongoing concern and long-term risk and performance. In 2011, the Sustainability Accounting Standards Board (SASB) was founded by Jean Rogers to enable companies to provide industry-based disclosures about sustainability-related risks and opportunities that could affect corporations' financial health. Investors globally recognize SASB as a standard for corporate comparable sustainability disclosures. In August 2022, the International Sustainability Standards Board (ISSB) of the International Financial Reporting Standards (IFRS) assumed responsibility for maintaining, evolving, and enhancing the SASB standards. While the Global Reporting Initiative (GRI) sets standards for companies to report on their economic, environmental, and social impact, SASB focuses on the financial materiality of sustainability issues.

SASB provides tools for companies to implement ESG reporting frameworks, such as the Taskforce for Climate-related Financial Disclosure (TCFD) and the International Integrated Reporting Council (IIRC). Available for 77 industries, the SASB Standards identify the sustainability-related risks and opportunities that could affect a company's financial metrics, like cash flows, access to financing, or cost of capital, i.e. the disclosure topics and metrics most helpful to investors. SASB groups such metrics into five "sustainability dimensions": (1) the environment, (2) human capital, (3) social capital, (4) business model and innovation, and (5) leadership and governance.

1.4. *Layered Structure of Global Initiatives, Standards, and Reporting Frameworks*

To illustrate the layered and interconnected structure of global initiatives, standards, reporting frameworks, and national regulations that collectively shape the ESG landscape, we created a visualization in the form of a layered pyramid, shown in Figure 2. Each layer of this pyramid builds upon the previous one, beginning at the base with global general initiatives that set broad sustainability goals. This foundation progresses to the middle tier, establishing more specific standards and reporting frameworks. The structure culminates at the apex, where detailed national regulations mandate compliance.

Our starting point for constructing the pyramid was the ESG Regulations and Reporting Standards Tracker developed by Sustainable

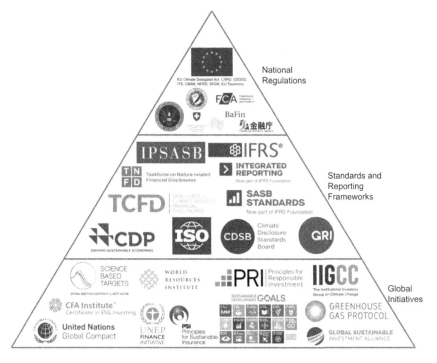

Figure 2. The layered and interconnected structure of global initiatives, standards, reporting frameworks, and national regulations shapes the ESG landscape

Fitch (Tisminetzky *et al.*, 2023). This tracker provides a detailed survey of the latest regulatory developments and standards related to ESG. Building on this groundwork, we have extended the range to encompass a more extensive collection of ESG-related standards and have explored a broader spectrum of global initiatives. This expansion allows for a more holistic representation of the ESG regulatory and framework ecosystem, capturing the details of the specific reporting standards and the overarching principles of global sustainability efforts.

At the pyramid's base are global initiatives that set the general principles for sustainability and governance. These encompass universal frameworks and coalitions such as the United Nations Global Compact (UNGC), the UN Sustainable Development Goals (SDGs), the Greenhouse Gas Protocol (GGP), the Global Sustainable Investment Alliance (GSIA), the Institutional Investors Group on Climate Change (IIGCC), and the

PRI. Their wide-reaching goals provide general guidance for sustainable practices across all sectors and geographies.

Moving up to the middle tier, we include more specific standards and reporting frameworks. These include the SASB, the IFRS, the Carbon Disclosure Project (CDP), the TCFD, the Climate Disclosure Standards Board (CDSB), GRI, the International Public Sector Accounting Standards Board (IPSASB), and the Taskforce on Nature-related Financial Disclosure (TNFD). These frameworks provide detailed methodologies and indicators for businesses to report their ESG performance consistently and comparably.

National sustainability-related regulations, tailored to each country's legal and economic contexts, are at the pyramid's apex. They provide a clear structure for compliance and accountability in ESG considerations. The national regulatory bodies enforce rules and guidelines that organizations must adhere to within their jurisdictions. The most notable regulations coming from the EU include the European Union's Climate Delegated Act, the Corporate Sustainability Reporting Directive (CSRD), the Non-Financial Reporting Directive (NFRD), the Sustainable Finance Disclosure Regulation (SFDR), and the EU Taxonomy. Similarly, other countries contribute to this apex tier with their regulatory agencies, such as the UK's Financial Conduct Authority (FCA), Germany's Federal Financial Supervisory Authority (BaFin), Japan's Financial Services Agency, and the United States' SEC.

2. Literature Review of Challenges and Opportunities in Applying AI to ESG Reporting

The application of AI in ESG reporting has attracted considerable interest in recent years. This area of research, marked by many academic papers, delves into the diverse ways AI can enhance ESG reporting. These studies mainly examine how AI technologies can facilitate data collection, increase accuracy in reporting, and provide deeper insights into ESG metrics. Integrating AI in this field assists in efficiently processing large volumes of ESG-related data. It enables more detailed and comprehensive analyses, thus leading to more informed and effective decisions in sustainable investing practices.

Aldridge and Martin (2022) examine the relationship between ESG mentions in corporate filings and subsequent financial performance.

Using a technique called Singular Value Decomposition (SVD), the authors analyze the impact of specific ESG topics on contemporaneous and forward-looking returns. The results suggest that certain ESG factors, such as data security and labor practices, positively correlate with future returns. In contrast, others, like product labeling and wastewater management, correlate negatively with returns. The study highlights the importance of considering ESG factors in investment decisions and the potential for using ML techniques to extract meaningful insights from corporate disclosures. Amel-Zadeh *et al.* (2021) explore using natural language processing (NLP) and machine learning techniques to measure corporate alignment with the United Nations SDGs. By analyzing text from corporate sustainability disclosures, the authors develop models to predict SDG alignment and explore how word-embedding techniques can enhance predictive accuracy. Their results suggest that NLP and ML can provide valuable insights for investors seeking to measure and manage their portfolios' social and environmental impact.

Burnaev *et al.* (2023) review practical applications of AI for solving ESG challenges. They identify successful use cases in areas such as carbon neutrality and ESG scoring. The paper also highlights challenges posed by AI, such as fake news generation and increased energy consumption. The authors conclude that while AI has the potential to revolutionize ESG, its full potential is yet to be realized. Crona, B. (2021) examines environmental aspects of ESG and risks and opportunities for using big data and AI to capture these in ESG ratings. He starts by outlining the difference between relative and absolute sustainability and argues that current ESG metrics and rankings are largely detached from causal connections to environmental sustainability. He suggests that while AI can process vast unstructured data, it can miss complex environmental issues. A hybrid approach, combining AI with human analysts, is proposed to better capture and evaluate sustainability outcomes. Zhang and Zhang (2023) state that while AI is poised to transform ESG, its full impact is still emerging. Machine Learning excels in handling complex, unstructured data. It outperforms traditional accounting methods in predictive accuracy and adaptability, making it ideal for evolving accounting challenges like fraud detection and financial forecasting.

Ehrhardt and Nguyen (2021) use NLP tools to detect coal activities in ESG and CSR reports. They train the MRE model for relation extraction and achieve comparable results to the state-of-the-art model SpERT. Finally, they created an NER-RE pipeline for joint entity and relation extraction that outperformed SpERT on the ClimLL dataset. Guo *et al.*

(2020) introduce ESG2Risk, a deep learning framework for assessing financial risk based on ESG news. The framework utilizes NLP and machine learning (ML) techniques to extract relevant information from ESG-related news articles. The study demonstrates the effectiveness of ESG2Risk in predicting stock price movements, highlighting the potential of AI in integrating ESG factors into financial risk management.

Arguing that AI can provide a more nuanced understanding of the risks and opportunities associated with ESG investing, Jain *et al.* (2023) propose a big data and AI framework to create more accurate and comprehensive ESG ratings. They explore the conjunction between big data and AI to assess the environmental components of ESG ratings. They propose AI-based solutions to overcome the weakness of the traditional ESG ratings, which are detached from environmental sustainability. In their study, Kang and El Maarouf (2022) describe the results of the FinSim4-ESG competition, consisting of two subtasks: ESG Taxonomy Enrichment and Sustainability Prediction. The approaches relied heavily on distributional methods for term and sentence similarity measures and classification tasks. The fine-tuned RoBERTa model on ESG data surpassed other models like BERT, Sentence-BERT, FinBERT, and LinkBERT, and linear classifiers outperformed nonlinear ones in both subtasks.

In Kannan and Seki (2023), the authors address extracting textual evidence to support ESG score ratings using Japanese annual securities reports. They construct a dataset of labeled sentences by defining labeling strategies for both ESG sentence types and their corresponding sentiments. They propose a method for extracting textual evidence of ESG scores using both ESG classification and sentiment analysis models. Experimental results confirm that their method can effectively identify textual evidence for companies with high ESG scores. Khoruzhy *et al.* (2022) explore the relationship between ESG investing and the development of AI. They argue that AI technologies have the potential to significantly impact ESG investing practices, both in terms of the opportunities they create and the challenges they pose. The authors analyze the existing literature on ESG investing in the AI era and identify several key themes, including the use of AI for ESG data analysis, the development of AI-powered ESG investment tools, and the challenges of ensuring the ethical use of AI in ESG investing.

The paper by Lee *et al.* (2022) proposes an integrated approach to analyzing ESG data via machine learning and deep learning algorithms. They argue that ESG data are complex and multifaceted and that traditional statistical methods are often insufficient to capture their full richness.

The authors propose an approach that combines multiple machine learning and deep learning algorithms to extract meaningful insights from ESG data. They evaluate their approach on various datasets, and demonstrate that it outperforms traditional statistical methods regarding accuracy and interpretability. Luccioni *et al.* (2020) introduce ClimateQA, a tool that leverages recent advances in NLP to analyze sustainability reports and identify climate-relevant sections based on a question-answering approach. They present their custom model and methodology, which involves pre-training on unlabeled data and fine-tuning on labeled data guided by the TCFD questions. The model demonstrates strong performance, with an average F1 score of 91.7% across various sectors.

The implications of AI and machine-readable data for sustainable investing and ESG data are explored by Macpherson *et al.* (2021). The authors discuss recent European regulations, such as the EU's SFDR and CSRD, emphasizing the importance of sustainability-related disclosures and digital tagging for improved transparency. They also examine the use of AI in ESG investing, emphasizing its potential to enhance portfolio decision-making and identify material ESG factors. However, the authors acknowledge the challenges of ESG data biases and the need for further work to address these issues and promote more accurate and comparable information. They conclude that technology and digitization will be crucial in standardizing ESG reporting and developing ESG audits to build investor confidence. To solve challenges with NLP tasks in the financial industry due to limited and different datasets, Nugent *et al.* (2021) propose two methods: domain-specific language models and data augmentation. Fine-tuning a language model with financial data and using a back translation technique for data augmentation improved classification accuracy in ESG controversy and UN SDG detection tasks. To improve ESG analysis, Pasch and Ehnes (2022) develop a method to fine-tune transformer-based language models, like BERT, for the ESG domain. This method combines ESG ratings with annual reports to train models that can predict the ESG behavior of companies. The trained models outperform traditional text classifiers, indicating their potential to enhance ESG analysis in the financial industry.

Perazzoli *et al.* (2022) present a comprehensive bibliometric analysis supported by NLP techniques on ESG-related topics from a systemic standpoint. They analyze a corpus of 55,000 publications from the Google Scholar database, identifying the main trends and challenges in the field.

The authors argue that despite the increasing attention being paid to ESG, there needs to be more standardization and regulation, particularly for the social and environmental criteria. They propose a framework to analyze and explain the systemic attributes of ESG based on the general systems theory perspective. The study provides valuable insights for researchers, practitioners, and policymakers interested in promoting sustainable development and responsible investment. Sætra (2012, 2022) proposes a framework for evaluating and reporting the ESG impacts of AI systems using the United Nations SDGs. The proposed framework is comprehensive and systematic. It considers the impacts of AI at the micro, meso, and macro levels. The framework helps identify and categorize potential sustainability benefits and harms related to AI, enabling companies to analyze and disclose their AI-related ESG impacts more effectively. The author demonstrates the application of the framework using Microsoft's sustainability reporting as an example.

To improve investors' ability to anticipate unforeseen ESG risks, Sokolov *et al.* (2021) propose state-of-the-art NLP techniques to identify ESG risks using social media data. They explore applications of such methodologies to ESG investing, index construction, and algorithm design to create a fully or semi-autonomous ESG rating system. In Visalli *et al.* (2023) propose an ESG data collection method based on an AI platform that utilizes deep learning algorithms for computer vision and natural language processing. The platform combines large language models (LLMs), human-in-the-loop AI techniques, continuous learning, and knowledge representation methods to implement machine reading comprehension techniques that turn unstructured documents into structured data. The method facilitates gathering documents and content from disparate sources, including annual reports, sustainability reports, news articles, and company websites. The authors demonstrate the method's effectiveness through experiments conducted on real-world documents, showing its potential to improve ESG data collection and extraction for various stakeholders. Zhang (2023) investigates the relationship between ESG initiatives and companies' market risk using natural language processing and machine learning techniques. He analyzes ESG-related reports and articles of 100 Chinese public companies to create an internal ESG score that is more accurate, comprehensive, and intuitive. The results show that ESG initiatives positively correlate with lower market risk and higher returns, and the constructed internal ESG scores can distinguish between high- and low-quality stocks.

To improve existing language models and include specific domain-related texts, Webersinke *et al.* (2021) developed the ClimateBERT, a transformer-based language model specifically pre-trained on climate-related texts. ClimateBERT is trained on a corpus of over 2 million paragraphs of climate-related text and outperforms existing language models on various climate-related downstream tasks, including text classification, sentiment analysis, and fact-checking. In their comparative analysis, Trajanov *et al.* (2023) examine the performance of ChatGPT against ClimateBert, fine-tuned for climate-related tasks. They find that for classification tasks, especially for climate-related texts, ClimateBert generally outperforms ChatGPT. However, in complex tasks like classifying climate change disclosure categories, ChatGPT's performance was comparable to ClimateBert's. The study also underscores the adaptability of general-purpose models like ChatGPT, which can handle unfamiliar tasks and data with above-average performance, in contrast to conventional classifiers that require specific pre-training and fine-tuning. Lazarev *et al.* (2023) evaluate the performance of two text classification models tailored explicitly for classifying climate change-related texts to analyze the impact of fine-tuning these models.

Trajanoska *et al.* (2023) explore the use of LLMs to create knowledge graphs from unstructured text automatically. They specifically examine the use of LLMs for joint entity and relation extraction, a crucial step in constructing knowledge graphs. The authors conduct experiments on a dataset of sustainability-related text and show that LLMs can achieve state-of-the-art performance on this task. They also explore the use of LLMs for the automatic creation of sustainability-related ontologies, which can be used to improve the accuracy and consistency of knowledge graphs.

Vodenska *et al.* (2022) present an AI methodology to detect inconsistencies between corporate disclosures and societal views on corporate social responsibility. This method employs NLP and sentiment analysis to evaluate both SEC corporate filings and reports from mainstream and social media. An ESG-focused knowledge graph is created to identify corporations whose practices are inconsistent with their stated ESG objectives and assess investment risks related to ESG factors. The authors further explore the challenges in harnessing ESG data and the potential advancements that machine learning could bring to ESG investment analysis.

3. Collecting and Preprocessing Global ESG Regulation Documents

For regulatory document analysis, we use the September 2023 update of the ESG Regulations and Reporting Standards Tracker by Sustainable Fitch (Tisminetzky *et al.*, 2023), which provides an overview of key regulatory developments in sustainable taxonomies, climate disclosures, and ESG fund requirements. It also monitors well-established reporting frameworks and standards, aiming to offer concise guidance for stakeholders in the ESG sector. The report is updated quarterly and currently focuses on four types of regulations: Sustainable Taxonomy, Corporate ESG Disclosure, Corporate Climate Disclosure, and ESG Fund Requirements/Disclosure. It also includes a list of primary global and regional disclosure standards that have a material impact on sustainable finance. Jurisdictions covered include a wide range: the Americas, Asia-Pacific, Europe, the Middle East, and Africa. The regulation status is tracked from the announcement to effectiveness, and updates are noted when the respective authorities update the regulations. Enforcement levels categorize regulations as mandatory, limited application/"comply or explain," voluntary, and guidelines. For Scope 1 and 2 GHG emission disclosures, the document states whether the disclosures are compulsory, voluntary, subject to certain conditions, or not applicable.

3.1. *Data Collection*

The "ESG Regulations and Reporting Standards Tracker" contains distinct tables for regulations and standards. Each row describes a document, with detailed information about the type of regulation or standard, region and jurisdiction where the regulation/standard is enforced, summary and details, announcement date, status, and the authority that issues the regulation/standard. Additionally, each document has a hyperlink that directs either to the PDF version or the website where the document is available for download.

The overview of taxonomy type and effectiveness status by jurisdiction is shown on the world map in Figure 3, where we can see whether the regulation is adopted/effective (China, Russia, Europe, South Africa, Mexico, and Japan), under development/in draft (Canada, the UK,

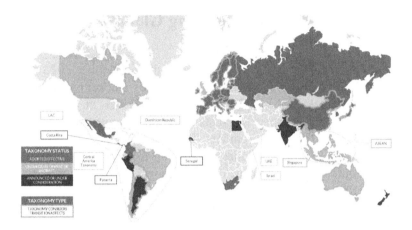

Figure 3.   Map of taxonomy status as of September 2023, based on Sustainable Fitch's ESG Regulation and Reporting Standards Tracker (Tisminetzky *et al.*, 2023)

Note: Taxonomy status as of September 2023.
Source: Sustainable Fitch's ESG Regulation and Reporting Standards Tracker.

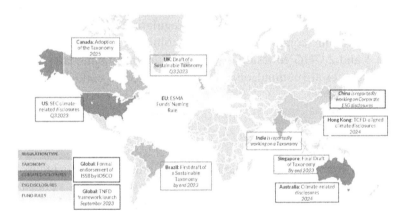

Figure 4.   Upcoming ESG Regulations (Tisminetzky *et al.*, 2023)
Source: Sustainable Fitch's ESG Regulation and Reporting Standards Tracker.

Australia, Kazakhstan, Brazil, ASEAN, and Singapore), or announced/ under consideration (Senegal, India, Egypt, Peru, Argentina, and New Zealand).

Figure 4 sheds light on the future of ESG regulation, indicating the planned or upcoming ESG regulations globally as taxonomies (Canada, Brazil, UK, Singapore, and India), climate disclosures (USA, Hong Kong, and Australia), ESG disclosures (China), or investment fund rules (EU, Western Balkans, Moldova, and Switzerland).

To speed up and automate the collection of regulatory documents, we developed a Python script for PDF document retrieval. The script processes each disclosure independently, identifies hyperlinks ending in .pdf, downloads them, and saves them in our centralized document repository. We successfully downloaded around 60% of the documents automatically. The remaining set of documents, which had a link to a website rather than a direct PDF, needed to be retrieved manually since the layout and the structure differed between the websites and posed a challenge to develop a universally effective automated script for all websites. As a result, manual retrieval procedures were employed to ensure accuracy and adaptability to the distinct characteristics of each website. The manual retrieval procedure consisted of two stages. The first step involved visiting the web pages where the disclosure standards are located, and the second step entailed classifying the documents based on their language and distinguishing between English and non-English texts. During each stage, we tracked which documents were downloaded and mapped each document to its respective row within the spreadsheet.

Following the initial retrieval procedure, we employed a post-processing procedure in which each document was translated and merged in the case of multi-document disclosure standards. The documents were translated using Google Translate, which required careful examination after the translation for quality assurance. We then merged the documents to ensure seamless integration in the analysis. After the final stage of the post-processing procedure, we successfully collected 107 out of 144 regulations. The excluded 37 documents were either press releases or contained non-functional links.

4. Methodology for AI-based Analysis of ESG Regulations

To analyze the collected regulations, we used the SASB Standard, one of the most detailed ESG-related standards. The SASB framework encompasses various sustainability-related risks and opportunities, organized into five key areas: (1) environment, (2) social capital, (3) human capital, (4) business model and innovation, and (5) leadership and governance. There are 26 specific SASB topics, and each area includes some of them, such as "GHG Emissions" for environmental concerns or "Business Ethics" for governance. Our analysis aims to determine whether all elements of the SASB framework are mentioned in the published global sustainability-related regulations. Through this analysis, we intend to map the disclosure standards onto SASB categories, providing a clearer perspective on the aspects of the sustainability landscape covered by the standard. We automate this analysis using two approaches: The first is a classical keyword-based search and the second is an AI-based model using the latest LLMs. We describe these distinct approaches in the following two sections.

4.1. *Keyword-based Analysis*

The first step in the keyword-based approach is identifying essential keywords for each topic to understand whether a document contains information about a specific issue. For instance, when investigating "GHG Emissions," we look for terms such as "carbon footprint" or "emission reduction." To make this approach more accurate, we created a list of five keywords for each of the 26 topics. The complete list of the five SASB categories and 26 topics is given in Table 1, showing the defined keywords for each topic.

To ensure consistency, we converted all the documents to lowercase letters. We then broke down the text into one-word, two-word, and three-word combinations, known as *n*-grams. This approach helps capture single keywords and phrases that carry specific meanings related to sustainability topics. We counted how often each keyword or phrase appears in the documents. This count gave us an idea of how much attention each sustainability topic received in the disclosure standards. After counting the keywords and phrases, we added them to see the bigger picture for each sustainability area to understand which areas were more present in the disclosure documents.

4.2. *Large Language Models-based Analysis*

In the recent era of advances in the field of AI and machine learning, a new innovative approach has been reshaping how information is created and gathered by AI systems and LLMs (Chang *et al.*, 2023). This new approach, called Retrieval Augmented Generation (RAG)

Table 1.   The predefined five keywords (key phrases) used in the keyword-based model for each category/topic from the SASB framework

Category	Topic	Keywords and Key Phases
Environment	GHG Emissions	• Greenhouse Gas Emissions • Carbon Footprint • Climate Change • Emission Reduction • Carbon Emission
	Air Quality	• Air Pollution • Particulate Matter • Air Quality Monitoring • Emissions Control • Air Quality Standards
	Energy Management	• Energy Efficiency • Energy Conservation • Renewable Energy • Energy Consumption • Energy Audit
	Water & Wastewater Management	• Water Conservation • Wastewater Treatment • Water Quality • Water Recycling • Water Management
	Waste & Hazardous Materials Management	• Waste Disposal • Hazardous Waste • Waste Recycling • Waste Reduction • Waste Management
	Ecological Impacts	• Ecological Conservation • Biodiversity • Ecosystem Impact • Natural Resources • Environmental Preservation
Social Capital	Human Rights & Community Relations	• Human Rights • Community Engagement • Social Responsibility • Community Development • Stakeholder Relations

(*Continued*)

Table 1.   (*Continued*)

Category	Topic	Keywords and Key Phases
	Customer Privacy	• Data Privacy • Customer Data Protection • Privacy Policy • Personal Data Security • Privacy Compliance
	Data Security	• Information Security • Data Protection • Cybersecurity • Data Breach Prevention • Security Measures
	Access & Affordability	• Accessibility • Affordable Services • Inclusivity • Equitable Access • Affordability Programs
	Product Quality & Safety	• Product Safety • Quality Assurance • Consumer Safety • Product Testing • Quality Standards
	Customer Welfare	• Customer Satisfaction • Customer Support • Consumer Welfare • Customer Well-being • Customer Service
	Selling Practices & Product Labeling	• Ethical Selling • Product Labeling Compliance • Marketing Practices • Consumer Information • Fair Trade
Human Capital	Labor Practices	• Labor Standards • Workplace Conditions • Employee Rights • Fair Labor Practices • Labor Compliance

Table 1. (*Continued*)

Category	Topic	Keywords and Key Phases
	Employee Health & Safety	• Occupational Health • Workplace Safety • Employee Well-being • Safety Training • Health and Safety Policies
	Employee Engagement, Diversity, & Inclusion	• Employee Engagement Programs • Diversity Initiatives • Inclusion Policies • Workforce Diversity • Employee Satisfaction
Business Model & Innovation	Product Design & Lifecycle Management	• Product Development • Lifecycle Analysis • Design Innovation • Product Sustainability • Product Lifecycle Strategies
	Business Model Resilience	• Resilience Strategies • Business Continuity • Adaptability • Crisis Management • Resilient Business Models
	Supply Chain Management	• Supply Chain Optimization • Supplier Relationships • Logistics Management • Supply Chain Efficiency • Value Chain
	Materials Sourcing & Efficiency	• Sustainable Sourcing • Resource Efficiency • Material Procurement • Supply Chain Sustainability • Resource Management
	Physical Impacts of Climate Change	• Climate Change Effects • Climate Resilience • Climate Adaptation • Extreme Weather Impact • Climate Risk Assessment

(*Continued*)

Table 1. (*Continued*)

Category	Topic	Keywords and Key Phases
Leadership & Governance	Business Ethics	• Ethical Business Practices • Corporate Ethics • Ethical Standards • Ethical Governance • Ethical Decision-Making
	Competitive Behavior	• Market Competition • Antitrust Compliance • Fair Competition • Competitive Practices • Market Dominance
	Management of the Legal & Regulatory Environment	• Regulatory Compliance • Legal Risk Management • Regulatory Governance • Compliance Programs • Legal Affairs
	Critical Incident Risk Management	• Risk Mitigation • Incident Response • Crisis Management • Emergency Planning • Disaster Preparedness
	Systemic Risk Management	• Systemic Risk Assessment • Risk Monitoring • Risk Analysis • Systemic Risk Factors • Risk Mitigation Strategies

(Lewis *et al.*, 2020), combines the capabilities of LLMs with the wealth of knowledge encapsulated within documents. With RAG, the knowledge base of the LLMs is extended by integrating external sources of data, such as documents, into the process of creating content and responses. Incorporating documents into the content generation process enhances context, accuracy, and factual integrity. This knowledge is extracted from documents rather than generated by the LLM, ensuring diverse and relevant knowledge integration by leveraging information from various domains. This approach allows these models to offer responses and information that shift from general knowledge models to more informed and accurate context-aware models.

Document processing begins with converting the text from the disclosure standards into smaller segments. Each segment is embedded or transformed into a dense vector, subsequently stored in an embedding index. This index represents the textual content in a numerical format tailored for AI comprehension and analysis. The creation of such an index is pivotal in facilitating the comparative assessment of textual data across various documents. For this study, we created a separate index for each disclosure standard. This approach ensures we only use information from that given document when evaluating a disclosure standard.

After the index generation, the study employed a structured prompt template for prompt engineering. This template is meticulously crafted to analyze references to specific ESG topics within the documents. Prompt engineering involves designing and crafting input queries or prompts to AI models to elicit desired responses or behaviors. It is essential because well-constructed prompts can significantly impact the quality and relevance of AI-generated outputs, making the technology more effective in specific tasks and applications. The AI responses are structured to encapsulate the presence or absence of the topic, contextual sentences, insightful commentary on the ESG impact, discussions around management or regulation of the topic, and the overarching tone of the narrative. The used prompt is given in Figure 5.

Each document undergoes a thorough querying process in which AI evaluates the content based on ESG-related questions. To comprehensively address the subject, we utilize the 26 topics from the SASB framework as a query string, generating prompts that gather the most relevant information from the index about the disclosure standard we are investigating. Initially, we begin with querying the index to identify and select the three most similar document segments, each comprising 300 words. These segments are crucial for establishing the context required for question answering by the LLM. Subsequently, we insert both the query string and the contextual information into the prompt template, resulting in a fully formed prompt submitted to the LLM. This study used the ChatGPT 3.5 turbo as our question-answering model.

The responses generated by the AI model are carefully analyzed to extract nuanced information. This analysis involves identifying the mentions of ESG topics, understanding their context, deriving insights about their ESG impact, and comprehending their management or regulatory discourse. The extracted data are then methodically compiled, typically in a Comma-Separated Values (CSV) format, enabling a systematic presentation of findings. This structured compilation includes document

```
Context information is below.
-------------------------------
{context_str}
-------------------------------
Given the context information and no prior knowledge, you need to analyze
mentions and discussions of '{query_str}' in the context of ESG
(Environmental, Social, and Governance).
The answer needs to be in JSON format, and it should include:
mention: yes or no
sentence: The sentence or paragraph where '{query_str}' or related terms are
mentioned.
insights: The insights on how the '{query_str}' is impacting ESG.
managementDiscussion: How '{query_str}' is managed or regulated in the
provided text.
OverallTone: The general tone of the discussion (e.g., concerned,
optimistic, critical).

The structure of the JSON output should be:
{{
    "mention": "yes/no",
    "sentence": "String",
    "insights": "String",
    "managementDiscussion": "String",
    "overallTone": "String"
}}
Answer:
```

Figure 5.   ChatGPT prompt that was used to find the mentions and the context of the SASB topics in the sustainability-related regulatory documents

names, queried topics, AI responses, and specific textual excerpts pertinent to the queries.

5. Results and Discussion

We first evaluate the performance of the ChatGPT-based model compared to enhanced keyword labeling. We then combine the results from the two models to create an ensemble model and use this model to analyze the ESG Regulations.

5.1. *Evaluation of ChatGPT vs. Keyword-based Model*

To make the comparison, we run both algorithms on all 107 regulation documents. For each document, we search for a specific keyword or analyze the answer from ChatGPT to see if it contains information about the specified topic.

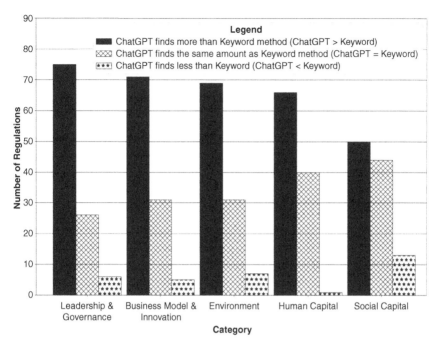

Figure 6. Comparison of the number of detected documents containing topics from the SASB framework. The black bars show the number of documents where ChatGPT finds more topics than the Keyword-based algorithm (ChatGPT > Keyword-based). The crossed-line bars show the number of documents where ChatGPT's performance is equivalent to the Keyword-based labeling (ChatGPT = Keyword-based), and the star-filled bars show the number of documents for which ChatGPT underperforms the Keyword-based model (ChatGPT < Keyword-based)

Figure 6 compares the performance of ChatGPT and Keyword-based labeling across five distinct categories: (1) environment, (2) social capital, (3) human capital, (4) business model and innovation, and (5) leadership and governance. The results show that ChatGPT finds most regulatory documents containing the SASB topics.

The complete number of topics detected in each document by ChatGPT vs. the keyword-based model is shown in Table 2, including the country code and the five SASB sustainability areas. The first digit shows the number of documents detected by ChatGPT and the second digit shows the number of documents detected by the keyword-based model.

Table 2.   Number of detected topics ChatGPT vs. Keyword-based model. The first number is related to ChatGPT and the second is related to the Keyword-based model

Disclosure Standard Name	Country Code	Env.	Soc. Cap.	Human Cap.	Bus. Mod. & Inn.	Lead. & Gov.
Sustainable Finance Taxonomy	AR	3/1	0/0	1/0	2/0	3/0
Corporate Governance Code	AR	0/0	1/1	1/0	0/1	1/1
ASEAN Taxonomy for Sustainable Finance	ASEAN	6/6	2/2	0/0	4/0	1/0
Climate-related Financial Disclosure Rule	AU	2/3	0/0	0/0	4/2	2/0
ESG Reporting Guide 2015	AU	5/4	5/2	3/2	3/1	1/0
ESG Reporting Guide	BH	4/4	2/3	3/1	4/1	3/0
Resolutions No. 4943 and 4944 (amendments to Resolution 4557 and 4606)	BR	5/0	2/0	1/0	2/0	0/0
Resolution CMN No. 4945 (Social, Environmental and Climate Responsibility Policy — PRSAC)	BR	3/1	1/0	0/0	1/0	1/0
Regulation No. 666/2022 Sustainability Requirements for Insurance Companies	BR	1/0	0/0	1/0	1/0	1/0
New Issuers Regulation — Annex B	BR	0/0	1/0	1/0	0/0	1/0
Resolution 4327 on Socio-environmental Responsibility	BR	1/0	0/0	0/0	0/0	0/0
Resolution No. 175	BR	1/0	1/0	0/0	0/0	1/0
Resolution No. 59	BR	2/0	0/0	2/0	0/0	2/0
Third Party Resource Management Code	BR	0/0	1/1	0/0	0/0	2/0
Sustainable Finance Taxonomy	BR	4/1	1/0	0/0	2/0	1/0
Staff Notice 81-334 ESG Related Investment Fund Disclosure	CA	2/5	2/2	0/0	0/0	2/0
A Primer for Environmental and Social Disclosure	CA	3/3	3/2	2/0	3/0	0/0
Green and Transition Finance Taxonomy	CA	3/3	2/1	2/0	3/2	1/1
Bill S-211 Fighting Against Forced Labor and Child Labor in Supply Chains Act	CA	0/0	2/1	2/0	1/0	2/0
Climate Risk Management	CA	1/1	0/1	0/0	2/2	0/2
Sustainability Reporting and Disclosure Guide	CL	3/1	1/0	1/0	2/0	2/0
Green Taxonomy	CL	6/1	1/0	1/0	3/0	1/0
Act 461	CL	2/0	4/0	2/0	2/1	2/0
Act 276 and Resolution 43	CL	0/0	0/0	1/0	0/0	0/0
Measures for Corporate Disclosures of Environmental Information	CN	4/0	0/0	0/0	1/0	1/0

Table 2.   (*Continued*)

Disclosure Standard Name	Country Code	Env.	Soc. Cap.	Human Cap.	Bus. Mod. & Inn.	Lead. & Gov.
China Green Bond Endorsed Project Catalogue (2021 edition)	CN	3/0	2/0	1/0	3/0	1/0
Common Ground Taxonomy-Climate Change Mitigation	EU-CN	5/5	2/1	2/0	2/1	1/0
Sustainable Finance Taxonomy	EG	6/3	0/0	0/0	1/0	0/0
Climate Delegated Act	EU	6/6	0/5	0/0	1/5	2/2
Environmental Delegated Act	EU	6/5	3/2	3/0	4/0	2/0
Corporate Sustainability Reporting Directive (CSRD)	EU	6/3	3/4	3/0	4/1	3/1
Implementing Technical Standards (ITS) on Pillar 3 Disclosures on Environmental, Social and Governance (ESG) Risks	EU	3/3	3/3	3/0	3/2	2/1
Carbon Border Adjustment Mechanism	EU	1/1	0/1	1/0	1/0	0/0
Complementary Climate Delegated Act	EU	6/5	3/1	1/0	3/3	1/1
Disclosures Delegated Act	EU	2/2	0/0	0/0	1/1	0/0
Non-Financial Reporting Directive (NFRD)	EU	4/2	2/1	3/0	1/0	1/0
Sustainable Finance Disclosure Regulation (SFDR)	EU	3/3	1/1	1/0	1/1	2/0
EU Taxonomy for Sustainable Activities	EU	6/5	3/2	2/0	3/1	2/0
Guidelines on Funds Names Using ESG or Sustainability-Related Terms	EU	2/4	1/1	0/0	0/2	2/0
Implementing Decree of Article 29 of the Law on Energy and Climate Law addressing non-financial reporting by market players	FR	3/2	1/0	0/0	3/2	1/0
Climate Change Risk Governance	FR	2/1	0/0	3/0	2/0	2/1
German Act on Corporate Due Diligence Obligations in Supply Chains	DE	3/0	1/1	2/1	4/0	3/1
Guidance Notice on Dealing with Sustainability Risk	DE	4/3	2/3	3/1	4/1	1/2
Sustainable Banking Principles and Guidelines	GH	6/6	4/4	3/1	2/1	2/3
The Climate Bonds Taxonomy	Global	5/4	1/0	1/0	3/0	0/0
Circular on Management and Disclosure of Climate-related Risks by Fund Managers	HK	2/1	0/0	0/0	1/0	0/0
HKEX Consultation Paper on Enhancement of Climate Disclosure under its ESG Framework	HK	2/4	0/5	0/1	4/3	0/0

(*Continued*)

Table 2.   (*Continued*)

Disclosure Standard Name	Country Code	Env.	Soc. Cap.	Human Cap.	Bus. Mod. & Inn.	Lead. & Gov.
Environmental, Social and Governance Reporting Guide	HK	5/4	5/3	2/1	2/0	1/0
Circular to management companies of SFC-authorized unit trusts and mutual funds — ESG funds	HK	2/1	1/0	0/0	0/0	1/0
Business responsibility and sustainability reporting by listed entities	IN	2/1	1/0	1/0	2/0	1/0
Revised Disclosure Requirements for Issuance and Listing of Green Debt Securities	IN	6/5	0/0	0/0	3/3	1/0
Consultation Paper on ESG Disclosures, Ratings and Investing	IN	5/4	2/0	3/1	3/0	0/0
OJK Regulation No. 51/POJK.03/2017	ID	6/1	5/0	3/0	3/0	1/0
Indonesia Green Taxonomy Edition 1.0	ID	6/1	2/0	0/0	1/0	2/0
Green Israeli Taxonomy	IL	6/6	1/2	1/0	3/2	0/1
Regulation No. 38/2018	IT	1/0	2/0	1/0	0/0	3/0
Update of the Corporate Governance Code	JP	1/1	1/1	2/0	1/1	2/2
Japan Corporate Climate Disclosures	JP	2/2	0/0	1/0	1/0	2/0
Taxonomy of Green Projects to be Financed through Green Bonds and Green Loans	KZ	6/0	4/0	3/0	5/0	4/0
Common Framework of Sustainable Finance Taxonomies for LAC	LAC	6/0	4/0	2/0	4/0	2/0
Simplified ESG Disclosure Guide (SEDG)	MY	6/5	6/3	3/2	4/2	3/1
Principle-Based Sustainability and Responsible Investment Taxonomy (SRI Taxonomy)	MY	6/4	6/3	3/1	3/1	1/0
Guidelines on Sustainable & Responsible Investment (SRI) Funds	MY	2/1	0/0	0/0	0/0	1/0
Climate Change and Principle-based Taxonomy (CCPT)	MY	6/5	2/1	1/0	3/2	2/2
Code of Professional Ethics — Sustainability Guide	MX	4/1	4/0	3/0	3/0	4/0
Sustainable Taxonomy	MX	6/1	3/1	3/0	3/0	1/0
Securities Market — Exhibit N	MX	3/0	2/0	2/0	3/0	1/0
Good Practice Integration of Climate-Related Risk Considerations into Banks' Risk Management	NL	3/3	0/0	0/0	1/1	1/2

Table 2. (*Continued*)

Disclosure Standard Name	Country Code	Env.	Soc. Cap.	Human Cap.	Bus. Mod. & Inn.	Lead. & Gov.
Development of Definitional Tools to Encourage Greater Investment in "Green" Projects	NZ	4/2	1/1	0/0	2/1	1/0
Mandatory Climate-related Disclosures	NZ	2/1	0/0	0/0	2/1	0/0
Sustainability Disclosure Guidelines	NG	6/3	4/1	3/0	4/2	2/1
ESG Reporting Guidelines	PA	6/1	4/1	3/0	2/0	1/0
Resolution	PE	0/0	0/1	1/0	0/0	1/0
Corporate Sustainability Reporting (Resolution 018-2020-SMV/01)	PE	0/0	0/0	0/0	0/0	0/0
Philippine Sustainable Finance Roadmap and Guiding Principles	PH	6/5	3/2	2/0	4/4	3/2
Sustainable Finance Roadmap and Guiding Principles on Sustainable Finance	PH	6/5	2/0	1/0	4/4	2/2
Green Fund Rules	PH	2/2	2/1	0/0	0/0	1/0
SEC Memorandum Circular No. 4 — Sustainability Reporting Guidelines for Listed Companies	PH	3/0	0/0	0/0	1/0	0/0
Principles of Responsible Investment	RU	5/2	1/1	3/1	2/0	0/0
ESG Disclosure Guidelines	SA	6/4	5/2	2/1	4/0	2/1
Sustainable Finance Taxonomy	SN	4/3	0/0	0/0	1/0	0/0
Public Consultation on Turning Climate Ambition into Action in Singapore	SG	3/2	1/1	2/1	4/2	2/0
GFIT Taxonomy	SG	6/6	3/2	0/0	3/4	1/0
Disclosure and Reporting Guidelines for Retail ESG Funds	SG	2/1	1/0	0/0	0/0	1/0
JSE Climate Change Disclosure Guidance	ZA	3/3	0/0	2/0	3/3	2/1
South African Green Finance Taxonomy	ZA	6/6	3/2	2/1	3/4	1/0
Ordinance on Climate Disclosure	CH	2/1	0/0	0/0	0/0	0/0
Greenwashing Prevention Fund Naming Rules	CH	1/1	2/0	0/0	1/0	2/0
Disclosure Banks and Disclosure Insurers Circulars	CH	0/0	0/0	0/0	0/0	0/0
Listed Company Sustainability Action Plan	TW	3/0	1/0	3/0	2/0	2/0
ESG Reporting Guide	TN	5/1	2/1	3/0	3/0	2/0
Sustainability Principles Compliance Framework (Communique No. II-17.1.a)	TR	6/4	3/3	3/3	1/1	2/0

(*Continued*)

Table 2.   (*Continued*)

Disclosure Standard Name	Country Code	Env.	Soc. Cap.	Human Cap.	Bus. Mod. & Inn.	Lead. & Gov.
Sustainability Guidelines for the Banking Sector	TR	6/4	2/2	3/3	3/1	2/0
Sustainability Disclosure Requirements	GB	6/5	3/2	2/0	3/1	1/0
Enhancing Banks and Insurers Approaches to Managing the Financial Risks from Climate Change	GB	0/2	0/0	0/0	2/0	0/1
PS21/23: Enhancing Climate-Related Disclosures by Standard Listed Companies	GB	5/1	0/0	3/0	3/2	1/0
PS21/24: Enhancing Climate-Related Disclosures by Asset Managers, Life Insurers and FCA-Regulated Pension Providers	GB	2/1	3/1	0/0	1/1	2/0
Limited Liability Partnerships (Strategic Report) (Climate-Related Financial Disclosure) Regulations 2022	GB	2/0	0/0	1/0	2/0	1/0
Companies (Strategic Report) (Climate-Related Financial Disclosure) Regulations 2022	GB	2/0	0/0	0/0	1/0	1/0
FSRA Fund Rules	AE	3/0	0/0	0/0	0/0	1/0
ESG Disclosure Guidance for Listed Companies	AE	3/2	1/2	3/1	1/0	2/1
Climate-Related Disclosures	US	4/5	1/2	0/0	4/3	2/1
Amendment to Rule 35d-1 — Fund Names Rule	US	0/1	2/2	1/0	0/0	3/0
Amendments to ESG Rules and Disclosures for Investment Advisers and Investment Companies	US	1/1	1/2	1/0	0/0	1/0
Climate Corporate Data Accountability Act	US	1/1	0/1	0/0	2/1	1/0
New York Stock Exchange ESG Guidance	US	6/0	4/0	3/0	5/0	3/0

5.2. *Coverage Analysis of SASB-defined Risks and Opportunities in Global Regulations*

To have more accurate results, we combine the two models to create a new ensemble model to analyze the coverage of the risks and opportunities defined in the SASB framework in the collected set of 107 global ESG-related regulations.

First, we calculate the number of topics covered in each of the regulations by a given jurisdiction that are effective/mandatory and effective/non-mandatory. Table 3 shows that the European Union, Nigeria, and

Table 3. Effective and mandatory regulations coverage by SASB category out of 26 topics in all five categories

Jurisdiction	Environment	Social Capital	Human Capital	Business Model & Innovation	Leadership & Governance	Total
EU	6	4	3	4	3	20
Nigeria	6	4	3	4	2	19
Saudi Arabia	6	5	2	4	2	19
Indonesia	6	5	3	3	1	18
Singapore	5	4	3	2	2	16
UK	5	3	3	3	2	16
Hong Kong	5	5	2	2	1	15
Brazil	5	2	2	2	2	13
Germany	3	1	2	4	3	13
Chile	2	4	2	2	2	12
China	4	2	1	3	1	11
Mexico	3	2	2	3	1	11
France	3	1	0	3	1	8
India	2	1	1	2	1	7
Italy	1	2	1	0	3	7
The Philippines	3	2	0	1	1	7
Japan	2	0	1	1	2	6
Argentina	0	1	1	1	1	4
New Zealand	2	0	0	2	0	4
Malaysia	2	0	0	0	1	3
Switzerland	2	0	0	0	0	2

Saudi Arabia are the most advanced in covering all aspects of the SASB framework. For example, EU regulations cover 20 of the 26 topics in effective and mandatory regulatory documents, while Nigeria and Saudi Arabia follow with 19 out of 26 topics covered.

In the effective and non-mandatory regulatory document category, the US is leading by covering 21 out of the 26 SASB topics in regulations, closely followed by Malaysia and Mexico with coverage of 20 SASB topics, each in their respective national sustainability-based regulations, as shown in Table 4.

Table 4.   Effective and non-mandatory regulations coverage by SASB category out of 26 topics in all five categories

Jurisdiction	Environment	Social Capital	Human Capital	Business Model & Innovation	Leadership & Governance	Total
US	6	4	3	5	3	21
Malaysia	6	6	3	3	2	20
Mexico	6	4	3	3	4	20
Ghana	6	4	3	2	3	18
LAC	6	4	2	4	2	18
The Philippines	6	3	2	4	3	18
Australia	5	5	3	3	1	17
Bahrain	4	3	3	4	3	17
South Africa	6	3	2	4	2	17
Türkiye	6	3	3	3	2	17
Germany	4	3	3	4	2	16
Panama	6	4	3	2	1	16
Canada	5	3	2	3	2	15
Tunisia	5	2	3	3	2	15
Indonesia	6	2	0	1	2	11
Russia	5	1	3	2	0	11
UAE	3	2	3	1	2	11
India	6	0	0	3	1	10
Chile	3	1	1	2	2	9
France	2	0	3	2	2	9
Japan	1	1	2	1	2	7
The Netherlands	3	0	0	1	2	6

In a subsequent analysis, we evaluate the extent to which regulatory documents cover various topics. Figure 7 shows that the topic of GHG emissions is the most extensively covered one, followed by Ecological Impacts and Energy Management. In contrast, Customer Welfare and Competitive Behavior received the least attention in the regulatory documents. While most of the topics are more present in the effective regulatory documents, Access and Affordability are equally present in both effective and not-yet-effective documents, which could signify that this category may become a front-runner in importance in the near future.

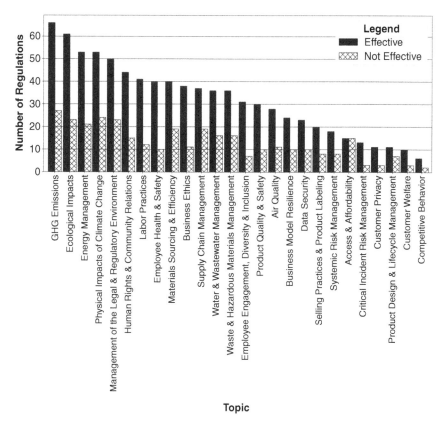

Figure 7. The number of sustainability-related regulations covering specific SASB topics

Figure 8 summarizes the granular analysis from Figure 7 at the SASB category level. The Environment category is the category most present in the regulations, and Leadership and Governance are the least present in the effective regulatory documents. Human Capital is the least mentioned in the not-yet-effective regulatory documents.

The relative relationship between the SASB's five sustainability dimensions — (1) Environment, (2) Business Model and Innovation, (3) Social Capital, (4) Human Capital, and (5) Leadership and Governance — and the four document types — (1) Corporate ESG Disclosure, (2) Sustainable Taxonomy, (3) Corporate Climate Disclosure, and (4) ESG Fund Requirements/Disclosure — is shown in Figure 9. Interestingly,

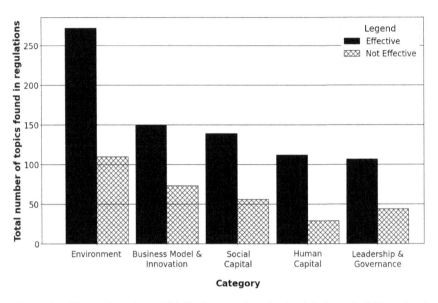

Figure 8.   The total number of SASB framework topics in global sustainability-related regulations is summarized by category

the ESG Fund Requirements/Disclosure documents contain the highest percentage of topics related to Leadership and Governance and the lowest proportion in the Business Model and Innovation category. Human capital is the most present category in the ESG Corporate disclosure regulatory documents. The highest overall proportion of documents belongs to the Corporate ESG Disclosure and the Sustainability Taxonomy categories.

6. Conclusions

This study uses AI to analyze over 100 global sustainability-related regulatory documents to determine how well SASB-defined material ESG issues are covered in global regulatory frameworks. The proposed AI-powered methodology shows that Large Language Models can be a valuable tool for understanding sustainability reporting better. The tool can be helpful to investors, regulators, and policymakers who can use AI to discern corporate dedication to addressing critical issues like climate change, social responsibility, and corporate governance. This chapter

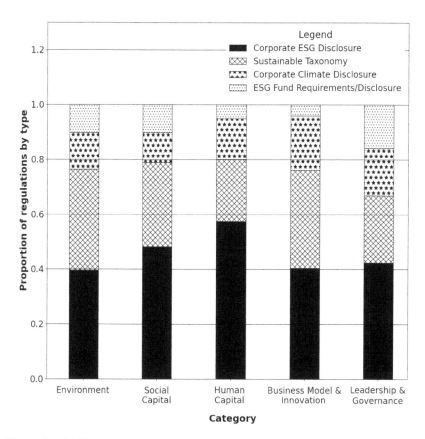

Figure 9. SASB categories' representation within different global sustainability-related regulatory document types

examines the role of AI in enhancing ESG reporting. We demonstrate how AI can improve data collection and reporting accuracy and thereby enhance insights into ESG metrics.

To showcase the power of the latest advances in NLP and AI, we developed a methodology that enables the coverage-analysis automation of categories and topics defined by the SASB standard within ESG regulations. The proposed model combines the classical keyword-based search methods with the latest developments in LLMs. A vital feature of this methodology is integrating the RAG approach, which enhances the capabilities of LLMs by incorporating external data sources. The RAG methodological extension significantly improves the contextuality and factual accuracy of the analysis.

The model was applied to 107 global ESG-related regulations, leading to several key findings. First, we quantified the number of regulations per country or union covering each SASB topic. This analysis detailed how extensively each SASB topic is addressed across the studied global sustainability-related regulations. Second, we summarized the coverage of SASB framework topics by category. This summary offered insights into categories within the SASB framework that are prominently featured in global ESG regulations. By aggregating the data at the category level, we were able to observe the broader trends and patterns in ESG regulation, offering a comprehensive overview of the regulatory landscape. Finally, we examined the relative relationship between the SASB categories and the regulation types.

The automated analysis results show that the EU is the most advanced in the effective and mandatory regulation area by covering 20 out of 26 SASB topics, closely followed by Nigeria and Saudi Arabia, which cover 19 topics each. In the effective and non-mandatory regulations, the US emerged as a leader by covering 21 of the 26 SASB topics, followed by Malaysia and Mexico, covering 20 topics each in their respective sustainability-related regulatory documents.

The Environment category is most frequently mentioned in sustainability-related effective regulations, and Leadership and Governance are the least present in the effective regulatory documents. Human capital is the most mentioned category in the ESG Corporate disclosure regulatory documents. Approximately 70% of all regulatory documents are Corporate ESG Disclosures or Sustainability Taxonomies.

This chapter highlights AI's critical impact on ESG reporting and regulation analysis, facilitating more informed, effective decision-making in sustainable investing. The advanced AI methodologies, such as RAG and ensemble modeling, offer a deeper, more nuanced understanding of the ESG regulatory environment, rapidly developing in new directions.

Future research considerations include the application of the automated topic retrieval analysis to other types of documents, including corporate disclosures, press releases, and news articles, to gauge the development trend of corporate responsibility and the directional dynamics of global sustainability-related regulations.

Acknowledgments

We would like to acknowledge the assistance of the students of the Faculty of Computer Science and Engineering at the Ss. Cyril and

Methodius University in Skopje, N. Macedonia, Gjorgji Kostadinov, David Stojanov, and Darko Pavicevic, in collecting the regulatory document data.

References

Aldridge, I. & Martin, P. (2022). *ESG in Corporate Filings: An AI Perspective.* Rochester, NY. Retrieved from https://doi.org/10.2139/ssrn.4279479.

Amel-Zadeh, A. *et al.* (2021). *NLP for SDGs: Measuring Corporate Alignment with the Sustainable Development Goals.* Rochester, NY. Retrieved from https://doi.org/10.2139/ssrn.3874442.

Basic v. Levinson, 485 U.S. 224 (1988). Retrieved from https://supreme.justia.com/cases/federal/us/485/224/.

Bender, J., He, C., Maggina, S., & Sun, X. (2023). Peeling back the onion: Understanding what goes into an ESG rating. *The Journal of ESG and Impact Investing*, 4(1), 11.

Buchanan, B. G. (2005). A (very) brief history of artificial intelligence. *AI Magazine*, 26(4), 53–53. Retrieved from https://doi.org/10.1609/aimag.v26i4.1848.

Burnaev, E. *et al.* (2023). Practical AI cases for solving ESG challenges. *Sustainability*, 15(17), 12731. Retrieved from https://doi.org/10.3390/su151712731.

CFA ESG. (2022). *Certificate in ESG Investing Curriculum: ESG Investing Official Training Manual* (3rd and 4th edns.). Charlottesville, VA: CFA Institute.

Chang, Y. *et al.* (2023). A Survey on Evaluation of Large Language Models. arXiv. Retrieved from https://doi.org/10.48550/arXiv.2307.03109.

Crona, B. (2021). *Sweet Spots or Dark Corners? An Environmental Sustainability Examination of Big Data and AI in ESG.* Rochester, NY. Retrieved from https://doi.org/10.2139/ssrn.4037299.

Ehrhardt, A. & Nguyen, M. T. (2021). Automated ESG report analysis by joint entity and relation extraction. In M. Kamp *et al.* (ed.), *Machine Learning and Principles and Practice of Knowledge Discovery in Databases* (pp. 325–340). Cham: Springer International Publishing (Communications in Computer and Information Science). Retrieved from https://doi.org/10.1007/978-3-030-93733-1_23.

Exchange Act of 1934. Retrieved from https://www.govinfo.gov/content/pkg/COMPS-1885/pdf/COMPS-1885.pdf.

Freshfields Bruckhaus Deringer. (2005). A Legal Framework for the Integration of Environmental, Social and Governance Issues into Institutional Investment. Report produced for the Asset Management Working Group of the UNEP Finance Initiative.

Guo, T. *et al.* (2020). ESG2Risk: A Deep Learning Framework from ESG News to Stock Volatility Prediction. arXiv. Retrieved from https://doi.org/10.48550/arXiv.2005.02527.

Hey, T. (2009). *The Fourth Paradigm: Data-Intensive Scientific Discovery* (1st edn.). S. Tansley & K. Tolle (eds.). Redmond, Washington: Microsoft Research. Retrieved from https://www.microsoft.com/en-us/research/publication/fourth-paradigm-data-intensive-scientific-discovery/.

Investment Advisers Act of 1940: Retrieved from https://www.govinfo.gov/content/pkg/COMPS-1879/pdf/COMPS-1879.pdf.

Jain, Y. *et al.* (2023). *Overcoming Complexity in ESG Investing: The Role of Generative AI Integration in Identifying Contextual ESG Factors*. Rochester, NY. Retrieved from https://doi.org/10.2139/ssrn.4495647.

Kang, J. & El Maarouf, I. (2022). FinSim4-ESG shared task: Learning semantic similarities for the financial domain. Extended edition to ESG insights. In C.-C. Chen *et al.* (eds.), *Proceedings of the Fourth Workshop on Financial Technology and Natural Language Processing (FinNLP)*. FinNLP 2022, Abu Dhabi, United Arab Emirates (Hybrid): Association for Computational Linguistics, pp. 211–217. Retrieved from https://doi.org/10.18653/v1/2022.finnlp-1.28.

Kannan, N. & Seki, Y. (2023). Textual evidence extraction for ESG scores. In C.-C. Chen *et al.* (eds.), *Proceedings of the Fifth Workshop on Financial Technology and Natural Language Processing and the Second Multimodal AI for Financial Forecasting*. Macao, pp. 45–54. Retrieved from https://aclanthology.org/2023.finnlp-1.4. (Accessed December 11, 2023).

Karl, T. R. & Trenberth, K. E. (2003). Modern global climate change. *Science*, 302(5651), 1719–1723. Retrieved https://doi.org/10.1126/science.1090228.

Khoruzhy, L. I. *et al.* (2022). ESG investing in the AI era: Features of developed and developing countries. *Frontiers in Environmental Science*, 10. Retrieved from https://www.frontiersin.org/articles/10.3389/fenvs.2022.951646. (Accessed December 11, 2023).

Lazarev, G., Trajanov, D., & Gramatikov, S. (2023). Comparing the performance of text classification models for climate change-related texts. Retrieved from https://repository.ukim.mk:443/handle/20.500.12188/27406. (Accessed December 15, 2023).

Lee, O. *et al.* (2022). Proposing an integrated approach to analyzing ESG data via machine learning and deep learning algorithms. *Sustainability*, 14(14), 8745. Retrieved from https://doi.org/10.3390/su14148745.

Lewis, P. *et al.* (2020). Retrieval-Augmented Generation for Knowledge-Intensive NLP Tasks. In *Advances in Neural Information Processing Systems* (pp. 9459–9474). Curran Associates, Inc. Retrieved from https://proceedings.neurips.cc/paper/2020/hash/6b493230205f780e1bc26945df7481e5-Abstract.html.

Luccioni, A., Baylor, E., & Duchene, N. (2020). Analyzing sustainability reports using natural language processing. arXiv. Retrieved from https://doi.org/10.48550/arXiv.2011.08073.

Macpherson, M., Gasperini, A., & Bosco, M. (2021). *Implications for Artificial Intelligence and ESG Data*. Rochester, NY. Retrieved from https://doi.org/10.2139/ssrn.3863599.

Nugent, T., Stelea, N., & Leidner, J. L. (2021). Detecting environmental, social and governance (ESG) topics using domain-specific language models and data augmentation. In *Flexible Query Answering Systems: 14th International Conference*, FQAS 2021, Bratislava, Slovakia, September 19–24, 2021, Proceedings 14 (pp. 157–169). Springer International Publishing.

Pasch, S. & Ehnes, D. (2022). NLP for responsible finance: Fine-tuning transformer-based models for ESG. In *2022 IEEE International Conference on Big Data (Big Data)*. *2022 IEEE International Conference on Big Data (Big Data)*, pp. 3532–3536. Retrieved from https://doi.org/10.1109/BigData55660.2022.10020755.

Perazzoli, S. *et al.* (2022). *Evaluating Environmental, Social, and Governance (ESG) from a Systemic Perspective: An Analysis Supported by Natural Language Processing*. Rochester, NY. Retrieved from https://doi.org/10.2139/ssrn.4244534.

PRI. (2023). ESG Integration in listed equity. ESG INTEGRATION IN LISTED EQUITY: A TECHNICAL GUIDE.

Sætra, H. S. (2021). A framework for evaluating and disclosing the ESG related impacts of AI with the SDGs. *Sustainability*, 13(15), 8503. Retrieved from https://doi.org/10.3390/su13158503.

Sætra, H. S. (2022). *The AI ESG Protocol: Evaluating and Disclosing the Environment, Social, and Governance Implications of Artificial Intelligence Capabilities, Assets, and Activities*. Rochester, NY. Retrieved from https://doi.org/10.2139/ssrn.4179536.

Securities Act of 1933: Retrieved from https://www.govinfo.gov/content/pkg/COMPS-1884/pdf/COMPS-1884.pdf.

Sokolov, A. *et al.* (2021). Building machine learning systems for automated ESG scoring. The *Journal of Impact and ESG Investing*, 1(3), 39–50. Retrieved from https://doi.org/10.3905/jesg.2021.1.010.

Tisminetzky, T., Smith, J., & Attwell, W. (2023). ESG Regulations and Reporting Standards Tracker — September 2023 Highlights. *Sustainable Fitch*. Retrieved from https://www.sustainablefitch.com/banks/esg-regulatory-reporting-standards-tracker-september-2023-highlights-18-09-2023.

Trajanoska, M., Stojanov, R., & Trajanov, D. (2023). Enhancing Knowledge Graph Construction Using Large Language Models. arXiv. Retrieved from https://doi.org/10.48550/arXiv.2305.04676.

Trajanov, D. *et al.* (2023). Comparing the Performance of ChatGPT and State-of-the-art Climate NLP Models on Climate-related Text Classification Tasks. In *E3S Web of Conferences*, 436, p. 02004. Retrieved from https://doi.org/10.1051/e3sconf/202343602004.

TSC Industries v. Northway Inc. 426 U.S. 438, 449 (1976). Retrieved from https://supreme.justia.com/cases/federal/us/426/438/.

Visalli, F. *et al.* (2023). ESG Data Collection with Adaptive AI. In *Proceedings of the 25th International Conference on Enterprise Information Systems*, pp. 468–475. Prague, Czech Republic: SCITEPRESS — Science and Technology Publications, Retrieved from https://doi.org/10.5220/0011844500003467.

Vodenska, I. *et al.* (2022). Challenges and Opportunities in ESG Investments. In T. Zlateva & R. Goleva (eds.), *Computer Science and Education in Computer Science*, pp. 168–179. Cham: Springer Nature Switzerland (Lecture Notes of the Institute for Computer Sciences, Social Informatics and Telecommunications Engineering). Retrieved from https://doi.org/10.1007/978-3-031-17292-2_14.

Webersinke, N. *et al.* (2021). ClimateBert: A Pretrained Language Model for Climate-related Text, arXiv.org. Retrieved from https://arxiv.org/abs/2110.12010v3.

Zhang, A. Y. & Zhang, J. H. (2023). Renovation in Environmental, Social and Governance (ESG) Research: The Application of Machine Learning. *Asian Review of Accounting*, (ahead-of-print). Retrieved from https://doi.org/10.1108/ARA-07-2023-0201.

Zhang, Y. (2023). *ESG-Based Market Risk Prediction and Management Using Machine Learning and Natural Language Processing*. NYU Shanghai. Retrieved from https://cdn.shanghai.nyu.edu/sites/default/files/yimeng_zhang_thesis_nyush_honors_2023.pdf.

Chapter 7

A Sneak Peek into Machine Learning Methods for ESG Factor Score Computation

Budha Bhattacharya[*,†] **and Maxime Kirgo**[†]

[*]*UCL Institute of Finance & Technology, London, United Kingdom*

[†]*Lombard Odier Asset Management, Geneva, Switzerland*

Abstract

Machine learning models, when applied to Environmental, Social, and Governance (ESG) data, can serve as an essential guide in assessing various aspects of sustainability for investing, financing, insurance, and even policymaking. They can be used for computing ESG thematic scores, carbon scores, water scores, etc. This chapter provides a "sneak peek" into some of the challenges related to the application of machine learning methods to compute an ESG thematic score based on a set of ESG parameters for a given entity. We start with a general presentation of how ESG thematic scores are computed, the data that we use, and the preprocessing steps that we suggest applying to the underlying data. Then, we explore how to generate ESG themes in an unsupervised manner via clustering algorithms and how to summarize the information contained in such a theme via dimensionality reduction techniques. Finally, we observe that traditional parametric models do not allow one to generalize a given ESG score to a large universe of entities. Our evaluation of these methodologies highlights the complexity of building ESG scores without prior supervision and the difficulty of generalizing available ESG scores to a broader universe.

1. Introduction

This chapter explores machines learning models that can be applied to an Environmental, Social, and Governance (ESG) dataset, to compute ESG factor scores or thematic scores, of any entity. Such scores not only aid in the understanding of a company's ESG disclosures but also help quantify the sustainability of a company or entity. ESG scores can be aggregated and manipulated further to compute scores to include various financial instruments (stocks and bonds), portfolios, funds, and economic sectors.

The machine learning models explored in this chapter are an excerpt from an upcoming broader and deeper study called, "Quantitative Methods to unravel Sustainability Signals," which will provide further insights into sustainability data. Machine learning models, when applied to ESG datasets, usually disclosed by companies as part of their Corporate Social Responsibility (CSR) reports or annual reports on their websites, serve as an essential guide in assessing various aspects of sustainability for investing, financing, insurance, and even policymaking. They can be used to compute an individual company's or entity's ESG score, carbon scores, gender inclusion scores, water safety scores, so on and so forth. Such a machine learning-based ESG scoring capability, at an entity level, is vital as it allows easy comparison of distinct levels of "ESGness" of entities without requiring the practitioner to dive into a complex set of parameters with great variability in type, scale, and overall interpretation. Moreover, since even the measure of ESG parameters lacks general methodological consensus (Berg *et al.*, 2022), aggregating relevant ESG parameters per ESG theme or ESG factor, rather than working with individual parameters, is a sound procedure not only from a sustainability perspective but also from a statistical point of view: This method prevents indeed any individual constituent of the average from overpowering the final score.

In this chapter, we present an overview of some of the challenges related to the automated creation of such global ESG scores by providing a set of straightforward methodologies.

1.1. *ESG Scoring Setup and Process Overview*

In its broadest sense, from a practitioner's point of view, ESG scoring aims at computing — in the most *independent and accurate fashion* — *a global ESG score of an entity.* To make this assessment, we assume that the practitioner has at his disposal a set of ESG parameters that are partly overlapping and/or correlated. Note that in the rest of this chapter, "ESG parameters" are interchangeably called "ESG metrics," "ESG factors," "ESG features," and "ESG variables."

We also assume that the practitioner wants to limit qualitative judgments as much as possible when computing the ESG scores. Henceforth, the number of such judgment is kept to the bare minimum throughout this chapter.

The standard practice for building an ESG score from ESG parameters is to *attribute to each parameter a weight*, which may be region/sector dependent, and *to use the weighted average of the parameters* as the final, global score. Some practitioners perform this score creation on a subset of thematic ESG parameters, e.g. carbon emissions or water use. The choice of both weights and thematic subsets relies greatly on qualitative (expert) judgment.

Once an ESG theme and the corresponding parameters have been defined, a preprocessing of the ESG parameters *prior to aggregation* is required. Indeed, ESG factors have a broad range of type: Some are continuous variables, given in absolute value for a given company (e.g. overall carbon emissions), others are continuous but scaled to the size of the company (e.g. carbon intensity), others are discrete absolute variables (e.g. number of fatalities), other are Boolean variables (e.g. the company has a diverse board), etc. The preprocessing depends on the type of underlying variable but usually *amounts to a standardization.*

Finally, a score can be computed by applying the weights to each ESG factor and summing each contribution together at an entity level. This score allows one to directly attribute a rank to each entity in the universe.

Although various rating agencies and practitioners follow their own methodologies, in general, an ESG score computation for entities, using a weighted average method, would involve the following main steps:

(1) Define an ESG theme.
(2) Define a subset of ESG factors corresponding to the theme.

(3) Preprocess the ESG factors so that they can be aggregated.
(4) Attribute weights to each ESG factor.
(5) Compute the thematic score by performing a weighted average.
(6) Attribute a rank to each company based on this score.

1.2. *Main Challenges Related to ESG Scoring*

The score construction process mentioned in the previous paragraph leads to a number of questions from a practical perspective:

- How does one define an "ESG theme?" (Q1)
- How can a set of ESG factors be associated with the chosen theme? (Q2)
- How should this set of factors be transformed to ensure additivity between parameters? (Q3)
- How can one determine a proper weighting scheme for these factors? (Q4)
- Is the ranking obtained by a weighted average of ESG factors meaningful? (Q5)

Ultimately, these qualitative elements of human judgments contribute largely toward the disparity of the resulting ESG ratings and create confusion. In the remaining sections of this chapter, we evaluate the ability of straightforward machine learning tools to address a subset of these issues.

To guide our exploration process, we consider two initial setups: either the practitioner has a reference score at his disposal on a subset of entities of the universe covered by his dataset (A) or he/she does not (B). (A) represents a *supervised learning* setup, where an external signal is available to guide the inference of unseen ESG scores, while (B) is an *unsupervised learning* setup, which is far more challenging due to the lack of guidance to rely upon.

Even though (B) corresponds to a more difficult setup, it also better corresponds to the starting point of most practitioners who aim to produce an ESG scoring system: No information is available outside the input ESG parameters. We therefore use (B) as our setup to treat questions (Q1) and (Q2). As explained in the associated sections in the following, the questions can be formulated, respectively, as a *clustering problem* and a *dimensionality reduction problem*.

Setup (A) is used to address a relaxed version of (Q4). Indeed, a supervised learning framework fits well with this problem as we will highlight in the dedicated section to follow.

Finally, (Q3) is treated in the section dedicated to *data preprocessing* as it applies to all methodologies described in this chapter.

1.3. *Chapter Overview*

This chapter is structured as follows:

- First, we *present the dataset* that we use to conduct our numerical experiments and treat (Q3) by proposing a *generic methodology to preprocess any ESG dataset*.
- Second, we apply standard clustering algorithm to automatically extract ESG themes from the input dataset to address (Q1).
- Third, we consider (Q2) by *comparing dimensionality reduction algorithms* related to an ESG theme.
- Fourth, we address (Q4) by benchmarking parametric models for ESG weighting scheme regression.

2. ESG Data Preprocessing: A Generic Methodology

In this section, we present a generic methodology that can be used to preprocess any ESG dataset by (i) briefly introducing the dataset that we use to conduct our experiments and (ii) providing preprocessing guidelines.

2.1. *Our ESG Dataset*

We use a dummy ESG dataset mimicking third-party company ESG data as of February 2023. It consists of 450 E and S parameters and 137 G parameters for over 10k companies identified by their International Securities Identification Number (ISIN). The dataset used is similar to company-level ESG data as of February 2023 and provides historical data for the selected parameters ranging between January 2018 and

January 2022. For all entities, the most recent data point was used without additional post-processing.

Each row of the dataset corresponds to a company, while each column represents an ESG parameter. Finally, we classified all the parameters using the framework described in Berg *et al.* (2022). The authors of this framework identified 64 sub-themes that are common across six different data provider agencies, namely, Sustainalytics, S&P Global, Refinitiv, Moody's ESGView and Morgan Stanley Capital International (MSCI). In order to align the 450 E and S parameters with the identified sub-themes, a manual mapping process was conducted based on all information available on each ESG parameter in our dataset.

2.2. *Preprocessing Guidelines*

An ESG parameter can be a real continuous number, a discrete number, or a Boolean value.

The *continuous real-valued parameters* represent measurements of various physical metrics pertaining to sustainability, such as the amount of carbon emissions, water usage, or the percentage of waste reduction achieved.

The *discrete parameters* are a measure on a scale or a score. In our dataset for instance, the strength of a biodiversity policy ranges from 1 to 5.

The *Boolean parameters* indicate the presence or absence of policies and disclosure data related to sustainability topics. Examples of Boolean parameters in our dataset include the existence of a biodiversity policy, implementation of quality management practices, and adoption of green building policies.

There are three fundamental steps to preprocess an ESG dataset:

(1) Removal of low-coverage parameters.
(2) Ensuring consistent parameter directionality.
(3) Normalization of values.

2.2.1. *Removal of low-coverage parameters*

The presence of missing values in parameters poses a significant challenge to the credibility of the parameter itself, its explanatory power, and the generalizability of models that rely on it. In our dataset, for instance, parameters exhibit on average approximately 85% empty values, indicating the high degree of sparsity of the dataset.

Various approaches can be taken to address missing values, with one common method being to replace them with an arbitrary value, typically zeros. Value padding unfairly penalizes companies in a specific feature and distorts the underlying statistical distribution of the parameter at hand. However, the presence of missing values signifies that the data provider either lacked the information or that the data itself was not available (NA). We therefore recommend removing parameters with insufficient coverage before any analysis.

To this aim, the following process can be applied:

(1) Sort the parameters based on coverage, from the smallest to the largest.
(2) Systematically assess the number of remaining companies in the dataset as each parameter with insufficient coverage is removed.

This iterative process optimizes the dataset by retaining a subset of parameters that provide an adequate number of data points while maintaining dataset completeness. It is important to note that the absence of certain information may not be material or relevant to the company's operations, such as a deforestation policy for an engineering services company. We provide an application of this procedure in the third section of this chapter.

2.2.2. Ensuring consistent parameter directionality

To ensure consistency in the interpretation of parameters, a unified "direction" for each parameter is required. Here, "direction" refers to the contribution of the parameter toward the overall score, and whether it positively influences the score by increasing or decreasing its value. It is crucial to address cases where parameters have opposite directionalities, as they can pose challenges when applying non-parametric models.

For instance, consider the example of two parameters with different directionalities: carbon emissions and the water usage policy score. For carbon emissions, lower values are considered desirable and have a positive effect on the overall score. On the other hand, the water usage policy score has an opposite interpretation: A low score indicates poor performance.

To overcome this challenge and ensure uniformity, *a qualitative assessment of each parameter's direction must be conducted*. For parameters that did not align with the desired direction, appropriate transformations were applied to attain consistency. Specifically, we recommend the two following simple transformations:

- $f(x) = -x$. By applying this transformation to continuous parameters, the parameters are inverted, effectively aligning them with the desired direction.
- $f(x) = 1 - x$. This transformation is preferred for Boolean parameters and those expressed in percentages, as they provide a meaningful value for the parameter in question (i.e. a Boolean parameter stays Boolean and a percentage stays a percentage).

By ensuring that all parameters have a unified direction, the dataset maintains internal coherence.

This in turn allows a straightforward aggregation of parameter contributions.

2.2.3. *Normalization*

The final phase of the data preprocessing stage involves the normalization of the parameters. The normalization step plays a crucial role in facilitating meaningful comparisons across parameters, as it eliminates the potential bias introduced by differences in the original scales of the parameters. There are different ways to normalize a dataset:

- **Min-Max Scaling:** Use this technique when the specific range of the data needs to be preserved, the data distribution is approximately linear, and extreme outliers are not present. It is suitable when the actual values of the data are meaningful and need to be retained.
- **Z-Score (Standardization):** Standardization is appropriate when the data distribution is approximately normal or close to normal. It is useful for comparing variables with different units or scales, identifying outliers, and preserving the mean and standard deviation of the data.
- **Log Transformation:** Log transformation is useful when the data have a highly skewed distribution or span a wide range of values. It reduces

the impact of extreme values and is useful when the relationship between variables is better represented on a logarithmic scale.

- **Unit Vector Scaling:** When the magnitude or relative importance of variables is significant, and there are different scales or units, unit vector scaling can be used. It allows for comparison based on the direction or angle between variables.
- **Robust Scaling:** When the data contain outliers or extreme values that could significantly affect normalization results, robust scaling is appropriate. It is useful when the median and interquartile range are more representative measures than the mean and standard deviation, and when the data distribution deviates from normality.

We recommend using a *standardization transformation*. This technique is suited to ESG data processing because it allows one to compare data that have different units while still preserving the standard deviation of each parameter.

3. ESG Theme Extraction

In this section, we study the soundness of ESG theme extraction in an unsupervised learning setup (see setup (B) in the introduction section). By "ESG theme," we designate any grouping of ESG parameters that relate to a similar topic. For example, "carbon emissions" or "water use" can be considered as ESG themes.

ESG theme definition is a fundamental step when using ESG data. Such a theme definition indeed allows one to group together factors of interest and supply a general overview of the performance of an entity with respect to the chosen theme. Despite its apparent simplicity, this process is, however, far from being trivial. The approach usually undertaken by practitioners is to use expert knowledge to group together scores that concern a similar area of interest (that we denote as a "meta-parameter" in the remaining of this section). This approach is used for example in Berg *et al.* (2022) to analyze the origin of divergence between overall ESG scores from different data providers.

There are, however, two drawbacks to this approach: (i) expert bias, lack of consensus, and errors; (ii) the process of grouping together metrics is time consuming and does not scale well when using multiple datasets. On the contrary, a completely unsupervised approach alleviates these limitations since (i) supervised learning does not rely on expert judgement as heavily and (ii) allows one to process different datasets efficiently provided that its generalization power is large enough.

The remainder of this section is organized as follows. First, we reformulate the problem of grouping ESG metrics together with an unsupervised learning lens. Then, we present the method that we use before presenting our numerical experiments. Our experiments consist in, first, assessing whether a basic clustering algorithm is suited for grouping together ESG scores via a pilot study and, second, conducting a broader study of clustering algorithms. Finally, we conclude the section and propose an outlook on future research.

3.1. *ESG Theme Extraction as a Clustering Problem*

In this section, our problem of interest consists in partitioning an initial set of ESG metrics in the absence of prior information on their relationships. From a machine learning perspective, this setup is best described as a *clustering problem*. The link between metric grouping and clustering has been treated in previous works. In the context of information retrieval from documents, Grimmer and King (2011) developed, for instance, a good argumentation on why clustering is relevant when attempting to extract unspecified "insights" from features. In a more general setup, Cai *et al.* (2010) derived a clustering algorithm specifically tailored to feature selection.

Moreover, since we place ourselves in an unsupervised setup, we do not have any objective function to optimize or reference clustering to guide the learning process. We therefore consider the correlation matrix between features using all observations available as the only reliable relationship between variables. We view the correlation matrix between features as a "distance/affinity matrix" that can be leveraged to group together similar features (i.e. features that are close together with respect to the distance matrix). We further detail the computation process of the distance matrix in the dataset and method section.

3.2. *Method*

In this section, we present the algorithms and the performance metrics that we use to perform the clustering of ESG scores.

3.2.1. *Preprocessing*

Each ESG parameter is standardized to have zero mean and unit variance.

We qualitatively divided the ESG parameters into six pillars: Environmental, Social, Governance, Energy, Water, and Carbon (there is an overlap between the Environmental category and the Energy, Water, and Carbon ones). This allowed us to reduce the dimensionality of the dataset used for the clustering and isolate important categories. We then remove ESG parameters that had 80% or more of NA values. Moreover, we estimate the correlation matrix between ESG parameters, using each company score measurement as an observation and keeping NA values. From the correlation matrix, we produce a distance (or affinity) matrix with entries d_{ij} by applying the following transform to each entry of the correlation matrix: corr_{ij}: $d_{ij} = 1 - |\text{corr}_{ij}|$. This modified correlation matrix constitutes the pairwise distance table used to fit our clustering models. The distance between factors will be small for highly correlated factors and large for highly uncorrelated factors.

3.2.2. *Clustering algorithms*

We compare the performances of the following algorithms:

- **K-medoids clustering:** *K*-means clustering leverages a pairwise distance matrix rather than distances between point embeddings.
- **BIRCH:** Reduces the input data to a set of sub-clusters which are obtained directly from the leaves of a tree called Clustering Feature Tree.
- **DBSCAN:** Algorithm views clusters as areas of high density separated by areas of low density.
- **OPTICS:** Algorithm that generalizes DBSCAN.
- **Agglomerative clustering:** Builds nested clusters by merging or splitting them successively.
- **Spectral clustering:** Performs a low-dimension embedding of the affinity matrix between samples, followed by clustering.

We choose these algorithms because they allow the direct implementation of a pairwise affinity matrix, which in our case is the modified correlation matrix as explained in the preprocessing section earlier.

3.2.3. *Performance measure*

Comparison measures: The quality of a clustering can be measured by comparing it to another cluster that demonstrated its relevance to the task at hand. The measures outlined in the following can be leveraged for this purpose. In our study, we always use the clustering conducted by Berg *et al.* (2022) as our reference clustering. Since our ESG factors dataset is different from the dataset used by Berg *et al.* (2022), we map each feature in our dataset to a category from Berg *et al.* (2022) according to our judgment and the available information on the variables. In the remainder of this chapter, we denote this clustering as "Berg *et al.*" In total, we retrieve 44 distinct categories that contain between 1 and 78 metrics.

Cluster purity C: This is a standard measure to compare two clusterings. Let A and B be two overlapping clusterings composed of clusters a_i and b_i, respectively. Let N be the total number of clusters. We define cluster purity as follows:

$$C(A,B) = \frac{1}{N} \sum_k \max_j \left| a_k \cap b_j \right| \tag{1}$$

We use the *average cluster purity* $\bar{C}$ as our performance measure:

$$\bar{C} = \frac{1}{2}\left(C(A,B) + C(B,A)\right) \tag{2}$$

Jaccard index J: Let A and B be two overlapping clusterings. We define the Jaccard index as follows:

$$J(A,B) = \frac{\left| A \cap B \right|}{\left| A \cup B \right|} \tag{3}$$

Intrinsic measures: These measures only depend on the selected cluster and can therefore be computed using the clustering itself. They constitute a mean to assess the quality of a clustering, independently of its end use.

Intra-cluster variance V: Let A be a set of clusters a_i:

$$V(A) = \frac{1}{\left| A \right|} \Sigma_k \Sigma_j \, \text{cov}\left(a_k, a_j\right) \tag{4}$$

Internal Validation V is a combined metric that uses the cohesion of a clustering and its separation:

$$Cohesion(C_k) = \frac{1}{n_k} \sum_{x \in C_k; y \in C_k} correlation(x, y) \qquad (5)$$

$$Cohesion = \frac{1}{m} \sum_{k}^{m} Cohesion(C_k) \qquad (6)$$

$$Separation(C_k, C_j) = \frac{1}{n} \sum_{x \in C_k; y \in C_j} Correlation(x, y) \qquad (7)$$

$$Separation = 1 - \left(\frac{1}{|\Omega|} \sum_{(k,j) \in \Omega} Separation(C_k, C_j) \right) \qquad (8)$$

$$V = \frac{1}{2}(Cohesion + Separation) \qquad (9)$$

where

- C_i is the ith cluster,
- n_k is the number of features in the cluster k,
- m is the total number of clusters,
- Ωs the set of 2-combinations of the clusters (i.e. if there are three clusters A, B, and C, then Ω is $\{AB, AC, BC\}$).

3.3. *Pilot Study: Semantic Clustering and K-medoids*

In this first experiment, we perform a comparison between the two most straightforward methods, allowing one to automatically cluster a set of ESG factors by relying solely on metric semantics or using a *K*-medoids algorithm. The *K*-medoids algorithm is a reformulation of the *K*-means algorithm that allows one to use a distance matrix as input instead of feature embedding. See Arora *et al.* (2016) for a comparison of both.

Semantic clustering from ChatGPT: As a first baseline clustering, we prompt ChatGPT to match each feature to a Berg *et al.* category. The clustering of features is therefore based solely on naming similarity. Once applied on our dataset, this method yields 46 clusters containing between 1 and 117 different metrics.

K-medoids clustering: As a second baseline, we perform K-means-like clustering on the correlation matrix. We set the number of clusters K to be equal to the number of categories that we identified in the reference clustering: K = 44. Since this approach requires a distance matrix as input, i.e. a positive definite matrix, we perform the following additional preprocessing step to the raw correlation matrix of standardized metrics.

Let C be the correlation matrix of standardized metrics. We define our distance matrix C_{dist} as follows:

$$C_{\text{dist}} = 1 - C \odot C/\max(C \odot C) \tag{10}$$

After performing this normalization, we remove NA values by replacing them with an arbitrary value of 10^7. Since this value is far greater than any entry in C_{dist}, it allows us to remove the influence of outliers.

Finally, we reconcile the obtained clustering with Berg *et al.* categories by replacing each K-medoids category with the Berg *et al.* category that overlaps most with it.

3.3.1. *Results*

We first assess the best method to reconstruct the Berg *et al.* Classification of the metrics in our dataset, considering both semantic clustering and K-medoids clustering as potential methods. The outcome is shown in Table 1.

The semantic approach provides vastly better results than the K-medoids approach. This result highlights two aspects.

First, the high performance of the semantic approach underlines the fact that the reference clustering proposed by Berg *et al.* can be reconstructed with high confidence using solely the name of the parameters. This is unsurprising as our reference clustering was partly produced using semantic cues solely (i.e. the name of each parameter).

Table 1.   Agreement between semantic clustering and K-medoids clustering to the Berg *et al.* classification

Clustering Method	Average Cluster Purity (%)	Jaccard Index(%)
Semantic	**80.00**	**83.67**
***K*-medoids**	43.79	10.14

Second, the weak performance of *K*-medoids shows that the features lying within the same category according to Berg *et al.* are not well approximated by the mean of its constituents.

Overall, our pilot study highlights that at first sight, simple clustering algorithms are insufficient to capture the complexity of an ESG factor dataset and automatically create ESG themes. On the other hand, the success of the methodology involving solely factor names indicates that a successful clustering approach of ESG factors can be created by leveraging only ESG factor names.

3.4. *Systematic Benchmark of Clustering Methods*

In this section, we perform a systematic overview of other clustering methods to further strengthen the analysis conducted in the previous section regarding the insufficiency of simple clustering algorithms. Our grouping criterion is based on the mutual correlation of ESG metrics as conducted previously: Two metrics that are highly correlated must be grouped together.

Moreover, given the poor performance of *K*-medoids in our pilot study, instead of considering the full set of ESG factors, we rely on subsets of the original dataset. Each subset comprises ESG metrics that are related to one another.

In terms of the *cohesion metric*, the outcome of this benchmark is provided in Table 2 for each algorithm.

We observe that DBSCAN performs the best compared to the other metrics, but with great variability between scores since the computation.

The computation of the *separation metric* provides the results in Table 3.

All tested algorithms *have high separation values*. This is unsurprising since we construct the clusters by requiring highly correlated clusters to be grouped. *Birch, Agglomerative Clustering, and K-medoids perform equally well.*

From the observation of the internal validation scores of the algorithms provided in Table 4, we deduce that DBSCAN allows the best maximization of intra cluster correlation and the best minimization of extra-cluster correlation as the internal validation score represents the average of the Cohesion and Separation measure of a clustering (see Eq. 9).

Table 2.   Cohesion metric obtained for each clustering algorithm (columns) for a given ESG parameter subset (rows)

	Birch (%)	Spectral Clustering (%)	Agglomerative Clustering (%)	DBSCAN (%)	Optics (%)	K-Medoids (%)
Energy	77	77	77	90	33	77
Water	75	69	75	75	57	75
Carbon	89	89	89	89	55	89
E	77	73	76	76	40	75
S	36	35	35	77	16	38
G	48	48	48	48	48	48
Average	67	65	67	76	41	67
Median	75	69	75	76	41	75

Table 3.   Separation metric obtained for each clustering algorithm (columns) for a given ESG parameter subset (rows)

	Birch (%)	Spectral Clustering (%)	Agglomerative Clustering (%)	DBSCAN (%)	Optics (%)	K-Medoids (%)
Energy	100	100	100	92	None	100
Water	99	80	99	99	99	99
Carbon	95	95	95	95	55	95
E	94	93	93	94	95	93
S	95	96	96	93	87	95
G	97	97	97	97	97	97
Average	97	93	97	95	87	97
Median	97	95	97	95	91	97

Table 4.   Internal validation scores for each clustering algorithm (columns) for a given cluster (rows)

	Birch (%)	Spectral Clustering (%)	Agglomerative Clustering (%)	DBSCAN (%)	Optics (%)	K-Medoids (%)
Energy	88.0	88.0	88.0	91.0	32.0	88.0
Water	86.0	74.0	86.0	86.0	77.0	86.0
Carbon	92.0	92.0	92.0	92.0	55.0	92.0
E	85.0	82.0	84.0	85.0	67.0	84.0
S	65.0	65.0	65.0	84.0	51.0	66.0
G	72.0	72.0	72.0	72.0	72.0	72.0
Average	81.3	78.8	81.2	85.0	59.0	81.3
Median	85.0	78.8	84.0	85.0	59.0	84.0

3.5. *Closing Remarks*

We analyzed how ESG themes can be extracted from a set of ESG parameters using a clustering perspective. The clustering was performed on normalized scores using a *distance function yielded by the correlation matrix* between ESG factors.

Our analysis shows vast differences between techniques. In particular, the purity of the obtained clusters when using a priori categorization of the metrics as a reference, e.g. as produced in Berg *et al.* (2022), is not preserved, i.e., the extracted themes do not correspond to themes with a semantic meaning. This result is not surprising in itself as no semantic queue was provided to the clustering algorithms, but it highlights the lack of interpretability of the automatically extracted themes. At this point, the most effective method to automatically group together ESG scores in a theme is to consider a methodology driven by the name of each ESG parameter.

As the next step, *a regional and sectoral split of the dataset* could be used to *detect discrepancies between clusters* under different assumptions regarding the underlying universe of companies. This could allow one to better fit clusters to region or sector specificities.

4. Summarizing an ESG Theme: Application of Dimensionality Reduction Techniques

In the previous section, we addressed the problem of grouping together ESG scores without prior information. Entity-level ESG scores are, however, often constructed around a given theme (or "pillar"), such as carbon emissions or water use. The interest of this type of thematic score is that it allows one to summarize the information contained in several ESG parameters under a single number. Moreover, aggregating together ESG parameters coming from the same theme is more likely to be meaningful as the parameters that compose a theme are more homogeneous than parameters covering vastly different topics.

In the following section, we propose an approach to summarize the parameters contained in an ESG theme via dimensionality reduction algorithms. We adopt a drastic dimensionality reduction target as an ESG theme, composed of many ESG parameters (i.e. dimensions), which must be summarized in a single dimension. We do so because reducing an ESG theme to a single dimension represents the simplest way to create a thematic score.

The rest of this section is organized as follows. We (i) present our methodology regarding data preprocessing and (ii) provide our main results by applying the methodology before (iii) concluding.

4.1. Dataset and Method

4.1.1. Water pillar dataset

Our benchmark is conducted on the "water use pillar" or "water pillar" of our dataset. The water pillar is composed of parameters that are related to water management, conservation, and performance.

We then conduct the preprocessing steps described in the first section of this chapter. More specifically, first, we systematically disregard water pillar parameters with significantly low coverage. To ensure accurate implementation of non-parametric models, a dense matrix is required.

Consequently, by applying the algorithm described in the first section of this chapter, we obtain a subset of twelve water-related parameters, which constitute approximately one quarter of the initial set of 42 parameters. The resulting subset comprises the following parameters: "totalWaterUse," "waterPolicy," "totalWaterWithdrawal," "waterUse-Withdrawal," "h2oUseWthdrlIntensSales," "h2oUseWthdrlIntensEmpl," "h2oUseWthdrlIntensAssets," "waterIntensityPerSales," "waterIntensity-PerEmployee," "waterIntensityPerAssets," "waterIntensityPerEnergy," "wastewaterManagementPolicy."

In Figure 1, we see that choosing twelve parameters as we do constitutes a fair compromise that allows one to still have a good number of features left and a large amount of data points (4,293) as the coverage of companies sharply drops toward 0 starting from 13 features.

We also ensure that all parameters have a consistent direction. For most water-related parameters, lower values are indicative of superior performance (e.g. lower water consumption signifies better water pillar performance). However, a few parameters deviate from this pattern. For instance, the presence of a water policy, represented by a Boolean parameter, signifies improved water performance, resulting in a high score (i.e. 1) denoting positivity, while a low score (i.e. 0) connotes negativity.

We finally normalize all parameter values to allow meaningful comparisons in terms of magnitude.

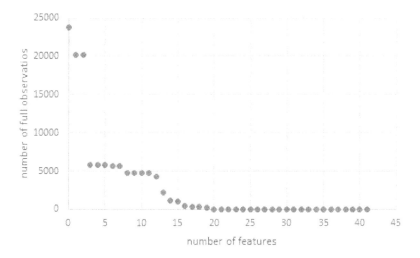

Figure 1. Number of full observations (i.e. rows where no column is NA) as a function of the number of features selected

4.1.2. *Reference score derivation*

After preprocessing our dataset, we compute the average of all parameters and execute a preliminary ranking of companies within the same sector of activity. The sectoral split is based on the Global Industry Classification Standard (GICS) one-sector classification (MSCI, 2024). This initial ranking serves as a benchmark against which subsequent scores can be evaluated.

In the remainder of this text, we designate this reference score as the "naive rank."

4.1.3. *Non-parametric score derivation*

To improve upon the naive ranking, we refine our approach using two well-known non-parametric dimensionality reduction algorithms: principal component analysis (PCA) and factor analysis (FA). The application of dimensionality reduction algorithms in our problem setup offers the following distinct advantages:

• It simplifies the input feature space to an orthogonal basis that explains most of the variance in the data.

Table 5.   Kendall's tau score for each pair of ranking methods

	Naïve Rank	PCA Rank
PCA rank	**0.692**	
FA rank	0.494	0.679

- This simplification allows an easier interpretation of the final score since there are fewer parameters to consider.
- It also allows one to consider redundant or minor factors that could bias the final score. Indeed, redundant factors give more weight to a single latent parameter, while minor factors may get a weighting that artificially increases their materiality.

4.2. Results

In order to compare the effectiveness of both dimensionality reduction methods, we employed Kendall's tau metric (Kendall, 1938), which serves as a measure of correspondence between two rankings. Kendall's tau value close to 1 signifies a strong agreement between the rankings, while a value close to -1 indicates a strong disagreement.

Table 5 shows the result of computing Kendall's tau score for each pair of ranking methods. All models produce a similar rank, except for the FA model and the naive rank that are more distant to one another.

From this comparison, we see that the PCA rank-based method is more robust and closer to our naive ranking approach than the FA method.

4.3. Parametric score derivation

To complement the above-mentioned experiments, we provide in this section a naive example of how a clustering of ESG factors as produced in the second section of this chapter can be used for dimensionality reduction. More specifically, we analyze whether a cluster of highly correlated ESG metrics can be well approximated using a most representative constituent.

To make this assessment, we apply the following procedure:

(1) *Most important ESG metric retrieval*: For each ESG cluster defined in Berg *et al.*, we extract the most important ESG metric by

conducting a PCA. More specifically, given the axis explaining the most variance in the dataset (i.e. the first component of the PCA), we retrieve the ESG metric that is the most colinear to it and define it as the most important ESG metric for the given category.

(2) *Regression of the most important ESG metric using the remaining ESG metrics as features*: We apply a linear regression model to the remaining ESG metrics in the cluster and fit the model to replicate as close as possible the most important ESG metric of the cluster.

(3) *Delta to actual computation*: Let y_i be the most important ESG metric in cluster i and let y_i be its estimate using the remaining ESG metrics X_i. We define the delta to actual measure Δ as follows:

$$\Delta = \frac{|y_i - y|}{|y_i + y|} \tag{11}$$

The results of this procedure are provided in Table 6.

We observe weak results as most delta values are close to 100%. However, GHG Emissions, Environmental Management System, and Business Ethics have much lower delta values with, respectively, 77%, 74%, and 35%. It is evident from the results that each parameter within a given cluster provides unique insights that cannot be regressed with the remaining set of parameters.

4.4. *Closing Remarks*

In this section, we studied dimensionality reduction methods to summarize the parameters from an ESG theme into a single ranking. The two methods retained produce rankings that are similar to one another. However, the PCA-based score is the only approach leading to a ranking close to the reference ranking and is therefore to be preferred to its FA counterpart.

This study could be extended in future work. First, our preprocessing requires removing empty fields from the initial dataset. As entities start disclosing more sustainability-related data, less imputation is going to be required, due to which the quantitative analyses are going to improve over time, catalyzed by regulatory and market forces. However, in the interim, using proxy data generated from the available data points, ideally in a sector–region-specific manner, to populate these missing data points appears to be a slightly improved direction in which to extract signals

Table 6.   Delta between the predicted and ground truth for each cluster provided by Berg *et al.* (Berg *et al.* Cat.) for the most important ESG metric in the cluster

Berg *et al.* Cat.	Delta to Actual (%)
Non-GHG air emissions	96
Corruption	100
Diversity	93
Employee development	86
Health and safety	98
Environmental policy	96
Human rights	87
Community and society	99
Energy	99
GHG policies	90
Board diversity	90
Lobbying	100
Business ethics	35
Toxic spills	99
Environmental fines	99
Water	102
Electromagnetic fields	100
Environmental mgmt. system	74
Forests	100
Waste	101
Resource efficiency	100
Reporting quality	95
ESG incentives	100
Audit	100
GHG emissions	77

from the dataset. Moreover, it would be interesting to conduct the same investigation on other ESG themes such as carbon emissions or governance aspects to see if the same conclusions apply in that case.

5. Benchmarking Parametric Models for ESG Weighting Scheme Regression

In this section, we provide elements supporting the fact that parametric analysis is not applicable for ESG score generalization.

The term "parametric method" has at least two definitions in the context of machine learning. It can be any method that models the following:

(i) *a population using a parameterized statistical distribution f_θ.* The parameters θ of the distribution are estimated from samples of the population. Each sample X is therefore drawn from f_θ: $X \sim f_\theta$.

(ii) *the relationship between two random variables X, Y using a model f_θ:* $Y = f_\theta(X)$. The parameters θ of the model are fitted using a "training set" of X, Y pairs. The random variable X is usually called the "independent variable" in statistics or the "feature vector" in machine learning. Y is called the "dependent variable" in statistics or the "output vector" in machine learning.

The definition (i) is not suited to our problem. Indeed, we are not interested in sampling from the underlying "true" probability distribution of the space of ESG factors for companies. Moreover, it is highly unlikely that this space admits any tractable parametric model. We therefore use the definition (ii) of parametric models in the remainder of this section.

From a pure machine learning perspective, there are several ways by which a ranking can be created using parametric models. In the following, we outline the easiest and most common approach.

5.1. *Rank Regression: A Basic Approach*

The following process can be used to generalize a rank provided on a limited number of entities to a broader universe via a supervised model.

First, we assign to each company in a list an ESG score using expert knowledge. For the sake of simplicity, the score is a real value ranging from 0 (lowest score) to 1 (highest score). This ESG score will constitute our dependent variable Y.

Second, the input ESG factors constitute the independent variables X. As discussed previously, X has to be preprocessed so that all factors are compatible with one another.

Finally, we can select a parametric model f_θ and fit it using $\{X, Y\}$ to obtain the optimal set of parameters $\hat{\theta}$.

Given a new list of unseen companies X_e, we can use the fitted model $f_{\hat{\theta}}$ to infer their ESG scores Y_e.

This approach can be refined by considering ordinal regression paradigms. The overarching process will remain the same as the above-mentioned one outlined, with variations in how the rank is constructed. For instance, one could choose to define the "low score," "medium score," and "high score" categories instead of a real value, consider as a correct prediction any output that correctly orders the elements without considering the absolute rank value, or perform only comparisons between pair of companies. For a more detailed review on ordinal regression, Gutiérrez *et al.* (2015) provide a good overview using traditional machine learning methods.

5.2. *Application*

To illustrate the methodology, we conduct a simple experiment using our ESG dataset as input variables from which we try to regress a dummy ESG score as the signal to generalize. Our preprocessing follows the general methodology in the first section of this chapter. It consists of the following steps:

(1) We select a set of 43 parameters containing at least 47% of the available companies.
(2) We remove rows containing empty parameter values. In the case where multiple rows are available for a single company, we select the most recent row.
(3) We standardize each feature.
(4) We randomly split the universe of companies into a training and testing dataset, with 80% of data for training and 20% for testing.

In total, the training dataset consists of 5,710 companies and the testing dataset of 1,428 companies.

We fit the following parametric regression models using the training dataset:

(1) Linear Regression with standard L2 penalty and with "ridge" penalty.
(2) Support Vector Machine (SVM) regression with linear, polynomial, and radial basis function kernel.
(3) Bayesian ridge regression.
(4) A Multi-Layered Perceptron (MLP) with a single hidden layer of 43 units and ReLu activation function.

This training process yields the results displayed in Table 7 when applying the models to the testing dataset.

All models have comparable performance. The best performing model is the SVM with a polynomial kernel by a small margin.

To balance this assessment, we also consider the regression output from a classification point of view by performing the following post-processing on the regression outputs: Multiply the output values by 10, rounding them to the closest integer and clamping the output between 0 and 9. This process effectively creates 10 classes depending on how high the reference dummy ESG score is. The outcome of this experiment is presented in Table 8.

All models have similarly weak performance. Three models perform better than the other models in two out of three metrics: SVM with a polynomial kernel, Bayesian Ridge, and MLP.

Table 7. Quantitative evaluation of parametric regression models (rows) according to performance metrics (columns). Best values are displayed in bold

	Mean Rel. Abs. Error (in % of max.)	Median Rel. Abs. Error (in % of max.)	Std Rel. Abs. Error (in % of max.)
SVM (linear kernel)	16	13	**13**
SVM (polynomial kernel)	**15**	**12**	**13**
SVM (radial basis Fun. kernel)	19	15	16
Linear regression	16	13	**13**
Ridge	16	13	**13**
Bayesian ridge	16	13	**13**
MLP	19	15	16

Table 8.   Quantitative evaluation of parametric classification models (rows) according to performance metrics (columns). Best values are displayed in bold

	Precision (%)	Recall (%)	F1-Score (%)
SVM (linear kernel)	30	**25**	25
SVM (polynomial kernel)	29	**25**	**26**
SVM (Radial Basis Fun. kernel)	30	24	25
Linear regression	30	**25**	25
Ridge	30	**25**	25
Bayesian ridge	**32**	**25**	25
MLP	30	**25**	**26**

Table 9.   Example of correct predictions obtained with our approach using different parametric regression models (in columns) for increasing reference scores (Ref. Score)

Ref. Score (%)	SVM (linear kernel) (%)	SVM (polynomial kernel) (%)	SVM (radial basis fun. kernel) (%)	Linear Regression (%)	Ridge (%)	Bayesian Ridge (%)	MLP (%)
2	9	10	10	9	9	9	9
10	51	34	32	51	51	52	37
20	41	28	42	41	41	42	33
50	96	97	87	93	93	93	101
70	73	75	75	72	72	71	75
89	63	70	71	63	63	63	63
100	91	93	79	89	89	89	79

Overall, the SVM with a polynomial kernel performs best when using regression and classification metrics.

Finally, to qualitatively illustrate this study, Tables 9 and 10 provide, respectively, an excerpt of good and bad results obtained for companies with different dummy ESG scores when using parametric regression models.

Remark: As the number of classes grows, the task at hand becomes increasingly difficult. It would be of interest to repeat the classification performance assessment when decreasing the number of classes.

To summarize, standard parametric methods are insufficient to correctly generalize an ESG score provided on a limited number of entities. While using more complex models, such as neural networks, combined

Table 10. Example of wrong predictions obtained with our approach using different parametric regression models (in columns) for increasing reference scores (Ref. Score)

Ref. Score (%)	SVM (linear kernel) (%)	SVM (polynomial kernel) (%)	SVM (radial basis fun. kernel) (%)	Linear Regression (%)	Ridge (%)	Bayesian Ridge (%)	MLP (%)
4	28	29	23	31	31	31	19
11	42	35	44	44	44	43	43
21	51	51	47	50	50	50	37
50	19	20	19	21	21	21	14
72	37	32	31	39	39	39	32
98	43	26	43	44	44	44	47

with more training data could allow for stronger regression performance of parametric models, the methodological complexity of such a process renders such an approach unlikely to be useful in practice.

6. Conclusion

In this chapter, we proposed a sneak peek into Machine learning methods for ESG factor score computation. We presented the challenges that are related to ESG score computation and proposed a general approach for preprocessing ESG parameters. We also highlighted the difficulty of regressing meaningful ESG themes via clustering algorithms and showed that applying standard dimensionality reduction algorithms allowed one to partially reconstruct a thematic score computed using a simple weighted average of ESG parameters. Finally, we showed that simple parametric models lack the representation power required to generalize a reference score from a small set of entities to a larger universe.

References

Arora, P. *et al.* (2016). Analysis of *k*-means and *k*-medoids algorithm for big data (1st International Conference on Information Security & Privacy 2015). *Procedia Computer Science*, 78, 507–512. Retrieved from https://doi.org/10.1016/j.procs.2016.02.095.

Berg, F., Koelbel, J. F., & Rigobon, R. (2022). Aggregate confusion: The divergence of ESG ratings. *Review of Finance*, 26(6), 1315–1344.

Cai, D., Zhang, C., & He, X. (2010). Unsupervised feature selection for multi-cluster data. *Proceedings of the 16th ACM SIGKDD International Conference on Knowledge Discovery and Data Mining*. Association for Computing Machinery, New York, NY, USA, pp. 333–342.

Grimmer, J. & King, G. (2011). General purpose computer-assisted clustering and conceptualization. *Proceedings of the National Academy of Sciences*, 108(7), 2643–2650.

Gutiérrez, P. A., Perez-Ortiz, M., Sanchez-Monedero, J., Fernandez-Navarro, F., & Hervas-Martinez, C. (2015). Ordinal regression methods: Survey and experimental study. *IEEE Transactions on Knowledge and Data Engineering*, 28(1), 127–146.

Kendall, M. G. (1938). A new measure of rank correlation. *Biometrika*, 30(1/2), 81–93.

MSCI. (2024). The global industry classification standard (GICS). Retrieved from https://www.msci.com/our-solutions/indexes/gics. (Accessed January 15, 2024).

https://doi.org/10.1142/9789811297786_0008

Chapter 8

Challenges in Analyzing ESG Data and Their Potential Solutions

Shaheen Contractor

Bloomberg Intelligence, Bloomberg, New York, USA

Abstract

In this chapter, we examine the challenges in extracting and analyzing Environmental, Social and Governance (ESG) data and their potential solutions. In particular, we focus on material ESG data relevant to companies and industries vs. a "one-size-fits-all" approach, highlighting examples where ESG has had a financial impact. We discuss how ESG metrics impact company performance, highlighting among others how ESG facets might impact risk, returns along with fundamentals. Furthermore, using the holdings of some of the largest US ESG funds, we discuss what characteristics drive ESG fund inclusion and what might be missed. Lastly, we discuss how ESG might not be that far removed from having a positive societal impact and discuss strategies that can drive this.

1. Introduction

The challenges in ESG data analysis have come to the forefront in recent years, as evidenced by increasing regulatory scrutiny. Following are four challenges and unanswered questions that are inherent in ESG analysis, along with potential solutions:

(1) **ESG data analysis: Problems and solutions:** This covers the many challenges which come from analyzing company-reported ESG data along with potential solutions to better understand risks and opportunities.

(2) **Understanding ESG impacts on performance:** The impacts of ESG on risk and returns are highly debated, with many studies showing different outcomes. We discuss Bloomberg Intelligence (BI) research on this topic, highlighting inferences reached and different ways in which the data can be used.

(3) **What metrics do fund managers look at and what's missed?** Given the swath of ESG metrics, understanding what matters to investors and gets factored into fund inclusion can be challenging. An analysis of some of the largest US ESG fund holdings by BI gives us a view into the ESG characteristics favored by fund managers, along with what might be missed.

(4) **When it comes to driving change, what has an impact?** Another common criticism and confusion around ESG is the concept of measuring and creating an impact. Through our research at BI, we detail how impact and ESG might not be that far removed from each other as one might think.

2. ESG Data Analysis: Problems and Solutions

Extracting and analyzing data can have multiple challenges, including comparability, availability and disparity, which lead to a lack of usefulness. Yet, ESG information and analysis can be useful in identifying risks and opportunities when some of these challenges can be overcome. Strategies such as going beyond just company-reported data and using forward-looking metrics can be potential solutions. In the following sections, we examine some of the most common challenges associated with the ESG analysis and some potential solutions, using practical examples from BI's research.

2.1. *The Challenge in the Breadth of ESG Metrics: Leaning on Materiality*

Analyzing ESG data can be overwhelming, and often, the most frequent question that gets asked is: Where to start, given there are hundreds of different metrics to choose from? ESG data span across multiple themes from environmental metrics such as carbon emissions to social metrics such as accident rates, and governance metrics such as board independence. Given the vast breadth of metrics, the biggest challenge is often identifying metrics that are decision-useful vs. those that are just noise. Identifying financially material ESG metrics can help narrow this down. Gone are the days where a one-size-fits-all approach is used, where one might consider the emissions from a healthcare company just as they would from a cement company. A focus on materiality has emerged as a way to narrow down into decision-useful data. For the cement industry, considered a hard-to-abate, emissions-heavy sector, measuring carbon emissions might be relevant. However, for healthcare, social issues might be more relevant.

Identifying material ESG metrics can help provide a holistic view into a company as opposed to relying only on financial metrics. The examples from BI's research in the following sections show how material ESG data in some industries can impact a company's financials.

2.1.1. *Metals and mining*

Material issue — Safety: The mining industry is one of the most dangerous, making accident and fatality rates important and material ESG metrics suitable for analysis. Weak safety measures may be a sign of higher operational risks and can lead to more downtime, production disruptions, regulatory oversight as well as fines and lawsuits. According to Contractor & Rua (2023a), Sibanye Stillwater, a mining company, has a three-year average fatality rate and a total recordable incident rate above the peer median, though the company has seen some improvements in 2022. Fatalities and incident rates when high and recurring can point to operational risk. As the research further discusses, for 2021, Sibanye forecasted gold production at the lower end of its range due to safety incidents and regulatory measures that led to closings.

Material issue — Carbon risks: For metals and mining, the amount of carbon emitted varies based on the type of metal being produced and companies involved in aluminum production generally have a carbon intensity (Tones GHG Emissions normalized by Sales) that is much higher than others in the industry, according to Contractor and Kane (2022a), subjecting them to country-specific risks related to carbon policy and regulation. Contractor and Rua (2022a) suggest that carbon costs for Europe's aluminum producers could reach 1.5% of EBITDA from 2020 to 2024 under the EU's Emissions Trading System. While this is relatively small, for other metals, it tapers off even further pointing to the differences in risk even within industries. Similarly, as per Contractor and Rua (2022b), for steel companies on the other hand, costs are much higher and could reach up to 9.5% of EBITDA over the same time frame. While costs are regional, the risk lies in carbon pricing and regulations expanding to other industries. Hence, within these carbon-intensive industries, efficient operations and ambitious carbon reduction goals might result in substantial cost savings, particularly in a regime where a company faces a carbon cost. The EU Emissions Trading Scheme is a cap-and-trade system that puts a price on carbon and is an example of such a cost, given prices have increased almost 8 times since 2017 according to Contractor and Kane (2022b). Given carbon is one of the most material ESG metrics for the steel industry, those companies with a lower carbon intensity (carbon per ton of crude steel) have outperformed higher intensity peers by 68% over the past five years, as per Stevenson (2023a). This is partially driven by the use of more recycled metal by companies with a lower carbon intensity, which can reduce supply chain disruptions, exposure to commodity price spikes and regulatory carbon costs.

2.1.2. *Utilities*

Material issue — Carbon risks: Utilities too remain a carbon-intensive sector, making metrics like the share of renewable production, carbon intensity and capex investments material in analyzing risks and opportunities. Stevenson (2023b) finds that US utilities such as Alliant and American Electric Power that have invested more capex toward clean energy have outperformed capex laggards by 43% over five years. This is driven by a higher rate of recovery for cleaner spending. Such companies stand to benefit from spending more on cost recovery capex like renewables and less on fuel and maintenance, which are pass-through costs. Similarly, utilities with the lowest carbon emissions per kilowatt-hour outperform their more CO_2-intensive peers by 58% over five years, as per

Figure 1. Materials industries low vs. high carbon intensity performance
Source: Bloomberg Intelligence.

Stevenson (2023c), showing that better returns can share the spotlight with cleaner power. The study goes on to state that those with a lower carbon intensity benefit, as the inputs for clean power, are largely paid for upfront, lowering fuel-cost risks related to supply-chain disruptions and commodity-price spikes.

2.1.3. *Materials: Cement, steel and aluminum*

Material issue — Carbon risks: Industries in the materials sector like cement, steel and aluminum have among the highest carbon intensities, making it a material risk. These three industries together account for 20% of global combustion greenhouse gas (GHG) emissions. Stevenson (2023a) finds that within these three industries, lower carbon intensity companies delivered 42–68% better performance at the industry level over five years. Combined, those with lowest emissions per ton of output outperformed peers by 56% over five years (see Figure 1).

2.1.4. *Gauging materiality across different industries*

Identifying ESG metrics that are material to a company can often be a challenge, given the varying impacts across industries and business models along with constantly evolving regulations. Bloomberg identifies material ESG issues through an assessment that looks at the probability, magnitude, and timing of financial impact along with referring to frameworks, such as the Sustainability Accounting Standards Board (SASB).[1] This analysis is then used to assign priorities to various issues that are relevant to the industry, which then feed into Bloomberg's ESG Scores. As made clear in Bloomberg's methodology industry guide for the metal and mining, and steel industry and the heat map of priorities,[2] GHG emissions management is among the highest priority environmental issues for the steel industry, given its high carbon intensity. This has been discussed in Section 2.1.1 which suggests that companies under the EU ETS could see costs up to 9.5% of EBITA. For the precious metals industry on the other hand, water management is one of the top priorities while GHG emissions management has a lower priority. Precious metals are not as carbon-intensive as steel and hence the magnitude of impact is likely to be smaller. Water use and scarcity, on the other hand, can have a more acute bearing on operations and community relations.

Analyzing which ESG factors are linked to executive pay can be another way for investors to identify risks that might be material to the industry. For example, within the gold mining industry, many companies link executive pay to safety, and Contractor and Rua (2023b) suggest that among the companies analyzed, 12% of annual bonuses on average are linked to safety, pointing to the relevance of the issue. However, this does not apply across the board. In steel, as discussed by Contractor and Rua (2023c), few companies link pay to emissions, despite the industry's high carbon intensity.

2.2. The Challenge of Relying on Company-Reported Data: Going Beyond It

One of the challenges in ESG data is relying on information that is reported by companies. These data, while useful, face several challenges including inconsistencies across regions and sectors. In addition, companies often choose to exclude information that might not be favorable, such

---

[1]Environmental, Social and Governance (ESG) Scores, Methodology and Field Information, Bloomberg LP. Available on the Bloomberg Terminal on BESG -> Bloomberg Scores.
[2]Environmental and Social Scores Methodology Industry Guide — Metals & Mining and Steel, Bloomberg LP. Available on the Bloomberg terminal at the link DOCS 2095548. Also, see the work of Contractor and Kane (2023).

as data around fines and lawsuits, resulting in investors trying to piece together information from various sources.

The extent to which data are reported and its quality often depend on the type of data and the sector. Resource-intensive industries like oil and gas, metals and mining or cement tend to see greater levels of disclosures and more standardization, while others like healthcare and technology trail in terms of both quality and quantity. The type of data also plays a role, with governance datasets often being the most complete and reliable, followed by data on issues such as carbon emissions and gender diversity at the board and executive levels. Following this, most data around water, waste and other ESG issues can be much harder to analyze, given significant gaps and quality issues.

While ESG data can be useful and challenging at the same time, one must not forget that ESG analysis also includes going beyond just company-reported ESG information.

For example, assessing the physical risks of climate change on a company often leverages geospatial analysis, in which asset-level data can be overlayed with climate-related data like floods or droughts. Extreme weather impacts not just a company's outputs — be it a product or service — but also disrupts supply chains and creates unforeseen costs. Typhoon Mangkhut in 2018 resulted in a 33-hour closure, costing the Macau casino industry over $200 million in revenue according to research published by Glazerman (2023). Another example from Kane and Rua (2023a) suggest that hospital corporations, including HCA and Community Health Systems, are exposed to the physical risks of climate change. Around 13% of HCA's net patient revenue and 26% of the company's total licensed beds are from facilities in Florida, based on the latest American Hospital Association (AHA) data; over 10% of Community Health net patient revenue and beds are in Florida. Such companies could face higher costs associated with enhancing resilience as well as lost revenue due to service disruptions. As an example of the cost, Hurricane Idalia resulted in HCA temporarily suspending operations in August 2023 at several facilities across Tampa Bay. In 2022, the company lost an estimated $85 million in revenue due to Hurricane Ian, largely at its Florida facilities. Tracking areas that are the most exposed to climate change and overlaying company analysis can be one way of analyzing impacts. Stevenson (2023d) calculates that climate damages have made up the equivalent of 4–10% of Texas, Florida and Louisiana's GDP since 2017. Companies with significant assets in such regions could continue to be exposed to the physical risks of climate change which include lost revenues, physical damages and supply chain disruptions. Such analysis doesn't necessarily rely on company-reported ESG data, providing useful insights into risks.

2.3. *The Challenge in ESG's Limited History and Reporting Frequency: Using Forward-Looking Metrics*

One of the main challenges when trying to decipher the risk and return implications of ESG includes limited historical data, along with data being reported once a year, often with a large time lag. This makes E and S data in particular a challenge to work with. While historical data has improved and is still incredibly important, forward-looking metrics are becoming increasingly valuable, a few examples of which are given in the following sections.

2.3.1. *Analyzing targets and goals*

Analyzing a company's ESG targets can help paint a picture of where a company is going, rather than a view from historical data which tell us where the company has been. Analyzing the most material issues a company faces along with the targets and goals to manage these issues can be useful in gauging risks. For example, climate targets have become an increasingly important and robust dataset and analyzing their level of ambition can help differentiate leaders from laggards. BI's carbon scores, which assess a company's forecasted carbon emissions based on stated goals and alignment with a 1.5-degree Celsius-aligned benchmark, are an example of such a dataset.[3] Analyzing such data can help identify companies that might face risks from being too slow to transition to a low-carbon economy. The cement industry is one where many companies have set or strengthened carbon targets in the last couple of years, yet many still fall short of reductions needed to limit warming to 1.5 degree Celsius. Based on an analysis of BI carbon scores, Contractor and Wentzel (2023) suggest that only four out of the 17 cement companies analyzed have set carbon reduction targets that are in line with the 2030 temperature aligned from

---

[3]BI Carbon Scores. Available on the Bloomberg terminal at {BI BESGG CO2SCORE K:S4W1NR46RMO7<GO>}, Bloomberg Intelligence, Bloomberg LP.

the International Energy Agency's Net Zero by 2050 scenario, as of April 24, 2023. This is less than 25% of the peer set, underscoring the risks companies might face if regulators seek to limit emissions and pointing to a long path the industry has ahead in meeting global climate goals. Understanding targets and goals can also help identify leaders that could potentially benefit from increased efficiency and carbon cost savings. As discussed in Section 2.1.1, in resource-intensive industries like steel, carbon costs under the EU Emissions Trading Scheme could reach up to 9.5% of EBITDA through 2024. Hence, those setting ambitious carbon goals could see substantial cost savings. SSAB, for example, is among a leader in the steel industry, setting an ambitious goal of being almost carbon-neutral in the next decade. According to Sporre and Olsha (2023), this could save millions of euros in CO_2 costs, adding an edge over rivals. Hence, analyzing carbon goals rather than just a company's current and historic carbon intensity can provide a more forward-looking view into the risks and opportunities a company might face.

2.3.2. *Analyzing ESG metrics linked to executive compensation*

Analyzing whether ESG is factored into executive compensation can provide a more forward-looking indicator into whether a company is managing related risks and opportunities through a direct monetary incentive on performance. Such an indicator may also point to greater corporate focus and oversight of ESG issues. For example, within the gold industry, on average, 12% of annual bonuses are linked to safety according to Contractor and Rua (2023d), one of the most material ESG issues given the dangers of mining. Such links between compensation and safety performance could help reduce accidents and the risk of a major safety incident, while for those who don't establish such links, oversight may be limited.

When analyzing such metrics, it's important to better understand whether the metric being linked to is material, related payout thresholds along with a few other factors as discussed in the following sections with examples from BI research.

2.3.2.1. Understanding the KPIs being linked to

Investors are best served when executive compensation is linked to material ESG issues, yet it often may be linked to issues that are non-material.

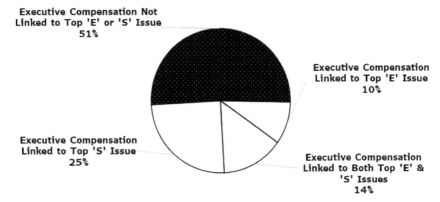

Figure 2.   Executive pay vs. financially material ESG issue

Note: Top issue defined as Issue Priority 1 or 2 in Bloomberg's ESG Scores.
Source: Bloomberg Intelligence.

According to Du Boff and Wentzel (2023), 51% of companies with ESG-linked compensation do not link it to significant material issues, with many linking compensation to carbon emissions, even in industries where Bloomberg doesn't view carbon as material, such as pharma or insurance (see Figure 2). In addition, while aligning pay with ESG can help drive accountability and performance, it is most effective when the ESG metrics linked to compensation are specific, quantifiable and well reported. While the number of companies linking ESG concepts to executive compensation is increasing, most of these concepts are linked to broad ESG performance, either third-party scores or a wide set of ESG issues, rather than specific KPIs. The study goes on to find that about a third of US companies link ESG to executive compensation, double the amount in 2016. Yet, of those with pay links, 34% include a "Broad ESG" goal.

2.3.2.2.   Understanding payout thresholds

The payouts received by executives usually depend on the extent to which they meet goals and thresholds for the KPI set. Understanding these thresholds in terms of how much of an improvement is being targeted vs. current levels, along with how it might compare to the industry standard, can provide insight into the level of oversight. For example, an executive may get top marks and a large share of his or her bonus payout if a company's safety threshold is met. However, if the threshold is not very different from the current safety rates and still worse off compared to peers, it is likely to be met easily and hence not a guidepost into improvements and effective oversight.

2.3.2.3. Understanding the extent to which KPIs are linked

Companies often include a mix of financial and non-financial indicators (i.e. ESG) as part of bonus payouts, with the proportion of each varying from company to company. Understanding the share of bonuses being linked to ESG can identify those where it might be more muted (perhaps less than 5% of bonuses being linked to ESG), while for others it might play a bigger role. According to Contractor and Rua (2023d), Eldorado Gold and Newcrest Mining are among the gold miners that link over 20% of annual bonuses to ESG measures.

Hence, looking at whether a company links ESG to executive compensation, whether the metrics being linked to are material and quantifiable, along with understanding nuances such as payout thresholds, can help provide a more forward-looking view into how a company is overseeing and managing ESG-related risks.

2.4. *The Challenge in the Comparability of ESG Metrics: Finding Workarounds*

One of the biggest challenges in ESG data is comparability which can vary greatly across regions. This can be driven by differences in calculations and even definitions.

Another challenge is data that is often adjusted by companies using different mechanisms, making the data inconsistent and incomparable. Data around the gender pay gap is an example of this, with one potential solution being the use of proxies or data points that might drive the metric being analyzed. For example, Contractor and Du Boff (2020) find that the gender pay gap is often driven by a pipeline issue where there are more women at the lower ends of the organization compared to the top. Looking at the share of female representation at different levels of the organization (non-managerial, managerial, executives) can be one way to evaluate the issue and dig deeper.

A further challenge is terminology, where phrases are often used interchangeably. ESG data tend to be of better quality when standards are provided by an industry body. For example, the World Steel Association has a set of sustainability indicators that members provide data on and as a result tends to be more comparable than others.[4] More such industry organizations adopting similar practices could further improve data consistency and comparability.

2.5. The Challenge in the Variability of ESG Scores: More Transparency

Another concern raised is around the lack of comparability between methodologies for ESG scores. Yet, perhaps the problem is not in the divergence of methodologies, but in the lack of transparency, in part. A comparison to credit ratings, which is often made, might not be the best as ESG seeks to evaluate a variety of things spanning from emissions and safety to a company's governance structure. Credit ratings on the other hand seek to measure largely one thing, a company's creditworthiness. A better comparison for ESG scores may be other facets like sell-side equity stock recommendations that often have varying price targets and buy/sell/hold recommendations for a company, depending on analyst inputs and assessments. Another similar comparison is macroeconomic models, with outcomes often differing depending on the assumptions and inputs used. What's useful and important in both sell-side and economic models is understanding the inputs and assumptions used, allowing the user to better understand the outputs. Transparency into ESG scores so that users can understand the input and see if they agree with the model outcomes is the need of the hour, not necessarily for all of them to point to the same outcome.

ESG data and reporting are still in their infancy, which does complicate analysis. While this should improve with the adoption of standards like the International Sustainability Standards Board (ISSB), trying to get something as subjective as ESG to point to the same outcome is likely to be quite difficult and perhaps unrealistic. Similar to sell-side stock recommendations that offer varying views of a company, ESG views that might vary can be useful, but only if the transparency and inputs can be understood. Rather than throwing the baby out with the bath water due to the

---

[4]World Steel Association, Sustainability Indicators 2023 report, https://worldsteel.org/steel-topics/sustainability/sustainability-indicators-2023-report/.

difference in methodologies, perhaps transparency is a more efficient solution.

3. Understanding ESG Impacts on Performance

Often, a lot of attention is paid to what ESG metrics to use, but less information is available on how to use such metrics and understand their impact on risk and returns. ESG metrics often have different thresholds at which risk and returns may be impacted and results can vary across industries. In the following sections, we highlight BI research that looks at the implications of ESG on companies' financial performance.

3.1. *ESG Scores and Metrics Work Differently Across Different Industries*

As made clear in the materiality analysis above, decision-useful ESG metrics differ from industry to industry as do the related risk and return implications. As per some of the examples, it's clear that while carbon metrics can create costs for industries like steel, they are less relevant for others.

Even for governance, which is one of the ESG pillars that is considered more industry-agnostic, implications for risk, returns, and fundamentals vary by industry.

For example, Contractor *et al.* (2023c) find that within the materials sector, companies in the chemicals and construction materials industries with high Bloomberg shareholder rights scores saw annual outperformance of over 1% vs. those with the worst scores over the period from July 2017 to September 2023, but the same wasn't observed in other industries like steel (see Table 1). Bloomberg's shareholder rights scores enable investors to assess how well company policies protect the interests of all shareholders, particularly minority shareholders, as well as how responsive company managers and directors are to the concerns of these shareholders.

3.2. *Metrics Have Different Thresholds and Don't Necessarily Work in a Linear Manner*

While many conversations focus on what metrics to use, few focus on how to use them. All too often metrics are ranked in a linear manner from

Table 1.   Shareholder Rights Scores Best vs. Worst Performance

Shareholder Rights: Best vs. Worst Scores		
Industries	**Higher Performance?**	**How Much?**
Metals & Mining	Y	0.3%
Chemicals	Y	1.3%
Steel	N	–0.1%
Cons Materials	Y	5.4%

Notes: Scores Bucket = 50% of the best and worst scores on a region and beta neutral basis.
Source: Bloomberg Intelligence.

best to worst, even though impacts on risk and returns might be felt only at certain thresholds.

One example is gender diversity, where Contractor *et al.* (2023a) find that in the US, companies with the lowest share of women on boards saw the lowest returns. The relationship between women on boards and returns, however, wasn't linear and ratcheting up board-level diversity didn't necessarily lead to better returns. However, stocks in the bottom quintile did post the lowest annualized returns, around 0.5% below the top quintile, as per the analysis from 2Q 2013 to December 20, 2022. This again suggests risks at the lower end of the metric, but perhaps not necessarily at the top.

Another example is chairman tenure, where Du Boff (2023a) finds that lack of refreshment can impact performance. Returns improved as a board chair gained experience, but those benefits peaked in the sixth year with an annualized return of 13%, based on a study of the trailing three-year return of the Bloomberg World Index. This suggests that companies must develop plans to refresh board leadership before it becomes too entrenched for effective governance and independence.

3.3. *ESG's Impacts on Risk Management*

ESG impacts not just returns but various aspects of risk. Contractor *et al.* (2023c) find that while those with better Bloomberg governance scores don't see consistent outperformance in materials industries, companies do see lower maximum drawdowns across most industries analyzed, suggesting that the strategy may reduce tail risk that can be associated with weak board composition, poor shareholder rights and audit practices. While topline governance scores did see lower drawdowns, digging a little deeper is important and the research found that strong shareholder rights, a subcomponent of governance sees the most benefits. As per the analysis, better scoring companies on shareholder rights saw maximum drawdowns lower by at least five percentage points across all industries in the materials sector (see Table 2).

This points to the benefits of effective shareholder checks and balances so that management continues to focus on value creation. The existence of dual share classes — two or more classes of shares with different voting rights — is an important metric in evaluating shareholder rights and risk is often skewed to the downside according to Du Boff (2021). For companies with below-average or negative returns, shares with lower voting power often see their discounts widen since poor governance can exacerbate underperformance in mismanaged operations. When a company is doing poorly, weak shareholder rights offer little recourse, leading to continued underperformance if management interests don't align with shareholders. A classic example of this is Meta (formerly Facebook) that, according to the research, underperformed peers for over a year following the 2018 Cambridge Analytica scandal, pointing to management's poor oversight and threats of additional regulation. Following the scandal, shareholder proposals that aimed to enhance corporate governance and risk management failed to gain significant traction, given public shareholders had limited voting rights.

3.4. *ESG Does Not Only Impact Risk and Returns: Fundamentals are Key Aspects*

While risk and returns are important pieces to analyze, they can often be driven by multiple factors such as news or market sentiment. Another helpful approach is to analyze the impacts of ESG metrics on the fundamentals of companies. For example, Contractor *et al.* (2023b) find that in the US, companies with high Bloomberg governance scores show tilts toward high profitability and low valuations, factors that tend to provide fundamental support. Companies in the top quintile of scores (sector adjusted) see an average return on invested capital (ROIC) of 11.6 vs. 7.1 for the worst quintile, as per an analysis from June 30, 2017, until April 27, 2023.

Table 2.   Maximum Drawdowns for Best vs. Worst Governance Scores

	Governance		Board Comp		Exec Comp		Shareholder Rights[*]		Audit	
Best vs. Worst Scores: Maximum Drawdowns										
Industries	Less?	How Much?	Less?	How Much?	Less?	How Much?	Less?	How Much?	Less?	How Much?
Metals & Mining	Y	4.8%	Y	14.4%	N	−0.1%	Y	8.2%	Y	0.6%
Chemicals	Y	1.2%	Y	2.8%	N	−3.4%	Y	6.2%	Y	3.2%
Steel	N	−0.4%	Y	0.3%	N	−0.9%	Y	5.9%	N	−1.7%
Cons Materials	Y	3.9%	N	−2.1%	N	−4.7%	Y	7.2%	Y	10.3%

Notes: Scores Bucket = Companies with top tercile vs. bottom tercile score's on metrics analyzed, on a region and beta neutralized basis. Shareholder rights had a unequal region distribution when using 3 buckets and hence is divided into 2 to improve the distribution.

Source: Bloomberg Intelligence.

In the U.S., similar results were found when analyzing women on boards according to Contractor *et al.* (2023a), and leaders (those in the top quintile) have an average return on equity (ROE) of 14.6% vs. 11.2% for laggards (bottom quintile) as per the analysis from 2Q 2013 to December 20, 2022.

It is also important to note that fundamental exposures can vary by industry. For global construction materials peers, those with a better director roles score see a profitability tilt, while for others like metals and mining, the trend isn't observed according to Contractor *et al.* (2023d). Bloomberg's director roles scores measure the extent to which board members have additional time commitments on other boards and highlight overboarding risks.

4. What Metrics Do Fund Managers Look at and What's Missed?

ESG metrics can range across dozens of different themes from gender to climate to governance. In this context, what actually matters to fund managers and ends up being considered for ESG fund inclusion remains a black box. Some of the other lingering and compelling questions include the following: What companies are ESG-friendly? Are certain sectors more compelling from an ESG perspective than others? Looking at the top-rated firms from ESG scoring providers can be one solution, though ESG scores often differ across multiple providers.

To solve for this, Contractor (2023) created portfolios of companies most and least held by US ESG funds and examined these to better understand what drives manager decisions. To create the high and low inclusion portfolios, 15 large US ESG funds that benchmark to a large cap index were selected and a company was scored based on how frequently it held funds and how overweight or underweight it was compared to the S&P 500. The ESG conviction scores, based on fund holdings, range from 0 to 2, with 2 being better. Those with the highest scores, i.e. the most held and most overweight companies, formed the ESG high conviction portfolio or the companies most included in ESG funds; those least held and most underweight formed the low conviction portfolio and companies that were in none of the funds analyzed formed the exclusionary portfolio. Each portfolio holds 53 stocks as per the analysis in May 2023.

These portfolios are used to represent fund managers' ESG stock convictions and their characteristics were then used to understand what drives managers' decisions. The following sections provide some examples from the research report that details the companies most and least held, sectors and characteristics preferred by ESG funds, and what might be missed.

4.1.   *What Companies Do Fund Managers Lean Toward?*

The research suggests that in the U.S., Microsoft, Alphabet and Mastercard are the most favored stocks in large ESG funds analyzed given their high conviction scores. These companies appear at the greatest frequency in ESG funds analyzed and have the highest average overweight positions compared to the S&P 500. An interesting case study is Tesla, on which the ESG community remains divided. While many suggest that Tesla is an ESG-friendly stock as its products contribute to mitigating climate change, others look at its social controversies and poor aspects of governance which point to ESG risks. As discussed by Contractor (2022), the S&P 500 ESG Index dropped Tesla as of a May 2, 2022 rebalance, citing concerns relating to poor working conditions and the company's handling of an investigation into injuries and deaths related to its autopilot vehicles. As per Kerber (2022), the company has since been reincluded back into the index after the electric car maker added environmental disclosures. Even though Tesla's status remains highly debated, it remains favored in ESG funds with a relatively high conviction score. This suggests that many fund managers consider it to be ESG-friendly despite its controversies.

4.2.   *What Companies Do Fund Managers Avoid?*

Companies like Meta, Wells Fargo and Chevron are less included in ESG funds and have a low conviction score. Meta takes one of the lowest spots, which may be driven by poor aspects of governance. Other large companies that have below-average conviction scores include Apple, Exxon Mobil, Walmart, Netflix and AT&T. Many like AES, Xcel Energy and United Air are excluded from all funds analyzed, which may be a missed opportunity given their ambitious carbon goals.

4.3. *What Does This Tell Us About Managers Sector and Industry Preferences?*

An analysis of companies most vs. least held in ESG funds suggests that ESG fund managers tilt toward resource-light sectors like technology while avoiding resource-intensive ones like utilities and energy. The ESG fund aggregate is on average most overweight tech and underweight energy, with differentials exceeding 2% for both (see Figure 3). Utilities too remain underweight in ESG funds, and an analysis of the exclusion portfolio suggests that 66% of S&P 500 utility constituents are excluded from all funds analyzed. A similar analysis conducted by Contractor and Zhou (2023) within the materials sector found that industries with a high carbon intensity like cement and steel are less likely to be included in ESG funds, with investors preferring those that are carbon-light. ESG fund inclusion was measured as the number of ESG funds a stock is in vs. all funds a stock is in and the analysis found an almost inverse relationship between the inclusion rate and carbon intensity. Less intensive industries within the materials sector like containers and packaging had a median ESG fund inclusion rate of over 10%, higher than carbon-intensive ones like cement and steel that had a rate of 6% or less.

Such sector and industry preferences can influence fund returns, and this likely contributed to ESG underperformance through parts of 2022,

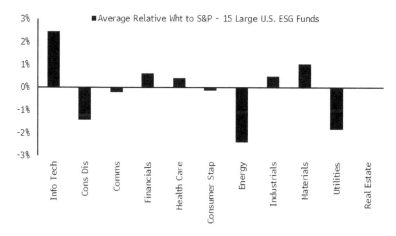

Figure 3.   ESG funds relative sector weights vs. S&P 500

Source: Bloomberg Intelligence.

as the energy sector, which is left out of ESG funds, saw outperformance. These typical sector allocations have come under criticism in recent years and perhaps a rethink around ESG being more of a fundamental decision, regardless of sector, will become increasingly important. These sector allocations otherwise will continue to influence returns, driving outperformance in some years and underperformance in others.

4.4. *What are the ESG Characteristics of the High vs. Low Conviction Portfolio and What Does That Tell Us About Fund Managers' ESG Preferences?*

An analysis of the ESG characteristics of companies most and least included in US ESG funds suggests that environmental factors play a large role in company selection, while social and governance factors get left behind.

Companies in the high-conviction ESG portfolio that is designed to represent companies most included in ESG funds have a median Bloomberg environmental score of 89, much higher than those in the low conviction or exclusions portfolio, at 53 and 64, respectively. The differential is much smaller for social and governance scores, suggesting they matter to a lesser extent in the ESG selection. This makes it clear that a company's environmental performance is related to its level of inclusion in ESG funds and those with higher scores are more heavily included. This is not evidenced for social and governance scores, and more companies included in ESG funds do not have a higher governance score than those less included, pointing to the disconnect. One reason for a preference for the E over the S could be that social factors are harder to measure and quantify compared to environmental factors. In addition to the 'E' being one of the most included, carbon intensity seems to be a differentiating factor and stocks in the high conviction portfolio have a carbon intensity of 13 tons CO_2 per million of sales, much lower than 163 for the exclusion portfolio. This supports the sector biases noted above, where ESG investors prefer industries that are carbon-light, steering capital away from some of the most resource-intensive sectors. The carbon intensity is calculated by using scope 1 + 2 data reported by companies and, if not, an estimate calculated by Bloomberg which is then normalized by sales.

4.5. *What Might Be Missed?*

The conviction portfolio analysis suggests that "S" and "G" factors are less considered by ESG funds as opposed to the "E" factor, overlooking risks that could potentially harm company performance. Our research above covers materiality in great detail, pointing to examples where social factors can be relevant, examples of which include industries like metals and mining where accident rates are of great importance.

Deemphasizing governance factors seems counterintuitive, given it is one of the most quantifiable factors and one that likely predates E and S as a focus of investment analysis. One of the reasons could be the fact that governance might be included in both ESG and non-ESG funds alike, such that the governance scores of companies in ESG funds are not substantially higher than those excluded from ESG funds.

Yet, a deeper dive into companies most included in ESG funds suggests that many have weak governance, going back to the rationale that governance remains overlooked. One of the clearest examples remains Tesla. The auto manufacturer remains highly favored in ESG funds, likely driven by its environmental impact, despite aspects of poor governance. Tesla scores a 2.91 out of 10 on Bloomberg's FY 2022 Shareholder Rights Score, a key governance theme, pointing to weak shareholder policies and challenges in aligning shareholder interests with management.[5] Section 2.3 that discusses ESG's impacts on risk provides ample evidence suggesting that strong shareholder rights can help avoid downside risk, pointing to the value of effective oversight and the protection of minority interest. Poor shareholder rights can often exasperate underperformance at mismanaged companies as there are limited options for recourse or levers to bring about change. Hence, while Tesla might fit an environmental or impact-focused fund, its poor governance makes its inclusion in ESG funds debatable. Many other examples of companies being highly favored in ESG funds despite poor governance exist. Salesforce stands out as a company often included in ESG funds, yet lags on Bloomberg's FY 2022 Board Composition Scores (5.47 out of 10).[6] Adequate board refreshment, independence and diversity along with limited overboarding (directors not

---

[5] Tesla's ESG Score, Available on the Bloomberg Terminal by loading the function{TSLA US Equity ESG SCORE}, Bloomberg LP.
[6] Salesforce ESG Score. Available on the Bloomberg Terminal by loading the function {CRM US Equity ESG SCORE}, Bloomberg LP.

serving on too many other boards such that they are stretched thin) are part of Bloomberg's board composition score and are important in providing effective oversight.

Other potential missed opportunities include some of the more resource-intensive industries, likely due to ESG investors' focus on carbon intensity. Industries and companies with high carbon intensity like cement and steel remain less likely to be included in ESG funds, despite the importance of such industries in the energy transition. In addition, Stevenson (2023e) suggests that steel, aluminum and cement companies with the lowest emissions per ton of output have outperformed peers by 56% over 5 years. Yet, many ESG funds have overlooked these industries. Many companies in such industries also have ambitious carbon reduction goals which remain missed. Utilities for example remain as one of the most excluded sectors, despite many companies having ambitious carbon reduction goals. AES and Xcel Energy, for example, have ambitious carbon goals, as suggested by above-average BI Carbon Scores, but are left out of ESG funds likely due to their high-current carbon intensity. Other examples include United Airlines and Alaska Air. ESG fund exclusion of industries due to their high carbon intensity could overlook those that play an important role in the energy transition, starving capital from those that need it the most.

5. When It Comes To Driving Change, What Has an Impact?

While ESG integration and impact investing are two separate strategies — the former seeking to measure and manage non-financial risks and opportunities specific to the company and the latter seeking to target a positive outcome or additionality — both are often confused and used interchangeably. Some of the challenges and unanswered questions include the following: Are ESG and impact two separate strategies? What metrics or strategies drive impact and how can one measure this? While the objective of an ESG strategy is managing non-financial risks and opportunities, when it comes to the outcome, it might not be that far removed from having a positive impact. Yet, ESG and sustainable investing are often criticized for not having an impact or not having enough of a means to measure and quantify impact. In the following sections, we synthesize BI research that helps understand what drives impact.

5.1. *Focusing on Financially Material Issues Can Help Drive Impact*

While ESG and impact investing might have two separate objectives, the outcomes might not be that divergent, with Kane and Rua (2023b) suggesting that one can have a positive impact by focusing on the most financially material metrics. For example, if carbon emissions are financially material to an industry like cement — given that the industry accounts for 7% of global emissions as discussed by Stevenson (2023f) — focusing on an analysis of emissions, targets and goals and driving change through engagement or other strategies can potentially lead to a net positive impact. On the other hand, a company's carbon emissions are likely not as material for a sector like healthcare, and focusing on them will likely have little impact. In other words, issues that are financially material and those that can lead to the greatest environmental or social impacts are often intertwined.

Kane and Rua (2023b) find that only 16% of companies in the Bloomberg ESG Coverage Index account for 83% of the index's total Scope 1 carbon emissions. These companies are selected by using Bloomberg's ESG scores to identify industries for which a materiality-based analysis determined GHG management to be the top environmental issue. Given how financially material emissions could be for these companies, those that are best managing the issue can not only lower financial risks associated with asset stranding, demand erosion and regulatory costs but also bring about a positive impact in terms of emission reductions. In contrast, for the other 84% of index constituents, the share of emissions was just 3%, suggesting finite financial risks and limited climate impacts.

Another example could be safety and accident rates. As discussed before, safety is among the most material issues in the mining industry, given how dangerous operations can be, and focusing on such issues through engagement or other means can help lower risks and also improve an organization's safety culture. Hence, while impact and ESG might be two separate approaches, a materiality-driven ESG analysis can help identify issues with the greatest financial risk and also the greatest positive impacts. The simplest way to put it is while the goal of ESG analysis is not to have an impact, the secondary implications can include a positive impact if a materiality-based lens is applied.

5.2. *Tying Executive Compensation to ESG Issues Can Drive Impact*

Linking ESG metrics to executive compensation can potentially drive impact by providing a monetary incentive on performance. Du Boff and Wentzel (2023) find that companies in the Bloomberg 1000 index that link pay to specific ESG objectives saw those issues improve to a larger extent than those that didn't tie pay to those metrics. For example, for those that include diversity metrics as part of pay packages, women make up 30% of senior executives, higher than the 26% for the Bloomberg 1000 index (see Table 3).

The study goes on to find that companies linking diversity efforts to executive pay also tend to be more transparent. One of the biggest challenges in analyzing racial diversity is the lack of self-reported data, and the research finds that for those that include diversity as part of executive pay, 45% of these companies disclose the ratio of racial and ethnic minorities in their workforce as opposed to 39% for the broader Bloomberg 1000 index. This extends to issues like safety and accident rates as well and those that

Table 3.   Impacts of DE&I-Linked Pay and Gender Diversity

	Women Execs		
	Companies w/DE&I Linked Pay	**Bloomberg 1000**	**Δ**
Health Care	34.9%	28.3%	*7%*
Communications	34.3%	30.6%	*4%*
Consumer Staples	34.2%	28.4%	*6%*
Financials	32.8%	25.2%	*8%*
Materials	31.7%	24.3%	*7%*
Utilities	31.4%	33.2%	*−2%*
Consumer Discretionary	28.9%	27.5%	*1%*
Technology	27.5%	25.6%	*2%*
Energy	24.5%	22.5%	*2%*
Industrials	23.3%	23.0%	*0%*
Real Estate	16.8%	23.3%	*−7%*
Total	29.5%	26.2%	*3%*

Source: Bloomberg Intelligence.

link health and safety to executive pay have total recordable injury rates (TRIR) of 0.98, lower than the 1.05 rate for the Bloomberg 1000 index. Yet, as we note in the previous sections, where we discuss executive compensation in more detail, metrics should be quantifiable, material to operations, and are most effective when they are as specific as possible.

5.3. *Incentivizing Impact Through Financing Costs*

Similar to linking ESG issues to executive pay, driving ESG through debt financing instruments can be another monetary incentive to drive change. According to Negoita (2022), companies like EQT and Iberdrola are among those that associate their debt-financing instruments with diversity goals. Such instruments known as sustainability-linked debt pay slightly higher interest if the issuers don't achieve intended sustainability targets. EQTs bond, for example, pays an extra 7.5 bps if the share of women among investment advisory professionals doesn't rise to 28% by 2026 (from 21% in 2020). Such instruments create a financial incentive for companies to meet sustainability goals by levying a penalty if missed. For example, as discussed by Ritchie (2023), Enel SpA, which has close to $11 billion in SLBs, is highly unlikely to meet a 2023 carbon-emissions goal following changes to European energy policy that resulted in coal plant phase-out delays, according to the Anthropocene Fixed Income Institute. This could result in an estimated $27 million of additional annual interest costs as per the AFII. When analyzing sustainability-linked bonds as one method to drive change, here too metrics are best served if they are specific, quantifiable, and measurable. The level of ambition too is important. For instance, Negoita (2022) discusses how Iberdrola's sustainability-linked credit line aims for women in leadership positions to be 30% by 2025 (vs. 28% in 2021).

5.4. *Engagement to Drive Impact*

Shareholder engagement has always been a strategy for driving change at companies, with Du Boff (2023b) suggesting that a record 336 environmental and social proposals were filed in the US in the 12 months till June 2023. Such resolutions can drive positive outcomes at companies, and Du Boff (2023c) suggests that those with successful shareholder votes saw their Bloomberg ESG scores improve significantly as opposed to peers in subsequent years. Companies that saw successful social proposals (over 50% support) saw their Bloomberg social scores improve by 16 percentile ranks on average over the three years after approval. Gains were even higher — at an average 31 points — for proposals that won over 80 support (see Figure 4).

The same applies to environmental proposals. Those with successful proxy votes saw their Bloomberg environmental pillar score climb an average 14 percentile ranks after three years (see Figure 5).

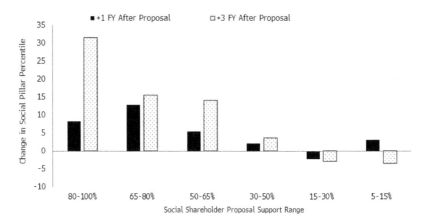

Figure 4.   Changes in social score after proposal

Source: Bloomberg Intelligence.

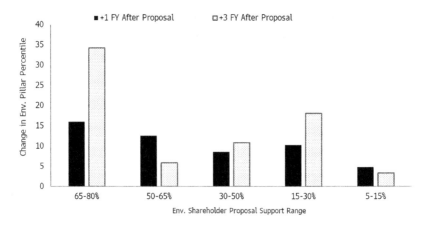

Figure 5.   Changes in environmental score after proposal

Source: Bloomberg Intelligence.

Even modest investor support (15–30%) has been enough to drive change. Exxon Mobil activists slowly made progress over several years, culminating in a 2021 proxy fight that drove significant change.

The research finds that proposals don't need full approval to drive corporate policies as often a sizable minority of key investors is enough to drive change. For example, Goldman Sachs agreed to adopt a proposal on mandatory arbitration in workplace harassment cases that failed by less than 1% in 2021. Similarly, in the same year, Citi relented on opposition to a racial-equity audit that had nearly 40% support.

6. Conclusion

As discussed in the previous sections, the ESG data come with many challenges, but applying a materiality lens, going beyond just company-reported data and using more forward-looking metrics can help overcome some of these challenges. While a lot of focus goes into which metrics to use, less goes into how to use and understand them, and we note that ESG metrics can have different thresholds. While ESG spans many metrics and topics, an analysis of companies most included in ESG funds suggests that managers prioritize the 'E', often overlooking risks in the 'S' and the 'G'. In addition, many companies in resource-intensive industries like utilities get screened out of funds, despite many having ambitious carbon reduction goals.

Lastly, one can drive positive societal outcomes by focusing on materiality, thus driving change through engagement along with monetary incentives, such as linked ESG to executive compensation and other financing mechanisms.

References

Contractor, S. (2022). Is tesla ESG? Many funds own it. We say it's not for everyone. Bloomberg Intelligence, Bloomberg LP. Retrieved from https://blinks.bloomberg.com/news/stories/rc6415t1um1a.

Contractor, S. (2023). ESG fund-conviction portfolios: What do managers lean toward? Bloomberg Intelligence, Bloomberg LP. Retrieved from https://blinks.bloomberg.com/news/stories/rvis6cdwlu69.

Contractor, S. & Du Boff, R. (2020). Women lag on pay even as more promoted: Gender equality index. Bloomberg Intelligence, Bloomberg LP. Retrieved from https://blinks.bloomberg.com/news/stories/q5c255t0afb7.

Contractor, S. & Kane, E. (2022a). Among metals, aluminum bears the brunt of carbon costs. Bloomberg Intelligence, Bloomberg LP. Retrieved from https://blinks.bloomberg.com/news/stories/rgc3m3t0afb4.

Contractor, S. & Kane, E. (2022b). Carbon price's surge may prove a headwind for aluminum. Bloomberg Intelligence, Bloomberg LP. Retrieved from https://blinks.bloomberg.com/news/stories/rgc3r5t0afb6.

Contractor, S. & Kane, E. (2023). Heat map on priority rankings helps explain materiality. Bloomberg Intelligence, Bloomberg LP. Retrieved from https://blinks.bloomberg.com/news/stories/rz7qaadwlu69.

Contractor, S. & Rua, M. (2022a). Among base metals, aluminum most at risk from carbon pricing. Bloomberg Intelligence, Bloomberg LP. Retrieved from https://blinks.bloomberg.com/news/stories/rabtd4t1um0w.

Contractor, S. & Rua, M. (2022b). Energy, climate, health, safety Drive E, S in steels' ESG. Bloomberg Intelligence, Bloomberg LP. Retrieved from https://blinks.bloomberg.com/news/stories/rcwbn7t1um0w.

Contractor, S. & Rua, M. (2023a). Sibanye trails, newmont leads gold peers on safety metrics. Bloomberg Intelligence, Bloomberg LP. Retrieved from https://blinks.bloomberg.com/news/stories/RZJ5E9T1UM0W.

Contractor, S. & Rua, M. (2023b). Harmony gold trails peers on ESG perfor Bloomberg Intelligence, Bloomberg LP. Retrieved from https://blinks.bloomberg.com/news/stories/rzxyl8dwx2pt.

Contractor, S. & Rua, M. (2023c). Energy, climate, health, safety Drive E, S in steels' ESG. Bloomberg Intelligence, Bloomberg LP. Retrieved from https://blinks.bloomberg.com/news/stories/rcwbn7t1um0w.

Contractor, S. & Rua, M. (2023d). ESG bonuses indicate priorities: 12% on aver-linked to safety. Bloomberg Intelligence, Bloomberg LP. Retrieved from https://blinks.bloomberg.com/news/stories/rzsel5dwrgg0.

Contractor, S. & Wentzel, M. (2023). CO_2 spells risk for cement yet many fall short: BI Carbon scores. Bloomberg Intelligence, Bloomberg LP. Retrieved from https://blinks.bloomberg.com/news/stories/rxm5x5t1um0x.

Contractor, S. & Zhou, Y. (2023). Carbon metrics keep ESG funds from tapping materials' potential. Bloomberg Intelligence, Bloomberg LP. Retrieved from https://blinks.bloomberg.com/news/stories/s3wbg8t0afb5.

Contractor, S., *et al.* (2023a). A benefit of board gender diversity could be reduced volatility? Bloomberg Intelligence, Bloomberg LP. Retrieved from https://blinks.bloomberg.com/news/stories/roz9u5dwrgg0.

Contractor, S., *et al.* (2023b). When does governance show benefits? screening for improvers? Bloomberg Intelligence, Bloomberg LP. Retrieved from https://blinks.bloomberg.com/news/stories/rz2htedwx2ps.

Contractor, S., *et al.* (2023c). Good governance helps avoid downside stock shocks in materials. Bloomberg Intelligence, Bloomberg LP. Retrieved from https://blinks.bloomberg.com/news/stories/s23ql6dwx2ps.

Contractor, S., *et al.* (2023d). Benefits of better governance for metals: Lower drawdowns. Bloomberg Intelligence, Bloomberg LP. Retrieved from https://blinks.bloomberg.com/news/stories/s2gp98dwlu68.

Du Boff, R. (2021). Facebook's low accountability lands it in hot water … Again. Bloomberg Intelligence, Bloomberg LP. Retrieved from https://blinks.bloomberg.com/news/stories/r054yht1um1n.

Du Boff, R. (2023a). Succession planning becoming a necessity. Bloomberg Intelligence, Bloomberg LP. Retrieved from https://blinks.bloomberg.com/news/stories/s4s6t8t0g1kx.

Du Boff, R. (2023b). US proxy season 2023: Lots of squeaky wheels, not much grease. Bloomberg Intelligence, Bloomberg LP. Retrieved from https://blinks.bloomberg.com/news/stories/rzuc66t0afb.

Du Boff, R. (2023c). ESG shareholder proposals can move needle even without passage. Bloomberg Intelligence, Bloomberg LP. Retrieved from https://blinks.bloomberg.com/news/stories/s5aphddwlu68.

Du Boff, R. & Wentzel, M. (2023). Linking pay can boost ESG performance, but materiality key. Bloomberg Intelligence, Bloomberg LP. Retrieved from https://blinks.bloomberg.com/news/stories/S3E46BT0G1KX.

Glazerman, G. (2023). Companies confront heat, typhoons, antitrust: ESG dollar & cents. Bloomberg Intelligence, Bloomberg LP. Retrieved from https://blinks.bloomberg.com/news/stories/s0k9i9dwrgg0.

Kane, E. & Rua, M. (2023a). Health care isn't immune from climate-change risks. Bloomberg Intelligence, Bloomberg LP. Retrieved from https://blinks.bloomberg.com/news/stories/s2b865dwlu68.

Kane, E. & Rua, M. (2023b). ESG myth-busting: Financial materiality, impact align. Bloomberg Intelligence, Bloomberg LP. Retrieved from https://blinks.bloomberg.com/news/stories/s315i4dwrgg0.

Kerber, R. (2022). Tesla returns to S&P 500 ESG index with more environmental disclosures. Reuters. Retrieved from https://www.reuters.com/sustainability/tesla-returns-sp-500-esg-index-with-more-environmental-disclosures-2023-06-21/.

Negoita, R. (2022). Incentivizing gender balance through financing costs. Bloomberg Intelligence, Bloomberg LP. Retrieved from https://blinks.bloomberg.com/news/stories/rknnr3t0g1kw.

Ritchie, G. (2023). Top issuer in $250 billion ESG bond market risks trigger event. Bloomberg LP. Retrieved from https://www.bloomberg.com/news/articles/2023-10-20/enel-seen-missing-key-target-linked-to-11-billion-of-esg-bonds.

Sporre, G. & Olsha, A. (2023). SSAB's safety, net-zero plan boosts ESG credentials: ESG outlook. Bloomberg Intelligence, Bloomberg LP. Retrieved from https://blinks.bloomberg.com/news/stories/S36EV6DWRGG0.

Stevenson, A. (2023a). Investors could gain material edge from low-intensity materials. Bloomberg Intelligence, Bloomberg LP. Retrieved from https://blinks.bloomberg.com/news/stories/s31588dwrgg0.

Stevenson, A. (2023b). Clean-spending utilities outperform laggards by 43% over 5 years. Bloomberg Intelligence, Bloomberg LP. Retrieved from https://blinks.bloomberg.com/news/stories/rrk656t0afb4.

Stevenson, A. (2023c). Low-carbon utilities light up sector, beat peer returns by 58%. Bloomberg Intelligence, Bloomberg LP. Retrieved from https://blinks.bloomberg.com/news/stories/S2B871DWX2PS.

Stevenson, A. (2023d). Tracking climate, the fastest growing sector of the US economy. Bloomberg Intelligence, Bloomberg LP. Retrieved from https://blinks.bloomberg.com/news/stories/s1lap8t1um12.

Stevenson, A. (2023e). Materials sector's climate leaders return 56% more than laggards. Bloomberg Intelligence, Bloomberg LP. Retrieved from https://blinks.bloomberg.com/news/stories/s203r6dwrgg1.

Stevenson, A. (2023f). Cement's 7% share of emissions a major challenge. Bloomberg Intelligence, Bloomberg LP. Retrieved from https://blinks.bloomberg.com/news/stories/S1QUU4T1UM0Z.

Part 2

Addressing Climate Change

https://doi.org/10.1142/9789811297786_0009

Chapter 9

Net-Zero Investing

Marcin Kacperczyk

Imperial College London, London, United Kingdom

Abstract

Net-zero portfolios (NZPs) aim to reduce their carbon footprint over time, typically until 2050, by mimicking scientific paths of decarbonization, and aggregate carbon budget, for the global economy. Their popularity among institutional investors has been growing over time, with more than $100 trillion of global assets under management currently covered by various net-zero (NZ) investing initiatives. The first part of the chapter provides a discussion of the construct of the NZP, its benefits, and its potential limitations for portfolio managers. The second part of the chapter outlines the role of the NZP in asset prices. The channels underlying the pricing are divestment and engagement. Contrary to common wisdom that focuses on divestment that is already happening, being associated with an NZP initiative does not necessarily imply that investors need to divest from high-emitting companies right away. It may also mean an expectation of such divestment in the future. Because the expectation of divestment allows for a dialogue between institutional investors and corporates, the framework is also a form of engagement.

Net-zero portfolios (NZPs) aim to reduce their exposure to carbon footprint over time, typically until 2050, by mimicking scientific paths of decarbonization for the global economy. Even though NZPs by themselves do not guarantee the decarbonization of the global economy, they aim to provide incentives for companies to do so. Companies that undertake emissions reduction are rewarded by being included in NZPs, and companies that are behind the decarbonization curve are penalized by being excluded from NZPs. The popularity of net-zero investing among institutional investors has been rapidly growing, with more than $100 trillion of global assets under management currently covered by various net-zero investment initiatives. The NZP initiative has also shaped discussions surrounding sustainable finance, as is the case for the EU Low-Carbon Benchmark Regulation, which establishes uniform rules for low-carbon investment benchmark indexes and sets their required decarbonization trajectories.

In this chapter, I first provide details that govern the construction of NZPs, building on the early work of Bolton *et al.* (2022). Next, I discuss the properties of such portfolios relative to a standard market portfolio benchmark. Finally, I discuss how the NZP framework can be applied to construct measures of carbon transition risk at the firm level, which offer conceptual improvements over measures in prior work by Bolton and Kacperczyk (2023).

1. Construction and Properties of Net-Zero Portfolios

Two elements are important in the NZP concept: (a) a dynamic carbon budget, applied by investors in their portfolio decisions, which is informed by scientific projections about climate scenarios and determines the maximum amount of emissions NZP can be exposed to at each point in time, and (b) the rule by which investors select companies into the NZP. In the following, I outline the key principles governing each of them.

1.1. *Dynamic Carbon Budget*

The starting point for constructing the portfolio budget is the global carbon budget. The global budget is defined as the amount of aggregate emissions that can be maximally produced to adhere to scientifically determined climate scenarios informed by temperature changes. In theory, many carbon budgets are possible, as long as different scenarios are being considered; in practice, some scenarios are more popular than others. For illustration in this chapter, I focus on one such scenario, in which the Intergovernmental Panel on Climate Change (IPCC), the leading provider of climate data, estimates that in order to limit the global temperature rise to below 1.5°C compared to pre-industrial levels, with 83% probability, one would need to limit global emissions to 300 GtCO$_2$ as of the beginning of 2020. To get a better sense of this number, the following thought exercise can be useful. The Global Carbon Project, a consortium of scientists, estimates that global emissions in 2020 reached 39.3 GtCO$_2$, which means that the remaining budget as of the beginning of 2021 is 260.7 GtCO$_2$. Assuming a scenario in which emissions stay constant into the near future, the remaining budget would be depleted within 6.6 years (260.7/39.3). These findings underscore the urgency of addressing emissions reduction to sustainably manage the finite carbon budget and to attain critical climate objectives.

Given the global carbon budget, one can construct the portfolio carbon budget as follows. First, we need to define the investable universe for investors. For that, I include stocks on all publicly traded firms for which we have emissions data. The source of such data is the S&P Trucost. Second, Scopes 1–3 emissions are summed up from all such firms in a given year. As an example, this number equals 25.5 GtCO$_2$e in 2020. Third, assuming that the rate of portfolio decarbonization is proportional to the rate of global decarbonization, the cumulative portfolio budget is equal to the portfolio emissions in 2020 times the number of 6.6 years left to exhaust the world cumulative budget as of that date. This procedure yields an estimate of a cumulative portfolio budget of 168.3 GtCO$_2$e.

Having pinned down the size of the total carbon budget for NZPs, the next step is to decide the pathway along which investors would decarbonize their portfolios. This step is flexible and allows one to consider several different choices of such decarbonization paths, all created at the discretion of investors: (a) investors immediately decarbonize their portfolios' footprint at a constant rate, (b) the budget is kept constant for some time and then investors decarbonize their portfolios' footprint at a constant but faster rate, (c) investors decarbonize their portfolios at a faster (slower) rate for the first half of the remaining period and then at a slower (faster) rate for the second half, or (d) investors follow a more sophisticated science-based decarbonization path.

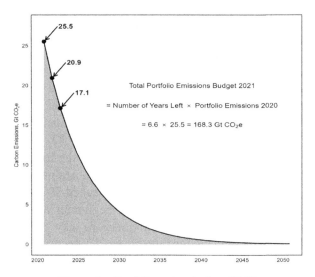

Figure 1.   Portfolio carbon budget (2020)

To provide a visual illustration of the portfolio budget's construction, Figure 1 zooms in on a constant-rate decarbonization pathway for the cohort starting in 2020. Specifically, global emissions in 2020 amount to 39.3 $GtCO_2e$, and the corresponding annual carbon footprint of the investable universe is 25.5 $GtCO_2e$. Using the proportionality rule, the remaining global emissions budget of 260.3 $GtCO_2e$ translates into a cumulative portfolio budget of 168.3 $GtCO_2e$. This proportionality rule applies not only to total emissions but also works for all individual yearly carbon budgets. For example, if we followed the constant-rate decarbonization pathway, from 2020, global emissions would need to drop to 32.2 $GtCO_2e$, and, correspondingly, our NZP would allow for a carbon footprint of 20.9 $GtCO_2e$ in 2021. Going forward, we can see that the carbon budget continues its exponential decline until 2050 when it reaches a value that is close to 0. Given that the budget gets progressively tighter over time, it is with that spirit that investors would become more restrictive in holding assets with different carbon footprints.

1.2. *NZP Selection Rules*

As a final step to obtaining NZPs, in this section, I describe the rules by which investors select companies for NZPs, such that their total emissions jointly do not exceed the yearly emissions budget. A broad principle being applied is that companies with greater decarbonization prospects should be given preference.

I consider three different rankings of such prospects, each subsequent one building on the previous one and thus being more comprehensive and more realistic for the objective function of the exercise. As a first and simple illustration of the ideas, I use companies' current total emissions, following the idea that such emissions are the best predictor of future decarbonization efforts. Next, to acknowledge the importance of looking at future data and thus in our second approach, I sort companies based on their predicted total emissions. Here, the basic principle is that decarbonization may take time, so what matters is where companies will be later on with their efforts, and not necessarily where they are today. Third, and most general, I select companies according to their combined efforts to decarbonize their activities, measured by a novel composite, the *Ambition Score*, originally introduced in the work of Cenedese *et al.* (2023). For the first two schemes, one can consider measures based on unconditional sorting, as well as measures sorted within a given 4-digit Global Industry Classification Standard (GICS-4) industry group. In turn, the third scheme is always industry neutral. All the measures utilize a wide range of data, starting with the emissions data, which are obtained from S&P Trucost, and then following with forward-looking climate-related indicators from the following databases: Refinitiv ESG, CDP, and Orbis Intellectual Property.

1.3. *Rule 1: Historical Carbon Emissions*

The first selection rule is based on the sum of all firm-level emissions. Companies with lower total emissions are preferred to those whose total emissions are higher. The construction of emissions data starts with all global firms in the S&P Trucost Environmental Data reported yearly between 2005 and 2021. Trucost reports firm-level absolute greenhouse gas emissions in tons of carbon dioxide equivalent (tCO_2e) for Scopes 1–3 upstream emissions. According to the Greenhouse Gas Protocol, Scope 1 emissions are emissions directly from sources that are owned or controlled by the company, Scope 2 emissions refer to emissions generated by a company consuming purchased electricity, heat, or steam, and Scope 3 emissions are indirect emissions produced by the company's value chain but occurring from sources not owned or controlled by the company.

1.4. *Rule 2: Forecasted Emissions*

The second scheme classifies companies based on the levels of their forecasted emissions, following the work of Cenedese *et al.* (2023). This means that for a given dynamic budget path, investors estimate total emissions for each point in time along the path, taking a given decarbonization cohort as a starting point for making predictions. Cenedese *et al.* (2023) rely on a fairly simple procedure to form predictions, a weighted average between pre-announced, self-reported firm commitments to decarbonize their efforts and past emissions trends.

The final forecasted emissions pathway is a weighted average of the decarbonization target-based path and the emissions trend path. Following the target credibility framework set out by the Glasgow Financial Alliance for Net Zero, a 75% weight is assigned to a target-based path if a firm meets two criteria: (1) its targets are approved by the Science Based Targets initiative (SBTi) and (2) it has targets for both the short-term and medium-to-long-term horizons. In the case in which a firm only meets one of the two criteria, a 50% weight is assigned to the target-based path. A 25% only weight is assigned to the target-based path if a firm only has medium-to-long-term targets that are not approved by SBTi. For all these three cases, the rest of the weights are assigned to the trend path. Finally, if a firm only has short-term targets, or does not have targets at all, the forecasts rely fully on the trend path.

1.5. *Rule 3: Ambition Score*

The third and most comprehensive classification scheme aims to capture both corporate intention and ability to decarbonize future activities. The basic idea is to integrate information from past decarbonization efforts with information that speaks to future efforts to do so. To this end, I use the Ambition Score of Cenedese *et al.* (2023), defined as a weighted average of the following three categories of variables: (1) historical emissions levels and their growth rates (50%), (2) historical emissions intensities and their growth rates (25%), and (3) forward-looking climate-related activity metrics (25%). Within each category, equal weights are assigned to individual characteristics. The weighting scheme to construct the score can be modified in a very flexible way. These specific weights have been chosen to reflect the importance of directly observed emissions in the prospects of decarbonization. The equal weights within each category are consistent with an uninformed prior regarding the importance of each individual corporate action. All three categories aim to predict firm-level decarbonization outcomes. Carbon emissions levels and their growth rates are useful to extrapolate current emissions trends into the future. Intensity-level metrics add an additional dimension of efficiency to carbon production, not directly linked to company size. Finally, forward-looking metrics summarize all the efforts undertaken by the company that relate to the company's ambition to reduce future emissions.

Specifically, within the first category, the size and the three-year moving-average simple growth rate of a company's absolute carbon emissions are included. Within the second category, the level and the three-year moving-average growth rate of a company's carbon intensities, measured as tons of CO_2 equivalent divided by the company's revenue in millions of dollars, are included. Within the third category, three aspects of decarbonization ambition measures are incorporated: (a) environmental variables from the company's Corporate Social Responsibility (CSR) report, (b) patent variables on green and brown innovations, and (c) variables on decarbonization commitments reported in the CDP survey. In Table 1, I present details for the Ambition Score using the example of Apple in 2020.

1.6. *Properties of NZPs*

Some of the typical concerns of the NZPs pertain to their properties relative to benchmark portfolios. I show in the following that such portfolios display characteristics that are favorable. First, in Figure 2, I show the evolution of the ex ante tracking error of the portfolio with a constant decarbonization rate relative to the MSCI Europe Index.

As can be seen, the NZP has a tracking error that is quite small and ranges between 0.08% in 2021 and 1.9% in 2050. This result indicates that portfolio decarbonization is feasible without losing diversification benefits. As another dimension, I have looked at the sectoral distribution of assets relative to the same MSCI Europe benchmark. The results of this analysis indicate that the NZP does not create a strong tilt away from any individual industries and instead is well balanced across sectors.

Overall, it becomes apparent that the NZP framework can offer a well-diversified portfolio that reduces exposure to the carbon footprint.

Table 1. Ambition score for Apple (2020)

Category	Category Weight	Data Source	Variables	Reported Value	Score Input	Standardized Value
Historical hard data	50%	Trucost	Carbon emission	39,453,087.42	39,453,087.42	165.24
			Emission growth	0.14	0.14	0.68
Historical soft data	25%	Trucost	Carbon intensity	143.72	143.72	−0.56
			Intensity growth	0.06	0.06	1.65
Forward-looking soft data	25%	CSR Report	Decarbonization target existence	Yes	0	−2.59
			Decarbonization policy existence	Yes	0	−1.75
			Emission disclosure	Reported	0	−1.94
			Sustainability committee existence	Yes	0	−2.08
			UNPRI signatory	No	1	NA
			SDG13 climate action	Yes	0	−2.63
		Orbis Patent	Green patent number	24	−24	−2.34
			Brown efficiency patent number	0	0	0.14
			Green patent citation number	264	−264	−16.1
			Brown efficiency patent citation number	0	0	0.11
			Green patent ratio	0.03	−0.03	0
			Brown efficiency patent ratio	0	0	0.08
		CDP Survey	SBTi participation	Submitted	1	−2.8
			Greenwashing indicator	0	0	3.18
			Abatement rate	5	−5	−6.35
			Target underperformance	18.96	18.96	−3.83
			Target impracticability	18.00	18.00	−3.78
					Final score	40.93

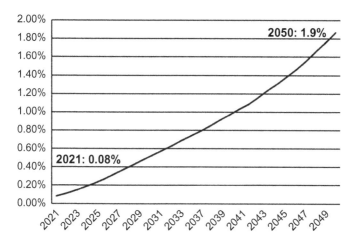

Figure 2.   Ex ante tracking error for NZP based on the MSCI Europe Index

2. Implications for Asset Prices

In this section, I show how the NZP framework can be applied to create measures of carbon transition risk. As the carbon budget gets progressively tighter, companies are more likely to exit NZPs unless they change their own absolute and relative decarbonization efforts. Companies for which the exclusion threat is greater face more pressure. Cenedese *et al.* (2023) measure such exposures using the distance in years until the expected exclusion from NZPs takes place and define them as distance-to-exit (DTE). They argue that DTE is a forward-looking measure of carbon transition risk implied by investor preferences, and thus investors should require compensation for bearing such risk.

There are at least three direct channels through which the pricing effect can operate. First, divestment by a significant fraction of investors can reduce risk sharing and thus affect equilibrium prices and returns. Second, the pricing effect can be induced by investors' expectations of future divestment, which could be non-trivial even if one does not observe significant portfolio movements today. Finally, through NZPs, investors can communicate expectations of future divestment to corporates and thus exert pressure on corporates to adjust their efforts to avoid potential penalties. This last communication channel suggests a new insight, namely, NZPs can be modes of both divestment and engagement. Notably, the strength of the three forces depends not only on the individual firm-level efforts but also on the behavior of other companies subject to similar pressures. This competition effect among companies is induced by the presence of an aggregate constraint imposed on the holdings.

Cenedese *et al.* (2023) study the main determinants of DTE using a large panel of global firms with emissions and other firm characteristics, sampled over the 2005–2021 period. They find that DTE is negatively correlated with firm emissions and monthly stock return volatility, consistent with the hypothesis that DTE captures equity risk. DTE is also negatively related to book leverage and dollar trading volume, but the correlations here get weaker for DTE based on the Ambition Score. All DTEs are positively related to firms' measures of property, plant, and equipment and firm age. When it comes to other firm characteristics, the results are more mixed. For example, DTE based on emissions is negatively related to firms' stock market capitalization and the book value of assets, but the correlation is positive for DTE based on the Ambition Score.

Cenedese *et al.* (2023) study whether DTE is priced by investors in the stock market. They first relate DTE to next month's stock returns. Their empirical specification is based on a pooled cross-sectional regression framework of Bolton and Kacperczyk (2021) and includes a host of firm-level characteristics, as well as country, industry, and time fixed effects. Across all specifications, they find a statistically strong negative association between DTE and stock returns. The results are economically large: A one-standard-deviation increase in DTE for a given cross section of firms is associated with an approximate 2.5–4.6 percentage point reduction in next month's annualized stock returns. They further find that while the predictive power of DTE declines with a longer lag, it remains considerably significant, even for one-year-ahead stock returns. These results support the hypothesis that companies with lower DTE are more risky and investors require higher compensation from them.

They also provide additional evidence using valuation regressions. The benefit of using this approach is that valuation ratios are less noisy than stock returns. Further, they can control for future cash flows, and thus the interpretation of our results is more aligned with the pure discount rate effect. In their tests, they consider three measures of firm value, price-to-earnings, price-to-book, and price-to-sales. They find a strong positive correlation between DTE and almost all measures of values. These results are consistent with the view that companies subject to stronger NZP pressure are priced with lower multiples than those for which the pressure is lesser.

In another test, they examine whether DTE premia also accrue on the extensive margin, that is, whether companies which never exit NZPs are priced differently than those that do exit at any point up to and including 2050. They find a very strong statistical difference in stock returns between the two groups of stocks, for five out of six measures of exit. The results are also economically large. Companies that exit have higher annualized returns by about 2.6–6.2 percentage points. Thus, the pressure from institutional investors matters both at an intensive and extensive margin.

These findings strongly support the risk-based explanation of the cross-sectional variation in stock returns. Given the nature of exit measures, the most natural interpretation is that of transition risk. This interpretation is further supported by a test in which the size of the exit premium is related to a shift in transition risk due to the Paris Agreement. This shock has been previously applied in studies of climate risk. The cross-sectional premium in stock returns roughly doubles when risk premia are measured using either stock returns or price-to-earnings ratios. The results are statistically weaker for exit measures based on the Ambition Score. Another finding that supports the transition risk interpretation is the strong correlation between DTE and other proxies of transition risk, such as emission levels, their growth, and the Ambition Score.

A natural question to ask is to what extent DTE captures the same variation as other climate-related measures. This question is answered with a baseline regression model with additional controls for such measures. As expected, some of the variation in DTE can be explained by the other variables. Nonetheless, the coefficients of DTE retain their sign. Moreover, statistical significance is preserved for our most comprehensive measure based on the Ambition Score. These results paint two important conclusions. First, DTE carries independent stock return variations, especially when we use the most comprehensive metric of decarbonization ambition. Second, the explanatory power of DTE stems from both the signals on which we sort stocks and the carbon budget that moderates the inclusion of stocks into NZPs.

The results are also robust to different specifications. First, they hold when Scope 3 emissions, which are sometimes regarded as more noisy, are excluded. Second, the effect of DTE on stock returns interacts with the firm-level decision to disclose climate data directly, but if anything, the decision to disclose emissions amplifies rather than mitigates the size of the return premium. Third, the results are robust to different choices of decarbonization paths. Here, a number of possibilities are considered: (a) The budget is kept constant for some time and then investors decarbonize their portfolios' footprint at a constant, but faster rate; (b) investors decarbonize their portfolios at a faster (slower) rate for the first half of the remaining period and then at a slower (faster) rate for the second half; or (c) investors follow a more sophisticated science-based decarbonization path. Very similar magnitudes of the return differences can be found among firms across all the paths.

3. Conclusions

This chapter introduces the concept of net-zero investing which has recently gained popularity among institutional investors. NZPs that implement the idea rely on the interaction of two elements: a carbon budget that is informed by scientific projections and an investor discretionary rule of selecting companies into portfolios. An important element of the NZP framework is its flexibility which allows the decision-makers to change their inputs according to their forecasts of climate effects. The chapter shows that NZPs maintain a healthy balance between portfolio diversification, manifested by the inclusion of representative sectors and risks, and the resulting decarbonization of the portfolio. NZPs maintain reasonable tracking errors not exceeding 2%. Finally, the chapter shows how the framework can be applied to construct measures of carbon transition risk implied by investors' preferences. The measure of risk, DTE, is significantly related to cross-sectional variation in stock returns and their valuation ratios. The variation in pricing is consistent with investors' revision of beliefs regarding climate change and is robust across different decarbonization choices.

Overall, I conclude that the NZP framework can be a useful tool in the process of exerting pressure on the corporate sector to decarbonize its activities. I expect that with the increasing pressure to address the climate crisis, more institutional capital will move in a direction consistent with this principle.

References

Bolton, P. & Kacperczyk, M. (2021). Do investors care about carbon risk? *Journal of Financial Economics*, 142, 517–549.

Bolton, P. & Kacperczyk, M. (2023). Global pricing of carbon-transition risk. *The Journal of Finance*, 78, 3677–3754.

Bolton, P., Kacperczyk, M., & Samama, F. (2022). Net-zero carbon portfolio alignment. *Financial Analysts Journal*, 78, 19–33.

Cenedese, G., Han, S., & Kacperczyk, M. (2023). Carbon-transition risk and net-zero portfolios. Working Paper Imperial College London. Retrieved from http://dx.doi.org/10.2139/ssrn.4565220.

Chapter 10

The Determinants of Scope 3 Disclosure among Large Corporations

Antoine Bonelli* and Guillaume Coqueret[†]

*AI Builders, Paris, France

[†]EMLYON Business School, Ecully, France

Abstract

A company's carbon impact extends across its entire value chain, both upstream and downstream. This is referred to as "Scope 3," and it is essential to address climate change and provide true estimates of corporations' carbon performance. However, the evaluation of Scope 3 emissions is a major challenge, because its calculation is poorly standardized and regulated. Publication trends vary widely across the globe and across sectors.

This chapter discusses the evolution of environmental practices over the last ten years across more than 6,000 listed companies based in 4 major regions of the world. In particular, we examine several determinants of Scope 3 disclosure, their links with environmental scores from environmental, social, and governance (ESG) data providers, and the disparities between regions, sizes, sectors, and other company characteristics.

We find that companies communicate strongly on value chain environmental policies both before and after Scope 3 publication. Disparities are very marked between regions of the world, particularly for less glo-balized and lower-capitalized companies. Moreover, companies publishing Scope 3 are generally those that already have a high environmental score and have been publishing Scope 1 data for several years.

1. Introduction

Climate change and the related carbon risks have become a major concern for investors (Bolton & Kacperczyk, 2021). The latter rely more and more on non-financial data to craft their portfolios,[1] especially on greenhouse gas (GHG) emissions, which are the main driver of global warming (Masson-Delmotte *et al.*, 2021). This, along with public opinion influence and regulatory frameworks (e.g. the European CSRD), puts pressure on corporations to communicate more on their social and environmental footprints. As an illustration of this trend, we produce in Figure 1 the number of firms that report sustainability-related data to the Carbon Disclosure Project (CDP).

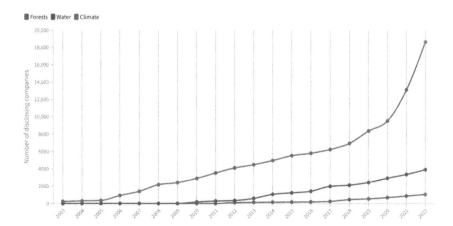

Figure 1.   Trends in willingness to disclose. This figure reports the number of firms that disclose information to the CDP (2003–2022), across three dimensions: climate, water, and forests

Source: https://www.cdp.net/.

---

[1] See Pedersen *et al.* (2021) and Coqueret (2022), for example.

Now, when it comes to GHG emissions, there are some subtleties because a firm's impact goes beyond its core activity and extends to the whole value chain. It is customary to split emissions into three groups, also called "*scopes*." The first one pertains to direct emissions and the second one to emissions that are generated by the energy consumption of the company. Lastly, the third scope encompasses emissions that are linked to suppliers and customers, i.e. along the whole value chain of the product or service that is sold. Now, the issue is that Scope 3 emissions are both the most important ones in volume (see, e.g. Anquetin *et al.*, 2022) and the hardest to accurately evaluate. They are therefore the most crucial value needed to tackle climate change and the most difficult to report, either because firms are not willing to disclose or because they are willing, but face technical hurdles in the calculations.

This is a serious issue, because accurate disclosure is key to transparency. In addition, several studies have shown the benefits of mandatory reporting on firm value and financial markets as a whole (Ioannou & Serafeim, 2017; Krueger *et al.*, 2023). In particular, disclosure is likely to favor the best-in-class (most durable) corporations (Grewal *et al.*, 2019). These are topics that we cover and review in the following.

This chapter is split into three parts. In Section 2, we briefly survey the literature on non-financial disclosure. In Section 3, we present the salient features of the data that we analyze throughout the chapter. Lastly, in Section 4, we document the drivers of Scope 3 reporting.

2. Related Literature

Non-financial reporting is a surprisingly old practice. While it may be difficult to trace back its exact origins, it is possible to claim that the creation of the Global Reporting Initiative (GRI) in 1997 represents a cornerstone. Its promises and challenges were, for instance, summarized quite early by Willis (2003). More generally, the pitfalls (vagueness and greenwashing) and opportunities (management engagement) of sustainability accounting were listed long ago by Schaltegger and Burritt (2010).

From a historical standpoint, since the 1990s, the GRI has been successful in inspiring corporations to disclose more information about their social and environmental footprint (Brown *et al.*, 2009). Since then, many other initiatives have blossomed (the CDP, Taskforce on climate-related financial disclosures (TCFD), Taskforce on Nature-related Financial Disclosures (TNFD), etc.). Similar to accounting and financial frameworks like the IFRS, the International Sustainability Standards Board (ISSB) seeks to propose uniform canvasses for environmental, social, and governance (ESG) reporting. The accumulation of data since 2010 has led to an increase of research papers on the matter. In particular, Roca and Searcy (2012) list the types of indicators that were disclosed at the beginning of the 2010 decade, long before reporting standards became compulsory in Europe.

The most frequently documented question pertains to the impact of disclosure on firm performance. For instance, Wang *et al.* (2020) find a positive association between disclosure and return on equity in the Chinese listed market. In Pakistan and in the pharmaceutical sector, Malik and Kanwal (2018) reach similar conclusions. Gholami *et al.* (2022b) also report that ESG reporting is positively linked to profitability, but there are strong sector discrepancies. In contrast, Qiu *et al.* (2016) conclude that prior good profitability drives higher sustainable disclosure. The conditionality of the link between disclosure and financial performance also holds for large vs. small firms (Gholami *et al.*, 2022a).

Disclosure is also linked to other financial attributes and behaviors. For instance, De Villiers *et al.* (2023) (respectively, Loh and Tan, 2020) document a positive relation between unexpected disclosure dividend payout (i.e. brand value) and using GRI data.[2] Negative associations are found with risk taking (measured as variability of annual Return On Assets (ROA)) in Menla Ali *et al.* (2023) and with idiosyncratic volatility (Perera *et al.*, 2023). Boulton (2023) and Chen *et al.* (2023) also document the risk of Initial Public Offering (IPO) underpricing linked to disclosure.

Is there a positive environmental effect to disclosure? The evidence is mixed. On the one hand, Kim *et al.* (2022) find that disclosing firms were virtuous after the climate change rule was enacted by the Securities and Exchange Commission (SEC) in 2010. They engaged in more pro-environmental policies. Similarly, in their study on the UK carbon disclosure mandate, Downar *et al.* (2021) document a decrease in emissions of 8%, compared to a control group of other European firms. Tomar (2023) comes to similar conclusions: Disclosure implies benchmarking which, in turn, spurs emissions reduction.

On the other hand, Shi *et al.* (2023) find that disclosure does not improve corporation behavior. The effect is not obvious though: Firms

---

[2]Axjonow *et al.* (2018) find limited effect on firm reputation, however.

that disclose tend to reduce their Scope 1 emissions, but compensate negatively by increasing their Scope 3 emissions. From a theoretical standpoint, Lu *et al.* (2023) propose a model in which firms invest in both polluting and non-polluting projects and the former are associated with negative externalities (social costs). Surprisingly, there are situations in which imposing disclosure leads to lower social welfare. At the macro level, Jackson *et al.* (2020) find that firms in countries in which non-financial reporting is mandatory engage in more CSR activities, which is beneficial to society.

Finally, a sizable chunk of the literature — to which the present chapter contributes — seeks to determine the drivers and characteristics of corporate disclosures. This topic is reviewed in Dienes *et al.* (2016) and Ali *et al.* (2017).

Non-financial reporting is positively linked to facets of governance as discovered through the studies of Peters and Romi (2014) (existence of a Chief Sustainability Officer), Tauringana and Chithambo (2015) (board size, director ownership, and ownership concentration), Gao *et al.* (2016) and Liao *et al.* (2015) (percentage of female directors on the board), and Eugster *et al.* (2023) (managerial extraversion). There are also various ways to report extra-financial information and Banerjee *et al.* (2023) compare disclosure via dedicated corporate sustainability reports or via frameworks such as the CDP.

There are three additional drivers of disclosure:

- **Industry:** Young and Marais (2012) find that firms in high-risk industries (energy, transportation, construction, mining, and industrials) report more than those in low-risk ones (healthcare, finance, retail, telecom, and entertainment). Moreover, Chithambo and Tauringana (2014) also conclude that industrial corporations are associated with a higher propensity to disclose, and so are companies in consumer services.
- **Firm size:** Large corporations have more resources to devote to reporting. Most contributions corroborate this intuition, e.g. Chithambo and Tauringana (2014), Drempetic *et al.* (2020), and Dobrick *et al.* (2023). However, Khan *et al.* (2020) report non-significant results both for firm size and hazardous industries (but the geographical scope of the study is limited to Pakistan).
- **Regulation:** It is external to companies, which makes disclosure much less *voluntary*. Indeed, in Europe in particular, the Non-Financial

Reporting Directive (NFRD) first and the Corporate Sustainability Reporting Directive (CSRD) subsequently progressively forced large and medium-sized entities to report on extra-financial matters, including their environmental footprint. This typically explains discrepancies between countries (e.g. France and Australia, as in Young and Marais, 2012). We refer to Tauringana and Chithambo (2015) (with a focus on the UK) and Cicchiello *et al.* (2023) for more details on the matter.

We also want to mention the work of Friedman *et al.* (2021). They propose a theoretical model on ESG reporting to investors. One of the intuitive predictions of the model is that the financial materiality of the report is positively linked to the magnitude of price reaction.

Lastly, closest to our contribution is the early seminal work of Hackston and Milne (1996) and Gray *et al.* (2001), and, more recently, of Christensen *et al.* (2021), though purely from a review standpoint,[3] and that of Delmas *et al.* (2022), which analyzes data from the World Economic Forum.

3. Data and Key Statistics

3.1. *Dataset Description*

We use several sources to collect the data. For company-level data, we resort to Refinitiv Eikon (Thomson Reuters) for accounting and financial information, CO_2 emissions, general information (sector, country, etc.), all variables pertaining to environmental policies and practices, and ESG scores. For country-level data, the information is retrieved from the public websites of the World Bank and the Organisation for Economic Co-operation and Development (OECD). Finally, we use data from the Science Based Target Initiative (SBTi) datasets, which are available as open data. The dataset we obtained from Refinitiv encompasses 6,610 companies and covers a 10-year period, from 2012 to 2021. It contains companies with a market capitalization ranging from $500 million to $2000 billion, spread across 11 sectors, 22 industrial groups, and 76 different industries (according to the GICS classification). It covers 31 countries in four different regions (North America: NA, Asia: AS, Europe: EU, and Oceania: OC).

---

[3]We also point to the purely topic-driven literature review of Tsang *et al.* (2022).

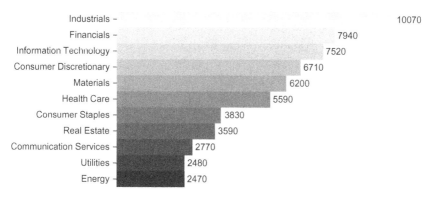

Figure 2. Firm-year observations per GICS sector in the dataset

The distribution of companies across sectors, capitalizations, and countries is unbalanced. For example, there are 10,070 company-year observations in the Industrials sector and 2,470 in the Energy sector, or 20,900 in the USA vs. 310 in the Philippines. The distribution of environmental ratings (from D− to A+) is broadly homogeneous, except at the two extremes, with an overrepresentation of D− ratings (6,900 company-years) and an underrepresentation of A+ ratings (880 company-years). In future analyses, depending on the samples selected, we will remove the most underrepresented sectors and countries (<30 unique companies). We provide in Figure 2 the breakdown of companies by sector, according to the GICS standard classification system.

3.2. *Key Statistics and Trends*

In this section, we carry out an exploratory analysis of the dataset in order to present macro trends: distributions of key environmental variables, temporal trends in company practices, sectoral and local differences, etc. The analysis was carried out on variables mainly related to general accounting information, environmental practices, ESG scores, and CO_2e emissions.

Environmental reporting practices have evolved over the last ten years, across all the regions studied (companies with a market capitalization of over $500 million in Asia, Oceania, North America, and Europe). However, these trends are highly heterogeneous. In this section, we therefore analyze some of these trends and their variations, in an attempt to

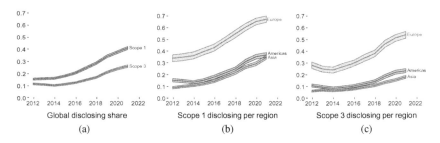

Figure 3.   Disclosing share, global and per region

understand the overall state of corporate environmental practices and to compare the dataset with the literature.

3.2.1. *Disclosure trends per market capitalization and region*

The total proportion of companies reporting Scopes 1, 2, and 3 has increased significantly over the last ten years, as is shown in Figure 3. Overall, in the regions studied, the percentage of companies publishing Scope 1 has risen from around 15% in 2012 to over 40% (a 166% relative increase). Scope 3 reporting has also risen sharply, albeit at a slower pace, from around 12% to over 25% (116% increase). There are, however, major disparities between regions, and trends in the publication of emissions data differ greatly between company types, regions, and emissions scopes. Overall, the total share of companies reporting Scope 1 (direct emissions) was 35% in Europe for 2012, compared with 15% for North America and 10% for Asia. These three regions have seen a sharp increase in the number of companies reporting emissions, reaching 70% in Europe, 40% in North America, and 35% in Asia by 2021. Overall, therefore, European companies publish significantly more Scope 1 than other regions, and the trends are very similar between Asia and North America.

Nevertheless, if we discriminate by size between very large companies (>$50 billion market capitalization) and companies <$50 billion, the trends are different, as is shown in Figure 4.

Regional trends for companies <$50 billion remain similar to overall trends. However, the trend by region for companies >$50 billion exhibits other patterns. In North America and Europe, Scope 1 publication trends are very similar. 90% of companies in Europe and 85% in North America

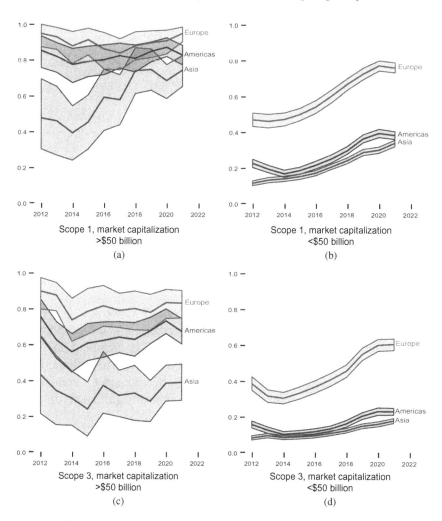

Figure 4. Scopes 1 and 3 disclosing share, depending on firm size

published Scope 1 in 2012, and this share has changed very little since then. In Asia, however, this figure has risen significantly, from 45% in 2012 to 75% in 2021. It can therefore be seen that, although the overall proportion of companies reporting Scope 1 is roughly the same in Asia and North America, and the trend is the same, very large companies were already reporting Scope 1 for the most part in Europe and North America in 2012, while very large companies in Asia were significantly less likely to do so.

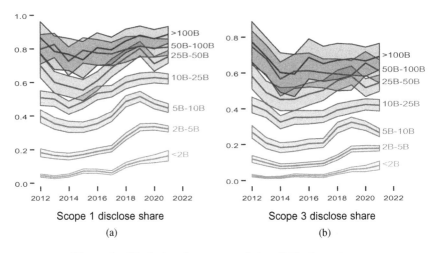

Figure 5.   Disclosing share, per market capitalization category

Similar trends can be observed in Scope 3 reporting. However, among large companies (>$50 billion of market cap), the proportions have changed very little between 2012 and 2021, including in Asia. Finally, Europe remains the clear leader in Scope 3 reporting (three times higher than in Asia and North America), both overall and for companies <$50 billion. European companies therefore publish significantly in both Scopes 1 and 3, particularly for smaller companies.

The proportion of companies communicating on the emissions reduction policy and a quantified target has also risen considerably overall in the last ten years. In 2012, only 20% of companies communicated an emissions policy, compared with over 60% in 2021. As for targets, around 7% of companies announced that they had set one in 2012, compared with over 35% in 2021. In line with trends in the publication of emissions data, companies in Europe and Oceania are much more likely to set targets than those in North America and Asia (60%, 62%, 33%, and 28%, respectively, in 2021). The size factor (measured here via average market capitalization in the year under review) plays a particularly important role. When we look at the share of companies publishing Scopes 1 and 3 by size (in Figure 5, broken down into 7 categories: <$2 billion, $2 billion to $5 billion, $5 billion to $10 billion, $10 billion to $25 billion, $25 billion to $50 billion, $50 billion to $100 billion, and >$100 billion), we see that the figures evolve in a strictly increasing manner with category/size. There are thus very significant gaps between the smallest companies in the dataset (>$2 billion), of which 16% published Scope 1 in 2021, and the very largest companies (>$100 billion), of which over 85% published it.

3.2.2. *Disclosing variations per country*

When looking at trends by country, we also document major differences, even within regions, as is shown in Figure 6. The high figures for Europe are explained in particular by current legislation requiring Scopes 1 and 2 to be published in a growing number of countries and for a certain number of sectors (in France, the UK, and Spain). This is also the case in Japan for large companies. There have been several other interesting developments.

First, the proportion of companies reporting Scope 1 based in Hong Kong, Singapore, and Malaysia has skyrocketed over the past 10 years, from 10–15% in 2012 to 60–75% in 2021, a proportion similar to many European countries (although these countries reported significantly more

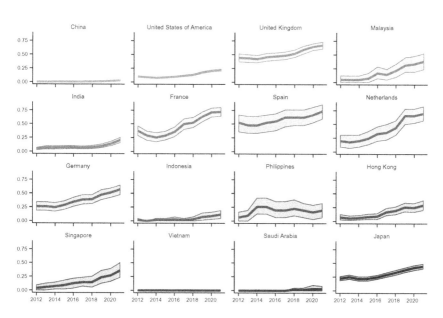

Figure 6. Trends in willingness to disclose Scope 3 per country, 2012–2022

in 2012) and higher than in the USA. Shares for companies based in India, Indonesia, Russia, or EMU also have risen from below 15% to over 30–45%, an increase analogous to the USA.

However, Scope 1 data from corporations based in China, Ireland, and Saudi Arabia is still scarce in 2021 (19%, 21%, and 16%, respectively). Overall, the trend in Scope 1 publication is in line with that of Scope 3. There are few outliers, with some countries having a higher share of Scope 3 publication than of Scope 1, for example. In almost all countries, Scope 3 publication remains significantly below that of Scope 1. In China, Saudi Arabia, and Vietnam, Scope 3 publication was still below 5% in 2021.

Plainly, the companies reporting the most on Scope 3 are all based in Europe — in Spain, the Netherlands, France, the UK, Germany, Denmark, Italy, and Sweden — with shares ranging from 57% to 74%. Finally, we note that 47% of Australian-based companies published Scope 3 data by 2021, a figure significantly higher than the USA (22%) and close to the European average (53%). Canadian companies are also more concerned by Scope 3 publication (39%) than their US counterparts.

Overall, median scores by country have changed little over the last ten years, as is shown in Figure 7. Many countries with a median

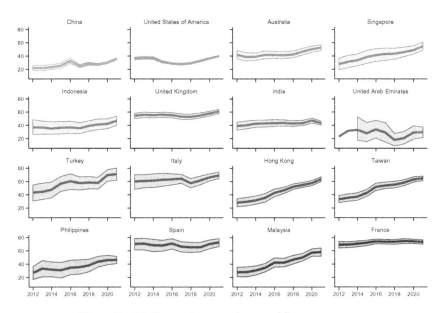

Figure 7.   Median environmental score of firms, per country

environmental score above 60 in 2021 already had a similar score in 2012. This is particularly true of European countries, such as Italy, France, the UK, and Germany. However, there are some countries where the score has risen significantly. These are, by and large, the same countries that have seen a sharp increase in the proportion of companies reporting Scope 1, mainly in Asia — the Philippines, Hong Kong, Singapore, Taiwan, and Indonesia. All these countries have gone from a median score below 20–30 in 2012 to a score above 50–60 in 2021 (100–200% increase).

This trend does not apply to Asia as a whole. In 2012, for example, Japanese companies already had a higher score. Conversely, the median score in China has also risen, from 17 to 34, an increase of exactly 100%, but remains significantly below (30–60%) the other countries mentioned. We also note that very few Vietnamese companies are rated, even though they are well represented in the dataset. Finally, we note that the only country to have seen a decrease in its median score is Saudi Arabia, with the score dropping from 20 in 2012 to 9 in 2021. It is also the country with the lowest score.

Figure 8 shows that the proportion of companies communicating an emissions reduction policy and the proportion communicating a

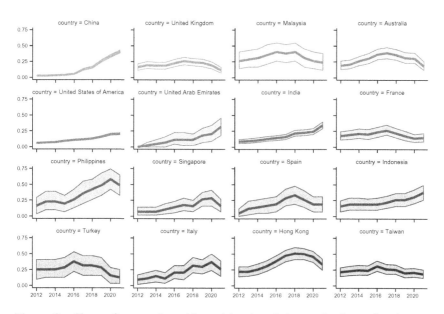

Figure 8. Share of companies with a claimed emissions reduction policy but no quantified targets announced

quantified target are moving in tandem. However, there is also a wide gap between these two metrics. Many companies communicate emissions reduction policies without communicating targets. Although some companies may undertake real reduction actions without having set targets, this type of action can be qualified as a form (among others) of "carbonwashing," where the commitment it represents can be qualified as symbolic and not very concrete.

We therefore propose to also study the proportion of companies with an emissions reduction policy but no targets, defined as having very different "behaviors" in the evolution over the period studied at country level. Many countries experienced a "peak," where the proportion of companies with this gap increased significantly, reaching a maximum before declining sharply. Other countries, on the other hand, have been increasing sharply for several years, and their peak, to date, is in the last year studied, i.e. 2021. One possible interpretation is that, when the trend to deal with emissions accelerates in a country, companies first make a purely symbolic commitment, via an announced policy, before quantifying and announcing targets (which may still be purely symbolic). In this case, we can see that not all countries are in the same phase.

We roughly observe four different phases into which countries could be classified:

(1) No transition underway: low proportion of companies announcing emissions policies.
(2) A first phase: a high proportion of companies announcing a policy but a low proportion announcing a target.
(3) A second phase: a high proportion of companies with both a policy and a target.
(4) A third phase: a high proportion of companies with a policy, a target, and initial results in terms of emissions reductions.

3.2.3. *Sector biases*

The dynamics of Scopes 1 and 3 reporting is similar across sectors, as is shown in Figure 9. There has been similar growth in the proportion of companies reporting Scope 1 across all sectors, although this varies considerably from one sector to another, ranging from 30% for Real Estate to over 60% for Utilities. A similar trend and distribution can be observed for

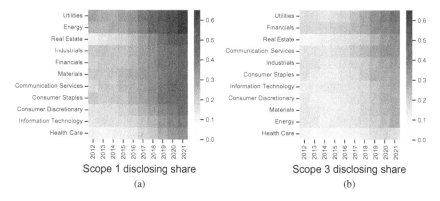

Figure 9. Disclosing share, per sector

Scope 3. On the whole, the same sectors that publish the least Scope 3 also publish the least Scope 1.

The sectors with the highest carbon dependency are also generally those with the best environmental performance, as calculated by Refinitiv (Energy, Utilities, Materials, and Industrials). Most median scores have changed little since 2012, as in shown in Figure 10. However, there have been some interesting dynamics. For example, the Real Estate sector almost doubled its median score between 2012 and 2021 (from 32 to 56). The Financials and Health Care sectors experienced a sharp drop in score between 2015 and 2018, before recovering almost to their 2012 levels. The worst-performing sectors are those with a high dependence on Scope 3: IT, Financials, Communication Services, and Health Care.

Overall, it is still the largest companies that have the most ambitious targets: The median is 40% reduction in GHG emissions for companies >$100 billion, compared with 25% for those <$2 billion. Within sectors, however, it is not necessarily the best-performing sectors in terms of environmental score that have the most ambitious targets. In fact, as represented in Figure 11, the Energy and Materials sectors (two of the sectors with the highest median environmental score) have the least ambitious targets (with medians of 25% and 26%, respectively). Conversely, the Communication Services sector, one of the worst in terms of environmental score, has a median reduction target of 45%. Overall, the sectors have an average reduction target of 30% (when set and communicated).

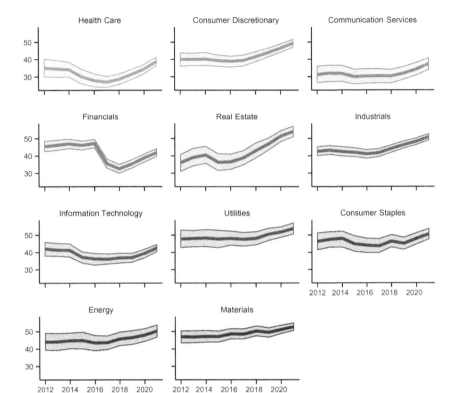

Figure 10.   Median environmental score of firms, per sector

3.3. *Scope 3 Accuracy and Reported Data*

The emissions data used to measure carbon performance and construct decarbonizing portfolios are mainly derived from Scopes 1 and 2, i.e. emissions linked to companies' direct activities. When considering direct emissions only, the primary sector (metals, minerals, and fossil fuels) is penalized in comparison to the secondary sector (industry), which is in turn penalized in contrast to the tertiary sector (services). This is due to the fact that, for many activities, a large proportion of direct emissions come from the extraction and transformation of resources, as well as the production and consumption of electricity. A significant proportion of emissions also occur when products are used by the consumer: electricity to run appliances, oil combustion to run transport, etc. However, these

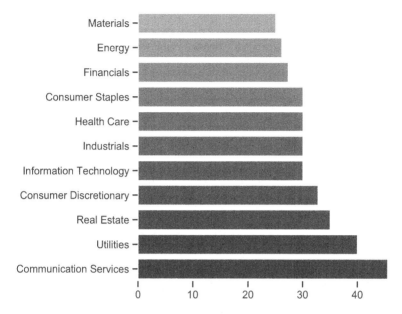

Figure 11. Median CO$_2$e reduction target between 2012 and 2021

primary activities are essential and provide the materials for the industrial sector. Similarly, the tertiary sector is heavily dependent on the primary and secondary sectors. This is why Scope 3 (indirect emissions upstream and downstream of a company's activities) is becoming increasingly important and is taken into account to measure a company's real dependence on emissions, as well as its real impact on the environment. Coeslier *et al.* (2016) show that taking Scope 3 into account is essential to address climate change.

The number of companies publishing Scope 3 emissions has risen sharply over the past ten years. However, the calculation of these emissions by companies is highly heterogeneous, relying mainly on internal methodologies and choices, which are rarely published (In and Schumacher, 2021). Although there are standards and guides for calculating Scope 3 (such as the GHG Protocol), many companies calculate only part of the 13 categories of Scope 3 (6 upstream + 7 downstream), and the figures, including intensity, vary widely from one company to another, as well as from one data provider to another (Anquetin *et al.*, 2022), due to very significant methodological differences. Blanco *et al.* (2016) conclude that many companies in all sectors significantly underestimate Scope 3,

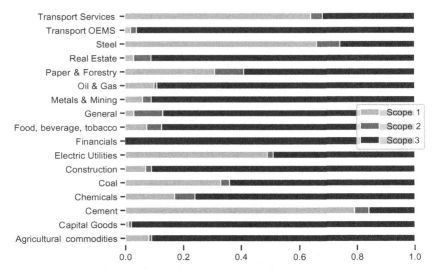

Figure 12. Typical relative share of scope in total carbon emissions per sector, provided by the CDP in April 2022

sometimes by a factor of 10 to 100. The growing need to integrate Scope 3 into the assessment of a company's environmental impact, as well as its actual carbon dependency, is therefore today constrained by strong issues of data quality and heterogeneity, in the publication of data, in the methodology for calculating emissions, and in the figures themselves. In a technical note published in April 2022, the CDP issued the results of a review of scientific literature on the importance of Scope 3 within high-impact sectors, as well as estimates of the total share represented by Scope 3 in a given sector. The big picture of this work is reproduced in Figure 12, where the total emissions of sectors are split into the three scopes.

When comparing the Scope 3 reported by ESG data providers (Refinitiv Eikon here) with the theoretical Scope 3 of the sector to which the company belongs (as reported by the CDP), we observe striking discrepancies. To do this, we calculate a theoretical (sector-based) Scope 3 from the industry proportions published by the CDP and from the Scopes 1 and 2 reported by the companies. For simplicity, we make two assumptions:

(1) The CDP's estimates of the proportions of each Scope are correct in terms of orders of magnitude.
(2) The Scopes 1 and 2 data published by companies and supplied by Refinitiv are accurate.

We therefore use the following formula to estimate a company's Scope 3 from its industry's aggregate values:

$$\hat{S}_{3,i} = \frac{\alpha_{3,s}}{\alpha_{1,s} + \alpha_{2,s}} \times (S_{1,i} + S_{2,i}), \tag{1}$$

where

- α_1, α_2, and α_3 are coefficients representing the proportion of Scopes 1, 2, and 3, respectively, for company i's industry, provided by the CDP;
- S_1, S_2, and S_3 are Scopes 1, 2, and 3, respectively, where Scopes 1 and 2 are supplied by a company i and Scope 3 is estimated.

Given that we know Scopes 1 and 2 and the respective proportions of Scopes 1, 2, and 3 in a given sector, we can infer the sector-based Scope 3, as if the sector was representative of the firm and vice versa. There are, of course, many reasons why this estimate is not valid at the company level. For example, a company relocating part of its emissions from Scope 1 to Scope 3 will see its Scope 1 emissions drop, which will also lower the estimate for Scope 3, while the real value increases (all other things being equal). Nevertheless, we can draw a number of conclusions from indicators that aggregate sufficient data, particularly with regard to trends over time.

We can then calculate the resulting error, i.e. the difference between the Scope 3 published by a company and the value inferred from the standards of its industry:

$$r_i = S_{3,i} - \hat{S}_{3,i}, \tag{2}$$

where S_3 represents the Scope 3 as published by the company and supplied by Refinitiv, and $\hat{S}_3$ represents the Scope 3 estimated by formula from Equation (1). We also calculate the *relative* difference between the published Scope 3 and the estimated Scope 3 using the following formula:

$$\Delta S_{3,i} = \frac{(S_{3,i} - \hat{S}_{3,i})}{\hat{S}_{3,i}}. \tag{3}$$

The result gives the proportion of "missing" or "surplus" emissions in the company's published emissions compared with the expected

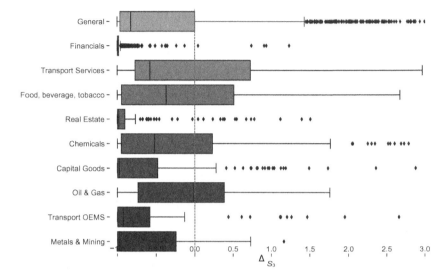

Figure 13.   Distribution (box plot) of ΔS_3 per sector. The rectangles mark the IQR and the outliers are shown after 1.5 times the IQR beyond the upper quartile

sector-based emissions. We plot in Figure 13 the distributions of ΔS_3 by sector, across all years. All sector medians are below 0. An interesting point concerns the width of the interquartile range (IQR). These boxes are very narrow for the Financials and Real Estate sectors, and are also very close to -1 and below -0.9. This indicates that for these two sectors, a majority of corporations publish Scope 3 figures that are 10 times lower than the sector-based Scope 3. Conversely, the Transport Services, Food, Beverage, & Tobacco, Chemicals, and Oil & Gas sectors have much wider IQR. Oil & Gas is the only sector where the median is close to 0. Finally, 4 out of 10 sectors have IQRs that encompass zero. Overall, with the exception of Oil & Gas and Food, Beverage, & Tobacco, the medians are below -0.5.

We then analyze the evolution of ΔS by company size. To do this, we categorize firms into 5 sizes according to average market capitalization for each year: <$5 billion, $5 to $10 billion, $10 to $25 billion, $25 to $50 billion, and >$50 billion. We compute the difference in total sums per size category, expressed as follows:

$$\frac{I(C) - \hat{I}(C)}{\hat{I}(C)}, \tag{4}$$

where

- I is the sum of all Scope 3 disclosed emissions for a market capitalization category C, using Refinitiv data.
- $\hat{I}$ is the sum of all Scope 3 estimated emissions for a market capitalization category C, using CDP proportions and Scopes 1, 2 published by Refinitiv.

We observe that for the highest categories, the differences have changed significantly between 2012 and 2021, as is shown in Figure 14. In particular, these differences changed relatively little between 2012 and 2017, then, in the space of a year, narrowed considerably: from −50% in 2017 to −8% in 2018 for companies >$50 billion in capitalization, and from −53% in 2018 to −6% in 2019 for companies between $25 billion and $50 billion in capitalization. The differences are then in the same order of magnitude over the period 2019, 2020, and 2021 for both categories (+5% to +12%). For more moderate-sized companies, the differences are still around 50% in 2021. It seems important to note that there are at least two biases in the analysis of these results, which we have observed

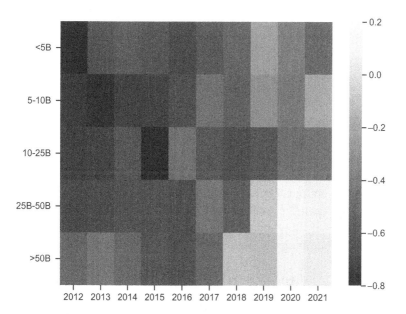

Figure 14. Evolution of relative differences (Equation 4) between estimated and published Scope 3 on total emissions of a market capitalization category

by looking at the distribution of observations by sector and size. Firstly, we observe that for the year 2021, we find a much higher share of the Capital Goods sector in the \$5–10 billion category than in the <\$5 billion and \$10–25 billion categories, a sector which has a lower average spread than the other sectors, potentially explaining the difference. Secondly, we find a very marked underrepresentation of the Real Estate sector in the very large companies (>\$50 billion), a sector in which we observe one of the highest average deltas, which may partially explain the difference between the >\$50 billion category and the other categories. The impact of these two biases seems limited, however, due to the significantly higher share of companies in the "General" and "Financials" sectors, which are present in all company size categories and in relatively homogeneous proportions (35–40% for General, 25–35% for Financials), whose differences are also very high.

In order to further analyze ΔS, we want to reduce the asymmetry of the distribution, which is strongly skewed. For this purpose, we use the Yeo–Johnson transform that Yeo and Johnson (2000) defined as follows:

$$\psi(\lambda, \Delta S3) = \begin{cases} \dfrac{(\Delta S_3 + 1)^{\lambda} - 1}{\lambda}, & \text{for } \Delta S_3 \geq 0, \lambda \neq 0 \\[2mm] \log(\Delta S_3 + 1), & \text{for } \Delta S_3 \geq 0, \lambda = 0 \\[2mm] -\dfrac{(-\Delta S_3 + 1)^{(2-\lambda)} - 1}{2 - \lambda}, & \text{for } \Delta S_3 < 0, \lambda \neq 2 \\[2mm] -\log(-\Delta S_3 + 1), & \text{for } \Delta S_3 < 0, \lambda = 2 \end{cases} \tag{5}$$

where λ is determined using Maximum Likelihood Estimation (MLE). This transform reduces skewness in the distribution, while retaining the sign of the original values. In particular, this is a generalization of the Box–Cox transform (Box and Cox, 1964) and equivalent to it for any $\Delta S_3 > -1$.

We therefore transform ΔS_3 after estimating λ. The lambda estimated for the global panel transformation of ΔS_3 is positive, different from 0 and 2 ($\lambda \approx -0.1587$), and the Yeo–Johnson transform for this case thus becomes the following:

$$\psi(\lambda, \Delta S3) = \begin{cases} \dfrac{(\Delta S_3 + 1)^{\lambda} - 1}{\lambda}, & \Delta S_3 \geq 0, \lambda \approx -0.1587 \\[2mm] -\dfrac{(-\Delta S_3 + 1)^{(2-\lambda)} - 1}{2 - \lambda}, & \Delta S_3 < 0, \lambda \approx -0.1587 \end{cases} \tag{6}$$

We then look at the annual evolution of the overall distributions (all sectors combined in Figure 15) of ψ. A similar trend to the one described previously can be observed: The median drops considerably between 2012 and 2021, as do the values of the first and third quartiles. We note that the decline is most visible from 2016/2017, indicating a potential change in overall behavior from this period. Part of the explanation could be, for example, due to the acceleration of policies on the subject following the COP21 (Paris Agreement) and the increase in media coverage on CO_2 emissions and climate change.

Our final analysis pertains to trends at the country level. We retain the 15 countries with the highest number of observations, where the minimum is 107 (the Netherlands). Clearly, we find that the evolution of ΔS again varies much from one zone to another. Countries such as South Korea, Taiwan, Switzerland, Spain, Australia, and the Netherlands have not seen a significant drop in their average gap between 2012 and 2021, while other countries such as Japan, France, and the USA have.

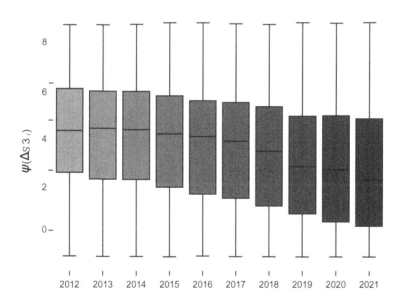

Figure 15. Global evolution of the distribution (box plot) of scaled ΔS. The rectangles mark the IQR and the outliers are shown after 1.5 times the IQR beyond the upper quartile

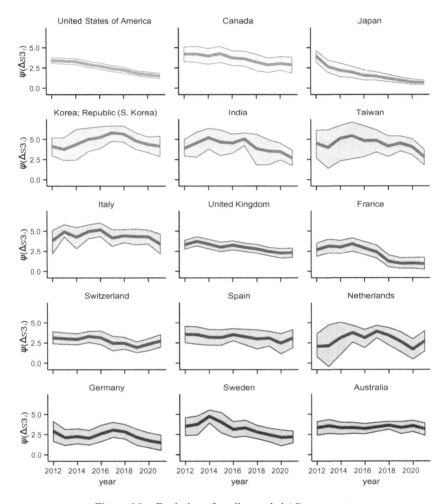

Figure 16.   Evolution of median-scaled ΔS per country

4. Determinants of Disclosure

4.1. *Variables*

This section studies the link between several company characteristics, including some of their environmental practices, and their propensity to publish Scope 3 data in their CSR reports. More precisely, we take a look at the relationship between Scope 3 disclosure and the following:

- The company's earnings (measured here with EBITDA);
- The number of years since Scope 1 has been published;

- The presence of environmental policies on activities directly linked to Scope 3 (supply chain for upstream Scope 3, minimizing the carbon impact of products for downstream Scope 3) during the previous year;
- The presence and quantity of environmental financial investments made during the previous year.

We retain a set of observations (company-years), keeping only observations from the initial dataset where all values are non-missing. We also remove CDP sectors where Scope 1 represents more than 70% of emissions (mainly primary sectors), being interested only in sectors where Scope 3 represents a significant share. Finally, we omitted the financial sector, which is not involved in manufacturing products or controlling its upstream supply chain (raw material purchases, etc.), and for which over 99% of emissions come from investments (CDP, 2023). To analyze this sector, other factors seem worth considering. We obtain a final sample of 10,388 company-years, with an underrepresentation of companies with a capitalization of less than $2 billion (although this does not significantly affect the distribution of environmental scores). We also note that the CDP Coal, Paper & Forestry, and Agricultural Commodities sectors have few observations (between 60 and 97). All indicators which we use as dependent variables are listed and described in Table 1.

Table 1. Variable description

Variable	Description	Type
Log (Market Cap)	Mean market capitalization in year t	Real
CSR Committee	Presence or absence of a CSR committee within the governance structure in year t	Boolean
Board Female	Percentage of women in corporate governance at year t	Percentage
Years S1	Number of years since Scope 1 > 0	Integer
Ebitda lag	Ebitda for year $t-1$	Percentage
Δ Revenue lag	Revenue evolution in year $t-1$	Percentage
Env. Supply lag	Presence of a supply chain environmental management policy in year $t-1$	Boolean
Log(Invest) Lag	Environmental investments made in year $t-1$	Real
Take-Back lag	Presence of a product take-back policy in year $t-1$	Boolean
Product min. lag	Presence of a policy to minimize the environmental impact of products in year $t-1$	Boolean

Table 2.   Descriptive statistics

Variable (num)	Count	Mean	Std.	Min	25%	50%	75%	Max
Log (Market Cap)	10,388	22.91	1.17	18.69	22.08	22.74	23.62	28.52
Log (Invest)	10,388	4.01	7.35	0.00	0.00	0.00	0.00	22.80
Years Scope 1	10,388	2.94	3.22	0.00	0.00	2.00	5.00	10.00
Delta Revenue	10,388	0.07	0.22	−0.58	−0.03	0.05	0.14	2.98
Ebitda	10,388	0.22	0.16	−0.49	0.11	0.18	0.30	0.75
Board Female	10,388	19.51	13.59	0.00	10.00	20.00	28.57	75.00

Variable (bool)	Count	False	True	% False	% True
Disclose Scope 3	10,388	5,947	4,441	57	43
CSR Committee	10,388	3,576	6,812	34	66
Take-back products	10,388	8,832	1,556	85	15
Product minimization	10,388	7,543	2,845	73	27
Env. Supp. chain monit.	10,388	6,181	4,207	60	40

Moreover, compared to the original global dataset presented earlier, we retain a set of observations (company-years), keeping only observations where all values are non-missing. We also remove CDP sectors where Scope 1 represents more than 70% of emissions, as we are only interested in sectors where Scope 3 represents a significant share. We end with a final sample of 10,388 company-years, with an underrepresentation of companies with a capitalization of less than $2 billion (although this does not significantly affect the distribution of environmental scores). When we look at the descriptive statistics for the whole sample (see Table 2), we can see that the dependent variable is well balanced (57% False, 43% True). We also note that almost two-thirds of observations also include a CSR committee. Finally, we note that most observations do not include any environmental investments (zero third quartile in the table).

4.2. *Model and Results*

The model we put forward is aimed at predicting the probability that a company will publish Scope 3 in year *t*. We work with the following logistic model:

$$D_{i,t} = \beta_1 Y_{i,t} + \beta_2 EP_{i,t-1} + \beta_3 CFP_{i,t-1} + \beta_4 CT_{i,t} + \gamma_f + \tau_t + \varepsilon_{i,t}, \qquad (7)$$

where

- $D_{i,t}$ is the dependent variable, equal to 1 if a company i discloses Scope 3 figures at year t.
- $Y_{i,t}$ is the number of years since a company i discloses Scope 1 figures.
- $EP_{i,t-1}$ is a vector composed of different environmental practices as described in the previous section, such as "Product Minimization," "Take-Back Products," "Environmental Supply Chain Monitoring," and the log of total environmental investments. All variables are lagged at $t-1$.
- $CFP_{i,t-1}$ is a vector composed of financial variables *Ebitda*, $\Delta Revenue$. All variables are lagged at $t-1$.
- $CT_{i,t}$ is a vector composed of control variables: *Log(Market Cap)*, *CSRCommittee*, and *BoardFemale*.
- γ_f represents the fixed effects on entities, via dummy variables. We use two different entity fixed effects, with two models: γ_f represents countries for the model 1 and CDP Sector represents countries for the model 2.
- τ_t represent the fixed effects on years, simulated with dummy variables. Years range from 2012 to 2021 (included).
- $\varepsilon_{i,t}$ is an error term.

Our results are gathered in Table 3. The fitted models have an R^2 of 0.36 (sector fixed effect) and 0.4 (country fixed effect). First of all, we observe that the time since first disclosure ($Y_{i,t}$) does have a positive effect on Scope 3 publication. Indeed, companies overwhelmingly tend to publish Scope 1 first.

The set of variables linked to past financial performance is not associated with statistically significant coefficients. On the contrary, all variables linked to environmental practices have statistical significant coefficients, for both model types. However, the effect size for environmental investments is rather small. There is nevertheless a strong influence of environmental practices (Product Minimization and Environmental Supply Chain Monitoring), indicating that companies tend to first implement sustainable practices (or at least communicate about them) before publishing their indirect CO_2e emissions linked to Scope 3.

Table 3.   Logistic regression output

Sector, Year	Fixed Effects					
Country, Year	X			X		
Variable	Odds Ratio	Z-Value	[2.5%, 97.5%]	Odds Ratio	Z-Value	[2.5%, 97.5%]
Controls						
Log (Market Cap)	1.16***	0.00	[1.10, 1.22]	1.46***	0.00	[1.39, 1.54]
CSR Committee	2.45***	0.00	[2.14, 2.81]	2.34***	0.00	[2.06, 2.66]
Board Female	1.02***	0.00	[1.01, 1.02]	1.02***	0.00	[1.02, 1.03]
Disclosure history						
Years ($Y_{i,t}$)	1.42***	0.00	[1.39, 1.45]	1.39***	0.00	[1.36, 1.42]
Finance (lagged $t-1$)						
Revenue	0.88	0.36	[0.67, 1.16]	1.09	0.51	[0.85, 1.40]
Ebitda	0.84	0.36	[0.57, 1.23]	1.25	0.16	[0.92, 1.72]
Env. Practices (lag $t-1$)						
Log (Invest)	1.02***	0.00	[1.01, 1.03]	0.99***	0.00	[0.98, 0.99]
Take-Back Products	1.35***	0.00	[1.15, 1.60]	1.25**	0.02	[1.04, 1.49]
Product Minimization	1.85***	0.00	[1.60, 2.13]	1.16**	0.04	[1.01, 1.33]
Env. Supp. Chain Monit.	1.61***	0.00	[1.43, 1.81]	1.42***	0.00	[1.26, 1.61]
Adjusted R^2	0.356			0.399		
Model (Method)	Logit (MLE)			Logit (MLE)		
Observations	10392			10392		
Log-Likelihood	−4566			−4878		
Ll-Null	−7093			−8117		
LLR P-Value	0***			0***		

Notes: *Z-value < 0.1; **Z-value < 0.05; ***Z-value < 0.01.

4.3. *Further Insights from Random Forests*

Finally, we also propose to analyze the impact of the different variables via a tree-based model. Tree-based methods have the advantage of being able to discover asymmetrical and nonlinear relationships in the data, unlike generalized linear models (GLM). They can also naturally incorporate categorical variables (such as company sectors and countries). This allows us to study in greater detail the dependence between company characteristics and Scope 3 publication, compare the results with fixed-effect logistic regressions, and propose additional interpretations.

We chose to work with Random Forests (RFs), which are a popular learning algorithm (Januschowski *et al.*, 2022) which has strong interpretability properties (see, e.g. Molnar, 2020). We split our sample (10,392 observations) into two sets, a training set to calibrate the model and a test set to interpret the results. We then train a model with 150 estimators (trees trained in parallel), with several of the following hyperparameters: a maximum depth for the trees of 6 and a sub-sampling proportion of 75% for each tree. We also set a random seed to guarantee reproducibility of our results.

Upon training, we obtain stable metrics, as shown in Table 4: Accuracy, precision, and recall are close both on the training (between 82.77% and 83.22%) and test (between 78.78% and 79.05%) datasets. In order to interpret the results, we resort to two canonical tools: feature importance and Shapley values (Rozemberczki *et al.*, 2022). Feature importance assesses by how much each variable improves the overall fit of the model.

In Figure 17, we show the relative importance of all predictors in explaining Scope 3 reporting, on test set data (20% of data, i.e. 2,079 observations). We see that prior Scope 1 publication is the variable with the greatest influence in the construction of the forest. The presence of a CSR committee, an environmental policy on supply chain management, the percentage of women in corporate governance, and market capitalization also have a significant impact. These results corroborate those presented in Section 4.2, however, policies that seek to minimize the carbon impact of products have less influence in this model.

We then turn to SHAP (SHapley Additive exPlanations) values (Lundberg and Lee, 2017). Shapley values seek to decompose the

Table 4. Random forest classifier metrics

Dataset	Accuracy (%)	Recall (%)	Precision (%)	F1-Score (%)
Train set	82.77	82.76	83.22	82.85
Test set	78.78	78.77	79.05	78.85

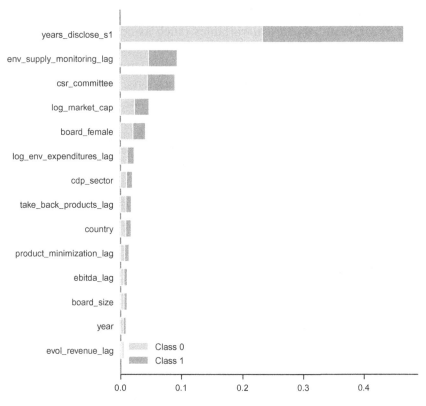

Figure 17. Feature importance. Class 0 (in light gray) refers to the absence of Scope 3 disclosure. Class 1 (in dark gray) pertains to observations with active Scope 3 reporting

importance of each variable for each individual observation in a given sample. In Figure 18, we depict the distribution of these impacts, where each point is an observation in the data (variables are scaled before the analysis is run to allow comparisons). We again conclude to the prominence of the number of years of Scope 1 publication, even though the effect is not always positive. This seems to indicate that companies publish Scope 3 without publishing Scope 1.

In addition, the presence of a CSR committee appears to be strongly correlated: In the fitted model, the presence of a CSR committee systematically increases the probability of publishing Scope 3, and its absence systematically decreases it. However, the impact is weak. The conclusion

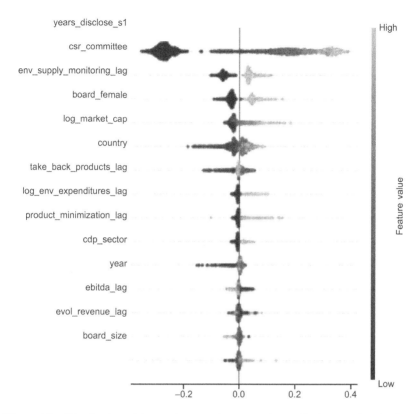

Figure 18. Distribution of feature impacts the propensity to disclose. Each point is an observation in the test set

is analogous for the presence of an environmental policy on supply chain management. Finally, we note an interesting effect on environmental investments: In the results of the fixed-effect logistic regression models, we noted an absence of link. However, here, we observe an asymmetrical relationship: The absence of investments in fact has an impact close to zero on Scope 3 publication, but the higher environmental investments are, the more pronounced the effect on individual observations. This indicates that companies with significant investments are more likely to publish Scope 3, but that many companies with no investments do, or do not, publish Scope The absence of environmental investments has no influence on Scope 3 publication, but a high amount does.

5. Conclusion

In this chapter, we detail the trends in Scope 3 reporting around the world. We provide evidence of extensive heterogeneity, especially across sectors and countries. Nevertheless, the proportion of firms disclosing emission information has steadily increased in the past decade. This tendency should continue in the coming years, especially in areas where regulation will impose non-financial reporting (e.g. in Europe).

We also seek to shed light on the determinants of voluntary Scope 3 disclosure. The main driver seems to be prior extra-financial reporting: Firms that were already reporting on their environmental footprint are more likely to start disclosing data on the emissions across the whole value chain. Other factors, such as CSR committees and gender parity in boards, are also linked to the propensity to disclose. These insights are useful to understand the potential hurdles and incentives linked to corporations' willingness to be transparent about their exhaustive ecological impact.

References

Ali, W., Frynas, J. G., & Mahmood, Z. (2017). Determinants of corporate social responsibility (CSR) disclosure in developed and developing countries: A literature review. *Corporate Social Responsibility and Environmental Management*, 24(4), 273–294.

Anquetin, T., Coqueret, G., Tavin, B., & Welgryn, L. (2022). Scopes of carbon emissions and their impact on green portfolios. *Economic Modelling*, 115, 105951.

Axjonow, A., Ernstberger, J., & Pott, C. (2018). The impact of corporate social responsibility disclosure on corporate reputation: A non-professional stakeholder perspective. *Journal of Business Ethics*, 151, 429–450.

Banerjee, S., Chen, A., Li, M., Mehrotra, V., & Vijayaraghavan, R. (2023). Voluntary climate disclosures: A tale of two venues. *SSRN Working Paper 4575733*.

Blanco, C., Caro, F., & Corbett, C. J. (2016). The state of supply chain carbon footprinting: Analysis of CDP disclosures by us firms. *Journal of Cleaner Production*, 135, 1189–1197.

Bolton, P. & Kacperczyk, M. (2021). Do investors care about carbon risk? *Journal of Financial Economics*, 142(2), 517–549.

Boulton, T. J. (2023). Mandatory ESG disclosure, information asymmetry, and litigation risk: Evidence from initial public offerings. *SSRN Working Paper 4399682*.

Box, G. E. & D. R. Cox (1964). An analysis of transformations. *Journal of the Royal Statistical Society Series B: Statistical Methodology*, 26(2), 211–243.

Brown, H. S., de Jong, M., & Levy, D. L. (2009). Building institutions based on information disclosure: Lessons from gri's sustainability reporting. *Journal of Cleaner Production*, 17(6), 571–580.

Carbon Disclosure Project. (2023). CDP technical note: Relevance of scope 3 categories by sector.

Chen, J. W., Khoo, E. S., & Peng, Z. (2023). Climate change disclosure and the information environment in the initial public offering market. *Accounting & Finance*, 63, 907–952.

Chithambo, L. & Tauringana, V. (2014). Company specific determinants of green-house gases disclosures. *Journal of Applied Accounting Research*, 15(3), 323–338.

Christensen, H. B., Hail, L., & Leuz, C. (2021). Mandatory CSR and sustainability reporting: Economic analysis and literature review. *Review of Accounting Studies*, 26(3), 1176–1248.

Cicchiello, A. F., Marrazza, F., & Perdichizzi, S. (2023). Non-financial disclosure regulation and environmental, social, and governance (ESG) performance: The case of EU and US firms. *Corporate Social Responsibility and Environmental Management*, 30(3), 1121–1128.

Coeslier, M., Louche, C., & Hétet, J.-F. (2016). On the relevance of low-carbon stock indices to tackle climate change. *Journal of Sustainable Finance & Investment*, 6(4), 247–262.

Coqueret, G. (2022). *Perspectives in Sustainable Equity Investing*. CRC Press.

De Villiers, C., Ma, D., & Marques, A. (2023). Corporate social responsibility disclosure, dividend payments and firm value–relations and mediating effects. *Accounting & Finance*, 64(1), 185–219.

Delmas, M. A., Clark, K., Timmer, T., & McClellan, M. (2022). The state of corporate sustainability disclosure. *SSRN Working Paper 4194032*.

Dienes, D., Sassen, R., & Fischer, J. (2016). What are the drivers of sustainability reporting? A systematic review. *Sustainability Accounting, Management and Policy Journal*, 7(2), 154–189.

Dobrick, J., Klein, C., & Zwergel, B. (2023). Size bias in refinitiv ESG data. *Finance Research Letters*, 55, 104014.

Downar, B., Ernstberger, J., Reichelstein, S., Schwenen, S., & Zaklan, A. (2021). The impact of carbon disclosure mandates on emissions and financial operating performance. *Review of Accounting Studies*, 26, 1137–1175.

Drempetic, S., Klein, C., & Zwergel, B. (2020). The influence of firm size on the ESG score: Corporate sustainability ratings under review. *Journal of Business Ethics*, 167, 333–360.

Eugster, F., Kallunki, J., Kallunki, J.-P., & Nilsson, H. (2023). Managerial extraversion and corporate voluntary disclosure. *Contemporary Accounting Research*, 41(1), 95–125.

Friedman, H. L., Heinle, M. S., & Luneva, I. M. (2021). A theoretical framework for ESG reporting to investors. *SSRN Working Paper 3932689*.

Gao, F., Dong, Y., Ni, C., & Fu, R. (2016). Determinants and economic consequences of non-financial disclosure quality. *European Accounting Review*, 25(2), 287–317.

Gholami, A., Murray, P. A., & Sands, J. (2022a). Environmental, social, governance & financial performance disclosure for large firms: Is this different for SME firms? *Sustainability*, 14(10), 6019.

Gholami, A., Sands, J., & Rahman, H. U. (2022b). Environmental, social and governance disclosure and value generation: Is the financial industry different? *Sustainability*, 14(5), 2647.

Gray, R., Javad, M., Power, D. M., & Sinclair, C. D. (2001). Social and environmental disclosure and corporate characteristics: A research note and extension. *Journal of Business Finance & Accounting*, 28(3–4), 327–356.

Grewal, J., Riedl, E. J., & Serafeim, G. (2019). Market reaction to mandatory nonfinancial disclosure. *Management Science*, 65(7), 3061–3084.

Hackston, D. & Milne, M. J. (1996). Some determinants of social and environmental disclosures in New Zealand companies. *Accounting, Auditing & Accountability Journal*, 9(1), 77–108.

In. S. Y. & Schumacher, K. (2021). Carbonwashing: ESG data greenwashing in a post-paris world. In T. Heller, A. Seiger (eds.), *Settling Climate Accounts: Navigating the Road to Net Zero*, pp. 39–58, Springer.

Ioannou, I. & Serafeim, G. (2017). The consequences of mandatory corporate sustainability reporting. *SSRN Working Paper 1799589*.

Jackson, G., Bartosch, J., Avetisyan, E., Kinderman, D., & Knudsen, J. S. (2020). Mandatory non-financial disclosure and its influence on CSR: An international comparison. *Journal of Business Ethics*, 162, 323–342.

Januschowski, T., Wang, Y., Torkkola, K., Erkkilä, T., Hasson, H., & Gasthaus, J. (2022). Forecasting with trees. *International Journal of Forecasting*, 38(4), 1473–1481.

Khan, M., Lockhart, J., & Bathurst, R. (2020). A multi-level institutional perspective of corporate social responsibility reporting: A mixed-method study. *Journal of Cleaner Production*, 265, 121739.

Kim, J.-B., Wang, C., & Wu, F. (2022). The real effects of risk disclosures: Evidence from climate change reporting in 10-Ks. *Review of Accounting Studies*, 28, 2271–2318.

Krueger, P., Sautner, Z., Tang, D. Y., & Zhong, R. (2023). The effects of mandatory ESG disclosure around the world. *SSRN Working Paper 3832745*.

Liao, L., Luo, L., & Tang, Q. (2015). Gender diversity, board independence, environmental committee and greenhouse gas disclosure. *British Accounting Review*, 47(4), 409–424.

Loh, L. & Tan, S. (2020). Impact of sustainability reporting on brand value: An examination of 100 leading brands in Singapore. *Sustainability*, 12(18), 7392.

Lu, T., Ruan, L., Wang, Y., & Yu, L. (2023). Real effects of GHG disclosures. *SSRN Working Paper 4561549*.

Lundberg, S. M. & Lee, S.-I. (2017). A unified approach to interpreting model predictions. *Advances in Neural Information Processing Systems*, 30.

Malik, M. S. & Kanwal, L. (2018). Impact of corporate social responsibility disclosure on financial performance: Case study of listed pharmaceutical firms of Pakistan. *Journal of Business Ethics*, 150, 69–78.

Masson-Delmotte, V., Zhai, P., Pirani, A., Connors, S. L., Péan, C., Berger, S., Caud, N., Chen, Y., Goldfarb, L., Gomis, M., *et al.* (2021). Climate change 2021: The physical science basis. In *Contribution of Working Group I to the Sixth Assessment Report of the Intergovernmental Panel on Climate Change 2*.

Menla Ali, F., Wu, Y., & Zhang, X. (2023). ESG disclosure, CEO power and incentives and corporate risk-taking. *European Financial Management*, 30(2), 961–1011.

Molnar, C. (2020). *Interpretable Machine Learning*. Lulu.

Pedersen, L. H., Fitzgibbons, S., & Pomorski, L. (2021). Responsible investing: The ESG-efficient frontier. *Journal of Financial Economics*, 142(2), 572–597.

Perera, K., Kuruppuarachchi, D., Kumarasinghe, S., & Suleman, M. T. (2023). The impact of carbon disclosure and carbon emissions intensity on firms' idiosyncratic volatility. *Energy Economics*, 128, 107053.

Peters, G. F. & Romi, A. M. (2014). Does the voluntary adoption of corporate governance mechanisms improve environmental risk disclosures? Evidence from green-house gas emission accounting. *Journal of Business Ethics*, 125, 637–666.

Qiu, Y., Shaukat, A., & Tharyan, R. (2016). Environmental and social disclosures: Link with corporate financial performance. *British Accounting Review*, 48(1), 102–116.

Roca, L. C. & Searcy, C. (2012). An analysis of indicators disclosed in corporate sustainability reports. *Journal of Cleaner Production*, 20(1), 103–118.

Rozemberczki, B., Watson, L., Bayer, P., Yang, H.-T., Kiss, O., Nilsson, S., & Sarkar, R. (2022). The shapley value in machine learning. *arXiv Preprint* (2202.05594).

Schaltegger, S. & Burritt, R. L. (2010). Sustainability accounting for companies: Catchphrase or decision support for business leaders? *Journal of World Business*, 45(4), 375–384.

Shi, Y., Tang, C. S., & Wu, J. (2023). Are firms voluntarily disclosing emissions greener? *SSRN Working Paper*.

Tauringana, V. & Chithambo, L. (2015). The effect of DEFRA guidance on greenhouse gas disclosure. *British Accounting Review*, 47(4), 425–444.

Tomar, S. (2023). Greenhouse gas disclosure and emissions benchmarking. *Journal of Accounting Research*, 61(2), 451–492.

Tsang, A., Frost, T., & Cao, H. (2023). Environmental, social, and governance (ESG) disclosure: A literature review. *British Accounting Review*, 55(1), 101–149.

Wang, S., Wang, H., Wang, J., & Yang, F. (2020). Does environmental information disclosure contribute to improve firm financial performance? An examination of the underlying mechanism. *Science of the Total Environment*, 714, 136855.

Willis, A. (2003). The role of the global reporting initiative's sustainability reporting guidelines in the social screening of investments. *Journal of Business Ethics*, 43, 233–237.

Yeo, I.-K. & Johnson, R. A. (2000). A new family of power transformations to improve normality or symmetry. *Biometrika*, 87(4), 954–959.

Young, S. & Marais, M. (2012). A multi-level perspective of CSR reporting: The implications of national institutions and industry risk characteristics. *Corporate Governance: An International Review*, 20(5), 432–450.

https://doi.org/10.1142/9789811297786_0011

Chapter 11

Venture Investment in Carbon Dioxide Removal Technologies: Current State and Outlook

Egor M. Muravev* and Alexander V. Chernokulsky†

*HSE University, Moscow, Russia

†A. M. Obukhov Institute of Atmospheric Physics, Russian Academy of Sciences, Moscow, Russia

Abstract

This paper examines venture investments in Carbon Dioxide Removal (CDR) technologies. It analyzes the main trends, challenges, and opportunities that exist in this sector, with a focus on three key technologies: Bioenergy with Carbon Capture and Storage (BECCS), Direct Air Carbon Capture and Storage, and Enhanced Weathering (EW). According to the Sixth Assessment Report of the Intergovernmental Panel on Climate Change (IPCC), CDR is an integral component in scenarios aiming to limit warming to 2°C or below by 2100. While "traditional" or "conventional" CDR methods, based on the CO_2 uptake capacity of forests and soils, remain the most widely used, there are limitations to their scalability. This underscores the importance of developing and implementing new CDR methods, many of which are still at a low level of technological maturity. In this context, venture investments often play a crucial role in the successful development and commercial application of technologies in the early stages due to a high tolerance for risk and a long-term investment horizon.

1. CDR Technologies and Their Role in Achieving the Paris Agreement Goals

1.1. *The Role of CDR in Achieving Carbon Neutrality*

The Paris Agreement was adopted at the 21st session of the Conference of the Parties to the United Nations Framework Convention on Climate Change. The goal of the Paris Agreement is to "hold the increase in the global average temperature to well below 2°C above pre-industrial levels, while pursuing efforts to limit the temperature increase to 1.5°C" (Paris Agreement, 2015). However, the current global temperature is already 1.2°C above the pre-industrial average (1850–1900) (World Meteorological Organization (WMO), 2022), and, given the current trajectory of greenhouse gas emissions, an increase of 2.7°C can be expected by 2100 (Climate Action Tracker, 2022).

Scientific research on mitigating anthropogenic climate impact, as summarized in the Sixth Assessment Report of the Intergovernmental Panel on Climate Change (IPCC) (contribution of Working Group III), indicates with high confidence that carbon dioxide removal (CDR) is a necessary component in scenarios that limit warming to 2°C (with a probability of >67%) or below by 2100. Specifically, the sustainable development scenario (SSP1), which aims to limit warming to the levels specified in the Paris Agreement, requires the removal of about 10 $GtCO_2$ yr^{-1} by 2050 and about 20 $GtCO_2$ yr^{-1} by 2100 (National Academies of Sciences, Engineering, and Medicine, 2019) (a fivefold and 10-fold increase from current levels, respectively). A similar capacity will be required if emissions peak after 2030. And, society is currently on this trajectory.

CDR refers to anthropogenic activities aimed at the intentional removal of carbon dioxide from the atmosphere and its long-term storage in geological, terrestrial, and oceanic reservoirs, or in products (UNFCCC, 2023a). It is not a single technology but a whole range of approaches from reforestation to direct carbon capture from the air (or ocean).

Three main roles of CDR in achieving the Paris Agreement goals can be identified: in the short term, it reduces net CO_2 emissions; in the medium term, it balances residual emissions to achieve zero emissions (especially in sectors such as metallurgy and agriculture); and, in the long term, it aims to achieve negative emissions. The Carbon Business Council highlights the following main principles of quality CDR: additionality, durability, lifecycle net negativity, verification, and equity and community engagement. However, the potential costs and externalities of these methods vary widely.

Currently, the most widely used CDR methods are based on the absorption capacity of forests and soils (so-called "traditional" or "conventional" methods), which capture about 2 Gt CO_2 per year. Such CDR methods account for over 99% of the total CDR volume and are expected to remain dominant, accounting for over 75% by 2030. However, these methods have scaling limits at the level of 5 $GtCO_2$ per year (Smith *et al.*, 2023). Other limitations of these methods include carbon releases from forest fires, windthrow, and biotic forest mortality.

At the same time, new CDR methods are being actively developed, including Bioenergy with Carbon Capture and Storage (BECCS), Direct Air Carbon Capture and Storage (DACSS), Enhanced Weathering (EW), and others. In the second half of the century, the capacity of new CDR methods is expected to exceed that of traditional CDR, with a 250–750-fold increase in new CDR methods (depending on the emissions scenario). By 2050, compared to 2020 levels, land-based absorption should roughly double for global warming trajectories below 1.5°C and increase by about 50% for trajectories below 2°C (Smith *et al.*, 2023).

Recently, a discussion has been rekindled regarding the relevance of new CDR technologies. One of the main points of contention is whether new CDR methods should be equated with emissions reductions. Specifically, a March 2023 note dedicated to the inclusion of CDR in Article 6.4 of the Paris Agreement expressed criticism of CDR based on the assumption that a focus on carbon removal could delay essential emissions reduction measures (UNFCCC, 2023b). In response, over 100 experts submitted a letter emphasizing the role of CDR as an integral part of limiting global warming to 1.5°C, citing the IPCC's 6th Assessment Report. The experts also called to move away from the term "engineering-based activities" in favor of assessing the applicability of each technology to Article 6.4 separately, based on the alignment of a particular solution with the core principles of quality CDR. In summary, the use of various CDR methods can be an effective complement to emissions reduction efforts. A more detailed description of some CDR methods is provided in the following.

1.2. *A Brief Overview of Existing CDR*

We performed a classification of different CDR technologies using several sources including expert reports (Smith *et al.*, 2023; Carbon Dioxide Removal Primer, 2021), approaches by corporations acquiring carbon credits created through CDR (Shopify, 2023; Frontier, 2023b), and investment activities of venture funds specializing in investments in ClimateTech and CDR (Orbuch, 2022; Aenu, 2023). As a result, we identified 12 main types of CDRs (Table 1). It is important to note that this study omits Carbon Capture, Utilization, and Storage (CCUS) technologies because they do not imply the actual removal of carbon from the atmosphere. CCUS technologies focus on reducing carbon dioxide emissions by capturing it during the combustion of fossil fuels, without addressing greenhouse gases already emitted by human activities. All CDR technologies are at different stages of development and vary in cost (Chernokulsky, 2022) (Figure 1).

Three technologies were selected for further analysis: BECCS, DACCS, and EW. They were selected based on evaluations by key market players and in accordance with innovation criteria, making them suitable for venture investment. Separately, it is worth noting that technologies with the maximum carbon storage duration (durability) were selected. Specifically, one of the largest CDR offset marketplaces, Supercritical (2023), rates the durability of biochar as medium, so it was not included in the further analysis.

Technologies and solutions that overlapped with those already considered were not included in the classification. For example, in the field of traditional CDR, there are start-ups that are engaged in remote forest monitoring or creating platforms for trading carbon units. Despite their importance and the technological component of the solutions, they function as auxiliary solutions. This study focuses on technologies directly related to the removal of carbon from the atmosphere.

1.3. *The Role of Venture Capital in Achieving the Paris Agreement Goals*

The presence of venture investment in the early stages of technology development often plays a key role in its successful development and commercial application. Venture investors are characterized by a high degree of risk tolerance and a long-term investment horizon. This makes

Table 1. Main types of CDR technologies

Type of CDR	Description
Conventional	
Afforestation/ reforestation	Planting forests (restoring old or planting new): enhancing photosynthesis.
Peatland and wetland restoration	Secondary watering of previously drained peatlands.
Soil carbon sequestration	A set of agricultural practices that allow part of the carbon to be retained in the soil.
Novel	
BECCS	Use of vegetation as biofuel. When burned: energy production, CO_2 capture, compression, and transportation to burial sites.
Biochar	Use of wood charcoal, obtained from biomass by pyrolysis, as a soil additive.
Coastal wetland/blue carbon	Preservation of carbon stored in coastal and marine ecosystems (mangroves, tidal marshes, seagrass).
DACCS	Capturing CO_2 from the air using various technologies: absorption (e.g. in amine solutions); adsorption (on solids); using membranes.
DOCCS (Direct ocean capture)	An electrochemical process for removing CO_2 from seawater, followed by injection for permanent geological storage.
Durable products	Storing carbon in long-lived products (e.g. concrete or wood buildings).
EW	Minerals that naturally absorb CO_2 (e.g. limestone, basalt) are crushed and sprayed on land.
Ocean alkalinization	Minerals that naturally absorb CO_2 (e.g. limestone, basalt) are crushed and sprayed into the ocean. Also causes alkalinization.
Ocean fertilization	Iron or other nutrients are added to the ocean, stimulating the growth of phytoplankton, which absorb CO_2 (photosynthesis). When plankton die, they fall to the deep layers of the ocean, removing carbon from the carbon cycle.

them important drivers of progress, especially in industries where significant initial R&D investment is required and where quick success is not guaranteed.

There is an economic concept called the "learning curve" that reflects the process by which productivity and efficiency increase through

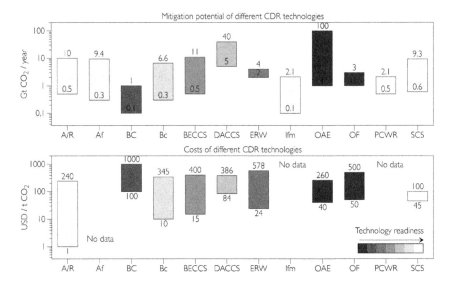

Figure 1.   Comparison of various CDR technologies in terms of the potential for climate change mitigation and cost.

Notes: Afforestation/Reforestation (A/R), Agroforestry (Af), Blue Carbon management in coastal wetlands (BC), Biochar (Bc), Bioenergy and Carbon Capture and Storage (BECCS), Direct Air Carbon Capture and Storage (DACCS), Enhanced Rock Weathering (ERW), Improved Forest Management (IFM), Ocean Alkalinity Enhancement (OAE), Ocean Fertilization (OF), Peatland and Coastal Wetland Restoration (PCWR), and Soil Carbon Sequestration (SCS)

Source: The figure is compiled by the authors and is based on estimates from IPCC (2022) for the following CDR technologies.

repetition and accumulated experience. It implies that with each new single product or service produced, the cost and time per unit of production or service decrease as the company or industry "learns" and improves. The concept also implies that investments made in the early stages of development can yield substantial returns in the future as technology costs decrease and efficiencies increase. This principle underlies the work of venture investors. One of the most striking examples of the role of venture capital (VC) in industry development can be found in the U.S. solar energy sector. From 2000 to 2004, government grants and VC were the primary funding sources for technology development in the solar sector. The period 2005–2007 saw a significant shift, with substantial public investment entering the sector. This influx of capital was notably influenced by the leverage effect of VC and private equity (PE) investments. Specifically, for every unit invested by VC and PE, there was a 15-fold increase in public equity and solar debt investment. This suggests that VC and PE were not just complementary, but instrumental in attracting larger pools of investment to the sector (George & Gupta, 2022). Although the cost per megawatt-hour of solar energy at that time was significantly higher than the cost of traditional fuels (>$450), it declined in subsequent years to levels comparable to traditional energy sources. New CDR technologies may follow a similar path of cost reduction.

2. Venture Investments in CDR: Current Status and Outlook

2.1. *Current State of the Venture Investment Market for CDR Technologies*

CDR technologies represent a segment of the broader ClimateTech market (technologies related to climate change mitigation and adaptation). In 2022, the global volume of venture investment in ClimateTech exceeded $40 billion worldwide, and the number of deals closed exceeded 1,000 (CTVC, 2023). Total funding volume decreased by 3% compared to 2021. At the same time, the broader VC market shrank by 35% (Teare, 2023). The high level of resilience during a crisis shows that investment in ClimateTech is a long-term trend. In the first quarter of 2023, investments remained at the same level as the first quarter of the previous year, at $11.2 billion (HolonIQ, 2023).

Seven main sectors of ClimateTech can be identified (CTVC, 2023):

(1) **Energy:** Subsector examples: new-generation technologies (e.g. nuclear, solar, and geothermal energy) and new types of fuels (e.g. hydrogen).
(2) **Transportation:** Subsector examples: electric vehicles (EV), EV charging and fleet management, electric micromobility, and car sharing.
(3) **Food and agriculture:** Subsector examples: alternative proteins, regenerative agriculture, and vertical farms.
(4) **Industry:** Subsector examples: low-carbon materials (e.g. cement, steel) and recycling and reuse of raw materials.

(5) **Climate change management:** Subsector examples: greenhouse gas emissions reporting and climate risk assessment.
(6) **Construction and real estate:** Subsector examples: sustainable construction materials and low-carbon heating and cooling.
(7) **Carbon:** Subsector examples: CDR and carbon credit marketplaces.

Investments in the segment related to carbon removal or emissions avoidance account for less than 3% of total investments for the period 2020–2022 (CTVC, 2023). In 2022, the Carbon segment grew faster than the others: The volume increased by 305% and the number of deals increased by 59% (see Table 2). Part of this growth can be explained by the largest funding round for Climeworks, which took place in April 2022 and amounted to 650 million euros (Rathi, 2022). Additionally, several VC funds specializing in CDR have emerged, such as Lowercarbon Capital and Carbon Removal Partners. All of this suggests that the market potential for CDR has become more apparent, and the segment is transitioning from the product creation stage to scaling its operations.

2.2. *Current State of Development of DACCS, BECCS, and EW Technologies*

DACCS is a collective term for a number of processes that extract carbon dioxide from the atmosphere, typically through various chemical

Table 2. Investment volumes in various ClimateTech segments [based on data from CTVC (2023)

ClimateTech Industry	Volume of Venture Investment, 2022, USD bn	Volume of Venture Investment, 2021, USD bn	Change in 2022 vs. 2021 (%)
Transportation	11.7	16.9	−31
Energy	11.3	9.0	+26
Food & Land use	6.1	8.9	−31
Industry	4.4	3.7	+18
Climate change management	2.3	1.6	+50
Construction and real estate	2.2	0.9	+151
Carbon	2.3	0.6	+305

Table 3. Top three start-ups in the DACCS field by funding volume

Start-Up Name	Year Founded	Total Investments (in millions of dollars)	Operational Capacity (planned), Tons CO_2 Year^{-1}
Climeworks	2009	777	4,000 (36,000)
Carbon engineering	2009	106	<100 (1,500,000)
Heirloom carbon	2020	54	n/a

reactions, adsorption, and absorption (Minx *et al.*, 2018). Burying or utilizing the extracted carbon dioxide is a challenge. In particular, CO_2 can be stored either in deep geological reservoirs, e.g. depleted oil wells (Carbon Engineering Ltd., 2023), or in durable materials, such as concrete (CarbonCure, 2023).

Several start-ups in the DACCS field can be highlighted (Table 3), where Climeworks has the largest volume of total investments. An example of the DACCS technology implemented by Climeworks is presented in its first carbon capture facility, Orca (Climeworks, 2023). Air being drawn in passes through a filter inside the collector that captures CO_2 particles. Once the filter is full of CO_2, the collector is closed and the temperature is raised to about 100°C. This releases the CO_2 from the filter, allowing it to be collected. The CO_2 can then be safely and permanently stored underground.

In general, existing DACCS technologies are rather energy intensive. Therefore, to achieve a negative net effect, i.e. more carbon removed than emitted, it is crucial to use renewable energy sources. The scalability of DACCS technologies is still in question.

BECCS is a hybrid carbon removal solution that integrates "traditional" natural processes on the one hand and new technological processes on the other. BECCS involves the capture of carbon dioxide in plants during photosynthesis, its subsequent combustion to produce electricity, heat, or fuel, the capture of CO_2 during this combustion, and its subsequent burial in rock formations or use in the production of carbon-based products.

There are many variations of BECCS (Table 4). One example is the technology employed by Charm Industrial (Charm Industrial, 2023). The first step is to collect biomass, including agricultural waste. The biomass is then converted into biofuel using a fast pyrolysis process (heating the biomass to 500°C for a few seconds in an oxygen-free chamber). The resulting biofuel can be stored in underground wells, used as a fuel, or used as an industrial chemical.

Table 4.   Top three start-ups in the BECCS sphere by funding volume

Start-Up Name	Year Founded	Total Investments (in millions of dollars)	Operational Capacity (planned), Tons CO_2 Year^{-1}
Charm industrial	2018	100	6,500 (n/a)
CO280	2022	6	<100 (30,000)
Arbor energy	2022	1	<100 (1,000)

Table 5.   Top three start-ups in the EW sphere by funding volume

Start-Up Name	Year Founded	Total Investments (in millions of dollars)	Operational Capacity (planned), Tons CO_2 Year^{-1}
Un-do	2022	13	6,750 (1,000,000)
Paebbl	2021	9	n/a (n/a)
Inplanet	2022	1	1,000 (n/a)

It is important to note that not all forms of BECCS result in net carbon removal. Many factors come into play, including the source and type of biomass, transportation requirements, the efficiency of the conversion process, and the final use of the captured carbon. Another important limiting factor for this technology is the use of agricultural land for biomass cultivation. Therefore, the role of biomass waste in BECCS is of paramount importance.

Chemical weathering is a natural process of carbon removal from the atmosphere that has been occurring for millions of years. However, current technologies can reduce this time frame from hundreds of thousands of years to just a few decades. This acceleration is called EW (Table 5).

EW technology works as follows: Carbon dioxide combines with rainwater to form carbonic acid. When such acid-diluted rainfall occurs, CO_2 interacts with rocks and soils (primarily with silicate and carbonate minerals), leading to the formation of bicarbonate ions (ions of calcium, magnesium, etc.). These ions either remain in the soil or enter the ocean through river runoff, where they recombine into various forms of carbonate minerals and settle on the ocean floor. This abiotic carbon cycle removes about 1 $GtCO_2$ per year from the atmosphere (Strefler *et al.*, 2021). This process can be amplified and accelerated by scaling, for instance, by increasing the surface area of minerals and crushing them, such as basalt rocks, followed by spraying. Importantly, it is quite challenging to reverse this reaction. CO_2 remains removed from the atmosphere for hundreds of thousands of years.

The primary side effects of EW (IPCC, 2022) include ecological concerns related to material extraction and transportation, potential release of heavy metals, and potential impacts on air quality (particulate matter load and health risks) and water quality, which could reduce biodiversity. In addition, mineral processing can be energy intensive.

2.3. Prospects for Venture Investments in CDR Technologies

The costs of various solutions vary substantially (Table 6) (Höglund & Niparko, 2022), making it challenging to determine which particular technology will be most in demand. A combination of technologies is most likely the answer.

It is worth noting that VC volume is often insufficient as a sole source of investment. Markets are prone to create bubbles, as seen in ClimateTech between 2005 and 2011 (Wan *et al.*, 2022). A prime example is the fact that by the end of 2022, most of the CO_2 removed was sold by Climeworks, a start-up that attracted the most funding in the CDR segment, although it delivered less than 1 $ktCO_2$ of actual carbon removal (Höglund & Niparko, 2022).

Much will also depend on government policies and the incentives they create. Governments are currently following the path of developing the sector as a whole, rather than specific selected technologies. For instance,

Table 6. Price range for individual CDR solutions (based on data from Höglund & Niparko (2022))

Removal Method	Min Price, USD	Average Price, USD	Max Price, USD
Biochar	179	11	600
DAC	1,113	225	2,345
Biooil	572	300	660
EW	339	75	1,370
Mineralization	540	170	1,316
Macroalgae	240	220	269
Electrochemical ocean CO_2 capture	1,662	1,370	1,953

the United States passed the Inflation Reduction Act, which provided significant incentives for the development of clean technologies. This act increased payments for each ton of carbon removed via DAC from $50 to $180 and also provided benefits for other technologies (BECCS, CCUS, etc.) (Hendrickson & Sims, 2023). In Europe, significant steps are being taken to support CDR technologies. In November 2022, the European Commission prepared the first draft of regulations in the area of voluntary CDR (European Commission's CDR Certification Framework). At the same time, the Swedish government announced plans to invest $3.3 billion in BECCS technology by 2045 (Biorecro, 2022).

Another driver is the demand for CDR solutions from the private sector. A prime example of a market signal is the Frontier alliance, which includes major companies (Alphabet, Shopify, Meta, etc.). For 2023, Frontier announced its willingness to purchase tons of carbon removed using CDR methods for more than $1 billion (Frontier, 2023a). Overall, the number of deals to purchase CDR credits and overall volume of carbon removal purchased increased by 533% in 2022 compared to 2021: 593 ktCO$_2$ vs. 94 ktCO$_2$ (Höglund & Niparko, 2022).

Among the barriers, cost is currently the primary constraint on the industry's growth. However, economic theory and the empirical experience of other industries (e.g. solar energy) suggest that economic factors will become secondary over time. Other barriers to scaling the CDR industry include the following (Merchant *et al.*, 2022):

(1) **Lack of standardization:** Current approaches do not yet provide a comprehensive list of CDRs with proven effectiveness. There is an ongoing debate about the role of new CDRs and "traditional" methods related to forests and soils.

(2) **Verification:** Expanding on point 1, there is a lack of consensus on how to verify and objectively assess the amount of carbon removed as a result of various CDR implementations.

(3) **Infrastructure issues:** The lack of a safe and efficient infrastructure for storing and transporting CO$_2$ can hinder the development of CDR.

(4) **Role of the public sector:** Despite stated support policies, few countries are taking action. In contrast, there is almost complete consensus in the global community to support renewable energy.

(5) **Role of the public:** Many environmental organizations and climate activists believe that CDR technologies allow large-scale emission reductions to be postponed.

Despite the above-mentioned barriers, the CDR segment has begun to scale, as evidenced by the increasing demand for such solutions. Supply is scaling in parallel, primarily due to government incentives and VC investments. It is crucial to emphasize the need for research in the CDR field to comprehensively evaluate the potential adverse effects and risks associated with the adoption and scaling of these technologies. The success of scaling CDR technologies also depends on transparent verification mechanisms, as this can increase industry confidence. Simultaneously, it is important to focus not only on the technical aspects but also on public engagement to provide transparent and objective information about the necessity, benefits, and limitations of CDR technologies.

3. Conclusions

Attention to the climate technologies sector has increased in recent years. However, the share of investments in CDRs remains low, accounting for less than 3% of the total ClimateTech investments in 2020–2022. However, the CDR segment shows substantial growth in 2022, with investment volume increasing by 305% and the number of deals increasing by 59%. Specialized VC funds are emerging, such as Lowercarbon Capital and Carbon Removal Partners, which focus specifically on CDR. Despite this, even the most notable start-ups in the field have not achieved significant scale in terms of carbon removal. In particular, their current capacity does not exceed 10,000 tons of CO_2 per year, with planned capacity reaching 1,500,000 tons of CO_2 per year. One of the main barriers to the development of the CDR sector at present is its cost. There are also challenges related to the lack of standardization, infrastructure, and verification issues. Despite these obstacles, it is clear that the CDR sector has begun to scale. Historical experience in other sectors, such as solar energy, suggests that the economic attractiveness of innovative solutions tends to increase over time. A similar trend for CDR will be driven by increasing corporate demand for CDR technologies and the expansion of supply, stimulated by government support and VC investment.

References

Aenu. VC Investor (2023). Portfolio. Retrieved June 16, 2023, from https://www.aenu.com/portfolio/.

Biorecro. (2022). Swedish government commits $3.3 billion to BECCS investment. Retrieved June 5, 2023, from https://www.biorecro.com/swedish-government-commits-3billion/.

Carbon Dioxide Removal Primer. (2021). The building blocks of CDR systems. Retrieved May 3, 2023, from https://cdrprimer.org/read/chapter-2.

Carbon Engineering Ltd. (2023). Direct air capture + storage. Retrieved May 27, 2023, from https://carbonengineering.com/direct-air-capture-and-storage/.

CarbonCure. (2023). Official website. Retrieved May 6, 2023, from https://www.carboncure.com/.

Charm Industrial. (2023). Official website. Retrieved May 29, 2023, from https://charmindustrial.com/.

Chernokulsky, A. (2022). The role of CCS in transitioning to negative emissions. Climate Platform. Retrieved May 30, 2023, from https://climate-change.moscow/article/rol-ccs-v-perehode-k-otricatelnym-emissiyam.

Climate Action Tracker. (2023). Temperatures. Retrieved May 20, 2023, from https://climateactiontracker.org/global/temperatures/.

Climeworks. (2023). Orca: The first large-scale plant. Retrieved June 13, 2023, from https://climeworks.com/roadmap/orca.

CTVC. (2023). $40B and 1,000+ deals in 2022 market downtick. Retrieved June 15, 2023, from https://www.ctvc.co/40b-and-1-000-deals-in-2022-market-downtick/.

European Commission. (2022). European Green Deal: Commission Proposes Certification of Carbon Removals to Help Reach Net Zero Emissions. Retrieved June 1, 2023, from https://ec.europa.eu/commission/presscorner/detail/en/ip_22_7156.

Frontier. (2023a). Frontier carbon removal commitment tops $1B with four new members: Autodesk, H&M Group, JPMorgan Chase, and Workday. Retrieved June 3, 2023, from https://frontierclimate.com/writing/new-members.

Frontier. (2023b). Portfolio. Retrieved June 5, 2023, from. https://frontierclimate.com/portfolio.

George, A. & Gupta, P. (2022). Venture capital and private equity: Catalysing the solar sector. *Solar Compass*, 3–4, 100030. ISSN 2772-9400.

Hendrickson, S. & Sims, B. (2023). IRA aims to give CCUS a boost, but will it take off? Modern Power Systems. Retrieved June 17, 2023, from https://www.modernpowersystems.com/features/featureira-aims-to-give-ccus-a-boost-but-will-it-take-off-10561869/#:~:text=The%20IRA%20substantially%20increases%20the,%2C%20up%20from%20%2450%2Fton.

Höglund, R. & Niparko, K. (2022). CDR.fyi 2022 year in review. Medium. Retrieved May 7, 2023, from https://medium.com/cdr-fyi/cdr-fyi-2022-year-in-review-d095acd9a1a0.

HolonIQ. (2023). $11.2B of climate tech venture funding for Q1 2023. Forecasting a $36B full year. Retrieved May 17, 2023, from https://www.holoniq.com/notes/11-2b-of-climate-tech-venture-funding-for-q1-2023.

IPCC. (2022). Climate change 2022: Mitigation of climate change. Contribution of Working Group III to the Sixth Assessment Report of the Inter-governmental Panel on Climate Change. Cambridge University Press, Cambridge, UK and New York, NY, USA.

Merchant, N., Chay, F., Cullenward, D., & Freeman, J. (2022). Barriers to scaling the long-duration carbon dioxide removal industry. Carbon Plan.

Minx, J. C., *et al.* (2018). Negative emissions — Part 1: Research landscape and synthesis. *Environmental Research Letters*, 13(063001), 5–6.

National Academies of Sciences, Engineering, and Medicine. (2019). *Negative Emissions Technologies and Reliable Sequestration: A Research Agenda.* Washington, DC: The National Academies Press.

Orbuch, R. (2022). Our carbon removal startup wishlist. LowerCarbonCapital. Retrieved May 27, 2023, from https://lowercarboncapital.com/2022/07/27/cdr-wishlist/.

Paris Agreement. (2015). United Nations Organization. Retrieved May 1, 2023, from https://www.un.org/en/climatechange/paris-agreement.

Rathi, A. (2022). Climeworks raises $650 million in largest round for carbon removal Startup. *Bloomberg*. Retrieved May 15, 2023, from https://www.bloomberg.com/news/articles/2022-04-05/climeworks-raises-650-million-in-largest-round-for-carbon-removal-startup.

Shopify. (2023). Partnering for the planet. Retrieved May 23, 2023, from https://www.shopify.com/climate/sustainability-fund/partners#product.

Smith, S. M. *et al.* (2023). The state of carbon dioxide removal — 1st edition. Retrieved June 14, 2023, from https://www.stateofcdr.org.

Strefler, J. *et al.* (2021). Carbon dioxide removal technologies are not born equal. *Environmental Research Letters*, 16(7), 074021.

Supercritical. (2023). Reach net zero with carbon removal. Retrieved May 29, 2023, from https://gosupercritical.com/.

Teare, G. (2023). Global funding slide in 2022 sets stage for another tough year. Crunchbase. Retrieved June 16, 2023, from https://news.crunchbase.com/venture/global-vc-funding-slide-q4-2022/.

UNFCCC. (2023a). Meeting the Goals of the Paris Agreement: Letter from 100+ Carbon Removal Experts. Retrieved June 10, 2023, from https://urldefense. proofpoint.com/v2/url?u=https-3A__www.carbonbusinesscouncil.org_ news_unfccc&d=DwMGaQ&c=slrrB7dE8n7gBJbeO0g-IQ&r=CPekRlIiK6

v83hOL1MBVGQ&m=yumyYGjHZqZs2ie--1DaS2wr1dFXwlBQ0
sVaV6ijeFvWr-JXvYvzP9wORWlK3QVn&s=2oZIgHaB9MUu1gEdscqkM
1nbyiu5tFjryi11uERyoLQ&e="https://www.carbonbusinesscouncil.org/
news/unfccc.

UNFCCC (2023b). Information note: "Summary of the views submitted by parties and observers on activities involving removals." Article 6.4 Mechanism, submissions, emission removal activities, methodologies. Retrieved June 10, 2023, from https://urldefense.proofpoint.com/v2/url?u=https-3A__unfccc. int_sites_default_files_resource_a64-2Dsb005-2Daa-2Da10v1.pdf&d=Dw MGaQ&c=slrrB7dE8n7gBJbeO0g-IQ&r=CPekRlIiK6v83hOL1MBVGQ& m=yumyYGjHZqZs2ie--1DaS2wr1dFXwlBQ0sVaV6ijeFvWr-JXvYvzP 9wORWlK3QVn&s=dUVhhi2l5sBD6SF7QLpxeu4NGDFrAd6EMS9SKqh AG4o&e="https://unfccc.int/sites/default/files/resource/a64-sb005-aa-a10v1.pdf.

Wan, C., Shue, M., Sarycheva, A., & Dadi, S. (2022). Eight lessons from the first climate tech boom and bust. BVP. Retrieved June 20, 2023, from https://www.bvp.com/atlas/eight-lessons-from-the-first-climate-tech-boom-and-bust.

World Meteorological Organization (WMO). (2022). Global temperatures set to reach new records in next five years. Retrieved June 1, 2023, from https://public.wmo.int/en/media/press-release/global-temperatures-set-reach-new-records-next-five-years.

Chapter 12

Optimizing Fuel Production in Carbon Trading: A Karush–Kuhn–Tucker Framework for Sustainable Balance

Bruno G. Kamdem

Department of Finance and Risk Engineering,
Tandon School Engineering,
Brooklyn, New York, USA
Lepton Consulting, LLC, New York, USA

Abstract

This paper addresses the urgent challenge of climate risks amid escalating temperatures in 2023 and forthcoming projections for 2024. Focused on the intersection of climate risk mitigation, carbon trading, and the Karush–Kuhn–Tucker (KKT) optimization framework, we utilize advanced mathematical models to enhance emission reduction strategies within carbon trading systems. Our research emphasizes the dynamic interplay between production quantity, fuel prices, and the energy sector, aiming to contribute to both environmental impact and economic viability. The central exploration involves the application of the KKT model to navigate the intricate landscape of fuel production. Linear inverse demand functions are employed to quantify market demand and address relationships between fuel price and production quantity. The KKT model facilitates the definition and optimization of production quantities, balancing consumer needs, economic feasibility, and environmental impact mitigation. Integration of carbon trading mechanisms considers costs and benefits related to emissions reduction, achieving a delicate equilibrium between market demands and the carbon footprint of fuel production. A distinctive aspect of our approach is the direct inclusion of individual fuel producers into the optimization model, transforming profit objectives into refined KKT constraints for market equilibrium. This methodology signifies a substantial advancement in understanding and optimizing fuel production dynamics. Leveraging the KKT model, our research contributes valuable insights to sustainable energy practices, providing a theoretical foundation for academia and practical guidance for industry stakeholders navigating the delicate balance between economic prosperity and environmental responsibility.

1. Introduction

As 2023 marked the hottest year on record and indications for 2024 suggest another scorcher, it is clear that climate risks present a significant challenge for the global community. The naturally occurring El Niño is likely to push up temperatures in much of the world and humans will keep pumping greenhouse gases into the atmosphere (see Figures A.2–A.4). That will very likely mean more extreme heat and more wildfires, like the ones that torched Canada, Europe, and North Africa. In order to address climate risks, it is imperative to implement innovative and effective strategies for reducing greenhouse gas emissions. Carbon trading systems have emerged as pivotal tools in fostering sustainable development by placing a financial value on emissions, encouraging cleaner practices and facilitating the transition toward a low-carbon economy (see Figure A.1). In the pursuit of optimal solutions within these systems, the integration of advanced mathematical models becomes crucial. In this paper, I explore the intersection of climate risk mitigation, carbon trading, and the Karush–Kuhn–Tucker (KKT) optimization framework (Kuhn & Tucker, 1951), (Karush, 1939).

The KKT model, rooted in mathematical optimization theory, provides a powerful methodology for solving constrained optimization problems. By incorporating this model into the dynamics of a carbon trading system, we aim to enhance the efficiency and effectiveness of emission reduction strategies. Our focus lies at the nexus of production quantity and fuel prices (P^t) within this framework, acknowledging the pivotal role of the energy sector in contributing to both environmental impact and economic viability. We aim to contribute to the theoretical foundation of climate risk management by providing insights into the interplay between optimization techniques, carbon trading systems, and the intricate dynamics of fuel production. Through a systematic exploration of these elements, we seek to advance research on sustainable practices, offering a framework that can inform policymakers, industry stakeholders, and researchers alike in the pursuit of a resilient and environmentally conscious future.

The central premise of our exploration is to illuminate how the KKT model, grounded in mathematical optimization theory, can be applied to navigate the multidimensional landscape of fuel production. Specifically, we aim to quantify market demand by assuming a linear inverse demand function. For some fuel types, polynomial or exponential relationships exist between the fuel price (P_i^t) and the production quantity of the fuel ($Q_{i,j}^t$). We use the KKT model to define and optimize production quantities, ensuring alignment with market demand. This sheds light on the intricate interplay between consumer needs, economic feasibility, and the imperative to mitigate environmental impact. We integrate carbon trading mechanisms into the optimization model by accounting for the cost (C_i^t) and benefits associated with emissions reduction. The KKT framework allows for the simultaneous consideration of economic variables and environmental objectives within a unified model. We investigate how the KKT conditions can guide decision-making to achieve sustainability objectives, striking a delicate balance between meeting market demands and minimizing the carbon footprint of fuel production. We examine the adaptability of the KKT model to real-world industrial complexities, considering factors such as varying fuel types, production constraints, and evolving market conditions. For example, we guarantee that the supply of fuel for gasoline and diesel generators corresponds to their respective annual demands. We ensure compliance with the Environmental Protection Agency (EPA) guidelines for the blend wall constraint, which represents the maximum permissible blending rate of gasoline or diesel substitutes allowed in the blending process for gasoline or diesel. We make a distinctive contribution by directly incorporating the fuel producer, denoted as j, into the optimization problem's objective function and constraints — a facet not explicitly addressed in previous studies (Hu & Chen, 2019). In contrast to prior research, our approach involves a direct consideration of the individual fuel producer (j) in the optimization solution.

This departure is pivotal, as it results in the transformation of the maximum profit objective function for each fuel producer into an equivalent KKT optimality constraint. The culmination of these refined KKT constraints facilitates the attainment of market equilibrium. The unique perspective and methodology constitute a significant advancement in understanding and optimizing fuel production dynamics, setting our research apart in contributing to the field. By unraveling the intricacies of fuel production optimization through the lens of the KKT model, we seek to contribute valuable insights to the ongoing discourse on sustainable energy practices. In doing so, we aim to offer a theoretical foundation that not only informs academic research but also provides pragmatic guidance for industry stakeholders navigating the delicate equilibrium between economic prosperity and environmental responsibility.

The next segment of the paper, Section 2, examines the existing research and scholarly contributions that form the foundation for our exploration. We review relevant studies, methodologies, and findings related to the intersection of the KKT model, carbon trading, and optimal fuel production. Building upon the insights gained from the literature, we transition to Section 3, where we present the conceptual framework and mathematical foundations underpinning our proposed approach. This section outlines the theoretical paradigm of the KKT model to address the complexities of determining optimal fuel production quantities within the intricate dynamics of a carbon trading prototype. In the last part of the article, Section 4, we synthesize key findings, discuss the implications of our model, and propose avenues for future research, thereby concluding our exploration.

2. Literature Review

The pressing challenges of climate change and the urgent need to reduce greenhouse gas emissions have spurred the development of innovative strategies, with carbon trading systems emerging as pivotal tools for fostering sustainable development. Research and scholarly contributions related to the intersection of the KKT optimization framework, carbon trading, and the optimization of fuel production within the context of climate risk mitigation exist but are sparse. Responding to the pressing demand for sustainable approaches in the energy industry aimed at alleviating environmental pollution and diminishing carbon emissions, Cao *et al.* (2023) propose a Stackelberg game strategy to optimize energy transactions for multiple virtual power plants (MVPPs), balancing environmental concerns and market interests. The authors introduce a ladder-type carbon price mechanism, reflecting the incorporation of carbon trading mechanisms. While acknowledging the suitability of KKT conditions for finding the optimal solution of a convex optimization problem, in their model, the operator serves as the leader in the Stackelberg game, guiding MVPP through price optimization. In our paper, we consider the role of fuel producers in a carbon trading system, explicitly incorporating individual fuel producers into the optimization model. We highlight the significance of strategic decision-making by key actors in achieving sustainability goals. To emphasize the importance of optimization strategies for achieving energy optimization and sustainability, Cao *et al.* (2022) introduce the KKT optimization framework within a two-stage scheduling strategy for virtual power plants (VPPs) with multi-timescale optimization, considering day-ahead and real-time scheduling. The authors discuss the role of the virtual power plant coordinator (VPPCO) in real-time energy complementation, leading to improved economic efficiency and the consumption of regional energy.

The application of optimization techniques to address complex problems in energy systems is an active and evolving area of research. Jia *et al.* (2022) discuss the establishment of a multi-objective bilevel optimization model and the introduction of the KKT condition to optimize the pricing strategy and business performance in power markets. They simplify the KKT optimization model and transform it into a mixed integer linear programming model. The ongoing research and applications of optimization techniques in energy systems aim to optimize energy systems, achieve economic efficiency, and systematically consider the roles of key actors, such as coordinators and agents, in the decision-making processes. The implementation of optimization models in energy systems also aligns with the exploration of carbon credit trading as an instrumental mechanism for achieving environmental targets. Hu and Chen (2019) utilize a mathematical program with an equilibrium constraint model (MPEC) and KKT optimality conditions to represent profit maximization. The paper explores the implications of the Low-Carbon Fuel Standard for fuel producers in California. They find that carbon credit trading can be used as a means for fuel producers to generate revenue and reduce carbon intensity. While Hu and Chen (2019) utilize a mathematical program with an equilibrium constraint model (MPEC) and KKT optimality conditions to represent profit maximization, in our paper, we extend the framework by directly incorporating fuel producers. Examining the integration of fuel producers into a mathematical program featuring an equilibrium constraint model (MPEC) and leveraging KKT optimality conditions for profit maximization constitutes a vital element in the overarching realm of Carbon Trading and Environmental Economics. A significant body of literature has explored the effectiveness of carbon trading systems in addressing climate change and promoting sustainable development. Scholars such as Helm (2017) and Zhang *et al.* (2020) emphasize the economic incentives embedded in carbon markets, providing a financial value for emissions and encouraging industries to adopt cleaner practices. The establishment of carbon markets as policy instruments has been widely discussed (Liu *et al.*, 2019), highlighting their potential to drive the transition toward a low-carbon economy. The integration of mathematical optimization models, such as the KKT framework, into environmental management strategies has also gained attention in recent literature. Guo *et al.* (2021) showcase the applicability of optimization techniques in designing environmentally sustainable systems. The KKT model, rooted in mathematical optimization theory, has proven to be particularly powerful in solving constrained optimization problems across various domains (Boyd & Vandenberghe, 2004).

Although the KKT model, firmly rooted in mathematical optimization theory, has shown impressive effectiveness in handling constrained optimization problems across various domains, there is currently a restricted research focus on optimizing fuel production within the context of carbon trading; however, this area is gradually gaining momentum. Yılmaz Balaman *et al.* (2019) present a framework for optimizing biofuel production under carbon pricing mechanisms, emphasizing the need to balance economic viability with environmental responsibility. However, the explicit incorporation of the KKT model into fuel production optimization remains an underexplored area. While the KKT model has been extensively applied in economics and optimization problems (Karush, 1939; Kuhn & Tucker, 1951), its specific application to environmental economics and carbon trading systems is less prevalent. Hu and Chen (2019) explore KKT conditions in the context of emission reduction, laying a foundation for incorporating optimization techniques into environmental policy design. The limited attention given to the explicit inclusion of individual fuel producers within optimization models is noteworthy. Most studies in fuel production optimization often focus on aggregate industry behavior, neglecting the distinct contributions and constraints faced by individual producers (e.g. Hu & Chen, 2019). In our paper, we depart from this trend by directly considering the fuel producer (j) in the KKT optimization and thereby uniquely contributing to the literature.

The adaptability of the KKT model to real-world complexities in fuel production optimization has been a subject of recent interest. In our article, by including factors such as varying fuel types, production constraints, and compliance with regulatory guidelines, we add a practical dimension to the theoretical framework (Hu & Chen, 2019).

3. Model Formulation

We consider the main decision variables $Q_{i,j}^t$ and $X_{i,j}^t$ where $Q_{i,j}^t$ is the production quantity of fuel type i by producer j in year t and $X_{i,j}^t$ is the quantity of carbon credits sold or purchased by producer j for fuel type i in year t:

$$X_{i,j}^t = \sum_k x_{ik}^t - \sum_k x_{ki}^t \tag{1}$$

where $k \in F_{-i}$ is an alternate type of transportation fuel. F is the index set of transportation fuels (gasoline, diesel, electricity, hydrogen, …) and F_{-i} is the index set of transportation fuels excluding fuels already produced. We define x_{ik}^t as the amount of carbon credits traded from fuel of type i to fuel of type k in year t and x_{ki}^t as the amount of credits traded from fuel of type k to type i in year t. In essence, Equation (1) stands for the net carbon credit sold (positive) or purchased (negative) by fuel producer j. The price of fuel (P_i^t),[1] the cost of fuel (C_i^t), and the unit price of carbon credit (P_R^t) are other inputs in the model. For the mandatory cap for fuel average carbon intensity (A_i^t)[2] and the index set of carbon intensity value for fuel transportation (I_i),[3] we must ensure the balance of carbon credits for each fuel producer in the following manner:

$$Q_{i,j}^t (A_i^t - I_i) \geq \sum_k x_{ik}^t - \sum_k x_{ki}^t \tag{2}$$

From Equation (1), we describe the objective function by

$$\begin{aligned} &P_i^t Q_{i,j}^t - C_i^t Q_{i,j}^t + P_R^t X_{i,j}^t \\ &= f^{-1}(Q_i) Q_{i,j}^t - C_i^t Q_{i,j}^t + P_R^t \left(\sum_k x_{ik}^t - \sum_k x_{ki}^t \right) \end{aligned} \tag{3}$$

---

[1] In dollars per metric ton of carbon dioxide equivalent ($ per Metric Ton CO2e).

[2] In grams of carbon dioxide equivalent per megajoule of energy (gCO2e/MJ).

[3] In grams of carbon dioxide equivalent per gallon (gCO2e per gallon).

In Equation (3), $P'Q'_f$ represents the fuel production revenue, $C'Q^t_{i,j}$ is the fuel production cost, P^t_R and $X^t_{i,j}$ is the revenue or cost of selling or purchasing carbon credits. Given T, the index set of time periods in years, we feasibly solve the problem and derive the following main optimization formulation by accounting for the objection function (3) and the constraint (2):

$$\max\left(f^{-1}(Q_i)Q^t_{i,j} - C^t_i Q^t_{i,j} + P^t_R\left(\sum_k x^t_{ik} - \sum_k x^t_{ki}\right)\right)$$

$$\text{s.t.} \quad Q^t_{i,j}(A^t_i - I_i) \geq \sum_k x^t_{ik} - \sum_k x^t_{ki} \tag{4}$$

$$Q^t_{i,j} \geq 0; t\in T; x^t_{ik}, x^t_{ik} \geq 0; i\in F; k\in F_{-i};$$

We assume that the demand for the fuel of type f is endogenously determined by its production quantity. Thus, we let $f^{-1}(Q_i)$ be the inverse demand function for fuel of type i where Q_i is the quantity of fuel of type i produced (Hu & Chen, 2019). Furthermore, we hold that the inverse demand function $f^{-1}(Q_i)$ flows in the following linear format for some constants A_i and B_i:

$$f^{-1}(Q_i) = A_i - B_i Q_i.$$

The objective function (3) is convex and continuous with respect to the decision variables $Q^t_{i,j}$ and $X^t_{i,j}$. For that matter, we can express the optimization problem (4) in terms of the following KKT optimality conditions:

$$\left(C^t_i - f^{-1}(Q^t_{i,j}) - f^{-1'}(Q^t_{i,j})Q^t_{i,j} - (A^t_i - I_i)\,\lambda_{t,i}\right) \perp Q^t_{i,j}$$

$$\left(Q^t_{i,j}(A^t_i - I_i) - \left(\sum_k x^t_{ik} - \sum_k x^t_{ki}\right)\right) \perp \lambda_{t,i}$$

$$(\lambda_{t,i} - P^t_R) \perp x^t_{ik}$$

$$C^t_i - f^{-1}(Q^t_{i,j}) - f^{-1'}(Q^t_{i,j})Q^t_{i,j} - (A^t_i - I_i)\lambda_{t,i} \geq 0 \tag{5}$$

$$\left(Q^t_{i,j}(A^t_i - I_i) - \left(\sum_k x^t_{ik} - \sum_k x^t_{ki}\right)\right) \geq 0\,(\lambda_{t,i} - P^t_R) \geq 0$$

$$Q^t_{i,j} \geq 0, x^t_{i,k} \geq 0, \lambda_{t,i} \geq 0$$

$$i\in F, k\in F_{-i}$$

The operator $x \perp y$ is the complementary condition equivalent to $x \cdot y = 0$. $\lambda_{t,i}$ is the Lagrange multiplier of fuel of type i at time period t and $f^{-1'}(Q_{i,j}^t)$ is the derivative of $f^{-1}(Q_{i,j}^t)$. It is possible to determine the equilibrium level of the market that would allow the fuel producer to maximize its profit. However, that level would only be attained if the supply of fuel in the gasoline and diesel categories meets its demand each year (6). Furthermore, as required by the EPA, the maximum blending rate of gasoline or diesel substitutes should be apportioned to blend in gasoline or diesel (7). The two new constraints can be expressed as follows:

$$\sum_{i \in F_G} Q_{i,j}^t \geq \Delta_G^t, \quad \sum_{i \in F_D} Q_{i,j}^t \geq \Delta_D^t, t \in T \tag{6}$$

$$\frac{\sum_{i \in R_G} Q_{i,j}^t}{\sum_{i \in F_G} Q_{i,j}^t} \leq \Theta_G, \quad \frac{\sum_{i \in R_D} Q_{i,j}^t}{\sum_{i \in F_G} Q_{i,j}^t} \leq \Theta_D, t \in T \tag{7}$$

$F_G = \{\text{Gasoline, } R_G\}$ and $F_D = \{\text{Diesel, } R_D\}$. Δ_G^t and Δ_D^t, respectively, describe the demand for gasoline and diesel fuels at time period t.[4] R_G is an index set of renewable gasoline substitutes such as corn ethanol, sugarcane ethanol, cellulosic ethanol, or pure gasoline. R_D is the index set of renewable diesel substitutes such as ultra-low sulfur diesel, biodiesel, and renewable diesel. Θ_G and Θ_D are successively the maximum renewable fuel blend percentage for gasoline and for diesel, respectively.[5] Equation (6) guarantees that the supply of fuel in the gasoline and diesel generators aligns with their respective demands each year. As stipulated by the EPA (2007), Equation (7) dictates the highest permissible blending rate of gasoline or diesel substitutes into gasoline or diesel.[6] For fuel producer j, the set of solutions that satisfies equation (3.5) along with conditions (3.6) and (3.7) represents the solution that achieves market equilibrium.

---

[4] The unit is in Gasoline Gallon Equivalent (GGE) per year.

[5] It is about 15% for gasoline and 20% for diesel.

[6] It represents the blend wall constraint.

4. Conclusion

The escalating threat of climate change, underscored by record-breaking temperatures in 2023 and ominous predictions for 2024, necessitates urgent and innovative strategies to mitigate climate risks. This paper addresses this imperative challenge by delving into the intersection of climate risk mitigation, carbon trading, and the utilization of the KKT optimization framework. Carbon trading systems have emerged as pivotal tools in fostering sustainable development by assigning a financial value to emissions, promoting cleaner practices, and facilitating the transition to a low-carbon economy. Within this framework, the KKT model, deeply rooted in mathematical optimization theory, stands out as a powerful methodology for solving constrained optimization problems. Our focus lies at the juncture of production quantity and fuel prices, recognizing the pivotal role of the energy sector in influencing both environmental impact and economic viability. This paper aims to contribute to the theoretical foundation of climate risk management, providing insights into the intricate dynamics of fuel production and advancing research on sustainable practices.

Central to our exploration is the application of the KKT model to navigate the multidimensional landscape of fuel production. The quantification of market demand, incorporating linear inverse demand functions, and the consideration of polynomial or exponential relationships between fuel price and production quantity illustrate the depth of our approach. Through the integration of carbon trading mechanisms, we address the associated costs and benefits of emissions reduction, aiming for a unified model that considers economic variables and environmental objectives simultaneously. The KKT conditions guide decision-making, achieving a delicate balance between meeting market demands and minimizing the carbon footprint of fuel production.

A distinctive contribution lies in the direct incorporation of individual fuel producers into the optimization model, departing from prior research paradigms. By transforming maximum profit objectives into KKT optimality constraints for each fuel producer, we facilitate the attainment of market equilibrium, marking a significant advancement in understanding and optimizing fuel production dynamics. This departure is particularly pivotal in navigating real-world industrial complexities, ensuring compliance with regulations such as the blend wall constraint and guaranteeing the supply of fuel for specific generators.

Appendix

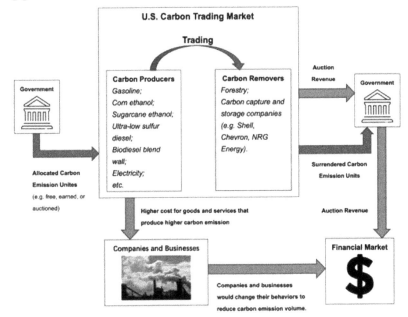

Figure A.1.   U.S. carbon trading market

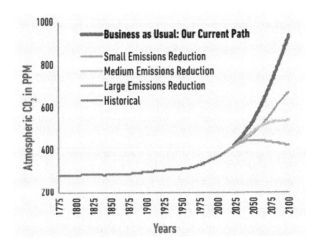

Figure A.2.   Global emissions scenarios

Source: Risky Business (2014).

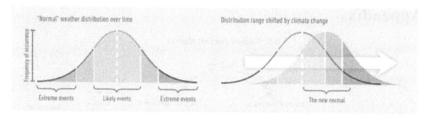

Figure A.3.   How extreme weather events become the norm
Source: Risky Business (2014).

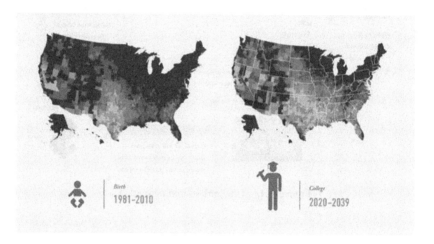

Figure A.4.   Average days over 95°F: Projections mapped over a lifetime
Source: Risky Business (2014).

References

Boyd, S. & Vandenberghe, L. (2004). *Convex Optimization*. Cambridge University Press, Cambridge, UK.

Cao, J. Yang, D., & Dehghanian, P. (2023). Co-optimization of multiple virtual power plants considering electricity-heat-carbon trading: A stackelberg game strategy. *International Journal of Electrical Power & Energy Systems*, 153(109294).

Cao, J., Zheng, Y., Han, X., Yang, D., Yu, J., Tomin, N., & Dehghanian, P. (2022). Two-stage optimization of a virtual power plant incorporating with demand response and energy complementation. *Energy Reports*, 8, 7374–7385.

EPA. (2007). *Guidance for Biodiesel Producers and Biodiesel Blenders*. Users Transportation and Regional Programs Division.

Guo, C., Luo, F., Cai, Z., & Dong, Z. Y. (2021). Integrated energy systems of data centers and smart grids: State-of-the-art and future opportunities. *Applied Energy*, 301(117474).

Helm, D. (2017). *Burn Out: The Endgame for Fossil Fuels*. Ed. by Yale University Press. SAGE Publications, New Haven, Connecticut.

Hu, K. & Chen, Y. (2019). Equilibrium fuel supply and carbon credit pricing under market competition and environmental regulations: A California Case Study. *Applied Energy*, 236, 815–824.

Jia, S., Peng, K., Zhang, X., Li, Y., & Xing, L. (2022). Dynamic pricing strategy and regional energy consumption optimization based on different stakeholders. *International Journal of Electrical Power & Energy Systems*, 141(108199).

Karush, W. (1939). Minima of functions of several variables with inequalities as side constraints. MA thesis. Chicago, Illinois: Department of Mathematics, University of Chicago.

Kuhn, H. W. & Tucker, A. W. (1951). Nonlinear programming. In *Proceedings of 2nd Berkeley Symposium*. MR 0047303. University of California Press, pp. 481–492.

Liu, X., Zhou, X., Zhu, B., He, K., & Wang, P. (2019). Measuring the maturity of carbon market in China: An entropy-based TOPSIS approach. *Journal of Cleaner Production*, 229, 94–103.

Risky Business. (2014). The economic risks of climate change in the United States. Technical report, National Report. Retrieved from https://riskybusiness.org/report/national/.

Yılmaz Balaman, Ş., Scott, J., Matopoulos, A., & Wright, D. G. (2019). Incentivising bioenergy production: Economic and environmental insights from a regional optimization methodology. *Renewable Energy*, 130, 867–880.

Zhang, W., Li, J., Li, G., & Guo, S. (2020). Emission reduction effect and carbon market efficiency of carbon emissions trading policy in china energy. *Energy*, 196(117117).

Part 3

Sustainable Investing Strategies

Chapter 13

Portfolio Management with News-Based Sustainability Scores

**Ron Große[*], Viet Hoang Le[†], Fei Liu[‡],
and Hans-Jörg von Mettenheim[‡]**

[*]*Norddeutsche Landesbank, Hannover, Germany*
[†]*Université Paris Saclay and Keynum Investments, Paris, France*
[‡]*IPAG Business School, Paris, France*

Abstract

In this chapter, we present a novel approach to produce Environmental, Social, and Governance (ESG) and Sustainable Development Goal (SDG) scores based on near-real-time news. Through the application of Natural Language Processing (NLP) techniques, we extract the relevant entities, topics, and likely effects of the news. The individual information is aggregated into scores on a regular time grid. Based on the scores, we build topic-oriented portfolios and compare them to a benchmark. The data have been provided in the AiData.green database that was co-developed by the authors of this chapter. In our studies, we cover mostly European and US markets. We find that substantial risk-adjusted outperformance of portfolios can be achieved by taking sustainability topics into account.

1. Introduction

In this chapter, we present an innovative approach to generating Environmental, Social, and Governance (ESG) and Sustainable Development Goal (SDG) scores through the analysis of near-real-time news data. Leveraging advanced Natural Language Processing (NLP) techniques, we extract key information — entities, topics, and anticipated impact — from news articles, aggregating these insights into scores on a regular time grid. The invaluable data source for our study is the AiData. green database, collaboratively developed by the authors of this chapter.

Our investigation initially centers on the European and US markets, specifically stocks in the STOXX600 and S&P500 indices, where we explore the profound influence of sentiment on market dynamics, investment decisions, and the creation of trading strategies. Drawing on previous research demonstrating the significance of sentiment indicators in the European stock market, particularly in explaining company returns and facilitating profitable trading strategies — especially with ESG-related and SDG-related news indicators — we set the stage for a broader examination.

Expanding our scope, we extend our analysis to the Vietnamese stock markets, an uncharted territory in the context of sentiment dynamics. Armed with an extensive database comprising around 8.6 million news articles from diverse sources, we meticulously examine various dimensions, including company-focused sentiment and specific topics, such as ESG themes and SDG themes. Notably, our chapter stands as the first to venture into the Vietnamese market in this regard.

Similar to our findings in the European and US markets that have established the potential for substantial risk-adjusted outperformance through the incorporation of sustainability topics into investment considerations, the Vietnamese market once again shows better performance of sustainability indicators. Unlike the European markets, preliminary results for Vietnam indicate that sentiment indicators such as Tone and Polarity do not exhibit significant relationships with stock returns. However, a noteworthy observation emerges — the quantity of positive and negative news articles carries substantial influence.

2. Literature Review

In examining sentiment analysis rooted in news data and its implications for finance, numerous studies have contributed valuable insights. Tuckett *et al.* (2014) and Shiller (2017) proposed that positive and negative sentiments extracted from newspapers can serve as indicators for economic cycles. Baker *et al.* (2016, 2020) introduced novel variables derived from news articles, shedding light on their relevance in explaining stock price volatility, investment rates, and employment growth. Fraiberger *et al.* (2021) and Colladon *et al.* (2020) utilized sentiment from *Reuters* and Italian news articles to predict emerging stock markets and Italian stock markets, respectively. Fronzetti Colladon and Elshendy (2017) and Tilly *et al.* (2021) extended their analysis to news data from the GDELT project, offering forecasts for macroeconomic indices. Additionally, studies by Kazemian *et al.* (2016) and Mudinas *et al.* (2019) explored applications of sentiment analysis in the trading domain.

While the Efficient Market Hypothesis (EMH) posits the efficiency of financial markets, incorporating all available information into stock prices rapidly, recent research challenges this notion, especially regarding topic-specific data such as ESG-related news Fama (1970). Schmidt (2019) highlighted a connection between ESG-related news and stocks' financial performance, challenging the EMH assumption. Capelle-Blancard and Petit (2019) found that firms facing negative events experience market value drops, while positive announcements have negligible impact. Chen *et al.* (2020) estimated stock-level ESG beta, considering economy-wide ESG concerns and stock return history. Kvam *et al.* (2022) generated ESG scores from sentiment extracted from Google Trends, Twitter, and the VIX index, revealing a negative relationship with stock returns that turns positive during ESG concerns.

The methodological landscape of sentiment extraction from text encompasses traditional approaches like the bag-of-words method and more sophisticated techniques like word embedding. Wang *et al.* (2014) employed sentiment analysis on StockTwits data using supervised learning on pre-classified "Bullish" or "Bearish" messages. Word embedding, a deep learning methodology, captures the order of information in text, encoding word meanings in real-valued vectors. This innovation facilitates the proximity of words with similar meanings in the vector space.

Despite the wealth of sentiment analysis research in finance, there remains a gap in studies focusing on the Vietnamese market. Chau *et al.* (2023) and Vu *et al.* (2023) investigated sentiment extraction from news and stock market reactions in Vietnam, but a specific exploration of trading strategies in the Vietnamese context was lacking. Our current research seeks to bridge this gap, offering insights into sentiment-driven trading strategies within Vietnamese stock markets. Building upon our previous study on the European market, where we identified significant relationships between sentiment indicators and stock returns, leading to profitable trading strategies, with a specific emphasis on ESG-related indicators (Goutte *et al.*, 2023), our work aims to enrich the literature by extending our analysis to the Vietnamese financial landscape.

3. Data Description

This section delineates the data employed in our study, encompassing news articles pertinent to stocks from the STOXX600, S&P500, and VN100 indices, spanning the periods from 2015 to 2023.

The STOXX600 and S&P500 datasets involves the collection of news data from Google Search, accumulating approximately 15 million articles from over a hundred countries, with an emphasis on the results from the US and European countries. Around 1.6 thousand diverse data sources were identified, with a notable presence in the US and UK. This dataset also includes news articles in languages other than English, especially translated for comprehensive analysis of the STOXX600 index.

The VN100 dataset comprises approximately 600,000 articles from around 500 online newspapers, with a primary focus on English-language news from Vietnam (90%) and additional contributions from US and UK websites. While our dataset predominantly centers on English news, it includes news articles in languages other than English, particularly Vietnamese in this study. To ensure language consistency, these non-English articles were translated into English. Similar to the STOXX600 and S&P500 dataset, each article in this dataset is equipped with a timestamp, title, and main text as specified in Table 1.

Both datasets leverage ElasticSearch, a NoSQL database software, for efficient organization and retrieval of massive text databases. The unstructured nature of the datasets necessitates ElasticSearch's real-time search capabilities, facilitating the identification of articles mentioning specific companies and topics of interest.

For sentiment analysis, all three datasets aim to assess sentiments related to the topic of sustainability. Articles are categorized into different subtopics based on either the three pillars ESG or the 17 Sustainable Development Goals (SDGs) established by the United Nations General Assembly in 2015. Sentiment is gauged using a lexicon-based approach, employing predefined dictionaries of tonal words. Sentiment scores, including positive tone, negative tone, overall tone, and polarity, are calculated for each article as described in Table 1.

Table 1.   Sentiment Fields from each article

Field	Description
Timestamp	The date time in YYYYMMDDHHMMSS format on which the article was published.
Companies	The list of all mentioned company and organization names found in the text of the article.
ESG Topics	The list of all ESG topics found in the text of the article.
SDG Topics	The list of all SDG topics found in the text of the article.
Positive Tone	The percentage of positive words in the article. Ranges from 0 to 100.
Negative Tone	The percentage of negative words in the article. Ranges from 0 to 100.
Tone	The average "tone" of the document as a whole. Ranges from –100 to 100.
Polarity	The indicator of how emotionally polarized the text of the article is. Ranges from 0 to 200.
Word Count	The total number of words in the document.

To consolidate individual news articles into monthly intervals, sentiment indicators are aggregated by averaging the sentiment variables of all articles mentioning a particular stock company during a given month. Additional fields, such as the total number of news articles, positive news articles, and negative news articles, are introduced for each month. Two ESG- and SDG-related counterparts are created for these fields which only consider news articles that are related to those topics. In total, 25 different monthly sentiment indicators are generated for both datasets as illustrated in Table 2.

Regarding stock price data, monthly price data (log return based on close prices) for stocks from the three indices are utilized which cover the period from January 2015 to November 2023. The composition of the indices and the stock price data are obtained from investing.com and Yahoo Finance, respectively.

4. Methodology

4.1. *Statistical Analysis*

A necessary condition for our sentiment indicators to be useful in predicting stock prices is that they exhibit some correlation with future prices.

Table 2.   Monthly Sentiment Indicators for each stock

Field	Description
Date	The timestamp for the month that is reflected by the indicator.
Tone	The average "Tone" of all articles that mention the stocks in that month.
Positive Tone	The average "Positive Tone" of all articles that mention the stocks in that month.
Negative Tone	The average "Negative Tone" of all articles that mention the stocks in that month.
Polarity	The average "Polarity" of all articles that mention the stocks in that month.
News Count	The total number of articles that mention the stocks in that month.
Positive News Count	The total number of positive articles that mention the stocks in that month.
Negative News Count	The total number of negative articles that mention the stocks in that month.
Word Count	The average number of words that each article contains in that month.
SDG Tone	The average "Tone" of SDG articles that mention the stocks in that month.
SDG Positive Tone	The average "Positive Tone" of SDG articles that mention the stocks in that month.
SDG Negative Tone	The average "Negative Tone" of SDG articles that mention the stocks in that month.
SDG Polarity	The average "Polarity" of all SDG articles that mention the stocks in that month.
SDG News Count	The total number of SDG articles that mention the stocks in that month.
SDG Positive News Count	The total number of positive SDG articles that mention the stocks in that month.
SDG Negative News Count	The total number of negative SDG articles that mention the stocks in that month.
SDG Word Count	The average number of words that each SDG article contains in that month.
ESG Tone	The average "Tone" of ESG articles that mention the stocks in that month.
ESG Positive Tone	The average "Positive Tone" of ESG articles that mention the stocks in that month.

Table 2. (*Continued*)

Field	Description
ESG Negative Tone	The average "Negative Tone" of ESG articles that mention the stocks in that month.
ESG Polarity	The average "Polarity" of all ESG articles that mention the stocks in that month.
ESG News Count	The total number of ESG articles that mention the stocks in that month.
ESG Positive News Count	The total number of positive ESG articles that mention the stocks in that month.
ESG Negative News Count	The total number of negative ESG articles that mention the stocks in that month.
ESG Word Count	The average number of words that each ESG article contains in that month.

To explore this possibility, we conducted a comprehensive regression analysis based on the Capital Asset Pricing Theory, examining the linear relationship between the sentiment indicators and the subsequent returns of stocks. The regression model is as follows:

$$R_{i,t} = \alpha + \beta_0 R_{M,t} + \beta_n \text{SentimentIndicator}_{i,t-1} + \varepsilon,$$

where $R_{i,t}$ represents the log return of each individual stock at time t and $R_{M,t}$ denotes the log return of the stock index at time t. Sentiment-Indicator$_{i,t-1}$ represents the value of each sentiment variable at time $t-1$ and ε is the error term. Following the approach in our previous work, Goutte *et al.* (2023), we used the Pooled Ordinary Least Squares (OLS) method for all three datasets. The results of our panel regression are presented in Tables 3–11 for the general sentiment indicators, the ESG-related indicators, and the SDG-related indicators of each universe.

4.2. *STOXX600 Dataset*

Table 3 exhibits the regression outcomes for four combinations of the eight general sentiment indicators applied to the STOXX600 dataset. In our prior study (Goutte *et al.*, 2023), we solely focused on the overall number of monthly news articles (News Count) for each stock and found no significant correlation with subsequent stock prices. In this study, we

Table 3.   STOXX600 — General sentiment indicators regression result

Dependent Variable	Log Return ($t+1$)									
	1	2	3	4	5	6	7	8	9	10
Positive News Count	-4.882E-06**		-4.882E-06**		-4.388E-06*			-4.388E-06*		
Negative News Count	1.64E-06		1.64E-06		8.24E-07			8.20E-07		
Positive Tone	3.194E-03***	3.151E-03***							3.136E-03***	
Negative Tone	-1.413E-03*	-1.358E-03*							-1.576E-03**	
Word Count	3.58E-07	3.58E-07	3.58E-07	3.58E-07	3.159E-07	3.65E-07				3.211E-07
News Count	-1.212E-06**	-1.212E-06**		-1.212E-06**						
Tone			2.304E-03***	2.255E-03***		2.368E-03***	2.356E-03***			
Polarity			8.90E-04	0.0008966		0.0007739	0.0007798			
Index Return	1.071E-00***	1.071E-00***	1.071E-00***	1.071E+00***	1.072E-00***	1.072E-00***	1.072E-00***	1.072E-00***	1.072E-00***	1.072E-00***
Const.	-2.29E-02***	-2.30E-02***	-2.29E-02***	-2.30E-02***	-1.725E-02***	-2.292e-02***	-2.26E-02***	-1.696E-02***	-2.26E-02***	-1.784E-02***

Note: ***99%; **95%; *90%.

Table 4. STOXX600 — ESG-related indicators regression result

Dependent Variable	Log Return ($t+1$)									
	1	2	3	4	5	6	7	8	9	10
ESG Positive News Count	-3.36E-06		-3.36E-06		-2.74E-06			-2.73E-06		
ESG Negative News Count	-1.07E-06		-1.07E-06		-2.23E-06			-2.24E-06		
ESG Positive Tone	**2.247E-03*****	**2.241E-03*****							**2.274E-03*****	
ESG Negative Tone	**-1.868E-03*****	**-1.879E-03*****							**-2.017E-03*****	
ESG Word Count	3.00E-07	3.00E-07	3.00E-07	3.00E-07	2.91E-07	3.05E-07				2.90E-07
ESG News Count		**-1.715E-06****		**-1.715E-06****						
ESG Tone			**2.058E-03*****	**2.060E-03*****		**2.150E-03*****	**2.146E-03*****			
ESG Polarity			0.0001894	0.0001813		0.0001026	0.0001284			
Index Return	1.072E-00***	1.072E-00***	1.072E-00***	1.072E-00***	1.072E-00***	1.072E-00***	1.072E-00***	1.072E-00***	1.072E-00***	1.072E-00***
Const.	-1.91E-02***	-1.91E-02***	-1.91E-02***	-1.91E-02***	-1.73E-02***	-1.917E-02***	-1.90E-02***	-1.706E-02***	-1.90E-02***	-1.780E-02***

Note: ***99%; **95%; *90%.

Table 5. STOXX600 — SDG-related indicators regression result

Dependent Variable	Log Return ($t+1$)									
	1	2	3	4	5	6	7	8	9	10
SDG positive News Count	**-8.096E-06****		**-8.096E-06****		**-7.508E-06****			**-7.498E-06****		
SDG negative News Count	2.25E-06		2.25E-06		1.223E-06			1.217E-06		
SDG Positive Tone	**2.202E-03*****	**2.150E-03*****							**2.185E-03*****	
SDG Negative Tone	**-1.67E-03*****	**-1.636E-03*****							**-1.82E-03*****	
SDG Word Count	3.04E-07	3.017E-07	3.04E-07	3.017E-07	2.915E-07	3.08E-07				2.884E-07
SDG News Count		**-1.818E-06****		**-1.818E-06****						
SDG Tone			**1.939E-03*****	**1.893E-03*****		**2.011E-03*****	**2.004E-03*****			
SDG Polarity			2.63E-04	2.57E-04		1.54E-04	1.81E-04			
Index Return	1.071E-00***	1.072E-00***	1.071E-00***	1.072E-00***	1.072E-00***	1.072E-00***	1.072E-00***	1.072E-00***	1.072E-00***	1.072E-00***
Const.	-1.94E-02***	-1.95E-02***	-1.94E-02***	-1.95E-02***	-1.72E-02***	-1.950E-02***	-1.93E-02***	-1.692E-02***	-1.93E-02***	-1.781E-02***

Note: ***99%; **95%; *90%.

Table 6.   S&P500 — General sentiment indicators regression result

Dependent Variable	Log Return ($t+1$)									
	1	2	3	4	5	6	7	8	9	10
Positive News Count	**1.649E-06*****		**1.649E-06*****		**1.631E-06*****			**1.631E-06*****		
Negative News Count	**−1.201E-06****		**−1.201E-06****		**−1.218E-06****			**−1.218E-06****		
Positive Tone	−9.16E-04	−8.11E-04							−8.10E-04	
Negative Tone	−3.23E-04	−4.03E-04							−4.00E-04	
Word Count	−1.13E-08	−1.88E-08	−1.13E-08	−1.88E-08	−4.00E-09	−1.90E-08				−1.21E-08
News Count		7.521E-09		7.52E-09						
Tone			−0.0002969	−0.0002037		−0.0002055	−0.0002053			
Polarity			−6.20E-04	−6.07E-04		−6.05E-04	−6.05E-04			
Index Return	1.069e+00***	1.069e+00***	1.069e+00***	1.069e+00***	1.069e+00***	1.069e+00***	1.069e+00***	1.069e+00***	1.069e+00***	1.068e+00***
Const.	1.63E-04	2.41E-04	1.63E-04	2.41E-04	−3.010E-03***	2.39E-04	2.19E-04	−3.014E-03***	2.19E-04	−2.823E-03***

Note: ***99%; **95%; *90%.

Table 7. S&P500 — ESG-related indicators regression result

Dependent Variable	Log Return ($t+1$)									
	1	2	3	4	5	6	7	8	9	10
ESG Positive News Count	2.01E-06**		2.01E-06**		2.03E-06**			2.03E-06**		
ESG Negative News Count	−1.38E-06		−1.38E-06		−1.43E-06*			−1.43E-06*		
ESG Positive Tone	−4.45E-04	−4.23E-04							−4.05E-04	
ESG Negative Tone	−1.96E-04	−2.04E-04							−2.66E-04	
ESG Word Count	8.70E-08	7.54E-08	8.70E-08	7.54E-08	8.14E-08	8.05E-08				7.54E-08
ESG News Count		−2.29E-07		−2.29E-07						
ESG Tone			−1.25E-04	−1.09E-04		−7.03E-05	−6.94E-05			
ESG Polarity			−3.21E-04	−3.14E-04		−3.37E-04	−3.36E-04			
Index Return	1.07E-00***	1.07E-00***	1.07E-00***	1.07E-00***	1.07E-00***	1.07E-00***	1.07E-00***	1.07E-00***	1.07E-00***	1.07E-00***
Const.	−1.45E-03	−1.25E-03	−1.45E-03	−1.25E-03	−3.05E-03***	−1.26E-03	−1.19E-03	−2.970E-03***	−1.19E-03	−2.906E-03***

Note: ***99%; **95%; *90%.

Table 8. S&P500 — SDG-related indicators regression result

Dependent Variable	Log Return ($t+1$)									
	1	2	3	4	5	6	7	8	9	10
SDG Positive News Count	**2.540E-06*****		**2.540E-06*****		**2.557E-06*****			**2.561E-06*****		
SDG Negative News Count	**-1.627E-06****		**-1.627E-06****		**-1.718E-06****			**-1.719E-06****		
SDG Positive Tone	-6.17E-04	-5.31E-04							-5.28E-04	
SDG Negative Tone	-4.61E-04	-4.89E-04							-5.31E-04	
SDG Word Count	-1.229E-07	-1.336E-07	-1.23E-07	-1.34E-07	-1.316E-07	-1.31E-07				-0.00000014
SDG News Count		-1.25E-07		-1.25E-07						
SDG Tone			-7.78E-05	-2.10E-05		1.24E-06	1.52E-06			
SDG Polarity			**-5.388E-04***	-5.10E-04		-5.27E-04	-5.29E-04			
Index Return	1.069E-00***	1.069E-00***	1.069E-00***	1.069E-00***	1.069e-00***	1.069e+00***	1.069E-00***	1.069E-00***	1.069E-00***	1.068E-00***
Const.	-1.50E-04	-0.00007806	-1.50E-04	-0.00007806	-2.86E-03***	-0.00006176	-0.0001856	-2.998E-03***	-0.0001856	-2.691E-03***

Note: ***99%; **95%; *90%.

Table 9. VN100 — General sentiment indicators regression result

Dependent Variable	Log Return (t+1)									
	1	2	3	4	5	6	7	8	9	10
Positive News Count	**-4.539E-04***		**-4.539E-04***		**-3.856E-04***			**-3.778E-04***		
Negative News Count	0.0002544		2.54E-04		0.0002016			0.000167		
Positive Tone	**2.084E-03***	1.73E-03							1.73E-03	
Negative Tone	6.36E-04	1.05E-03							8.24E-04	
Word Count	**1.682E-06***	**1.668E-06***	**1.682E-06***	**1.668E-06***	**1.709E-06***	**1.701E-06***				**1.707E-06***
News Count		-5.52E-05		-5.523E-05						
Tone			0.0007242	0.0003419		0.0003623	0.0004534			
Polarity			1.36E-03	1.39E-03		1.31E-03	1.28E-03			
Index Return	1.127E-00***	1.128E-00***	1.127E-00***	1.128E-00***	1.128E-00***	1.128E-00***	1.129E-00***	1.129E-00***	1.129E-00***	1.128E-00***
Const.	-6.38E-03	-6.77E-03	-6.38E-03	-6.77E-03	-5.33E-05	-7.051E-03*	-4.91E-03	2.10E-03	-4.91E-03	-1.03E-03

Note: ***99%; **95%; *90%.

Table 10.   VN100 — ESG-related indicators regression result

Dependent Variable	Log Return ($t+1$)									
	1	2	3	4	5	6	7	8	9	10
ESG Positive News Count	-5.762E-04**		-5.762E-04*		-4.810E-04*			-0.0004541		
ESG Negative News Count	3.64E-04		3.64E-04		0.0002619			0.0002136		
ESG Positive Tone	1.18E-03	7.15E-04							9.00E-04	
ESG Negative Tone	-3.78E-04	0.0000869							-6.016E-06	
ESG Word Count	1.763E-06**	1.713E-06*	1.763E-06**	1.713E-06*	1.862E-06**	1.736E-06*				1.804E-06**
ESG News Count		-5.89E-05		-5.89E-05						
ESG Tone			7.78E-04	3.14E-04		3.29E-04	4.53E-04			
ESG Polarity			4.01E-04	4.01E-04		3.27E-04	4.47E-04			
Index Return	1.128E-00***	1.128E-00***	1.128E-00***	1.128E-00***	1.128E-00***	1.128E-00***	1.129E-00***	1.129E-00***	1.129E-00***	1.128E-00***
Const.	-2.07E-03	-2.25E-03	-2.07E-03	-2.25E-03	-1.91E-04	-2.47E-03	-1.03E-03	1.99E-03	-1.03E-03	-1.03E-03

Note: ***99%; **95%; *90%.

Table 11. VN100 — SDG-related indicators regression result

Dependent Variable	Log Return (t+1)									
	1	2	3	4	5	6	7	8	9	10
SDG Positive News Count	-3.44E-04		-3.44E-04		-0.0002781			-0.0002541		
SDG Negative News Count	1.15E-04		1.15E-04		8.53E-05			4.36E-05		
SDG Positive Tone	1.07E-03	0.0008684							0.00101	
SDG Negative Tone	2.07E-04	3.69E-04							2.50E-04	
SDG Word Count	1.482E-06*	1.465E-06*	1.482E-06*	1.465E-06*	1.591E-06**	1.494E-06*				1.579E-06**
SDG News Count		-6.37E-05		-6.37E-05						
SDG Tone			0.0004297	0.0002496		0.0002659	0.0003799			
SDG Polarity			6.36E-04	6.19E-04		5.17E-04	6.30E-04			
Index Return	1.128E-00***	1.129E-00***	1.128E-00***	1.129E-00***	1.128E-00***	1.128E-00***	1.129E-00***	1.129E+00***	1.129E-00***	1.128E-00***
Const.	-0.002956	-0.003041	-2.96E-03	-3.04E-03	-0.000316	-3.17E-03	-1.81E-03	0.001727	-0.001813	-0.0009555

Note: ***99%, **95%, *90%.

delve deeper by dissecting the News Count into Positive News Count and Negative News Count, allowing for a more nuanced examination of how news sentiment impacts stock prices.

Positive News Count pertains to news articles highlighting positive events related to a stock, such as favorable financial results or strategic partnerships. A higher count signifies increased investor confidence and the potential for elevated stock prices. Conversely, Negative News Count encompasses articles spotlighting adverse events like poor financial performance or legal issues, potentially leading to diminished investor confidence and subsequent stock price declines.

By separately scrutinizing positive and negative amounts of news each month, we gain a comprehensive understanding of how market sentiment influences stock returns. This analytical approach aids in identifying the factors that drive both positive and negative sentiments, facilitating informed decision-making and the anticipation of market shifts.

Within the table, we present 10 distinct combinations of sentiment indicators. Since Tone and Polarity can be derived from Positive Tone and Negative Tone, and News Count can be derived from Positive and Negative News Count, they are not simultaneously regressed. Similar to our findings in the European market (Goutte *et al.*, 2023), we identify a significant relationship between News Count and Tone concerning stock returns in the STOXX600 index ($p < 0.05$ for News Count and $p < 0.01$ for Tone). While Tone emphasizes the overall sentiment, the Polarity is intended to describe how extreme the sentiment is. These two variables can be further broken down into smaller components, such as Positive News Count, Positive Tone, and Negative Tone, all exhibiting some significance ($p < 0.05$ for Positive News Count, $p < 0.01$ for Positive Tone, and only $p < 0.1$ for Negative Tone). Notably, the negative coefficient of Positive News Count may seem counterintuitive. However, as we observed, negative coefficients for News Count, this can be explained by the fact that stocks with more news (international news in this case, as most of our news is in English) generally have a higher market cap and more popular stocks, which typically offer lower returns than smaller stocks. It is plausible that the Positive News Count variable suffers from similar effects. Regarding the coefficients of Tone, Positive Tone, and Negative Tone, the results are rational, featuring positive coefficients with Tone and Positive Tone and a negative relationship with Negative Tone.

This observed phenomenon extends to the ESG- and SDG-related indicators (Tables 4 and 5), with minor differences, such as ESG Positive

News Count not being significant or Negative Tone being more significant when considering only ESG and SDG news. Nevertheless, overall, the regression results remain quite similar, regardless of the news topic.

4.3. *S&P500 Dataset*

Regarding the regression outcomes for the US stock market, notable distinctions emerge when compared to the European market. As delineated in Tables 6–8, we observe that only the variables Positive News Count and Negative News Count exhibit significance. Particularly noteworthy is that Positive News Count consistently manifests smaller p-values ($p < 0.01$) in most cases, unlike the ESG-related Negative News Count indicators, which show significance at $p < 0.05$ or even prove non-significant.

An intriguing observation arises with the SDG-related Polarity, exhibiting weak significance in a single instance. However, this significance is contingent on the variable being regressed in conjunction with Positive News Count, Negative News Count, and Word Count. This significance dissipates when regressed alone or when Positive News Count and Negative News Count are excluded. Remarkably, News Count alone fails to attain significance. This could imply that the correlation between the number of news articles and the market cap/popularity of stocks in the US market is comparatively weaker. This interpretation aligns with the fact that our news sources primarily feature English-language content from the US where stocks in the S&P500 index are already widely known. Consequently, there might be minimal variance in the volume of news coverage for these stocks.

In contrast to the European stock markets, the coefficients of Positive News Count and Negative News Count in the US stock markets exhibit more logical patterns, demonstrating a positive relationship with Positive News Count and a negative relationship with Negative News Count. As discussed earlier, the negative impact of News Count (reflecting the relationship between more news, a higher market cap, and lower returns) appears to be less pronounced in the US context, allowing Positive News Count and Negative News Count coefficients to convey rational implications.

4.4. *VN100 Dataset*

Tables 9–11 present the regression findings for the Vietnamese stock markets, revealing a notable decrease in the significance levels of the variables. Notably, only Positive News Count, Positive Tone, and Word Count emerge as statistically significant, with a substantially weaker level of significance — most p-values barely surpass the 0.1 threshold. This diminishing significance might be attributed to Vietnam's status as an emerging market, coupled with the predominance of English-language news sources. It is reasonable to infer that sentiment indicators derived from English news may wield less influence compared to indicators grounded in the local language.

Additionally, the performance of ESG- and SDG-related variables falls short of the general indicators, suggesting that the impact of sustainability-related topics may not be as pronounced in an emerging market like Vietnam compared to more established markets.

However, a noteworthy similarity between the Vietnamese and European stock markets lies in the coefficients of Positive News Count and Negative News Count, both exhibiting irrational patterns with negative and positive coefficients, respectively. Similarly, the coefficients of Positive Tone, though often non-significant, consistently show a logical positive direction. The following question then arises: What commonalities between the European and Vietnamese stock markets set them apart from the US stock market? Our hypothesis centers on the news sources. In both the European and Vietnamese markets, where news sources are predominantly English, the language of the news articles used to formulate sentiment indicators is not the local language. Consequently, factors such as the impact of more news, a higher market cap, greater visibility, and lower returns should be taken into account. This is further emphasized by the presence of the negative coefficients of News Count in all regression cases in the Vietnamese market, aligning with observations in the European market, but notably absent in the US stock market, as discussed earlier.

5. Trading Experiments

Given the paramount significance of sentiment variables, specifically Positive News Count, Negative News Count, Positive Tone, and Negative Tone, we crafted a straightforward trading strategy based on their coefficients. Our approach involves utilizing the previous month's criteria to select the next month's investment portfolio. We devised three distinct trading strategies:

- **Long-only strategy:** This conventional strategy involves taking long positions in the top n stocks with the highest selected sentiment variable for positive coefficients (or the lowest for negative coefficients).

- **Long-index strategy:** This is a market-neutral approach where we long the top n stocks and, instead of shorting individual stocks, we short the (Exchange Traded Fund) ETF representing the corresponding index.
- **Long-short strategy:** Another market-neutral strategy, this entails taking long positions in the top n stocks with the highest selected sentiment variable and short positions in the bottom n stocks with the lowest variable.

It is important to note that we excluded Short-Only strategies due to the complexities associated with shorting, especially in emerging markets like Vietnam, where shorting individual stocks may be restricted or unavailable. Additionally, even in well-established markets like Europe and the US, finding shares to borrow for shorting can be challenging, causing one to incur high borrowing fees or face liquidity issues and potentially higher costs compared to more liquid and diversified ETFs.

Due to these limitations, the long–short strategy's performance primarily serves to illustrate the effectiveness of sentiment indicators conceptually, rather than being a recommended investment strategy for real-world trading.

Instead, our focus lies on the long-index and long-only strategies, which are more practical and feasible in most markets. The long-index strategy, which involves shorting the ETF representing the corresponding index, allows us to explore the impact of sentiment variables on a market-neutral approach while avoiding the challenges of shorting individual stocks. The long-only strategy, reflecting a traditional investment approach, enables us to assess the effectiveness of sentiment indicators in selecting a long portfolio of stocks with potentially positive sentiment signals.

For each type of strategy, we conducted experiments using different values of n. In the European and US stock markets, where the number of constituents is substantial (600 and 500 stocks, respectively), we chose 5 different values of n (10, 30, 50, 70, and 90 stocks), with the largest number being around 20% of the total stocks in each universe. As the Vietnamese stock index comprises fewer stocks (100), we selected 4 different sets of values (5, 10, 15, and 20), with the highest number again representing approximately 20% of the total stocks. To evaluate the performance of these strategies, we focus on key metrics, primarily the Sharpe ratio for each type of strategy (long-only, long-index, and long-short), along with the maximum drawdown. The Sharpe ratio acts as the primary metric for assessing strategy performance, measuring the excess return of a strategy per unit of risk taken. A higher Sharpe ratio indicates better risk-adjusted performance, with values above 1 generally considered good and above 2 considered excellent.

6. Result and Discussion

Tables A.1–A.3 illustrate the detailed performance metrics of our strategies for each different market. The tables provide the Sharpe ratio for each type of strategy as well as the max drawdown that we discussed in Section 4.2, which is sorted based on the number of stocks in the portfolio. The last row of each table also provided the performance metrics of the corresponding index during the same period as the context for comparison.

6.1. *STOXX600 Dataset*

Table A.1 delves into the nuanced performance metrics of each strategy, aligning with the significant variables outlined in Section 4 for the European market. Given the market's richness in significant variables, the table encapsulates an extensive array of 70 distinct trading strategies (210 when treating long-only, long-index, and long–short as independent strategies). Due to the vast number of strategies, we provide a concise overview of the top five for each type in Figures 1–3.

The visualization of the top five long-only strategies for the European market (Figure 1) reveals a consistent outperformance over the STOXX600. Notably, regardless of the number of stocks or sentiment variables, our top five long-only strategies surpassed the STOXX600 in raw return throughout the study period. Among these top performers, 4 out of 5 strategies are rooted in ESG- or SDG-related sentiment indicators. The best-performing strategy, ESG News Count with 10 stocks, achieved a Sharpe ratio of around 0.94 and a max drawdown of 29.2%, showcasing superior performance compared to the index, which only attained a Sharpe ratio of 0.107 during the same period. However, it is important to note that these strategies are not market neutral, making them susceptible to drawdowns in bear markets, as evidenced by a significant drop in performance in the first few months of 2020.

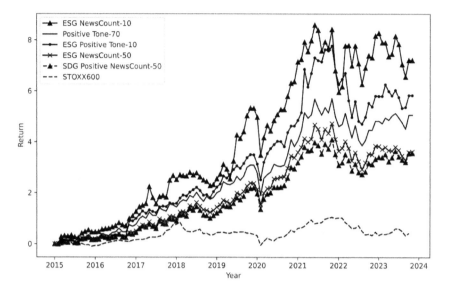

Figure 1.   Long-only STOXX600 — Top 5 strategies

Figure 2 explores the top five long-index strategies, emphasizing their market-neutral nature. These strategies continued to outperform the STOXX600, even after adjusting for returns subtracted from the index. Among the top five, three strategies are based on ESG- and SDG-related sentiment indicators. The graph highlights that the strategy based on ESG Positive Tone is consistently above other lines, indicating superior return. However, it is noteworthy that the strategy with the highest Sharpe Ratio (1.10) is based on Positive Tone. The market-neutral nature of these strategies mitigated the impact of the substantial drawdown in 2020.

Finally, Figure 3 illustrates the performance of long–short strategies and their corresponding metrics in the third column of Table A.1. The superiority of these strategies over the benchmark index is less evident. Among the top five, only the first two consistently outperformed the index, with the highest line based on ESG News Count providing the best return. However, the top-performing strategy in terms of risk-adjusted return is based on Positive Tone, boasting a Sharpe ratio of 0.88.

As the three graphs only show the result of the top strategies, Table 12 presents the average performance of the top strategies based on

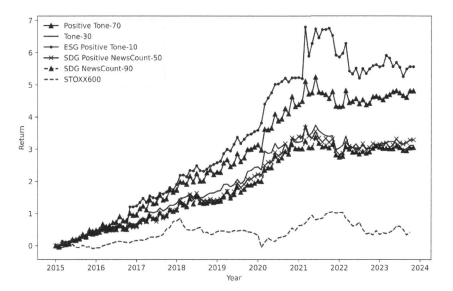

Figure 2.   Long-index STOXX600 — Top 5 strategies

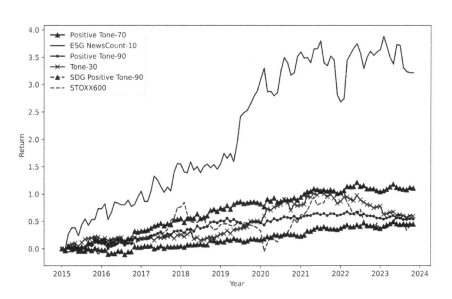

Figure 3.   Long–short STOXX600 — Top 5 strategies

Table 12. STOXX600 — Sentiment type performance comparison

Sentiment Type	Sharpe Ratio — LO	Sharpe Ratio — Index	Sharpe Ratio — LS	Max Drawdown (%)
General	0.733	0.893	0.113	−31.43
ESG	0.750	0.912	0.060	−31.38
SDG	0.742	0.903	0.048	−31.69
STOXX600		0.107		−28.67

each type of sentiment data (General, ESG-, or SDG-related news articles). The table underscores that the majority of our long-only and long-index strategies significantly outperformed the index. However, in long–short strategies, the average performance aligns more closely with the index. Examining each strategy type, those rooted in sentiment indicators related to sustainability topics (ESG and SDG) consistently outperformed those derived from all news (General), with the exception of long–short strategies.

6.2. S&P500 Dataset

Mirroring the structure of the STOXX600 dataset, Table A.2 meticulously presents the performance metrics of strategies applied in the US stock market. The table encapsulates insights from 35 distinct trading strategies, with Figures 4–6 offering a visual representation of the top 5 strategies for each strategy type.

In parallel with the European market, the dominance of the top long-only strategies becomes evident when compared to the S&P500 performance over the same period. Despite the S&P500 outperforming the STOXX600 with a Sharpe Ratio of 0.67 compared to 0.107, the top strategies exhibit comparable performance, displaying a narrower range of variation. Notably, all top-performing strategies are rooted in SDG-related indicators, setting them apart from other sentiment indicators.

For long-index strategies, the narrative takes a different turn, with most top strategies showcasing performance within a similar range as the S&P500 index. The S&P500, however, appears more volatile compared to our strategies. Similar to long-only strategies, the top-performing

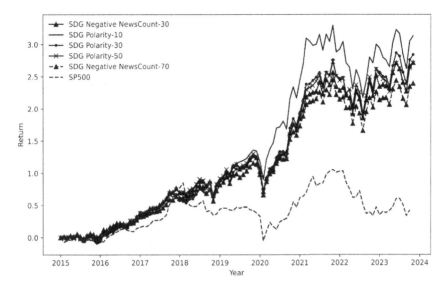

Figure 4.   Long-only S&P500 — Top five strategies

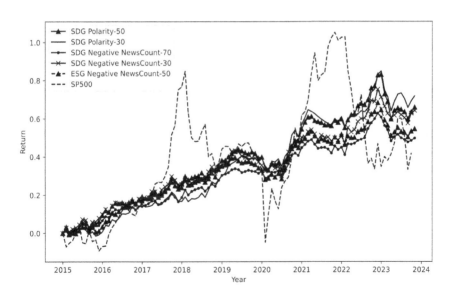

Figure 5.   Long-index S&P500 — Top five strategies

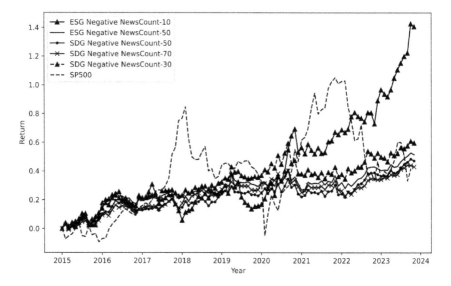

Figure 6.   Long–short S&P500 — Top five strategies

long-index strategies are exclusively based on sustainability sentiment indicators, specifically SDG and ESG. Despite being market neutral, these strategies show slight susceptibility to the bear market in 2020, but not so much in the early months of 2023.

The long–short strategy performance in Figure 6 reveals a striking resemblance to long-index results, with top-performing strategies closely aligned. Interestingly, all leading strategies are grounded in Negative News Count indicators, exclusively derived from sustainability news articles (three based on SDG and two on ESG). Given the consistently negative coefficients associated with these variables, the outcomes suggest that the smaller number of negative news articles related to sustainability topics correlates with better company performance in the US stock market.

Table 13 delves into the intersection of sustainability topics and stock market returns, offering the average performance of strategies categorized by sustainability topics. Here, the dominance of sustainability-related strategies is apparent across various metrics. SDG-based strategies consistently outperform others in every metric. ESG-based strategies also outshine those derived from all types of news in three out of four metrics. Notably, most long-only performances surpass the S&P500 index, all exhibiting positive average Sharpe Ratios, indicating overall profitability of our strategies.

Table 13. SP500 — Sentiment type performance comparison

Sentiment Type	Sharpe Ratio — LO	Sharpe Ratio — Index	Sharpe Ratio — LS	Max Drawdown (%)
General	0.761	0.502	0.199	−26.1
ESG	0.762	0.508	0.247	−26.3
SDG	**0.800**	**0.599**	**0.298**	**−25.1**
S&P500		**0.670**		**−25.5**

7. VN100 Dataset

Much like our analyses of the European and US stock markets, we present the performance metrics of our strategies applied to the Vietnamese stock market in Table A.3. The final row in the table outlines the performance metrics of the VN100 index during the same period, acting as a benchmark for comparison.

Figure 7 vividly portrays the cumulative return of our top five long-only strategies from February 2015 to November 2023. Notably, regardless of the number of stocks or sentiment variables employed, all these strategies outperformed the VN100 in raw return during the study period. Exhibiting a Sharpe ratio ranging from 0.86 to 0.95, the top five long-only strategies showcased almost triple the level of performance compared to the VN100 index (0.297). Three out of the five strategies leverage sustainability indicators, reinforcing the trend observed in the European and US markets. In line with Section IV, where Word Count emerged as a significant variable in this market, it is unsurprising that the top-performing strategies are based on this criterion. The best-performing strategy, relying on Word Count with only two stocks, achieves an annual Sharpe ratio of 0.95.

Transitioning to long-index strategies, their superiority over the benchmark index remains apparent, albeit not as pronounced as long-only strategies. Figure 8 shows that almost all top strategies outperformed the VN100 index. Table 14 confirms this, with the average Sharpe ratio of all long-index strategies exceeding 1, more than three times the Sharpe ratio of the VN100 during the study period. Table A.3. demonstrates that not a single portfolio has a Sharpe ratio lower than the index (0.297). The Sharpe ratios of other portfolios range from 0.51 to 1.25, surpassing the best strategies from every market investigated thus far. Once again, Word Count proves effective as a portfolio selection criterion, with

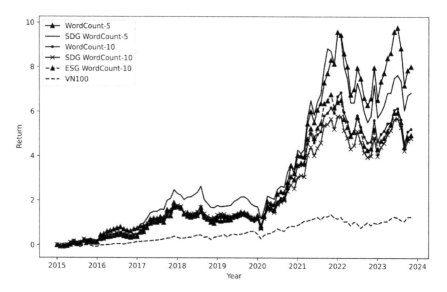

Figure 7.   Long-only VN100 — Top 5 strategies

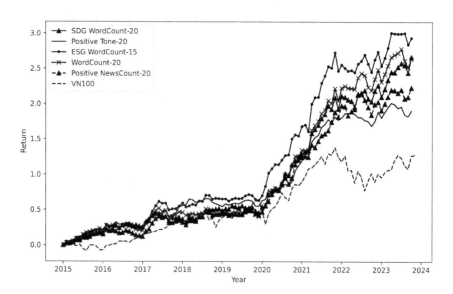

Figure 8.   Long-index VN100 — Top 5 strategies

three out of five best-performing strategies relying on this indicator. Other criteria such as Positive Tone and Positive News Count also appear in the top five.

The last type of strategy, long–short, appears to perform less favorably than the previous two types. Figure 9 indicates that only the ESG Positive News Count-based strategy stays above the VN100 line, while most other strategies remain below the index. This implies that most cannot outperform the index in pure return. However, in terms of risk-adjusted return, Table 14 confirms that, on average, long–short strategies outperformed the market during the study period. As mentioned in Section IV, caution is advised in interpreting results from this type of strategy due to the current impossibility of shorting the Vietnamese stock market.

In alignment with the European and US stock markets, Table 14 reveals that strategies based on SDG and ESG criteria outperformed those based on general criteria, with the exception of long–short strategies. SDG-based strategies provide the best average performance in three out of four performance metrics and rank second in the third metric. Strategies based on all articles, however, exhibit the worst performance in three out of four metrics. Nonetheless, when compared to the index, all strategies outperformed the index in every metric.

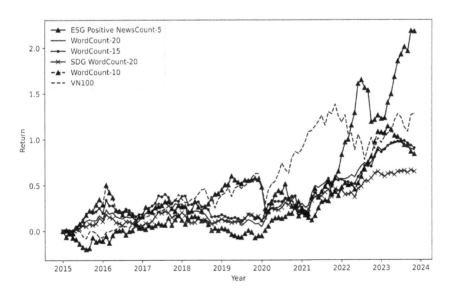

Figure 9. Long–short VN100 — Top five strategies

Table 14.   VN100 — Sentiment type performance comparison

Sentiment Type	Sharpe Ratio — LO	Sharpe Ratio — Index	Sharpe Ratio — LS	Max Drawdown (%)
General	0.739	1.088	**0.428**	−43.1
ESG	0.763	1.097	0.315	−41.1
SDG	**0.861**	**1.275**	0.355	**−38.0**
VN100		**0.297**		**−48.4**

In conclusion, our sentiment-based trading strategies, regardless of the market, demonstrate generally good performance when compared to their corresponding market in the same time period, particularly the long-only and long-index types of strategies. Even in the US stock market, where the S&P500 index showed strong performance, our portfolios composed of its constituents outperformed it significantly in risk-adjusted return. Despite some differences in coefficients and the significance of variables between the three markets, we observe better performance of sentiment indicators created based on sustainability-related news (especially based on the topic of SDG) compared to indicators created from all news.

8. Conclusion

In this chapter, we introduced an innovative methodology for generating ESG and SDG scores derived from near-real-time news using NLP techniques. Our approach involves extracting pertinent entities, identifying topics, and gauging the likely impact of news, with the aggregated information forming scores on a regular time grid. Utilizing these scores, we constructed portfolios centered on specific topics, subsequently comparing their performance against established benchmarks.

Our exploration covered primarily European and US markets, with additional insights gained from the Vietnamese market, drawing data from the AiData.green database co-developed by the authors. Through our studies, we made notable observations. Across all markets, we discerned a consistent pattern of substantial risk-adjusted outperformance in portfolios that incorporated sustainability topics. The findings underscore the efficacy of our sentiment-based trading strategies, particularly in the long-only and long-index categories. Even in the robust US stock market, where the S&P500 index exhibited considerable strength, our portfolios, composed of its constituents, demonstrated significant outperformance in risk-adjusted returns.

The success of our approach underscores the significance of integrating ESG and SDG considerations into investment strategies, transcending geographical boundaries. The ability to leverage near-real-time news for informed decision-making showcases the potential of NLP techniques in the financial domain. The AiData.green database stands as a valuable resource, providing a rich dataset for researchers and practitioners alike.

Our results point toward a promising avenue for sustainable investing. By incorporating timely information on ESG and SDG factors, investors can achieve risk-adjusted outperformance, aligning their portfolios with sustainable and responsible investment practices. This chapter contributes to the growing body of literature advocating for the integration of environmental and social considerations into financial decision-making, emphasizing the tangible benefits in terms of portfolio performance across diverse markets.

Appendix

Table A.1. STOXX600 strategies detailed performance

Score Type	No. of Stocks	Sharpe Ratio	Sharpe Ratio — Index	Sharpe Ratio — LS	Max Drawdown (%)
SDG Tone	10	0.67	0.85	0.06	−38.2
SDG Positive Tone	10	0.81	0.94	0.06	−33.4
Tone	10	0.74	0.92	0.30	−41.8
News Count	10	0.73	0.83	0.36	−29.9
ESG Positive Tone	10	0.91	1.08	0.00	−35.0
Positive News Count	10	0.46	0.49	−0.12	−46.2
ESG News Count	10	**0.94**	1.03	0.80	−29.2
SDG News Count	10	0.63	0.73	0.23	−35.8
ESG Tone	10	0.70	0.93	0.16	−33.6
SDG Positive News Count	10	0.69	0.77	−0.13	−47.5
SDG Negative Tone	10	0.55	0.57	−0.13	−32.3
Positive Tone	10	0.78	0.95	−0.13	−40.0
Negative Tone	10	0.42	0.44	−0.14	−33.1

(*Continued*)

Table A.1. *(Continued)*

Score Type	No. of Stocks	Sharpe Ratio	Sharpe Ratio — Index	Sharpe Ratio — LS	Max Drawdown (%)
ESG Negative Tone	10	0.54	0.59	−0.15	−29.3
SDG Tone	30	0.61	0.79	−0.17	−30.7
SDG Positive Tone	30	0.70	0.88	0.03	−33.7
Tone	30	0.82	1.08	0.50	−29.5
News Count	30	0.75	0.88	−0.34	−29.1
ESG Positive Tone	30	0.65	0.81	−0.38	−34.7
Positive News Count	30	0.69	0.80	−0.43	−26.1
ESG News Count	30	0.85	1.03	−0.01	−33.7
SDG News Count	30	0.79	0.98	−0.21	−33.0
ESG Tone	30	0.52	0.67	−0.42	−32.4
SDG Positive News Count	30	0.77	0.92	−0.25	−31.1
SDG Negative Tone	30	0.57	0.67	−0.30	−33.4
Positive Tone	30	0.80	1.04	0.34	−34.9
Negative Tone	30	0.60	0.72	0.30	−32.5
ESG Negative Tone	30	0.62	0.77	−0.29	−31.6
SDG Tone	50	0.78	1.03	0.17	−30.5
SDG Positive Tone	50	0.83	1.00	0.43	−29.2
Tone	50	0.77	1.02	0.22	−32.3
News Count	50	0.86	1.04	0.02	**−25.6**
ESG Positive Tone	50	0.80	0.96	0.25	−30.3
Positive News Count	50	0.79	0.94	−0.04	−25.4
ESG News Count	50	0.86	1.05	−0.01	−31.3
SDG News Count	50	0.79	0.99	−0.05	−32.8
ESG Tone	50	0.74	0.95	−0.12	−30.7
SDG Positive News Count	50	0.86	1.07	−0.01	−26.7
SDG Negative Tone	50	0.62	0.74	−0.04	−31.5
Positive Tone	50	0.80	1.00	0.44	−30.2
Negative Tone	50	0.60	0.71	−0.09	−33.4
ESG Negative Tone	50	0.70	0.85	0.10	−30.9

Table A.1. (*Continued*)

Score Type	No. of Stocks	Sharpe Ratio	Sharpe Ratio — Index	Sharpe Ratio — LS	Max Drawdown (%)
SDG Tone	70	0.77	1.00	0.23	−28.9
SDG Positive Tone	70	0.85	1.03	0.43	−27.3
Tone	70	0.73	0.96	0.10	−32.3
News Count	70	0.84	1.04	0.10	−27.2
ESG Positive Tone	70	0.79	0.96	0.27	−28.5
Positive News Count	70	0.75	0.91	−0.12	−25.7
ESG News Count	70	0.84	1.04	0.00	−32.6
SDG News Count	70	0.79	0.98	−0.03	−32.4
ESG Tone	70	0.76	0.95	0.08	−30.7
SDG Positive News Count	70	0.84	1.04	0.00	−27.5
SDG Negative Tone	70	0.63	0.75	−0.08	−30.9
Positive Tone	70	0.91	**1.10**	**0.88**	−29.4
Negative Tone	70	0.66	0.78	−0.07	−31.9
ESG Negative Tone	70	0.71	0.86	0.12	−30.4
SDG Tone	90	0.80	0.99	0.44	−29.5
SDG Positive Tone	90	0.84	1.01	0.48	−27.8
Tone	90	0.78	0.99	0.37	−32.6
News Count	90	0.81	1.00	0.01	−28.2
ESG Positive Tone	90	0.77	0.93	0.38	−29.1
Positive News Count	90	0.76	0.91	−0.02	−26.6
ESG News Count	90	0.82	1.03	0.00	−33.2
SDG News Count	90	0.84	1.06	0.00	−28.3
ESG Tone	90	0.76	0.93	0.20	−28.8
SDG Positive News Count	90	0.83	1.02	0.08	−29.5
SDG Negative Tone	90	0.66	0.76	−0.03	−30.3
Positive Tone	90	0.82	1.01	0.53	−30.7
Negative Tone	90	0.65	0.76	−0.15	−31.2
ESG Negative Tone	90	0.70	0.83	0.23	−31.7
STOXX600			**0.107**		**−28.7**

Table A.2.   S&P500 strategies detailed performance

Score Type	No. of Stocks	Sharpe Ratio	Sharpe Ratio — Index	Sharpe Ratio — LS	Max Drawdown (%)
Negative News Count	10	0.74	0.42	0.53	−32.4
SDG Polarity	10	0.92	0.75	0.08	−26.1
ESG Negative News Count	10	0.87	0.68	**0.78**	−30.1
SDG Negative News Count	10	0.75	0.41	0.54	−27.1
ESG Positive News Count	10	0.64	0.27	0.14	−30.4
Positive News Count	10	0.68	0.32	0.00	−28.0
SDG Positive News Count	10	0.65	0.26	0.04	−26.0
Negative News Count	30	0.85	0.67	0.44	−24.6
SDG Polarity	30	0.91	**0.90**	0.49	−23.7
ESG Negative News Count	30	0.83	0.61	0.31	−26.5
SDG Negative News Count	30	**0.93**	0.83	0.62	−24.7
ESG Positive News Count	30	0.69	0.38	0.13	−27.6
Positive News Count	30	0.73	0.55	0.10	−29.9
SDG Positive News Count	30	0.64	0.22	−0.12	−27.8
Negative News Count	50	0.86	0.71	0.55	−24.6
SDG Polarity	50	0.90	0.89	0.63	−25.4
ESG Negative News Count	50	0.88	0.81	0.65	−25.6
SDG Negative News Count	50	0.86	0.72	0.63	−24.1
ESG Positive News Count	50	0.71	0.47	0.12	−25.0

Table A.2. *(Continued)*

Score Type	No. of Stocks	Sharpe Ratio	Sharpe Ratio — Index	Sharpe Ratio — LS	Max Drawdown (%)
Positive News Count	50	0.71	0.48	−0.01	−24.7
SDG Positive News Count	50	0.72	0.49	−0.04	−24.5
Negative News Count	70	0.84	0.67	0.52	−24.0
SDG Polarity	70	0.83	0.76	0.46	−24.6
ESG Negative News Count	70	0.86	0.78	0.58	−24.3
SDG Negative News Count	70	0.89	0.84	0.63	**−22.9**
ESG Positive News Count	70	0.67	0.28	−0.16	−24.9
Positive News Count	70	0.70	0.32	−0.16	−24.2
SDG Positive News Count	70	0.70	0.35	−0.09	−24.0
Negative News Count	90	0.85	0.71	0.38	−24.2
SDG Polarity	90	0.77	0.60	0.42	−25.4
ESG Negative News Count	90	0.82	0.65	0.26	−24.1
SDG Negative News Count	90	0.84	0.72	0.47	−24.8
ESG Positive News Count	90	0.64	0.16	−0.35	−25.1
Positive News Count	90	0.65	0.17	−0.37	−24.5
SDG Positive News Count	90	0.68	0.25	−0.31	−24.7
S&P500			**0.67**		**−25.5**

Table A.3.   VN100 strategies detailed performance

Score Type	No. of Stocks	Sharpe Ratio	Sharpe Ratio — Index	Sharpe Ratio — LS	Max Drawdown (%)
ESG Positive News Count	5	0.78	0.98	**0.78**	−45.0
Positive News Count	5	0.53	0.51	0.38	−49.8
Positive Tone	5	0.60	0.71	0.50	−51.9
ESG Word Count	5	0.75	0.88	−0.28	−41.3
Word Count	5	**0.95**	1.21	0.27	−35.4
SDG Word Count	5	0.91	1.11	0.21	−40.1
ESG Positive News Count	10	0.67	0.87	0.34	−43.6
Positive News Count	10	0.68	0.92	0.29	−44.0
Positive Tone	10	0.64	0.93	0.39	−45.6
ESG Word Count	10	0.86	1.26	0.12	**−33.8**
Word Count	10	0.89	1.28	0.53	−36.1
SDG Word Count	10	0.87	1.24	0.22	−37.0
ESG Positive News Count	15	0.68	0.96	0.25	−43.6
Positive News Count	15	0.70	1.01	0.33	−44.3
Positive Tone	15	0.67	1.15	0.28	−44.6
ESG Word Count	15	0.86	1.36	0.38	−38.2
Word Count	15	0.84	1.29	0.67	−40.0
SDG Word Count	15	0.84	1.30	0.36	−36.9
ESG Positive News Count	20	0.74	1.17	0.42	−42.3
Positive News Count	20	0.80	1.30	0.46	−37.9
Positive Tone	20	0.75	1.40	0.30	−45.3
ESG Word Count	20	0.77	1.29	0.52	−40.8
Word Count	20	0.81	1.35	0.73	−41.8
SDG Word Count	20	0.83	**1.45**	0.63	−37.8
VN100			**0.297**		**−48.4**

References

Baker, S. R., Bloom, N., & Davis, S. J. (2016, July). Measuring economic policy uncertainty. *The Quarterly Journal of Economics*, 131, 1593–1636. doi:10.1093/qje/qjw024.

Baker, S. R., Bloom, N., Davis, S. J., & Terry, S. J. (2020, April). COVID-induced economic uncertainty. NBER Working Papers, National Bureau of Economic Research, Inc. Retrieved from https://ideas.repec.org/p/nbr/nberwo/26983.html.

Capelle-Blancard, G. & Petit, A. (2019). Every little helps? ESG news and stock market reaction. *Journal of Business Ethics*, 157, 543–565.

Chau, N. T., Kien, L. V., & Phong, D. T. (2023). Stock price movement prediction using text mining and sentiment analysis. In N. H. Phuong & V. Kreinovich (eds.), *Deep Learning and Other Soft Computing Techniques: Biomedical and Related Applications*, pp. 167–179. Cham: Springer Nature Switzerland. doi:10.1007/978-3-031-29447-1_15.

Chen, Y., Kumar, A., & Zhang, C. (2020). Dynamic ESG preferences and asset prices. *Capital Markets: Market Efficiency eJournal*.

Fama, E. (1970). Efficient capital markets: A review of theory and empirical work. *Journal of Finance*, 25, 383–417. Retrieved from https://EconPapers.repec.org/RePEc:bla:jfinan:v:25:y:1970:i:2:p:383-417.

Fraiberger, S. P., Lee, D., Puy, D., & Ranciere, R. (2021). Media sentiment and international asset prices. *Journal of International Economics*, 133, 103526. https://doi.org/10.1016/j.jinteco.2021.103526.

Fronzetti Colladon, A. & Elshendy, M. (2017 July). Big data analysis of economic news: Hints to forecast macroeconomic indicators. *International Journal of Engineering Business Management*, 9, 1–12. doi:10.1177/1847979017720040.

Fronzetti Colladon, A., Grassi, S., Ravazzolo, F., & Violante, F. (2020). Forecasting financial markets with semantic network analysis in the COVID-19 crisis. *Journal of Forecasting*, 42, 1187–1204.

Goutte, S., Grosse, R., Le, H.-V., Liu, F., & Von Mettenheim, H.-J. (2023). Portfolio management with ESG news sentiment. *Bankers, Markets & Investors*, 172–173, 72–84. Retrieved from https://www.cairn.info/revue-bankers-markets-et-investors-2023-1-2-page-72.htm.

Kazemian, S., Zhao, S., & Penn, G. (2016, August). Evaluating sentiment analysis in the context of securities trading. In *Proceedings of the 54th Annual Meeting of the Association for Computational Linguistics* (*Volume 1: Long Papers*), pp. 2094–2103. doi:10.18653/v1/P16-1197.

Kvam, E., Molnár, P., Wankel, I., & Ødegaard, B. A. (2022). Do sustainable company stock prices increase with ESG scrutiny? Evidence using social media. *SSRN Electronic Journal*. Available at SSRN 4057988.

Mudinas, A., Zhang, D., & Levene, M. (2019). Market trend prediction using sentiment analysis: Lessons learned and paths forward. *CoRR, abs/1903.05440*. Retrieved from http://arxiv.org/abs/1903.05440.

Schmidt, A. (2019). Sustainable news — A sentiment analysis of the effect of ESG information on stock prices. *Political Economy — Development: Environment eJournal*.

Shiller, R. J. (2017). Narrative economics. *The American Economic Review*, 107, 967–1004. Retrieved from http://www.jstor.org/stable/44251584. (Accessed May 31, 2022).

Tilly, S., Ebner, M., & Livan, G. (2021, February). Macroeconomic forecasting through news, emotions and narrative. *Expert Systems with Applications*, 175, 114760. doi:10.1016/j.eswa.2021.114760.

Tuckett, D., Ormerod, P., Smith, R. E., & Nyman, R. (2014). Bringing social-psychological variables into economic modelling: Uncertainty, animal spirits and the recovery from the great recession. *Economic Growth eJournal*.

Vu, L. T., Pham, D. N., Kieu, H. T., & Pham, T. T. (2023, June). Sentiments extracted from news and stock market reactions in Vietnam. *Preprints*. doi:10.20944/preprints202306.2192.v1.

Wang, G., Wang, T., Wang, B., Sambasivan, D., Zhang, Z., Zheng, H., & Zhao, B. Y. (2014). Crowds on wall street: Extracting value from social investing platforms. In *CSCW '15: Proceedings of the 18th ACM Conference on Computer Supported Cooperative Work & Social Computing*. February 2015, pp. 17–30.

Chapter 14

Optimizing Sustainable Performance: A Strategic Approach to Value Creation and Impactful Investing

Heiko Bailer

*Head Quantitative Investments & Research,
Stuttgart, Germany*

Abstract

This chapter thoroughly examines eight long-only MSCI style factors, nine long-only sustainable theme factors, and four long–short sustainable theme factors. Backtests against the historic MSCI World benchmark from September 2019 to November 2023, using MSCI's Barra Portfolio Manager, reveal that the low active risk and low turnover long-only portfolios performed in line with their MSCI World benchmark. Meanwhile, sustainable themes as well as the MSCI style factor ESG exhibited significantly higher sustainable performance. Testing the 17 long-only factors in a restricted universe, simulating the stringent 2023 Paris-aligned sustainability law of Baden-Württemberg, Germany, showed that stringent universe exclusions negatively impacted performance, increased portfolio size without lowering active risk but reducing emissions, and improved the overall Sustainable Development Goals (SDGs) scores. Remarkably, the long–short sustainable factors exhibit significant risk sustainability-adjusted outperformance compared to the MSCI World benchmark. These findings challenge the conventional notion that sustainability for investors depends mainly on universe exclusions.

Moreover, they demonstrate that steering portfolios with sustainable factors not only broadens the universe and diversifies across industries but also reduces concentration risk without compromising performance. This approach seamlessly integrates with impact investing, enabling the pursuit of explicit positive objectives, such as advancing SDGs or facilitating the transition from Brown to Green, potentially serving as an engine for EU Sustainable Finance Disclosure Regulation (SFDR) Article 9 funds.

1. Introduction

Assuming the reader's familiarity with traditional factor investing and the use of optimization techniques in portfolio construction, this chapter is focused on techniques and factors that lead to portfolios with low active risk to a benchmark and low turnover while demonstrating significantly improved sustainable performance. Increased sustainable regulations such as exclusions or emissions caps pose a heightened challenge for portfolio managers in the task of stock selection while concurrently meeting performance expectations. As Scherer (2022) noted, sustainable portfolio managers act like all other rational investors in the initial "Value Creation" phase up to a certain threshold of required sustainability. Exceeding this threshold, without greenwashing, leads to mere value alignment and a trade-off between sustainability and performance (see Scherer, 2022, p. 7). At this point, the use of modern optimization tools can help to incorporate regulatory requirements and risk preferences while steering the portfolio toward higher sustainability, thereby elevating the "Value Creation" phase to a higher threshold.

Before delving into portfolio construction, establishing a shared understanding of sustainable performance is crucial. Despite the shift of sustainable investing from the periphery to mainstream adoption, the linchpin for defining sustainable performance lies in comprehending the concept of double materiality: the recognition that companies are influenced by and, in turn, influence the two interrelated dimensions of financial materiality and environmental, social, and governance (ESG) materiality. Financial materiality means that institutional investors, asset managers, and corporations increasingly recognize the materiality of ESG factors in assessing long-term financial performance as measured by ESG

Ratings, even though there is little agreement between various research providers (Berg *et al.*, 2022), in contrast to high consensus of credit ratings, while both sharing the common objective of assessing the impact of external factors on a company's financial performance (this chapter does not delve into the debate on whether ESG Ratings contribute alpha to portfolios through enhanced financial materiality and increased flows into ESG products, or serve as a confounding variable). ESG materiality refers to the impact of the company's financial activities on the broader environment, society, and governance structures, both positive and negative, to sustainable development and societal well-being. The measurement of ESG materiality, currently based on non-mandatory non-financial disclosures, is still in the early stages with the aim of standardization by means of efforts such as the International Sustainability Disclosure Standards (IFRS) developed by the International Sustainability Standards Board (ISSB).

In the meantime, research houses such as MSCI Inc. have begun to provide a variety of new metrics, including estimates such as Scope Emissions, Implied Temperature Rise, Climate VaR, Carbon Transition, and SDG alignment for a large universe of companies (Table 2). While these emerging data types are still in the process of standardization, they are conceptually more forward looking and specifically oriented toward gauging the positive or negative impact of company operations on external factors (the world). This makes them well suited for the measurement of sustainable performance. As research data of this nature become more accessible, one can anticipate a rise in applications and research studies, as seen from the works on ESG-efficient portfolios by Schmidt (2020) and Pedersen (2021), and a recent paper by Robeco's Blitz *et al.* (2023) introducing the concept of "3D Investing," where return, risk, and sustainability are jointly optimized. Although intriguing, it is worth noting that this chapter takes a different approach by utilizing sustainable factors as drivers for returns, optimizing sustainability and risk within a traditional optimization framework.

The following sections are structured as follows: data and analytics introduces the MSCI style, sustainable research variables, sustainable theme factors, and the optimization setup. It further describes the computation of the alpha scores as the sole differentiator between the strategy backtests, and states that the alpha score and weights tend to have a positive relationship called "steering." Backtesting of strategies shows, for lack of space, an extract illustrating the traditional and sustainable performance of the 17 long-only factors, both with and without exclusions, alongside the results of the 4 long–short backtests. The final sections conclude.

2. Data and Analytics

In 2010, MSCI Inc. launched the Barra Portfolio Manager (BPM), a platform for backtesting and rebalancing portfolios, with an integrated optimization engine and a range of risk models. Over the past 10+ years, it has developed into an institutionally trusted platform for the out-of-sample backtesting and rebalancing of investment strategies. The platform is also supplied with comprehensive index and market data as well as several modules covering sustainable research data such as scope emissions, implied temperature rise, and net alignment to sustainable development goals (SDGs).

2.1. *MSCI Style Factors* (8)

Bonne *et al.* (2018) introduced the MSCI FaCS, as a classification standard and framework for analyzing and reporting style factors in equity portfolios, based on the Barra Global Total Market Equity Model for Long-Term Investors (GEMLT, Morozov *et al.*, 2016). The standard organizes 16 style factors of GEMLT into eight style factor groups: Yield, Growth, Size, Volatility, Momentum, Quality, Value, and Liquidity. In April 2020, MSCI launched a version of the GEMLT that added ESG as the 17th style factor (Cano & Minovitsky, 2021). The resulting GEMLTESG (Minovitsky & Bonne, 2020) risk model was constructed using the industry-adjusted scores from the MSCI ESG Ratings as the raw ESG exposures. This chapter uses the eight MSCI style factor groups as described in Table 1 and provided through BPM.

2.2. *Sustainable Theme Factors* (9)

The nine long-only sustainable theme factors and the four long–short sustainable theme factors, described in Table 4, are based on MSCI sustainable research and standard data, as described in Table 2 and provided through BPM.

Table 1.   MSCI style factors (8) used as "Input Scores" in the optimization (Table 3)

Style Factor Group	Factor Composition
Value "Inexpensive"	30% Book-to-Price, 60% Earning Yield, 10% LT Reversal
Size "Smaller MarketCap"	10% Mid-Cap, 90% Size
Momentum "Rising returns"	100% Momentum
Quality "Sound balance sheet"	12.5% Leverage, 25% Investment Quality, 12.5% Earnings Variability, 25% Earnings Quality, 25% Profitability
Yield "Cash flow paid out"	100% Dividend Yield
Volatility "Lower volatile, beta"	60% Beta, 40% Residual Volatility
Growth "Better growth prospects"	100% Growth
ESG "Resilience to LT ESG risks"	100% ESG

Table 2.   MSCI sustainable research and standard data & description

Sustainable Research Data	Description
Industry-Adjusted Scores "ESGRatings"	ESG ratings (adjusted by industry peers) converted to scores. (Score: 0 to 10, since August 1999) MSCI ESG Research (August 2023)
Implied Temperature Rise "ImplTempRise, ITR"	A forward-looking quantitative assessment of companies' alignment with global temperature goals, in °C, based on projected emissions, considering emissions reduction targets relative to its share of the global carbon budget. (Score: 1.3–10, since June 2021*) MSCI ESG Research (August 2023)
Sustainable Revenue "SustainRev"	The total percentage of all revenues derived from thirteen social and environmental impact themes (Sustainable Impact Solutions Max Percentage). (Score: 0–100%, since August 2017) MSCI ESG Research (2023)

(Continued)

Table 2. (*Continued*)

Sustainable Research Data	Description
Scope 123 Intensity "Emissions"	A company's estimated total Scope 1, 2, and 3 emissions normalized by the most recently available enterprise value including cash (EVIC**) in million USD. (Score: 0–550,000, since May 2020*) MSCI ESG Research (August 2023)
Climate VaR 1.5°C "ClimateVaR.1.5"	The stressed market value of a stock under the climate change scenario of 1.5°C. It aggregates exposure from policy risk, technology opportunities, and physical climate risk. (Score: −100–100%, since January 2020*) MSCI ESG Research (August 2023)
Low Carbon Transition "CarbonTrans"	A company's alignment to the low-carbon environment. Higher Low-Carbon Transition scores are more aligned. (Score: 0–10, since October 2013) MSCI ESG Research (August 2023)
SDG Net Alignment Scores "SDG"	Assesses companies' alignment with the 17 United Nations Sustainable Development Goals (SDGs). (Score: −10 to +10, since January 2020*) MSCI ESG Research (October 2023)
Assets	Number of portfolio constituents at a given point in time or average over a time frame.
MarketCap	Weighted market capitalization of a portfolio at a given point in time or average over a time frame.
Beta	Weighted beta of a portfolio at a given point in time or average over a time frame.
Female Director "FemDir"	Weighted percentage of portfolio female board members. For companies with a two-tier board, the calculation is based on members of the Supervisory Board only. (Score: 0–100%, since June 2019). Governance Metrics.
Female CEO "FemCEO"	Percentage of portfolio with female CEOs. (Score: 0–100%, since June 2019). Governance Metrics.
Female CFO "FemCFO"	Percentage of portfolio with female CFOs. (Score: 0–100%, since June 2019). Governance Metrics.

Notes: *Time series extended to September 2019 by backfilling the first available data value. **Enterprise Value Including Cash (EVIC).

3. Analytics and Optimization Setup

All strategies are backtested using the same optimization setup and constraints as described in Table 3. The constraints are even very similar between the long-only and long–short strategies. Since the MSCI styles are risk indices, all long-only strategies were also run without factoring in trading costs. The low turnover reduces the impact of trading costs greatly, still allowing a reasonable benchmark comparison. For the long-short strategies, trading costs were applied (see Table 3).

The "Input Score" in Table 3 is the sole differentiator between the strategies analyzed in this chapter. Table 4 describes the input scores on a high level. MSCI style factors (8) (Table 1) are based on MSCI research. The sustainable theme factors (9 + 4) are based on LBBW AM research and are only a proxy for the respective themes in order to keep the number of parameters as low as possible.

Table 3.   Optimization setup and constraints

Constraints	Long-only	Long–short
Currency	USD	USD
Benchmark	MSCI World	MSCI World
Sector constraint	Benchmark + −4%	No constraints
Minimum assets	100	100
Maximum weight	5%	No constraints
Rebalance	Close of first day of month	Close of first day of month
	1	2
Leverage	3.5%	3.5%
Turnover	0	6 bps
Trading costs	Yes	Yes, USD-neutral
Fully invested		

Risk Model* *Minovsky and Bonne (2020)	**GEMLTESG = GEMLT + ESG** 17 style, 87 country, 45 industry, and 72 currency factors
Alpha Scores* *Grinold and Kahn (1999)	**Volatility * Information Coefficient * "Input Score"** **"Input Score"** as described in Table 4. **Other parameters:** Proportional to volatility; IC = 0.05; weights corrected for size bias; standardized with GICS sectors.

Table 4.   The "Input Scores" for the MSCI styles and sustainable theme factors serve as the foundation for calculating the alpha scores within the optimization process

MSCI Style Factors (8)	
Yield	Respective MSCI style factor scores as described in Table 1.
ESG	
Growth	
Size	
Volatility	
Momentum	
Quality	
Value	

Sustainable Theme Factors* (9)	
Biodiversity	Average SDG 2, 6, 12, 13, 14, 15 scaled by ITR
Climate	Average SDG 7, 9, 11, 13, 14, 15 scaled by ITR
ESGRatings	Average ESG ratings (Industry-Adjusted Scores mapped)
FemaleAlpha	Average SDG 5, 8, 19, 17 & % Females C-Level and Board
SustainDevGoals	Average SDG
SustainRev	Average Sustainable Revenues
ClimateVaR.1.5	Climate VaR at 1.5°C (loss probability)
ImplTempRise	Implied Temperature Rise
Emissions	Scope 123 Intensity (scaled by EVIC)

Long/Short Sustainable Theme Factors* (4)	
LS.Emissions	Emissions (L/S ranked bottom/top, alpha score across)
LS.ESGRatings	ESG Ratings (L/S ranked top/bottom, alpha score across)
LS.ImplTempRise	ImplTempRise (L/S ranked bottom/top, alpha score across)
LS.CarbonTrans	CarbonTrans (L/S ranked top/bottom, alpha score across)

Note: *Themes (simplistic) were built based on LBBW AM research.

3.1. *Universe Exclusions*

Besides comparing the traditional and sustainable performance of the 17 long-only strategies (MSCI styles (8) and sustainable themes (9)), this chapter also evaluates the impact of reducing the available universe by a comprehensive set of "sustainable" exclusions, as described in Table 5, for each of the 17 strategies, resulting in 34 long-only strategies.

3.2. *Sustainable Steering and Portfolio Weights*

Following the conversion of "Input Scores" into alpha scores, the optimizer endeavors to maximize these alpha scores. This process takes into

Table 5.   Universe exclusions based on sustainable research

Variable Names	Description	Exclusions per Nov 2023
No Exclusions		
Scope 3 Intensity	<500,000	**11 out of 1509***
Exclusions Similar to German BaWü Law NaFiBWG (2023)		
Scope 3 Intensity	<500,000	**339 out of 1509***
Tobacco	No	
Genetic Aggr. Engineering	No	
No Nuclear Power	No	
No Nuclear Weapons	No	
Controversial Weapons	No	
Max % Rev Thermal Coal	≤ 1%	
Max % Rev Conv Oil & Gas	≤ 10%	
UNGC Compliance	No Fail	
SDG 7, 9, 11, 13, 14, 15	>−2 "Climate focused"	

Note: *On November 30, 2023, the MSCI World had 1509 constituents.

account the risk model and additional optimization constraints (see Table 3). Thus, higher alpha scores are expected to correspond to higher weights or scores (see Figures 1 and 2). Since the alpha scores are standardized within GICS sectors (Table 3), the positive relation between alpha scores and weights can best be seen at the sector level.

Given that the alpha scores for the sustainable theme factors (9) rely solely on sustainable research factors, the composition of the portfolio is driven (steered) by factors emphasizing sustainable performance. This marks a notable departure from traditional performance drivers. This distinctive approach places sustainability at the forefront of portfolio construction, establishing it as the primary portfolio objective and opening the doors to impact investing.

4.   Backtesting of Strategies (17 * 2 + 4)

The MSCI BPM platform was used to calculate the out-of-sample performance of a total of **17 * 2 + 4 = 38** strategies, with the historic constituents of the MSCI World as their universe: long-only MSCI styles (8) and sustainable themes (9), and long–short sustainable themes (4), using the same optimization settings and only differing in their respective alpha scores

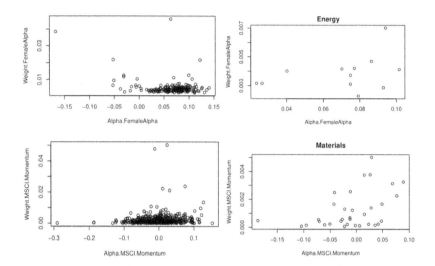

Figure 1. Examples of alpha scores vs. strategy weights by sector for FemaleAlpha and MSCI Style Momentum, as of November 2023

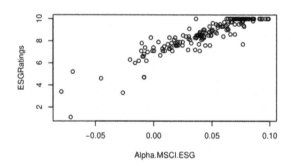

Figure 2. Alpha scores of the MSCI Style ESG vs. ESGRatings (scores), as of November 2023, show a clear positive relationship

(see Tables 3 and 4). The long-only strategies (17) were also backtested using a more restricted universe, as specified in Table 5. All backtests were run over from September 2019 through November 2023.

4.1. *Performance (Traditional, Long-only)*

Figures 3, 4 and 5 show selected backtests for two of the long-only sustainable themes of Biodiversity (Figure 3) and FemaleAlpha (Figure 4), as

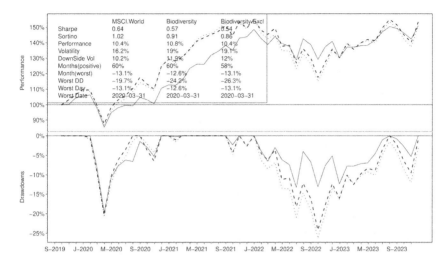

Figure 3. Biodiversity with and without universe exclusions vs. benchmark

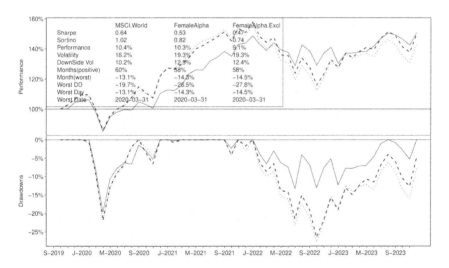

Figure 4. FemaleAlpha with and without universe exclusions vs. benchmark

well as for the MSCI style theme of Growth (Figure 5). Each figure shows the MSCI World benchmark and the sustainable theme with and without universe exclusions (see Table 5).

With sector constraints near the benchmark sectors (see Table 3), the strategies closely track the benchmark performance, occasionally exhibiting robust outperformance. The active risk for all strategies is well

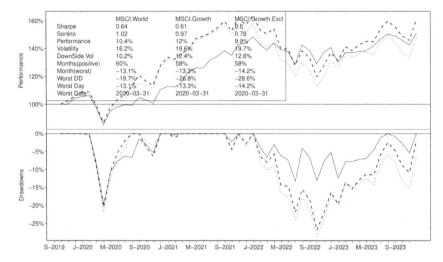

Figure 5.   MSCI Growth style with and without universe exclusions vs. benchmark

below 3%. Notably, strategies based on a universe with stringent exclusions always underperform.

4.1.1. *Fama–French and Carhart Factor Exposures*

All backtested strategies underwent testing for various Fama–French factor exposures and their extensions (Fama & French, 1992, 1993; Carhart, 1997; Fama & French, 2014). Appendix Table A.3 shows that all long-only strategies have a significant market factor with an adjusted $R^2 > 80\%$, which is expected by design of the sector constraints in the optimization (see Table 3). However, most other factor exposures are insignificant due to the risk reduction facilitated by the MSCI Risk Model GEMLTESG (see Table 3). Only the long–short strategies have a significant and positive alpha. A deeper analysis is left for further research.

4.2. *Performance (Sustainable, Long-only)*

In general, sustainable performance has demonstrated an upward trend over time, as illustrated in Figure 6 for the examples of Biodiversity and FemaleAlpha.

Table 6 presents sustainable statistics encompassing the backtests conducted from September 2019 through November 2023 (for detailed

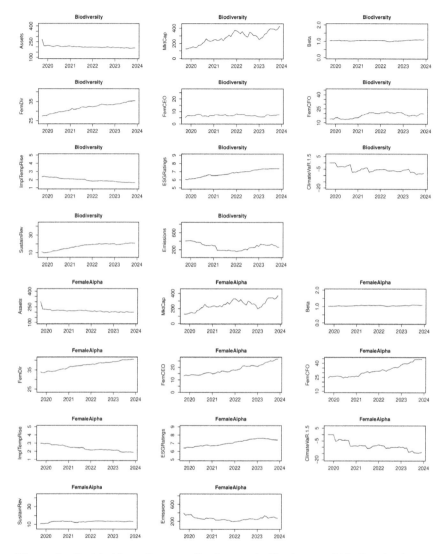

Figure 6. Sustainable performance for the sustainable themes of biodiversity (upper panel) and FemaleAlpha (lower panel)

statistics of the month of November 2023, please find the summaries in the Appendix, Tables A.1 and A.2).

Table 6 yields various insights across the MSCI styles and sustainable themes. Additionally, it provides a basis for comparison with the MSCI World benchmark.

Table 6. Performance statistics spanning September 2019 to November 2023 for MSCI styles (8*2), sustainable themes (9*2), and the MSCI World benchmark

	Total. Ret	Ret	SD	SR	ARisk	Assets	Mkt-Cap	Beta	Fem-Dir	Fem-CEO	Fem-CFO	ESG-Ratings	Impl-TempRise	Sustain-Rev	Emissions	Climate-VaR.1.5
MSCI.Yield	46.1	10.8	19.2	0.56	2.3	206.65	294.71	1.04	31.89	8.53	15.3	6.49	2.54	12.78	386.34	−9.38
MSCI.Yield.Excl	32.8	8.6	19.3	0.44	2.5	220.24	115.63	1.03	31.4	6.47	16.01	6.83	2.42	11.35	285.35	−8.75
MSCI.ESG	55.4	12.3	19.3	0.64	2.3	226.8	286.35	1.05	33.77	6.85	17.87	8.3	2.38	13.8	286.86	−6.82
MSCI.ESG.Excl	44.5	10.6	19.5	0.54	2.5	222.88	119.55	1.05	33	6.91	17.88	8.44	2.2	12.17	187.37	−5.24
MSCI.Growth	60.5	13.1	19.6	0.67	2.4	212.37	270.45	1.07	29.86	3.44	15.97	6.2	2.42	11.04	389.19	−9.28
MSCI.Growth. Excl	48	11.2	19.7	0.57	2.6	233.94	101.54	1.07	29.35	3.92	15.61	6.39	2.31	10.38	239.93	−6.87
MSCI.Size	40.1	9.8	19.3	0.51	2.3	303.55	206.97	1.04	29.81	5.56	13.38	6.02	2.75	9.48	359.44	−9.75
MSCI.Size.Excl	28	7.8	19.8	0.39	2.6	287.08	56.44	1.06	29.31	5.11	13.04	6.16	2.65	8.58	263.27	−7.57
MSCI.Volatility	47.1	10.8	18.3	0.59	2	296.04	281.41	0.95	32.21	5.66	14.42	6.53	2.4	10.55	317.01	−8.81
MSCI.Volatility. Excl	42	9.9	18.2	0.54	2.1	298.73	105.62	0.94	31.02	6.03	15.46	6.63	2.23	9.21	205.38	−6.47
MSCI.Momentum	54.2	12.1	19.4	0.62	2.3	333.2	297.02	1.05	31.77	6.39	15.42	6.42	2.43	10.73	344.74	−7.96
MSCI.Momentum. Excl	45.3	10.8	19.8	0.54	2.4	336.04	117.45	1.06	30.71	4.87	14.3	6.66	2.31	10.25	220.88	−6.31
MSCI.Quality	47.2	10.9	18.8	0.58	2.2	364.24	282.61	1.04	31.4	5.47	16.54	6.3	2.55	11.45	498.67	−11.64
MSCI.Quality. Excl	38.3	9.4	19	0.5	2.4	237.63	98.56	1.04	30.38	5.53	17.8	6.61	2.39	10.29	309.51	−8.69
MSCI.Value	49	11.2	19	0.59	2.2	239.29	288.36	1.06	31.02	6.97	15.29	6.25	2.47	14.11	619.86	−13.09
MSCI.Value.Excl	38.8	9.6	19.2	0.5	2.5	236.06	99.41	1.07	30.07	5.64	14.26	6.52	2.42	13.22	347.54	−8.63
MSCI.World	51	11	16.2	0.68	0	1558.73	293.48	1.06	31.87	5.57	13.47	6.45	2.47	12.09	360.65	−8.51

Biodiversity	53.5	11.9	19	0.63	2.2	200.39	277.79	1.05	31.9	6.81	18.11	6.81	1.97	17.21	276.85	−5.28
Biodiversity.Excl	50.8	11.5	19.1	0.6	2.4	237.88	115.61	1.07	31.4	4.61	16.8	7.09	1.97	15.57	192.66	−4.85
Climate	51.5	11.7	19.4	0.6	2.3	212.43	260.6	1.06	32.41	6.14	17.9	6.98	1.91	15.86	214.18	−4.21
Climate.Excl	42.9	10.3	19.3	0.53	2.5	362	106.93	1.07	31.74	4.52	17.48	7.08	1.94	13.73	178.99	−5.23
ESGRatings	50.9	11.6	19.4	0.6	2.3	211.33	278.84	1.06	33.35	5.9	18.54	8.29	2.45	14.54	305.05	−6.45
ESGRatings.Excl	45.9	10.8	19.7	0.55	2.5	241.2	114.68	1.07	32.9	6.31	18.03	8.46	2.26	13.18	202.48	−4.96
FemaleAlpha	50.4	11.5	19.3	0.59	2.3	212.61	248.32	1.06	37.35	18.46	32.35	7.05	2.37	12.99	266.75	−8.74
FemaleAlpha. Excl	44	10.4	19.3	0.54	2.4	263.69	102.22	1.07	36.48	13.76	27.26	7.15	2.28	11.28	215.3	−7.57
SustainDevGoals	49.3	11.3	19.2	0.59	2.2	187.84	271.45	1.06	32.75	4.71	17.54	6.89	2.41	15.47	339.61	−7.74
SustainDevGoals. Excl	40.2	9.8	19.1	0.51	2.4	289.63	114.26	1.07	32.03	4.62	16.01	7.06	2.22	14.06	228.55	−5.6
SustainRev	44.7	10.3	18	0.57	2.2	173.94	289.66	1	30.94	2.91	20.77	6.91	2.59	39.05	384.91	−1.6
SustainRev.Excl	38.1	9.2	18.1	0.51	2.3	194.1	115.97	1	30.11	4.37	18.74	7.07	2.52	36.99	219.7	−0.98
ClimateVaR.1.5	52.1	11.6	18.7	0.62	2.2	183.35	287.74	0.99	30.54	4.42	15.85	6.1	2.59	11.7	230.41	−2.83
ClimateVaR.1.5. Excl	37.3	9.3	19.5	0.48	2.6	222.96	78.4	0.98	27.48	4.8	15.48	6.05	2.38	9.28	175.5	−1.38
ImplTempRise	58.1	13	21.1	0.62	2.5	142.08	306.54	1.04	32.7	6.29	18.58	6.76	1.99	11.33	303.02	−8.04
ImplTempRise. Excl	47	10.8	18.6	0.58	2.2	249.61	119.5	1.02	31.85	6.32	15.43	6.93	1.73	8.81	139.44	−5.25
Emissions	41.9	10.2	19.9	0.51	2.5	162.92	283.49	1.05	32.28	5.76	18.15	6.35	2.28	10.3	109.2	−4.53
Emissions.Excl	34.6	9	20.1	0.45	2.8	178.18	112.1	1.03	31.7	6.4	17.55	6.66	2.01	9.5	66.16	−3.05
MSCI.World	51	11	16.2	0.68	0	1558.73	293.48	1.06	31.87	5.57	13.47	6.45	2.47	12.09	360.65	−8.51

4.2.1. *Universe Exclusions (see Table 5)*

- Have a negative impact on performance (see also Figures 3–5).
- Result in larger portfolios, even slightly increasing active risk.
- Result in over 40–50% decrease in portfolio MarketCap (more smaller size stocks).
- Have significantly higher SDG performance vs. the twin without exclusions.
- Sustainable performance related to Emissions and ClimateVar.1.5 increases.
- The selection of the alpha score is still the main driver for sustainable performance.

The remainder of this section delves into backtests conducted on the entire historic MSCI World universe without universe exclusions as summarized in Table 6.

4.2.2. *Both MSCI Styles (8) and Sustainable Themes (9)*

- Can have a positive effect on performance compared to the benchmark.
- Have similar portfolio sizes and low active risk.
- Have portfolio MarketCap similar to the benchmark.

4.2.3. *MSCI Styles (8)*

- MSCI Quality and Value have the worst Emissions, ImplTempRise, and ClimateVar.1.5.
- None of the MSCI styles, besides ESG, have notable sustainable performance.
- Only the MSCI ESG style shows improved sustainable performance compared to the benchmark as measured by lower Emissions, lower ImplTempRise, better ClimateVar.1.5, and more Female Executives — all while delivering the second highest performance of the styles.

4.2.4. *Sustainable Themes (9)*

Table 7 extracts from Table 6 and adds the 17 SDG statistics, taking a closer look at the sustainable theme performance.

Table 7 shows that the selection of the alpha score theme (Table 4) has a clear impact on the type of sustainable outperformance.

Table 7. Traditional and sustainable performance of the sustainable themes (9): sustainable research variables (upper panel), 17 SDGs (lower panel)

	Total. Ret	Ret	SD	SR	ARisk	Assets	Mkt-Cap	Beta	Fem-Dir	Fem-CEO	Fem-CFO	ESG-Ratings	Impl-TempRise	Sustain-Rev	Emissions	Climate-VaR.1.5
Biodiversity	53.5	11.9	19	0.63	2.2	200.39	277.79	1.05	31.9	6.81	18.11	6.81	1.97	17.21	276.85	−5.28
Climate	51.5	11.7	19.4	0.6	2.3	212.43	260.6	1.06	32.41	6.14	17.9	6.98	1.91	15.86	214.18	−4.21
ESGRatings	50.9	11.6	19.4	0.6	2.3	211.33	278.84	1.06	33.35	5.9	18.54	8.29	2.45	14.54	305.05	−6.45
FemaleAlpha	50.4	11.5	19.3	0.59	2.3	212.61	248.32	1.06	37.35	18.46	32.35	7.05	2.37	12.99	266.75	−8.74
SustainDevGoals	49.3	11.3	19.2	0.59	2.2	187.84	271.45	1.06	32.75	4.71	17.54	6.89	2.41	15.47	339.61	−7.74
SustainRev	44.7	10.3	18	0.57	2.2	173.94	289.66	1	30.94	2.91	20.77	6.91	2.59	39.05	384.91	−1.6
ClimateVaR.1.5	52.1	11.6	18.7	0.62	2.2	183.35	287.74	0.99	30.54	4.42	15.85	6.1	2.59	11.7	230.41	−2.83
ImplTempRise	58.1	13	21.1	0.62	2.5	142.08	306.54	1.04	32.7	6.29	18.58	6.76	1.99	11.33	303.02	−8.04
Emissions	41.9	10.2	19.9	0.51	2.5	162.92	283.49	1.05	32.28	5.76	18.15	6.35	2.28	10.3	109.2	−4.53
MSCI.World	51	11	16.2	0.68	0	1558.73	293.48	1.06	31.87	5.57	13.47	6.45	2.47	12.09	360.65	−8.51

	SDG-01	SDG-02	SDG-03	SDG-04	SDG-05	SDG-06	SDG-07	SDG-08	SDG-09	SDG-10	SDG-11	SDG-12	SDG-13	SDG-14	SDG-15	SDG-16	SDG-17	SDG. Sum
Biodiversity	0.04	0.21	−0.07	−0.22	1.62	1.37	1.13	1.07	0.52	0.52	0.23	1.82	1.4	−0.07	−0.22	−0.27	−0.2	6.7
Climate	0.41	0.04	0.06	−0.06	1.77	0.95	1.32	1.42	1.17	1.17	0.39	1.58	1.55	−0.07	−0.16	0.19	0.31	8

(Continued)

Table 7. (Continued)

	SDG-01	SDG-02	SDG-03	SDG-04	SDG-05	SDG-06	SDG-07	SDG-08	SDG-09	SDG-10	SDG-11	SDG-12	SDG-13	SDG-14	SDG-15	SDG-16	SDG-17	SDG. Sum
ESGRatings	0.3	0.06	-0.01	-0.11	1.78	0.96	0.65	1.29	0.93	0.93	0.07	0.88	0.84	-0.27	-0.3	0.03	0.16	5.7
FemaleAlpha	0.57	0.09	0.1	0	2.03	0.96	0.58	1.51	1.32	1.32	0.01	0.69	0.73	-0.23	-0.25	0.3	0.47	6.4
SustainDevGoals	0.29	0.09	0.11	-0.11	1.78	1.07	0.7	1.19	0.82	0.82	0.14	1	0.83	-0.18	-0.28	-0.08	0.09	5.7
SustainRev	0.44	0.17	0.2	-0.12	1.53	1.08	0.68	1.25	0.77	0.77	0.55	1.69	0.87	-0.21	-0.37	-0.15	-0.12	6.8
ClimateVaR.1.5	-0.27	-0.03	-0.21	-0.27	1.51	0.83	0.63	0.76	0.24	0.24	-0.12	0.67	0.82	-0.29	-0.35	-0.6	-0.38	3.2
ImplTempRise	-0.16	-0.03	-0.2	-0.24	1.63	0.82	0.51	0.9	0.42	0.42	-0.02	0.72	0.74	-0.3	-0.36	-0.42	-0.24	3.8
Emissions	-0.13	-0.01	-0.31	-0.26	1.5	0.76	0.25	0.89	0.45	0.45	-0.03	0.4	0.49	-0.27	-0.34	-0.27	-0.23	3.2
MSCI.World	-0.22	-0.05	-0.25	-0.29	1.54	0.74	0.46	0.72	0.24	0.24	-0.22	0.46	0.64	-0.4	-0.5	-0.56	-0.4	2.6

- Traditional performance is close to benchmark performance with low active risk.
- Sustainable performance beats the benchmark's sustainability overall and on most individual variables.
- Sustainable performance differs distinctly between sustainable themes.
- **Biodiversity** outperforms the benchmark, has the second best ImplTempRise and SustainRev, and excels in SDGs 2, 6, 7, 12, 13, 14, and 15 with the third highest total SDG.
- **Climate** outperforms the benchmark, has the best ImplTempRise, and excels in SDGs 2, 7, 8, 9, 10, 11, 12, 13, 14, and 15 with the highest total SDG.
- **ESGRatings** performed as the benchmark and has the highest ESG Ratings close to AAA (adjusted industry score between 8.571 and 10) (per November 2023, only ESGRatings.Excl reaches AAA, see Appendix Table A.1).
- **FemaleAlpha** slightly underperformed the benchmark and has by far the highest number of female board directors, CFOs, and CEOs (per November 2023, the percentage of female CEO rises to 44%, see Appendix Table A.1).
- **SustainDevGoals** slightly underperformed the benchmark but exhibited the most evenly distributed high SDGs.
- **SustainRev** underperformed the benchmark, but has by far the highest SustainRev, the best ClimateVaR.1.5, and the second highest total SDG.
- **ClimateVaR.1.5** outperforms the benchmark with the second lowest ClimateVaR.1.5. Its relatively high ImplTempRise indicates that it is a brown-to-green strategy.
- **ImplTempRise** strongly outperforms the benchmark and has the third lowest ImpTempRise (per November 2023, **ImplTempRise.Excl** reaches 1.5°C, see Appendix Table A.1).
- **Emissions** underperforms the benchmark and has less than 30% of the benchmark's emissions (per November 2023, **Emissions** and **Emissions. Excl** reach 25% and 12.4% of benchmark emissions, respectively, see Appendix Table A.1), while still being fairly sector neutral (also somewhat a brown-to-green strategy).

4.3. *Performance (Long–Short Theme Factors)*

In contrast to the long-only style and theme factors, Figure 7 shows that the long–short sustainable theme strategies (4) outperform the MSCI World, after trading costs. A Fama–French factor analysis

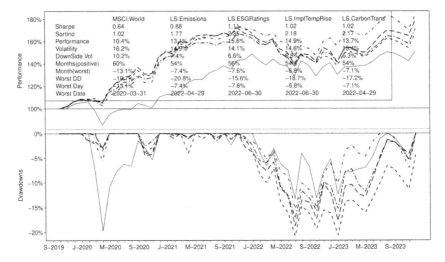

Figure 7. Long–short theme factors vs. long-only benchmark

(Appendix Table A.3) of the long–short strategies shows a significant positive intercept, indicating additional alpha not explained by the factors, which is further confirmed by a fairly low adjusted R^2 of below 70%.

Table 8 presents the monthly and annual performance of the MSCI World alongside the backtested sustainable long–short theme strategy LS.ESGRatings (long–short ESG ratings after transactions and lending costs, as detailed in Table 3).

Table 9 displays the summary statistics for the long–short theme strategies (4) spanning September 2019 to November 2023.

4.4. *Key Takeaways*

Long–short Strategies

- Outperform the MSCI World (Figure 7 and Table 9) with less than 3.5% monthly turnover.
- Are on average USD neutral (NetLong close to zero, Table 9).
- Have a low (Barra) beta (0.7–0.8) against the MSCI World and a slight net large cap bias (MedLongCap exceeding MedShortCap, Table 9).
- Are cooling the planet and have a positive ClimateVaR.1.5 (Table 9) with the optimized strategies having the respective highest sustainable performance.

Table 8. Performance comparison of MSCI World (upper panel), LS.ESGRatings (middle panels), and LS.Emission (lower panels)

	Jan	Feb	Mar	Apr	May	Jun	Jul	Aug	Sep	Oct	Nov	Dec	Annual
2019										0.2	4	1.2	5.5
2020	0.7	−7.6	−13.1	11.2	3.3	1.7	−0.4	5.5	−1.5	−2.4	9.9	1.9	6.8
2021	−0.3	2.7	6.8	2.2	−0.1	4.7	1.8	3	−2.3	5.8	0.6	3.3	31.8
2022	−3.9	−2.7	3.8	−3.2	−1.4	−6.3	10.7	−2.8	−6.9	6.3	2.7	−7.6	−12.3
2023	5.2	0	0.7	0.2	2.6	3.7	2.3	−0.8	−1.9	−2.7	6		15.9
Average	0.4	−1.9	−0.4	2.6	1.1	0.9	3.6	1.2	−3.1	1.4	4.6	−0.3	10.4

	Jan	Feb	Mar	Apr	May	Jun	Jul	Aug	Sep	Oct	Nov	Dec	Annual
2019										2.7	3.5	2.5	8.9
2020	−1.6	−0.3	−3.5	8.2	3.2	4.8	0	6.7	−4.1	0.4	13	4.3	34.2
2021	0.8	7.1	−0.9	2.9	1.8	−0.1	−1.5	1.5	1	5	−1.8	0.3	16.9
2022	−1.6	−2.2	1.9	−4.5	−0.9	−7.6	6.5	−1.6	−3.9	8	2.4	−4.6	−8.9
2023	7.6	1.2	−1.8	−0.7	3.3	3.7	3.3	−1	−2.8	−3.3	7.6		17.7
Average	1.3	1.4	−1.1	1.5	1.8	0.2	2.1	1.4	−2.5	2.5	4.9	0.6	15.6

	Jan	Feb	Mar	Apr	May	Jun	Jul	Aug	Sep	Oct	Nov	Dec	Annual
2019										2.3	4.1	2	8.6
2020	0.3	0.4	−3.5	11.1	4.5	3	0.8	5.5	−3.8	1	12	3.8	39.6
2021	−0.4	6.7	−4	5.6	−1.1	2.2	0	1.4	−1.2	5.2	−1.1	−2.6	10.5
2022	−4.9	−1.7	3.2	−7.4	−2.5	−5.6	7.7	−1.9	−3.5	4.6	−0.7	−5.3	−17.6
2023	8.5	0.5	−1.6	−1.4	3.7	3.4	3.9	−0.9	−2.1	−2.3	8.3		21
Average	0.9	1.5	−1.5	1.9	1.2	0.7	3.1	1	−2.7	2.2	4.5	−0.5	13.1

- Even LS.ESGRatings, without an optimized climate bias, has a low emission value of 10.5 compared to the MSCI World with 360.6 (Table 9).
- Fama–French regressions (Appendix Table A.2) confirm significant alpha with an adjusted R^2 of below 70% and factor exposures mimicking portfolios with large cap bias, negative profitability (RMW < 0), and aggressive investments style (CMA < 0).

5. Conclusions

The amplification of regulatory constraints, coupled with an expanding array of universe exclusions, forms an unfavorable concoction restraining the potential for significant "Value Creation" in sustainable investing.

Table 9.   Traditional and sustainable performance of the long–short themes (4)

	Total. Ret	Ret	SD	SR	ARisk	Assets	Mkt-Cap	USD-Long	USD-Short	Beta	Fem-Dir	Fem-CEO	Fem-CFO	ESG-Ratings	Impl-TempRise	Sustain-Rev	Emissions	Climate-VaR.1.5
LS.Emissions	67.1	13.2	14.9	0.89	3.1	631.76	169.38	195.97	−26.58	0.75	5.9	5.28	14.41	0	−0.93	−4.39	−527.57	19.98
LS.ESG-Ratings	83.1	15.3	14.1	1.09	2.9	701.92	98.28	124.82	−26.54	0.7	10.28	5.14	14.3	4.07	−0.22	0.41	10.47	8.71
LS.Impl-TempRise	78.6	14.7	14.6	1.01	3	644.69	167.25	190.9	−23.65	0.8	8.31	5.17	15	0.58	−3.03	−6.43	−296.94	8.41
LS.Carbon-Trans	71.1	13.6	13.4	1.01	3.2	627.29	125.04	154.43	−29.39	0.74	6.52	5.46	14.43	0.8	−1.22	3.06	−452.3	22.11
MSCI.World	57.3	12.1	16.6	0.73	0.8	1558.73	293.48	293.48	0	1.06	31.87	5.57	13.47	6.45	2.47	12.09	360.65	−8.51

This circumstance results in a low sustainability threshold, shifting sustainable portfolio construction toward a predominantly "Value Alignment" strategy, albeit at the substantial cost of traditional performance. Addressing these challenges, this chapter tackles two key issues: the importance of double materiality in measuring sustainable performance, facilitated by forward-looking research variables exemplified by those provided by the MSCI, and the significance of portfolio construction through quantitative optimization, steered by sustainable alpha scores and optimized by a comprehensive risk factor model. As the results suggest, it is feasible to achieve a significant enhancement in sustainable performance relative to benchmark sustainability, all while maintaining low active risk and comparable benchmark performance. This indicates a significant pickup in "Value Creation." Since the approach incorporates explicit positive and sustainable objectives in portfolio construction, such as advancing biodiversity, promoting SDGs, or facilitating the transition to a low-carbon environment (from Brown to Green), it aligns with the principles of impact investing, potentially serving as an engine for EU Sustainable Finance Disclosure Regulation (SFDR) Article 9 funds.

Appendix

Performance statistics for the Month of November 2023

Table A.1 describes the performance statistics for the month of November 2023 of the sustainable themes (9*2) and the MSCI World benchmark."

Table A.2 describes the SDG performance statistics for the month of November 2023 of the sustainable themes (9*2) and the MSCI World benchmark."

Fama–French and Carhart Factors

Table A.3 describes the established Fama-French. Leveraging the established Fama–French factors and their extensions, as outlined in the references (Carhart, 1997; Fama & French, 1992, 1993, 2014), the findings in Table A.3 show a significant market factor as expected by construction of the sector constraints (see Table 3). Most other factor exposures appear to be statistically insignificant. Only the long–short theme strategies (4) have positive alpha (positive and significant intercept). A more in-depth analysis is deferred for future research.

Table A.1. Performance statistics for the month of November 2023 of the sustainable themes (9*2) and the MSCI World benchmark.

	Assets	MktCap	Beta	FemDir	FemCEO	Fem-CFO	ESG-Ratings	ImplTemp-Rise	Sustain-Rev	Emissions	Climate-VaR.1.5
Biodiversity	189	428.71	1.11	35.41	7.41	19.58	7.38	1.66	20.83	257.98	−8.29
Biodiversity.Excl	197	241.1	1.11	35.81	5.58	18.78	7.7	1.63	19.21	173.56	−6.58
Climate	201	397.37	1.12	35.7	7.46	23.38	7.52	1.61	17.53	216.03	−6.45
Climate.Excl	427	217.83	1.11	35.6	6.56	19.44	7.74	1.63	15.02	151.47	−7.18
ESGRatings	211	411.31	1.11	35.73	6.16	19.91	8.44	1.92	14.42	319.55	−11.52
ESGRatings.Excl	233	229.34	1.11	36.46	8.58	19.31	8.78	1.71	13.27	170	−7.94
FemaleAlpha	199	371.95	1.1	40.45	26.63	44.22	7.39	1.87	13.1	274.58	−13.95
FemaleAlpha.Excl	227	221.48	1.12	39.74	20.26	39.65	7.64	1.82	12.17	174.86	−11.8
SustainDevGoals	152	412.18	1.12	35.81	3.95	21.71	7.24	2.06	17.47	409.84	−13.58
SustainDevGoals.Excl	275	229.23	1.12	35.91	6.55	19.27	7.71	1.8	18.01	222.95	−7.38
SustainRev	160	432.7	1.05	34.03	4.38	24.38	7.22	1.93	39.46	304.84	−4.08
SustainRev.Excl	169	234.78	1.05	33.79	5.92	21.3	7.46	1.95	39.3	218.14	−2.08
ClimateVaR.1.5	156	437.11	1.03	32.91	5.77	18.59	6.4	2.29	13.44	178.86	−4.14
ClimateVaR.1.5.Excl	144	119.92	0.92	26.44	8.33	16.67	5.78	1.73	9.53	127.03	−1.86
ImplTempRise	138	442.64	1.11	35.26	7.25	21.74	7.02	1.72	13.78	301.43	−12.43
ImplTempRise.Excl	224	238.53	1.05	36.15	9.38	19.2	7.48	1.51	9.91	119.4	−7.68
Emissions	161	418	1.13	36.13	9.94	21.74	6.89	1.67	13.58	90.77	−6.44
Emissions.Excl	161	218.19	1.12	36.61	12.42	21.12	7.21	1.6	12.88	44.85	−3.83
MSCI World	1507	442.06	1.12	34.71	6.9	16.46	6.9	2.07	12.8	361.74	−12.69

Table A.2. SDG performance statistics for the month of November 2023 of the sustainable themes (9*2) and the MSCI World benchmark.

	SDG-01	SDG-02	SDG-03	SDG-04	SDG-05	SDG-06	SDG-07	SDG-08	SDG-09	SDG-10	SDG-11	SDG-12	SDG-13	SDG-14	SDG-15	SDG-16	SDG-17	SDG. Sum
Biodiversity	-0.45	0.2	-0.12	-0.67	1.14	1.43	1.05	0.59	0.29	0.29	0.14	2	1.34	-0.04	-0.2	-0.68	-0.62	5.7
Biodiversity.Excl	0.38	0.14	0.28	0	1.89	1.43	1.53	1.43	1.29	1.29	0.35	2.51	1.78	0.04	-0.07	0.19	0.29	14.8
Climate	-0.03	0.03	0.01	-0.43	1.39	0.99	1.18	0.96	0.94	0.94	0.33	1.59	1.43	-0.04	-0.14	-0.17	-0.07	8.9
Climate.Excl	0.62	0.03	0.28	0.16	2.06	0.95	1.55	1.66	1.7	1.7	0.37	1.98	1.77	0.01	-0.05	0.57	0.64	16
ESGRatings	-0.05	0.02	-0.06	-0.51	1.41	1.04	0.64	0.88	0.74	0.74	0.04	0.97	0.88	-0.22	-0.31	-0.3	-0.24	5.7
ESGRatings.Excl	0.52	0.03	0.22	0.11	2.09	1.01	1.29	1.56	1.48	1.48	0.22	1.85	1.5	0.02	-0.05	0.4	0.48	14.2
FemaleAlpha	0.14	0.1	-0.07	-0.33	1.68	0.91	0.58	1.13	1.17	1.17	0.01	0.86	0.79	-0.18	-0.22	0.03	0.11	7.9
FemaleAlpha.Excl	0.75	0.07	0.26	0.21	2.25	0.93	1.2	1.81	1.8	1.8	0.12	1.65	1.41	0	-0.05	0.66	0.71	15.6
SustainDevGoals	-0.1	0.17	0.05	-0.51	1.37	1.04	0.59	0.77	0.7	0.7	0.14	1.06	0.76	-0.12	-0.25	-0.4	-0.24	5.7
SustainDevGoals.Excl	0.74	0.09	0.47	0.17	2.07	1.23	1.4	1.71	1.63	1.63	0.32	2.1	1.59	0.01	-0.06	0.59	0.57	16.3
SustainRev	0.11	0.2	0.11	-0.51	1.21	1.22	0.84	0.92	0.72	0.72	0.47	2.11	1.05	-0.17	-0.31	-0.47	-0.42	7.8
SustainRev.Excl	0.91	0.25	0.65	0.18	1.92	1.35	1.38	1.83	1.62	1.62	0.86	2.84	1.53	0.04	-0.08	0.32	0.38	17.6
ClimateVaR.1.5	-0.54	-0.03	-0.27	-0.64	1.11	0.98	0.74	0.45	0.26	0.26	-0.08	0.92	0.97	-0.22	-0.28	-0.7	-0.59	2.3
ClimateVaR.1.5.Excl	0.41	0.04	0.23	0.1	1.51	0.73	1.08	1.12	1.08	1.08	0.12	1.31	1.26	-0.01	-0.02	0.46	0.37	10.9
ImplTempRise	-0.74	-0.06	-0.26	-0.67	1.28	0.8	0.51	0.36	0.03	0.03	-0.26	0.87	0.82	-0.31	-0.54	-0.98	-0.72	0.2
ImplTempRise.Excl	0.26	-0.04	0.09	-0.01	1.88	0.9	1.24	1.34	1.27	1.27	0.16	1.59	1.49	-0.01	-0.05	0.24	0.31	11.9
Emissions	-0.35	-0.06	-0.29	-0.62	1.24	0.7	0.31	0.59	0.3	0.3	-0.09	0.44	0.56	-0.25	-0.3	-0.55	-0.47	1.5
Emissions.Excl	0.55	-0.04	0.22	0.09	1.93	0.67	1.18	1.45	1.29	1.29	0.12	1.44	1.41	0	-0.04	0.39	0.42	12.4
MSCI.World	-0.64	-0.08	-0.39	-0.71	1.15	0.75	0.44	0.28	0.08	0.08	-0.36	0.51	0.67	-0.39	-0.54	-0.95	-0.79	-0.9

Table A.3.   Fama–French and Carhart factor exposures

	Intercept	Mkt.RF	SMB	HML	RMW	CMA	Intercept	Mkt.RF	SMB	HML	RMW	CMA	aR2
Biodiversity	-0.003	1.083	0.057	-0.042	-0.054	0.332	-1.4	42.7	-0.5	0.2	0.6	2.8	81.7
Climate	-0.003	1.092	0.094	-0.064	-0.02	0.305	-1.4	34.8	0.2	-0.3	1	1.8	81
ClimateVaR.1.5	-0.002	1.052	0.062	-0.024	-0.071	0.283	-1	36.6	-0.4	0.5	0.1	1.7	79.9
Emissions	-0.004	1.116	-0.002	-0.06	-0.031	0.222	-2.2	35.2	-1.5	-0.2	0.7	0.5	78.9
ESGRatings	-0.003	1.083	0.102	-0.041	0.006	0.291	-1.5	35.4	0.3	0.2	1.4	1.7	80.7
FemaleAlpha	-0.003	1.08	0.103	-0.054	0.009	0.278	-1.6	36.9	0.4	-0.1	1.6	1.5	81.4
ImplTempRise	-0.003	1.166	0.153	0.014	-0.012	0.243	-0.8	29.2	1	1.1	1.1	0.5	82.6
SustainDevGoals	-0.003	1.083	0.072	-0.028	-0.078	0.24	-1	28.5	0	0.3	0.2	0.6	81.6
SustainRev	-0.003	1.026	0.065	-0.087	-0.036	0.344	-1.6	30.5	-0.1	-0.9	0.8	2.4	81.4
MSCI.ESG	-0.003	1.081	0.07	-0.046	0.022	0.285	-1.2	34.7	-0.2	0	1.7	1.5	80.9
MSCI.Growth	-0.001	1.083	0.086	-0.058	-0.034	0.216	-0.5	41.8	-0.2	-0.2	0.7	0.7	78.9
MSCI.Momentum	-0.003	1.101	0.006	-0.04	-0.017	0.234	-1.5	45.4	-1.7	0.2	1.3	0.9	80.9
MSCI.Quality	-0.004	1.053	0.083	0.016	0.011	0.284	-1.8	34.6	0.1	1.4	1.6	1.6	82
MSCI.Size	-0.004	1.051	0.176	-0.009	0.044	0.222	-2.6	36.1	1.6	0.9	2.1	0.7	81.7
MSCI.Value	-0.004	1.044	0.13	0.059	0.062	0.299	-1.7	31.1	0.9	2.2	2.2	1.7	82.8
MSCI.Volatility	-0.004	1.051	-0.003	-0.018	0.024	0.259	-2.2	40.8	-1.4	0.7	2.2	1.4	83.4
MSCI.Yield	-0.004	1.067	0.077	0.047	0.061	0.323	-2	31	0.1	1.9	2.2	1.9	82.4
LS.CarbonTrans	0.007	0.575	0.229	0.013	-0.374	-0.098	2.7	9.2	1.6	0.4	-2.6	-1.6	67.5
LS.Emissions	0.006	0.657	0.193	-0.036	-0.38	-0.187	2.6	11.5	1.2	-0.1	-2.9	-2.5	71.3
LS.ESGRatings	0.007	0.638	0.25	0.029	-0.276	0.059	2.6	10.1	1.6	0.6	-1.8	-0.4	65.7
LS.ImplTempRise	0.007	0.665	0.132	0.06	-0.378	-0.126	2.6	10.1	0.6	0.9	-2.4	-1.8	65.6

	Intercept	Mkt.RF	SMB	HML	MOM	ST_Rev	LT_Rev	Intercept	Mkt.RF	SMB	HML	MOM	ST_Rev	LT_Rev	aR2
Biodiversity	-0.003	1.061	-0.117	-0.088	-0.115	-0.115	0.26	-1.4	39.8	-2.7	-0.3	-2.1	-1.6	2.1	81.2
Climate	-0.003	1.092	-0.044	-0.047	-0.099	-0.144	0.173	-1.1	32.5	-1	0.5	-1.3	-1.8	0.2	80.2
ClimateVaR.1.5	-0.003	1.037	-0.054	-0.032	-0.117	-0.141	0.174	-1	35.3	-1.3	0.9	-1.9	-2.2	0.4	79.3
Emissions	-0.004	1.08	-0.144	-0.079	-0.092	-0.042	0.14	-2	32.8	-2.6	-0.1	-1	0	-0.3	78.3
ESGRatings	-0.003	1.079	-0.053	-0.021	-0.112	-0.133	0.165	-1.2	32.9	-1.1	1	-1.6	-1.7	0.1	80
FemaleAlpha	-0.003	1.063	-0.054	-0.023	-0.11	-0.098	0.139	-1.1	33.7	-1.2	1	-1.6	-1	-0.3	80.5
ImplTempRise	-0.003	1.115	-0.055	-0.036	-0.111	0.001	0.242	-0.6	26.9	-0.9	0.6	-1.3	1.1	1	82.4
SustainDevGoals	-0.003	1.049	-0.055	-0.076	-0.178	-0.138	0.191	-1.1	28.3	-1	-0.1	-3.1	-1.5	0.6	82
SustainRev	-0.004	1.024	-0.083	-0.094	-0.105	-0.159	0.221	-1.4	28.2	-1.5	-0.4	-1.5	-2	1.1	80.7
MSCI.ESG	-0.003	1.075	-0.085	-0.016	-0.117	-0.129	0.138	-0.7	32.4	-1.6	1.1	-1.7	-1.6	-0.3	80.2
MSCI.Growth	-0.002	1.072	-0.038	-0.074	-0.101	-0.1	0.158	-0.4	40	-1.1	0	-1.4	-1.5	0	78.5
MSCI.Momentum	-0.003	1.1	-0.088	-0.018	-0.05	-0.094	0.106	-1	43.4	-2.2	1.4	0	-1.1	-1.2	80.1
MSCI.Quality	-0.004	1.054	-0.079	0.015	-0.145	-0.165	0.178	-1.5	34.1	-1.7	1.8	-2.7	-2.4	0.4	82
MSCI.Size	-0.004	1.047	0.069	0.095	-0.051	-0.062	0.039	-1.7	33.2	0.9	3.3	-0.1	-0.3	-1.9	80.4
MSCI.Value	-0.004	1.053	-0.085	0.046	-0.161	-0.172	0.224	-1.3	29.9	-1.6	2.1	-2.9	-2.2	1.1	83
MSCI.Volatility	-0.004	1.047	-0.148	-0.012	-0.076	-0.093	0.142	-1.5	36.6	-3.2	1.3	-1	-0.8	-0.2	82.7
MSCI.Yield	-0.004	1.07	-0.136	0.044	-0.14	-0.15	0.213	-1.5	28.4	-2.2	2	-2.2	-1.6	0.8	82
LS.CarbonTrans	0.005	0.51	0.374	-0.136	-0.122	-0.05	0.132	1.8	7.2	2.9	-0.9	-1.2	-0.2	0.4	63.7
LS.Emissions	0.004	0.568	0.325	-0.22	-0.118	0.035	0.113	1.5	8.5	2.5	-1.6	-1.1	0.5	0.2	66.9
LS.ESGRatings	0.004	0.6	0.262	-0.129	-0.17	-0.133	0.259	1.9	9	2.1	-0.8	-1.8	-1.1	1.4	66.7
LS.ImplTempRise	0.004	0.595	0.193	-0.227	-0.141	-0.019	0.28	1.5	8	1.4	-1.6	-1.3	0.1	1.4	63.4

References

Berg, F., Koelbel, J., & Rigobon, R. (2022). Aggregate confusion: The divergence of ESG ratings. *Review of Finance*, 26(6), 1315–1344.

Blitz, D., Chen, M., Howard, C., & Lohre H. (2023). 3D Investing: Jointly optimising return, risk, and sustainability. SSRN 4670534.

Bonne, G., Roisenberg, L., Subramanian, R. A., & Melas, D. (2018). MSCI FaCS methodology. Retrieved from https://www.msci.com/documents/10199/275765e9-d631-4222-b4aa-520f7fa7d830.

Cano, G. & Minovitsky, S. (2021). Factoring in ESG. *MSCI Blog Post*. Retrieved from https://www.msci.com/www/blog-posts/factoring-in-esg/02343304664.

Carhart, M. M. (1997). On persistence in mutual fund performance. *The Journal of Finance*, 52(1), 57–82.

Fama, E. F. & French, K. R. (1992). The cross-section of expected stock returns. *The Journal of Finance*, 47(2), 427–465.

Fama, E. F. & French, K. R. (1993). Common risk factors in the returns on stocks and bonds. *Journal of Financial Economics*, 33(1), 3–56.

Fama, E. F. & French, K. R. (2014). A five-factor asset pricing model. *Journal of Financial Economics*, 116, 1–22.

Grinold, R. C. & Kahn, R. N. (1999). *Active Portfolio Management: A Quantitative Approach for Producing Superior Returns and Selecting Superior Returns and Controlling Risk*. McGraw-Hill Library of Investment and Finance.

Minovitsky, S. & Bonne, G. (2020). MSCI Global Equity Factor Model + ESG Model Insight.

Morozov, A., Minovitsky, S., Wang, J., & Barrera, D. (2016). Barra global total market equity model for long term investors, empirical notes. MSCI Model Insight.

MSCI ESG Research. (2023, October). *MSCI SDG Alignment Methodology*. https://fm.baden-wuerttemberg.de/de/finanzen/haushalt/nachhaltig-anlegen https://www.msci.com/documents/1296102/15233886/MSCI+SDG+Alignment+Methodology.pdf.

MSCI ESG Research. (2023, August). *MSCI ESG and Climate Symbols and Definitions*.

MSCI ESG Research. (2023). *MSCI ESG Sustainable Impact Metrics*. Retrieved from https://www.msci.com/zh/esg-sustainable-impact-metrics.

NaFiBWG. (2023). *Gesetz für nachhaltige Finanzanlagen*. Financial Ministry of the German State of Baden Württemberg. Retrieved from https://fm.baden-wuerttemberg.de/de/finanzen/haushalt/nachhaltig-anlegen.

Pedersen, L. H., Fitzgibbons, S., & Pomorski, L. (2021). Responsible investing: The ESG-efficient frontier. *Journal of Financial Economics*, 142, 572–597.

Scherer, B. (2022). Was Investoren über E(SG) wissen müssen! *Deutsche Pensions & Investment Nachrichten (DPN-Magazin)*. https://fm.baden-wuerttemberg.de/de/finanzen/haushalt/nachhaltig-anlegen http://dx.doi.org/10.2139/ssrn.4242585.

Schmidt, A. B. (2020). Optimal ESG portfolios: An example for the Dow Jones index. *Journal of Sustainable Finance and Investment*, 12(2), 529–535.

Chapter 15

The Portfolio Costs of Sustainability and Three-Dimensional Trade-offs

Aston S. K. Chan

Impact Cubed
London, United Kingdom

Abstract

This chapter presents a three-dimensional investment framework that combines factor investing techniques and factorized sustainability data to enable investors to quantitatively connect the sustainability dimension to the risk-and-return dimensions when constructing sustainable investment portfolios. We demonstrate how the portfolio costs of sustainability objectives, in terms of risk-and-return implications, can be modeled, followed by insights into how sustainability can be approached in risk budget terms with an examination of the potential degree of diversification available when multiple sustainability outcomes are targeted.

1. Introduction

Inflows into sustainable investment products have increased significantly in recent years across all major regions and asset classes. This significant asset flow is taking place through both new sustainability-focused investment funds and existing funds that started incorporating sustainable elements in their investment policies. However, sustainable investing in its many forms ("socially responsible," "ESG," "climate," etc.) is far from a new concept. Religious value-based or ethical funds were early examples of investment products that explicitly controlled or targeted non-financial characteristics of a portfolio through exclusionary policies.

In many respects, this controlling or targeting of sustainability characteristics of portfolios is similar to other popular investment disciplines such as factor investing. In the case of factor investing, the investor seeks to control or target financial or "style" factors, instead of environmental, societal, or governance metrics. Given this similarity between sustainable investing and factor investing, it is surprising that typical implementations of these two popular branches of investment are often radically different.

It is interesting to note that the manipulation of company characteristics in factor investing is typically closely integrated with intentional risk-and-return considerations. This integration can be executed through a number of well-established quantitative frameworks. In contrast, the field of sustainable investing so far lacks this quantitative integration, with relatively few examples of modern portfolio theory being applied rigorously (Pedersen *et al.*, 2021; Schmidt, 2020). The absence of a robust quantitative framework connecting sustainability with risk and return has hampered investors' ability to integrate sustainability objectives in an efficient manner, in terms of both policy setting and portfolio implementation.

This chapter presents a framework that combines portfolio engineering techniques commonly used in factor investing with sustainability data constructed as factors in order to quantitatively integrate the sustainability dimension with the traditional risk-and-return dimensions. This quantitative framework allows investors to (1) customize the definition of sustainability by selectively including and targeting sustainability factors that represent their values and (2) quantify the trade-offs in risk and return as incremental units of this set of sustainability factors are implemented in the portfolio.

To provide readers with a brief background on how factor investing techniques can enhance sustainable investing practices, this chapter first highlights the differences between the typical investment frameworks of sustainable investment products and factor investing products, then offers brief explanations of possible reasons for these disparities. In the process of observing these differences, several shortcomings of common sustainable investing processes emerge.

A simplified version of Impact Cubed's[1] quantitative sustainable investment framework that combines advanced factor investing techniques with our in-house sustainability factor data is then described. This investment framework enables investors to meet their sustainability objectives with an optimal set of risk-and-return trade-offs. We use this framework to demonstrate how investors can gain a three-dimensional understanding of the relationship between sustainability, risk, and return, by showing how expected risk and return change with incremental units of a sample set of sustainability preferences being introduced into a global equity portfolio.

We believe this three-dimensional framework addresses a shortcoming of current common sustainable investment approaches that lack clarity on how sustainability interacts with risk and return, which in turn impairs the ability of investors to calibrate their sustainability objectives effectively and to construct optimal portfolios.

In this chapter, the terms "sustainable" and "sustainability" can be interpreted interchangeably with other commonly used terms such as "ESG," "socially responsible," and "climate." As the reader will see, the investment framework described can incorporate a wide array of characteristics that are commonly understood to fall under one or more of these terms. Furthermore, while this investment framework is equally applicable to equities and fixed-income investments, for simplicity, this chapter focuses on equity investing when more detailed processes and modeling are described.

2. Key Differences between Sustainable and Factor Investing Methodologies

Security exclusion is the most prominent methodology used in sustainable investing products to manipulate portfolio-level and/or holdings-level sustainability characteristics. This is followed by "best in class" which is a process that targets better sustainability results by over- and under-weighting securities within a sector, without affecting the overall sector weight. Thematic strategies typically use "selection" as their main

---

[1] Impact Cubed is a specialist sustainable investing advisor based in London. It specializes in providing advanced custom sustainable investment solutions as well as data and analytics services to the asset owner and asset management markets.

methodology, by only holding securities that satisfy a certain set of sustainability requirements. However, selection is in fact a form of exclusionary methodology. "Selecting only companies with over 30% revenue aligned with climate positive solutions" is operationally the same as "excluding all companies in the eligible universe with climate positive solutions revenue alignment equal to or below 30%." Finally, a small proportion of ESG indices or benchmarks combines exclusions and optimization to create climate indices that target specific metrics such as carbon intensity, while excluding companies involved in controversial activities.

When it comes to the information to which these exclusionary policies typically apply, the sustainability market has historically been dominated by ESG scores or ratings published by major index providers or credit ratings agencies. These scores and ratings often combine a number of underlying indicators into a scoring system with discrete values. As an example, a "Climate Risk score" will have possible outcomes of 1, 2, 3, 4, or 5.

Furthermore, these scores or ratings can be generated by rule-based systems, either weighting each underlying indicator in predetermined allocations or being subjectively decided by analysts applying an agency-specific evaluation framework. Most current scoring and ratings published by major index providers and credit risk agencies are the latter type.

Factor investing started in the early 1990s, after the seminal three-factor (market, size, and value) papers published by Eugene F. Fama and Kenneth French (Fama & French, 1993). Since then, other factors such as momentum, quality, and volatility have been added. Factor investing is sometimes known as Smart Beta and typically targets quantifiable company characteristics to achieve certain return-and-risk objectives.

Most likely due to its academic origin, factor investing is predominantly a quantitative investment discipline, where non-discrete factor data and a risk model are used to optimally weight stock holdings. Additionally, the determination of the "tilt" toward a certain factor is often expressed as a risk target, in the form of ex ante volatility.

While there are a wide variety of investment frameworks within the sustainable investing and factor investing disciplines, the above-mentioned passage briefly summarizes the features that are representative of these disciplines and Table 1 highlights the differences between them. These differences permit us to identify the shortcomings and untapped

Table 1. Summary of differences in the typical features of each investment product group

Typical Feature	Sustainable Investing	Factor Investing
Motivation	Asset owner sustainability policy and regulation	Outperformance and risk control
Underlying data	Discrete value scoring based on analysts' evaluation and, to a lesser extent, continuous ESG metrics	Continuous factor data on company financial characteristics
Risk model and optimization used in portfolio allocation	Seldom	Most often
Extent of exposure or "tilt" toward company characteristics	Determined by qualitative ESG policy	Determined by ex ante risk targets
Implementation	Multiple, discreet sequential steps of exclusions and "best-in-class" allocations	Multiple portfolio allocation operations performed in a single optimization step
Individual securities outcome	Binary: in or out, over- or under-weighted vs. sector peers	Weights determined according to risk-and-return expectations with a wide range of possible outcomes depending on position constraints and covariance

potential of sustainable investing, and they motivate the development of Impact Cubed's three-dimensional sustainable factor approach to investing.

3. Possible Reasons for Such a Divergence in the Two Practices

As discussed earlier, these two investment disciplines manipulate portfolio and holdings characteristics in very different ways. One potential explanation for this is the origins of these investment disciplines. Factor investing grew out of academic research that is supported by advanced quantitative techniques while sustainable investing has its roots in investment policy settings.

Furthermore, reliable and granular ESG data with good coverage were not available for the investment community until recently, while factor investing has enjoyed strong data availability for a long time, which in turn has facilitated factor investing's widespread utilization of more advanced portfolio engineering techniques.

Lastly, while achieving better returns is certainly part of every sustainable investor's objective, investment choices in sustainable investing must also accommodate binary in/out treatments of companies based on ESG criteria. This dual purpose complicates the investment process and introduces non-financial variables that are not well handled by systematic processes. This issue is likely the reason why quantitative sustainable investment is relatively rare in today's market. Instead, this dual purpose is currently more easily accommodated in a discretionary portfolio management process.

4. Establishing the Links Among Sustainability, Risk, and Return

By adopting factor investing techniques and using Impact Cubed's objective, factorized sustainability data, we are able to provide a quantifiable and flexible framework that connects risk and return to sustainability preferences. A simplified version of this investment framework can be demonstrated by the following hypothetical example:

Imagine an investor who has a simple objective of reducing the carbon intensity of her long-only passive global equity portfolio, tracking a global cap-weighted benchmark. This can be achieved by some reallocations from higher-emitting companies to lower-emitting companies. For a certain degree of decarbonization, let's say a 20% reduction in carbon intensity, there are a number of combinations of over- and under-weighting that can meet the overall portfolio target given the large number of companies in the investment universe.

Among these many possible combinations of over- and under-weighting of individual companies, the investor can be assumed to prefer the combination that has the lowest expected tracking error against the underlying benchmark. For any level of target decarbonization, we can construct the most tracking-error-efficient portfolio, by undertaking an

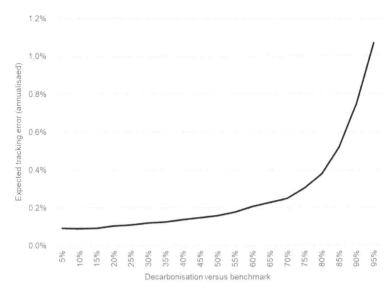

Figure 1. Decarbonization vs. expected tracking error (global developed market large and mid-cap equities; Scopes 1 and 2 revenue-based carbon intensity reduction targets).

optimization with an objective of meeting the decarbonization target with the lowest expected tracking error (see Table 2).[2]

The resulting relationship between decarbonization and portfolio tracking error (shown in Figure 1) is intuitive. Increasing tracking error is incurred as more decarbonization is specified for the portfolio. This rate of increase rises as the decarbonization target goes up, a consequence of a larger deviation from the benchmark being needed to achieve higher targets.

It is possible to calculate an expected return for each of the portfolios in Table 2. For simplicity, we use the first process of the Black–Litterman approach (Black & Litterman, 1991) to generate market-implied equilibrium returns for each company in the index by reverse optimization, using

---

[2]Data specification: Global developed market equities universe as of October 21, 2023; Scopes 1 and 2 carbon emission per USD revenue.

Table 2.   Decarbonization vs. expected tracking error (global developed market large and mid-cap equities; Scopes 1 and 2 revenue-based carbon intensity reduction targets)

Decarbonization Target (%)	Expected Annualized Tracking Error vs. Benchmark (%)
10	0.091
20	0.105
30	0.120
40	0.137
50	0.159
60	0.208
70	0.249
80	0.390
90	0.751

Table 3.   Market-implied equilibrium returns for the minimum tracking error portfolios vs. benchmark

Decarbonization Target (%)	Market-Implied Equilibrium Returns Deviation from Benchmark (%)
10	0.00000
20	0.00001
30	0.00017
40	0.00004
50	−0.00005
60	−0.00016
70	−0.00074
80	−0.00191
90	−0.00585

the cap weighting of the benchmark and a covariance matrix based on historic returns (see Table 3).

We observe a reduction of expected returns at an increasing rate as the decarbonization target rises (as shown in Figure 2). It is important to note that the use of market-implied equilibrium returns from the Black–Litterman approach implicitly assumes that the market portfolio, i.e. the

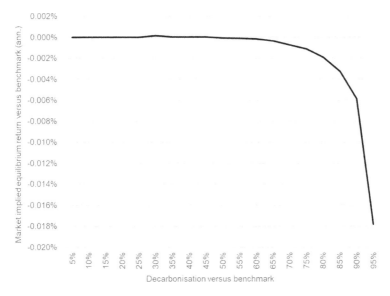

Figure 2. Market-implied equilibrium returns for the minimum tracking error portfolios vs. benchmark.

cap-weighted benchmark, is efficient. Therefore, the fact that expected return declines with increasing decarbonization can fairly be described as intentional. In practice, the full 3D modeling framework used to create client portfolios takes into account the clients' return views supported by other sustainability investment research. When these views are incorporated, the relationship between decarbonization and returns will take different, and often surprising, shapes. Layering investor sustainable return views over "neutral" Black–Litterman expected returns is beyond the scope of this chapter, due to the complexity involved.

The process described earlier represents the basic framework to quantitatively integrate the three dimensions: sustainability, risk, and return (see Figure 3). This simplified process starts by first creating an optimal relationship between one sustainability factor and risk, which then connects to the return dimension by observing changes in expected returns based on a "neutral" set of return expectations. It is possible to connect the three dimensions in other ways and in other orders. For example, investors can start with a specific tracking error budget and then maximize

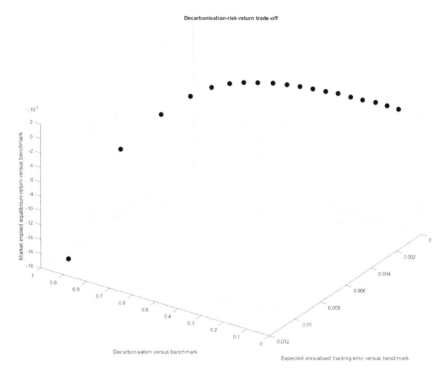

Figure 3.   A three-dimensional plot of the decarbonized portfolios as detailed in Tables 2 and 3.

returns and/or decarbonization. Finally, the return dimension can be observed, as in the previous example, or it can be intentionally targeted, leading to new portfolios with different risk-and-return trade-offs with the same decarbonization target. This will produce a three-dimensional surface or efficient frontier representing another advanced application of Impact Cubed's investment solutions.

5.   Observing the Portfolio "Costs" of Sustainability Implementation

Using Impact Cubed's sustainability factor dataset, we can calculate the sustainability and risk trade-offs in the same way as the example in the earlier section for over 300 sustainability data points across

Table 4. Improvements in individual sustainability factors for a given risk budget (25, 50, 75, and 100 basis points in annualized tracking error)

Risk Budget	Sustainability Improvement Delivered for A Given "Risk Budget" in Annualized Tracking Error (basis points, bps)			
	25 bps (%)	50 bps (%)	75 bps (%)	100 bps (%)
Scopes 1 & 2 carbon intensity	70	82	90	93
Scope 3 carbon intensity	45	65	75	82
Water usage	93	97	98	99
Water scarcity avoidance	8	13	17	21
Waste generation	95	99	100	100
Gender equality	10	17	24	30
Board independence	6	10	13	15
Executive pay ratio	18	31	43	50
Economic development	8	15	21	26
Tax gap	30	53	65	74
Employment	9	17	24	29
SDG environmental good revenue alignment	60	110	165	210
SDG environmental harm revenue alignment	46	71	90	100
SDG social good revenue alignment	55	99	141	173
SDG social harm revenue alignment	86	100	100	100

environmental, societal, governance, regulatory, biodiversity, and SDG alignment factors.

Table 4 shows the percentage improvements for each incremental 25-basis-point risk budget[3] for a subset of Impact Cubed sustainability factors.

As with the previous simplified example, the results are intuitive. The first 25 basis points of risk budget produce more sustainability improvements than the second, incremental, 25 basis points, and so on. This is

---

[3]Expressed as annualized tracking error against a global developed market equities benchmark.

expected as the optimizer has less freedom to produce the desired out-come as the total targeted improvement rises.

Furthermore, we observe stark differences in the improvement that each unit of risk budget can buy for different factors. For most of the environmental factors (Scope 1–3 carbon intensity, waste generation, and water usage), the first 25-basis-point risk budget can remove a significant amount of environmental impact. On the other hand, for governance factors (gender equality, board independence, and executive pay ratio), only relatively small improvements can be achieved for the same risk budget. This contrast is explained by the underlying distribution of factors. Environmental factors tend to be highly concentrated in a relatively small number of outlier companies and sectors such as mining and oil produc-tion. Hence, targeting the under-weighting of a smaller number of compa-nies and sectors yields a relatively low tracking error and produces significant improvements. In contrast, governance factors tend to follow a more normal distribution. This has the opposite effect on the amount of improvement available for a given risk budget. These extreme and vary-ing factor distributions made it very difficult to find a statistical method for estimating factor tracking error costs, which therefore dictates that a more empirical approach, using a portfolio optimizer, is needed.

As a point of clarification, for factors where zero is the best possible sustainability outcome (i.e. lower is better or more sustainable), such as for carbon emissions, 100% improvement is the theoretical maximum achiev-able (meaning all carbon emissions have been removed). For factors where higher is better, or more sustainable, such as environmentally good SDG revenue alignment, it is possible for improvements to be above 100% since it is possible to more than double such revenue alignment. Therefore, the SDG-defined environmental and social good revenue alignment can yield improvements of over 100% when a sufficient risk budget is spent.

By measuring improvements in risk budget units, investors can approach sustainability allocations in a way similar to how factor invest-ing would consider factor allocation, e.g. a 1% risk allocation to the value factor. This way of thinking can enhance investors' ability to set sustain-ability goals that are better aligned with risk exposures.

6. Portfolio Benefits of Sustainability

So far, the primary framing of the trade-offs among sustainability, risk, and return in the chapter has been in terms of costs. This makes sense since any deviation from the starting benchmark would cost something in risk and/or return terms. A good sustainable investing framework achieves a given sustainability outcome with the least cost to risk and return.

However, just as in factor investing and portfolio construction in general, diversification is available. A key strength of the factor investing technique adopted is the ability to target multiple factors simultaneously. So, what happens to the risk-and-return trade-offs when an investor implements multiple unit improvements in different factors at the same time?

Table 5 shows the portfolio tracking errors when improvements in all 15 factors are implemented by the optimizer. To clarify, "Unit portfolio 1" is a portfolio that uses the same global equities benchmark as the

Table 5. Portfolio tracking error when combining "unit" improvements of all 15 factors simultaneously

	Sustainability Improvement Delivered for A Given Risk Budget of Annualized Tracking Error (basis points, bps)			
	Unit Portfolio 1	Unit Portfolio 2	Unit Portfolio 3	Unit Portfolio 4
Risk Budget	25 bps (%)	50 bps (%)	75 bps (%)	100 bps (%)
Scopes 1 & 2 carbon intensity	70	82	90	93
Scope 3 carbon intensity	45	65	75	82
Water usage	93	97	98	99
Water scarcity avoidance	8	13	17	21
Waste generation	95	99	100	100
Gender equality	10	17	24	30
Board independence	6	10	13	15
Executive pay ratio	18	31	43	50
Economic development	8	15	21	26
Tax gap	30	53	65	74
Employment	9	17	24	29
SDG environmental good revenue alignment	60	110	165	210
SDG environmental harm revenue alignment	46	71	90	100
SDG social good revenue alignment	55	99	141	173
SDG social harm revenue alignment	86	100	100	100
Portfolio tracking error	**1.10**	**2.95**	**7.57**	**17.50**

Table 6. Changes in expected tracking error and returns for a given unit of sustainability (defined in Table 5) being inserted into a global equity benchmark

Unit Portfolio	0.0 (%)	0.5 (%)	1.0 (%)	1.5 (%)	2.0 (%)	2.5 (%)	3.0 (%)
Expected tracking error vs. benchmark	0.00	0.43	1.10	1.81	2.95	4.36	7.57
Market-implied equilibrium return vs. benchmark	0.000	−0.004	−0.011	−0.026	−0.040	−0.082	−0.224

previous examples. It targets the 25 basis points of risk budget for factor improvement across all 15 factors simultaneously. It can be thought of as a sustainability factor risk parity portfolio.

Here, we observe that there is indeed significant diversification among this wide selection of sustainability factors. Combining 15 lots of 25 basis points of risk budget improvements simultaneously in an optimizer incurred a portfolio tracking error of only 1.1%. This understanding can encourage investors to incorporate increasingly larger sets of complementary sustainability factors into their portfolios.

Lastly, we show in Table 6 how the three-dimensional trade-offs evolve as we implement increasing amounts of this risk parity sustainability in a global equity portfolio.

The general shape of the three-dimensional trade-offs remains similar to the first simplified example this chapter presented. We see both rising risk and falling expected returns at increasing rates (see Figures 4 and 5). Given the Black–Litterman reverse optimization assumptions and the general operations of portfolio optimization, these results are intuitive.

A three-dimensional plot with all three axes shown in Figure 6.

7. Conclusion

This chapter sets out an investment framework that explicitly and quantitatively connects the three key dimensions of sustainable investing: risk, return, and sustainability. This three-dimensional framework improves on common existing sustainable integration methodologies by incorporating techniques from factor investing processes. By combining these advanced factor investing techniques with Impact Cubed's factorized sustainability data, we are able to approach sustainability integration in a more optimal

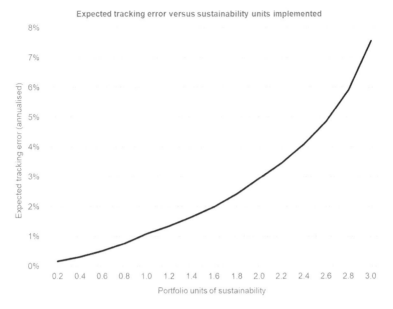

Figure 4. Changes in expected tracking error when increasing amounts of sustainability are incorporated into the global equity benchmark as detailed in Table 6.

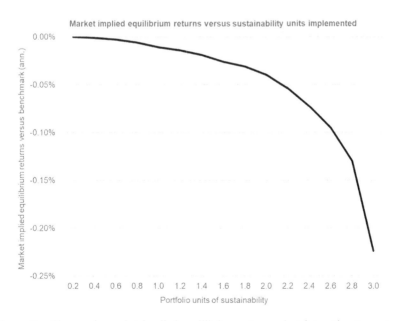

Figure 5. Changes in market-implied equilibrium returns when increasing amounts of sustainability are incorporated into the global equity benchmark as detailed in Table 6.

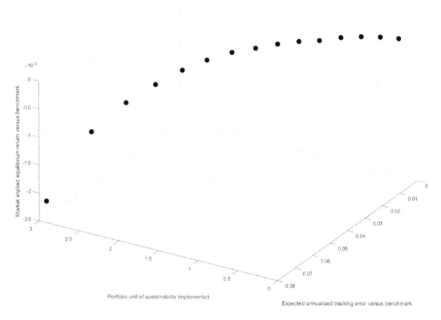

Figure 6. A three-dimensional plot of the portfolios with increasing sustainability implementation as detailed in Table 6.

manner, permitting investors to more intentionally manage the unavoidable trade-offs among the three dimensions. The ability to, for example, manage sustainability factors in risk budget terms or optimize multiple sustainability targets simultaneously represents a significant advancement in the field of sustainable investing.

It is important to point out that this framework is not simply theoretical. A more advanced version of this framework is in use to build investor portfolios. As outlined in this chapter, investors can learn the quantitative risk-and-return consequences of any individual sustainability requirement, as well as any combination of sustainability requirements. We used a sample 15-factor sustainability set to demonstrate the three-dimensional trade-offs. In practice, the sustainability factors that investors consider vary significantly. While most investors include environmental externality factors in their sustainability target mix, these are complemented by social factors in some use cases and by SDG revenue alignment improvements in other cases. The ability to manage these varying sustainability mixes is a key strength of this framework.

Another advantage of this framework is that it is flexible in terms of accommodating key elements of existing common tools such as stock exclusions, where such requirements can simply be handled by the optimizer as specific constraints.

This framework is also valuable in investment policymaking. The ability to connect the sustainability dimension to both risk and returns enables trustees and committees to better perform their fiduciary duties by constructing measurable, multi-year progressive sustainable investment policies.

Lastly, as highlighted in an earlier section, this factor investing-inspired framework enables investors to understand and take advantage of the diversification benefits available when combining sustainability targets. This in turn encourages investors to expand their sustainability objectives over time, further contributing to a more sustainable future through intelligent allocation of capital.

References

Black, F. & Litterman, R. (1991, September). Asset allocation combining investor views with market equilibrium. *Journal of Fixed Income*, 1(2), 7–18.

Fama, E. F. & French, K. R. (1993). Common risk factors in the returns on stocks and bonds. *Journal of Financial Economics*, 33, 3–56.

Pedersen, L. H., Fitzgibbons, S., & Pomorski, L. (2021). Responsible investing: The ESG-efficient frontier. *Journal of Financial Economics*, 142, 572–597.

Schmidt, A. B. (2020). Optimal ESG portfolios: An example for the Dow Jones index. *Journal of Sustainable Finance and Investment*, 12(2), 529–535.

https://doi.org/10.1142/9789811297786_0016

Chapter 16

Post-investment Strategies for Impact Investing

Mathieu Joubrel

ValueCo, Paris, France

Abstract

This chapter provides a comprehensive guide to post-investment strategies for impact investing tailored for sustainable investment professionals. Engagement and stewardship are pivotal post-investment strategies to steer companies toward sustainable practices that align with investors' environmental, social, and governance (ESG) goals. They encompass active dialogue with company management, exercising voting rights, and participating in collaborative initiatives. We also introduce tools and metrics for measuring ESG performance improvements, such as ESG ratings and monitoring of ESG controversies, and explore the use of advanced analytics to assess the real-world extra-financial impact of portfolio companies. We discuss the inherent risks and opportunities in post-investment strategies, including company resistance, resource constraints, and the potential for short-termism. Conversely, there are numerous opportunities in influencing corporate behavior, enhancing long-term value creation, and aligning investments with broader societal and environmental objectives. By effectively understanding and implementing these strategies, asset managers can contribute to the transition toward a more sustainable future while meeting their clients' financial and extra-financial objectives.

1. Introduction

The evolution of impact investing has witnessed a significant shift from the traditional focus on upfront investment selection to a heightened emphasis on post-investment strategies to ensure sustained impact. This transition stresses the recognition that realizing sustainable impact is not solely determined by the initial investment decision but rather by the ongoing engagement and stewardship activities after the investment. Historically, the primary focus of investment professionals was the initial selection of investments based on financial performance and risk considerations. While financial metrics remain crucial, the contemporary landscape of impact investing recognizes the imperative of extending the investment horizon to encompass the post-investment phase.

Post-investment strategies rely on continuous monitoring, evaluation, and active management to drive positive environmental and social outcomes. Investment professionals increasingly acknowledge that effective stewardship of capital post-investment is essential for maximizing the long-term impact of investments. This shift in focus aligns with the broader understanding that sustainable finance is not merely about allocating capital to responsible companies but also about actively influencing corporate behavior and driving positive change within investee companies.

The concept of active ownership is fundamental to the understanding of the underpinnings of post-investment strategies. Active ownership encompasses the proactive approach investors adopt to influence the behavior and performance of the companies they invest in. It goes beyond traditional shareholder rights and responsibilities, emphasizing the active exercise of ownership rights to drive positive social and environmental impact alongside financial returns. Active ownership is rooted in recognizing that investors have a significant role in shaping their investee companies' sustainability practices and long-term value creation. Active ownership is a cornerstone for post-investment strategies in impact investing, enabling investment professionals to engage with companies on environmental, social, and governance (ESG) issues actively. This engagement can take various forms, including direct dialogue with company management, participation in shareholder meetings, and the exercise of voting rights on ESG-related resolutions. By actively engaging with companies, investment professionals can influence corporate behavior, promote sustainable business practices, and address systemic ESG challenges, thereby driving positive change within the corporate landscape.

The growing emphasis on post-investment strategies reflects a more profound commitment to active ownership, where investment professionals are not passive stakeholders but proactive agents of change. Investment professionals can influence corporate decision-making, promote sustainable business practices, and address systemic ESG challenges by engaging with companies on extra-financial issues. This proactive approach to stewardship is essential for fostering transparency, accountability, and long-term value creation within investee companies, thereby contributing to achieving global sustainability goals. This shift also acknowledges the dynamic and evolving nature of sustainability challenges, where the impact of investments is contingent on the adaptability and responsiveness of investment professionals to emerging trends and risks. By integrating post-investment strategies into their investment practices, professionals can proactively position themselves to draw on new opportunities, mitigate potential risks, and contribute to the advancement of sustainable finance. By embracing post-investment strategies, sustainable investment professionals can play a transformative role in addressing global sustainability challenges and achieving meaningful impact.

2. Understanding Stewardship in Sustainable Finance

2.1. *Stewardship and Active Ownership Drive Social and Environmental Change*

Stewardship in sustainable finance encompasses the responsible and active management of investments to drive positive ESG outcomes. It involves integrating sustainability considerations into investment decision-making and ongoing engagement with investee companies to promote long-term value creation. Stewardship goes beyond traditional notions of financial management. It includes the fiduciary duty of investment professionals to act in the best interests of their beneficiaries while also considering the broader impact of their investment decisions on society and the environment. The significance of stewardship in enhancing long-term investment value lies in its potential to mitigate risks, drive sustainable growth, and achieve positive societal and environmental outcomes. By actively engaging with companies on ESG issues, investment professionals can influence corporate behavior, promote sustainable business practices, and address systemic ESG challenges, fostering long-term resilience and value creation within their investment portfolios.

Stewardship fosters transparency, accountability, and responsible governance within investee companies. By actively exercising ownership rights, such as voting on ESG-related resolutions and participating in shareholder meetings, investment professionals can influence corporate decision-making and promote adopting sustainable practices. By integrating stewardship practices into investment strategies, professionals can systematically monitor and evaluate their investments' sustainability performance, identify improvement areas, and actively collaborate with companies to drive positive ESG outcomes.

The recognition that investment professionals have a significant role in influencing corporate behavior and driving positive societal and environmental outcomes underpins the relationship between stewardship and impact investing. This proactive approach to stewardship aligns with the broader shift toward impact-driven investment strategies, where the pursuit of financial returns is coupled with a commitment to generating positive social and environmental impact. The significance of active ownership in stewardship is evident in its potential to drive systemic change within investee companies. By actively engaging with companies on ESG issues, investment professionals can influence corporate decision-making, promote sustainable business practices, and address systemic ESG challenges. It aligns with the broader goals of impact investing, which seeks to generate positive societal and environmental outcomes alongside financial returns.

2.2. *Stewardship Strategies Improve Financial and ESG Outcomes Alike*

The effectiveness of stewardship strategies in improving ESG outcomes has been a subject of extensive academic inquiry. Studies have delved into the impact of stewardship activities on corporate financial performance, providing valuable insights for investment professionals seeking to enhance the sustainability performance of their portfolios.

The correlation between stewardship activities and corporate financial performance has been the subject of extensive academic research. Prior *et al.* (2008) explored the relationship between earnings management and corporate social responsibility, highlighting the instrumental stakeholder theory, which argues that positive relationships with critical stakeholders improve financial performance. This study sheds light on the potential influence of stewardship activities on financial performance through the lens of corporate social responsibility. Kyere and Ausloos (2020) surveyed corporate governance in the United Kingdom, highlighting the positive impact of good corporate governance on financial performance. It provides valuable insights into the role of governance in driving financial performance, offering a foundation for understanding the potential influence of stewardship activities on corporate economic outcomes.

Additionally, Christensen *et al.* (2010) examined the relationship between corporate governance and company performance in Australia, providing frameworks for board evaluation planning and diagnosing the effectiveness of boards. Davis *et al.* (2010) explored stewardship perceptions in family businesses, demonstrating that stewardship behaviors are an essential component of the competitive advantage of family businesses. This study highlights the potential influence of stewardship behaviors on the performance of family businesses, offering valuable insights into the role of stewardship in driving sustainable business performance. Al-Saidi and Al-Shammari (2013) studied board composition and bank performance in Kuwait, showing a link between board composition and firm performance.

On the other hand, Makni *et al.* (2008) investigated the causality between corporate social performance and financial performance in Canadian firms, finding no significant relationship between a composite measure of corporate social performance and financial performance for Canadian firms. Their research provides a nuanced perspective on the relationship between social and economic performance, offering insights into the complexities of assessing the impact of stewardship activities on financial outcomes. Myšková and Hájek (2019) examined the relationship between corporate social responsibility in corporate annual reports and the financial performance of US companies, highlighting the challenges of defining and measuring corporate social responsibility. This study offers insights into the complexities of assessing the impact of social responsibility on financial performance.

Overall, academic research has provided valuable insights into the effectiveness of stewardship strategies in improving ESG outcomes, offering investment professionals a robust foundation for integrating evidence-based stewardship practices into their post-investment strategies. Numerous results support the theory of a correlation between stewardship activities and corporate financial performance. However, there is still a need to bring a definite answer to the relationship between these two concepts. Depending on the proxy used to assess the CSR performances of firms and the region in which the study is carried out, the results vary between no correlation and a positive one.

2.3. *Practical Considerations for Implementing Effective Stewardship Practices*

Implementing effective stewardship practices is essential for investment professionals seeking to drive positive social and environmental impact within their portfolios. This implementation involves a proactive and engaged approach to ownership, encompassing a range of actionable steps to influence corporate behavior and promote sustainable business practices. It establishes regular communication channels with company management to discuss ESG issues, sustainability strategies, and long-term value creation. By fostering open dialogue, investment professionals can gain insights into the company's approach to sustainability and guide best practices, influencing corporate behavior and driving positive change. Responsible investors must integrate ESG considerations into investment decision-making processes to anticipate proper stewardship action post-investment. This process involves conducting thorough ESG due diligence, monitoring the sustainability performance of investments, and actively collaborating with companies to address ESG issues.

In addition to direct engagement, implementing stewardship practices relies on formulating clear voting policies. Asset managers can use their voting rights to influence corporate decisions on ESG-related matters, such as climate change initiatives, diversity and inclusion policies, and executive compensation structures. By aligning voting policies with sustainable objectives, investment professionals can actively support resolutions that promote long-term value creation and positive societal impact.

The implementation of stewardship practices may also include the establishment of collaborative initiatives with other investors. Investment professionals can amplify their impact and address systemic ESG challenges more effectively by forming investor coalitions or engaging in collaborative engagement efforts. Collaborative engagement allows investors to leverage collective influence to drive positive change within companies, encouraging the adoption of sustainable practices and aligning corporate strategies with global sustainability goals. This approach fosters a unified voice among investors, enhancing their ability to advocate for sustainable business practices and drive meaningful impact.

3. Transparency and Accountability in Stewardship Activities

3.1. *Transparency and Accountability Build up Investor Trust and Value Creation*

Transparency and accountability are fundamental in building investor trust and fostering long-term value creation. They form the bedrock of responsible and impactful investment practices. By providing clear and comprehensive information about engagement activities, voting decisions, and integrating ESG factors, they enhance the credibility of stewardship activities and contribute to the long-term sustainability of investment portfolios. By openly disclosing the rationale behind engagement strategies, voting decisions, and the integration of ESG considerations, asset managers and institutional investors demonstrate a commitment to responsible and sustainable investment practices. This transparency fosters trust among stakeholders, assuring them that stewardship activities align with sustainable objectives and stand for a genuine commitment to positive impact. It enhances the effectiveness of engagement efforts by promoting open dialogue and collaboration with investee companies. Clear and transparent communication about the objectives and expectations of engagement activities fosters constructive relationships with firms, encouraging them to address ESG issues and drive positive change. This transparency creates an environment of mutual understanding and cooperation, enabling investee companies to respond proactively to investor concerns and work toward sustainable business practices.

Moreover, transparency contributes to the accountability of investment professionals, ensuring that their actions align with the best interests of their clients and the broader society. By providing clear and accessible information about engagement priorities, voting policies, and the outcomes of stewardship activities, investment professionals are held accountable for their decisions and actions. It contributes to the broader goal of market integrity and stability by providing investors and the public with insights into the responsible management of investment portfolios. By openly sharing information about engagement priorities, voting decisions, and the integration of ESG considerations, investment professionals contribute to the transparency and integrity of financial markets. This transparency enhances market confidence and contributes to the overall stability and resilience of the financial system.

3.2. *Transparency Influences Investor Behavior and Company Performance*

As academic research shows, transparency is pivotal in shaping investor behavior and influencing company performance. Ponce *et al.* (2022) conducted a compliance analysis to assess the readiness of IBEX35 companies to submit ESG reports through their communication and web transparency, aiming to determine whether such ESG information is related to these companies' financial indicators. This study sheds light on the relationship between transparency in ESG reporting and economic indicators, providing insights into the potential impact of transparency on investor decision-making and company performance. Gelos and Wei (2003) highlighted empirical studies that measure the degree of herding among funds, emphasizing the influence of transparency on international investor behavior. This research underscores the significance of transparency in shaping investor behavior and market dynamics.

Malau (2019) conducted a study on financial performance to examine the effect of earnings persistence and transparency on company performance, applying panel data analysis to assess the relationship between transparency and financial performance. Li *et al.* (2019) examined the moderating role of political embeddedness in the relationship between corporate public transparency and financial performance, highlighting the influence of transparency on company performance. These research articles contribute to the understanding of the multifaceted impact of transparency on financial performance, offering investment professionals valuable insights into the implications of openness for company accountability and performance.

Jeriansyah and Mappanyukki (2020) conducted a study to examine the effect of accountability and transparency of regional financial management on local government performance, looking into the implications of transparency for local government accountability and performance. Katelouzou and Klettner (2020) highlighted the potential of stewardship to promote the incorporation of ESG factors into both financial and business decision-making, emphasizing the role of stewardship in driving sustainable practices and ESG improvements. This research provides perspectives on the potential impact of stewardship on sustainable finance and ESG integration.

Academic research has also delved into the effectiveness of different transparency and accountability frameworks regarding stewardship. For instance, Withers *et al.* (2015) examined the combined adoption of stewardship policies and stakeholder cooperation to maximize resource and environmental benefits, delivering a more competitive, circular, and sustainable European economy. This study emphasizes the importance of interactive policies and harmonized approaches in maximizing the benefits of stewardship. Kosack and Fung (2014) explored the impact of transparency on international investor behavior, providing insights into the influence of transparency on market dynamics and investor decision-making. Their research underscores the significance of transparency in shaping investor behavior and market dynamics.

3.3. *Best Practices Enhance Transparency in Stewardship Activities*

To ensure effective stewardship reporting, asset managers and issuers must adhere to best practices that promote transparency and accountability in their engagement and voting policies. By implementing these best practices, they can enhance the credibility of their stewardship activities and contribute to the overall integrity of the investment process. One of the essential best practices for asset managers and issuers is to establish clear and comprehensive reporting standards for their stewardship activities.

This involves providing detailed information about the rationale behind engagement decisions, the objectives of voting policies, and the outcomes of stewardship activities. By offering transparent and accessible reports, asset managers and issuers can demonstrate their commitment to responsible and sustainable investment practices, building stakeholder trust and confidence.

It is also essential for asset managers and issuers to communicate their engagement and voting policies effectively to their clients and stakeholders. Such communication clearly explains the criteria used to determine engagement priorities, the process for making voting decisions, and the mechanisms for holding investee companies accountable for their ESG performance. Asset managers and issuers should consider the adoption of standardized reporting frameworks, such as the Principles for Responsible Investment (PRI) Reporting Framework or the EU Sustainable Finance Disclosure Regulation (SFDR). These frameworks provide a structured approach to reporting on stewardship activities, enabling asset managers and issuers to align their reporting with industry best practices and enhance the credibility of their sustainability efforts. They can strengthen transparency and accountability by engaging in regular dialogue with their clients and stakeholders about their stewardship activities. These dialogues include providing opportunities for feedback, addressing concerns, and soliciting input on engagement priorities and voting decisions. By fostering open communication, asset managers and issuers can demonstrate their commitment to responsible stewardship and ensure that their activities align with the best interests of their clients and the broader society.

4. Executive Compensation and ESG Performance

4.1. *Executive Compensation Structures Influence Corporate Behavior*

The role of shareholders in influencing executive compensation to align with ESG goals is a crucial aspect of active ownership. Shareholders can advocate incorporating ESG metrics into executive compensation packages, influencing corporate governance and sustainability practices. This shareholder activism promotes sustainable behaviors within organizations and aligns organizational incentives with long-term sustainability objectives. When executives' compensation is tied to ESG metrics and sustainability targets, it directly aligns with financial rewards and achieving non-financial objectives. This alignment can motivate executives to prioritize ESG considerations in their strategic planning and operational activities, leading to improved sustainability performance. Performance-based compensation components, including bonuses and stock options, reward executives based on their ability to deliver on ESG-related objectives.

The design of executive compensation packages can influence the time horizon over which corporate leaders evaluate performance and make decisions. For instance, long-term incentive plans, such as equity-based awards with extended vesting periods, can encourage executives to adopt a more forward-looking perspective that encompasses the long-term implications of their actions on ESG factors. By linking compensation to long-term ESG goals, companies can foster a culture of sustainable decision-making that transcends short-term financial gains. Furthermore, it can alter risk-taking behavior and the management of ESG-related risks within organizations. By incorporating ESG criteria into performance evaluations and incentive structures, companies can encourage executives to proactively identify and mitigate ESG risks, thereby reducing the potential for environmental or social incidents that could harm the company's reputation and long-term value.

4.2. *Managing Executive Compensation Helps Optimize ESG Outcomes*

A review of academic research reveals a fragmented landscape, with studies offering diverse perspectives on the interplay between executive compensation and ESG performance. Cohen *et al.* (2023) examined the international evidence on executive compensation tied to ESG performance, shedding light on the potential implications of ESG variables as leading indicators of future financial performance. Sarikas *et al.* (2019) investigated the sustainability methodologies and sustainability-linked senior management compensation policies, revealing the potential impact of executive compensation incentives related to sustainability on ESG scores. Rath *et al.* (2020) explored the effect of the executive pay gap on ESG disclosure, shedding light on the potential influence of executive compensation structures on ESG transparency. These studies contribute to the understanding of the relationships between executive compensation and ESG outcomes, emphasizing the need for comprehensive frameworks that integrate ESG considerations into executive compensation structures.

Similarly, Kartadjumena and Rodgers (2019) explored the relationship between executive compensation; sustainability, climate, and environmental concerns; and company financial performance, revealing varying findings indicating both positive and negative correlations between executive compensation and ESG outcomes. Eccles *et al.* (2012) delved into the impact of corporate sustainability on organizational processes and performance, shedding light on the potential influence of executive compensation incentives based on short-term metrics or long-term value creation. These studies underscore the complexity of the relationship between executive compensation and ESG outcomes, highlighting the need for a nuanced approach to aligning compensation structures with sustainable objectives.

Academic research has also explored the effectiveness of various compensation models in driving ESG performance and developed performance measures for executive pay, as evidenced by the work of Matemane *et al.* (2022) or Cohen *et al.* (2023). Hong *et al.* (2015) investigated the impact of corporate governance and executive compensation on CSR, highlighting the potential influence of executive compensation incentives on long-term value creation and sustainable practices. Keddie and Magnan (2023) investigated the effectiveness of ESG performance-based incentives in driving sustainable practices, emphasizing the need for comprehensive frameworks that integrate ESG considerations into executive compensation structures. These studies contribute to the understanding of the interplay between executive compensation and sustainable objectives, emphasizing the need to align compensation structures with ESG goals.

4.3. *Aligning Compensation Structures with Sustainable Objectives in Practice*

Designing executive compensation packages that incentivize sustainable practices and ESG improvements is critical to aligning corporate incentives with long-term sustainability objectives. Practical strategies for developing executive compensation packages that incentivize sustainable practices often incorporate ESG performance metrics into variable pay components, such as bonuses and long-term incentives. Companies can encourage sustainable behaviors and decision-making by linking executive incentives to specific ESG targets. Additionally, integrating ESG metrics into executive compensation can drive organizational cultural change, aligning executive behavior with sustainable objectives and long-term value creation.

Investment professionals can advocate for adopting compensation models prioritizing ESG improvements by engaging directly with companies. Shareholder activism has a significant role in supporting the integration of ESG considerations into executive compensation structures. This advocacy serves as a mechanism for driving positive change within organizations, aligning executive incentives with sustainable practices and ultimately enhancing the integration of ESG considerations into corporate strategies. Even where they are not leading the movement, sustainable investment professionals can promote the alignment of executive incentives with sustainable objectives by participating in existing or collective shareholder engagement initiatives. The influence of shareholders in aligning executive compensation with ESG goals extends beyond individual companies, contributing to broader systemic change within the investment landscape. By advocating for sustainable compensation practices across their investment portfolios, sustainable investment professionals can drive positive impact and promote the integration of ESG considerations into corporate strategies. This collective effort is not to be overlooked when assessing the impact of asset managers on their portfolio companies' sustainable practices.

5. Integrating Digital Transformation for Enhanced ESG Performance

5.1. *Digital Technologies Can Improve ESG Data Collection, Analysis, and Reporting*

As technological advancements continue to reshape the business landscape, integrating digital tools and platforms offers a transformative opportunity for investment professionals to leverage advanced specialized tools and platforms to streamline ESG data processes, improve analytical capabilities, and enhance the transparency and accuracy of sustainability reporting. Using application programming interfaces (APIs), web scraping tools, and data integration platforms, investment professionals can efficiently aggregate ESG data from various internal and external sources, including regulatory filings, company reports, and third-party databases. This automated data collection process not only saves time and resources but also ensures real-time access to comprehensive ESG information and enhances the speed and accuracy of sustainability reporting. Digital technologies also enable advanced analytical capabilities for processing and interpreting large volumes of ESG data. Artificial intelligence, machine learning algorithms, natural language processing, and data visualization tools can extract valuable insights from complex ESG datasets, identify emerging trends, and assess the materiality of ESG factors for investment portfolios. These analytical tools empower investment professionals to understand companies' ESG performance better and develop proactive sustainability strategies.

Digital transformation facilitates ESG reporting practices by providing robust platforms for transparent and standardized disclosure of sustainability information. Cloud-based reporting systems, integrated sustainability management software, and blockchain-enabled platforms offer secure and auditable frameworks for compiling, validating, and disseminating ESG reports to stakeholders. This technology provides a safe and transparent framework for tracking and verifying sustainability data, enabling investment professionals to ensure the integrity and authenticity of ESG information. Blockchain infrastructures hold the potential to strengthen sustainability reporting and assurance, providing stakeholders with immutable and auditable records of sustainability performance. These digital reporting solutions ensure the accuracy and reliability of sustainability disclosures and enable real-time access to ESG information, fostering greater transparency and accountability in investment practices.

These digital communication channels foster greater transparency and accountability, enabling investment professionals to build trust with stakeholders and effectively communicate the positive impact of their sustainability efforts. Integrating digital technologies into ESG data collection, analysis, and reporting presents opportunities for enhancing the accessibility and usability of sustainability information. Interactive dashboards, online portals, and mobile applications can provide stakeholders with intuitive and user-friendly interfaces for navigating and visualizing ESG data. This enhanced accessibility empowers investors, asset managers, and other stakeholders to engage with ESG information more effectively, promoting accountability and trust. Digital transformation offers opportunities to improve the scalability and accessibility of sustainability initiatives. Through the development of online training programs, webinars, and digital resources, investment professionals can educate stakeholders, including employees, clients, and the broader public, on sustainability best practices and the importance of ESG considerations. This scalable approach to sustainability education fosters a culture of sustainability within and beyond the organization, driving positive impact and systemic change.

5.2. *Leveraging Digital Transformation for Sustainable Outcomes*

The intersection of digital transformation and sustainability has garnered significant attention in academic research, mainly focusing on implications for ESG performance. Studies have delved into the multifaceted relationship between digital transformation initiatives and their influence on ESG outcomes. Research by Buallay (2019) emphasizes the growing support for sustainability reporting, particularly the disclosure of ESG factors, to improve transparency and establish the link between financial performance and sustainability. This article stresses the importance of leveraging digital transformation to streamline the reporting and integration of ESG considerations into corporate strategies. Zhou *et al.* (2023) have conducted notable studies examining the impact of ESG performance on sustainability outcomes, particularly in emerging economies such as China and Brazil. Their research emphasizes the need for digital transformation to mediate the relationship between ESG performance and overall sustainability.

The successful implementation of digital tools to drive ESG improvements has also been a subject of extensive research. For instance, Warner and Wäger (2019) have emphasized the ongoing strategic renewal process by building dynamic capabilities for digital transformation, highlighting the pivotal role of digital tools in enabling organizations to adapt and respond to evolving ESG challenges. Camodeca and Almici (2021) have provided evidence from Italian-listed firms, demonstrating the convergence of digital transformation toward the Sustainable Development Goals. Ulez'ko *et al.* (2022) have delved into the utilization of digital platforms to form the technological basis of digital agriculture, offering insights into the practical application of digital tools to enhance environmental sustainability and resource management. Chen *et al.* (2023) have investigated the role of digital transformation in managing executive compensation to optimize ESG performance, providing empirical evidence of the link between digital tools and sustainable corporate governance.

Regarding the limitations of digital technologies in handling data and reporting for impact investing applications, Alsayegh *et al.* (2020) have highlighted the interchangeable use of terms such as CSR, ESG, and Economic, Governance, Social, Ethical, and Environmental (EGSEE) sustainability within the academic community. They underscore the need for clear frameworks and standards to report and communicate, as the increasing volume of available data compels practitioners to use digital technologies and automation to keep up to date. Li and Pang (2023) have explored the impact of digital inclusive finance on corporate ESG performance, underscoring the need for digital transformation to drive inclusive and sustainable financial practices that align with ESG objectives. Li and Fei (2023) have explored the moderating effect of top managerial cognition on the relationship between network embeddedness, digital transformation, and enterprise performance, providing insights into the nuanced interplay between digital tools and ESG outcomes. Their research highlights the need for a comprehensive understanding of the cognitive factors influencing the successful integration of digital tools to drive ESG improvements. Overall, academic research frames the role of digital transformation in shaping ESG performance and sustainability outcomes but emphasizes the need for innovative digital strategies to drive comprehensive and impactful sustainability practices within organizations.

5.3. *Challenges Related to the Adoption of Digital Tools*

Investment professionals should prioritize selecting digital tools that align with their ESG objectives and investment strategies. This selection entails conducting a comprehensive assessment of available technologies to identify those that best cater to the unique ESG considerations of their investment portfolios. Integrating advanced ESG data analytics and artificial intelligence tools enables tasks like real-time ESG data collection and analysis. However, these models often operate in black boxes and can be hard to interpret for non-specialists. Using them often means sacrificing some of the transparency and lowering the level of understanding of the inner working of the models. More complex models are often more efficient and more challenging to explain and interpret, which can cause problems as transparency and accountability are vital components of a successful stewardship strategy. Investment professionals must ensure that the digital solutions chosen for ESG monitoring and management comply with industry standards and regulatory requirements. This verification involves thorough due diligence to verify the digital tools' reliability, accuracy, and ethical implications in capturing and interpreting ESG data.

One of the primary challenges is the complexity of data integration and interoperability. As sustainability data are often sourced from diverse systems and formats, ensuring seamless integration and compatibility of digital tools with existing data infrastructure can be daunting. This challenge necessitates investment in robust data management systems and interoperable technologies to facilitate aggregating and analyzing disparate ESG data sources. The need for skilled personnel proficient in data management and analytics is crucial to effectively harness the potential of digital technologies for ESG monitoring and management. Moreover, cybersecurity and data privacy are critical concerns in integrating digital technologies into sustainability practices. The sensitive nature of ESG data requires stringent cybersecurity measures to safeguard against potential cyber threats and data breaches. Investment professionals must prioritize the implementation of robust cybersecurity protocols and compliance with data privacy regulations to mitigate the risks associated with digital data management. Relevant measures include encryption, access controls, and regular security audits to uphold the integrity and confidentiality of ESG-related information.

The dynamic nature of digital technologies introduces the challenge of staying abreast of technological advancements and ensuring continuous adaptation. Given the rapid pace of technological innovation, sustainable investment professionals must remain vigilant in updating their digital tool kits to leverage the latest advances in data analytics, machine learning, and visualization techniques. It requires a proactive approach to technology adoption and ongoing investment in training programs to equip professionals with the necessary skills to navigate the evolving digital landscape. Investment professionals should prioritize ongoing training and capacity building to ensure their teams possess the essential skills and competencies to leverage digital solutions effectively for ESG monitoring and management. This training may involve organizing workshops, seminars, and knowledge-sharing sessions to enhance the digital literacy of investment professionals and empower them to leverage digital tools for comprehensive ESG analysis and reporting. By fostering a culture of continuous learning and adaptation, investment firms can harness the full potential of digital transformation.

6. Collaborative Engagement for Sustainable Impact

6.1. *Collaborative Engagement Amplifies the Impact of Individual Investors*

Collaborative engagement involves investors, asset managers, and other stakeholders working together to drive sustainable change and create meaningful social and environmental impact. Collaborative engagement recognizes that the scale and complexity of global sustainability challenges require coordinated and collective action, leveraging the influence and resources of multiple stakeholders to effect positive change. The importance of collaborative engagement lies in its potential to magnify the impact of individual investor actions, transcending the limitations of isolated efforts and driving systemic change. By pooling resources, expertise, and influence, collaborative engagement enables investors to address complex ESG issues that may be beyond the scope of individual initiatives.

One of the primary benefits of collaborative engagement is the ability to address systemic ESG challenges that require coordinated and collective action. For instance, issues such as climate change, human rights violations, and supply chain sustainability often transcend the boundaries of individual companies or investors. By collaborating, stakeholders can develop comprehensive strategies to address these challenges, leveraging their combined influence to drive meaningful change. This collective approach fosters a shared responsibility and collaboration culture, enabling stakeholders to address pressing ESG challenges more effectively and drive sustainable impact at scale.

Collaborative initiatives may include establishing stakeholder advisory groups, joint projects with local communities, or partnerships with non-governmental organizations and industry peers. These initiatives provide a platform for stakeholders to contribute their expertise, insights, and perspectives, enriching investment professionals' ESG strategies and decision-making processes. They can lead to the establishment of industry-wide standards, the adoption of best practices, and the alignment of investment strategies with global sustainability goals.

Collaborative engagement provides a platform for knowledge sharing, innovation, and capacity building, enabling stakeholders to learn from each other's experiences, leverage diverse perspectives, and develop innovative solutions to complex sustainability challenges. By fostering a collaborative environment, investors can share best practices, exchange insights on emerging ESG trends, and collectively develop strategies to address shared challenges. This collaborative learning process enhances the effectiveness of individual investor actions, enabling stakeholders to stay abreast of evolving sustainability practices and drive continuous improvement in their sustainable investment strategies. It can lead to forming investor coalitions and partnerships, amplifying the influence of individual investors and enabling them to engage with companies to drive positive change collectively. Investor coalitions can leverage their collective ownership stakes to advocate for ESG improvements, engage in dialogue with investee companies on sustainability issues, and influence corporate decision-making more significantly.

6.2. *Academic Insights into Collaborative Engagement Dynamics and Strategies*

Rau and Yu (2023) have conducted a survey to provide an overview of the academic literature on ESG and corporate sustainability. Their survey emphasizes the need for a holistic approach to collaborative engagement strategies. Espahbodi *et al.* (2019) have explored the relationship between sustainability priorities, corporate strategy, and investor behavior, offering valuable insights into the dynamics of stakeholder engagement and its implications for ESG integration. Their research stresses the need for a comprehensive understanding of the interplay between sustainability priorities, corporate strategy, and investor behavior to effectively leverage collaborative engagement for sustainable impact. Diener and Habisch (2022) have emphasized the importance of developing an impact-focused typology of socially responsible fund providers, shedding light on the diverse ESG integration and collaborative engagement approaches. Lai *et al.* (2014) have examined the role of integrated reporting as a legitimation strategy for corporate sustainable development, shedding light on the potential of integrated reporting to enhance stakeholder engagement and transparency.

Analyzing the dynamics of investor coalitions and their influence on corporate behavior is essential for understanding the impact of collaborative engagement on ESG goals. Chen *et al.* (2020) and Dyck *et al.* (2015) have investigated the influence of institutional shareholders on CSR, shedding light on the driving forces behind joint engagement initiatives. Katelouzou and Klettner (2020) have highlighted the significance of integrating ESG factors when making investment decisions, emphasizing the role of institutional investors in promoting sustainable finance and stewardship. Keeley *et al.* (2022) have examined the ultimate ownership of ESG investments, shedding light on the complexities of targeting the actual flow and ownership structure of ESG investment through ESG ratings. These articles provide valuable insights into the dynamics of investor coalitions and their potential to influence corporate behavior, emphasizing the role of institutional investors in promoting stakeholder engagement and driving corporate social responsibility.

6.3. *Practical Guidance for Implementing Collaborative Engagement Initiatives*

Investment professionals should follow a structured road map to initiate and manage collaborative engagement initiatives effectively. The first essential step is identifying common sustainability goals and forming a coalition of like-minded investors. It involves conducting thorough research to identify potential partners who share similar ESG objectives and are willing to collaborate on driving sustainable change. Once the coalition is established, the next step involves setting clear and measurable sustainability objectives and aligning the collective efforts of the investors toward a common purpose. This process requires open dialogue and consensus building to ensure the coalition's goals are well defined and achievable.

After the coalition is formed, its members must design a strategic engagement plan outlining the actions and initiatives the coalition will undertake to influence corporate behavior and drive ESG improvements. This plan should include a comprehensive assessment of the material ESG issues facing investee companies and a targeted approach to engagement, such as direct dialogue with company management, shareholder resolutions, or collaborative advocacy efforts. The engagement plan should be tailored to the unique characteristics of the investee companies and the industry in which they operate, ensuring that the strategies are context specific and impactful. Ideally, the engagement plan would leverage the collective influence of the coalition members to engage with investee companies effectively. This plan involves coordinating the efforts of the coalition to maximize the impact, such as through joint statements, coordinated voting on ESG-related resolutions, or the establishment of industry-wide sustainability standards. By aligning their actions, investors can amplify their influence and encourage companies to adopt more sustainable business practices.

Finally, engagement efforts must be monitored and sustained over time until the coalition reaches the targets set at its formation or until it fulfills a predetermined stopping condition. The coalition members need to manage the ongoing monitoring and evaluation of their efforts to assess their effectiveness and adjust their strategy as needed. This monitoring involves tracking key performance indicators related to ESG outcomes, such as changes in corporate policies, improvements in ESG disclosures, or advancements in sustainability practices. Regular communication and knowledge sharing among coalition members are essential to ensure that the engagement efforts remain aligned with the coalition's objectives and that participants share best practices.

7. Impact Measurement and Reporting

7.1. *Impact Measurement and Reporting Cannot be Overlooked*

Robust impact measurement and reporting are essential components that enable investment professionals to assess the effectiveness of their strategies, track progress, and demonstrate accountability and transparency to their clients, beneficiaries, and the broader investment community. Reporting impact metrics provides a clear and tangible representation of the real-world impact of sustainable investment practices, enabling professionals to communicate the outcomes of their investments effectively. This evidence is crucial for building trust and confidence among stakeholders, including investors, clients, and the public, and showcasing the real-world impact of sustainable investment practices.

As the focus on ESG considerations continues to intensify, investors and stakeholders are increasingly seeking clear and comprehensive information on the impact of their investments. Straightforward and consistent impact metrics are essential for meeting the growing demand for transparency and accountability. By systematically collecting and analyzing impact data, investment professionals can gain valuable insights into their investments' performance, identify improvement areas, and make informed decisions to optimize their strategies.

Impact measurement and reporting are also essential for fulfilling regulatory and reporting requirements. As sustainable finance regulations evolve and reporting standards become more stringent over time, investment professionals must adhere to these guidelines and provide accurate and reliable impact data. Reliable impact measurement and reporting practices enable professionals to comply with regulatory frameworks, demonstrate compliance with industry standards, and uphold their commitment to responsible and sustainable investment practices.

7.2. *Impact Measurement Methodologies and Reporting Frameworks*

Bengo *et al.* (2022) present a comprehensive framework for social impact measurement practices in the context of EU financial regulations, emphasizing the need for tools and methodologies that consider sustainability across social, environmental, and governance dimensions. Gambelli *et al.* (2021) introduce a novel method that combines the balanced scorecard framework with importance-performance analysis to assess firm sustainability, showcasing the diverse applications of impact measurement tools in different sectors. However, the proper way to carry out these impact measurements depends on the context of the engagement effort: The profile of the company and its shareholders, the regulatory landscape, and market conditions must be considered. Ayuso *et al.* (2007) have conducted an empirical analysis of the stakeholder approach to corporate governance, shedding light on the complexities of maximizing stakeholders' interests and the implications for impact reporting. Ting-Hua *et al.* (2022) highlight the evolving landscape of financial technologies and their influence on sustainable development. These studies underscore the need for tailored methodologies that capture the multidimensional nature of sustainability and align with diverse financial contexts.

Moreover, investment professionals seeking to quantify the holistic impact of their investment decisions must evaluate the effectiveness of their metrics and impact reporting standards. Bengo *et al.* (2022) have developed a comprehensive framework on finance for sustainable development, addressing the need for standardized social impact measurement practices. Brueton *et al.* (2014) have proposed a framework and methods to identify evidence of impact in methodological research, providing insights into the diverse indicators and sources used to demonstrate the broad implications of research. Yi and Duval-Couetil (2021) have emphasized the importance of standards for evaluating impact in entrepreneurship education research, highlighting the need for methodological rigor and transparency in impact assessment. Jensen and Berg (2011) have examined the determinants of traditional sustainability reporting vs. integrated reporting, shedding light on the institutional pressures that lead to adopting different reporting standards.

7.3. *Selecting Impact Measurement Tools and Frameworks Still Proves Challenging*

When selecting impact measurement tools and reporting frameworks, investment professionals should consider the specific objectives of their investments and the nature of the impact they seek to achieve. It is crucial to align the selection process with the overarching goals of the investment strategy, whether it pertains to environmental conservation, social development, governance enhancement, or several of these targets. For instance, if the investment aims to address climate change, professionals may consider tools that focus on carbon footprint measurement, renewable energy deployment, or climate risk assessment. Integrating impact measurement tools with other reporting frameworks, such as ESG ratings and sustainability reporting standards, can provide a comprehensive view of investment performance.

The challenges of impact measurement in sustainable finance are numerous and require careful consideration to ensure the accuracy and reliability of assessments. One of the primary challenges is the complexity of measuring non-financial impacts, such as social and environmental outcomes, which often need more standardized metrics and can be challenging to quantify. This complexity arises from the variability of what is considered impactful and material across different sectors and geographies. It makes it difficult to develop universal measurement tools that adequately capture the nuances of impact across various contexts. The interconnectedness of effects across different dimensions, such as social, environmental, and economic factors, further complicates the measurement process. The dynamic nature of impact presents additional challenges in capturing the long-term effects of investments. Many social and environmental impacts may unfold over extended periods, requiring investment professionals to adopt a forward-looking approach to impact measurement. Predicting and quantifying the long-term effects of investments, especially in areas such as climate change mitigation or community development, present inherent uncertainties and complexities.

Another significant challenge is the availability and quality of data. Impact measurement relies on robust and comprehensive data sources to provide accurate assessments. However, accessing high-quality data, especially for non-financial impacts, can be challenging. In many cases, impact data may need to be more cohesive, consistent, or available, making it difficult to conduct thorough impact assessments. The lack of standardized reporting frameworks and data collection methodologies across industries and regions can further hinder the comparability and reliability of impact data. Addressing these challenges requires a multifaceted approach. Investment professionals can leverage quantitative and qualitative methods to capture data assessing the diverse dimensions of impact. These methods may involve using a mix of financial metrics, such as return on investment and cost–benefit analysis, alongside qualitative assessments, including stakeholder interviews and case studies, to provide a comprehensive view. Collaboration and standardization within the industry are essential to address the challenges of impact measurement. Engaging with industry peers, stakeholders, and regulatory bodies to develop standardized impact measurement frameworks and reporting standards can help improve the consistency and comparability of impact data. Initiatives such as the Impact Management Project and the Global Impact Investing Network have driven industry-wide collaboration and standardization efforts in this direction.

8. Navigating the Future of Impact Investing

8.1. *Looking Ahead: Technology, Regulation, and Stewardship*

As sustainable investment professionals navigate the ever-evolving landscape of impact investing, exploring potential future directions for post-investment strategies and their implications for sustainable finance is essential. The future of impact investing is likely to be shaped by a confluence of factors, including technological advancements, regulatory developments, and shifting investor preferences, which will significantly influence the trajectory of post-investment practices.

The emergence of new digital tools has revolutionized impact investing, offering innovative tools and platforms that enhance the efficiency of sustainable finance initiatives. The integration of advanced data analytics, artificial intelligence, and machine learning technologies has empowered investment professionals to gain deeper insights into the ESG performance of their portfolios. A potential future direction for post-investment strategies is the increasing integration of these technologies to enhance impact measurement and reporting. Applying these technologies can streamline the quantification and communication of the positive impact generated by investments, offering a more reliable assessment of both financial and extra-financial outcomes.

In parallel, regulatory changes are significantly shaping the impact investing landscape, with policymakers and standard-setting bodies introducing new guidelines and frameworks to govern sustainable finance practices. As they increasingly emphasize integration and transparency, investment professionals must adapt their post-investment strategies to comply with their requirements. Implementing standardized impact reporting frameworks is likely to become more prevalent, shaping how impact investors measure, report, and communicate the extra-financial value created by their investments. The emergence of mandatory ESG disclosure requirements in various jurisdictions should drive greater accountability and comparability in impact reporting.

Finally, the future of post-investment strategies may see an increased emphasis on stakeholder engagement and collaborative initiatives as drivers of sustainable impact. As the importance of stakeholder perspectives in shaping ESG strategies becomes more pronounced, investment professionals may need to refine their engagement practices further to incorporate a broader range of stakeholder interests. Collaborative engagement efforts, such as investor coalitions and multi-stakeholder partnerships, will likely gain prominence as vehicles for addressing systemic ESG challenges and driving collective action.

8.2. *Call to Action for Practitioners*

The knowledge and strategies presented in this chapter will hopefully catalyze sustainable investment professionals to drive positive change and achieve global sustainability goals. As we look to the future of impact investing, it is essential to emphasize its pivotal role in driving systemic change and achieving global sustainability goals. Post-investment practices have a transformative potential in shaping the trajectory of sustainable finance and fostering positive social and environmental impact. By applying these strategies, sustainable investment professionals can advance the broader sustainability agenda and drive meaningful corporate and systemic change.

Integrating digital transformation for enhanced ESG performance offers sustainable investment professionals the opportunity to leverage innovative technologies to improve ESG data collection, analysis, and reporting. By adopting digital solutions for ESG monitoring and management, professionals can enhance the efficiency and effectiveness of sustainability initiatives, thereby contributing to advancing global sustainability goals. The strategic implementation of digital tools and frameworks enables professionals to gain deeper insights into the impact of their investments, fostering transparency and accountability in the process.

As the industry evolves, practitioners must remain agile and responsive to emerging trends and future directions in impact investing. The application of impact measurement and reporting frameworks, as well as the translation of academic research findings into actionable strategies, enables practitioners to quantify the positive impact of their investments from both a financial and an extra-financial point of view. By aligning compensation structures with sustainable objectives and integrating ESG ratings with other impact measurement tools, professionals can ensure that their investments generate positive outcomes across financial, social, and environmental dimensions. A mindset of continuous improvement and innovation can position them to capitalize on new opportunities, mitigate potential risks, and contribute to the advancement of sustainable finance.

References

Al-Saidi, M. & Al-Shammari, B. (2013). Board composition and bank performance in Kuwait: An empirical study. *Managerial Auditing Journal*, 28(6), 472–494. Retrieved from https://doi.org/10.1108/02686901311329883.

Alsayegh, M., Rahman, R., & Homayoun, S. (2020). Corporate economic, environmental, and social sustainability performance transformation through

ESG disclosure. *Sustainability*, 12(9), 3910. Retrieved from https://doi.org/10.3390/su12093910.

Ayuso, S., Ariño, M., Garcia-Castro, R., & Rodríguez, M. (2007). Maximizing stakeholders' interests: An empirical analysis of the stakeholder approach to corporate governance. *SSRN Electronic Journal*. Retrieved from https://doi.org/10.2139/ssrn.982325.

Bengo, I., Boni, L., & Sancino, A. (2022). EU financial regulations and social impact measurement practices: A comprehensive framework on finance for sustainable development. *Corporate Social Responsibility and Environmental Management*, 29(4), 809–819. Retrieved from https://doi.org/10.1002/csr.2235.

Brueton, V., Vale, C., Choodari-Oskooei, B., Jinks, R., & Tierney, J. (2014). Measuring the impact of methodological research: A framework and methods to identify evidence of impact. *Trials*, 15(1). Retrieved from https://doi.org/10.1186/1745-6215-15-464.

Buallay, A. (2019). Is sustainability reporting (ESG) associated with performance? Evidence from the European banking sector. *Management of Environmental Quality an International Journal*, 30(1), 98–115. Retrieved from https://doi.org/10.1108/meq-12-2017-0149.

Camodeca, R. & Almici, A. (2021). Digital transformation and convergence toward the 2030 agenda's sustainability development goals: Evidence from Italian listed firms. *Sustainability*, 13(21), 11831. Retrieved from https://doi.org/10.3390/su132111831.

Chen, L., Mao, C., & Gao, Y. (2023). Executive compensation stickiness and ESG performance: The role of digital transformation. *Frontiers in Environmental Science*, 11. Retrieved from https://doi.org/10.3389/fenvs.2023.1166080.

Chen, T., Dong, H., & Lin, C. (2020). Institutional shareholders and corporate social responsibility. *Journal of Financial Economics*, 135(2), 483–504. Retrieved from https://doi.org/10.1016/j.jfineco.2019.06.007.

Christensen, J., Kent, P., & Stewart, J. (2010). Corporate governance and company performance in Australia. *Australian Accounting Review*, 20(4), 372–386. Retrieved from https://doi.org/10.1111/j.1835-2561.2010.00108.x.

Cohen, S., Kadach, I., Ormazabal, G., & Reichelstein, S. (2023). Executive compensation tied to ESG performance: International evidence. *Journal of Accounting Research*, 61(3), 805–853. Retrieved from https://doi.org/10.1111/1475-679x.12481.

Davis, J., Allen, M., & Hayes, H. (2010). Is blood thicker than water? A study of stewardship perceptions in family business. *Entrepreneurship Theory and Practice*, 34(6), 1093–1116. Retrieved from https://doi.org/10.1111/j.1540-6520.2010.00415.x.

Diener, J. & Habisch, A. (2022). Developing an impact-focused typology of socially responsible fund providers. *Journal of Risk and Financial Management*, 15(7), 298. Retrieved from https://doi.org/10.3390/jrfm15070298.

Dyck, I., Lins, K., Roth, L., & Wagner, H. (2015). Do institutional investors drive corporate social responsibility? International evidence. *SSRN Electronic Journal*. Retrieved from https://doi.org/10.2139/ssrn.2708589.

Eccles, R., Ioannou, I., & Serafeim, G. (2012). The impact of corporate sustainability on organizational processes and performance. Retrieved from https://doi.org/10.3386/w17950.

Espahbodi, L., Espahbodi, R., Juma, N., & Westbrook, A. (2019). Sustainability priorities, corporate strategy, and investor behavior. *Review of Financial Economics*, 37(1), 149–167. Retrieved from https://doi.org/10.1002/rfe.1052.

Gelos, G. & Wei, S. (2003). Transparency and international investor behavior. *SSRN Electronic Journal*. Retrieved from https://doi.org/10.2139/ssrn.424462.

Hong, B., Li, Z., & Minor, D. (2015). Corporate governance and executive compensation for corporate social responsibility. *SSRN Electronic Journal*. Retrieved from https://doi.org/10.2139/ssrn.2553963.

Jensen, J. & Berg, N. (2011). Determinants of traditional sustainability reporting versus integrated reporting. An institutionalist approach. *Business Strategy and the Environment*, 21(5), 299–316. Retrieved from https://doi.org/10.1002/bse.740.

Jeriansyah, W. & Mappanyukki, R. (2020). The effect of accountability and transparency of regional financial management on local government performance. *International Journal of Asian Social Science*, 10(12), 721–729. Retrieved from https://doi.org/10.18488/journal.1.2020.1012.721.729.

Kartadjumena, E. & Rodgers, W. (2019). Executive compensation, sustainability, climate, environmental concerns, and company financial performance: Evidence from Indonesian commercial banks. *Sustainability*, 11(6), 1673. Retrieved from https://doi.org/10.3390/su11061673.

Katelouzou, D. & Klettner, A. (2020). Sustainable finance and stewardship: Unlocking stewardship's sustainability potential. *SSRN Electronic Journal*. Retrieved from https://doi.org/10.2139/ssrn.3578447.

Keddie, S. & Magnan, M. (2023). Are ESG performance-based incentives a panacea or a smokescreen for excess compensation? *Sustainability Accounting Management and Policy Journal*, 14(3), 591–634. Retrieved from https://doi.org/10.1108/sampj-11-2022-0605.

Keeley, A., Li, C., Takeda, S., Gloria, T., & Managi, S. (2022). The ultimate owner of environmental, social, and governance investment. *Frontiers in Sustainability*, 3. Retrieved from https://doi.org/10.3389/frsus.2022.909239.

Kosack, S. & Fung, A. (2014). Does transparency improve governance? *Annual Review of Political Science*, 17(1), 65–87. Retrieved from https://doi.org/10.1146/annurev-polisci-032210-144356.

Kyere, M. & Ausloos, M. (2020). Corporate governance and firms financial performance in the United Kingdom. *International Journal of Finance and Economics*, 26(2), 1871–1885. Retrieved from https://doi.org/10.1002/ijfe.1883.

Lai, A., Melloni, G., & Stacchezzini, R. (2014). Corporate sustainable development: Is 'integrated reporting' a legitimation strategy? *Business Strategy and the Environment*, 25(3), 165–177. Retrieved from https://doi.org/10.1002/bse.1863.

Li, W. & Pang, W. (2023). The impact of digital inclusive finance on corporate ESG performance: Based on the perspective of corporate green technology innovation. *Environmental Science and Pollution Research*, 30(24), 65314–65327. Retrieved from https://doi.org/10.1007/s11356-023-27057-3.

Li, Y. & Fei, G. (2023). Network embeddedness, digital transformation, and enterprise performance — The moderating effect of top managerial cognition. *Frontiers in Psychology*, 14. Retrieved from https://doi.org/10.3389/fpsyg.2023.1098974.

Li, Y., Miao, X., Zheng, D., & Tang, Y. (2019). Corporate public transparency on financial performance: The moderating role of political embeddedness. *Sustainability*, 11(19), 5531. Retrieved from https://doi.org/10.3390/su11195531.

Makni, R., Francœur, C., & Bellavance, F. (2008). Causality between corporate social performance and financial performance: Evidence from Canadian firms. *Journal of Business Ethics*, 89(3), 409–422. Retrieved from https://doi.org/10.1007/s10551-008-0007-7.

Malau, M. (2019). The effect of earnings persistence and earnings transparency on company performance with corporate governance as moderating variable (empirical study in manufacturing company that listed in Indonesia stock exchange in 2014–2016. *EAJ: Economics and Accounting Journal*, 2(2), 86. Retrieved from https://doi.org/10.32493/eaj.v2i2.y2019.p86-94.

Matemane, R., Moloi, T., & Adelowotan, M. (2022). ESG performance measures for executive pay: Delphi inquiry strategy and experts' opinion. *Acta Commercii*, 22(1). Retrieved from https://doi.org/10.4102/ac.v22i1.1072.

Myšková, R. & Hájek, P. (2019). Relationship between corporate social responsibility in corporate annual reports and financial performance of the US companies. *Journal of International Studies*, 12(1), 269–282. Retrieved from https://doi.org/10.14254/2071-8330.2019/12-1/18.

Ponce, H., González, J., & Serrat, N. (2022). Disclosure of environmental, social, and corporate governance information by Spanish companies: A compliance analysis. *Sustainability*, 14(6), 3254. Retrieved from https://doi.org/10.3390/su14063254.

Prior, D., Surroca, J., & Tribó, J. (2008). Are socially responsible managers really ethical? Exploring the relationship between earnings management and corporate social responsibility. *Corporate Governance an International Review*, 16(3), 160–177. Retrieved from https://doi.org/10.1111/j.1467-8683.2008.00678.x.

Rath, C., Kurniasari, F., & Deo, M. (2020). CEO compensation and firm performance: The role of ESG transparency. *Indonesian Journal of Sustainability*

Accounting and Management, 4(2), 278. Retrieved from https://doi.org/10.28992/ijsam.v4i2.225.

Rau, P. & Yu, T. (2023). A survey on ESG: Investors, institutions and firms. *China Finance Review International*. Retrieved from https://doi.org/10.1108/cfri-12-2022-0260.

Ulez'ko, A., Kurnosova, N., & Kurnosov, S. (2022). Digital platforms as a tool to form the technological basis of digital agriculture. *IOP Conference Series Earth and Environmental Science*, 1069(1), 012003. Retrieved from https://doi.org/10.1088/1755-1315/1069/1/012003.

Warner, K. & Wäger, M. (2019). Building dynamic capabilities for digital transformation: An ongoing process of strategic renewal. *Long Range Planning*, 52(3), 326–349. Retrieved from https://doi.org/10.1016/j.lrp.2018.12.001.

Withers, P. J., van Dijk, K. C., Neset, T. S., Nesme, T., Oenema, O., Rubæk, G. H., Schoumans, O. F., Smit, B., & Pellerin, S. (2015). Stewardship to tackle global phosphorus inefficiency: The case of Europe. *Ambio*, 44(S2), 193–206. Retrieved from https://doi.org/10.1007/s13280-014-0614-8.

Yi, S. & Duval-Couetil, N. (2021). Standards for evaluating impact in entrepreneurship education research: Using a descriptive validity framework to enhance methodological rigor and transparency. *Entrepreneurship Theory and Practice*, 46(6), 1685–1716. Retrieved from https://doi.org/10.1177/104225 87211018184.

Zhou, S., Rashid, M., Zobair, S., Sobhani, F., & Siddik, A. (2023). Does ESG impact a firm's sustainability performance? The mediating effect of firm innovation performance. Retrieved from https://doi.org/10.20944/preprints 202303.0058.v1.

Chapter 17

Fixed-Income ESG Strategies

Ulf Erlandsson

Anthropocene Fixed Income Institute,
Stockholm, Sweden

Abstract

Fixed income is the biggest asset class in global financial markets, spanning capital provision for all types of entities from sovereign to private corporates, and with a direct cost-of-capital effect through primary market capital supply. This article discusses a holistic perspective on applying climate and ESG-type investment preferences on fixed-income portfolios. We discuss how these types of strategies then can be implemented in a portfolio context to generate a well-diversified impact and risk/return profile. Due to the asymmetrical risk–return profile of fixed income, applying a multi-threaded, well-diversified approach is argued to be a fiduciary-aligned approach to managing any fixed-income portfolio.

1. Overview and Background

Fixed income as an asset class sits at around US$125 trillion[1] in size, slightly above equities (US$100 trillion in 2022), and with alternative asset markets (estimated US$25 trillion) being substantially smaller.

---

[1]The number is time varying, estimated at 122.7 trillion in Q2 2022, see Greenwich Associates and SIFMA Insights (2023).

It is also special in that fixed-income exposures are integrated into almost all economic agents: A government, a public company, a municipality, and a private corporation will all be likely to tap into the fixed-income market either directly — through bonds or public loans — or indirectly — through bank-provided fixed-income products. This makes the role of fixed-income investors — those who are supplying this capital — and their application of ESG more complex than compared to public equity markets: A strategy that may work for public companies may be unsuitable for sovereigns or private companies. For a further introduction, see Sjöström and Erlandsson (2020).

This chapter discusses a holistic perspective on applying climate and ESG-type investment preferences on fixed-income portfolios. The approaches can be structured as supplying capital for green and transition projects predominantly through the labeled bond space; shorting and raising cost of capital for non-aligned activities in portfolio efficient ways; relative value approaches for leaders and laggards; and non-pecuniary and engagement approaches. Due to the asymmetrical risk–return profile of fixed income, applying a multi-threaded, well-diversified approach is argued to be a fiduciary-aligned approach to managing any fixed-income portfolio.

Our focus in this chapter will be on a number of practical, impactful ways to apply ESG in such a manner. It is not a fit-for-all approach but aims at broadly designing a strategy under the assumption that fixed-income allocating drives cost of capital and a relatively free investment mandate. The first section discusses the relationship between ESG and cost of capital in the context of fixed income; it looks at a non-parametric approach to measure ESG impact and how this has performed historically, followed by a summary of investment strategies across long risks (labeled bonds), curve trades, relative value, and finally outright shorting. We then overlay this with non-financial approaches in terms of various engagement strategies. The final section concludes.

2. The Concept of Cost of Capital

In order to understand the implications of selecting one security over another, in terms of ESG impact, a natural question to ask is the following: What is the fundamental effect on a company if I buy their security X (or not)? From a purely financial perspective, this will be reflected in how an investor changes the company's cost of capital. A company with plenty of capital has a lower cost and is more likely to invest in good (or bad) real economy projects than one that is facing a higher cost of capital.

Investors' impact on cost of capital varies through either a primary or secondary channel. In a primary market channel, the investor supplies capital directly to the issuer, with a direct link between the size of supply, the quantity demanded, and the price required to put supply and demand in equilibrium. In a secondary channel, investors exchange issuer capital with each other, setting a secondary market price of the capital, if the issuer would hypothetically need to get more (or reduce, like in an equity buyback) capital.

This leads to a key difference between fixed-income and public equities: Fixed-income securities have a fixed maturity, and as they roll down and mature, they will need to be refinanced through primary market operations. Thus, a very substantial proportion of fixed-income decisions (also in terms of ESG) will be in terms of primary effect. If we assume an FI asset base of US$125 trillion and an average maturity of 5 years, US$25 trillion will need to be refinanced in the primary market every year. Contrast this with equities where initial public offerings amounted to US$180 million in 2022 and share buybacks of US$1.7 trillion[2]: US$25 trillion in primary vs. US$2 trillion.

The nature of the primary focus on fixed income is also a relevant point when discussing the ubiquitous critique of ESG that "one's seller is another's buyer." That is a more valid critique in the equities space than in fixed income. Company Y may not care if Investor A sells bonds to Investor B at a certain price. But, if Investor A does not want to buy Company Y's bonds in a primary market offering, Company Y will have to increase the offered interest rate on the bond (inversely, lower the price) to entice Investor B to replace Investor A. That is a baseline cost (higher interest rate) to the company, which will eventually translate into (reduced) investment rates.[3]

---

[2] "Global IPO activity cut nearly in half in 2022," S&P Global Market Intelligence, January 12, 2023; "Global stock buybacks hit record high in 2022," *ibid.*, May 25, 2023.
[3] See Gilchrist and Zakrajsek (2007).

How do we estimate the elasticity between demand and supply in terms of fixed-income capital? This is an extremely difficult question, especially if one is to calibrate it to the small proportions of outstanding bond issuances that investors would normally be considering. To start with, it is analytically clear that there is a positive correlation between investment quantity and the price (and inversely, the yield of a security).[4] In practice, we can observe the extremes in the pricing of coal-related fixed-income securities, e.g. see Zhout *et al.* (2021),[5] but much work still remains to be done in order to calibrate a structural model for how much a certain size bond trade affect the market price and yield of a bond. And without knowing that relationship, it is also treacherous to try to be specific on a total portfolios impact on ultimate real-economy investment decisions.

2.1. *Risk-based ESG Exposure Measurement*

An alternative approach to structural modeling is to look at ESG impacts of the portfolio through the lens of risk contributions, as in Erlandsson (2017). The logic is that investors in a company are contributing capital at risk without which the company could not operate. The first question in this context is how to distribute this risk between different parts of the capital structure: How much should go into the equity side and how much into the debt side? We will conveniently follow fixed-income market practice and assume that this is based on the distribution ESG impact only on the debt structure. If we do so, duration-based or duration-times-spread-based measures are apt weighting factors for the ESG impact/footprint, where the following equation describes the contribution w of bond i at time t in a duration-only measurement system:

$$w_t^i = \frac{N_t^i \cdot d_t^i}{\sum_k^K N_t^k \cdot d_t^k},$$
(1)

---

[4]This is the basis of central banks' quantitative easing policy, where bonds are bought in order to drive prices up and yields down.

[5]See Zhou *et al.* (2021).

where N is the nominal owned in the bond and d is the duration of the bond. This may strike the reader as a rather simplistic percentage measure of bond exposure, but even with this simple definition, some important effects are achieved. Consider a company that has a carbon footprint allocated to its debt capital structure of 100 Mt and it has two bonds outstanding: one 2-year bond with a nominal of US\$1 billion and a duration of 1.5, and one 30-year bond with a nominal of US\$250 million and a duration of 20. A bond trader would consider a trading ratio of $20/1.5 = 13.33$ as "duration neutral," i.e. if the bond spread widened by 1bp across the whole issuer bond curve, holding 13.33 million of the 2-year bond would give the same P&L as holding 1 million of the 30-year bond. Arguably, that risk perception is reflected upon in the same way for the issuer: They will find 13.33 million of the 2-year bond issuance equivalent to being able to issue 1 million of the 30-year bond. Under this assumption, the total amount of duration risk in the debt stack becomes the following:

$$1 \times 1.5 + 0.25 \times 30 = 6.5$$

and the attribution of duration risk to the 2 year becomes $(1 \times 1.5)/6.5 = 23\%$ and for the 30 year $(0.25 \times 30)/6.5 = 77\%$. Hence, buying 1 million of the 30-year bond gives a carbon footprint of $(1/250) \times 77\% \times 100$ Mt $= 0.31$ Mt, and buying 1 million of the 2-year bond gives 0.023 Mt. This should be contrasted with a nominal amount approach where the 2 year/30 year 1 million position would have a footprint of 0.08 Mt. The difference in outcomes between the two approaches is striking and there clearly is an opportunity for a "carbon footprint arbitrage" for a portfolio manager applying a duration risk-based portfolio management approach, but using nominal weighting schemes for ESG factors: Buy long-dated bonds to retain your credit risk allocation to carbon-intensive names in order to minimize your carbon footprint. Such a system will drive the allocation of money into the long end of a "bad" issuer. Indeed, Jarnmo and Richardson (2023) show a higher degree of differentiation in credit spreads in the short end vs. the long end of the oil-and-gas sector, which could be interpreted as a result of such an allocation.

Our cost-of-capital approach has clear implications for more advanced approaches in credit, such as short positioning. If we accept that a long position, i.e. increasing the demand for a bond and thus increasing the price, drives cost of capital down for the issuer, then the reverse must also be true: A short sale increases the cost of capital. This is a point of contention, where one can note that a hedge fund type of investment vehicle could be positioned such that it is carbon negative, putting long-only type of managers into ESG mandates in a difficult ESG competitive position. Erlandsson (2021) discusses this at length, also looking at how leverage affects the net ESG position of a fund. It should not be controversial that a manager whose benchmark allocation into an oil company bond is €10 million, but only carries €5 million in the actual portfolio, should have a lesser footprint from that actual position compared to if she had held the benchmark position. Also, it seems logical that curve trades (further elaborated upon in the following) should be able to net long vs. short positions. The general recommendation on long vs. short position accounting of ESG footprint is to present all numbers in terms of gross as well as netted exposures.

3. Portfolio Design and ESG Optimization

Portfolio design under an ESG strategy quickly runs into difficult optimization trade-offs: Maximization of return under a volatility and ESG constraint requires a definition of how much 1 unit of ESG is worth relative to 1 unit of volatility.

First, we need to consider what that unit of ESG is and how we measure it and allocate it among the bonds and other positions in the strategy. Many market participants use structural approaches, where, for example, the carbon footprint of a company is assumed to be spread out across all outstanding bonds, and thus the owner of the bond owns that percentage of the footprint. However, beyond ignoring the duration risk component discussed earlier, this also ignores what should be allocated to other capital providers of the company such as equity investors and bank lenders. Even within bonds, there will be different seniorities and the potential for labeled ("green") bonds. For these exercises, there is currently little practical methodology.

As an alternative, Erlandsson (2017) introduced an ordinal ranking framework, ECOBAR, that uses a non-parametric approach to score the portfolio position and be able to aggregate individual positions into a total portfolio score. The methodology in broad terms is based on scoring sectors according to their carbon footprint on a scale of 1, 2, and 3 and then scoring issuers within each sector; individual issuers are ranked 1, 2, and 3. The resulting ECOBAR score is then the product of the two, i.e. in the range (1, 2, 3, 4, 6, 9). These issuer scores are then aggregated by using the duration weighting mechanism for individual bond and derivatives positions in Equation (1), with adjustments for green bonds (giving a score of 0) and an inversion of the score for outright short positions (a short on a 9 company becomes a 1 score).

Arguably, the outcome, a number between 0 and 9, may be superficially less informative for end investors, but it seems like something that is a better tool in terms of managing the portfolio and it makes more modest claims on having exactly measured the climate effect of a portfolio. Also, it provides meaningful time series that can be used to test hypotheses on whether the ESG factor contributes to or reduces (excess) returns.

The next step in terms of designing an ESG strategy will be to look at how to reduce a portfolio score (or footprint) while also retaining a risk–return profile. Figure 1 illustrates two different approaches. On the left, the active strategy in Erlandsson (2017) is illustrated in terms of excess returns vs. the portfolio ECOBAR score. This strategy in some ways is reflected in Table 1. On the right-hand side, the excess return of an ECOBAR portfolio rebalancing strategy is illustrated: An S&P investment-grade corporate bond index is compared to a "carbon-efficient" one, where the latter has allocations adjusted according to issuers'

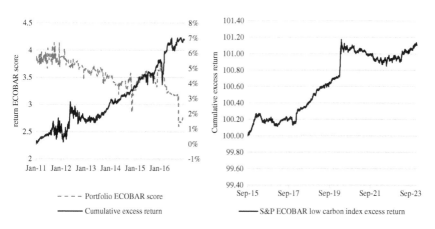

Figure 1. Left panel: Active credit portfolio excess return (solid line) vs. ECOBAR score (dotted) at AP4, 2011–2017. Right panel: S&P carbon-efficient corporate bond index excess return vs. standard index, duration neutral, 2015–2023

Source: Author, AFII, S&P.

Table 1.   Categories of fixed-income ESG strategies

Category	Implementation	Cost-of-Capital Impact	Target ECOBAR
Long positions	Labeled bonds, long position in "leaders"	Lower CoC on aligned credits	1
Curves	Steepeners, flatteners, forwards	CoC delta on time horizons where the issuer is aligned or not	2
Relative value	Pair trades, trades vs. index	Change relative CoC between individual leaders and laggards	2.5
Beta hedging	Index or ETFs	Change relative CoC on baskets of aligned vs. non-aligned credits	3
Short selling	Underweights, outright shorts	Increase CoC on non-aligned credit	2
Duration, FX hedging	Interest futures, swaps, FX spot and forward	Neutral	NA
Engagement	Direct issuer engagement, Labeled bond reverse enquiry, active counterparty management	Dynamic	NA

ECOBAR scores. The advantage of a scoring methodology becomes clear in this context as it allows for a wide range of strategies to be implemented, without the ESG dimension acting as a constraint.

4. Portfolio Sub-strategies

Establishing the underlying cost-of-capital argument and then applying some sort of measurement system — like ECOBAR — provide a baseline for designing various types of portfolio ESG strategies within the fixed-income portfolio. Table 1 presents the main categories, their implementation, and the potential cost-of-capital and ESG impact, assuming a focus on a credit portfolio as a subset of a broader fixed-income portfolio.[6]

---

[6]In this chapter, we will assume that duration and FX components of the portfolio are neutral in terms of ESG impact.

The strategies range from long-only, seeking to lower cost-of-capital for "good" issuers and instruments, to short positions, seeking to raise cost-of-capital. In parallel with this, engagements strategies are applied, as well as traditional FX and and interest rate hedging with no or only marginal ESG impact. The subsequent section provides a general introduction for each of the sub-strategies, except the rates and FX hedging component.

4.1. *Long Positions: Labeled Bonds*

Analogous to an equity strategy, the most straightforward ESG implementation in FI is to simply buy bonds of companies that score well on the ESG spectrum, which in our ECOBAR interpretation will be reflected in picking names with a low absolute score.

One of the advantages of ESG strategies in fixed incomes is that there are opportunities to express long risk views not only on issuers ("this company is making the world a better place") but also in terms of specific dimensions of an issuer: either in terms of their assets or in terms of their ESG strategy targets. The former will be in "use-of-proceeds" (UoP) types of bonds and the latter in terms of "general corporate purpose" (GCP) sustainability-linked bonds. From the perspective of the ECOBAR scoring methodology, as a general rule, green bonds will score as 0s, and sustainability-linked bonds will be up-notched one sector rank and one intra-sector rank (e.g. a $3 \times 3 = 9$-scored issuer will improve sector rank to 2 and intra-sector rank to $2 => 2 \times 2 = 4$ as the ECOBAR score). This is a general rule and has to be applied on a case-by-case basis in terms of determining the credibility of the labeled bond, with the discretion to downgrade the score if the label is considered a greenwash.

4.1.1. *Use of proceeds/green bonds*

First, the UoP format, for example, green bonds, ties investments in bonds to particular capital expenditure allocations by the issuer. This is typically not contractual, but rather a gentleman's agreement between the issuer and the investor. Although this may sound like a weak conditionality, it actually works well for certain types of issuers, especially those where there is a lot of repeat issuance. The different features of green and other UoP labeled bonds are discussed at length in Flammer (2020). With the market currently having grown to around US$2 trillion, it has been a successful route to start integrating ESG risks into portfolios in a practical way.

The feature that a green bond is able to theoretically separate green vs. gray activities gives a different angle to a fixed-income strategy compared to a public equity strategy, where such distinctions are not possible.

A recurring debate, important to strategy design, is whether there is a differential in the pricing of green bonds vs. similar traditional bonds. Green bonds are *pari passu*, equal in rank in case of default, to gray bonds. Essentially, the risk profile from a strict cash flow point of view is the same for the two bonds, limiting how far away they can trade from each other from a pure arbitrage viewpoint. This difference, the "greenium," is usually referred to as non-pecuniary, or in other words relating to a non-financial appreciation of the instrument. Zerbib (2019) is a standard reference in the literature discussing this "greenium." However, a financial motivation for this greenium may be that it exists due to lower volatility (or alternatively, higher liquidity) in green vs. gray bonds. Erlandsson (2020) looks at how to test this by measuring conditional volatility in the (Generalized Autroregressive Conditional Heteroskedasticity) GARCH type of models and also how to use cointegration to test if two bonds should be compared at all ("twin bonds"), noting that many greenium studies are comparing bonds that are structurally quite different.

As it happens, there is a natural experiment going on in terms of green bond premiums, through the German sovereign's issuance of twin bonds in August 2020. These bonds are issued with identical structural features and thus provide perfect comparability, allowing a deduction of the greenium. We illustrate this in Figure 2, which shows a time variability in the greenium, and at times a fairly substantial greenium. Interestingly, the greenium seems if anything to be positively correlated with volatility, which would imply that green bonds underperform when volatility increases. However, there could also be technical factors behind this: There are few very liquid green bonds such as the Bund, and thus green bond investors may be more inclined to sell their green bunds in a market drawdown.

4.1.2. *Sustainability-linked bonds* (*SLBs*)

Another format was introduced in 2019, called sustainability-linked bonds. These bonds tie some sort of target (sustainability performance target, SPT) to adjustments in the interest rate of the bond. A key difference between the UoP bond and the SLB is that the latter is gGCP: It does not prescribe to the issuer how it is going to reach a target, but instead focuses on the outcome. SLBs are generally targetting changes in ESG factors, for example setting _reduction_ of CO_2 emissions as a target,

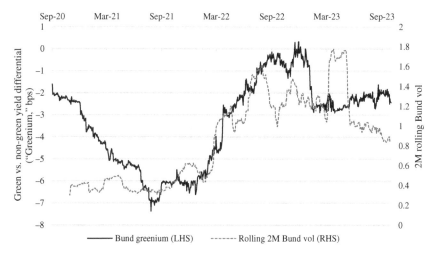

Figure 2. The yield differential in the green vs. gray German government 2030 bonds, vs. volatility

Source: Bloomberg.

rather than just capital allocation to some already existing low carbon asset. This makes it a good contender for labeled issuance from transition types of industries, where the starting point might not be strong enough to use a green bond format, but the incremental improvement might be even higher than for already "green" assets.

SLBs have been documented to have a number of attractive structural features but have also come under critique for lacking material targets and financial implications for missing/hitting those.

SLBs can be pricied using a risk-neutral, no-arbitrage relationship as shown in Erlandsson *et al.* (2022). The value of the coupon change is priced as the probability-weighted and risk discounted difference between an equivalent vanilla bond- and the stepped SLB coupon streams. This means that, as illustrated in Figure 3, an SLB will have an initial, fixed coupon below/above the equivalent vanilla bond if it is a step-up/step-down structure. Importantly, this also means that SLBs can be designed to provide lower cost-of-capital for issuers when successful in terms of target achievement. Mielnik and Erlandsson (2022) further prices SLBs as a binary options using the Black–Scholes framework. This can be expressed as follows:

$$\sum_{i=0}^{t-1} \Phi_i \cdot (C^{\text{EVB}} - C^{\text{SLB}}) = \pi_1 \cdot \sum_{i=t}^{T} \Phi_i \cdot (C^{\text{SLB*}} - C^{\text{EVB}}) - \pi_2 \cdot \sum_{i=t}^{T} \Phi_i \cdot (C^{\text{EVB}} - C^{\text{SLB}}),$$

(2)

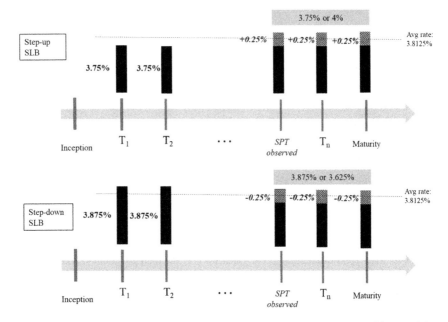

Figure 3. Coupon structures for step-up and step-down SLBs. In a no-arbitrage, risk-neutral framework, the equivalent vanilla bond to the SLB would price with a coupon at the average rate, assuming a 50% step probability.

Source: AFII.

where C indicates coupons for the Equivalent Vanilla Bond (EVB) and the SLB, Φ_i is a risky discount factor at time i, and $\pi_1 = (1 - \pi_2)$ is the probability of a step happening. Equation (2) can be used to find the right strike level for a coupon (in the primary market) or yield/spread level (in the secondary market) given a certain step structure and more importantly an investor view on the probability that an issuer will hit or miss their SPT.

4.2. Curves

As suggested in the section on cost of capital, one of the key differences between equities and fixed income is the potential to express time-contingent views on a company and their ESG alignment (under the assumption

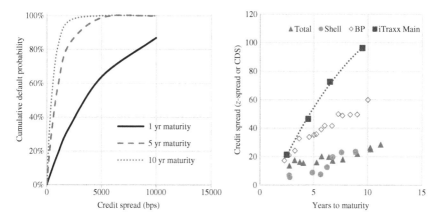

Figure 4. Left: Credit spreads and implied cumulative default probabilities. Right: Credit curves from cash bonds of oil majors and CDS market curvature

Source: AFII, Bloomberg.

of non-zero correlation between company value and such alignment). Fixed-income valuations indicate the market estimate of underlying default probabilities (see Figure 4, left panel) over time, and the investor can express views on this.[7] There can also be substantial discrepancies between curve shapes in different sectors and across different types of instruments: The right-hand panel of Figure 4 illustrates the flatness of oil major cash bonds in EUR vs. the general corporate curve expressed in CDS in the late 2010s. In that case, the interpretation of market pricing would be that long-dated oil company risk is low relative to short-dated risk, which an ESG-minded investor might not agree with.

If an investor believes that a company's long-term default probability is underpriced by the market (spread is too low/tight), vs. its short-term (spread in the short end is relatively too high), she would call the curve "too flat." This would imply that the right position is a steepener: buying front-end risk and shorting long-end risk. A useful metric for this calculation (is a curve spread high or low?) is the calculation of the credit forward: "If I were to buy five years of credit risk five years from now,

---

[7]For a detailed analysis of credit curves, see Rennison *et al.* (2007).

what is the current market implied price?"[8] An approximation of the forward credit spread risk is given by the following:

$$F_T^{t+i,t+k} = \frac{S_t^{t+k} \cdot D_t^{t+k} - S_t^{t+i} \cdot D_t^{t+i}}{1 - D_t^{t+k} \cdot D_t^{t+i}}.$$

As example of this pricing from the Bloomberg terminal is available in the following illustrating how the market is pricing the Morocco forward risk to be $300/135 = 2.2\times$ of the current risk, following the large earthquake effects of 2023. Is this appreciation of risk correct? Of course, this has to be weighted by factors such as the willingness of global concessionary finance institutions to provide capital for Morocco, which again will relate to some sort of ESG analysis.

In terms of portfolio scoring impact, as alluded to in the introductory sections, curve trades will be ESG weighted according to their total risk contribution to the portfolio. This means that DV01 neutral trades will neither add nor subtract from the ECOBAR score of a portfolio, as they are designed to neutralize risk contribution in terms of delta. Forwards, usually expressed as notional neutral curve trades, will generate changes to the total ECOBAR score according to their directionality.

4.3. *Relative Value Trades*

Curve trades are effectively long–short combinations within the same capital structure, meaning that they should have a market beta very close to 1 (or equivalently, be similarly dependent upon idiosyncratic company factors). A relative value trade is usually designed so as to be long company X, and short company Z, in a way that isolates the performance of the trades to the fundamental differential. An ideal example would be being long–short the CDS of two structurally similar utility companies, so as to achieve a trade combination that is approximately market neutral but will change in P&L as the relative spread differential between the companies moves. Indeed, full-scale portfolio strategies can be built upon, such as the DIEM strategy explained in Rennison *et al.* (2007). An example of an implementation of this is provided in Figure 5.

---

[8]A credit forward can be constructed by buying short dated protection (e.g. buy 5y CDS protection) and selling longer dated (e.g. sell 10y CDS protection). This would be a long risk position as described in the example.

ScoreCard	DIEM		Spread bucket	6,7	Date	2019-05-31				
Long risk candidates										
Company name	CDS spread	Equity ticker	Equity momentum	Equity Vol	DIEM signal	DIEM rank	dDIEM	ECOBAR_R	ECOBAR_S	ECOBAR
DR Horton Inc	81	DHI US	3.7%	32%	0.110	+2		2	3	6
Enbridge Inc	83	ENB CN	-1.9%	23%	-0.085	+2		3	2	6
Carrefour SA	84	CA FP	-1.0%	28%	-0.037	+2		1	2	2
Kinder Morgan Inc/DE	86	KMI US	3.5%	22%	0.154	+2		3	2	6
Viacom Inc	87	VIAB US	-0.3%	30%	-0.011	+2		2	1	2
McKesson Corp	87	MCK US	0.7%	27%	0.024	+2		1	2	2
Conagra Brands Inc	93	CAG US	6.2%	36%	0.162	+2		2	2	4
Yum! Brands Inc	94	YUM US	5.5%	16%	0.327	+2		2	2	4
Enel SpA	95	ENEL IM	3.0%	18%	0.166	+2		3	2	6
Advanced Micro Devices	108	AMD US	11.7%	69%	0.152	+2		3	1	3
MGIC Investment Corp	113	MTG US	4.3%	28%	0.148	+2				

Short risk candidates										
Company name	CDS spread	Equity ticker	Equity momentum	Equity Vol	DIEM signal	DIEM rank	dDIEM	ECOBAR_R	ECOBAR_S	ECOBAR
Marathon Petroleum Co	74	MPC US	-29.5%	32%	-0.913	-2		3	2	6
Metsa Board OYJ	76	METSB FH	-34.8%	42%	-0.836	-2		2	2	4
Bayerische Motoren Wei	78	BMW GR	-17.0%	23%	-0.740	-2		2	2	4
HOCHTIEF AG	79	HOT GR	-22.9%	24%	-0.950	-2		2	2	4
Accor SA	80	AC FP	-13.6%	21%	-0.637	-2		1	3	3
Eastman Chemical Co	82	EMN US	-18.1%	26%	-0.695	-2		3	3	9
Arrow Electronics Inc	94	ARW US	-21.2%	27%	-0.788	-2		2	3	6
Nokia OYJ	96	NOKIA FH	-14.9%	27%	-0.553	-2		1	2	2
Stora Enso OYJ	97	STERV FH	-18.8%	36%	-0.522	-2		2	3	6
Imperial Brands PLC	101	IMB LN	-31.2%	24%	-1.279	-2		2	1	2
Bayer AG	105	BAYN GR	-18.8%	34%	-0.559	-2		1	3	3
Cardinal Health Inc	107	CAH US	-14.6%	28%	-0.521	-2		1	2	2

Figure 5. Example of an implementation of a relative value strategy with ESG influence. The DIEM rank goes from −2 to +2 where −2 is a short risk signal and +2 is a long risk signal. Solid highlighted names could form a long risk basket vs. dashed highlighted names forming a short basket

Source: Bloomberg.

The ECOBAR score calculation for the equal-weighted long–short basket in Figure 5 is as follows:

$$1/6 \times [(2 + 2 + 3) + (1 + 2 + 4)] = 14/6 = 2.33,$$

where (2 + 2 + 3) refers to the scoring of the long positions (Carrefour, McKesson, AMD) and (1 + 2 + 4) refers to the inverted scores of the shorts (Eastman, 9; Stora, 6; Bayer, 3). The total ECOBAR score of this basket is then consequently 2.33.

4.4. *Underweights and Outright Shorting*

One of the most challenging trades in fixed income is outright shorting. At the core is the fundamental issue that the only time you lose money

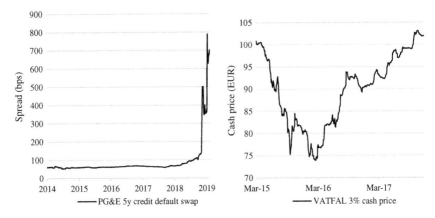

Figure 6. (Left) Pacific Gas & Electric (PG&E) 5y CDS spreads before and after the Californian wildfires in 2019. (Right) Vattenfall hybrid bond cash prices from new issue and the following 2015 write downs of lignite assets in Germany

Source: MarkIT, Bloomberg.

(on a hold-to-maturity basis) in fixed incomes is in case of default. If there is no default, all bonds pull to par, i.e. go back to nominal repayment. So, outright shorting is essentially betting on defaults to happen and the credit spread is the premium you pay for betting on this. Furthermore, in the case of outright shorting, there are substantial costs involved in repo as well as the non-zero risks of so-called short squeezes, where short sellers are scrambling to buy bonds to deliver into their repos, thus pushing prices upward significantly and incurring outsized losses on their short positions.

In terms of ESG strategy, short selling can be viewed as an impact trade (driving up cost of capital) and/or a risk decisions trade (looking at situations where ESG risk is not priced in). Two examples are provided in Figure 6. PG&E (left panel) is a typical example of ESG risks being underpriced, in this case the company's liabilities for starting forest fires with decrepit power lines as California was hit by severe drought conditions. In the right-hand panel, Vattenfall — a Swedish state utility — issued bonds without a clear plan for decommissioning lignite assets in Germany. However, as markets piled on the pressure, the company started facing a higher cost of capital: The initial bond coupon was around 3%, but markets started pushing yields toward 6% due to the lignite exposure.

This then led to a change in strategy of the company, with faster divestment from lignite coal.

5. Engagement Strategy

Traditionally, active investor engagement in ESG has been the remit of equity holders, where the natural engagement route has been through board appointments and communications. However, fixed-income investors have outsized and often underused opportunities to engage, where the "bond vigilantes" of history have probably been some of the most engaged investors across any asset class.

5.1. *Deal Roadshow Engagement: Due Diligence*

As mentioned in the introduction, investors will make a large number of primary market allocation decisions, and for many issuers, a bond issuance will be preceded by more or less extensive investor presentation, either in a physical roadshow format or through virtual means ("NetRoadShow"). This is an opportunity for investors to engage the issuers on important ESG topics and sometimes build investor coalitions around important questions.

One key aspect of this engagement is to conduct due diligence in terms of the issuer presenting key aspects of their ESG impact. Issuers will generally show an idealized version of their organization. The task of the investor is to try to clean out the cupboards that the issuer might hide, requesting full transparency. The following is a surprisingly effective question to ask in meetings (for the investor): "What is the worst thing on your balance sheet that I should be aware of?" (This is sometimes referred to as the "The Skeleton in the Cupboard" question.) The issuer will have to consider the risk of either not disclosing things that the investor might actually already know about, and thus losing credibility, or they will actually have to talk about the downside issues that might be the most relevant for the investor.

One particular type of intervention for investors can be in terms of asking for improved disclosures around ESG-related risks in the bond prospectus. Although it may be hard to drive litigation against poor risk disclosures in prospectuses, the experience is that regulators and lawyers alike are taking the bond prospectus more seriously. ESG has grown into something that can make or break an investor's decision to invest or not invest, and thus, not disclosing material factors (within reason) that would be relevant to that decision may be considered fraudulent. A recent example of this is the discussion around disclosure of an Indian coal company's sustainability-linked bond issuance in 2021, as mentioned in Hay (2021).

5.2. *Labeled Bond/Structure Reverse Enquiry*

Investors can also play important roles in terms of providing issuers with information about their own targets when it comes to outcomes. An ESG strategy might be promising a hypothetical 5% reduction in its carbon footprint per annum: such a strategy should engage and steer companies that it invests in to reach that target, given that they will be unvestable otherwise. We have discussed the sustainability-linked bond structure earlier as an example of this. A very natural, and constructive, engagement route for investors is of course to request SLB structures to reflect their investment preferences. A special case can be when investors have credit rating requirements, where engagement with credit enhancement providers, such as development finance institutions, can be productive to make certain higher-risk ESG bond investments possible.

5.3. *Counterparty Selection*

Banks play a central role as intermediaries in the fixed-income space but are hard to influence in terms of being an individual bond holder, as their debt capital structures are typically very large and individual investors are small. An alternative approach as an investor is to use the power one has a client to banks rather than as an investor in their securities, what is referred to as "counterparty selection." The investor simply gives preference in business relationships to banks that are aligned with the investor's own ESG strategy.

As an example of this, The Anthropocene Fixed Income Institute (2021a) introduced a framework to select counterparties based on the net fee generation from debt-capital market (DCM) activities from "green" vs. "fossil" issuers. The framework called 'The Box' suggests removing a bottom few of banks that are heavily engaged on a relative basis in

Table 2.   Sample spot and forward CDS spread matrix for Morocco sovereign

Forward Start Date	Spread (bps)	Years Forward						
		1	**2**	**3**	**4**	**5**	**7**	**10**
1	36	80	135	180	233	327	284	
2	62	109	158	207	282	336	277	
3	88	132	183	248	301	317	274	
4	111	156	218	269	294	306		
5	**135**	188	239	268	289	**300**		
7	186	215	245	268	284			
10	205							

Source: Bloomberg.

fossil fuel bond capital raisings. A sample of this is provided in Table 2, which lists a number of the larger fixed-income trading banks, ranking them based on net fees as produced in the Anthropocene Fixed Income Institute (2022).

Based on a list like the one provided in Table 3, investors are in practice, albeit at a modest scale so far, adjusting their counterparty exposures and thus fee generation for banks (e.g. see St. Clair (2022)). This is also reflexive and perhaps even more effective on the issuer side. An issuer pursuing to issue a green bond or an SLB may realize that they their traction with investors may be impeded by using banks that are concentrated on fossil fuel provisioning deals. A bank that executed the SUEK 2021[9] deal on a Tuesday may not be the issuing bank for a green bond on the Wednesday: The credibility it provides in terms of the gravitas of the green bond structuring might be impeded. The auto-regressivity in this comes in where issuers anticipate lower investor demand if they are too engaged in fossil fuel deals.

This may sound like a theoretical exercise, but in practice, banks are sensitive to investor sentiment and are good at pricing it in terms of fees. Running a controversial deal will generate a request for higher fees, and thus eventually lead to a higher cost of capital (in fixed income).

[9]See Anthropocene Fixed Income Institute (2021b) for an overview of the SUEK transaction. SUEK, a Russian thermal coal mining company, did an inaugural benchmark US dollars deal in 2021.

Table 3. Net green/fossil funding syndication fee league tables, Dec22

Bank	Rank	Chg vs. Sep-22	vs. Dec-2021	vs. Dec-2020	Net Green/Fossil Fees pct (%)	Total Fees US$ (in million)	Net Green/Fossil Revenue US$ (in million)	Chg in Fossil Fees vs.-20/21 (%)	SLB Fees of Total (%)	Net Fees (green+SLB)/Fossil (%)
UBS	1	1 ↑	1 ↑	0 ~	7.5	603.8	45.2	–85	0.7	8.2
Credit Agricole CIB	2	–1 →	–1 →	2 ↑	5.7	1 009.2	57.8	–37	1.1	6.8
HSBC	3	0 ~	2 ↑	3 ↑	4.2	1 227.8	51.0	–48	1.6	5.7
BNP Paribas	4	0 ~	–1 →	4 ↑	3.6	1 441.9	52.2	–45	1.9	5.5
Credit Suisse	5	2 ↑	2 ↑	–2 →	2.3	910.2	21.0	–59	1.5	3.8
Goldman Sachs	6	2 ↑	4 ↑	–1 →	1.5	1 445.3	21.5	–56	1.4	2.9
Societe Generale	7	2 ↑	2 ↑	2 ↑	1.4	715.9	9.9	–47	1.9	3.3
Deutsche Bank	8	–3 →	–4 →	–1 →	1.2	1 374.4	16.7	–8	0.9	2.1
Morgan Stanley	9	3 ↑	2 ↑	–7 →	1.2	1 192.7	14.1	–48	1.7	2.9
Barclays	10	0 ~	2 ↑	1 ↑	1.1	1 400.2	15.4	–61	0.9	2.1
Sumitomo Mitsui Financial	11	–5 →	–5 →	7 ↑	–0.6	747.9	–4.2	–47	0.7	0.1
BofA Securities	12	–1 →	–4 →	0 ~	–0.7	2 768.5	–20.7	–25	0.6	–0.1
JP Morgan	13	1 ↑	0 ~	– →	–1.5	2 672.3	–41.0	–47	0.9	–0.7
Citi	14	–1 →	0 ~	– →	–1.6	2 005.8	–31.9	–37	1.0	–0.6
Mizuho Financial	15	0 ~	0 ~	– →	–2.4	886.4	–21.4	–19	1.2	–1.2
Mitsubishi UFJ Financial Group I	16	2 ↑	0 ~	1 ↑	–6.1	896.7	–55.1	–22	0.9	–5.2
Wells Fargo	17	–1 →	1 ↑	–1 →	–6.8	1 434.4	–98.0	–12	0.4	–6.4
RBC Capital Markets	18	–1 →	–1 →	–3 →	–8.4	1 011.5	–85.3	7	1.0	–7.4

Source: Anthropocene Fixed Income Institute, Bloomberg.

6. Conclusion

Assuming cost-of-capital effects of fixed-income positions, this chapter has briefly introduced a number of sub-strategies that can be deployed in order to drive such cost-of-capital effects in a fixed-income strategy. The approach taken has been one that is focused on being able to understand and apply traditional credit trading strategies in terms of ESG impact rather than the other way around, making it suitable for main-stream managers rather than dedicated funds. This is important, we believe, as dedicated funds will remain a relatively small proportion of the market for the foreseeable future, and it is thus important to crowd in mainstream money to achieve a broader ESG impact.

We propose sub-strategies broadly defined as long-only (leaders and labeled bonds), relative value (curves and outright relative value), and shorts (underweights and outright shorts), as well as complementary engagement strategies. Applying a broad set of ESG strategies across a mainstream fixed income is likely to improve impact effectiveness over time, especially in the context of credit valuation ebb and flows. Furthermore, new instruments such as SLBs and related engagement seems to be strong candidates for driving change and transition in material ESG factors.

References

Anthropocene Fixed Income Institute. (2021a). The box. Retrieved from https://anthropocenefii.org/fossil-lending/the-box (Accessed December 13, 2023).

Anthropocene Fixed Income Institute. (2021b). Banking on coal: SUEK bond review. Retrieved from https://anthropocenefii.org/bond-spotlight/banking-on-coal-suek-bond-review (Accessed December 13, 2023).

Anthropocene Fixed Income Institute. (2022). Net green/fossil bond syndication league table — December 22. Retrieved from https://anthropocenefii.org/fossil-lending/net-green-fossil-bond-syndication-league-table-dec22 (Accessed December 13, 2023).

Erlandsson, U. (2017). Credit Alpha and CO_2 reduction: A portfolio manager perspective. Retrieved from http://dx.doi.org/10.2139/ssrn.2987772.

Erlandsson, U. (2020). Green bond risk premiums: A twin-bond ULFP approach. Retrieved from http://dx.doi.org/10.2139/ssrn.3624591.

Erlandsson, U. (2021). Carbon negative leveraged investment strategies. Retrieved from http://dx.doi.org/10.2139/ssrn.3906531.

Erlandsson, U., Mielnik, S., Richardson, J., & Rimaud, C. (2022). Notes on risk-neutral pricing of SLBs and step-down structures. Retrieved from http://dx.doi.org/10.2139/ssrn.4258897.

Flammer, C. (2021). Corporate green bonds. *Journal of Financial Economics*, 142(2), 499–516.

Gilchrist, S. & Zakrajsek, E. (2007). Investment and the cost of capital: New evidence from the corporate bond market. NBER Working Paper 13174. Retrieved from http://www.nber.org/papers/w13174 NATIONAL BUREAU OF ECONOMIC RESEARCH 1050 Massachusetts Avenue Cambridge, MA 02138 June 2007.

Greenwich Associates and SIFMA Insights. (2023). Understanding fixed-income markets in 2023. Retrieved from https://www.sifma.org/resources/research/understanding-fixed-income-markets-in-2023/ (Accessed December 13, 2023).

Hay, J. (October 21, 2021). Banks hit by 'fraud' complaint to SEC over Adani SLB coal links. Global Capital. Retrieved from https://www.globalcapital.com/article/297sitz2boxhpl0ffm29s/sri/banks-hit-by-fraud-complaint-to-sec-over-adani-slb-coal-links.

Jarnmo, J. & Richardson, J. (2023). *Oil & Gas: Climate Performance and the Cost of Capital*. Anthropocene Fixed Income Institute. Stockholm: Sweden.

Mielnik. S. & Erlandsson, U. (2022). An option pricing approach to sustainability-linked bonds. Retrieved from http://dx.doi.org/10.2139/ssrn.4582574.

Rennison, G., Erlandsson, U., & Ghosh, A. (2007). *CDS Curve Trading Handbook*. Barclays Capital. London: UK.

Sjöström, E. & Erlandsson, U. (2020). *The Bond Market: Its Relevance and Functionality for the Climate Transition*. Stockholm Sustainable Finance Centre/Anthropocene Fixed Income Institute. Stockholm Sweden.

St. Clair, B. (2022). Can ESG trading and best execution coexist? *Risk.Net*. Retrieved from https://www.risk.net/our-take/7921611/can-esg-trading-and-best-execution-coexist (Accessed December 13, 2023).

Zerbib, O. D. (2019). The effect of pro-environmental preferences on bond prices: Evidence from green bonds. *Journal of Banking & Finance*, 98, 39–60.

Zhou, X., Wilson, C., & Caldecott, B. (2021). The energy transition and changing financing costs. Oxford Sustainable Finance Programme. Retrieved from https://www.smithschool.ox.ac.uk/sites/default/files/2022-02/The-energy-transition-and-changing-financing-costs.pdf (Accessed December 13, 2023).

Chapter 18

Portfolio Performance Measures for Sustainable Investing

Anatoly B. Schmidt

*Finance and Risk Engineering, NYU Tandon School,
New York, USA*

Abstract

The portfolio performance measure generally used in classical finance is based on the volatility risk-adjusted return (Sharpe ratio). Unfortunately, applying this measure in sustainable investing may yield some confusion since portfolios with higher environmental, social, and governance (ESG) ratings may not outperform their ESG-neutral peers. Moreover, correlations between the corporate ESG ratings and stock returns in some portfolios can be negative. Since the ESG factors represent non-pecuniary risks, it is suggested in this work that socially responsible investors should include the ESG metrics explicitly in the portfolio performance measures. This idea is closely related to deriving optimal ESG portfolios (OESGPs) that are simultaneously optimized in terms of their return, volatility risk, and ESG value. Another important issue discussed here is that investors may prefer ESG ratings customized according to their preferences rather than simple averages of the E, S, and G categories that are offered by various ratings agencies. In this work, both problems are addressed using OESGPs formed with the constituents of nine major US equity sector Exchange-Traded Funds (ETFs). It is found that the main OESGP holdings are not very sensitive to the ESG metrics and hence can be promising leads for future investments.

1. Introduction

According to classical finance, rational investors are focused on increasing their wealth and minimizing their investment risks. For equity investors, stock price volatility risk is their major concern. As a result, the portfolio volatility risk-adjusted return (the famous Sharpe ratio *Sh*) is the most widely used portfolio performance measure. Markowitz (1952) developed the theory of the mean-variance portfolio in which the optimal portfolio weights are estimated by simultaneously maximizing portfolio return and minimizing portfolio volatility.

While there has been a dramatic growth in the sustainable investing that incorporates environmental, social, and governance (ESG) factors in the investment selection process, several important problems with this practice have been discussed in the literature. First, there are unfounded claims that ESG-based investing delivers excess alpha (Kumar, 2019; Cornell & Damodaran, 2020; La Torre *et al.*, 2020; Berchicci & King, 2022; King & Pucker, 2022). It should be noted that the very popularity of some ESG-based investments might temporarily drive their price up (van der Beck, 2021), particularly in light of the inelastic market hypothesis (Gabaix & Koijen, 2021). Moreover, correlations between the stock returns and ESG ratings in some portfolios can be very low or even negative. As a result, portfolio Sharpe ratio may decline with increasing portfolio ESG value (PESGV) (Schmidt, 2020; Schmidt & Zhang, 2023).

Various ESG factors represent various non-pecuniary investment risks. Therefore, Schmidt (2020) suggested that socially responsible investors should use a portfolio performance measure that is determined not only by portfolio return and price volatility risk but also by PESGV, specifically, *the ESG-tilted Sharpe ratio*:

$$Sh\_ESG = Sh(1 + PESGV). \qquad (1)$$

In (1), PESGV is defined as the sum of the portfolio constituents' weighted ESG ratings. Similar ESG-dependent performance measures were proposed by Chen and Mussalli (2020) and Alessandrini and Jondeau (2021). This idea can be naturally incorporated into the mean-variance portfolio (MVP) framework in which the portfolio is simultaneously optimized in terms of return, volatility risk, and PESGV (Pedersen *et al.*, 2021; Schmidt, 2020). Importantly, *Sh*_ESG may have a maximum at intermediate PESGVs, which can serve as a criterion for the optimal ESG portfolio (OESGP).

While high ESG ratings point to corporate "goodness," a similar approach can be used to account for corporate "sinfulness." For example, Schmidt (2023) introduced the notion of the greenhouse gas (GHG) aversion (GHGA). The portfolio GHGA (PGHGA) is assumed to be a weighted sum of the portfolio holdings' GHG emission intensities. Then, the GHGA-tilted Sharpe ratio is

$$Sh\_GHGA = Sh*(1 - PGHGA). \tag{2}$$

Note that PESGV in (1) and PGHGA in (2) have the opposite signs, contrasting the corporate "goodness" and "sinfulness" measures.

Another problem addressed in this work is deriving the ESG ratings. At present, these ratings may differ significantly among their providers (Berg *et al.*, 2022; Christensen *et al.*, 2022; Lioui & Tarelli, 2022; Schmidt & Zhang, 2023). One reason for these discrepancies is that the ESG ratings are based mostly on corporate self-reporting, which can be subjected to "greenwashing" (e.g. Amenc *et al.*, 2022; King & Pucker, 2022; Pastor *et al.*, 2023). Also, the ways in which the ratings agencies mix their generally incompatible environmental (E), social (S), and governance (G) scores into the aggregate ESG ratings are inevitably subjective.

Schmidt (2021) suggested that investors should be able to define the ESG ratings according to their own priorities. In recent years, some agencies started offering news-based (as opposed to self-reporting-based) ESG scores for 26 individual Sustainability Accounting Standards Board categories (see SASB, 2023) or 17 United Nations Sustainable Development Goals (see United Nations Department of Economic and Social Affairs, 2023). In this methodology, the relevant news is collected using natural language processing algorithms from thousands of independent information sources and hopefully represents more objective corporate ESG metrics than self-reporting does. This approach allows investors to easily specify customized ESG ratings.

In this work, I consider OESGPs formed by the constituents of nine major US equity sector ETFs using the news-based TrueValue Labs (TVL) scores. Specifically, we compare the results for TVL scores based on the aggregated 26 SASB categories (denoted further ESG), single ecological impact (Eco) score, and single greenhouse gas emission (GHG) score. Note that the news for the Eco and GHG categories does not overlap: Ecological impact scores are determined from news on water pollution, environmental project lifecycles, and impacts on biodiversity. GHG scores are determined from news about GHG emissions, sustainable transportation, fuel costs, renewable energy, and climate lawsuits.

In the next three sections, we describe the OESGP framework, the data used in this work, and the results, respectively. The discussion concludes this chapter.

2. The Framework for Optimal ESG Portfolios

MVP theory is based on minimizing the objective function (see, e.g. Elton *et al.*, 2009)

$$U_{\text{MVP}} = 0.5\lambda\sigma_p^2 - r_p. \tag{3}$$

In (3), λ is the risk aversion parameter that is usually chosen for yielding either the minimum variance portfolio or the maximum Sharpe portfolio. We use the latter in this work. Portfolio variance σ_p^2 equals

$$\sigma_p^2 = \sum_{i,j=1}^{N} w_i w_j \sigma_{ij}, \tag{4}$$

where w_i are portfolio weights, $i = 1, 2, ..., N$; $\sum_{i=1}^{N} w_i = 1$, σ_{ij} are covariances between asset returns i and j, r_p is mean portfolio return

$$r_p = \sum_{i=1}^{N} w_i r_i, \tag{5}$$

and r_i are mean portfolio asset returns. The Sharpe ratio is defined as

$$Sh = (r_p - r_f)/\sigma_p, \tag{6}$$

where r_f is the risk-free rate of return (neglected in this work).

When OESGPs are considered, U_{MVP} is expanded with PESGV as

$$U_{\text{ESG-MVP}} = U_{\text{MVP}} - \gamma\text{PESGV}, \tag{7}$$

where γ is the ESG strength parameter, which is the investors' choice depending on how important PESGV is for them. PESGV is assumed to be a weighted sum of the portfolio constituents' ESG scores δ_i:

$$\text{PESGV} = \sum_{i=1}^{N} w_i \delta_i. \tag{8}$$

Then, the derivation of a long-only OESGP represents the following quadratic programming problem:

$$\min \left[0.5\lambda \sum_{i,j=1}^{N} w_i w_j \sigma_{ij} - \gamma \sum_{i=1}^{N} \delta_i w_i \right], \tag{9}$$

$$\text{s.t. } \sum_{i=1}^{N} w_i r_i = r_p, \tag{10}$$

$$\sum_{i=1}^{N} w_i = 1, \tag{11}$$

$$w_i \geq 0; \quad i = 1, 2, ..., N. \tag{12}$$

We consider long-only OESGPs with the constraint (12) since unconstrained MVPs may have large short positions undesirable for most investors (see, e.g. Jacobs *et al.*, 2013).

Another specificity of this work is that portfolio covariance is estimated using both Pearson's correlations and partial correlations. The latter are conditioned on the state of the economy (mimicked for the US equity market with the S&P 500 index). The motivation for introducing partial correlations-based MVP (PartMVP) as an alternative to Pearson's correlations-based MVP (PearMVP) is that stock returns generally follow the equity market trend according to the capital asset pricing model, which increases Pearson's correlations between stocks. On the other hand, partial correlations conditioned on market returns describe co-movements of the excess asset returns unaffected by the market momentum. As a result, partial correlations are lower than the corresponding Pearson's correlations, and PartMVPs are more diversified than PearMVPs. It was found that PartMVPs may outperform PearMVPs and equal-weight portfolios out of sample (Nadler & Schmidt, 2014; Cai & Schmidt, 2019).

Another advantage of PartMVP is that while the PearMVP weights change frequently over time, the PartMVP weights outside the bear market effects can be almost constant.

The partial correlation coefficient, $\rho_{ij|k}$, between variables X_i and X_j that is conditioned on variable X_k measures the correlation between residuals of linear regressions of X_i on X_k and X_j on X_k (Johnston & DiNardo, 1997). It can be expressed in terms of partial covariance (Whittaker, 1990):

$$\sigma_{ij|k} \equiv \text{cov}(X_i, X_j | X_k) = \text{cov}(X_i, X_j)$$
$$- \text{cov}(X_i, X_k)\,\text{cov}(X_j, X_k)/\text{var}(X_k) = \rho_{ij|k}\,\sigma_{i|k}\,\sigma_{j|k}. \qquad (13)$$

In (12), partial variance $\sigma_{i|k}^2 \equiv \text{cov}(X_i, X_i | X_k)$ equals

$$\sigma_{i|k}^2 = \sigma_i^2 - \sigma_{ik}^4/\sigma_k^2. \qquad (14)$$

The partial correlation coefficient can be calculated using Pearson's correlations:

$$\rho_{ij|k} = \frac{\rho_{ij} - \rho_{ik}\rho_{jk}}{\sqrt{1-\rho_{ik}^2}\,\sqrt{1-\rho_{jk}^2}}. \qquad (15)$$

Portfolio variance in terms of partial covariance equals

$$\sigma_p^2 = \sum_{i,j=1}^{N} w_i w_j \sigma_{ij|k}. \qquad (16)$$

Hence, to derive PartMVP, Equation (16) should be used instead of Equation (4).

The choice of the OESGP is implemented in two steps. First, maximum Sharpe portfolios are estimated using minimization protocol (9)–(12) for various values of the ESG strength parameter γ. Then, the OESGP that yields the maximum value of the ESG-tilted Sharpe ratio *Sh_ESG* (1) is chosen.

3. The Data

In this work, OESGPs formed with the constituents of the following major US equity sector ETFs in 2021 were considered: Materials (ticker XLB), Energy (XLE), Finance (XLF), Industrials (XLI), Technology (XLK),

Table 1.   Statistics of the ESG ratings for the Materials (XLB), Energy (XLE), and Utilities (XLU) ETFs

ETF	Std. Dev				Correlation with TVL		
	MSCI	SPGI	SUST	TVL	MSCI	SPGI	SUST
XLB	0.25	0.25	0.09	0.08	0.14	0.51	−0.33
XLE	0.24	0.17	0.08	0.05	0.48	0.15	−0.30
XLU	0.20	0.22	0.08	0.06	0.29	−0.07	−0.08

Consumer Staples (XLP), Utilities (XLU), Healthcare (XLV), and Consumer Discretionary (XLY). To address the survival bias, only the stocks that were publicly traded during the entire OESGP calibration period of June 1, 2019–December 31, 2021 were included. We used the adjusted closing daily prices available on *finance.yahoo.com*. Generally, the TVL scores are compiled on a daily basis with an age-dependent weighting of the relevant news for the last six months, and we used the scores published on December 31, 2021. We scaled the TVL scores to bring their values into range [0, 1] and assigned the neutral value of 0.5 to those Eco and GHG scores that were absent in the TVL database.

The variations (Std. dev) of the TVL ESG ratings are notably lower than the scores of the MSCI and S&P Global (SPGI), but closer to those from Sustainalytics (SUST) (see an example in Table 1). The MSCI ratings, which in contrast to the other agencies' ratings are literal (from the worst CCC to the best AAA), were converted to the numeric ones by mapping them onto a linear grid within the range [0, 1] (Schmidt, 2020). Note that the SUST scores describe the ESG risk rather than the ESG value. Therefore, the correlations between the SUST scores and the scores of the other ratings providers are negative.

4. The Results

4.1. *Consumer Staples Select Sector SPDR ETF* (XLP)

The specifics of the XLP constituents are that the correlations between all three TVL scores (ESG, Eco, and GHG) and returns in 2021 were negative (see Table 2). The results for XLP reflect a general pattern of the TVL scores for the US equity ETF constituents in that the variations of the Eco scores are notably higher than the variations of the ESG and GHG scores.

Table 2.   Statistics of the TVL scores for XLP

Scores	Mean	Std. Dev	Max	Min	Corr. with Return 2021
ESG	0.573	0.055	0.637	0.396	−39.0%
Eco	0.618	0.141	0.930	0.376	−26.0%
GHG	0.644	0.058	0.731	0.477	−7.0%

Note: ESG — Scores based on all 26 SASB categories; Eco — Ecological impact score; GHG — GHG score.

The performance statistics and the weights of the XLP-based optimal ESG/Eco/GHG portfolios are listed in Table 3. All three ESG/Eco/GHG-optimal PartMVPs had higher *Sh*-ESGs than their ESG-neutral peers. As for PearMVPs, the ESG/GHG-optimal (Eco-optimal) portfolios had higher (lower) *Sh*-ESGs than the ESG-neutral portfolio. Note that the ESG-neutral PartMVP is much more diversified that the ESG-neutral PearMVP, which is typical for other MVPs. Unfortunately, OESGPs (both PearMVP and PartMVP) are much more concentrated than their ESG-neutral peers. In fact, some OESGPs may have only one or two constituents that have both high returns and high ESG scores (Schmidt & Zhang, 2023).

Some XLP constituents, such as Archer-Daniels-Midland (ticker ADM), Costco (COST), Estée Lauder (EL), and Kroger (KR) had significant weights in all three ESG/Eco/GHG-optimal portfolios. This shows that the protocol for deriving OESGPs can be used for filtering out the portfolio constituents that are "overall good" in terms of the three criteria: return, volatility risk, and various SASB categories (or their aggregated scores).

4.2. *Healthcare Select Sector SPDR ETF* (XLV)

For the XLV constituents, the ESG and Eco (GHG) TVL scores are positively (negatively) correlated with returns (see Table 4).

The performance statistics of the ESG-optimal portfolios based on the XLB constituents are listed in Table 5. With the exception of the GHG-optimal PearMVP, the ESG/Eco/GHG OESGPs outperform their ESG/Eco/GHG-neutral peers.

Table 3.   Performance statistics and weights of the XLP-based OESGPs

Portfolio		# Weights	Sh	PESGV	Sh-ESG	ADM	CHD	COST	EL	KR	LW	MNST	PM	STZ	SYY	TSN
ESG-neutral	PearMVP	4	1.78	0.52	2.71	0.03	0.00	0.56	0.19	0.22	0.00	0.00	0.00	0.00	0.00	0.00
	PartMVP	10	1.48	0.54	2.27	0.19	0.00	0.35	0.18	0.04	0.01	0.10	0.02	0.07	0.02	0.01
ESG-opt	PearMVP	3	1.78	0.53	2.72	0.00	0.00	0.51	0.26	0.23	0.00	0.00	0.00	0.00	0.00	0.00
	PartMVP	4	1.52	0.56	2.38	0.25	0.00	0.25	0.41	0.09	0.00	0.00	0.00	0.00	0.00	0.00
ESG-neutral	PearMVP	4	1.78	0.50	2.67	0.03	0.00	0.56	0.19	0.22	0.00	0.00	0.00	0.00	0.00	0.00
	PartMVP	10	1.48	0.53	2.26	0.19	0.00	0.35	0.18	0.04	0.01	0.10	0.02	0.07	0.02	0.01
Eco-opt	PearMVP	3	1.75	0.53	2.69	0.00	0.00	0.43	0.34	0.23	0.00	0.00	0.00	0.00	0.00	0.00
	PartMVP	5	1.54	0.58	2.44	0.18	0.02	0.31	0.43	0.06	0.00	0.00	0.00	0.00	0.00	0.00
GHG-opt	PearMVP	4	1.78	0.64	2.92	0.03	0.00	0.54	0.23	0.20	0.00	0.00	0.00	0.00	0.00	0.00
	PartMVP	6	1.52	0.66	2.52	0.22	0.00	0.40	0.27	0.01	0.00	0.00	0.08	0.00	0.02	0.00

Note: # weights — number of weights ≥ 0.01; PearMVP (PartMVP) — Pearson's (partial) correlation-based mean-variance portfolio.

Table 4.   Statistics of the TVL scores for XLV

Scores	Mean	Std. Dev	Max	Min	Corr. with Returns 2021
ESG	0.521	0.107	0.778	0.199	8.0%
Eco	0.537	0.139	0.901	0.137	20.1%
GHG	0.607	0.104	0.817	0.255	−20.7%

Table 5.   Performance statistics of the XLV-based OESGPs

Portfolio		# Weights	Sh	PESGV	Sh-ESG
ESG-neutral	PearMVP	6	2.21	0.573	3.48
	PartMVP	25	1.75	0.530	2.67
ESG-opt	PearMVP	6	2.20	0.581	3.49
	PartMVP	5	2.00	0.635	3.26
Eco-neutral	PearMVP	6	2.10	0.669	3.51
	PartMVP	25	1.71	0.538	2.64
Eco-opt	PearMVP	5	2.19	0.696	3.72
	PartMVP	5	2.05	0.769	3.62
GHG-neutral	PearMVP	6	2.21	0.512	3.34
	PartMVP	25	1.75	0.607	2.81
GHG-opt	PearMVP	7	2.20	0.522	3.35
	PartMVP	11	1.84	0.654	3.04

Note: # weights — number of weights ≥ 0.01; PearMVP (PartMVP) — Pearson's (partial) correlation-based mean-variance portfolio.

The XLV holdings of DaVita (DVA), DexCom (DXCM), West Pharmaceutical Services (WST), and, to a lesser extent, CVS (CVS) and Lilly (LLY) corporations had notable presence in all three ESG/Eco/GHG-optimal portfolios. The GHG-optimal PartMVP is the most diversified in comparison with the ESG- and Eco-optimal portfolios (11 constituents).

4.3. *Materials Select Sector SPDR ETF* (XLB)

For the XLB constituents (on par with XLP), all three TVL scores were negatively correlated with returns (see Table 6). Somewhat surprisingly, the minimum GHG score for the XLB constituents was higher than 0.5,

Table 6. Statistics of the TVL scores for XLB

Scores	Mean	Std. Dev	Max	Min	Corr. with Returns 2021
ESG	0.582	0.077	0.695	0.326	−1.3%
Eco	0.544	0.160	0.850	0.164	−2.4%
GHG	0.644	0.058	0.794	0.529	−15.1%

Table 7. Performance statistics of the XLB-based OESGPs

Portfolio		# Weights > 0.01	Sh	PESGV	Sh_ESG
TVL ESG-neutral	PearMVP	5	1.68	0.55	2.60
	PartMVP	10	1.50	0.59	2.38
Util ESG-neutral	PearMVP	5	1.68	0.48	2.48
	PartMVP	9	1.50	0.49	2.23
TVL ESG-opt	PearMVP	5	1.67	0.56	2.62
	PartMVP	9	1.48	0.61	2.38
Util ESG-opt	PearMVP	5	1.68	0.48	2.49
	PartMVP	4	1.54	0.51	2.33
TVL Eco-opt	PearMVP	5	1.65	0.57	2.60
	PartMVP	5	1.52	0.67	2.53
Util Eco-opt	PearMVP	4	1.66	0.44	2.39
	PartMVP	3	1.60	0.47	2.35
TVL GHG-opt	PearMVP	5	1.68	0.64	2.76
	PartMVP	12	1.48	0.66	2.47
Util GHG-opt	PearMVP	4	1.68	0.47	2.46
	PartMVP	5	1.51	0.52	2.29

Note: # weights — number of weights ≥ 0.01; PearMVP (PartMVP) — Pearson's (partial) correlation-based mean-variance portfolio.

which implies that only "good" GHG news was available for these companies in the 2nd half of 2021.

The performance statistics of the ESG-optimal portfolios based on the XLB constituents are listed in Table 7.

With the exception of the Eco-optimal PartMVP, ESG optimization does not improve the performance of the XLB-based MVPs. Albemarle (ALB), Freeport-McMoRan (FCX), Newmont (NEM), Nucor (NUE), and Sherwin-Williams (SHW) corporations are present in all three XLB-based OESGPs.

4.4. *Energy Select Sector SPDR ETF* (XLE)

For the XLE constituents, the ESG and Eco scores have positive correlations with returns, while the correlation for GHG is slightly negative (see Table 8). Similar to XLB, the minimum GHG score for the XLI constituents was higher than 0.5, i.e. only the "good" news was recorded in the 2nd half of 2021.

However, the combination of high returns and TVL scores yields the same two securities for all three XLE-based ESG/Eco/GHG OESGPs: Devon Energy (DVN) and Marathon Petroleum (MPC) (see Table 9).

4.5. *Finance Select Sector SPDR ETF* (*XLF*)

The XLF constituents' Eco scores have a small negative correlation with returns, while the ESG and GHG scores have positive ones (see Table 10).

Table 8.   Statistics of the TVL scores for XLE

Scores	Mean	Std. Dev	Max	Min	Corr. with Returns 2021
ESG	0.560	0.043	0.649	0.496	8.9%
Eco	0.430	0.149	0.748	0.199	27.0%
GHG	0.637	0.036	0.686	0.572	−2.0%

Table 9.   Performance statistics and weights of the XLE-based OESGPs

Portfolio		# Weights	Sh	PESGV	Sh_ESG	Weights DVN	MPC
ESG-neutral	PearMVP	2	0.74	0.58	1.17	0.73	0.27
	PartMVP	2	0.73	0.56	1.14	0.53	0.47
ESG-opt	PearMVP	2	0.74	0.59	1.18	0.83	0.17
	PartMVP	2	0.73	0.61	1.18	0..97	0.03
Eco-opt	PearMVP	2	0.74	0.61	1.19	0.77	0.23
	PartMVP	2	0.74	0.61	1.19	0.87	0.13
GHG-opt	PearMVP	2	0.74	0.67	1.24	0.79	0.21
	PartMVP	2	0.74	0.67	1.24	0.75	0.25

Note: # weights — number of weights ≥ 0.01; PearMVP (PartMVP) — Pearson's (partial) correlation-based mean-variance portfolio.

Table 10.   Statistics of the TVL scores for XLF

Scores	Mean	Std. Dev	Max	Min	Corr. with Returns 2021
ESG	0.516	0.098	0.756	0.199	26.8%
Eco	0.546	0.146	0.911	0.258	−5.3%
GHG	0.621	0.128	0.967	0.364	15.5%

Table 11.   Performance statistics of the XLF-based OESGPs

		# Weights	Sh	PESGV	Sh-ESG
ESG-neutral	PearMVP	4	2.30	0.48	3.41
	PartMVP	11	1.57	0.55	2.43
ESG-opt	PearMVP	4	2.26	0.54	3.49
	PartMVP	9	2.02	0.67	3.37
Eco-neutral	PearMVP	5	1.50	0.63	2.45
	PartMVP	12	1.37	0.59	2.17
Eco-opt	PearMVP	5	1.49	0.67	2.48
	PartMVP	7	1.42	0.67	2.37
GHG-neutral	PearMVP	5	1.50	0.71	2.56
	PartMVP	12	1.37	0.61	2.21
GHG-opt	PearMVP	4	1.50	0.73	2.59
	PartMVP	5	1.46	0.74	2.53

Note: # weights — number of weights ≥ 0.01; PearMVP (PartMVP) — Pearson's (partial) correlation-based mean-variance portfolio.

All three XLF-based ESG/Eco/GHG OESGPs had higher *Sh-ESG*s than their ESG-neutral peers (see Table 11).

MSCI, Nasdaq (NDAQ), SVB Financial (SIVB), and to a lesser extent Morgan Stanley (MS) had significant weights in most of the XLF-based optimal portfolios.

4.6. *Technology Select Sector SPDR ETF* (XLK)

For the XLK constituents, both the ESG and GHG scores have small negative correlations with their returns, while the Eco score has a slight positive one (see Table 12).

Table 12.   Statistics of the TVL scores for XLK.

Scores	Mean	Std. Dev	Max	Min	Corr. with Returns 2021
ESG	0.562	0.094	0.754	0.279	−5.8%
Eco	0.587	0.114	0.844	0.255	2.6%
GHG	0.640	0.124	0.843	0.269	−4.7%

Table 13.   Performance statistics of the XLK-based OESGPs.

Portfolio		# Weights	Sh	PESGV	Sh-ESG
ESG-neutral	PearMVP	7	2.30	0.481	3.41
	PartMVP	28	1.57	0.550	2.43
ESG-opt	PearMVP	7	2.26	0.543	3.49
	PartMVP	6	2.02	0.665	3.37
Eco-neutral	PearMVP	7	2.30	0.48	3.41
	PartMVP	28	1.57	0.55	2.43
Eco-opt	PearMVP	6	2.26	0.62	3.67
	PartMVP	7	2.04	0.68	3.42
GHG-neutral	PearMVP	7	2.30	0.64	3.77
	PartMVP	28	1.57	0.66	2.61
GHG-opt	PearMVP	8	2.27	0.69	3.83
	PartMVP	7	1.95	0.79	3.49

Note: # weights — number of weights ≥ 0.01; PearMVP (PartMVP) — Pearson's (partial) correlation-based mean-variance portfolio.

All three XLK-based OESGPs had higher *Sh-ESG*s than their ESG-neutral peers (see Table 13).

Apple (APPL), Enphase Energy (ENPH), Nvidia (NVDA), and to a lesser extent Fortinet (FTNT), Norton LifeLock (NLOK), and Zebra Technologies (ZBRA) had significant weights in most of the XLK-based optimal portfolios.

4.7. *Industrials Select Sector SPDR ETF* (XLI)

The specifics of the TVL scores for the XLI constituents are extremely low Eco scores for Illinois Tool Works (ITW) of 0.041 and Equifax (EFX) of 0.064 (overwhelmingly, the ESG/Eco/GHG TVL scores for the constituents of the US equity sector ETFs are above 0.2). It may be explained by the fact that both companies had some problems in the past ("stale" news), but their negative coverage had never been balanced by positive news later on. Also, the minimum GHG score for the XLI constituents was 0.5, which implies that only neutral or "good" GHG news was available for these companies in the 2nd half of 2021 (see Table 14).

All three XLI-based ESG/Eco/GHG OESGPs had higher *Sh-ESG*s than their ESG-neutral peers (see Table 15).

Eaton (ETN), Generac Holdings (GNRC), and Old Dominion Freight Line (ODFL) corporations had a significant presence in the ESG- and

Table 14.   Statistics of the TVL scores for XLI.

Scores	Mean	Std. Dev	Max	Min	Corr. with Returns 2021
ESG	0.576	0.087	0.750	0.352	20.4%
Eco	0.537	0.149	0.822	0.041	−10.6%
GHG	0.637	0.087	0.761	0.500	32.9%

Table 15.   Performance statistics of the XLI-based OESGPs.

Portfolio		# Weights	Sh	PESGV	Sh-ESG
ESG-neutral	PearMVP	5	2.18	0.609	3.50
	PartMVP	20	1.76	0.578	2.78
ESG-opt	PearMVP	4	2.19	0.624	3.56
	PartMVP	9	1.93	0.650	3.18
Eco-neutral	PearMVP	5	2.18	0.366	2.97
	PartMVP	20	1.76	0.478	2.60
Eco-opt	PearMVP	5	2.19	0.400	3.07
	PartMVP	10	1.88	0.600	3.01
GHG-neutral	PearMVP	5	2.18	0.366	2.97
	PartMVP	20	1.76	0.478	2.60
GHG-opt	PearMVP	3	2.19	0.781	3.91
	PartMVP	3	2.19	0.787	3.92

Note: # weights — number of weights ≥ 0.01; PearMVP (PartMVP) — Pearson's (partial) correlation-based mean-variance portfolio.

Eco-based OESGPs. Quanta Services (PWR) had an outsized weight (greater than 50%) in both GHG-optimal portfolios (PearMVP and PartMVP) due to its high TVL score.

4.8. *Utilities Select Sector SPDR ETF* (XLU)

The specifics of XLU are relatively high minimum values (and, as a result, low variations) of all three ESG/Eco/GHG TVL scores (see Table 16). Also, no fortunes of the constituents of the US equity ETFs changed as dramatically in 2021 as those of XLU (cf. correlations of the TVL scores for the 2nd half of 2021 with returns for June 2019–December 2021 and correlations with returns in 2021).

On par with XLB and XLE, the minimum GHG score for XLU is higher than 0.5, which implies that only "good" GHG-related news was available for the XLU constituents in the 2nd half of 2021.

The performance statistics and the weights of the XLU-based OESGPs are listed in Table 17.

Besides the Eco-optimal PearMVP, the XLU-based ESG/Eco/GHG OESGPs had higher *Sh*-ESGs than their ESG-neutral peers. Note that both Eco-optimal PearMVP and PartMVP had a single constituent, NextEra Energy (NEE), with a weight of 100% due a combination of its high return and high Eco score.

4.9. *Consumer Discretionary Select Sector SPDR ETF* (XLY)

For the XLY constituents in 2021, the Eco scores had a negative correlation with returns, while the correlations for the ESG and GHG scores were positive (see Table 18).

Table 16. Statistics of the TVL scores for XLU.

Scores	Mean	Std. Dev	Max	Min	Corr. with Returns 2021	Corr. with Returns 2019–2021
ESG	0.628	0.058	0.739	0.479	−47.6%	25.6%
Eco	0.562	0.075	0.696	0.439	31.0%	20.2%
GHG	0.733	0.057	0.823	0.579	−30.6%	−4.6%

Table 17.   Performance statistics and weights of the XLU-based OESGPs.

Portfolio		Sh	PESGV	Sh_ESG	# Weights > 0.01	Weights > 0.01			
						AES	AWK	NEE	NRG
TVL ESG-neutral	PearMVP	1.03	0.700	1.75	3	0.14	0.09	0.77	0.00
	PartMVP	1.00	0.687	1.69	4	0.24	0.19	0.49	0.07
Util ESG-neutral	PearMVP	1.03	0.495	1.54	3	0.14	0.09	0.77	0.00
	PartMVP	1.00	0.487	1.49	4	0.24	0.19	0.49	0.07
TVL ESG-opt	PearMVP	1.03	0.709	1.77	2	0.15	0.00	0.85	0.00
	PartMVP	1.01	0.714	1.74	2	0.28	0.00	0.72	0.00
Util ESG-opt	PearMVP	1.03	0.495	1.54	3	0.11	0.10	0.78	0.00
	PartMVP	1.01	0.500	1.53	2	0.00	0.06	0.94	0.00
TVL Eco-opt	PearMVP	1.02	0.634	1.66	1	0.00	0.00	1.00	0.00
	PartMVP	1.02	0.634	1.66	1	0.00	0.00	1.00	0.00
Util Eco-opt	PearMVP	1.02	0.374	1.42	3	0.09	0.12	0.79	0.00
	PartMVP	1.02	0.380	1.41	3	0.12	0.26	0.62	0.00
TVL GHG-opt	PearMVP	1.03	0.773	1.83	2	0.14	0.00	0.86	0.00
	PartMVP	1.01	0.775	1.80	2	0.28	0.00	0.72	0.00
Util GHG-opt	PearMVP	1.03	0.494	1.54	2	0.14	0.00	0.86	0.00
	PartMVP	1.01	0.500	1.50	3	0.27	0.00	0.66	0.07

Note: # weights — number of weights ≥ 0.01; PearMVP (PartMVP) — Pearson's (partial) correlation-based mean-variance portfolio.

Table 18.   Statistics of the TVL scores for XLY.

Scores	Mean	Std. Dev	Max	Min	Corr. with Returns 2021
ESG	0.536	0.085	0.709	0.340	5.1%
Eco	0.539	0.137	0.842	0.196	−27.3%
GHG	0.612	0.116	0.880	0.058	16.7%

The performance statistics and weights of the XLU-based ESG/Eco/GHG OESGPs are listed in Table 19.

All three XLY-based OESGPs had higher *Sh-ESG*s than their ESG-neutral peers. Only Target (TGT) and Tesla (TSLA) were present in all XLY-based OESGP constituents.

Table 19.   Performance statistics of the XLY-based OESGPs.

Portfolio		# Weights	Sh	PESGV	Sh-ESG
ESG-neutral	PearMVP	6	2.57	0.511	3.88
	PartMVP	20	1.83	0.512	2.76
ESG-opt	PearMVP	6	2.50	0.568	3.92
	PartMVP	10	2.15	0.613	3.46
Eco-neutral	PearMVP	6	2.57	0.511	3.88
	PartMVP	20	1.83	0.512	2.76
Eco-opt	PearMVP	6	2.55	0.529	3.91
	PartMVP	6	2.19	0.66	3.65
GHG-neutral	PearMVP	6	2.57	0.511	3.88
	PartMVP	20	1.83	0.512	2.76
GHG-opt	PearMVP	6	2.56	0.608	4.12
	PartMVP	7	2.22	0.74	3.87

Note: # weights — number of weights ≥ 0.01; PearMVP (PartMVP) — Pearson's (partial) correlation-based mean-variance portfolio.

5. Discussion

First, our results demonstrate that increasing PESGV does not guarantee a better portfolio performance in terms of the classical Sharpe ratio since the correlations between corporate returns and ESG ratings in some portfolios can be very low or even negative. This supports the opinion (Schmidt, 2020) that socially responsible investors need to adopt portfolio performance measures that explicitly depend on PESGV, e.g. the ESG-tilted Sharpe ratio (1).

The OESGP framework is a promising tool not only for deriving portfolios that are optimal in terms of return, volatility risk, and PESGV but also for filtering out companies that are the best both in terms of their market performance (returns and volatility risk) and various SASB categories. In other words, one may not necessarily implement OESGP, but simply choose its dominant holdings as promising leads for the future investments.

Our results show an advantage of news-based ESG scores available for various SASB categories that can be used for implementing customized ESG ratings aligned with investor priorities. The TVL scores are convenient for tracking the dynamics of the ESG ratings since they are updated on a daily basis. However, news-based scores have some drawbacks, too. First, it is "stale" news that may sometimes notably affect the company's scores even though the news may not be relevant anymore. Also, it is telling that such environmentally sensitive sectors as Energy, Utilities, and Materials had only "good" GHG news in the 2nd half of 2021. Undoubtedly, the companies in these sectors make efforts to improve their carbon footprint. But, the recent "good" news does not change the nature of their business. Therefore, news-based ESG scores are better suited for comparative analysis of companies within the same industry.

References

Alessandrini, F. & Jondeau, E. (2021). Optimal strategies for ESG portfolios. *The Journal of Portfolio Management*, 47(6), 114–138.

Amenc, N., Goltz, F., & Liu, V. (2022). Doing good or feeling good? Detecting greenwashing in climate investing. *The Journal of Impact and ESG Investing,* 2(4), 57–68.

Berchicci, L. & King, A. A. (2022). Corporate sustainability: A model uncertainty analysis of materiality. *Journal of Financial Reporting*, 7(2), 43–74.

Berg, F., Kölbel, J., & Rigobon, R. (2022). Aggregate confusion: The divergence of ESG ratings. *Review of Finance*, 26, 1315–1344.

Cai, H. & Schmidt, A. B. (2020). Comparing mean–variance portfolios and equal-weight portfolios for major US equity indexes. *Journal of Asset Management*, 21, 326–332.

Chen, M. & Mussalli, G. (2020). An integrated approach to quantitative ESG investing. *The Journal of Portfolio Management*, 46, 65–74.

Christensen, D. M., Serafeim, G., & Sikochi, S. (2022). Why is corporate virtue in the eye of the beholder? The case of ESG ratings. *The Accounting Review*, 97(1), 147–175.

Cornell, B. & Damodaran, A. (2020). Valuing ESG: Doing good or sounding good? *The Journal of Impact and ESG Investing*, 1, 76–93.

Elton, E. J., Gruber, M. J., Brown, S. J., & Goetzman, W. N. (2009). *Modern Portfolio Theory and Investment Analysis*. Hoboken: John Wiley and Sons.

Gabaix, X. & Koijen, K. S. J. (2021). In search of the origins of financial fluctuations: The inelastic markets hypothesis. NBER Working Paper 28967. Retrieved from: https://www.nber.org/papers/w28967.

Guillot, J. (2020). What is the connection between SASB and the SDGs? Retrieved from: https://sasb.ifrs.org/blog/what-is-the-connection-between-sasb-and-the-sdgs/ (Accessed on March 14, 2024).

Jacobs, H., Müller, S., & Weber, M. (2013). How should individual investors diversify? An empirical evaluation of alternative asset allocation policies. *Journal of Financial Markets*, 19, 62–85.

Johnston, J. & DiNardo, J. (1997). *Econometric Methods*. New York: McGraw-Hill.

King, A. A. & Pucker, K. P. (2022, February 25). ESG and alpha: Sales or substance? *Institutional Investor*. Retrieved from https://www.institutional investor.com/article/b1wxqznltqnyzj/ESG-and-Alpha-Sales-or-Substance (Accessed on November 30, 2023).

Kumar, R. (2019). ESG: Alpha or duty? *The Journal of Index Investing*, 9(4), 58–66.

La Torre, M., Mango, F., Cafaro, A., & Leo, S. (2020). Does the ESG index affect stock return? Evidence from the Eurostoxx50. *Sustainability*, 12(16), 6387.

Lioui, A. & Tarelli, A. (2022). Chasing the ESG factor. *Journal of Banking & Finance*, 139, 106498.

Markowitz, H. (1952). Portfolio selection. *The Journal of Finance*, 7, 77–91.

Nadler, D. & Schmidt, A. B. (2014). Portfolio theory in terms of partial covariance. Retrieved from http://ssrn.com/abstract=2436478.

Pastor, L., Stambaugh, R. F., & Taylor, L. A. (2023). "Green tilts" Jacobs Levy equity management center for quantitative financial research. Retrieved from https://ssrn.com/abstract=4464537.

Pedersen, L. H., Fitzgibbons, S., & Pomorski, L. (2021). Responsible investing: The ESG-efficient frontier. *Journal of Financial Economics*, 142, 572–597.

SASB. (2023). SASB conceptual framework. Retrieved from https://www.sasb.org/wp-content/uploads/2019/05/SASB-Conceptual-Framework.pdf?source=post_page (Accessed on November 30, 2023).

Schmidt, A. B. (2020). Optimal ESG portfolios: An example for the Dow Jones index. *Journal of Sustainable Finance and Investment*, 12(2), 529–535.

Schmidt, A. B. (2021). The ESG conundrum: An outsider's view. Retrieved from https://papers.ssrn.com/sol3/papers.cfm?abstract_id=3942572.

Schmidt, A. B. (2024). An impact of greenhouse gas aversion on optimal portfolios. Retrieved from https://ssrn.com/abstract=4453686.

Schmidt, A. B. & Zhang, X. (2024). Optimal ESG portfolios: Which ESG ratings to use? In Andrey Itkin (ed.), *Annual Reviews in Modern Quantitative Finance*. World Scientific. 189–208.

Statman, M. (2019). *Behavioral Finance. The Second Generation.* CFA Institute Research Foundation. Forthcoming in *The Journal of Energy Markets*.

United Nations Department of Economic and Social Affairs. (2023). Sustainable development. Retrieved from https://sdgs.un.org/goals (Accessed on November 30, 2023).

van der Beck, P. (2021). Flow-driven ESG returns. Swiss Finance Institute Research Paper No. 21–71. Retrieved from https://ssrn.com/abstract=3929359.

Whittaker, J. (1990). *Graphical Models in Applied Multivariate Statistics*. Hoboken: Wiley.

Index

Printed in the United States
by Baker & Taylor Publisher Services